AMERICAN BREWERIES

BY
DONAL BULL
MANFRED FRIEDRICH
ROBERT GOTTSCHALK

BULLWORKS
P.O. BOX 106
TRUMBULL, CONNECTICUT, 06611
1984

Library of Congress Catalogue Card Number 83-073558
ISBN 0-9601190-6-X

Printed in the United States of America

Published by

Bullworks, P.O. Box 106, Trumbull CT 06611

On the cover: The Jacob Schmidt Brewing Company, St. Paul, Minnesota about 1900

CONTENTS

Notes on the text	4
Preface	5
Chronology of the American Brewing Industry	6
State/City lists of breweries	11
Alabama (12 breweries)	11
Alaska (38 breweries)	11
Arizona (57 breweries)	13
Arkansas (4 breweries)	15
California (454 breweries)	15
Colorado (129 breweries)	38
Connecticut (63 breweries)	44
Delaware (7 breweries)	48
District of Columbia (21 breweries)	48
Florida (17 breweries)	49
Georgia (15 breweries)	50
Hawaii (8 breweries)	51
Idaho (100 breweries)	51
Illinois (376 breweries)	56
Indiana (162 breweries)	78
Iowa (249 breweries)	86
Kansas (53 breweries)	98
Kentucky (59 breweries)	100
Louisiana (28 breweries)	104
Maine (5 breweries)	105
Maryland (174 breweries)	106
Massachusetts (94 breweries)	116
Michigan (287 breweries)	121
Minnesota (210 breweries)	136
Mississippi (no breweries)	149
Missouri (207 breweries)	150
Montana (62 breweries)	162
Nebraska (57 breweries)	165
Nevada (57 breweries)	169
New Hampshire (14 breweries)	171
New Jersey (154 breweries)	172
New Mexico (19 breweries)	181
New York (724 breweries)	182
North Carolina (8 breweries)	220
North Dakota (19 breweries)	220
Ohio (364 breweries)	221
Oklahoma (7 breweries)	243
Oregon (104 breweries)	243
Pennsylvania (865 breweries)	249
Rhode Island (26 breweries)	295
South Carolina (6 breweries)	296
South Dakota (26 breweries)	296
Tennessee (29 breweries)	298
Texas (96 breweries)	299
Utah (40 breweries)	303
Vermont (4 breweries)	305
Virginia (26 breweries)	306
Washington (122 breweries)	307
West Virginia (33 breweries)	314
Wisconsin (542 breweries)	315
Wyoming (17 breweries)	349
Alphabetical index to brewing names	352
Addenda	396
Bibliography and Acknowledgments	397
Recommended reading list	399

NOTES ON THE TEXT

Abbreviations and symbols used:

c = circa or approximate year
aka = also know as
dba = doing business as
? = year unknown
NP = No federal permit issued. A number of breweries were listed in the 1934 BREWERY DIRECTORY AND SUPPLIES INDEX by Atlas Publishing Co. These breweries were not issued a federal permit and probably did not reach the production state. They are listed for identification purposes as advertising material and prototype production material may be found for these breweries. Several examples of this also appear in directories of later years and they are listed with the NP code.

When a "brewer" is not a brewer:

Since the publication of THE REGISTER, many inquiries have been received concerning "brewers'" names on bottles which were not listed in the book. Prior to 1890 bottling of beer was prohibited on the premises of a brewing concern. The law stated that "bottling must be done in a building entirely distinct and separate from the brewery or warehouse." The law led many brewers who wanted to supply bottled beer to enlist the services of bottling houses. Their beer was therefore kegged and transported to the bottler for bottling. Many of these bottlers used their own name on the bottles as the brewers of the contents. These should not be construed as "brewers" and therefore are not listed in this work. Examples of the bottlers brewers used are:

Anheuser-Busch introduced Budweiser in 1876 which was bottled by C. Conrad.
Pabst of Milwaukee turned over bottling to Stamm & Meyer.
Windisch-Muhlhauser of Cincinnati used the Lion Bottling Co. of Haskill and Thornton.

In 1890 the law was changed to allow the construction of pipe lines from storage cellars on the brewery premises to bottling houses. This did not negate the ruling on separation of brewing and bottling departments but it paved the way to a less complicated method of getting bottled beer to market. Many brewers still piped beer to bottling concerns right up to national prohibition.

"Brewing Company" names on cans:

A great deal of confusion is caused by brewing company names shown on cans. "Playmate Brewing Co." appears on cans of "Playmate" beer in 1967. There was never a "Playmate Brewing Co." This was a name used by the Sunshine Brewing Co. of Reading, PA to market the product (see PA 714f). Many additional "aka" listings will be found throughout the book. As brewing concerns folded over the years, brand names and rights to use company names have been purchased by other breweries to continue the traditionally recognized names in strong market areas. Rheingold never had a brewery in Philadelphia or Cleveland yet the name appears on cans a a result of C. Schmidt & Sons of Philadelphia purchasing the rights to the name (see PA 396g and OH 142d).

State/city alpha-numeric listings:

In order to assist the collector and researcher to date brewery artifacts, alpha-numeric listings are changed when one of the following events occurs:

1. Name change as a result of incorporation, merger, or purchase by another party or brewing concern.
2. Address change due to renaming or renumbering of streets.
3. Address change due to physical removal of the concern to another location.
4. A gap in production due to closure of the brewery for prohibition periods.
5. A gap in production due to closure as a result of fire, bankruptcy, or temporary loss of marketing capability.

If the brewery is a branch of a brewing concern in another location, reference to that concern is included in the listing. If the brewery operated under more than one name, additional names are listed with years of usage. Periods listed in the right hand column are the actual years in which the concern listed operated as a brewer. Addresses are not repeated when there is no change.

Alpha-numeric listing in the Alphabetical Index refer to Alpha-Numeric assignments in the state/city section. The first two letters are the state abbreviation.

PREFACE

In 1976 Manfred Friedrich and I compiled the two volumes of THE REGISTER OF UNITED STATES BREWERIES 1876-1976. Since 1976 a tremendous amount of research has gone into compiling AMERICAN BREWERIES. Experts in various areas of the country have contributed their knowledge which was coordinated by long-time brewery historian Robert Gottschalk. The efforts of scores of individuals gives us the present work which now goes back to the beginning of brewing in America.

We begin with a chronology of the American brewing industry. Reading through this will give the researcher a quick overall view of the development of the industry. It will show him the growth of the industry from East to West as well as the decline in the number of breweries due to such forces as taxation, syndication, and prohibition.

The next section of the book is the state/city lists of breweries. In each listing we have attempted to find the founding company name and address. The first listing under each numerical entry reflects the founding year after the name. This is followed by the year the company went out of business or changed name or address. There may also be gaps in the years when the company was closed for prohibition or other reasons. No year in the right hand column is an indication that the company is still one of the survivors. Each name change is listed after the original name and the periods of use of these subsequent names are shown at right. Additional reasons for changes in the alpha-numeric entries will be found under the notes on the text.

The alphabetical index to brewing names begins on page 352. In THE REGISTER each company was listed alphabetically by the first name in the concern with cross reference to the state and city listings. In this volume all surnames which appear in the brewing concern name are listed. For example, all of the names in the Maryland brewing concern of Gottlieb-Bauernschmidt-Straus (MD 79h) are listed in the index. This will assist the researcher in tracing brewing family names.

Finally, we come to the Bibliography and Acknowledgments which was compiled by Robert Gottschalk. There are hundreds of people who are deserving of our gratitude for their assistance. Bob has listed but a few of them and I echo his appreciation for their fine efforts. We look forward to working with them and the present readers of this material on future projects in the brewing industry field.

Every effort has been made to achieve accuracy in the listings in this book. If any errors or omissions are noted by the reader, we would appreciate hearing from you.

Robert Gottschalk
115 Peachtree Road
Penfield, NY 14526
USA

Donald Bull
P.O. Box 106
Trumbull, CT 06611
USA

Manfred Friedrich
D6900 Heidelberg
Zahringerstrasse 3
West Germany

Donald Bull, Trumbull, CT, USA. March, 1984

1587 Virginia colonists brew some ale by using corn.

1607 First shipment of beer arrives in the Virginia colony from England.

1609 American "Help Wanted" advertisements appear in London seeking brewers for the Virginia Colony.

1620 Pilgrims arrive in Plymouth in the Colony of Massachusetts aboard the Mayflower. Beer is extremely short on board ship and the seamen force the passengers ashore to ensure that they will have sufficient beer for their return trip to England.

1632 The West India Company builds a brewery on Brewers' Street in New Amsterdam (New York) led by Governor Van Twiller.

1633 Peter Minuit establishes the first public brewery in American at Market Field on Manhattan Island.

1634 Samuel Cole is the first to be licensed in Boston to operate a tavern.

1637 First authentically recorded brewery in the Massachusetts Bay Colony under the control of Captain Sedgwick.

1639 Sergeant Baulston is placed in charge of a brewhouse in Providence, Rhode Island.

1670 Samuel Wentworth of Portsmouth obtains the first license to brew beer in New Hampshire.

1683 William Penn's colony erects a brewery in Pennsbury near Bristol, Pennsylvania.

1685 William Frampton erects the first brewery in Philadelphia on Front St. between Walnut and Spruce.

1737 George Washington enters a beer recipe in his notebook.

1762 The Theory and Practice of Brewing by Michael Combrune is published. This is the first attempt to establish rules and principles for the art of brewing.

1772 A mixture of dark to light malts called "Porter" is concocted in England. Exports begin to America but it fails to gain popularity.

1775 Revolutionary War measures by Congress include rationing to each soldier one quart of Spruce Beer or Cider per man per day.

1789 George Washington presents his "buy American" policy indicating he will only drink porter made in America.

1789 Massachusetts passes an Act encouraging the manufacture and consumption of beer and ale.

1792 New Hampshire agrees not to tax brewing property.

1793 Philadelphia produces more beer than all the other seaports in the country.

1795 George Shiras founds the first brewery in Pittsburgh, Pennsylvania.

1808 Members of the Congregational Church in Moreau, Saratoga County, New York form a temperance society.

1810 132 operating breweries produce 185,000 barrels of beer. Population of the country is 7 million.

1810 Jacques Delassas de St. Vrain begins brewing in St. Louis, Missouri (brewery destroyed by fire in 1812). (See Bellefontaine).

1815 The American Brewer and Malster by Joseph Coppinger is published.

1819 A steam engine built by Thomas Holloway is installed in the brewery of Frances Perot in Philadelphia. This is the first engine to be used in beer production in America.

1819 Nathan Lyman starts the first brewery in Rochester, New York.

1820 Brewers report business off due to increased consumption of whiskey.

1826 American Society for the Promotion of Temperance formed in Boston (also known as the American Temperance Society).

1829 American Temperance Society has 100,000 members.

1830 Jacob Roos builds the first brewery in Buffalo, New York.

1832 Secretary of War Lewis Cass cancels the ration of liquor to the military.

1833 William Lill & Co. (Haas & Sulzer) start the first commercial brewery in Chicago and produce 600 barrels of ale in the first year.

1833 Membership in the country's five thousand temperance societies exceeds one and one quarter million.

1836 United States Temperance Union meets in Saratoga, New York and changes name to American Temperance Union. Principle of total abstinence or "Teetotalism" is introduced.

1837 Rice and Kroener establish the first brewery in Evansville, Indiana.

1840 Philadelphia brewer John Wagner introduces lager beer.

1844 The Fortmann and Company Brewery introduces lager beer to Cincinnati.

1844 Jacob Best starts a brewery in Milwaukee which later becomes Pabst Brewing Co.

1846 John Roessle starts a lager beer brewery in Boston.

1846 Maine passes prohibition law.

1847 John Huck and John Schneider start the first lager beer brewery in Chicago.

1848 Unrest in Germany causes many Germans to emigrate to America.

1849 August Krug forms a brewery in Milwaukee which evolved into the Schlitz Brewery.

1849 Adam Schuppert Brewery at Stockton and Jackson Streets in San Francisco becomes California's first brewery.

1850 Mathias Frahm establishes Davenport, Iowa's first brewery.

1850 431 breweries in the country produce 750,000 barrels of beer (31 gallons per barrel). The population is 23 million.

1852 George Schneider starts a brewery in St. Louis, Missouri. This brewery is the seed of the Anheuser-Busch Brewery.

1852 San Francisco has 350 barrooms to serve the hard-drinking population of 36,000.

1852 Henry Saxer starts a brewing business (City Brewery) in Portland, Oregon Territory. This brewery was later owned by Henry Weinhard.

1852 Prohibition comes to Vermont.

1852 Prohibition adopted in Massachusetts (repealed in 1868).

1852 Rhode Island enacts prohibition (repealed in 1863)

1852 Territory of Minnesota enacts a short-lived prohibition.

1853 Prohibition voted in for Michigan.

1854 Prohibition begins in Connecticut.

1855 German brewer William Menger starts a lager beer brewery in San Antonio, Texas. This is the first brewery in that city.

1855 Prohibition adopted in New York, New Hampshire, Delaware, Indiana, Iowa, and the Nebraska Territory.

1857 The largest brewery in the West is the Chicago brewery of William Lill and Michael Diversey.

1859 Solomon, Tascher & Co. start Colorado's first brewery, the Rocky Mountain Brewery.

1860 1269 breweries produce over one million barrels of beer for a population of 31 million. New York and Pennsylvania account for 85% of the production.

1861 Internal Revenue System introduced.

1862 Ernest Weisgerber builds Idaho's first brewery (in Lewistown).

1862 Internal Revenue Act taxes beer at the rate of one dollar per barrel to help finance the government during the Civil War.

1862 37 New York brewers from an association which would officially become the United States Brewers Association in 1864.

1863 161,607 barrels of beer are produced in the New England states.

1863 Thomas Smith founds the first brewery in Montana (Virginia City).

1865 Mathew Vassar, a prominent Poughkeepsie, New York brewer, founds Vassar College, the first privately endowed school for women.

1865 National Temperance Society and Publication House formed in Saratoga, New York.

1866 Internal Revenue issues stamp regulations requiring application of tax stamps to barrels of beer leaving the brewery.

1867 Prohibition efforts in Iowa and New York fail.

1867 3700 breweries in operation in America producing 6 million barrels of beer.

1868 John Siebel opens a brewing school which later becomes the Siebel Institute of Technology.

1868 Publication of the monthly magazine The American Brewer begins in January.

1869 Prohibition Party organized in Chicago.

1869 Another prohibition in Massachusetts (repealed 1875)

1869 Best Brewing Co. (later Pabst) begins expansion in Milwaukee with the purchase of Charles T. Melms' Brewery.

1871 A number of Chicago breweries destroyed by fire started by Mrs. O'Leary's cow: Doyle & Co., Huck, Jerusalem, Lill & Diversey, Metz, Mueller, Sands, and K. G. Schmidt.

1872 Anheuser adopts A and Eagle trademark.

1872 First brewery workers' strike in New York City.

1872 Prohibitionist presidential candidate James Black draws 5608 votes.

1873 4131 breweries (record number) produce 9 million barrels of beer.

1873 Adolphus Busch begins bottling of beer for large scale shipments at the Anheuser Brewery in St. Louis (bottling was not new - only the magnitude of this venture).

1874 Woman's Christian Temperance Union formed.

1875 First lager beer in California brewed by Boca Brewing Co. in Boca.

1876 Louis Pasteur publishes "Studies on Beer" showing how yeast organisms can be controlled.

1877 George Ehret of New York is the largest brewer in the country.

1879 Ballantine adopts three ring trademark.

1880 Frederick Salem authors Beer, Its History and Its Economic Value as a National Beverage. The book is his argument for beer as a temperance measure. It offers the motto "Beer against Whisky."

1880 Internal Revenue Department records indicate 2830 ale and lager breweries in operation.

1880 U. S. Brewers Academy established.

1880 -1910 Number of breweries declines. Improved methods of production and distribution mean fewer breweries can manufacture more beer. By 1910 number of breweries drops to around 1500.

1882 National Brewers' and Distillers' Association formed.

1884 Adolphus Busch of St. Louis and Otto Koehler establish the Lone Star Brewing Co. in San Antonio, Texas.

1886 National Union of the Brewers of the United States established.

1887 Master Brewers' Association organized.

1887 Tuscarora Advertising Company formed in Coshocton, Ohio producing a wide variety of advertising items.

1888 Standard Advertising Company founded by H. D. Beach in Coschocton, Ohio in competition with Tuscarora Advertising.

1888 Brewery employees strike in New York, Chicago, and Milwaukee.

1888 A British syndicate under the name New York Breweries Co. is formed through the purchase of H. Claussen & Son Brewing Co. and Flanagan, Nay & Co.

1889 One of the first big brewery mergers takes place. Franz Falk Breiwng Co. and Jung and Borchert in Milwaukee merge to form Falk, Jung & Borchert Brewing Co. This brewery was taken over four years later by Pabst.

1889 A British syndicate proposes a plan to merge Schlitz, Pabst, and Blatz in Milwaukee. Schlitz and Pabst decline the offer. Blatz sells part of its business to Milwaukee and Chicago Breweries Ltd.

1889 Eighteen St. Louis breweries merge into the English syndicate St. Louis Brewing Association.

1890 Six New Orleans brewers combine to form the New Orleans Brewing Co.

1892 British syndicates start price wars. Prices in Chicago decrease from $6.00 per barrell to $3.50 and $4.00 per barrel.

1892 Crown cap invented by William Painter of Crown Cork and Seal Co. in Baltimore.

1892 Wood pulp coaster invented by Robert Smith of Dresden, Germany.

1893 Anti-Saloon League founded by Rev. Howard Hyde Russell with the goal of suppressing the saloon.

1898 Beer barrel tax raised to $2.00 during Spanish American War. Beer sales decline.

1899 The Pittsburgh Brewing Company formed by the consolidation of twenty one Pittsburgh brewers.

1900 Woman's Christian Temperance Union member Carrie Nation does a hatchet job on the Carey Hotel in Wichita, Kansas.

1901 Ten Boston brewers merge into Massachusetts Breweries Company, Ltd.

1901 Sixteen Baltimore brewers consolidate into the Gottlieb-Bauernschmidt-Straus Brewing Company.

1901 Barrel tax on beer reduced to $1.60.

1902 Barrel tax on beer reduced to $1.00.

1905 Independent Brewing Company formed by fifteen Pittsburgh breweries.

1909 United States Brewers Association yearbook discusses the problems of poor conditions in saloons and the need for a cleanup.

1912 Nine states vote dry.

1913 Webb-Kenyon bill passed prohibiting the interstate shipment of alcoholic beverages to dry states.

1914 Resolution to prohibit liquor through a constitutional amendment loses in the House due to lack of required two-thirds majority vote (197 for, 190 against).

1914 Fourteen states dry.

1914 Secretary of Navy Josephus Daniels orders prohibition of alcohol on Naval ships and Naval installations.

1916 Twenty-three states dry.

1916 Six San Francisco breweries consolidate.

1917 District of Columbia passes a prohibition law.

1917 Distilleries closed by Food Control Law.

1919 18th Amendment to the U.S. Constitution ratified on January 16 calling for national prohibition to take effect one year from the date of ratification.

1919 House of Representatives Bill No. 6810 presented in May by Rep. Volstead establishing the apparatus for the enforcement of prohibition. The bill was passed October 10, vetoed by President Wilson on October 27, and the veto was subsequently overridden by Congressional vote.

1920s Near beers brewed during prohibition: Pablo by Pabst, Famo by Schlitz, Vivo by Miller, Lux-O by Strohs and Bevo by Anheuser Busch.

1920 Association Against the Prohibition Amendment organized by William H. Stayton.

1921 300 million gallons of "near beer" produced.

1922 Prohibitionist Volstead defeated in Minnesota elections.

1922 Anthony & Kuhn Brewery of St. Louis sold to a laundry.

1923 The Moderation League is formed.

1926 Montana votes to repeal the state prohibition enforcement law. Other states follow suit.

1929 The Women's Organization for National Prohibition Reform started.

1930 The Crusaders formed protesting the lawlessness, crime, and corruption brought on by Prohibition.

1930 American Brewers Association formed.

1931 American Legion votes for a referendum of national prohibition.

1932 86 million gallons of near beer produced.

1933 The Cullen Bill is passed in March allowing states which did not have state prohibition laws to sell 3.2% beer. It also instituted a $5.00 per barrel tax on beer. On April 7, 1933 the relegalization of beer takes effect via the 21st Amendment repealing the 18th.

1933 31 brewers back in operation by June.

1934 756 brewers back in operation.

1935 Canned beer introduced by American Can Company and Krueger Brewing Co. of Newark, New Jersey on June 24.

1935 Schlitz introduces cone top can produced by Continental Can Company.

1935 Falstaff Brewing Co. of St. Louis leases the Krug Brewing Company of Omaha, Nebraska. This touches off a wave of acquisitions by large brewers.

1936 United Brewers Industrial Foundation formed.

1936 Brewing Industry, Inc. formed.

1940 Beer production at level of pre-prohibition years with half the numbers of breweries in operation in 1910.

1940 Barrel tax raised from $5.00 to $6.00.

1941 All brewers' associations united under the United States Brewers' Association.

1943 Brewers are required to allocate 15% of their production for military use.

1944 Barrel tax raised to $8.00.

1949 -1958 185 breweries close down or sell out.

1950 407 breweries in operation.

1951 Anheuser-Busch of St. Louis builds a new brewery in Newark, New Jersey starting a trend for expansion of breweries.

1951 Barrel tax raised to $9.00.

1953 Anheuser-Busch buys the St. Louis Cardinals baseball team.

1954 First 16oz can introduced by Schlitz.

1959 Aluminum can introduced by Coors of Golden, Colorado.

1960 Aluminum can top introduced.

1961 230 breweries in operation. Only 140 are independently run.

1962 Tab top can introduced by Pittsburgh Brewing Company.

1965 "Ring Pull" can introduced.

1969 Canned beer outsells bottled beer for the first time.

1971 Philip Morris Co. acquires Miller Brewing Co.

1972 State of Oregon becomes the first state to adopt a container deposit law.

1983 In January 51 brewing concern are operating a total of 80 breweries.

1983 The top six breweries (Anheuser-Busch, Miller, Heileman, Stroh, Coors, and Pabst) control 92% of U. S. beer production.

1984 AMERICAN BREWERIES published.

ALABAMA

Birmingham

AL	1a	Birmingham Brewing Co. (Ave. D & 22nd St.)	1889-1891
	1b	Adler, Morris & Co.	1891-1893
	1c	Isidore Newman	1893-1897
	1d	Alabama Brewing Co.	1897-1907
AL	2a	Philip Schillinger (Ave. E Btw. 21st & 22nd Sts.)	1884-1888
	2b	Philip Schillinger Brewing Co.	1888-1908

Brownsville

AL	3	Willauer & Koenneker	1885-1885

Cullman

AL	4	Frank Anthe	1874-1875

Huntsville

AL	5	Christ. Fromm	1874-1875

Mobile

AL	6	Bienville Brewing Co. aka Bienville Brewery (St. Joseph & Bloodgood Sts.)	1901-1908
AL	7	Charles W. Gelbke	1874-1884
AL	8a	Mobile Brewing (Adams & 331 Waters Sts.)	1890-1893
	8b	Mobile Brewing Co.	1893-1896
	8c	Mobile Brewery	1896-1915
	8d	Mobile Brewery (330 N. Water St.)	NP 1934-1934
AL	9	Carl Thomas	1874-1875

Montgomery

AL	10a	Montgomery Brewing Co. (Hull St.)	1888-1896
	10b	Montgomery Brewery	1896-1903
	10c	Capitol Brewing and Ice Co.	1903-1915

Phoenix City

AL	11a	Chattahoochee Brewing Co.	1890-1896
	11b	Dixie Brewery	1896-1901

Sheffield

AL	12	Sheffield Brewing and Ice Co.	1902-1906

ALASKA

Anchorage

AK	1	Prinz Brau Alaska, Inc.	1976-1979

Circle

AK	2	E. Hegner	1899-1900
AK	3	C. S. Levante	1899-1900
AK	4	G. Rieffenstein	1899-1900

Dawson City

AK	5	Klondike Brewery	c1916

Douglas

AK	6	Ernest Beihl	1899-1899
AK	7	John Egan	1898-1900
AK	8a	Douglas City Brewery	1902- ?
	8b	Douglas City Brewing Co.	? -1904
	8c	Douglas City Brewery	1904-1906
AK	9	John Kreuzner	1896-1897

Dyea

AK	10	Alaska Brewing Co.	1898-1899
AK	11	Dabszinsky & Babler	1898-1898
AK	12	Geo. L. Rice & Co.	1898-1904

Eagle

AK	13	Eagle Brewing Co.	1902-1903

Fairbanks

AK 14	Barthel Brewing Co.	1906-1919
AK 15	Fairbanks Brewing Association, Inc. (103 1st Ave.)	1934-1935
AK 16	(The) Pioneer Brewing Co., Inc. (Garden Island)	1934-1942
AK 17a	Tanana Brewing Co.	1905- ?
17b	Fairbanks Brewing Co.	? -1908
17c	Arctic Brewing Co.	1908-1910

Fort Wrangel

AK 18	August Brettler	1903-1904
AK 19	Eureka Brewing Co.	1898-1899
AK 20a	Henry Uhler	1891-1895
20b	Estate of Henry Uhler	1895-1896
20c	Uhler & Greif	1896-1898
20d	Bruno Greif	1898-1902

Juneau

AK 21a	Abraham Cohen (First brewery in Alaska)	? -1888
21b	M. J. Cohen & Co.	1888-1893
21c	Marcus J. Cohen	1893-1904
AK 22	John F. Gray & Co.	1888-1898
AK 23a	Matlock & Fisher	1899- ?
23b	Juneau Alaska Brewing and Malting Co.	? -1902
23c	Alaska Brewing and Malting Co.	1902-1904
23d	Eagle Brewing Co.	1904-1919
AK 24	Annie D. Petersen	1899-1902

Ketchikan

AK 25a	Pilsener Brewing Co. of Alaska (1651 Cliff Ave.)	1935-1940
25b	Pilsener Brewing Co. of Alaska (1651 Tongass Ave.)	1940-1942

Nome

AK 26	Alaska Brewing Co.	1900-1901
AK 27	Cape Nome Brewing and Trading Co.	1900-1900
AK 28	Nome Brewing and Bottling Co.	1905-1919

Rampart

AK 29	Rampart City Brewing Co.	1899-1900

Sitka

AK 30a	Levi, Cohen, Fuller & Co.	1874-1875
30b	Aaron Cohen	1875-1891
30c	Robert Witz, Alaskan Brewery	1891-1902

Skagua

AK 31	Herman Barthel	1903-1904

Skagway

AK 32	Arctic Brewing Assn.	1898-1899
AK 33	Frederich Gansneder	1899-1899
AK 34	Miller & Co.	1899-1899
AK 35	Chas. A. Saake	1898-1902
AK 36a	Skagway Brewing Co.	1899-1902
36b	Skagway Brewery	1902-1908
36c	Eagle Brewery	1908-1910

Unga

AK 37	George Voelker	1898-1899

Valdez

AK 38a	Valdez Brewing Co.	1904- ?
38b	Valdez Brewing and Bottling Co.	1909-1919

ARIZONA

Alexandra
AZ 1 Jos. Minger, aka Jos. Minger & Bros. (1880) 1878-1882

Arivaca
AZ 2 Machaltz & Ruckelhausen 1882-1884

Bisbee
AZ 3a Al Sieber 1880-1882
3b Seiber & Tribaldt (or Tribolet) 1882-1884
3c Dubacher Bros. (Henry & Frank) 1884-1888
3d Henry Dubacher 1888-1891
3e Dubacher & (Joseph) Muheim 1891-1893

Charleston (Fort Huachuca)
AZ 4a Andreas Joerger 1888-1897
4b Andreas Joerger (Fort Huachuca) 1897-1900
4c Frank Joerger, Ransom Canyon Brewery 1900-1905

AZ 5 Smith & McDowell 1879-1880

Chricohua (or Chiricahua)
AZ 6 A. L. Stahl 1882-1882

Clifton
AZ 7 Adolph Gerhardt 1884-1884

Dos Cabezos
AZ 8 C. Graner 1884-1884

Douglas
AZ 9 Copper City Brewing Co. 1905-1914

Flagstaff
AZ 10a Carl & Stemmer 1884- ?
10b J. F. Dages, Flagstaff Brewery ? -1886
10c Gruner & Dillman, Flagstaff Brewery 1886-1888
10d Dillman, Powers & Streit, Flagstaff Brewery 1888-1889

Florence
AZ 11a Peter Will & Co. 1870-1884
11b Peter Will 1884-1888

Galeyville
AZ 12 Jacob Strohl 1882-1882

Gillett
AZ 13a P. Arnold 1878-1882
13b Cook & Co. 1882-1882

Globe
AZ 14 Bosche & Knight, aka G. Bosch & Co. (1882) 1882-1884

AZ 15a Fred Medler & Co. (Bissig & Pieper), Pinal Brewery 1878-1879
15b Bissig & Pieper 1879-1880
15c Hayes, Bissig & Pieper 1880-1884
15d Pieper, Bissig & Soyer 1884-1888

AZ 16a Chas. Banker, St. Louis Brewery (N. Broad St.) 1884-1890
16b Banker & Soyer, St. Louis Brewery 1890-1892
16c Chas. Banker, St. Louis Brewery 1892-1904

Harshaw
AZ 17 Danguire & Co. 1882-1882

AZ 18 Chas. Daucher & Co. 1882-1882

AZ 19 Jules Flin 1882-1882

AZ 20 S. P. Nelson 1882-1884

Lutrell (also known as LaNoria and Lochiel)
AZ 21 John Deckert 1882-1882

Payson
AZ 22 Ernest F. Pieper c1880-1890

Phoenix

AZ 23a Arizona Brewing Co. (1141-1143 E. Madison St.) 1933-1942
23b Arizona Brewing Co., Inc. 1942-1949
23c Arizona Brewing Co. (150 S. 12th St.) 1949-1964
23d Carling Brewing Co., Inc. 1964-1966
23e The National Brewing Co. (Western Div.), aka Dutch Treat Brewing Co. and Van Lauter Brewing Co. (1970-1975) 1966-1975
23f Carling National Breweries, Inc., aka Dutch Treat Brewing Co. 1975-1979
23g G. Heileman Brewing Co., aka Carling National Breweries, Inc. and Dutch Treat Brewing Co. 1979-

AZ 24a Gustav Becher & A. H. Sayles, United States Brewery 1878-1880
24b F. Becher 1880-1882

AZ 25 Matt Cavaness (First brewery in Phoenix) c1870

AZ 26a (C. A.) Luke & (J.) Thalheimer, Arcade Brewery 1878-1882
26b C. A. Luke 1882-1884
26c Wurch & Luke 1884-1888

AZ 27 Phoenix Brewing Co. 1901-1901

AZ 28 Tri-State Brewery Co. (Glendale Ave.) NP 1934-1934

AZ 29 Michael Wurch 1882-1884

Pinal (also known as Picket Post)

AZ 30 Fredk. Jensen 1884-1884

AZ 31a Warnke & Werner 1882-1883
31b E. F. Warnke 1883-1884
31c August Werner 1884-1888

Pioneer

AZ 32 Thompson & Deckert 1882-1885

Prescott

AZ 33a Arizona Bry., John Littig & Co. 1868-1869
33b Arizona Brewery, Max Simonsen & George Frommer 1869-1869
33c Arizona Brewery, Cal. Jackson & Co. (Sol & Jess Jackson) 1869-1872
33d Arizona Brewery, Julius Rodenburg & Gray Foster 1872-1877
33e Arizona Brewery, Julius N. Rodenburg 1877-1880
33f Arizona Brewery, Vefer & Co., aka G. Urfer & Co. 1880-1882
33g Arizona Brewery, F. Jacoby 1882-1882
33h Arizona Brewery, Aumuller & Jacoby 1882-1884
33i Arizona Brewery, Rodenburg & Aumiller 1884-1885

AZ 34 Arizona Brewing Co. 1905-1914

AZ 35 Blackburn & Co., City Brewery 1878-1879

AZ 36 A. T. Cornish 1892- ?

AZ 37 Louis Dugas, Excelsior Brewery 1879-1879

AZ 38 A. H. Hauch & Co. 1898-1898

AZ 39 Prescott Brewing Co. c1900

AZ 40a Pacific Brewery, John Raible & Philip Sheerer 1867-1872
40b Pacific Brewery, John Raible 1872-1879
40c Pacific Brewery, John Raible & Charles Wurth 1879-1884
40d Pacific Brewery, John Raible 1884-1888
40e Pacific Brewery, Raible & Waller 1888-1890

Rio Verde

AZ 41a Fish & Schrope 1874-1875
41b Schrope & Arnold 1875-1875
41c William Horn 1875-1884

Solomonville

AZ 42 Barnaby Palm (Wilcox-Globe Road) 1880-1884

Tip Top

AZ 43 Peter Arnold 1882-1888

Tombstone

AZ 44	Bernhardt & (Herman) Lepstein (or Leptein), Arizona Brewery	1882-1884
AZ 45	Kirker & Schrey	1882-1882
AZ 46	A. Ubel & Co.	1882-1882
AZ 47a	(Frederick) Wehrfritz & (Geofrey) Tribolet, Golden Eagle Brewery, (Allen & 5th Sts.)	1880-1882
47b	Tribolet & Berger	1882-1882
47c	S. Tribolet	1882-1884

Total Wreck

AZ 48	Lake & Root	1884-1884
AZ 49	Julius Lindenmeyer	1884-1884

Tucson

AZ 50	Paul Abadie, French Brewery	1874-1876
AZ 51a	(Alex) Levin & Co., Pioneer Brewery	
	with Frank Hodges (115-121 Camp St.)	1866-1869
	with Julius Goldtree (Main & Pennington Sts.)	1869-1870
	with J.W. Hopkins (315 Main St., Near Pearl St.)	1870-1871
51b	Alex Levin, Pioneer Brewery	1871-1872
51c	Zenona (& Alex) Levin, Park Brewery (Foot of Pennington St.)	1872-1880
51d	Joseph Bayer & Louis Schwartz, Park Brewery	1880-1882
51e	Louis Schwartz, Park Brewery	1882-1882
51f	Columbus Glasmann, Park Brewery	1882-1883
51g	Hugo Dorn, Park Brewery	1883-1885
51h	Patterson & Levin, Park Brewery	1885-1885
51i	Ernest Hartman, Park Brewery	1885-1886
51j	Jacob Martin & Henry Weick, Park Brewery	1886-1886
AZ 52a	Sales (aka Sayles & Siegel) & Smith, Opposition Brewery	1870-1870
52b	J. Neugass & Co.	1870-1870
AZ 53	Conrad Mundelius, Excelsior Brewery	1880-1882

Vulture

AZ 54	Jas. F. Marvin	1882-1882

Wickenburg

AZ 55	Abe H. Peeples, Magnolia Brewery	1868-1871

Williams

AZ 56	Williams Brewery, G. H. Barney	1900-1900

Yuma

AZ 57a	N. Watry	1874-1875
57b	F. C. Arnold	1875-1875

ARKANSAS

Fort Smith

AR 1	Joseph Freiseis	1878-1879

Little Rock

AR 2	Arkansas Brewery Corp. (in process of formation)	NP 1954-1954
AR 3	Little Rock Brewery Co. (Wallace Bldg.)	NP 1934-1934
AR 4	Little Rock Brewing and Ice Co. (2nd & Byrd Sts.)	1898-1915

CALIFORNIA

Adin

CA 1a	Jonas & Bofinger	1878-1879
1b	Bedford & Bofinger	1879-1884
1c	C. A. Bofinger	1884-1891

Alameda

CA 2a	Victor Ruthardt	1874-c1877
2b	Alameda Brewery	c1877-1879
2c	Dietzel & Adloff	1879-1882
CA 3a	Henry Schuler, Palace Brewery	1882-1891
3b	Lorenz L. Schuler, Palace Brewery (Central Ave.)	1891-1907
3c	Geo. F. Goerl, Palace Brewery	1907-1910

Altaville

CA 4a	John Becker	1874-1880
4b	Elizabeth Becker	1880-1893
4c	William Becker	1893-1900

Alturas

CA 5a	A. W. Goose	1882-1884
5b	Fred Bogner	1884-1895
5c	Joseph Dannhauser	1895-1909
5d	John Perry Bowers	1909-1911
5e	Wm. F. Werner	1911-1915

Amador City

CA 6	John Hirschle	1895-1895

Anaheim

CA 7a	Fred Erick Conrad, Anaheim Brewery	1872-1904
7b	Union Brewing Co.	1904-1920
CA 8a	S. Goldstein	1874-1875
8b	Theo Reiser	1875-1875
8c	J. Goodale	1875-1880
8d	J. P. Hinde	1880-1884

Angels Camp

CA 9	Angels Brewery	NP 1934-1934
CA 10	Ernst F. Hubler, Angels Brewery	1893-1905

Arcadia (see Los Angeles)

Auburn

CA 11a	Kaiser Brothers (Samuel & Frank)	1855-1862
11b	Frederick Grohs	1862-1879
11c	Kraus & Roll	1879-1884
11d	Roll & Weber	1884-1888
11e	Julius Weber	1888-1897
11f	Ferdinand Rechenmacher	1897-1908
CA 12	Placer Brewing Co.	NP 1979-1979
CA 13	Schuler & Hohl	1874-1875

Azusa

CA 14a	Lucky Lager Brewing Co. (branch of San Francisco)	1949-1963
14b	General Brewing Corp., California Southern Div.	1963-1966
14c	Miller Brewing Co. (branch of Milwaukee)	1966-1981

Bakersfield

CA 15	Bakersfield Brewery	NP 1934-1934
CA 16a	Bakersfield Brewing Co.	1911-1920
16b	Kern Brewing Co. (2720 Union Ave. at Oregon)	1938-1939
CA 17	E. G. Miller	1882-1884

Benicia

CA 18a	John Rueger (H Street)	1874-1880
18b	Benicia Brewery	1880-1884
18c	Gustav Gnauck	1884-1920
18d	Benicia Brewing Co.	NP 1934-1934

Benton (Partzwick)

CA 19	Adolph Gerckens	1882-1890
CA 20	John Kremkow, Partzwick Brewery	1874-1888

Berkeley (West Berkeley)

CA 21	Mrs. Catherine Christ	1884-1884
CA 22a	Hofburg Brewing Co.	1888-1890
22b	Hofburg Brewing Co.(branch of San Francisco Breweries Ltd.)	1890-1899
CA 23	Japan Brewing Co.	1902-1906
CA 24	Mt. Tamalrais Brewery	c1981

Berkeley (cont.)

CA 25	L. Neller & Co.	1884-1884
CA 26	Numano Sake Co. (708 Addison Street)	1979-
CA 27a	Joseph Raspiller	1893- ?
27b	Jos. Raspiller & Co., American Brewery	1897-1902
27c	Raspiller Brewing Co.	1902-1910
27d	Golden West Brewing Co.	1910-1915
CA 28	The Thousand Oaks Brewing Co. (444 Vassar Ave.)	1981-

Big Pine

CA 29	Joseph Schalten	1882-1884

Bishop Creek

CA 30a	Munzinger, Philippay & Co.	1878-1890
30b	L. & C. Munzinger	1890-1895
30c	Munzinger & Co.	1895-1899

Boca

CA 31	Boca Brewing Co. (1st California Lager Beer - 1875)	1875-1892

Bodie

CA 32a	A. A. Carion (see also North San Juan)	1878-1879
32b	Mrs. N. Carion	1879-1884
32c	Nicholas Carion	1884-1899
32d	Mulgren & McKenzie	1899-1901
32e	McKenzie & McAlpin	1901-1906
32f	John J. McKenzie	1906-1915
CA 33	Fahey & McVey	1882-1882
CA 34a	Frankenberger & Davison	1878-1880
34b	William Davison	1880-1882
34c	Davison & Waldenmeier	1882-1884

Bovinebar

CA 35a	Benjamin Gausner	1878-1879
35b	C. Gausner	1879-1882
35c	Benjamin Gausner	1882-1884

Brooklyn

CA 36	Keller & Stephan	1875-1875

Calexico

CA 37	Mexicali Brewing Co. (branch of Mexicali, Mexico)	NP 1934-1934

Camp Independence

CA 38	C. A. Walter, Star Brewery	1874-1884

Carters

CA 39	Benjamin Dannert	1901-1906

Caspar (Grove Pine)

CA 40a	Martin Brinzing (see also Pine Grove)	1898-1904
40b	Margaret Brinzing	1904-1920

Castroville

CA 41a	Lauck & Meyer	1874-c1877
41b	George Lauck	c1877-1880

Cedarville

CA 42	Stough & Weber	1884-1884

Cherokee

CA 43a	Charles Bader	1870-1882
43b	Elizabeth Bader	1882-1897
43c	H. F. Bader	1897-1903

Chico

CA 44a	Charles Croissant	1874-1891
44b	Michael Popp (Broadway)	1891-1899
44c	John D. Scholl	1899-1900
44d	Chico Brewery, Henry F. Bader & Wm. Fitch	1900-1902
CA 45	Sierra Nevada Brewing Co. (2539 Gilman Way)	1980-

Chollas Valley

CA 46 C. Doblin 1878-1882

Clayton

CA 47 Wm. A. Faig c1890

CA 48a J. Rapp 1874-1875
48b Joseph Ruscher ? -1888

Cloverdale

CA 49a Charles Cropp 1874-c1877
49b Schaeffer & Auker c1877-1880
49c Ignatz Schaeffer 1880-1884
49d Vital Reger, Cloverdale Brewery 1884-1908

Cobb (see Middletown)

Columbia

CA 50 Albert Baier 1896-1896

CA 51a Joseph Bixel 1875-1884
51b Paul Bixel 1884-1888
51c Mary Jane Bixel 1888-1891
51d A. C. Nelson, Columbia Brewery 1891-1910

CA 52 Charles Indeweiss 1896-1897

CA 53 Tobener Bros. 1896-1898

Colusa

CA 54a Henry C. Stillmayer 1874-c1877
54b G. Kammerer & Co. c1877-1882

Concord

CA 55 Jacob Kugel 1905-1906

Copperopolis

CA 56 G. B. Zaiss 1874-1875

Crescent City

CA 57a Frank Crusius 1895-1895
57b Gottlob Hess 1895-1897
57c Herman Kuebler 1897-1906

CA 58a Joseph Mayhoffer 1874-1888
58b G. W. Mayhoffer 1888-1890

CA 59 Geo. W. Wakefield 1908-1908

Crystal Peak

CA 60 William Rehfuss 1882-1882

Davisville

CA 61 William Faber 1874-1884

Darwin

CA 62 Jacob Jacobson 1884-1884

Dixon

CA 63a Thomas Berry 1874-c1877
63b Sieber & Oberholzer c1877-1880
63c Schomer & Oberholzer 1880-1895

Downieville

CA 64a Ferdinand Bosch 1874-1897
64b John S. Woessner 1897-1915

CA 65a Nessler & Blohm 1874-c1877
65b L. Nessler c1877-1891

Dutch Flat

CA 66a Mitchell & Rablin 1874-c1877
66b Wm. Mitchell c1877-1884
66c Pleitner & Meyer 1884-1889
66d Mallows & Trausdale, Placer Brewery 1889-1892

El Centro

CA 67 Maggio Bros. Co. NP 1934-1934

Elmhurst

CA 68 London Porter Brewery 1905-1908

Emeryville

CA 69 Japan Brewing Co. 1907-1907

Etna Mills

CA 70 Charles Kappler, Etna Brewery 1867-1920

CA 71 Charles Peters 1862- ?

Eureka

CA 72 Bonham & Co. 1893-1893

CA 73a Fischer & Wickstrom 1903-1904
73b Axel Johnson 1904-1904

CA 74a John U. Haltinner, aka Haltinner & Hendrickson (1901) (First St.) 1896-1903
74b Humboldt Brewing Co. (405 First St.) 1903-1920
74c Humboldt Malt and Brewing Co. (3150 Broadway St.) 1933-1940

CA 75 Jas. Harper 1878-1882

CA 76 Simon Woelfel 1888-1891

CA 77a M. Wanger 1874-c1877
77b Huck & McAllenan c1877-1880
77c Chas. Huck 1880-1882
77d P. McAleenan 1882-1898

Fall River Mills

CA 78 Florin & Bros. 1874-1875

Fairfield

CA 79a Anheuser-Busch, Inc. (branch of St. Louis) (3101 Magellan Rd.) 1976-1978
79b Anheuser-Busch, Inc. (branch of St. Louis) (3101 Busch Drive) 1979-

Fiddletown

CA 80 Schuler & Schroder 1874-1875

Folsom

CA 81 Peter Yaeger 1874-1882

Foresthill

CA 82a Joseph Andres 1874-1884
82b Maulbach & Beckstrum 1884-1893
82c John G. Beckstrum 1893-1900
82d John Finning 1900-1906
82e Smith & Anderson 1906-1908

Fort Bidwell

CA 83a M. Fulcher 1878-1879
83b Fulcher & Weilmunster 1879-1882
83c Fulcher & Tonningsen 1882-1884
83d Max Fulcher (Main St.) 1884-1909

Fortstown

CA 84 Walser & Rutishauser 1895-1895

Fredericksburg

CA 85 Henry Hogrefe 1899-1902

Fresno

CA 86 J. L. Erpelding 1878-1880

CA 87a Fresno Brewing Co. 1900-1920
87b Fresno Beverage Co. (Prohibition) 1920-1933
87c Fresno Brewing Co., Inc. (100 M. St.) 1933-1942
87d Grace Bros., Inc., dba Fresno Brewing Co. 1943-1944
87e Fresno Brewing Co. (affiliated with Grace Bros. Brewery, Ltd., Los Angeles) 1944-1949

CA 88 Yosemite Brewing Co., Inc. (1312 Blackstone Ave.) 1934-1939

Garrote (see Groveland)

Germantown

CA 89a	A. Miller & Co.	1878-1880
89b	Peter Matzen	1880-1884
89c	Backman & Henke	1884-1888

Gibsonville

CA 90	Jacob Bressel	1880-1893
CA 91	F. J. Kling	1874-1875

Gilroy

CA 92a	Adam Riehl	1874-c1877
92b	Adam Herold	c1877-1882
92c	Adam Herold & Co.	1882-1884
92d	Michael Casey	1884-1905
92e	Gilroy Brewery	1905-1906

Graniteville

CA 93	Wm. Hartman	1874-1875

Grass Valley

CA 94	Joseph Amberg	1874-1875
CA 95a	D. Binklemann	1874-1893
95b	Sophie Binklemann	1893-1900
95c	Binklemann & Wilhelm	1900-1901
95d	David J. Binkleman	1901-1920
95e	D. J. Binkleman Brewery	NP 1934-1934
CA 96a	John Frank	1874-1884
96b	Mrs. Catherine Frank	1884-1893
96c	Frank Bros.	1893-1900
96d	Frederick Frank	1900-1920
CA 97a	Charles Fritz	1874-1884
97b	Fritz & Hall	1884-1891
CA 98a	Thomas Hodge & Co.	1874-1893
98b	W. F. Mitchell	1893-1895
98c	Wm. F. Mitchell & Co.	1895-1899
98d	Michael Popp	1899-1905
98e	Wilhelm & Meier	1905-1906
98f	Geo. Wilhelm	1906-1909
CA 99	Charles Mitchell	1884-1884

Greenville

CA 100	Casper Schmitt	1882-1884

Greenwood

CA 101a	Wm. Fehrenbacher	1884- ?
101b	Frederica Halz	1890-1891
CA 102	McGonagle & Co.	1874-1875
CA 103a	Mrs. Nancy Muhlbach	1868-1903
103b	John Muhlbach	1903-1904

Groveland (Garrote)

CA 104a	Eugene Muller, Garrote Brewery	1874-1905
104b	Pauline C. Mueller, Garrote Brewery	1905-1911

Grove Pine (see Caspar)

Guadalupe

CA 105a	A. Tomasini	1874-c1877
105b	Tomasini & Tognini	c1877-1882
105c	Celestino Tognini	1882-1884
105d	Alberto Bonetti	1884-1888

Half Moon Bay

CA 106a	A. Schubert	1874-1875
106b	Edward Schubert	1875-1891

Havilah

CA 107a	Fred. Ehrich	1874-c1877
107b	Bernhard Neff	c1877-1882

Hayward

CA 108a Booken & Herman (A Street) 1875-1880
108b John Booken 1880-1891
108c Ulrichs & Sorensen 1891-1893
108d Charles Anderson & Son 1893-1895
108e Peter Butt 1895-1897
108f John Booken 1897-1904

CA 109a Charles Lyons, Lyon's Brewery 1862-1880
109b Leopold Palmtag, Lyon's Brewery 1880-1890
109c (Charles) Lyons & (Julius) Heyer, Lyon's Brewery 1890-1890
109d Palmtag & Heyer, Lyons Brewery (Castro St.) 1890-1905
109e Palmtag & Heyer Brewing and Malting Co. 1905-1910
109f Palmtag & Heyer Brewery (branch of Golden West Brewing Co., Oakland) 1910-1914

Healdsburg

CA 110 Carl Mueller (West & North Streets) 1874-1907

Hollister

CA 111a Henry Varcoe 1874-1884
111b Emil Buscher 1884-1891
111c Hollister Brewing Co. (631 San Benito St.) 1891-1920

Hollywood (see Los Angeles)

Hornitos

CA 112a Henry Lessmann 1875-1882
112b Mrs. Elizabeth Lessmann 1882-1888

Hot Springs

CA 113 Edward Fantz 1878-1882

CA 114 Henry Rahn 1882-1882

Howland Flat

CA 115a F. R. Becker 1874-1875
115b J. X. Becker 1875-1880
115c F. X. Becker 1880-1884

CA 116 John Wolf (see also Sacketts Gulf and Sears) 1897-1897

Independence

CA 117 Joseph Fernbach 1874-1884

CA 118 Philip Gehrig 1903-1920

Indian Valley

CA 119 M. Knoll 1874-1884

Ione City

CA 120a C. Raab & Co. 1874-c1877
120b C. Raab c1877-1884
120c Joseph Herschle 1884-1891
120d Albert Burkhardt 1891-1893
120e Joseph Herschle 1893-1897

Iowa City

CA 121a Kotter, Ravensburg & Kruse 1888- ?
121b Louis Kotter ? -1891

Iowa Hill

CA 122 John Schmidt 1874-1880

Irwindale

CA 123 Miller Brewing Co. (branch of Milwaukee, Wisconsin) (15801 E. 1st St.) 1980-

Jackson

CA 124a Beiser & Schroeder (Main St.) 1878-1880
124b Kuchler Bros. 1880-1884
124c John Strohm, Jackson Brewery 1884-1920

Jamestown

CA 125 Kleiner & Werner 1898-1898

CA 126 Sierra Brewery, Solomon Lehmann 1916-1918

Johnsville

CA 127a August Grazer 1880- ?
127b Grazer & Savana ? -1882
127c Grazer & Daly 1882-1884
127d Stephen Savana 1884-1885
127e Aug. Grazer 1885-1891
127f John E. Meyer 1891-1893
127g John C. Werner 1893-1895

CA 128 Peter Laurenzi 1888-1893

Kelseyville

CA 129 Swan Brewing Co. 1906-1910

Kernville

CA 130 Wm. Cook 1878-1888

CA 131 R. R. Wroesch 1874-1879

Knight's Ferry

CA 132 Victor Dolling 1874-1884

Lakeport

CA 133 R. O. Smith 1878-1893

La Porte

Ca 134 J. H. Robertson 1874-1875

Livermore

CA 135a Schwerin & Schobel 1873-1874
135b Wendell Jordan, Livermore Brewery (1st St.) 1874-1900
135c Dennis F. Bernal 1900-1907

Lone Pine

CA 136a Lubken & Meyer 1874-c1877
136b John Lubken c1877-1891

CA 137a Munzinger & Dodge 1878-1880
137b Van Briesen & Co. 1880-1882
137c D. Williams & Co. 1882-1883
137d Philip Gehrig 1883-1884

Long Beach

CA 138 Schinner-Hoffman (Long Beach Blvd.) NP 1934-1934

Loomis

CA 139 K. Igarashi Brewery 1934-1934

Lorin

CA 140 Charles Willmott & Co. 1896-1898

Los Alamos

CA 141 Frederick Beck 1888-1891

Los Angeles (includes Arcadia, Hollywood, Marvilla Park & Vernon)

CA 142a Acme Brewing Co.(branch of San Francisco) (2080 E. 49th St.) 1935-1954
142b Rheingold Brewing Co. 1954-1957
142c Theo. Hamm Brewing Co. (branch of St. Paul, MN) 1958-1972
aka Theodore Hamm Co. (1969-1972)

CA 143 Ambassador Brewing Co. (1281-93 E. 6th St.) 1933-1940

CA 144a American Sake Brewing Co. (2444/46 E. 8th St.) 1934-1935
144b Asahi Wine Mfg. Co. 1935-1935

CA 145 Anheuser-Busch, Inc. (branch of St. Louis) (15800 Roscoe Blvd.) 1954-

CA 146 Arrowhead Brewing Co., Ltd. (2207 Derde Oak Dr.) NP 1934-1934

CA 147a Berlin Weiss Beer Brewing Co. (250 Ave. 39) 1907-1911
147b California Weiss Beer Brewing Co. 1911-1912

CA 148 Fred Binder (Banning St.) 1882-1884

CA 149a Catalina Brewing Co. (671 S. Rio St.) NP 1934-1934
149b Rio Brewing Company 1934-1937
149c Grace Bros. Brewery Ltd., 1937-1951
aka Southern Brewing Co. (1940s - 1951)

Los Angeles (cont.)

149d	Grace Bros Brewery dba Southern Brewing Co. aka North Bay Brewing Co. (1955-1956) aka Buffalo Brewing Co. (1955-1956)	1951-1956
149e	Southern Brewing Co., Bohemian Brewery Corp. of Cal.	1956-1958
CA 150	Central Sake Brewing Co. (1144 S. Central Ave.)	1948-1950
CA 151a	Consolidated Brewing Corp.	NP 1933-1933
151b	West Coast Breweries (749-750 E. 15th St.)	1933-1937
151c	The Rollison Brewery, Charles W. Rollison	1937-1939
CA 152a	John J. DiMarco (10706/08 Burbank Blvd., N. Hollywood)	1947-1947
152b	California Sake Brewery Co.	1947-1949
CA 153	Duquesne Brewing Co. (Albion & E. Main Sts.)	1908-1909
CA 154a	Louis Eckert Brewing Co. (664/668 Gibbons St., Vernon)	1934-1943
154b	Stewart McKee & Co.	1943-1948
154c	Eckert Brewing Co., aka Tivoli Brewing Co.	1948-1949
CA 155	Fritz & Diesing	1874-1875
CA 156	Hauser Brewing Co. (11th St. & Sante Fe Ave.)	NP 1934-1934
CA 157a	Ferd. Heim Brewing Co. (1834/56 N. Main St.)	1901-1903
157b	Mathie Brewing Co.	1903-1920
157c	Mathie Brewing Co.	1933-1933
157d	Balboa Brewing Co.	1933-1937
157e	Monarch Brewing Co.	1937-1941
CA 158a	Home Brewing Co. (202-204 S. Mednik Ave., Marvilla Park) aka Imperial Brewing Co. (1934)	1933-1934
158b	X. L. Brewing Co., Inc.	1934-1935
158c	Gutsch Brewing Co., Inc.	1935-1937
CA 159	Ernst Hubler	1893-1893
CA 160a	Koch Brewing Co., Inc. (7000 Romaine St., Hollywood)	1934-1934
160b	Hollywood Brewing Co.	1934-1935
CA 161	James Larquier	1898-1898
CA 162	Lauth & Stecker	1882-1884
CA 163	Joseph Leiber	1875-1875
CA 164a	Henry Lemmert	? -1874
164b	Schwartz & Lemmert	1874-c1877
164c	Louis Schwartz	c1877-1879
CA 165a	Los Angeles Brewing Co. (1920/2026 N. Main St.)	1897-1920
165b	Los Angeles Brewing Co., Inc., Eastside Brewery aka Mission Brewing Co. (1934-1953)	1933-1953
165c	Pabst Brewing Co. (branch of Milwaukee, WI.)	1953-1979
CA 166	Los Angeles Sake Brewing Co. (716 E. 5th St.)	1947-1949
CA 168a	D. Mahlstedt & Co., Philadelphia Brewery (440 Aliso St.)	1875-1882
168b	Maier & Zobelein	1882-1907
168c	Maier Brewing Co.	1907-1920
168d	Maier Brewing Co.(500 E. Commercial St.) aka A.B.C. Brewing Co. (1952-1957)	1920-1971
168e	General Brewing Co.	1971-1974
CA 169	Monterey Brewing Co., Inc. (859 E. 60th St.)	1934-1937
CA 170	New York Brewery	1878-1880
CA 171	Ed. A. Preuss & Co.	1874-1875
CA 172	Schmidt Brewing Co. (606 S. Hill St., Arcadia)	NP 1934-1934
CA 173	Sierra Brewing Co., Ltd. (620 Antonio Ave.)	NP 1934-1934
CA 174	U. Teshima (2222 Barry Ave.)	1934-1935
CA 175	Tischhauser-Braun Brewing Co.	1897-1897
CA 176	U.S. Brewery	1878-1880

Los Angeles (cont.)

CA 177	Wm. Westerhagen & Co.	c1890
CA 178a	Vernon Brewing Co. (5151 Sante Fe Ave., Vernon)	1933-1942
178b	Rainier Brewing Co. (branch of San Francisco)	1943-1949

Lower Lake

CA 179	Leighmann	c1890
CA 180a	Mather & Linck	1875-1879
180b	C. F. Linck	1879-1898
CA 181a	Philip Trap	1902- ?
181b	William Menke	? -1903

Lundy

CA 182a	Becker & Hayenah	1882-1884
182b	John Becker	1884-1888

Lynwood

CA 183	Lynwood Brewing Co., Inc. (10857 Drury Lane)	1934-1937

Mariposa

CA 184	John Weiler	1875-1879

Marysville

CA 185a	Gottlieb Lieber	1854-1880
185b	G. & L. Lieber	1880-1884
185c	Louis Sieber	1884-1897
185d	California Brewery, Michael Reissinger	1897-1920
185e	Capital Brewing Co.	NP 1934-1934

Mayfield (San Mateo)

CA 186a	Ducker Bros.	1874-c1877
186b	Ducker & Co.	c1877-1882
186c	Fritz Meyer	1882-1884
186d	Ducker & Co.	1884-1891
186e	Christopher Ducker, Mayfield Brewery	1891-1904
186f	C. Ducker & Co.	1904-1906
186g	Mayfield Brewing Co. (305 Lincoln Ave.)	1906-1920

Mendocino

CA 187a	M. Brinzing	1874-c1877
187b	J. C. Sarowski	c1877-1903

Merced

CA 188a	Heinerath & Gossner	1878-1880
188b	Joseph Gossner	1880-1882

Middletown (Cobb)

CA 189a	Munz & Scott	1874-1880
189b	Marcus Munz	1880-1897
CA 190	E. W. Schwartz Brewery (Lake County)	1914-1920

Modesto

CA 191a	Michael Braun	1875-1884
191b	Gottfried Baier	1884-1888
CA 192	Modesto Brewery, Inc. (708/10 Tenth St.)	1934-1938
CA 193a	Sorensen & Peterson	1878-1888
193b	R. A. Sorensen	1888-1904

Mokelumne Hill

CA 194a	Disbrow & Co.	1874-1880
194b	Disbrow & Newton	1880-1884
CA 195a	Himminghofer & Suessdorf, Mokelumne Hill Brewery	1874-1898
195b	Augusta L. Suessdorf	1898-1899
195c	Suessdorf & Layman	1899-1901
195d	Andrew J. Layman	1901-1904

Monitor

CA 196a	N. Piequet	1874-c1877
196b	John Scossa	c1877-1879

Monterey		
CA 197a	William Bergschicker, Monterey Brewery	1884-1906
197b	Monterey Brewery, Bergschicker & Carpenter	1906-1911
197c	Fred F. Straub	1911-1913
197d	Monterey Brewery, Bergschicker & Carpenter	1913-1915
CA 198	Theodore Beck	1884-1884
CA 199	Frank X. Hauser	1874-1875
Moore's Flat		
CA 200a	O. E. Pueschel	1882- ?
200b	Charles E. Pueschel	? -1884
Napa		
CA 201a	California Brewing Association	1907-1909
201b	Napa Valley Brewing Co.	1909-1911
CA 202	Jas. H. Goodman & Co.	c1910
CA 203	Lang & Co.	1880-1880
CA 204	Napa City Brewery	c1910
CA 205a	Philip Pfeiffer	1874-1879
205b	G. Barth	1879-1882
CA 206a	Gottfried Wagner (1st St.)	1880-1900
206b	Wm. Hoffmeier	1900-1920
National City		
CA 207	Great Western Brewing Co. - under construction 1962	NP 1962
Nevada City		
CA 208a	John Blasauf	1874-c1877
208b	Mrs. Mary Blasauf	c1877-1882
208c	Richards & Blasauf	1882-1884
CA 209a	L. W. Dreyfuss	1874-1880
209b	Geo. Gehrig	1880-1900
209c	Horan & Gehrig	1900-1901
209d	Geo. Gehrig Jr.	1901-1902
209e	Simon Hieronimus (see also North Bloomfield)	1902-1911
209f	Nevada Brewery, S. C. Hieronimus	1911-1920
CA 210	Casper Fogeli	1874-1893
CA 211	F. L. Harryhousen	1884-1884
CA 212	Paul Hoffman	1904-1904
CA 213a	Israel Hoskin	1882-1900
213b	Sierra Nevada Brewing Co.	1900-1903
213c	F. L. Fischer	1903-1904
CA 214	Jos. L. Rausch (Spring St.)	1910-1920
CA 215	Emil Weiss	1874-1891
North Bloomfield		
CA 216	Simon Hieronimus (see also Nevada City)	1878-1902
CA 217	Valentine Weiss	1874-1884
North Fork		
CA 218	John Meckel & Bro.	1874-1875
North San Juan		
Ca 219	A. Carion (see also Bodie)	1874-1875
CA 220a	G. W. Koch	1874-1884
220b	Ben R. Brown	1884-1904
Novato		
CA 221	Debakker Brewing Co. (70 Commercial Blvd.)	1979-1981

Oakland		
CA 222a	Bredhoff & Gieschen	1874-1875
222b	Chas. Bredhoff	1875-c1877
222c	Bredhoff & Co.	c1877-1882
222d	Bredhoff & Westermann	1882-1884
222e	Schmidt & Schoenfelder	1884-1888
222f	John Schoenfelder, Brooklyn Brewery	1888-1890
222g	Brooklyn Brewery (branch of San Francisco Breweries Ltd.) (corner E. 14th St. & 18th Ave.)	1890-1920
CA 223a	unknown	1856- ?
223b	Welscher & Westermann	1878-1880
223c	Welscher & Braun	1880-1884
223d	Westermann, Graber & Henke	1884-1885
223e	Westermann & Co. (corner 5th & Kirkham Sts.)	1885-1891
223f	Chas. Helmke & Co., Washington Brewery	1891-1899
223g	Helmke & Kaelin, Washington Brewery	1899-1901
223h	Washington Brewing and Malting Co.	1901-1910
223i	Washington Brewery Branch (Golden West Brewing Co.)	1910-1911
223j	Golden West Brewing Co. (7th & Kirkham Sts.)	1911-1920
223k	Golden West Brewing Co. (533 Kirkham St.)	1933-1950
223l	Goebel Brewing Co. of California (branch of Detroit, Mich.)	1950-1954
223m	Goebel Brewing Co.	1954-1955
223n	Pacific Brewing, Inc.	1958-1959
CA 224	Cardes & Co.	1882-1882
CA 225a	Independent Brewing Co. (487 Clifton St. at Claremont St.)	1911- ?
225b	Independent Brewing and Malting Co.	1915-1920
CA 226a	Kramm & Dieves (Telegraph Ave. & Durant St.)	1874-1890
226b	Oakland Brewery, Kramm & Warnholtz (San Francisco Breweries Ltd.)	1890-1895
CA 227a	Chas. H. Kramm, Anchor Brewery (49th St. & Shattuck Ave.)	1894-1899
227b	Anchor Brewery, Estate of Chas. H. Kramm	1899-1902
227c	Anchor Brewery, Augusta Simons	1902-1905
227d	Anchor Brewery, Jos. W. Kramm	1905-1910
227e	Anchor Brewery Branch (Golden West Brewing Co.)	1910-1911
CA 228a	Oakland Brewing and Malting Co. (26th, Linden & Chestnut Sts.)	1907-1920
228b	Wunder Brewing Co. (2119 Linden St.) NP	1934-1934
CA 229a	Ringgenberg & Newkorn	1882- ?
229b	Rudolph Ringgenberg aka Landregan & Ringgenberg (1896)	1888-1897
229c	Ringgenberg & Co.	1897-1898
CA 230	Samarkand Brewing Co. (Office: 843 Folsom St., San Francisco) NP	1934-1934
CA 231	San Jose Sake Brewery (5101 E. 15th St.)	1934-1935
CA 232	Swan Brewing Co. (Brown St.)	1902-1903
Oleta		
CA 233	Henry Schroder	1878-1891
Oroville		
CA 234	Chico Brewery	c1910
CA 235a	Schneider & Heintz	1874-c1877
235b	Wm. Schneider	c1877-1882
235c	Geo. Gerst	1882-1891
235d	Chas. A. Huelsman (Meyers St.)	1891-1897
Pajaro		
CA 236a	C. Werner	1874-c1877
236b	Dulla & Werner	c1877-1880
236c	Charles Dulla	1880-1882
236d	Charles Werner	1882-1884
Panannit		
CA 237	Munzinger, Lubkin & Meyer	1874-1875

Partswick (see Benton)

Petaluma

CA 238	Edward Fantz	1874-1875
CA 239a	Michelie & Co.	1874-c1877
239b	Michelie & Griess	c1877-1882
239c	George Griess	1882-1884
239d	Geo. J. Greiss, Petaluma United States Brewery	1884-1916
CA 240a	Geo. Robinson	1874-c1877
240b	Geo. Robinson & Co.	c1877-1880
240c	Geo. Robinson	1880-1884
240d	J. H. L. Gerckens	1884-1888

Pine Grove

CA 241	Martin Brinzing (see also Caspar)	1890-1897
CA 242a	C. D. S. Luss	1874-c1877
242b	C. D. F. Sass	c1877-1884

Placerville

CA 243a	Fred Collins	1874-1884
243b	Michael Popp	1884-1890
243c	Giebenhain Bros.	1890-1910
243d	Frank Giebenhain	1910-1920
CA 244a	Jacob Zeiss	1874-1884
244b	George Zeiss	1884-1888

Point Arenas

CA 245	John Schlachter	1874-1891

Point Richmond

CA 246	Solomon Lehmann	1905-1906

Port Costa

CA 247a	Frederick Braun & Co.	1896-1899
247b	Contra Costa Brewery, J.P. Casey	1899-1901
247c	Contra Costa Brewery	1901-1920

Porterville

CA 248	John Mann	1874-1875

Port Wine

CA 249	Michael Wolff	1874-1875

Quincy

CA 250a	Wm. Schlatter	1874-1897
250b	John C. Werner, Buckhorn Brewery	1897-1920

Red Bluff

CA 251a	W. F. Bofinger	1874-1880
251b	Bofinger & Krauss	1880-1882
251c	John Krauss	1882-1884
CA 252a	Red Bluff Brewing Co.	1937-1940
252b	United States Brewing Corp.	1942-1948

Redding (see Shasta)

Redwood City

CA 253	Diercks & Co.	1882-1884
CA 254	Eureka Brewery	1878-1880
CA 255	F. Fuerstahl & Co.	1896-1897
CA 256	Chas. N. W. Kreiss	1884-1884
CA 257	Michael Kreiss	1874-1893
CA 258a	(G.) Plumb & (J.) Offermann	1870-1873
258b	Offermann & Hadlee	1873-c1877
258c	C. Hadler	c1877-1884
258d	Claus Hadler & Co.	1884-1888
258e	Claus Hadler	1888-1891
258f	Albert Freyer (Main St.)	1891-1897
258g	Spoerl & Bitzer	1897-1899
258h	Max Spoerl, Eureka Brewery	1899-1900
258i	Redwood Brewing Co.	1900-1903

Redwood City (cont.)

CA 259	San Mateo Brewing Co.	1906-1906

Rosemead

CA 260a	Bailey Brewing Co., Inc. (2215 E. Valley Blvd.)	1934-1934
260b	Imperial Brewing Co.	1934-1937
260c	Old Tyme Brewing Corp.	1937-1937

Roseville

CA 261	Hohl & Co.	1882-1884

Sackett's Gulch

CA 262	John Wolf (see also Sears & Howland Flat)	1878-1893

Sacramento

CA 263a	Buffalo Brewing Co. (21st & 22nd Sts.)	1890-1897
263b	Buffalo Brewery (branch of Sacramento Brewing Co.)	1897-1920
263c	Buffalo Brewing Co.	1934-1942
263d	Buffalo Brewery, Inc. (owned by Grace Bros. Brewing Co., Santa Rosa) (1717 21st St.)	1942-1942 1945-1949
CA 264a	E. Gruhler & Co. (cor. 6th & K Sts.)	1874-c1877
264b	E. & C. Gruhler	c1877-1882
264c	Christ. Wahl	1882-1890
264d	Columbus Brewing Co.	1890-1891
CA 265	Capital Brewing Co. (Alhambra Blvd. & C St.)	1933-1934
CA 266a	Hilbert & Borchers	1859-1865
266b	Borchers & Schwartz, City Brewery	1865-1880
266c	W. F. Borchers, City Brewery	1880-1881
266d	Ruhstaller & Schuler, City Brewery (12th & H Sts.)	1881-1887
266e	Frank Ruhstaller, City Brewery	1887-1892
266f	Frank Ruhstaller (branch Sacramento Brewing Co.)	1892-1897
266g	Sacramento Brewing Co., City Brewery, Ruhstaller Brewery	1897-1920
CA 267a	Kerth & Nicolaus (Cor. 12th & I Sts.)	1874-1884
267b	Louis Nicolaus	1884-1891
267c	L. Nicolaus (branch Sacramento Brewing Co.)	1891-1893
CA 268a	L. Knauer & Son (9th & P Sts.)	1874-c1877
268b	F. C. Knauer	c1877-1891
268c	F. C. Knauer (branch Sacramento Brewing Co.)	1891-1897
CA 269a	George Ochs (20th & O Sts.)	1874-c1877
269b	M. Ochs	c1877-1880
269c	Jacob Gebert	1880-1891
CA 270	River City Brewing Co. (2508 LaGrande Blvd.)	1980-
CA 271	Joseph Schamberger	1897-1897
CA 272a	Philip Scheld & Co. (2800 M & 28th Sts.)	1874-c1877
272b	Philip Scheld	c1877-1891
CA 273	Standard Brewing Corp. (3030 Q St.)	1937-1937

Saint Helena

CA 274a	Geo. Daeweritz, St. Helena Brewery	1898-1913
274b	Daeweritz Brewery	1913-1914
274c	Saint Helena Brewery (D. F. Tillman)	1914-1920
274d	Saint Helena Brewery	NP 1934-1934
CA 275a	Fautz & Binder	1874-1875
275b	Edward Fautz	1875-1893
275c	Emil Waeckerling	1893-1897

Salinas

CA 276	Otto Diesing	1874-1875
CA 277a	Lurz & Hagner	1874-c1877
277b	Lurz & Menke	c1877-1891
277c	J. H. Menke (San Juan St.)	1891-1904
277d	Salinas Brewing Co.	1904-1920
277e	Salinas Brewing and Ice Co. (347 N. Main St.)	1934-1938
277f	Monterey Brewing Co.	1938-1942

San Andreas

CA 278a John Bloom 1874-1884
278b Joseph Bartholdus 1884-1884
278c Mary A. Bartholdus 1884-1888
278d Rudolph Rathgeb 1888-1898

San Bernardino

CA 279 John Anderson 1874-1884

CA 280a Arrowhead Brewing Co. 1910-1910
280b Thode Brewery 1910-1912

CA 281 Bear State Brewing Co. (347 N. Main St.) NP 1934-1934

CA 282 Henry Mauer 1895-1895

CA 283 San Bernardino Brewing Co. (514 East St.) NP 1934-1934

San Buena Ventura

CA 284 Fridolin Hartman 1875-1891

San Diego

CA 285a Aztec Brewing Co. (2301 Main St.) 1933-1948
285b Altes Brewing Co. (branch of Detroit, Mich.) 1949-1953

CA 286a Bay City Brewing Co. 1912-1912
286b Mission Brewing Co. (Hancock & Harasidy Sts. - affiliated with San Diego Consolidated Brewing Co.) 1912-1916

CA 287a Christian Dobler 1874-1882
287b Mrs. Martha Dobler 1882-1884

CA 288a Ritz Brewing Co. (808 Imperial Blvd.) 1933-1933
288b Balboa Brewing Co. 1933-1934

CA 289a San Diego Brewing Co. (32nd & Bay Front Sts.) 1895-1907
289b San Diego Consolidated Brewing Co. 1907-1920
289c San Diego Consolidated Brewing Co. NP 1934-1934
289d San Diego Brewing Co. (2002/02 S. 32nd St.) 1936-1942

CA 290a Philip Wedel 1874-1877
290b Otto Walter 1877-1879
290c John Diehl 1879-1888

San Francisco

CA 291a Acme Brewing Co. (1401 Sansome St. and Greenwich St.) 1907-1916
291b California Brewing Association, Acme Plant 1916-1920
291c Globe Brewing Co., Inc. 1933-1938

CA 292 James Albrecht (623 Braman St.) 1878-1879

CA 293 James Armstrong 1874-1875

CA 294 John Bauer (120 Fillmore St.) 1878-1884

CA 295a Bay Brewery, G. Lurmann (612-616 7th St.) 1868-1880
295b Milwaukee Brewery, Lurmann & Co. 1880-1891
295c Milwaukee Brewery, Lurmann & Co. (432/36 10th St.) 1891-1895
295d Milwaukee Brewery of San Francisco, Lurmann & Co. 1895-1902
295e Milwaukee Brewery of San Francisco 1902-1920
295f Milwaukee Brewery of San Francisco 1933-1935
295g San Francisco Brewing Corp. 1935-1956
295h Burgermeister Brewing Corp. 1956-1961
295i Burgermeister Brewing Co., a div. of Jos. Schlitz Brewing Co. (branch of Milwaukee) 1961-1964
295j Jos. Schlitz Brewing Co. 1964-1969
295l Burgermeister Brewing Co. (branch of Meisterbrau, Chicago) 1969-1971
295m Falstaff Brewing Corp. 1971-1975
295n Falstaff Brewing Corp. (affiliated with General Brewing Co.) 1975-1978

CA 296 Frederick Breckle (Point Lobos Rd. & Boice St.) 1896-1897

CA 297a George Breckle, Golden City Brewery (1431 Pacific St.) 1874-1884
297b Estate of George Breckle, Golden City Brewery 1884-1888
297c Fred. Breckle, Golden City Brewery 1888-1891
297d Co-operative Brewing Co. 1891-1893
297e F. A. Lux 1893-1895
297f Anchor Brewery, Baruth & Schinkel 1895-1906

San Francisco (cont.)

CA 298a	Broadway Brewery, Jacob Adams (637 Broadway)	1874-1891
298b	Broadway Brewery, Jacob Adams & Co.	1891-1895
298c	Broadway Brewery, Adams & Rohrer (3151/3185 19th St. at Treat)	1895-1898
298d	Broadway Brewery, Jacob Adams	1898-1905
298e	Broadway Brewing Co.	1905-1916
CA 299	Christian Brunig (6 Stevenson St.)	1890-1891
CA 300a	J. H. Burnell, Albion Brewery (9th Ave. & G St.)	1875-1881
300b	J. H. Burnell & Bro., Albion Brewery	1881-1884
300c	J. H. Burnell, Albion Brewery	1884-1893
300d	Estate of J. H. Burnell, Albion Brewery	1893-1895
300e	J. H. Burnell & Co., Albion Brewery	1895-1908
300f	Albion Ale and Porter Brewery	1908-1911
300g	Albion Ale and Porter Brewery (Innes Anve. & Griffin St.)	1911-1920
CA 301	Fred. Burns & Co.	1875-1875
CA 302a	Buss & Hensler (209-211 Treat Ave.)	1878-1879
302b	Hensler & Fredericks	1879-1884
302c	Fredericks & Wack	1884- ?
CA 303	California Brewing Co. (111/123 Douglas St. between 17th & 18th)	1892-1915
CA 304a	California Sake Brewery Co. (432 Clay St.)	1934-1935
304b	Nippon Sake Brewery Co., Inc.	1935-1937
CA 305a	Chicago Brewery, H. Ahrens & Co. (1420/1434 Pine St.)	1876-1882
305b	Chicago Brewing Co.	1882-1890
305c	Chicago Brewing Co. (San Francisco Breweries Ltd.)	1890-1893
305d	Chicago Brewery (San Francisco Breweries Ltd.)	1893-1906
CA 306	John Christ (25th St.)	1875-1884
CA 307	Continental Brewing Co. (927 Market St.)	1902-1902
CA 308a	Eagle Brewery, Carl A. Tornberg (2213-2229 Harrison St.)	1899-1901
308b	Eagle Brewing Co.	1901-1911
308c	Eagle Brewing Co. (5050 Mission St.)	1911-1920
308d	El Rey Brewing Co., Inc.	1933-1937
308e	Albion Brewing Co., Inc.	1937-1941
308f	Eagle Brewing Co., Inc.	1941-1942
CA 309	Empire Brewery, John Harold (416 Chestnut St.)	1876-1884
CA 310a	Fauss & Kleinclaus (19th & Mission Sts.)	1874-c1877
310b	Willows Brewery, O. Fauss & Co.	c1877-1890
310c	The Willows Brewery (San Francisco Breweries Ltd.)	1890-1906
CA 311a	Fortman & Graber (271 Tehama St.)	1875-c1877
311b	Fortmann & Co., Pacific Brewery	c1877-1890
311c	Pacific Brewery (San Francisco Breweries Ltd.)	1890-1891
CA 312a	Philip Frauenholz & Co. (Jacob Gundlach 1852-1856, Wm. Davidson 1856-1858)	1852-1858
312b	Philip Frauenholz, Bavarian Brewery, aka Scherhold & Frauenholz- 1874-1875 (Vallejo & Green Sts.)	1858-1884
312c	Frauenholz Estate, Bavarian Brewery, aka Anna Maria Frauenholz, Bavaria Brewery	1884-1886
312d	Frederick Schultz & Son, Bavaria Brewery (Vallejo St. and Montgomery Ave.)	1886-1896
312e	Louis Schultz, Bavaria Brewery (Greenwich & Scott Sts.)	1896-1897
312f	Bavaria Brewing Co.	1897-1898
312g	Wunder Brewing Co.	1898-1909
CA 314a	Wm. A. Frederick, Jackson Brewery (1428 Mission St.)	1874-1884
314b	Jackson Brewery, Wm. Frederick & Co.	1884-1897
314c	Jackson Brewing Co.	1897-1906
314d	Jackson Brewing Co. (351 11th St. at Folsom)	1906-1920
314e	Jackson Brewery (1849 Folsom St.)	NP 1934-1934

San Francisco (cont.)

CA 315a	General Brewing Corp. (2601 Newhall St.)	1934-1948
315b	Lucky Lager Brewing Co.	1948-1963
315c	General Brewing Corp.	1963-1969
315d	Lucky Breweries, Inc.	1969-1972
315e	General Brewing Co.	1972-1975
315f	General Brewing Co. (affiliated with Falstaff Brewing Co.)	1975-1978
CA 316	Golden Gate Brewery, S. Lehmann (Lynn St.)	1907-1908
CA 317a	Grogan & Anstell, Lafayette Brewery	1875-1882
317b	A. Anstell & Co., Lafayette Brewery	1882-1888
317c	Lafayette Brewery	1888-1891
317d	Baruth & Kroenke, Lafayette Brewery	1891-1895
317e	Henry C. Kroenke, Lafayette Brewery	1895-1899
CA 318a	F. Hildebrandt & Co., Enterprise Brewery (2015/2085 Folsom St.)	1873-1892
318b	(U.) Remensperger & (P.) Windeler, Enterprise Brewery	1892-1892
318c	Enterprise Brewing Co.	1892-1914
318d	Enterprise Brewing Co. (1 Enterprise St.)	1914-1920
CA 319a	Christian Hess, Union Brewery (326 Clementina St.)	1875-c1877
319b	Hess & Co., Union Brewery	c1877-1880
319c	Christian Hess, Union Brewery	1880-1884
319d	Thode & Weirich, Union Brewery	1884-1886
319e	Henning Thode, Union Brewery	1886-1896
319f	Union Brewing Co.	1896-1897
319g	Columbia Brewing Co.	1897-1905
CA 320a	August Hoelscher & Co., South San Francisco Brewery (Railroad Ave. & 14th St.)	1855-1879
320b	Hoelscher, Pillig & Co., South San Francisco Brewery	1879-1880
320c	A. Hoelscher & Co., South San Francisco Brewery	1880-1884
320d	Waldenmeier & Co., South San Francisco Brewery	1884-1890
320e	South San Francisco Brewery (San Francisco Breweries Ltd.)	1890-1899
CA 321	Max Hornier	1875-1875
CA 322	Japan Brewing Co. (207 Battery St.)	c1904
CA 323a	Thos. J. Kirby, Phoenix Brewery (528 Noe St.)	1877-1904
323b	Estate of T. J. Kirby, Phoenix Brewery	1904-1906
CA 324a	Albert Koster	1854- ?
324b	Union Brewing Co. (18th & Florida Sts.)	1896-1902
324c	Union Brewing and Malting Co.	1902-1916
CA 325	J. F. Lafrantz	1874-1875
CA 326	Lee & Perkins	1882-1882
CA 327	A. H. Lochbaum & Co. (521 15th St.)	1893-1893
CA 328	Lyon & Co.	1874-1875
CA 329a	Aiji Matsuo (489 Bryant St.)	1934-1937
329b	Matsuo Sake Brewing Co.	1937-1941
CA 330	Maehl & Weber (1008 Pierce St.)	1882-1882
CA 331a	Samuel Marks, Marks Brewery (735 Tehama St.)	1878-1879
331b	John C. Sauter	1879-1884
CA 332	Mrs. Lucy Marks (537 McAllister St.)	1882-1882
CA 333a	Mason & Co. (527 Chestnut St.)	1874-c1877
333b	Mason's Brewery, John Mason	c1877-1884
CA 334	Mehrer & Cruse aka Balthazar Mehrer	1874-1875
CA 335	Merrifield & Rosiner	1875-1875
CA 336	Chas. Metzler, Golden Gate Brewery (713 Greenwich St.)	1874-1884
CA 337a	Mission Brewery, Schnitzer & Haibel (Visitacion Ave. & San Bruno Rd.)	1897-1900
337b	Mission Brewing Co.	1900-1904

San Francisco (cont.)

CA 338a	National Brewery, John F. Glueck & Charles E. Hansen (Fulton & Webster Sts.)	1861-1877
338b	National Brewery, Mrs. Elizabeth Glueck & Charles E. Hansen	1877-1880
338c	National Brewery, Chas. E. Hansen	1880-1884
338d	National Brewing Co. (722 Fulton St. at Webster St.)	1884-1916
338e	California Brewing Association, National Plant	1916-1920
338f	Cereal Products Refining Corp. (762 Fulton & Webster Sts.)	1923-1936
338g	Acme Breweries dba California Brewing Association	1936-1943
338h	California Brewing Association	1943-1954
338i	California Brewing Co. (branch of Liebmann Breweries, Brooklyn, New York)	1954-1958
CA 339	New York Brewery, L. J. Kirby (Shotwell St.)	1878-1879
CA 340	J. Nibbe & Co.	1874-1875
CA 341a	Noethig & Funk (1839 Mission St.)	1875-c1877
341b	Noethig & Turk, Humboldt Brewery	c1877-1880
341c	Wm. Noethig, Humboldt Brewery	1880-1884
CA 342a	North Star Brewing Co. (3310/3314 Army St.)	1897-1920
342b	North Star Brewing, Inc. (188 Filbert St. at Sansome St.)	1934-1935
CA 343	M. Nunan, Hibernia Brewery (1225/1267 Howard St.)	1874-1920
CA 344a	Pacific Brewing and Malting Co. (675-77 Treat Ave.)	1916-1920
344b	Regal Products Co.	1933-1935
344c	Regal Amber Brewing Co.	1935-1950
344d	Regal Amber Brewing Co. (3250 20th St.)	1950-1954
344e	Regal Pale Brewing Co.	1954-1962
CA 345	Pacific Syphon Beer. Co.	1915-1915
CA 346a	Thomas F. Pfether, American Railroad Brewery (423/427 Valencia St. between 15th & 16th Sts.)	1858-1870
346b	Fred P. Schuster, American Railroad Brewery	1870-1899
346c	Schuster & Kroenke, American Railroad Brewery merged with 324	1899-1902
346d	Union Brewing and Malting Co.	1902-1904
CA 347a	Rainier Brewing Co. (1550 Bryant St.)	1916-1920
347b	Rainier Brewing Co. (aka Tacoma Brewing Co. c1939)	1933-1953
347c	Theo Hamm Brewing Co. (branch of St. Paul, Minn. aka Theodore Hamm Co., Buckhorn Brewing Co., Burgie Brewing Co. 1969-73)	1953-1973
347d	Brewer's Unlimited, Inc.	1973-1975
CA 348	Theo. N. Rantzau	1874-1875
CA 349a	Schneider & Wachter, Sierra Nevada Brewery (1524 Pacific St.)	1882- ?
349b	L. Wachter, Sierra Nevada Brewery	1890-1891
349c	Wilmott, Willoh & Behlmer, Sierra Nevada Brewery	1891-1893
349d	Henry Behlmer, Sierra Nevada Brewery	1893-1895
349e	Saint Louis Brewery, Henry Behlmer	1895-1898
349f	Saint Louis Brewery, Behlmer & Freyer	1898-1904
CA 350a	Schultz & Geitner (26th & Bryant Sts.)	1878-1882
350b	Henry Schultz, California Brewery	1882-1888
CA 351	A. Schuppert (Stockton & Jackson Sts.) (1st brewery in Cal.)	1849- ?
CA 352a	Joseph Schwartz, North Beach Brewery (Powell & 420/428 Chestnut Sts.)	1874-1904
352b	Jos. Schwartz Brewing Co. (North Beach Brewery)	1904-1914
352c	Dieter's Brewery, Conrad Otto Dieter	1914-1916
352d	Carl A. Tornberg	1916-1920
CA 353a	J. & S. Schweitzer (235 1st St.)	1874-c1877
353b	Schweitzer & Bro., Eureka Brewery	c1877-1880
353c	S. Schweitzer, Eureka Brewery	1880-1884
CA 354a	Katsuzo Shioji (342 5th St.)	1934-1934
354b	San Francisco Sake Brewery	1934-1935
CA 355	Wm. D. Smith (1776 Folsom St.)	1875-1882

San Francisco (cont.)

CA 356a	South San Francisco Stock Brewing Co. (2118 Powell St.)		1876-1880
356b	San Francisco Stock Brewery		1880-1897
356c	Saint Louis Brewing Co.		1897-1906
CA 357a	Claus Spreckles, Albany Brewery (71/75 Everett St.)		1858-1870
357b	Spreckles & Co., Albany Brewery		1870-c1877
357c	F. Hagemann & Co., Albany Brewery		c1877-1882
357d	Albany Brewing Co.		1882-1888
357e	Hagemann Brewing Co.		1888-1895
357f	Hagemann Brewing Co. (271 Natoma St.)		1895-1900
357g	Hagemann Brewing Co., Albany Brewery (405/415 8th St.)		1900-1920
CA 358a	J. J. Streuli, Swiss Brewery (414/416 Dupont St.)		1875-1880
358b	Streuli Bros.		1880-1884
358c	Arnold & Hensler		1884-1884
CA 359a	Stuber & Weikert (Geary & Baker Sts.)		1888-1897
359b	Jacob Stuber		1898-1899
359c	Jacob Stuber & Co.		1899-1903
359d	Red Lion Brewery, Chas. W. Lutz		1903-1907
359e	Red Lion Brewery, Alfred C. Goscinsky		1907-1908
359f	Red Lion Ale and Porter Brewing Co.		1908-1911
359g	August Lang Brewing Association		1911-1912
CA 360	Swan Brewing Co. (15th & Dolores Sts.)		1878-1880
CA 361	Tacoma Brewing Co. (364 Central St.)	NP	1934-1934
CA 362	Carl A. Tornberg, Consumers Brewery aka Consumer's Brewing and Bottling Co.		1905-1913
CA 363	G. A. Trenschel		1874-1875
CA 364a	Viking Brewing Co. of San Francisco (18th & Hampshire Sts.)		1895-1897
364b	Anchor-Shasta Brewing Co.		1907-1908
364c	Anchor Brewing Co.		1908-1920
364d	Anchor Brewing Co. (1610 Harrison St.)		1933-1934
364e	Anchor Brewing Co. (398 Kansas St. & 1th St.)		1934-1959
364f	Anchor Steam Beer aka Steam Beer Brewing Co. (541 8th St.)		1961-1977
364g	Anchor Brewing Co.		1977-1979
364h	Anchor Brewing Co. (1705 Mariposa St.)		1979-
CA 365a	Wahlmuth & Meyer (512 Grove St.)		1875-c1877
365b	Wahlmuth & Co., Hayes Valley Brewery		c1877-1882
365c	Henry Wahlmuth, Hayes Valley Brewery		1882-1884
365d	Bose & Jungens, Hayes Valley Brewery		1884-1903
CA 366a	Wanemacher & Kronenberg (Franklin & McAllister Sts.)		1875-1876
366b	F. Kronenberg & Co., United States Brewery		1876-1884
366c	United States Brewery, F. Kronenberg & Co. (311/323 Fulton St.)		1884-1890
366d	United States Brewing Co. (San Francisco Breweries Ltd.)		1890-1893
366e	United States Brewery (San Francisco Breweries Ltd.)		1893-1906
CA 367a	Weickert & Blondberg, Alabama Brewery (819 Alabama St.)		1898-1902
367b	P. Blondberg, Alabama Brewery		1902-1905
CA 368	Weyand & Kasche		1874-1875
CA 369a	John Wieland, Philadelphia Brewery (228/246 2nd St.)		1856-1887
369b	John Wieland Brewing Co.		1887-1890
369c	John Wieland Brewing Co. (San Francisco Breweries Ltd.)		1890-1893
369d	John Wieland Brewery (San Francisco Breweries Ltd.)		1893-1920
369e	Wieland's, Inc.		? -1932
369f	John Wieland Brewery	NP	1934-1934
CA 370a	Charles Wilmot (324 Green St.)		1856-1870
370b	Elliott, Wilmot & Bugbee		1870-c1877
370c	Wilmot Brewing Co.		c1877-1879
CA 371a	Claus Wreden, Washington Brewery (723/725 Lombard & Taylor St.)		1859-1870
371b	Claus Wreden & Co., Washington Brewery		1870-1899
371c	Claus Wreden Brewing Co., Washington Brewery		1899-1916

San Jose

CA 372a Philip Doerr, San Jose Brewery 1875-1880
372b A. W. Bode (4th & Williams Sts.) 1880-1884
372c Philip Doerr 1884-1888
372d Geoffroy Bros. 1892-1903
372e Garden City Brewing Co. 1903-1906
372f Garden City Brewing Co. (Bassett & San Pedro Sts.) 1906-1920
372g Garden City Brewing Co., aka Geoffroy Bros. & Co. (353 N. San Pedro & Bassett Sts.) NP 1934-1934

CA 373a (John) Joseph Hartmann, Eagle Brewery (Market & San Carlos St.) 1851-1879
373b Geo. Scherrer 1879-1897
373c (L. H.) Hartmann & (Mrs. George) Scherrer 1897-1906
373d Eagle Brewery, Inc., Hartmann & Scherrer 1906-1920

CA 374 K. Hayashi, Sake Brewery 1916-1916

CA 375 A. Herman 1878-1890

CA 376a (Gottfried) Krahenberg, Fredericksburg Brewery 1856-1872
376b Krahenberg & Co., Fredericksburg Brewery 1872-1877
376c Schramm & Schnabel, Fredericksburg Brewery 1877-1880
376d Schnabel & Denicke, Fredericksburg Brewery 1880-1889
376e Fredericksburg Brewing Co. (San Francisco Breweries Ltd.) 1889-1893
376f Fredericksburg Brewery (San Francisco Breweries Ltd) (Cinnabar & Alameda Sts.) 1893-1920
376g Pacific Brewing and Malting Co. 1933-1951
376h Wieland's Brewery Co. (1025 Cinnabar St.) 1951-1952
376i Falstaff Brewing Corp. (branch of St. Louis, Mo.) 1952-1963
376j Falstaff Brewing Corp. (branch of St. Louis, Mo.) (1025 W. Julian St.) 1963-1973

CA 377a Louis Krumb (377 2nd St.) 1874-c1877
377b Krumbs' Brewery c1877-1880
377c Louis Krumb 1880-1888

CA 378 St. Claire Brewing Corp. (1090 W. Salvador) 1933-1940

CA 379a San Jose Sake Brewery (291 Jackson St.) 1934-1935
379b The Nippon Sake Brewery, Inc. 1935-1940

CA 380a Sugita Bros. (569 E. Taylor St.) 1905-1906
380b J. Sugita 1906-1908
380c K. Iida, Rice Beer Brewery 1908-1909
380d K. Kawaguchi & Co., Rice Beer Brewery 1909-c1915

San Juan

CA 381a Bentler & Beck 1874-1884
381b Albert Bentler 1884-1888
381c Wisser & Sanders 1888-1890
381d Taixe & Abbe 1890-1892

San Leandro

CA 382a Rantzau & Thayson 1875-c1877
382b T. H. Rantzau, Columbia Brewery c1877-1880
382c A. Theysohn 1880-1891

San Luis Obispo

CA 383a Hauser & Williamson 1878-1879
383b E. Fink 1879-1882
383c Michael Wurch 1882-1884
383d Otto Tullman 1884-1888

CA 384a Julius Lindenmeyer 1874-1879
384b Weigand & Keller 1879-1909

San Mateo (see Mayfield)

San Rafael

CA 385a	Boyen & Co.	1871-c1877
385b	Bagen & Goerl	c1877-1884
385c	Fritz Goerl	1884-1898
385d	Fritz Goerl & Co.	1898-1899
385e	San Rafael Brewery, F. Goerl	1899-1900
385f	San Rafael Brewery, F. Goerl & Son.	1900-1905
385g	San Rafael Brewery, Chapman, Huckle & Fryman	1905-1907
385h	San Rafael Brewery, Inc. (7 Greenwood Ave.)	1907-1920
385i	San Rafael Beverage Co.	NP 1934-1934
CA 386	California Steam Beer Brewing Co. / Brewery (135 Paul Dr.)	1978-1981

Santa Ana

CA 387	Reuter & Goldkaefer	1884-1884

Santa Barbara

CA 388a	H. Mueller & Bro.	1875-1884
388b	H. Mueller & Co.	1884-1888
388c	Max Hoefle	1888-1893
388d	H. R. Muller	1893-1897
388e	City Brewing and Bottling Works	1897-1899
388f	Santa Barbara City Brewery	1899-1901

Santa Clara

CA 389a	Gottfried (Fred) Krahenberg	? -1870
389b	Herman Leibe, Santa Clara Brewery (Alviso & Benton Sts.)	1870-1880
389c	Geo. Lauck	1880-1897
389d	Geo. Lauck Brewing Co., Santa Clara Brewery	1897-1913
389e	Louis Klein, Santa Clara Brewery	1913-1920

Santa Cruz

CA 390a	Henry Bausch	1874-1884
390b	Peter & Walti	1884-1893
390c	Bausch & Co.	1893-1908
CA 391a	Carl Beck, Big Trees Brewery (Market St.)	1894-1906
391b	Santa Cruz Brewing Co.	1906-1920
CA 392a	Theodore Beck (merged with CA 393)	1882- ?
392b	Beck & Koehm	? - 1884
392c	Pepin & Keym	1884-1890
392d	Henry A. Keym	1890-1891
CA 393	Ferdinand Koehn (merged with CA 392)	1882-1882
CA 394	Matt & Puegg	1875-1875
CA 395	Mendenhall Brewing Ltd. (1560 Mansfield Rd.)	1980-

Santa Rosa

CA 396a	Willima Metzger, Santa Rosa Steam Brewery (118 2nd St.)	1872-1873
396b	Joast & Metzger	1873-c1877
396c	Metzger & Haltinner	c1877-1884
396d	Jacob Haltinner	1884-1895
396e	Estate of Jacob Haltinner	1895-1897
396f	Grace Bros. Brewing Co. (Joseph T. & Frank P.)	1897-1916
396g	Grace Bros. Brewery	1916-1920
396h	Grace Brothers Brewing Co., Inc. aka North Bay Brewing Co. (1946-1952)	1933-1952
396i	Grace Brothers Brewing Co.	1958-1967
396j	Grace Bros. Brewing Co. (branch of Maier Brewing Co., Los Angeles)	1967-1969
CA 397	Sonoma Valley Brewing Corp. (7 College Ave.)	NP 1934-1934

Scales Diggings

CA 398a	John Rutishauser	1874-1895
398b	Wm. Rugg	1895-1900

Sear's

CA 399	John Wolff (see also Sacketts Gulf & Holland Flat)	1875-1875

Sehachepi

CA 400 Bernhard Neff 1884-1884

Shasta (later Redding)

CA 401a Behrle & Litsch 1874-1884
401b V. G. Kegley 1884-1888

CA 402 Frank Bucher, Shasta Brewery 1900-1908

Sheep Ranch

CA 403 Philip Gehring c1890

CA 404a W. Hauselt 1882-1888
404b John W. A. Hauselt 1888-1897

Sierra City

CA 405a Fischer & Junkert 1882-1882
405b F. L. Fischer 1882-1891

CA 406a Casper Joos 1884-1893
406b Joos & Kieffer 1893-1897

Sisson

CA 407a Peter Mugler 1890-1901
407b Albert Mugler 1901-1915

Six Mile Canyon

CA 408a Louis Reich (office at Virginia City, Nevada) 1874-1893
408b John & Virginia Reick 1893-1895
408c John & Rosina Reick, aka J. R. Reick (1898) 1895-1905
408d Albert Schnitzer 1906-1920

Sonoma

CA 409 New Albion Brewing Co. (20330 8th Ave. E.) 1976-

CA 410a Sonoma Brewing Co. 1905-1913
410b Sonoma Ice and Brewing Co. (2nd St. E. & Turkey) 1913-1916

Sonora

CA 411 Louis Baccigalapi 1875-1880

CA 412 John Bauman 1866-1907

Stockton

CA 413a C. Boemer & Bro. (American St. & Weber Ave.) 1874-c1877
413b Boemer & Wirth c1877-1880
413c Yost & Wirth 1880-1884

CA 414a Bush & Denlacker (Park & Stanislaus Sts.) 1855-1858
414b Daniel Rothenbusch 1858-1891
414c D. Rothenbusch & Son. 1891-1893
414d El Dorado Brewing Co. (Park & American Sts.) 1893-1920
414e El Dorado Brewing Co. (617 N. Stanislaus St.) 1933-1955

CA 415a Elizabeth Neistrath 1875-1879
415b Mrs. E. Elbreder 1879-1884

Surprise Valley

CA 416 Fulcher & Weilmunster 1874-1875

Susanville

CA 417 C. A. Bofinger 1893-1893

CA 418 Joachim Kroeger, Susanville Brewery 1906-1920

CA 419a J. W. Smith 1875-1882
419b Frank Runge 1882-1890
419c T. C. Hamann 1890-1893

Sutter Creek

CA 420a L. Rabolt 1874-1891
420b John Raddatz 1891-1911
420c Sutter Creek Brewery, Mosey & Williams 1911-1920

Sutterville

CA 421a Theilen & Futterer 1874-1875
421b N. Theilen 1875-1884

Table Rock

CA 422	John Wolff	1890-1900

Ten Mile River

CA 423	Franz & Bader	1878-1879

Tracy

CA 424a	Tracy Brewing Co.	1893-1896
424b	Tracy Brewery, Henry Schmidt	1896-1907
424c	Tracy Brewing Co.	1907-1910

Truckee

CA 425	Grazer & Stoll	1874-1888
CA 426a	Kielhofer & Woods	1896-1897
426b	Louis Kielhofer	1897-1898
426c	Truckee Brewing Co.	1898-1899
CA 427	Paul Menk	1874-1884
CA 428a	Charles Thomas, Eureka Brewery	1899-1904
428b	Eureka Brewery	1904-1911

Ukiah

CA 429a	Ukiah Brewing Co.	1907-1908
429b	Ukiah Brewing and Ice Co.	1908-1920
CA 430	S. Wurtenburg	1874-1884

Vallecito

CA 431a	Henry Tuchen, Vallecito Brewery	1874-1880
431b	H. H. Tuchen	1880-1890
431c	Mrs. Elizabeth Tuchen	1890-1895
431d	H. H. Tuchen	1895-1900

Vallejo

CA 432a	Fred Deininger, Vallejo Brewery	1870-1891
432b	Jacob Deininger, Vallejo Brewery	1891-1892
432c	Deininger & Rechenmacher, Vallejo Brewery	1892-1892
432d	Jacob Deininger, Vallejo Brewery	1892-1909
432e	Vallejo Brewing and Bottling Co.	1909-1915
CA 433	E. McGettigan	1874-1884
CA 434a	P. & J. Smith	1878-1884
434b	Minahan & Plagemann	1884-1898
434c	Daniel Minahan	1898-1904
CA 435a	Widenmann & Rothenburg	1874-1891
435b	Charles Widenmann (514 Marin St.)	1891-1904
435c	Solano Brewing Co. (Chas. Widenmann, President)	1904-1920
435d	Vallejo Brewing Co.	1933-1934

Van Nuys

CA 436	Jos. Schlitz Brewing Co. (branch of Milwaukee, Wis.) (7521 Woodman Ave. at Schlitz Ave.)	1954-

Visalia

CA 437a	Michael Mooney, Mooney's Brewery	1875-1884
437b	Joseph Hammer	1884-1888
437c	Andrew Hammer	1888-1891
CA 438a	J. B. O'Connor	1875-c1877
438b	Empire Brewery	c1877-1880
438c	M. Esteven	1880-1884

Volcano

CA 439a	Geo. Griesbach	1874-1880
439b	Frank T. Zehender	1880-1884
CA 440	David Schuler	1882-1882
CA 441	Peter Seible	1874-1875

Watsonville

CA 442a	Nicholas Burton	1890-1899
442b	Albert Graf	1899-1904

Watsonville (cont.)

CA 443a	Dullea & Mahoney	1874-c1877
443b	C. Kuhlitz	c1877-1882
443c	Charles Dullea	1882-1884
CA 444a	Christian Palmtag	1874-1880
444b	Mrs. Fredericka Palmtag	1880-1884
444c	F. Palmtag	1884-1896
444d	Palmtag & Heyer	1896-1901
444e	Pajaro Brewery, Mrs. C. Palmtag	1901-1911
444f	Pajaro Brewery, Wm. F. Palmtag	1911-1915
444g	Pajaro Brewery (Acme Distributing Co.)	1915-1920
444h	Ikuta Hashimoto (110 Union St.)	1936-1938
444i	Hiroshi Hashimoto	1938-1940
CA 445	Tamasaki & Murata, Sake Brewery	1907-1907

Weareville

CA 446	H. Harvey	1875-1875

Weaverville

CA 447a	Frederick Walter	1852- ?
447b	John Meckel	1879-1888
447c	Meckel Bros., Pacific Brewery	1888-1920

West Berkeley (see Berkeley)

West Point

CA 448	Bader & Frommer	1882-1882

Willows

CA 449	Willows Brewery	1880-1884

Woodland

CA 450a	Schuerley & Miller	1874-1880
450b	Joseph Germershausen	1880-1882
450c	Germershausen & Kuhn	1882-1888
450d	Geo. Goeppert & Co.	1888-1920
450e	Yolo Brewing Co.	NP 1934-1934
CA 451a	Geo. L. Wirth	1874-1882
451b	Estate of Geo. L. Wirth	1882-1884

Yreka

CA 452a	Gottfried Gambell, Pacific Brewery (Oregon St.)	1858-1870
452b	Charles Junker, Pacific Brewery	1870-1900
452c	Jos. Steinacher, Pacific Brewery	1900-1902
452d	Jos. Steinacher & Son, Pacific Brewery	1902-1908
452e	Jos. Steinacher, Pacific Brewery	1908-1911
CA 453a	Charles Peters	c1860-1884
453b	Peters & Co.	1884-1888

Yuba City

CA 454a	Hartman & Klempp	?- 1874
454b	Fred. Klempp	1875-1901
454c	Adolph Meyn, Yuba City Brewery	1901-1903

COLORADO

Alamosa

CO 1a	Alamosa Brewing Co.	1896-1898
1b	Alamosa Brewery	1898-1904
CO 2	William Bingle Brewery	c1879-1882

Aspen

CO 3a	Good & Mack	1885-1887
3b	Jacob Mack	1887-1891
3c	John Good	1891-1898
3d	Christ. Sanders	1898-1903

Black Hawk

CO 4	Conrad B. Elliott, Chase Gulch Brewery	c1862-1865

Black Hawk (cont.)

CO	5a	Samuel Haubrich, Chicago Brewery (Gregory St.)	1873-1884
	5b	F. Haubrich	1884-1885
CO	6	Kirby & Barnes Brewery	1877-1878

Boulder City (see note under CO 94)

CO	7	W. G. Cook Brewery (Rear Pearl St. between 12th & 13th)	1870-1872
CO	8a	Keller & Zuelfehofer	1875-1876
	8b	Weisenhorn & Voegtle (Arapaho between 9th & 10th Sts.)	1876-1884
	8c	Frank Weisenhorn	1884-1890
	8d	Fischer & Bercher	1890-1891
	8e	Boulder City Brewing Co. (Arapahoe Ave.)	1891-1897
	8f	Crystal Springs Brewing and Ice Co. (954 Arapaho St.)	1897-1911

Caribou

CO	9	Hugh Goodfellow	1875-1876

Central City

CO	10a	Wm. Lehmkuhl	1866-1891
	10b	Lehmkuhl Bros.	1891-1895
	10c	John H. Lehmkuhl	1895-1897
CO	11a	Jacob Mack & Co.	1862-1867
	11b	Jacob Mack	1867-1881
	11c	Mathias Mack	1882-1885
	11d	Jacob Mack	1885-1886
	11e	Mathias Mack	1897-1890
	11f	Martin Mack	1890-1897
	11g	Chas. & John Mack	1897-1898
CO	12	J. W. Pitts	1867-1876
CO	13a	Richards & Wickett	1878-1879
	13b	Wm. Richards	1879-1880
CO	14	Chr. Stamm (or Staum)	1878-1879

Colorado City

CO	15	Fred Behrle	1874-1875
CO	16	William Bingle	1879-1879
CO	17	Hill & Drake	1883-1884

Colorado Springs

CO	18a	F. Holderer	1875- ?
	18b	El Paso County Brewing Co., aka El Paso Brewing Company and Stockbridge & Fisher Brewing Co.	1878-1879
	18c	El Paso County Brewing Co., aka Stockbridge & Elwell-1879-1883, Mrs. Annie Stockbridge- 1884, El Paso Brewing Co. 1880-1881	1879-1884
CO	19	F. Haman	1881-1881

Creede

CO	20	Creede Brewery	1891-1892

Columbia (see Telluride)

Del Norte

CO	21a	Wm. Bingel	1873-1881
	21b	Wm. Bingel & Co.	1881-1882
	21c	Wm. Bingel	1882-1891
	21d	(Erich von) Buddencrock & Bingel	1891-1893
	21e	Del Norte Brewing Co.	1893-1897
	21f	San Luis Brewing Co.	1897-1899
	21g	San Luis Brewery	1899-1913
CO	22	Henry Weiss	1874-1880

Denver

CO	23a	B & Y Sales Co. (2845 Walnut St.)	1945-1947
	23b	Colorado Sake Brewing Co.	1947-1949

Denver (cont.)

CO 24 Geo. Bendleburg 1878-1879

CO 25 Berlin Brewing Co. 1900-1900

CO 26 Block & Rush 1875-1875

CO 27 Brown & Foster 1875-1875

CO 28 Colorado Brewing Co. 1876-1879

CO 29a Consumers Brewing Co., Mile High Brewery (2701 Wazee & 36th) 1909-1910
29b Capitol Brewing Co. 1910-1915

CO 30a Alex Davidson (Wazee & H -later 17th Sts.) 1870-1872
30b Barber & Castle 1872-1875

CO 31a Denver Ale Brewing Co. (6th & Cheyenne Sts.) 1869-1871
31b Denver Brewing Co., aka Denver Ale Brewing Co. 1871-1874
31c Denver Brewing Co. (9th & Lawrence Sts.) 1874-1895
aka Bates & Johnson (1874-1876)

CO 32 Denver Brewing Co., Inc. (1611 Platte St.) 1945-1950

CO 33 Denver Weiss Beer Brewery, Richard Boercherdt 1880-1880

CO 34 Eagle Brewery (1855 Arapahoe St.) 1891-1891

CO 35a Hugh Goodfellow (Wynkoop & Wewatta) 1872-1874
35b Hugh Goodfellow (213 Holladay St.) 1874-1875
35c Hugh Goodfellow (383 Champa St.) 1875-1884

CO 36a Joseph Gotto (713 Holiday St.) 1874-1876
36b George Pendlebury 1877-1878

CO 37 Gregory, Clough & Co. 1875-1875

CO 38 Charles Heinze 1880-1880

CO 39 Hoyt & Bagley 1874-1874

CO 40 Lion Brewing Co. (Larimer & 8th Sts.), aka Lion Brewing and
Bottling Association 1879-1884

CO 41a Max Melsheimer, aka Max Melsheimer & Co. (223 Larimer St.) 1879-1888
41b Milwaukee Brewery Co., Max Melsheimer (1336-1348 10th St.
at 223-227 Larimer St.) 1888-1895
41c Milwaukee Brewery Co., Max Melsheimer & John Mack 1895-1900
41d John Good, Tivoli Brewery (10th & Larimer Sts.) 1900-1901
41e Tivoli-Union Brewing Co. (aka John Good Brewery 1901-1904) 1901-1915
41f The Western Products Co. 1932-1933
41g The Tivoli Union Co. 1933-1953
41h The Tivoli Brewing Co. (aka Mountain Brewing Co. 1958-1964) 1953-1969

CO 42a One Horse Brewery, Louis Hessner & Henry Graff (Blake & H Sts.) 1864-1866
42b One Horse Brewery, Louis Hessner 1866-1868
42c One Horse Brewery, Gilbride 1868-1872
42d One Horse Brewery, Leonhard Summer 1872-1874

CO 43 Lyman Parkhurst & Bro. (Larimer & H - later 17th) 1870-1872

CO 44a Rocky Mountain Brewery, (F. Z.) Solomon & (Chas.) Tascher & Co.
(7th St. & Platte River, Highlands)(First Colorado Brewery) c1859-1860
44b Rocky Mountain Brewery, Solomon & Co. 1860-1861
44c Rocky Mountain Brewery, (Jim) Endlich & (John) Good 1861-1865
44d Rocky Mountain Brewery, John Good 1865-1870
44e Rocky Mountain Brewery, Philip Zang 1870-1880
44f Philip Zang & Co. (7th & Water Sts.) 1880-1888
44g Philip Zang Brewing Co. 1888-1915
44h Philip Zang Brewing Co. (7th & Water Sts.) NP 1934-1934

CO 45a City Brewery, Chas. Schriber & Co. (2431-2437 17th St.) 1871-1872
45b City Brewery, George F. Oppenlander aka Oppenlander & Co.
(1874-1875) 1872-1889
45c Union Brewery, George Oppenlander 1889-1892
45d Union Brewing Co. (merged with CO 41d) 1892-1901
45e Tivoli-Union Brewing Co., Union Brewery 1901-1904

Denver (cont.)

CO	46	Moritz Sigl, Colorado Brewery (1336-1348 10th St.)	1864-1875
CO	47a	Lorenz Stumpf	1874-1875
	47b	Aull & Stumpf	1875-1876
CO	48	Leonhard Summer (Blake & H. St.)	1869-1871
CO	49	C. F. Tesch (1849-1851 Lawrence St.)	1887-1887
CO	50a	Western Brewery, John Dostal (12th & Raritan)	1890-1892
	50b	Neef Brothers (1201 S. 5th St. & W. 12th Ave.)	1892-1896
	50c	Neef Brothers Brewing Co.	1896-1915
CO	51	William Wisch (1826 Stout St.)	1893-1893

Durango

CO	52a	Durango Brewing Co. (1320 2nd St.)	1887-1893
	52b	Smelter City Brewing Association	1893-1901
	52c	Durango Beer and Ice Co.	1901-1906
CO	53	Jos. Strasser	1882-1882

Empire

CO	54	Paul Lindstrom	1862-1880
CO	55	Zurwelme & Stumpf	1874-1875

Evans

CO	56	Fritz Niemeyer	1878-1878

Fairplay

CO	57	Adam Lechsmger	1880-1881
CO	57a	Wm. Molitor	1875-c1877
	57b	Leonard Summer	c1877-1891

Florence

CO	58	(O. P.) Townsend Brewing Co.	1887-1888

Fort Garland

CO	59	Jos. Hoffman	1874-1875

Fort Logan

CO	60	Malt Pop Co.	1893-1893

Georgetown

CO	61	Fred Aldinger	1878-1883
CO	62	Saunders & Reichart	1874-1875
CO	63	Albert Selak	1868-1875
CO	64a	John Wehr	1874-1875
	64b	John Summer & Bro. (Louis)	1875-1880
	64c	John Summer	1880-1884

Gilfin County

CO	65	Samuel Hanbrick	1874-1875
CO	66	Jacob Mack	1874-1875

Glenwood Springs

CO	67	Home Brewing Co.	1913-1915

Golden

CO	68	Otto Boche	1874-1875
CO	69a	Dorman & Woltmann, aka Eagle Brewing Co.	1889-1896
	69b	Colorado Brewing Co.	1896-1897
CO	70a	Golden City Brewery, Rudolph Koenig (Ford & Water Sts.)	1868-1870
	70b	Golden City Brewery, Christian Koenig & Luke Bron	1870-1871
	70c	Golden City Brewery, Luke Bron	1871-1874
CO	71	Herman Koenemann	c1891

Golden (cont.)

CO	72a	(Jacob) Schueler & (Adolph) Coors, Golden Brewery	1873-1880
	72b	Adolph Coors, Golden Brewery aka Adolph Coors Co., Golden Brewery (1909-1913)	1880-1913
	72c	Adolph Coors Brewing and Malting Co., Golden Brewery	1913-1915
	72d	Adolph Coors Co.	1933-

Grand Junction

CO	73	Grand Junction Brewing Co.	1905-1908

Granite

CO	74a	John Gaster & Co.	1874-1875
	74b	Mesch & Gerter	1875-1879
	74c	Gerster & Jesse	1879-1880

Gunnison

CO	75a	Fischer & Co., aka Fischer & Riley, Gunnison Brewery	1881-1882
	75b	James Riley & Co.	1882-1883
CO	76	M. Fritz	1888-1890
CO	77	Gunnison Brewing Co.	1882-1882
CO	78	Yule & Fritz	1882-1883

Howardsville

CO	79	Chas. Fischer	1880-1884

Idaho Springs

CO	80a	O. L. Barnes	1869-1875
	80b	Henry W. Gaw	1875-1877
CO	81	Fred Ullrich	1870-1881

Lake City

CO	82	Fisher & Co., aka Fischer, Lawyer & Co.	c1877-1879
CO	83	Charles Hirt	1878-1886
CO	84	Herman Mayer	1897-1897

Las Animas

CO	85a	William Vollert	1874-1875
	85b	Vollert & Fisher	1875-1875

Leadville

CO	86	Colorado Columbine Brewing Co. (103 Harrison Ave.)	1906-1915
CO	87	C. Feuerstein (10 Mile Rd. at Arkansas River)	1879-1880
CO	88a	Henry W. Gaw	1878-1879
	88b	(Mrs.) Elizabeth J. Gaw	1879-1895
CO	89	Gill & Martin (112 Chestnut St.)	1881-1881
CO	90a	John Good	? -1888
	90b	Mack & Bausch	1888-1891
CO	91	Gower's Brewery	1890-1893
CO	92a	Leadville Brewery, Koch & Lichter	1879-1880
	92b	Leadville Brewery, Gottlieb Mack Jr. & Jacob Bausch	1880-1884
	92c	Leadville Brewery, Vincent Albus	1885-1891
CO	93	Stockbridge & Elwell (106 E. 2nd St.)	1881-1881

Longmont

CO	94	Boulder Brewing Co. (15555 N. 83rd St.) Note: Building new brewery in Boulder for completion 1984	1980-

Malta

CO	95	Leo B. Hossle	1891-1891
CO	96a	John Ruedi	1879-1879
	96b	Ruedi & Martin	1879-1880
	96c	Gill & Martin	1880-1882
CO	97	V. H. Sponagel	1879-1880

Manitou

CO	98	F. Herman	1882-1882

Montrose

CO 99	Anton Hagely	1883-1884

Nevadaville

CO 100	Andy Bitzenhofer	1869-1871
CO 101	E. Wall	1880-1880

Ouray

CO 102a	D. Geiger	1879-1882
102b	Ouray Brewing Co. (2nd St. & 7th Ave.)	1882-1891
102c	Moelle Brewing Co. & Bottling Works	1891-1893
CO 103a	Conrad Miller Brewing Co.	1890-1891
103b	Jacob Keilhofer	1891-1893
CO 104	Ouray Beer & Ice Co.	1894-1900
CO 105	I. N. Simpson & Co.	1890-1890

Pool

CO 106	Saddle Mountain Brewing Co.	1904-1905

Pueblo

CO 107	Aull & Stumpf	1874-1875
CO 108	Wm. Bingle & Co.	1874-1875
CO 109a	Carl Roth & Co., aka Pueblo Brewing Co. (1891-1893)	1889-1893
109b	Louis Frisch Breing Co. (225 Sante Fe)	1893-1895
109c	Bohemian Brewing Co., aka Frisch Brewing Co.	1895-1898
109d	(Martin) Walter Brewing Co. (500 N. Sante Fe Ave.)	1898-1916
109e	The Walter Brewing Co. (Hickory & LaCrosse Sts.) aka Hoffman Brewing Co.(1951-1956) aka Metz Brewing Co.(1963-1966) aka Kol Brewing Co., Gold Label Brewing Co., Tivoli Brewing Co.	1933-1971
109f	General Brewing Co., dba Walter Brewing Co. (branch of San Francisco, Cal.)	1971-1975
CO 110	Otto Tubbs	1880-1881
CO 111a	Henry Weiss (1st & Sante Fe)	1868-1873
111b	Elias Merz	1875-1884
111c	John Bauer	1884-1888

Rosita

CO 112a	O. P. Townsend	1874-1881
112b	Rosita Brewing Co.	1882-1890

Saguache

CO 113	William Bingle	1885-1886

Salida

CO 114	Munn & Munn	1893-1893

San Bernardo

CO 115	Guenther & Campbell	1893-1893

Sedgewick

CO 116	D. T. Jameson	1882-1882
CO 117	Klear, Curtheth & Co.	1882-1882

Silver Cliff

CO 118	Seidensticker & Co.	1880-1882

Silver Plume

CO 119	Otto Boche	1869-1888

Silverton

CO 120a	Silverton Brewing Co., aka Mullholland & Peckham (1881-1882)	1880-1882
120b	Lutz & Reiber (or Reiver)	1882-1884
120c	Chas. Fischer	1884-1902
120d	William Schulz	1902-1907
120e	Faden & Oppenlander	1907-1910
120f	Chas. Faden	1910-1916

Telluride (previously Columbia)

CO 121a	Hippler & Langendorf, City Brewery	1888-1891
121b	Charles Langendorf	1891-1892
121c	Muller & Walter	1895-1898
121d	Conrad Muller, City Brewery	1898-1903
121e	Wichmann & Lagershausen, City Brewery	1903-1915
121f	Clemens Wichmann, City Brewery	1915-1916
121g	Wichman Brewing & Mfg. Co.	? -1934
121h	Telluride Brewery	1934-1935
121i	Telluride Brewing Co.	1935-1937
121j	Telluride Brewery	1937-1938
CO 122	H. Pamperein	1882-1885

Trinidad

CO 123	Vincent Albus (Main & Bridge Sts.)	1869-1875
CO 123a	Kerchner & Mair (or Kirchmer & Maier)	1874-1875
123b	Martin Kirchmer	1875-1876
CO 124	Peter Kler (foot of Bridge St.)	1870-1873
CO 125	Frank Meyer & Co. (foot of Church St.)	1873-1874
CO 126	Pells Brewing and Ice Co. (Arapahoe St.)	1910-1915
CO 127a	Henry Schneider (Convent & Plum Sts.)	1873-1889
127b	Ph. Schneider & Co.	1889-1892
127c	Ph. Schneider Brewing Co.	1892-1915
127d	Ph. Schneider Brewing Co. (204-243 N. Convent St.)	1933-1941
127e	The Walter Brewing Co.	1944-1948
127f	Colorado Brewing Corp.	1951-1952
127g	Schneider Brewery, Inc.	1953-1955
127h	Bohemian Brewery Corp. of Colorado	1955-1957
CO 128	J. Schroeder	1877-1877

Westcliff

CO 129a	Carl & Daemgen, Wet Mountain Brewery	1893-1897
129b	Carl & Hallauer, Wet Mountain Brewery	1897-1898
129c	Fuchs & Wissler, Wet Mountain Brewery	1898-1900
129d	Daemgen & Wissler	1900-1903
129e	Wissler & Becker, Wet Mountain Brewery	1903-1905

CONNECTICUT

Ansonia

CT 1a	Michael O'Brien	1888-1890
1b	James Ryan	1890-1891

Bridgeport

CT 2a	John Benz, City Brewery (76 N. Washington Ave.)	1856-1871
2b	Albert Wintter, City Brewery	1871-1882
2c	Albert Wintter & Co.	1882-1890
2d	Albert Wintter & Co. (Connecticut Breweries Co.)	1890-1897
2e	Connecticut Breweries Co., Wintter Brewery (270 Housatonic & 182 N. Washington Aves.)	1897-1920
2f	The Connecticut Breweries (Housatonic Ave.) NP	1934-1934
2g	The Bridgeport Brewing Co. (1575/1591 Railroad Ave.)	1934-1941
CT 3a	Alonzo D. Davis (18/22 Island Brook Ave.)	1894-1904
3b	Luippold & Walz Brewing Co.	1904-1906
CT 4	Eckart Bros. (202 North Ave.)	1865-1920
CT 5	Christian Knoedler	1878-1882
CT 6a	Louis Kutscher (729 State St.)	1874-1880
6b	F. Kutscher	1880-1884
6c	Louis Kutscher	1884-1888
6d	Kutscher Bros.	1888-1895
6e	Wm. F. Kutscher	1895-1903
CT 7	Geo. B. Montague	1874-1875

Bridgeport (cont.)

CT	8a	(Frederick) Seiler & (John) Mentzel	1852-1854
	8b	John Mentzel	1854-1858
	8c	(John) Conrad & Mentzel	1858-1867
	8d	Frederick Klaus	1867-1883
	8e	Bridgeport Brewing Co.	1883-1888
	8f	Chas. H. Hartmann (127 Hamilton St.)	1888-1897
	8g	Hartmann Brewing Co.	1897-1898
	8h	Hartmann Brewing Co. (224 Hallam St.)	1898-1911
	8i	Home Brewing Co.	1911-1920
	8j	The Burroughs Brewing Co., aka Algonquin Brewing Co.	1934-1934
	8k	The Barnum Brewing Co. (224 Hallam St.)	1934-1936
CT	9	John G. Simon	1874-1875
CT	10a	Joseph Noway	? -1865
	10b	John M. Speidel	1865-c1877
	10c	C. Loehr	c1877-1879
	10d	C. Stoehr	1879-1882
	10e	Estate of Christ. Stoehr	1882-1884
CT	11	Henry Speiser	1882-1884

Bristol

CT	12	Oskar Anderson	1896-1897

Danbury

CT	13	Jean Hornig & Co. (Main & Elm Sts.)	1893-1893
CT	14	Louis Neiss & Co.	1874-1875

Derby

CT	15a	Derby and Ansonia Brewing Co.	1898-1903
	15b	Derby and Ansonia Brewery	1903-1920
	15c	The Old England Brewing Co., Inc. (324/32 Derby Ave.)	1933-1941

Enfield (see Thompsonville)

Hartford

CT	16	Hartford Union Brewery	c1890
CT	17a	Charles Herold (52/62 Bellevue St.)	1865-1879
	17b	Herold Capitol Brewing Co.	1879-1896
	17c	Columbia Brewing Co.	1896-1900
	17d	Aetna Brewing Co. (52/62 Bellevue St.& 537/49 Windsor St.)	1900-1920
	17e	Aetna Brewing Co. (130 Bellevue St.)	1933-1939
	17f	Dover Brewing Co. (130 Bellevue St. & 529 Windsor St.)	1939-1947
CT	18a	Paul Link (110 Albany Ave.)	1874-1886
	18b	Suss & Sichler	1886-1888
	18c	Lena Sichler	1888-1891
CT	19a	New England Brewing Co. (503 Windsor St.)	1897-1920
	19b	The New England Brewing Co. (503/529 Windsor St.)	1936-1943
	19c	New England Brewing Co. (branch of Largay Brewing Co, Waterbury)	1944-1947
CT	20a	J. B. Russell Jr.	1874-1875
	20b	George Sichler	1875-1880
CT	21a	Shannon & McCann (232/242 Sheldon & Front Sts.)	1874-1084
	21b	Michael McCann	1884-1888
	21c	Hargrave Brothers	1888-1890
	21d	Hartford Brewing Co.	1890-1891
	21e	Chute	1891-1892
	21f	(Edgar L.) Ropkins & Young	1892-1893
	21g	Ropkins & Co.	1893-1920
CT	22a	George Sichler & Co. (315/327 Park St.)	1879-1886
	22b	Hubert Fischer	1886-1894
	22c	Hubert Fischer Brewery	1894-1920
	22d	Hubert Fischer Brewery	NP 1934-1934

Meriden

CT	23	The Meriden Brewery	1875-1875
CT	24a	Meriden Brewing Co. (137/157 S. Colony St.)	1887-1890
	24b	Meriden Brewing Co. (Connecticut Breweries Co.)	1890-1904
	24c	Meriden Brewery (Connecticut Breweries Co.)	1904-1920
	24d	The Connecticut Valley Brewing Corp.	1933-1935
CT	25a	Charles Schabel (Piedmont Ave.)	1892- ?
	25b	Albert Schabel	? -1904
	25c	Charles Schabel, Eagle Brewery	1904-1910
	25d	John J. Quinn	1910-1911
	25e	Luby & Walsh	1911-1912

Middletown

CT	26a	Jas. Bartholomew	? -1875
	26b	Frank Miller	1875-c1877
	26c	Hopke & Wilkins Jr.	c1877-1879

Naugatuck

CT	27	August Weber	1891-1902

New Britain

CT	28a	Health Beer Brewing Co. (Belden St.)	1903-1904
	28b	Cremo Brewing Co.	1905-1920
	28c	Cremo Brewing Co., Inc.	1933-1934
	28d	The Cremo Brewing Co., Inc., aka Diplomat Brewing Co.	1934-1955
CT	29	Joseph Kossuth	1875-1875

New Haven (includes Orange & West Haven)

CT	30	Benjamin & William Bakewell	1798-1804
CT	31a	Geo. A. Basserman (21 Rock Road.)	1869-1884
	31b	Basserman Rock Brewing Co. (74 Church St.)	1884-1891
CT	32	Sergeant Baulston	1638- ?
CT	33a	Ph. Fresenius (488 Congress Ave.)	1852-1884
	33b	Ph. Fresenius' Sons	1884-1906
	33c	Ph. Fresenius' Sons (800/820 Congress Ave.)	1906-1920
	33d	The Hull Brewing Co., aka Diamond Spring Brewing Co., Park Row Brewing Co.	1933-1977
CT	34a	Wm. Hull & Son (14/22 Whiting St.)	1870-1914
	34b	Hull Brewing Co.	1914-1920
	34c	Elm City Brewing Co., Inc.	1933-1936
CT	35	A. Kutscher	1880-1884
CT	36a	Frederick Kutscher (Broadway)	1867-1879
	36b	Mrs. Frederick Kutscher	1879-1882
CT	37a	Charles Nicklas (Oak St.)	1859-1883
	37b	Joseph Weibel (322 Oak St.)	1883-1894
	37c	Weibel's Brewery, Theresa F. H. Weibel	1894-1898
	37d	Weibel Brewing Co. (C. R. Nicklas, President)	1898-1920
	37e	The Weibel Brewing Co.	1933-1936
CT	38a	J. J. Phelps & Co. (25 Chapel St. at East St.)	1862-1873
	38b	The Burton Brewing Co.	1873-c1879
	38c	E. H. Gaylord	1882- ?
	38d	New Haven Brewing Co. (391 Chapel St.)	? -1890
	38e	Elm City Brewing Co.	1890-1891
	38f	Geo. Ringler & Co.	1891-1895
CT	39a	Rex Brewing Co. (368 Davenport Ave.)	1933-1934
	39b	The Staehly Brewing Co. (376 Davenport Ave.)	1937-1937
CT	40	Frederick Rupthuer	1875-1875
CT	41a	Schleippmann & Spittler (Ferry, Pearl & River Sts.)	1882-1885
	41b	Quinnipiac Brewing Co.	1885-1902
	41c	Yale Brewing Co.	1902-1920
	41d	New Haven Brewing Co. (branch of Chr. Feigenspan, Newark, N.J., 26 River St.)	NP 1934-1934

New Haven (cont.)

CT	42a	John Schultheis (14 Barclay)	1875-1876
	42b	John Schultheis (21 Auburn St.)	1877-1878
CT	43	John Solly (State St.)	1862-1865
CT	44	Sprenger & Co. (Orange)	1882-1884
CT	45	Frederick Stark (Orange)	1874-1875
CT	46	Taylor Bros. (20 Oak St.)	1882-1884
CT	47a	Thalheimer (59 Church)	1870-1871
	47b	Thalheimer (Grand Ave.)	1871-1872
	47c	Thalheimer (Temple St.)	1872-1872
CT	48	Topping & Hall	1874-1875
CT	49a	Henry Weidemann (Campbell Ave., Allington)	1884-1888
	49b	Henry Weidemann Brewing Co.	1888-1895
	49c	M. Weidemann & Co.	1895-1897
	49d	Henry Weidemann Co.	1897-1901
	49e	Lion Brewery Corp. (Orange)	1901-1904
	49f	Weidemann Brewing Co.	1904-1920
	49g	Weidemann Brewery (West Haven)	? -1933
	49h	The Wehle Brewing Co. (1093 Campbell Ave., West Haven)	1933-1943
CT	50a	Richard Zastrow (aka Zastrow Bros.)	1878-1884
	50b	Paul Wolter	1884-1890

New London

CT	51a	New London Brewing Co., Yale Brewery	1899-1903
	51b	American Brewing Co. (Winthrop & Mill Sts.)	1903-1904
	51c	Pequod Brewing Co.	1904-1910
CT	52	Yale Brewing Co.	NP 1934-1934

Norwich

CT	53	George Whiteley	1874-1875
CT	54	Connecticut Brewing Co. (99 Chestnut St.)	NP 1934-1934

Preston

CT	55	Sophia E. Marx	1874-1874

Rockville

CT	56	Jacob Kirchner	1880-1884
CT	57	Erhardt Link	1874-1880

South Meriden (see Meriden)

Thompsonville

CT	58a	Mathewson & Grey	1860-1872
	58b	John Mathewson	1872-1879
	58c	Estate of John Mathewson	1879-1885
	58d	Mathewson Bros. & Co.	1885-1898
	58e	Connecticut Valley Brewing Co.	1898-1915

Torrington

CT	59a	Thos. J. Stone	1907-1908
	59b	Thos. J Stone Brewing Co.	1908-1915

Union City

CT	60a	August Weber	1893-1909
	60b	Louise S. Weber	1909-1915
	60c	Weber's Weiss Beer Brewery	1915-1920

Waterbury

CT	61a	Eagle Brewing Co. (Riverside Park)	1904-1920
	61b	Eagle Brewing Co. (100 Eagle St.)	1934-1934
	61c	The Waterbury Brewing Co.	1934-1938
	61d	The Eastern Brewing Corp.	1938-1939

Waterbury (cont.)

CT	62a	Frederick Nuhn (1090 Bank St.)	1874-c1877
	62b	Hellmann & Kipp	c1877-1889
	62c	Hellmann & Martin	1889-1892
	62d	Mrs. Martin Hellmann	1892-1895
	62e	Hellmann Brewing Co.	1895-1920
	62f	Largay Brewing Co., Inc.	1933-1948

DELAWARE

Wilmington

DE	1a	Nebecker & Son	? -1870
	1b	A. Bickta & Co.	1870-1876
	1c	Stoeckle & Bickta (5th & Adams Sts.)	1876-1876
	1d	Jos. Stoeckle	1876-1893
	1e	Johanna S. Stoeckle	1893-1902
	1f	Joseph Stoeckle Brewing Co., Diamond State Brewery	1902-1920
	1g	Diamond State Brewery, Inc.	1936-1954
DE	2a	Hartmann & Fehrenbach (4th & French Sts.)	1865-1885
	2b	Hartmann & Fehrenbach Brewing Co. (Lovering Ave. & Scott St.)	1885-1920
DE	3a	John G. Schaefer (17th & Union Sts.)	1880-1891
	3b	Mary E. Schaefer	1891-1908
	3c	Edward Krause	1908-1910
	3d	Stanley L. Sobocinski	1910-1915
DE	4a	Carl Specht (5th & Dupont Sts.)	1878-1879
	4b	Specht & Spahn	1879-1884
	4c	Excelsior Brewing Co.	1884-1888
	4d	John A. Lengel, Bavarian Brewery	1888-1898
	4e	Bavarian Brewing Co.	1898-1920
	4f	Bavarian Luxburger Brewing Co. (506 N. Dupont St.)	1934-1935
	4g	Delmarva Brewing Co.	1938-1944
	4h	Krueger Brewery Co., Delaware (branch of Newark, N.J.)	1944-1951
DE	5	Joseph Stoeckle (rear of 223/25 King St.)	1859-1870
DE	6a	Wilmington Brewing Co. (French St.)	1901-1902
	6b	Henry Blouth	1902-1910
	6c	Wilmington Brewing Co.	1910-1915

Wooddale

DE	7a	C. F. Wurster	1882-1884
	7b	Biedermann & Weidmair	1884-1886
	7c	Geo. J. Biedermann	1886-1905
	7d	Spring Hill Brewery Co.	1905-1911

DISTRICT OF COLUMBIA

Washington, D.C.

DC	1a	John Albert (25th & F & G Sts.)	c1870-1895
	1b	Albert Brewing Co.	1895-1898
	1c	Abner & Drury	1898-1901
	1d	Abner-Drury Brewing Co.	1901-1917
	1e	Abner-Drury Brewing Co. (2424 G. St., N.W.)	1933-1937
	1f	Washington Brewery, Inc.	1937-1938
DC	2	John G. Cook (45 N St.)	1874-1880
DC	3a	Simon Deutz (38/40 Green St.)	1874-c1877
	3b	Catherine Deutz	c1877-1884
DC	4	Chris. Dickson (719 4½ St.)	1874-1884
DC	5	Julius Eisenbeiss (8th & L Sts., S.E.)	1890-1893
DC	6a	Geo. Juenemann (400 E St., N.E.)	c1850-1884
	6b	Mrs. Geo. Juenemann	1884-1886
	6c	Albert Carry	1886-1889
	6d	Washington Brewery Co.	1889-1917

Washington, D.C. (cont.)

DC	7	Kenilworth Brewing Co.	NP 1934-1934
DC	8a	George Kernwein (124 N St., N.W.)	1874-1884
	8b	George Kernwein's Son	1884-1900
	8c	Anton Danhakl	1904-1910
DC	9	J. Kozel	1874-1875
DC	10a	Geo. Kozel (43 N St.)	1880-1881
	10b	L. Ewald	1881-1882
DC	11	W. N. H. Maack & Co.	1874-1875
DC	12	John Nass	1874-1875
DC	13	Dewitt M. Ogden	1874-1875
DC	14a	Richter (13th, 14th, D & E Sts.)	1850-1870
	14b	Alexander Adt	1870-1873
	14c	F. J. Adt	1873-1882
	14d	John E. Guethler	1882-1884
	14e	Eisenmenger & Rabe	1884-1886
	14f	Henry Rabe	1886-1890
	14g	National Capital Brewing Co. (1337/53 D St., S.E.)	1890-1917
DC	15a	Jacob Roth (318 1st St., N.W.)	1874-1884
	15b	Henry G. Roemheldt	1884-1888
DC	16	Charles H. Sawyer	1874-1875
DC	17a	George Schnell	1864-1872
	17b	(Christian) Heurich & (Paul) Ritter	1872-1873
	17c	Christian Heurich (1229 20th St.)	1873-1890
	17d	Ch. Heurich Brewing Co.	1890-1896
	17e	Chr. Heurich Brewing Co. (25th, 26th, O & Water Sts.)	1896-1917
	17f	Chr. Heurich Brewing Co.	1933-1956
DC	18	L. Schoeplen	1875-1875
DC	19	Aug. Vogelberger	1882-1882
DC	20	Jos. Widman (624 11th St., N.E.)	1890-1891
DC	21	Wm. Zanner (526 4½ St., S.W.)	1874-1879

FLORIDA

Auburndale

FL	1a	Duncan Brewing Co., Inc., aka Fischer Brewing Co. (202 Gandy Road)	1973-1980
	1b	Duncan Brewing Co. (owned by G. Heileman, LaCrosse, WI)	1980-1980
	1c	Florida Brewing Co. (owned by G. Heileman, LaCrosse, Wi)	1980-

Hialeah

FL	2a	Hialeah Brewing Co. (699 Palm Ave.)	1934-1934
	2b	Miami Brewing Co.	1934-1937
	2c	Gold Top Brewing Co.	1937-1938
FL	3	Old Munich Brewing Co. (16500 N.W. 52nd Ave.)	1972-1974

Jacksonville

FL	4	Anheuser-Busch, Inc. (111 Busch Drive, branch of St. Louis)	1969-
FL	5a	Jacksonville Brewing Co. (Myrtle Ave. & 16th St.)	1913-1919
	5b	Jax Ice & Cold Storage Co. (1429-1701 W. 16th St. at Barnett)	1933-1940
	5c	Jax Brewing Co.	1940-1956

Miami

FL	6	Flamingo Brewing Co. (1199 N.W. 22nd St.)	1933-1935
FL	7	Miami Brewing Co. (720 Olympia Building)	NP 1934-1934
FL	8a	Wagner Brewing Co. (637 N.W. 13th St.)	1934-1938
	8b	American Brewing Co. (branch of New Orleans, LA)	1938-1958
	8c	Anheuser-Busch, Inc. (branch of St. Louis, MO)	1958-1961
	8d	The National Brewing Co., Southern Div. aka Florida Brewing Co.(1962-1964); Orbit Brewing Co. (1964-1967) Regal Brewing Co.; S.C. Brewing Co.	1961-1975

Orlando

FL 9a Atlantic Co. (1171 N. Orange Ave., branch of Atlanta, GA) 1937-1954
9b Marlin Brewing Corp. 1954-1956
9c The National Brewing Co. (branch of Baltimore, MD) 1956-1961

Pensacola

FL 10a The Spearman Brewing Co. (1600 S. Barrances Ave. at I St.) 1935-1964
aka Embassy Club Brewing Co. (1958-1963)
aka Quality Brewing Co. (1958-1962)
aka Regent Brewing Co. (1958-1964)
aka Sewanee Brewing Co. (1957-1964)
owned by Metropolis Brewing Co., Trenton, NJ (1960-1964)

Tampa

FL 11a Anheuser-Busch, Inc. (3000 Temple Terrace Hwy., Br. St. Louis) 1959-1968
11b Anheuser-Busch, Inc. (3000 August A. Busch Jr.) 1968-

FL 12 De Soto Brewing Co. (1202 N. Howard Ave.) 1934-1935

FL 13 Fette Brewing Co. (1013 32nd Ave.) NP 1934-1934

FL 14a Florida Brewing Co. (5th Ave. & 13th St.) 1897-1919
14b Tampa Florida Brewery, Inc. 1933-1961

FL 15a Jos. Schlitz Brewing Co. (11111 30th St., branch of Milwaukee) 1959-1982
15b Jos. Schlitz Brewing Co. (branch of Stroh Brewery, Detroit, MI) 1982-1983
15c Pabst Brewing Co. (branch of Miwaukee, WI) 1983-

FL 16a Southern Brewing Co. (Zack & Pierce Sts.) 1934-1957
16b International Breweries, Inc.(branch of Detroit, MI) 1957-1963
aka Kol Brewing Co. (1960-1962)
aka Stolz Brewing Co. (1960-1962)

West Palm Beach

FL 17a The Sunshine Brewery (419 2nd St.) 1934-1937
17b Gould Brewing Co. 1937-1939
17c Tona Brewing Co. 1939-1939

GEORGIA

Albany

GA 1 Miller Brewing Co. (405 Cordele Rd., branch of Milwaukee) 1980-

Atlanta

GA 2 Carling Brewing Co., Inc. (3599 Browns Mill Road, S.W.) 1958-1973

GA 3a Fechter, Kreis & Co. 1868-c1877
3b Atlanta City Brewing Co. c1877-1890
3c Atlanta Brewing and Ice Co. (Courtland & Harris Sts.) 1890-1918
3d Atlanta Ice and Bottling Co.(247 Courtland St.) 1933-1935
3e Atlanta Ice and Coal Co. 1935-1937
3f Atlantic Co. 1937-1955

GA 4 Southern States Breweries, Inc. (Healey Bldg.) NP 1934-1934

Augusta

GA 5 Augusta Brewing Co. (Fenwick, Nelson & 13th Sts.) 1888-1918

Brunswick

GA 6 Brunswick Brewing and Ice Co. 1891-1893

Columbus

GA 7 Dixie Brewery and Ice Factory (Front & 6th Sts.) 1903-1908

Macon

GA 8a Macon Brewing Co. (Bay & Hammond Sts.) 1891-c1899
8b Acme Brewing Co. c1899-1918

GA 9 Russell & Peter 1874-1875

Pabst (formerly Perry)

GA 10a Pabst Brewing Co. (Georgia Hwy. 247, branch of Milwaukee, WI) 1971-1983
10b G. Heileman Brewing Co. (branch of La Crosse, WI) 1983-

Savannah

GA 11 Consumers Brewing Co. 1913-1913

GA 12 Savannah Brewing Co. (Indian St.) 1889-1918

GA 13 Savannah Beverage Co. (Ray & Jefferson Sts.) NP 1934-1934

Savannah (cont.)

GA	14a	Herman Winter	1901-1902
	14b	Herman Winter Brewing Co. (leased by GA 10)	1902-1902
GA	15a	P. H. Wolters Brewing Co. (73/83 Bay St.)	1893- ?
	15b	Georgia Brewing Association (201/17 Bay St., leased by GA 10)	1897-1902

HAWAII

Hilo

HI	1	Hilo Brewery, Ltd. (Omao & Kaumana Rds.)	1937-1942
HI	2a	Nichibel Shuzo Kabushiki Kaisha, Ltd. (1965 Kamehameha Ave.)	1935-1942
	2b	Kokusui Co., Ltd.	1948-1957

Honolulu (includes Aiea)

HI	3a	Hawaii Brewing Corp., Ltd. (721 Kapiolani Blvd. at Cooke St.)	1934-1962
	3b	Hawaii Brewing Co.	1962-1964
	3c	Jos. Schlitz Brewing Co. (98-051 Kamehameha Hwy., branch of Milwaukee, WI)	1964-1976
	3d	Hawaii Brewing Co. (branch of Jos. Schlitz Brewing Co.)	1976-1979
HI	4	Hawaii Seisko Kwaisha Ltd.	1915-1915
HI	5a	Honolulu Brewing Co. (535 Queen St.)	1898-1900
	5b	Honolulu Brewing and Malting Co., Ltd.	1900-1920
	5c	American Brewing Co., Ltd.	1933-1962
HI	6	Honolulu Sake Brewery and Ice Co., Ltd. (2106/66 Booth Road)	1934-1942
HI	7a	Kanda Shokai, Ltd. (539 Cooke St.)	1934-1935
	7b	Fuji Sake Brewing Co., Ltd.	1935-1942
	7c	Fuji Sake Brewing Co., Ltd.	1948-1965

Kula, Maui

HI	8	Maui Sake Brewery Co., Ltd.	1935-1942

IDAHO

Albion

ID	1	John Botzett	1888-1893

Atlanta

ID	2a	Wilmer & Motlow	1878-1879
	2b	Nelson Davis	1879-1890
ID	3	J. H. Casey	1886-1887
ID	4	Guidorff	1886-1887

Bellevue

ID	5	Farnsworth & Co.	1882-1882
ID	6	Pioneer Bottling and Soda Co. (Main St. between Pine & Oak)	1888-1892
ID	7a	Anton Spielmann	1882-1887
	7b	H. Spielman & Co., aka Henry Spielman, Idaho Brewery (Main St. between Cottonwood & Cedar)	1887-1890
	7c	Aug. A. Fischer	1890-1891
ID	8	Wm. Pearson	1889-1890

Boise

ID	9	(A. B.) Ford & Co., Central Brewery and Bakery	? -1865
ID	10	L. P. Grunbaum	1910-1911
ID	11a	John Krall (Main St.)	1867-1875
	11b	John Brodbeck (Main St. between 6th and 7th)	1875-1900
	11c	Idaho Brewing Co. (N. 6th between West Main and Idaho Sts.)	1900-1905
	11d	Idaho Brewing and Malting Co.	1905-1916
	11e	Bohemian Breweries, Inc. (601 Idaho St. & 111 N. 6th St.)	1933-1956
	11f	Bohemian Breweries, a Div. of Atlantic Brewing Co., Chicago	1957-1960
ID	12	John Lemp, Boise Brewery (Main St. between 3rd and 4th) aka Felix Collins, Boise Brewery (1865) aka Adolph & Lemp (1866)	1863-1907
ID	13	Jas. H. Misselt	1874-1875

Boise (cont.)

ID	14	Peter Stuzenacker	1866-1866

Bonanza City

ID	15a	John Hepburn & Co.	1878-1879
	15b	John Hepburn	1879-1884
	15c	Michael Spahn	1884-1892

Buena Vista Bar

ID	16	Jacob Gans, City Brewery	? -1865

Centerville

ID	17	M. Zapp & J. Hevenin (Clark St.)	? -1865

Challis

ID	18	Ferdinand Klug & George Fuchs	c1886
ID	19	Frederick Albiez	1879-1890

Clayton

ID	20a	Koeniger Bros. & Co.	1889-1891
	20b	Koeninger Bros.	1891-1895
	20c	Kopp & Koeninger	1895-1898
	20d	Koeninger & Fantino	1898-1900
	20e	Herman Koeninger	1900-1903

Couer d'Alene

ID	21a	Coeur d'Alene Brewing Co.	1908-1909
	21b	Panhandle Brewing Co. (Government Way btwn. Mariner & Fort Sts)	1912-1915
ID	22	Henry Reiniger (branch of Rathdrum, ID)	1889-1890

Cottonwood

ID	23a	Schober & Hendricks	1896-1897
	23b	Schober & Peterson, Cottonwood Brewery (Main St. nr. Broadway)	1897-1903
	23c	Joseph Schober, St. Albert's Brewery (Front, Lewiston, and Coram Sts.)	1903-1910

Council Valley

ID	24	George Winckler	1886-1887

Custer City

ID	25	F. Gindroff	1880-1885
ID	26	Mosler & Co.	1880-1882

Delta

ID	27	Delta Brewing Co.	1886-1887

Franklin

ID	28	Sylvester Werneth	1884-1890

Genesee

ID	29a	(Joseph) Geiger & (Matt) Kambich (Tamarack St. between Chestnut & Pine.)	1889-1902
	29b	Joseph Geiger, Genesee Brewery	1902-1904
	29c	Paul Reck, Genesee Brewery	1904-1909

Gibsonville

ID	30a	Hogl, Demont & Kern	1895-1898
	30b	Demont & Kern	1898-1906

Grangeville

ID	31a	Grangeville Brewing and Malting Co. (Main & C St.)	1900-1905
	31b	Grangeville Brewing Co., Ltd.	1905-1910
	31c	Idaho Brewery, aka Leonhard Becker-Jurgen	1910-1915
ID	32a	William Von Berge, Eagle Brewery (Main & Mill Sts.) aka Von Berge & Schultz (1889-1890)	1887-1906
	32b	William Von Berge & Co.	1906-1908
	32c	William Von Berge	1908-1909

Hailey

ID	33	Harvey & Eggleston	1910-1910
ID	34a	Geo. W. Kohlepp	1882-1887
	34b	August Exner	1887-1905
	34c	Hailey Brewery, Jos. Chod	1905-1908

Hailey (cont.)

ID 35 John Nisch 1910-1910

ID 36a Mrs. Agnes E. Norberg 1882-1884
36b John Hendel 1884-1893
36c Charles Sonnleitner 1893-1904

ID 37 Star Brewery, Maria Utsch (River & Bullion) 1888-1915

Hump

ID 38 Hump Brewing Co. 1905-1905

Idaho City

ID 39 Fisher & Meydenbaur 1866- ?

ID 40a Nicholas Haug 1874-1884
40b Mary Haug 1884-1890
40c John Rost 1890-1891
40d Rost & Rood 1891-1897
aka John Rost (1896)

ID 41 C. Hoeflein, Idaho Brewery ? -1865

ID 42 Ignas Huber, Pacific Brewery ? -1865

ID 43 Knauer & Co., Miner's Brewery & Bakery (Main St. between Wall and Smith) ? -1865

ID 44 A. W. Spielman, Idaho Brewery (Main St.) ? -1865

Idaho Falls (formerly Eagle Rock)

ID 45a Heath & Keefer 1882- ?
aka W. W. Kiefer (1886-1887)
45b Kurt Brewing Co. ? -1895
45c Blum & Co. 1895-1896
45d Eagle Rock Brewing Co., Hyram Edwards & Co. (Capital Ave. near Hill St.) 1896-1901
45e Kremer & Edwards 1901-1905
45f Bannock Brewing Co. 1905-1906
45g Milwaukee Weiss Beer Co. 1906-1907

ID 46 Idaho Falls Brewing Co., Ltd. 1904-1910

ID 47a Pilsener Brewing Co. of Idaho Falls (Oneida & Short Sts.) 1935-1937
47b Idaho Falls Brewing Co. 1937-1939

ID 48a Wm. H. Thomas ? -1888
48b Eagle Rock Brewery 1888-1890
48c M. Weimann 1890-1893

Jordan Creek

ID 49 Frank & Gundorf 1878-1879

Juliaette

ID 50a Juliaetta Brewing Co., aka Deetsen & Wartemburg (Water & 3rd) 1891-1895
50b Milwaukee Brewing Co., aka Diamond Howarth 1895-1895
50c Jacob Howarth, aka Juliaetta Brewing Co. 1895-1897
50d Wisser & McGlynn, Milwaukee Brewery 1897-1900
50e Albert Wisser, Milwaukee Brewery 1900-1903
50f Christ. Berner, Milwaukee Brewery 1903-1904

ID 51 Meingassner Brewery c1883

Kellogg

ID 52 George Bittner 1908-1908

Ketchum

ID 53a Mitchell & Brugg 1882-1884
53b Thomas Mitchell, Leadville Brewery 1884-1889
53c Robert Koeniger, aka Koniger Bros. 1889-1902

ID 54 Schaeffer & Hildebrandt 1882-1882

Lewiston

ID 55a Brown & (Godfrey) Gambel 1862-1863
55b Gambel & (Ernest) Weisgerber 1863-1869
55c Weisgerber Bros. (Ernest, John & Christ) 1869-1871
55d Weisgerber Bros. (John & Christ) 1871-1889
55e Christ. Weisgerber 1889-1912

Lewiston (cont.)

ID 56 California Brewery ? -1865

ID 57 George Seiser & Constantine Baker 1864-1864

ID 58 Ernest Weisgerber 1862-1863

Malad City

ID 59a A. W. Vanderwood 1884-1886
59b W. G. Jenkins 1886-1887
59c Blume & Dill 1887-1890

McAuley

ID 60 John Hermann 1889-1890

Moscow

ID 61a Fries & Co., aka Otto Fries & Joseph Niederstadt (Main & A St.) 1882-1886
61b Joseph Niederstadt 1886-1890
61c Niederstadt & Schober 1890-1891
61d Koehler & Hermann, aka F. L. Koehler (c1895) 1895-1898
61e Frank Louis Koehler 1898-1901
61f Herman Nicola 1901-1902
61g Ferdinand Frankl, Moscow Brewery 1902-1908

ID 62 Idaho Brewing Co., aka Neiderstadt, Schober & Koehler (Main & C Sts.) 1891-1894

Mountain Home (see South Mountain)

Murray

ID 63 Carl Mallon 1884-1889

ID 64 Carl Mueller 1888-1888

ID 65a Rammelmeyer & Seelig 1886-1887
65b Ernest Rammelmeyer 1887-1888

Nampa

ID 66a Crescent Brewing Co. (D St. at Railroad) 1906-1916
66b Overland Beverage Co., Inc. (15 9th Ave. at Railroad Ave.) 1934-1950

Oxford

ID 67 F. K. Walker 1886-1887

Payette

ID 68a Stirm & Miller 1888-1889
68b Stirm & Hoffman 1889-1890
68c W. F. Stirm (Front St.) 1890-1891

Pioneer City

ID 69 G. Borhaeser ? -1865

ID 70 L. Haubrich ? -1865

ID 71 H. Imkamp ? -1865

ID 72 Jos. Stadtmiller 1874-1880

Placerville

ID 73 Joseph Helmuth, Boise Brewery 1865-1866

ID 74 Charles Kohny 1874-1888

Pocatello

ID 75a American Brewing Co., aka Hayes, Franklin & Fleigner 1902-1904
75b Franklin & Hayes Brewing Co. 1904-1913
75c East Idaho Brewing Co., Inc. (633 S. 1st Ave.; operated by Columbia Breweries, Inc., Tacoma, WA) 1935-1954

Rathdrum

ID 76 Henry Reiniger, aka City Brewery 1886-1899

Rocky Bar

ID 77 Jacob Ulrich 1888-1890

ID 78a Waymin & Waymin 1896- ?
78b Clarence H. Waymire ? -1891

Ruby City

ID 79 Schrader & Hosp 1866- ?

Saint Anthony

ID 80 St. Anthony Brewing Co. (6th St. between Main & California) 1901-1909

Salmon City

ID 81 X. Nutz 1886-1887

ID 82a Michael Spahn 1874-1897
82b Spahn & Langendorf 1897-1898
82c Freda & Warnecke 1898-1899
82d William Warnecke 1899-1903

Shoshone

ID 83 Frank Plentz, City Brewery 1886-1890

Silver City

ID 84 A. Goodman & Bro. 1866- ?

ID 85a Frederick Grete Sr. 1888-1903
85b George Rambour 1903-1904
85c Fritz Schleifer, Owyhee Brewery 1904-1915

ID 86 J. T. Hunt 1890-1891

ID 87a Sommercamp & Bray 1866- ?
87b W. F. Summercamp, aka Summercamp & Co. 1874-1884

ID 88 Williams & Slagle 1866- ?

Soda Springs

ID 89a Largilliere & Schmidt 1884-1886
89b August Largilliere 1886-1904

South Mountain (later Mountain Home)

ID 90 Jacob & John Lemp 1874-1875

Victor

ID 91 Adelbert L. Rice 1899-1904

Wallace

ID 92 Carl Mallon (Bank St. Extension) 1889-1902

ID 93a Sunset Brewing Co. (710/718 Hotel St.) 1901-1915
93b Sunset Mercantile Co., Inc. 1934-1937
93c Sunset Brewing Co. 1937-1939
93d The Sunset Mercantile Co. 1939-1943
aka Gem State Brewery (1939-1941)
93e Sunset Mercantile Co. 1945-1946
93f DeLuxe Brewing Co. 1946-1949

Wardner

ID 94 Otto Arnold 1886-1887

ID 95 Geo. Gleim 1890-1896

ID 96 Pelkes & Swift 1888-1893
aka John Pelkes, South Fork Brewery (1892)

ID 97 Scott & Lingley 1888-1888

Warrens Diggings

ID 98 J. J. Manuel 1866- ?

Washington

ID 99 Raymund Saux 1874-1875

Weiser City

ID 100a John O. Peters 1884-1886
100b Sylvester Werneth 1886-1890
100c Mrs. Sylvester Werneth 1891-1902

Alton

IL	1a	George Yackel	1842- ?
	1b	Jeckel Brewing Co. (1421 Pearl St.)	? -1882
	1c	Bluff City Brewing Co.	1882-1891
	1d	Bluff City Brewery, Wilhelm Netzhammer	1891-1911
	1e	Bluff City Brewery, Katherine Netzhammer	1911-1920
	1f	Bluff City Brewery, Inc.	1933-1952
IL	2a	Philip Peters	1874-1877
	2b	Jehle & Peters	1877-1880
	2c	John Jehle	1880-1890
	2d	Anton Reck	1890-1893
	2e	Alton Brewing Co.	1893-1895
	2f	Alton Brewery, Anton Reck (215 E. 15th St. at Easton St.)	1895-1910
	2g	Anton Reck Brewing Co., Alton Brewery	1910-1920
IL	3	B. Runzi & Co.	1874-1875

Amboy

IL	4	Stein & Halm	1874-1875

Arcadia

IL	5	Arcadia Brewing Co.	1934-1934

Arenzville

IL	6	M. Koerner	1874-1891

Aurora

IL	7a	J. P. Dostal (212 N. River St.)	1886-1890
	7b	Aurora Brewing Co.	1890-1920
	7c	Aurora Brewing Co.	1934-1939
IL	8	John Knell	1878-1884
IL	9a	J. O. McInhill	1874-1877
	9b	J. V. McInhill	1877-1884

Beardstown

IL	10a	Joseph Stehlin	1845- ?
	10b	Anton Rink (Main & Lafayette Sts.)	1874-1912

Belleville

IL	11a	George L. Neuhoff, Star Brewery	1854-1858
	11b	Neuhoff & Bressler, Star Brewery	1858-1863
	11c	Neuhoff & Loeser, Star Brewery	1863-1866
	11d	Loeser & Eucker, Star Brewery	1866-1867
	11e	Loeser & Hartmann, Star Brewery	1867-1872
	11f	Hartmann Bros., Star Brewery (326 E. Main St.)	1872-1887
	11g	Star Brewery Co. (from 1905: 1125 Lebanon Ave.)	1887-1920
	11h	Star-Peerless Brewery Co.	1934-1958
IL	12a	(Philip) Neu & (Peter) Gintz	1851-1873
	12b	Philip Neu	1873-1875
	12c	Western Brewery Co. (Gold & N. 4th St.)	1875-1904
	12d	Western Brewery Co. (Gold & D. Sts)	1904-1920
	12e	Griesedieck Western Brewery Co. (1201/1225 W. E St.)	1933-1954
	12f	Carling Brewing Co., aka Stag Brewery	1954-1975
	12g	Carling National Breweries, Inc., aka Stag Brewery	1975-1979
	12h	G. Heileman Brewing Co., aka Carling National Breweries, Inc.	1979-
IL	13	Normann & Gehler	1874-1875
IL	14	Fidel Stoegle (also Stoelzle)	1874-1884

Belvidere

IL	15a	John Waldeck	1875-1879
	15b	J. Heywood	1879-1880
	15c	Frederick Finder	1880-1888
	15d	Geo. J. Schlenk (N. State St.)	1891-1907

Bloomington

IL	16a	Chris Markgraf (S. Main St.)	? -1861
	16b	(Anton) Mayer & (F. X.) Wochner	1861-1902
	16c	Meyer Brewing Co.	1902-1920

Blue Island

IL	17a	John Bauer & Co.	1874-1877
	17b	Henry Bauer	1877-1884
IL	18a	Busch & Brand	1853-1871
	18b	Val. Busch	1871-1874
	18c	R. Brand, Blue Island Brewery	1874-1878
	18d	Busch & Brand	1878-1882
	18e	Louis Busch	1882-1891
	18f	Louis Busch & Co.	1891-1893
	18g	August Koenecke	1893-1895
	18h	Blue Island Brewing Co. (280 Gregory & York Sts.)	1895-1898
	18i	Blue Island Brewing Co. (branch of United Breweries Co., Chic.)	1898-1902
IL	19	G. H. Hausberg (280 Gregory St.)	1896-1896
IL	20a	Metz & Schwachow	1878-1879
	20b	Pilsen Brewing and Malting Co.	1879-1884
	20c	Chicago Co-operative Brewing Association	1884-1888

Bowmanville

IL	21	W. Volmer	1874-1884

Bushnell

IL	22	E. D. C. Haines	1874-1875

Cairo

IL	23	Cairo Brewing Co. (4th & 304 Commercial Ave.s)	1905-1920
IL	24	Feuchter & Schwanitz	1874-1875

Calumet City (West Hammond until 1924)

IL	25a	Chas. H. Mayer	1893-1908
	25b	West Hammond Brewing Co.	1916-1923
	25c	Great Lakes Brewing Co. (540/550 W. State St.)	1933-1939

Canton

IL	26a	M. Koebel	1874-1877
	26b	L. Koebel	1877-1888
	26c	John E. Johnson	1888-1891

Carlinville

IL	27a	Geo. P. Deibel	1874-1877
	27b	G. P. Deibel & Bros.	1877-1879
	27c	Susan Deibel	1879-1880
	27d	G. P. Deibel & Co.	1880-1884

Carlyle

IL	28	Joseph Krother	1874-1875

Casaquias

IL	29	Beauvais	1765- ?

Centralia

IL	30a	Frederick Finger	1884-1893
	30b	John Thoebes	1893-1897
IL	31	Chas. Storms	1874-1875

Centreville

IL	32	Val. Brenfleck	1874-1875
IL	33	D. Schuff	1874-1875

Champaign

IL	34	Louis Buschmann	1874-1875

Chicago (including Hyde Park & South Chicago - both annexed in 1889)

IL	35	Albrecht & Finkler, Home Brewery (1709 Lincoln Ave.)	1901-1902
IL	36	American Brewing Co. (922 N. Ashland Ave.)	1890-1901
IL	37	Augsberg Brewing Co. (3024 W. 30th St.)	NP 1934-1934
IL	38	Adam Baierle (34-38 N. Market)	1863-1869
IL	39	Banner Brewing Co. (1088/1092 Wilcox Ave.)	1896-1897

Chicago (cont.)

IL	40a	Bartholomae & Leicht, Eagle Brewery (684-706 Sedgwick St.)	1873-1877
	40b	Bartholomae & Leicht Brewing Co.	1877-1889
	40c	Bartholomae & Leicht Brewing Co. (United States Brewing Co.)	1889-1890
	40d	Bartholomae & Leicht Brewing Co. (Milwaukee and Chicago Breweries Co., Ltd.), aka United States Brewing Co.	1890-1911
IL	41	John Behringer (157 Orchard near Willow)	1861-1869
IL	42a	Bemis & Rindge	1862-1864
	42b	Downer, Bemis & Co. (23rd & Kankakee Ave.)	1864-1866
	42c	Downer, Bemis & Co. (23rd & South Park Ave.)	1866-1869
	42d	Downer & Bemis Brewing Co.	1869-1882
	42e	Bemis & McAvoy Brewing Co.	1882-1887
	42f	McAvoy Brewing Co. (91 S. Park Ave.) (merged with Wacker & Birk)	1887-1889
	42g	McAvoy Brewing Co. (Chicago Breweries, Ltd.)	1889-1920
	42h	McAvoy Co., aka Wacker & Birk Brewing & Malting Co.	1920- ?
IL	43a	Berliner Weiss Beer Brewery, Ferdinand Harke (82 Willow, Rear)	1874-1875
	43b	Berliner Weiss Beer Brewery, August Harke	1875-1876
IL	44a	Matthias Best (Indiana Ave. near 12th & The Lake)	1858-1863
	44b	Killian or Christian Schott (Indiana Ave. near North Halleck)	1863-1865
	44c	Martin Best (721 Indiana Ave.)	1865-1866
IL	45a	M. Best (foot of 14th St.)	1852-1854
	45b	Conrad Seipp	1854-1855
	45c	Conrad Seipp (foot of 27th St.)	1855-1858
	45d	Conrad Seipp & Co. (Lakeshore near Northern, Rio Grande, Hardin Pl.), aka Conrad Seipp	1858-1860
	45e	Seipp & Lehmann	1860-1872
	45f	Conrad Seipp	1872-1876
	45g	Conrad Seipp Brewing Co. (merged with West Side Brewery Co. and City Brewery Co.) (Lakeshore foot of 27th)	1876-1890
	45h	Conrad Seipp Brewing Co. (City of Chicago Consolidated Brewing & Malting Co., Ltd.)	1890-1933
IL	46a	Binz & LaParle (Cottage Grove Ave. betweeen 27th & 28th Sts.)	1866-1868
	46b	F. Binz Brewery aka (Michael) Keeley Brewery (1876-1878)	1868-1878
	46c	Keeley Brewing Co.	1878-1920
	46d	Keeley Brewing Co. (516 E. 28th St.)	1933-1953
IL	47a	Blattner & Seidenschwanz, aka Blattner & Co. (Hinsdale St. between Rush & Pine Sts.)	c1850-1857
	47b	Seidenschwanz & Wacker	1857-1858
	47c	Wacker & Seidenschwanz, aka Wacker & Co. (N. Franklin St. near Green Bay, Asylum Place, Dyer & Sophia)	1858-1865
	47d	Frederick Wacker (848 N. Franklin St. - later Webster Ave.)	1865-1867
	47e	F. Wacker (in malting business with others)	1867-1882
	47f	(Frederick) Wacker & (Jacob) Birk Brewing & Malting Co. (Des Plaines & Indiana Sts.) (Merged with McAvoy Brewing Co.)	1882-1889
	47g	Wacker & Birk Brewing & Malting Co. (Chicago Breweries Ltd.)	1889-1918
IL	48a	Bohemian Brewing Co. of Chicago (680/706 Blue Island Ave.)	1891-1896
	48b	Atlas Brewing Co. aka Atlas Brewing Co. of Chicago (1896-1902)	1896-1920
	48c	Atlas Beverage Co.	1920-1929
	48d	Atlas Brewing Co. (2107 Blue Island Ave.)	1929-1944
	48e	Atlas Brewing Co. (affiliated with Schoenhofen-Edelweiss Brewing Co.)	1944-1951
	48f	Atlas Brewing Co., branch of Drewry's Ltd., South Bend, IN	1951-1962
IL	49	William Bohn (651 37th St.)	1893-1893
IL	50a	Brand Brewing Co. (1251 Elston Ave.)	1899-1909
	50b	Brand Brewing Co. (2530 Elston Ave.) aka Producers Brewing Co. (1916-1920)	1909-1922
	50c	Brand Co. aka Prima Products Co. (1932) aka Royal Brewing Co. (1934)	NP 1932-1935

Chicago (cont.)

IL 51a (Charles) Brand & (Ernest) Hummel Brewing Co. (Ave. L & 100th St., Hyde Park) 1880-1887
51b South Chicago Brewing Co. 1887-1895
51c South Chicago Brewing Co. (Ave. N & 100th St.) 1895-1897
51d South Chicago Breiwng Co. (United Breweries Co.), aka South Chicago Brewery 1897-1922

IL 52a Michael Brand (Elston Ave. near W. Fullerton) 1878-1879
52b Michael Brand & Co. (Elston Ave. & Snow St.) 1879-1886
52c The Michael Brand Brewing Co. 1886-1889
52d United States Brewing Co. of Chicago, aka Michael Brand Brewing Co. 1889-1890
52e United States Brewing Co. of Chicago, aka Michael Brand Brewing Co. (1890-1915) (Milwaukee and Chicago Breweries Ltd.) (Elston Ave. & Snow St.) 1890-1927
52f United States Brewing Co. 1932-1955

IL 53a Brewer & Hofmann Brewing Co. (41/55 S. Green St.) 1886-1902
53b George J. Cooke (41/55 S. Green St. & Madison St.) 1905-1910
53c Goerge J. Cooke Co. (14/30 N. Green) 1910-1922

IL 54a Brisach & Hessemer (Oak St. near Green Bay) 1858-1859
54b Joseph Brisach (foot of Oak St.) 1859-1860

IL 55 Broadway Brewing Co. (5245 Broadway) NP 1934-1934

IL 56a Bucher & Hiller (Green Bay Road) 1858-1866
56b Geo. Hiller (9104 N. Clark & Green Bay near Franklin) 1866-1868

IL 57a George Burroughs c1850
57b Frederick Burroughs (144 W. Lake near Union) c1854-1862

IL 58a Valentin Busch (31 Cedar St. near Green Bay & Wolcott) 1851-1858
58b Busch & (Michael) Brand 1858-1873
58c Busch & Brand Brewing Co. 1873-1879

IL 59a Calumet Brewing Co., aka Calumet Brewery (10555/10557 Torrance Ave.) 1901-1909
59b Calumet Brewing & Malting Co. (Torrance Ave. & 106th St.) 1909-1911
59c Bessemer Brewing Co. 1911-1913

IL 60a James Carney (39-63 S. Water St. btwn. State & Wabash Sts.) 1840-1855
60b John O'Neill 1855-1860

IL 61 Castle Brewery Co. (E. Chicago Ave. & River St.) 1896-1896

IL 62 Chicago Ale and Malt Co. (S. Water & Clark, Lake Ave & Pier) 1861-1867

IL 63a Chicago Brewing Co. (64/80 W. North St.) 1888-1898
63b Chicago Brewing Co. (United Breweries Co.) 1898-1909
63c Chicago Brewery (United Breweries Co.) (1269 W. North St.) 1909-1919

IL 64a Chicago Union Brewing Co., aka Union Brewing Co., Patrick O'Neill (27th St. & Johnson Ave.) 1867-1885
64b Cooke & Stenson 1885-1887
64c Cooke Brewing Co. (Brewery Ave. & 521 E. 27th St.) 1887-1910

IL 65a Citizens Brewing Co. (Archer Ave. & Main St.) 1893-1898
65b Citizens Brewing Co. (United Breweries Co.), aka Citizens' Brewery (Archer Ave. & Throop St.) 1898-1920
65c Bismarck Brewing Co. (2738-2762 Archer Ave.) aka Hunter's Brewery, Inc. (1940-1941) 1933-1941
65d Prima-Bismarck Brewing Co. 1941-1951

IL 66a Columbus Brewing Co. (297 Cornell & Noble Sts.) 1902-1910
66b Lutz Brewing Co. 1910-1910
66c Atlantic Brewing Co. (1401 Cornell St.) 1910-1912

IL 67a Corper & Nockin (101/109 Webster Ave.) 1886-1891
67b Birk Bros. Brewing Co. (Edward & Frank Birk) 1891-1909
67c Birk Bros. Brewing Co. (1315/1325 Webster Ave.) 1909-1923
67d Birk Bros. Brewing Co. (2117 N. Ward St. & Webster Ave.) 1933-1936
67e Birk Bros. Brewing Co. (2117 N. Wayne St. - formerly Ward St.) 1936-1950

IL 68a Carl Corper Brewing Co. (41st St. & Union Ave.) 1903-1904
68b Globe Brewing Co. 1904-1910
68c Brand Brewing Co., No. 2 (4057 Union Ave.) 1910-1913

Chicago (cont.)

IL 69a Carl Corper Brewing and Malting Co. (39th St. & Union Ave.) 1893-1898
69b Carl Corper Brewing and Malting Co. (United Breweries Co.) 1898-1900

IL 70 Matthew Cziner (18 Canalport Ave.) 1874-1875

IL 71a Francis J. Dewes (764 W. Chicago & Hoyne Aves.) 1882-1885
71b F. J. Dewes Brewery Co. 1885-1890
71c F. J. Dewes Brewery Co. (City of Chicago Brewing and Malting Co.) 1890-1898
71d City Brewery Co. (Chicago Consolidated Brewing and Malting Co.) 1898-1906
aka Malt Sinew Co. (1901-1906)

IL 72a Arah P. Dickinson (Cass & Michigan) 1858-1859
72b Dickinson & Bemis (Cass & Kinzie) 1859-1860
72c Arah. P. Dickinson, aka North Star Brewery 1860-1864

IL 73 Thomas Donovan (Pine & Pearson Sts.) c1860

IL 74 (Corydon) Downer, (H. V.) Bemis & Co., Ale & Porter Brewery (16th St. at the Lake, Palo Alto & Douglas Ave.) 1860-1864

IL 75a Morgan Doyle (423 Wolcott Nr. Scott) 1863-1864
75b Doyle & Brother (State St.) 1864-1866
75c Doyle & Brother (423 N. State St. formerly Wolcott) 1866-1878
aka Doyle & Co. (1874-1875)
75d John Devereaux (or Deverix) 1878-1879

IL 76a Eagle Brewing Co. (1469/1479 N. Western Ave.) 1901-1909
76b Eagle Brewing Co. (2608/2631 N. Western Ave.) 1909-1927

IL 77 Simon Eichenseher (Larrabee St.btwn Willow & Center) 1858-1866
aka Eichenseher & Schreiber (1863)

IL 78a Endlich & Saladin (164-168 Archer Ave.) 1858-1860
78b William Saladin 1860-1870
78c Matheus Gottfried 1870-1882
78d Gottfried Brewing Co. (2249 Archer & Stewart Aves.) 1882-1924

IL 79a Ernst Bros. Brewing Co. (47/67 Larrabee St.) 1884-1889
79b Ernst Bros. Brewery (Milwaukee and Chicago Breweries aka United States Brewing Co.) 1889-1900

IL 80 Errickson & Berquist (123 S. Edgwick) 1874-1875

IL 81 Julius Fahrenbach (449 W. Fullerton Ave.) 1898-1902

IL 82a Ernst Fecker, Jr. (863-869 Dudley St. at Bloomingdale Road) 1894-1895
(an ale & porter brewery - IL 83 is a lager brewery)
82b George J. Stadler Brewing Co. (863-869 N. Winchester Ave. formerly Dudley) 1895-1899
82c Stenson Brewing Co. 1899-1909
82d Stenson Brewing Co. (1748 N. Wincester Ave.) 1909-1923
82e Stenson Brewing Co. 1933-1943

IL 83a The Fecker Brewing Co., Ernst Fecker, Jr. (871-75 Dudley St.) 1890-1895
83b The Fecker Brewing Co., Ernst Fecker, Jr. (871-75 Winchester) 1895-1898
83c The Fecker Brewing Co. (United Breweries Co.) 1898-1901

IL 84 F. C. Feigel (721 Indiana Ave.) 1875-1876

IL 85 August Fischer (20 S. Des Plaines St.) 1888-1888

IL 86 William Fleming (Hinsdale St. near Green Bay Road) 1858-1876

IL 87a William Fleming & Co. (Wolcott near Church) 1861-1863
87b Excelsior Brewery, William Fleming (110 Grand Haven) 1863-1868
aka Fleming & Conway (1863-1864)

IL 88a Fortune & Co. (62 Oakwood near the Lake) 1864-1865
88b Schmidt & Katz 1865-1866
88c Schmidt, Katz & Leverens 1866-1867
88d Schmidt, Katz & Co. 1867-1869

IL 89a Fortune Bros. (Peter & John) (138/144 W. Van Buren St.) 1857-1881
89b Fortune Brothers Brewing Co. (225 Des Plaines & Van Buren St.) 1881-1920
89c Fortune Bros. Brewing Co. (725 Van Buren St.) 1936-1948

Chicago (cont.)

IL 90a E. Funk & Co. (144/146 Willow St.) 1874-1877
90b Ernst Funk 1877-1884
90c Ernst Funk (50 Clyde St.) 1884-1891
90d Ernst Funk (50 Osgood St. formerly Clyde) 1891-1909
90e Ernst Funk (1921 Osgood St.) 1909-1911

IL 91a Gambrinus Brewing Co. (1525/1547 Fillmore St. at Albany Ave.) 1900-1909
91b Gambrinus Brewing Co. (3032/3058 Fillmore St.) 1909-1922
91c Gambrinus Brewing Co. 1933-1935
91d Gambrinus Co., Inc. 1935-1936
91e Patrick Henry Brewing Co., Inc. 1936-1939

IL 92 Garden City Brewing Co. (868 Hoyne St.) 1890-1890

IL 93a Garden City Brewing Co. (21st Pl. & S. Albany Ave.) 1901-1902
93b Garden City Brewery 1902-1925
93c Garden City Brewery (2111/2123 S. Albany Ave.) 1933-1951

IL 94 Jacob Gauch (Indiana St. between Pine & St. Clair) c1845

IL 95 Gauch & Brahm (Rush St. & Chicago Ave.) 1855-1856

IL 97 Joseph Geeman (Clybourn near Larrabee, Rees) 1862-1865

IL 98a Gillen, Schmidt& Co. (404/416 E. 25th St.) 1878-1880
98b Henry F. Gehring, aka Bavarian Brewing Co. 1880-1884
98c Bavarian Brewing Co.,aka O'Donnell & Duer 1884-1891
98d Cantwell & Ryan Eagle Brewing Co. 1891-1893
98e Cantwell Eagle Brewing Co. 1893-1897

IL 99a (Matheus) Gottfried & (Peter) Schoenhofen (178 W. 12th & Jefferson Sts.) 1860-1864
99b Gottfried & Schoenhofen (34/50 Sewar St., Canalport Ave. & 18th) 1864-1867
99c Peter Schoenhofen 1867-1879
99d Peter Schoenhofen Brewing Co. (merged with National Brewing) 1879-1925

IL 100 Gutsch Brothers (160/169 West Lake St.) 1859-1865

IL 101 Haas & Powell (27/31 W. Madison) 1870-1871

IL 102a Peter Hand Brewery Co. (37/59 Sheffield Ave.) 1891-1909
aka Peter Hand Brewing Co. (1891)
102b Peter Hand Brewery Co. (1612/1632 Sheffield Ave.) 1909-1920
102c Peter Hand Brewery Co. 1933-1967
102d Meister Brau, Inc. (1000 W. North Ave.) 1967-1972
aka Warsaw Brewing Co. (1971-1972)
102e Peter Hand Brewing Co. 1973-1978

IL 103 Thomas G. Hanson (28 Chicago Ave. near the Bridge) 1862-1867

IL 104 Healy & Regitz (129/131 Fullerton Ave.) 1887-1888

IL 105a Henn & Gabler Brewing Co. (35th & Ullman Sts.) 1892-1895
105b Henn & Gabler Brewing Co. (34th & Courts Sts. & S. Centre Ave.) 1895-1898
105c Henn & Gabler Brewery, North Western Brewery (United Breweries Co.) 1898-1901
105d Northwestern Brewery No. 2 (United Breweries Co.), aka Henn & Gabler Brewery) 1901-1908

IL 106 Matthew Hitz (Green Bay & Cedar near Wolcott) 1855-1862

IL 107a Jos. Hladovec Brewing Co. (1090/1118 W. 21st St. & Western) 1890-1892
107b Monarch Brewing Co. 1892-1898
107c Monarch Brewing Co., aka Monarch Brewery (United Breweries) 1898-1909
107d Monarch Brewery (2419/2443 W. 21st St.) 1909-1922
107e Monarch Beverage Co. 1923-1932
107f Monarch Brewing Co., Inc. 1932-1936
107g Monarch Brewing Co. 1936-1958
107h Van Merritt Brewing Co. 1958-1967
aka Bohemian Brewing Co. (1958-1967)
aka House of Augsburg (1959-1967)
aka Monarch Brewing Co. (1958-1967)

Chicago (cont)

IL 108a	John L. Hoerber (216/224 W. 12th St.)	1864-1882
108b	Bartholomay & Burgweger Brewing Co.	1882-1887
108c	William Ruehl Brewing Co.	1887-1898
108d	William Ruehl Brewing Co., aka Ruehl Brewery (United Breweries Co.)	1898-1907
IL 109a	John L. Hoerber (186 Griswold St.)	1858-1864
109b	Hoerber & Gastriech	1864-1865
109c	John L. Hoerber	1865-1865
109d	Michael Sieben (186/188 Pacific Ave. formerly Griswold & Polk)	1865-1876
IL 110a	John L. Hoerber (646/662 Hinman & 22nd Sts.)	1882-1885
110b	John L. Hoerber Brewing Co. (646/662 W. 21st Place)	1885-1909
110c	John L. Hoerber Brewing Co. (1617/1629 W. 21st Place)	1909-1927
110d	The Hoerber Brewing Co.	1934-1941
IL 111a	Hofmann Bros. (Alves, George & Valentine) Brewing Co. (107 W. Monroe & Rockwell Sts.)	1896-1909
111b	Hofman Bros. Brewing Co. (2606/2626 W. Monroe St.)	1909-1925
111c	Peter Fox Brewing Co.	1933-1955
IL 112	Home Brewery (2654/2670 Elston Ave.)	1910-1920
IL 113	Home Brewing Co. (1294 W. 61st St.)	1895-1895
IL 114	Home Weiss Beer Brewery aka Home Brewery (2702 N. 40th St.)	1913-1916
IL 115a	(John) Huck & (John) Schneider (Chicago Ave. & Division Sts.)	1847-1855
115b	John A. Huck, Eagle Brewery (Wolcott near Division, Bank & Church Sts.)	1855-1860
115c	Huck's Chicago Brewing Co.	1860-1869
115d	John A. Huck Brewing Co. (445/449 N. State St. formerly Wolcott)	1869-1871
IL 116a	Illinois Brewing and Malting Co. (38th St. & S. Centre Ave.)	1901-1910
116b	White Eagle Brewing Co. (3735 S. Centre Ave.)	1910-1913
116c	White Eagle Brewing Co. (3735/3757 S. Racine Ave. formerly Centre)	1913-1925
116d	Mid-West Products Co.	1926-1932
116e	White Eagle Brewing Co.	1933-1950
IL 117a	Independent Brewing Association (586/612 N. Halstead St.) aka Prima Tonic Co. (1905-1907)	1890-1909
117b	Independent Brewing Association (1440/1472 N. Halstead St.)	1909-1915
117c	Independent Brewing Association (821/825 Blackhawk & Halstead)	1915-1920
117d	Primalt Products Co.	1920-1925
117e	The Prima Co. (merged with IL 65)	1933-1938
IL 118a	Joseph Jerusalem (Foot of Elm St.)	1868-1871
118b	Joseph Jerusalem (357/365 Rush St.)	1872-1887
118c	Ulrike Jerusalem (562/564 N. Halstead & 126 Rees Sts.)	1888-1891
118d	Gustav Eberlein	1891-1903
118e	Ulrike Eberlein aka Eberlein Weiss Beer Brewery (1904-1908)	1903-1908
IL 119a	Joseph Junk (3700/3710 S. Halstead & 37th Sts.)	1883-1887
119b	Magdalena Junk aka Junk's Brewery (1890-1892)	1887-1904
119c	Jos. Junk Brewing Co.	1904-1909
119d	South Side Brewing Co.	1909-1921
119e	South Side Ice & Beverage Co.	1922-1926
119f	South Side Brewing Co. aka Frederick Bros. Brewing Co. (1934-1937)	1934-1937
119g	Ambrosia Brewing Co. aka Frederick Bros. Brewing Co. (1937-1941)	1937-1959
119h	Atlantic Brewing Co., plant 2 (827 W. 37th Place)	1959-1965
IL 120	Henry Kassens (Hyde Park)	1884-1884
IL 121	Goerge Keller	1867-1869

Chicago (cont.)

IL 122a Kerber & Stege (583 N. Clark near Schiller & 53 N. LaSalle) 1864-1866
122b Herman Spanknebel 1866-1867
122c Edward Stege 1867-1868

IL 123a Klockgeter & Co. (1317 Fletcher & Herndon Sts.) 1885-1886
123b Kagebein & Folstaff, Lakeview Brewery 1886-1889
123c Alvin Greiner 1889-1891
123d Best Brewing Co. of Chicago, aka Best Brewing Co. 1891-1915
123e Best Brewing Co. of Chicago (1301/1329 Fletcher St.) 1915-1928
123f Best Brewing Co. of Chicago 1932-1950
aka Best Brewing Co. (1933-1934)
aka National Brewing Co. (1933-1935)
123g Best Brewing Corp. 1950-1961
aka Malt Marrow Brewing Co. (1953-1960)

IL 124 William Knight (Hubbard between Lincoln & Roby) 1861-1863

IL 125 Koch & Poggensee (455/457 W. North Ave.) 1905-1906

IL 126a Koch & Reyber (Hyde Park) 1888- ?
126b Louis Wagner ? -1891

IL 127 Koller Brewing Co., Inc. (39th St. & Pershing Road) 1933-1953

IL 128 A. G. Kurth (1049 N. Oakley Ave.) 1888-1888

IL 129a Louis Lamm (941/943 N. Western Ave.) 1897-1898
129b Germania Brewing Co. 1898-1899
129c Germania Brewing Co. (588 N. California Ave.) 1899-1900

IL 130a William Lill & Co. (West Side) 1833-1839
130b William Lill & Co. (Pine St. & Chicago Ave.) 1839-1842
130c Lill & (Michael) Diversey 1842-1871
aka Chicago Brewery (1863-1871)
aka Lill's Chicago Brewery (1867-1869)

IL 131 Joseph (or James) Ludwick & Co. (31 Green Bay Road near Hinsdale & Pearson Sts.) 1858-1863

IL 132a Charles B. Mader (347 Milwaukee Ave.) 1884-1888
132b Mader & Bartelme 1888-1890
132c Charles B. Mader 1890-1893
132d C. B. Mader & Co. 1893-1895
132e Siegler & Schiemann Brewing Co. 1895-1897
132f Imperial Brewing and Bottling Co. 1897-1898
132g Globe Brewing Co. 1898-1901
132h Charles B. Mader 1901-1902
132i Chicago Consolidated Bottling Co. 1902-1904
132j Koch & Poggenseee 1904-1907

IL 133a Manhattan Brewing Co. (39th St. & 3901 Emerald Ave.) 1893-1933
aka Malt Maid Products Co. (1923-1932)
aka Malt Maid Co. (1923-1932)
aka Fort Dearborn Products Co. (1925)
133b Manhattan Brewing Co. (3900/3950 S. Union Ave. & 39th St.) 1933-1947
133c Canadian Ace Brewing Co. 1947-1968
aka Ace Brewing Co. (1958-1962)
aka Ace Hi Brewing Co. (1958-1962)
aka Allied Brewing Co. (1954-1957)
aka Berlin Brewing Co. (1964-1965)
aka Bismarck Brewing Co. (1963-1968
aka Cold Brau Brewing Co. (?)
aka Crest Brewing Co. (1961-1964)
aka Empire Brewing Co. (1959-1963)
aka Essex Brewing Co. (1957-1961)
aka Essex Brewery, Ltd. (1957-1961)
aka Gipps Brewing Co. (1956-1963)
aka Gold Brau Brewing Co. (1958-1968)
aka Hapsburg Brewing Co. (1964-1967)
aka Jester Brewing Co. (1953-1957)
aka Kings Brewing Co. (1959-1962)
aka Koenig Brau Brewing Co. (1955-1967)

Chicago (cont.)

aka Kol Brewing Co.
aka Leisy Brewing Co. (1960-1964)
aka Lubeck Brewing Co. (1960-1964)
aka Malt Marrow Brewing Co.
aka 9 - 0 - 5 Brewing Co. (1962-1965)
aka Old Missouri Brewing Co.
aka Old Vienna Brewing Co. (1952-1964)
aka Pilsen Brewing Co. (1962-1968)
aka Prima Brewing Co. (1955-1964)
aka Prima-Bismarck Brewing Co. (1956-1960)
aka Royal Brewing Co. (1964-1966)
aka Schultz Brewing Co.
aka Star Union Products Co. (1963-1968)
aka Superior Brewing Co. (1963-1965)
aka Tudor Brewing Co.
aka United States Brewing Co.
aka Westminster Brewing Co. (1958-1962)
aka Westminster Brewery, Ltd. (1958-1962)
aka Windsor Brewing Co. (1956-1960)

IL 134 MacDonald Brewery (1300/1308 McKinley Ave.) 1935-1935

IL 135 Frank McDermott Brewing Co. (3435/3441 S. Racine Ave.) 1925-1937
aka Beverly Brewing Co. (1937)
aka Hunters Brewery, Inc. (1934)
aka Frank McDermott

IL 136 Metropolitan Weiss Beer Brewing Co. (3802 Armour Ave.) 1898-1898

IL 137a Mette & Vogt (471 E. 26th St.) 1888-1889
137b John Vogt (467/473 26th St.) 1889-1892
137c Vogt & Sweeney aka Vogt & Sweeney Brewing Co. 1892-1895
137d Mullen Brewing Co. 1895-1904
aka James J. Mullen (1895)

IL 138a George Metz, Union Brewery (401/403 Wolcott & Scott Sts.) c1850-1869
aka George Metz & Killian Schott (1862-1863)
aka Metz & Brand (1863-1864)
138b Metz & Steges, Union Brewery (401/403 N. State St., formerly Wolcott) 1869-1875
138c George Metz, Jr. 1875-1877

IL 139a Miller & Son (State St. between Goethe & Division) 1863-1870
139b Seipp & Lehmann 1870-1871

IL 140a H. B. Miller & Son (Wolcott & Grand Haven Slip) 1865-1865
140b H. B. Miller & Son (420/440 N. State St., formerly Wolcott) 1866-1868

IL 141 John B. Miller (Larrabeee between North & Blackhawk) 1859-1862

IL 142 Timothy Mitchell (Hyde Park) 1882-1884

IL 143 Moser Bros. (62/64 Hurlburt) 1866-1868

IL 144 Mueller Bros. aka The Star Brewery & The Mueller Bros. Star Brewery (Foot of Elm near the Lake) 1867-1871
aka Charles Sheer (1870)

IL 145a Mueller Bros. (1131-1137 Fulton & Rockwell Sts.) 1887-1890
145b The Star Brewery Co., aka Star Brewery 1890-1898
aka The Star Brewery of Chicago (1896-1898)
145c The Star Brewery branch of United Breweries Co. 1898-1902
aka Star Brewery of Chicago (1898-1900)

IL 146a Mueller Brothers (Adolph & Henry) (28 S. Des Plaines St.) 1884-1888
146b Mueller Brothers' Brewing Co. 1888-1890

IL 147a A. & G. H. Mueller, aka Mueller Bros. (152 W. Randolph) 1859-1862
147b Mueller Bros. (308 W. Madison St.) 1862-1865

IL 148a Simon Munger (212 W. Chicago Ave.) 1888- ?
148b Henry P. Caldwell ? -1891

Chicago (cont.)

IL 149a John Nangle (Lydia between N. Union & N. Halstead) 1861-1864
149b John Nangle (154 N. Reuben near Indiana) 1864-1868

IL 150a National Brewing Co. (846/860 W. 18th & N. Lincoln Sts.) c1889-1909
aka National Malt Tonic Co. (1900-1909)
150b National Brewing Co. (1900/1910 W. 18th St.) 1909-1925
150c Schoenhofen Co., aka National Brewing Co. 1925-1933
aka National Malt Tonic Co. (1925-1928)
150d Schoenhofen Edelweiss Co. (1900/1956 W. 18th St.) 1933-1944
150e Schoenhofen Edelweiss Co. (affiliated with Atlas Brewing Co.) 1944-1951
150f Schoenhofen Edelweiss Co. (branch of Drewry's, Ltd., U.S.A, South Bend, IN) 1951-1966
aka Atlas Brewing Co. (1951-1966)
aka Barbarossa Brewing Co. (1959-1966)
aka Drewry's Ltd., USA (1962-1966)
aka Great Lakes Brewing Co. (1957-1964)
aka 9 - 0 - 5 Brewing Co. (1960-1962)
aka Prost Brewing Co. (1961-1965)
aka Trophy Brewing Co. (1960-1964)
150g Schoenhofen Edelweiss Co. (branch of Associated Brewing Co., Detroit, MI) 1966-1971
aka Associated Brewing Co. (1970-1971)
aka B. B. Brewing Co. (1966-1971)
aka Drewry's Ltd. USA (1966-1971)

IL 151a Mutual Brewing Co.(3324 W. 22nd St. & Spalding Ave.) 1907-1924
aka The New Brewery (1907)
151b Mutual Ice & Beverage Co. (22nd & Troy Sts.) NP 1933-1933

IL 152 Non-Alcoholic Beer Co. (54 Clybourne Ave.) 1893-1893

IL 153a North Western Brewing Co. (781/831 Clybourne Ave.) 1888-1898
153b North Western Brewing Co. (United Breweries Co.) 1898-1909
aka North Western Brewery
153c North Western Brewery (United Breweries Co.) (2270/2332 Clybourn Ave.) 1909-1921
aka North Western Co. (1918-1921)

IL 154a O'Donnell & Duer, aka Bavarian Brewing Co. (3937 Walker & 40th Sts.) 1892-1904
154b Muller Brewing Co. 1904-1917
154c National Brewing Co. (branch of IL 150b) 1917-1918

IL 155a Chas. F. Ogren (W. Division & Wood Sts.) 1886-1888
155b Chas. F. Ogren (625/629 Shober St.) 1888-1892
155c Chas. F. Ogren Brewing Co. 1892-1895
155d Chas. F. Ogren Brewing Co. (625/629 N. Irving Ave., formerly Shober) 1895-1909
aka Ogren Brewing Co. (1908)
aka Charles F. Ogren & Co. (1898-1909)
155e Charles F. Ogren & Co., aka Ogren Brewing Co. (1222/1228 N. Irving Ave.) 1909-1913

IL 156 Old Abbey Brewery Corp. (4539/4541 Armitage Ave.) 1936-1941

IL 157a John O'Neill Brewery (Cedar St.) ? -1860
157b Dickinson & Bemis 1860-1862

IL 158 John Parker, Garden City Brewery (115/117 Dearborn near Ohio) c1854-1856

IL 159a William Pfeifer (499 Milwaukee Ave.) 1888-1891
159b William Pfeifer (339/347 N. Leavitt St.) 1892-1909
aka Berlin Weiss Beer Co. (1892-1905)
aka William Pfeifer Weiss Beer Co. (1892-1905)
aka Pfeifer's Berlin Weiss Beer Co. (1905-1909)
159c William Pfeifer, aka Pfeifer's Berlin Weiss Beer Co. (718/742 N. Leavitt St.) 1909-1918
159d Superior Brewing Co. 1933-1941
aka Hunters Brewery, Inc. (c1936)

Chicago (cont.)

IL 160a	John Pforr (147/149 Fullerton Ave.)	1888-1892
160b	Catherine Pforr	1892-1895
160c	Catherine Pforr, aka John Pforr (74 Perry St.)	1895-1897
160d	John Pforr aka Catherine Pforr (1898-1900) aka Catherine Pforr Estate (1901-1903) aka J. Pforr & Co. (1903-1904) aka Pforr Weiss Beer Brewery (1904-1908)	1897-1908
160e	Edw. J. Birk & Bro. (2341 Perry St.)	1910-1912
IL 161a	Phoenix Brewing Co. (53/63 W. Division St.)	1896-1898
161b	Phoenix Brewing Co. (United Breweries Co.)	1898-1901
IL 162a	Pilsen Brewing Co. (368 W. 26th St. & Albany Ave.)	1903-1909
162b	Pilsen Brewing Co. (3043/3065 W. 26th St.)	1909-1920
162c	Pilsen Brewery Co. aka Pilsen Products Co. (1933-1936)	1933-1962
IL 163a	Pohl Bros. (27/35 Cooper St.)	1881-1882
163b	(Paul) Pohl & (Reinhold) Henry	1882-1884
163c	Paul Pohl	1884-1905
163d	Paul Pohl Brewing Co. (2335/2344 Cooper St.)	1905-1913
163e	Tabor Brewing Co.	1913-1915
163f	North American Brewing Co. aka Bosworth Products Co. (1927-1932)	1915-1932
163g	Bosworth Products Co. (2336 Bosworth Ave., formerly Cooper)	1932-1933
163h	Atlantic Brewing Co. (1545/1549 W. Fullerton & Bosworth Aves.) aka Champagne Velvet Brewing Co. (1960-1965) aka C. V. Brewing Co. (1960-1965) aka Excell Brewing Co. aka Lederer Brewing Co. (1958-1965) aka Red Top Brewing Co. (1960-1964) aka Savoy Brewing Co. aka Tuxedo Brewing Co.	1933-1965
IL 164	Quist & Carlson (895 Sheffield Ave.)	1908-1908
IL 165a	Jacob Rehm & Co. (333/337 W. 12th & Brown Sts.)	1865-1866
165b	Rehm & Bartholomae	1866-1868
165c	Bartholomae & Co.	1868-1873
165d	Bartholomae & Roesing	1873-1888
165e	Bartholomae & Roesing Brewing & Malting Co.	1888-1890
165f	Bartholomae & Roesing Brewing & Malting Co. (Milwaukee and Chicago Breweries Co., Ltd., aka United States Brewing Co.)	1890-1909
165g	Bartholomae & Roesing Brewing & Malting Co. (Milwaukee and Chicago Breweries Co., Ltd.) (908/920 W. 12th St.)	
IL 166	Joseph Reidelberger (Green Bay Rd. near Franklin)	1864-1865
IL 167	Reiser & Portmann (223 Michigan St.)	1859-1860
IL 168	Riverside Brewing Co. (4511 S. Kedzie Ave.) NP	1938-1938
IL 169a	Henry F. L. Rodemeyer (368/370 Ohio St. near the Lake)	1858-1859
169b	Schock, Devry & Co.	1859-1860
IL 170a	Charles Rooth (336 State St.)	1859-1860
170b	Thies & Bouland	1860-1862
IL 171a	Ruehl Bros. Brewing Co. (2646 Harvard St. & Washtenaw Ave.)	1901-1915
171b	Ruehl Bros. Brewing Co. (2630/2660 Arthington St., formerly Harvard)	1915-1925
171c	Roosevelt Brewing Co.	1933-1938
IL 172a	J. S. Saberton (Wolcott & Church nr. N. Division & Lakeshore) aka Saberton Brewery aka Truman Downer aka North Star Brewery (1854-1857) aka J. A. Irvin (1855) aka Isaac Irvin (1856)	1854-1857
172b	Arah P. Dickinson, North Star Brewery, aka Dickinson & Downer, North Star Brewery	1857-1858
172c	James McDonald	1859-1860
172d	J. S. Saberton	1861-1864

Chicago (cont.)

IL 173a	J. J. Sands, Columbia Brewery (Pearson & Pine Sts.)	1855-1863
173b	Sand's Ale Brewing Co., Columbia Brewery aka Hiram Wheeler & Sons (1869-1871)	1863-1871
IL 174a	Scanlon & Prinderville (251 Kinzie)	1862-1864
174b	John Scanlon	1864-1867
IL 175	(Henry) Scheffel & Co. (18/20 Hawthorne Ave.)	1891-1899
IL 176	Schmidt & Bender (509/511 Larrabee)	1866-1870
IL 177	H. Schmidt & Co. (358 S. Clark St.)	1859-1860
IL 178	Schoenhofen Edelweiss Co. (branch of IL 150f - 2132/2146 Laflin St.)	1954-1962
IL 179	Fred. Seibt (785 N. Halsted St.)	1882-1884
IL 180a	Michael Sieben (172/180 Clybourn Ave.)	1896-1898
180b	Michael Sieben (United Breweries Co., aka Sieben Brewery)	1898-1905
IL 181a	Michael Sieben (335/345 Larrabee St.)	1876-1895
181b	Excelsior Brewing Co.	1895-1898
181c	M. Sieben's Brewery (1454/1478 Larrabee St.)	1911-1914
181d	Sieben's Brewery Co.	1914-1920
181e	Mid-City Brewery Co.	1920-1924
181f	Sieben's Brewery Co.	1933-1967
IL 182a	(William) Siebert & (Kaspar) Schmidt, aka Siebert & Co. (221 N. Clark St. between Chicago Ave. & Superior St.)	1860-1864
182b	Siebert & Schmidt (Asylum Pl. near N. Clark & Green Bay Sts.)	1864-1866
182c	K. G. Schmidt (9/35 Grant Pl. & Cleveland Ave.)	1866-1871
182d	Schmidt & Glade	1871-1882
182e	K. G. Schmidt Brewing Co.	1882-1890
182f	K. G. Schmidt Brewing Co. (Milwaukee and Chicago Breweries Co., Ltd., aka United States Brewing Co.)	1890-1909
182g	K. G. Schmidt Brewing Co. (415/445 Grant Pl.)	1909-1917
IL 183	Siebert & Woelffer (32/38 Chicago Ave.)	1866-1868
IL 184a	The Standard Brewery (W. 12th & 571/600 S. Campbell Ave.)	1892-1920
184b	The Standard Products Co.	1920-1923
IL 185a	Edward R. Stege (702/712 S. Ashland Ave. & 15th St.)	1890-1905
185b	Edward R. Stege Brewery (1467/1508 S. Ashland Ave.)	1905-1923
IL 186	John Stutz (245 Cottage Grove Ave.)	1865-1867
IL 187a	N. P. Svenson (18 Huron)	1866-1867
187b	Henderson & Vedell	1867-1868
IL 188	Ernst Tosetti Brewing Co. (Wright, Butler & 40th Sts.)	1886-1915
IL 189a	Adolph Wagner (70/72 Clyde St.)	1886-1887
189b	Katherine Wagner	1887-1888
189c	Robert Seyer (or Seeger)	1890-1890
189d	Columbia Weiss Beer Brewing Co. (70/72 Osgood St., formerly Clyde)	1893-1896
189e	Martin J. Schnitzins,Columbia Weiss Beer Brewery	1896-1905
IL 190	E. A. Wagner & Co. (80 Willow St.)	1882-1882
IL 191	Louis Wagner (567 96th St. & Commerical Ave.)	1895-1897
IL 192	Louis or Ludwig Wagner (942 N. Clark St.)	1867-1883
IL 193a	Frank Walther Brewing Co., aka Frank Walther (402/416 Paulina & Augusta Sts.)	1878-1881
193b	East Side Brewery Co., aka West Side Brewing Co.	1881-1890
193c	West Side Brewery Co. (City of Chicago Consolidated Brewing and Malting Co., Ltd.) (916 N. Paulina St.) aka The Malt Sinew Co. (1907)	1890-1919
IL 194a	Westminster Brewing Co. (4160/4182 S. Union Ave.)	1935-1938
194b	Prima Brewing co., operating as Prima Co., aka Old Missouri Sales Co.	1938-1941

Chicago (cont.)

IL 195a White Eagle Brewing Co. (18th St. & 792 S. Ashland Ave.) 1900-1909
195b White Eagle Brewing Co. (1703 S. Ashland Ave.) 1909-1910

Chicago Heights

IL 196a Chicago Heights Brewing Co. 1908-1912
196b Home Brewery 1912-1915
196c Chicago Heights Brewery (1230 McKinley Ave.) 1933-1934

IL 197 King Cole Breweries, Inc. (Hanover & 17th Sts.) 1934-1947

Cicero

IL 198 Lincoln Brewing Co. (2101 S. 54th Ave. & 21st St.) 1933-1936

Colehour

IL 199 Louis Wagner 1893-1893

Columbia

IL 200a John Gundlach, Monroe Brewery (Main St.) 1874-1880
200b Klausmann Brewing Co. 1880-1884
200c John Gundlach & Son 1884-1895
200d John Gundlach & Co. 1895-1897
200e Leonhard Schoppe & Son 1897-1898
200f Leonhard Schoppe Jr. 1898-1900
200g Weisenstein & Co. 1900-1903
200h Edward Herman Gundlach 1903-1906

IL 201 Old Monroe Brewing Association NP 1934-1934

Danville

IL 202a Danville Brewing and Ice Co.(325/341 E. North St.) 1894-1906
202b Fecker Brewing Co. 1906-1920
202c Fecker Brewing Co. 1933-1939

IL 203 John Stein (441 E. Van Buren St.) 1874-1899

Decatur

IL 204a (John) Koehler & (Adam) Keck 1855-1860
204b Edward Harpstrite 1860-1862
204c Harpstrite & Shlaudeman 1862-1884
204d Henry Shlaudeman 1884-1888
204e Decatur Brewing Co. (604 E. Cantrell St.) 1888-1916

De Kalb

IL 205 Thos. Corkings 1874-1884

Dixon

IL 206 Blackhawk Brewing Co. NP 1934-1934

IL 207a Brady & Dee (170 E. River St.) 1867-1872
207b Clear's Dixon Brewery 1872-1875
207c Jas. B. Clears 1875-1888
207d Clears Brewing Co., aka Clear's Dixon Brewery 1888-1900
207e J. B. Clears & Son (422/430 E. River St.) 1900-1905

IL 208a Christian Plein (Jackson Ave. & 7th St.) 1874-1877
208b Nicholas Plein 1877-1904
208c Dixon Brewing Co. 1904-1908
208d La Salle City Brewing Co. 1908-1909
208e Dixon Brewing Co. 1909-1911

IL 209 William Thorp 1874-1875

Dunleith

IL 210 L. A. Rhomberg 1874-1875

East St. Louis

IL 211a Central Brewing Co. (18th St. & E. Broadway) 1901-1906
211b Central Brewing Co. (branch of Independent Breweries Co., St. Louis, Mo.) 1906-1909
211c Central Brewery (branch of Independent Breweries Co., St. Louis, Mo.) 1909-1920
211d Central Breweries, Inc. (1800/1816 Broadway) 1933-1939
211e Wm. J. Lemp Brewing Co., aka Lemp Brewery Co. 1939-1945
211f Ems Brewing Co. 1945-1947
211g Columbia Brewing Co. 1947-1948
211h Falstaff Brewing Corp. (branch of St. Louis, Mo.) 1948-1949

East St. Louis (cont.)

IL 212 East St. Louis Brewing Co. 1891-1891

IL 213a E. Schroeder & Co. 1891-1893
213b George Schroeder (919 Illinois Ave.) 1893-1901
213c Hartmann Bottling Works (234 N. 5th St.) 1901-1902
213d East St. Louis Bottling Works and Weiss Beer Brewery 1902-1903

IL 214a Siemon & Krug 1860-1870
214b F. Heim & Bro. (Ferdinand & Michael) 1870-1880
214c Heim's Brewery Co. (10th St. & Illinois Ave.) 1880-1889
214d Heim Brewery, branch of St. Louis Brewing Association 1889-1920

Edwardsville

IL 215 Henry Mick 1874-1880

Effingham

IL 216 Mary Berning 1874-1875

Elgin

IL 217 Elgin National Brewing Co. (151/161 Brook Ave. at Dexter Ave.) 1906-1915

IL 218a Charles Tazewell, Eagle Brewery 1849-1868
218b C. Althen & Co., Eagle Brewery 1868-1877
218c Caspar Althen 1877-1891
218d Caspar Althen & Sons (347/379 N. State St.) 1891-1894
218e Elgin Eagle Brewing Co. 1894-1920

Ellington

IL 219 F. X. Schill 1880-1882

El Paso

IL 220 Fix & Co. 1874-1875

Fayetteville

IL 221a Louis Hedwig 1875-1877
221b P. & F. Luers 1877-1878

Freeburg

IL 222a Aug. Meyer 1878-1879
222b J. Reichert 1879-1884

Freeport (formerly Silver Creek)

IL 223a Knipschlid 1845- ?
223b Haegele & Roth 1874-1904
223c Louis J. Roth 1904-1907
223d Yellow Creek Brewery 1907-1920

IL 224a McGee Brothers (Adams & Jackson Sts.) 1849-1854
224b Wade 1854-1856
224c Hertrich 1858-1869
224d Baier & Seyfarth 1869-1891
224e Baier & Ohlendorf 1891-1912
224f B. & O. Brewery, Wm. Ohlendorf 1912-1920
224g Ohlendorf Brewery (13½ Main) NP 1934-1934

IL 225a Jos. Milner & Bros. (Chicago St. & Oak Pl.) 1864-1884
225b George Milner & Co. 1884-1904
225c W. C. Milner & Co. 1904-1905
225d Bear Brewing Co. 1905-1910

IL 226a M. Schmich & Co. (422/430 N. Galena St.) 1885-1896
226b Franz Bros. 1896-1898
226c Franz Bros. Brewing Co. 1898-1920

IL 227a M. Schmich & Co. (293/321 E. Stephenson St.) 1888-1896
227b Schmich Bros. Brewing Co. 1896-1904
227c Schmich Bros. 1904-1920
227d Fritz Brewing Co. 1934-1937
aka Schmick Brewery Co. (1934)
227e Sterling Brewers, Inc. 1937-1939

Freiburg

IL 228 Jac Reichert 1874-1875

Galena		
IL 229a	Martin Blum (Franklin St.)	1891-1908
229b	Martin Blum Brewing Co.	1908-1920
IL 230	City Brewery, John Gun	c1850-1852
IL 231a	Gund & Wetzel	1850-1850
231b	Wetzel	1850-c1853
IL 232	Hony & Metzger	1874-1884
IL 233a	John Maser	1874-1877
233b	Rudolph Speier	1877-1880
IL 234a	Meller & Haser	1874-1884
234b	Haser & Son	1884-1888
IL 235a	Math. Meller (605 Prospect & Spring Sts.)	1874-1885
235b	Casper Eulberg & Sons	1885-1920
235c	Galena Brewing Co.	1934-1936
IL 236	Specht	1843- ?
IL 237a	Volz & Glueck	c1850- ?
237b	John F. Glueck	c -1861
Geneseo		
IL 238a	Geo. Geisser & Co.	1874-1884
238b	Geneseo Brewing Co.	1884-1895
Gilman		
IL 239	G. Rosenberger	1875-1875
Gilmer (see Mundelein)		
Golconda		
IL 240	J. V. Linder	1874-1875
Granite City		
IL 241a	Wagner Brewing Co. (2101/2119 Adams St. at 21st St.)	1905-1906
241b	Wagner Brewing Co. (br. of Independent Breweries Co., St. Louis, MO)	1906-1909
241c	Wagner Brewery (br. of Independent Breweries Co.)	1909-1920
241d	Wagner Brewing Co. (br. of City Ice & Fuel Co., Cleveland, OH)	1933-1938
241e	American Brewing Co. (br. of New Orleans, LA)	1938-1940
Harlem		
IL 242	Huber & Co.	1880-1884
IL 243	M. & M. Steffen	1874-1875
Hartland		
IL 244	Capital Breweries Inc. (10 S. LaSalle St.)	NP 1934-1934
Harvard		
IL 245	John Huebner	1878-1879
Havana		
IL 246a	Hoffman & Dehm	1874-1875
246b	Dehm & Reichel	1875-1877
246c	Dehm & Mack	1877-1882
246d	John L. Dehm	1882-1884
246e	Joseph Dehm	1884-1888
Highland		
IL 247a	Gerhard Schott	1855-1856
247b	Martin & Christian Schott	1856-1870
247c	Martin J. Schott	1870-1885
247d	Highland Brewing Co.	1885-1920
247e	Schott Brewing Co. (412/422 W. 13th St. at Mulberry St.)	1933-1940
247f	Schott Breweries, Inc.	1940-1947
247g	Gast St. Louis Brewing Co. (br. of St. Louis, MO)	1947-1949
Huntley		
IL 248	(The) Huntley Brewing Co. (Mill St. & Railroad Ave.)	1934-1936
Jacksonville		
IL 249a	Henry Rick & Son	1874-1877
249b	H. Rick & Sons	1877-1884

Joliet

IL 250a	Braun & Braun (Bridge & Summit Sts.)	1865-1868
250b	Joseph Braun & Co.	1868-1870
250c	Fred Sehring, Columbia Brewery	1870-1883
250d	Fred. Sehring Brewing Co.	1883-1902
250e	Fred. Sehring Brewing Co. (Scott & Clay Sts.)	1902-1920
250f	Acme Brewing Co., aka Acme Brewing Co. of Joliet, Ill. (412/472 Scott St.)	1933-1939
IL 251a	Citizens Brewing Co.	1904-1905
251b	Joliet Citizens Brewing Co. (Collins St.)	1905-1920
251c	Joliet Citizens Brewing Co. (100/108 Collins St.)	1933-1948
251d	Bohemian Brewing Co. aka Van Merritt Brewing Co. (1955-1958)	1948-1958
IL 252	Joliet Rye Pabst Co. (River St.)	1893-1893
IL 253a	Edwin Porter (138 S. Bluff St.)	1858-1891
253b	E. Porter Brewing Co.	1891-1920
253c	E. Porter Brewing Co. (142/300 S. Bluff St.)	1933-1935
IL 254a	Hillside Brewing Co. (515 Summit St.)	1933-1934
254b	Pioneer Brewing Co.	1934-1948
IL 255	Scheidt Bros. (208/210 S. Bluff St.)	1902-1910
IL 256a	(Anthony) Scheidt & (Joseph) Stephens	1862-1870
256b	Henry Eder (acquired by IL 224)	1870-1883

Jonesboro

IL 257	Peter Hofmann	1874-1875

Kankakee

IL 258	Martin Andres	1858-1861
IL 259a	Jacob Hanly	1860-1865
259b	Fred Beckman	1865-1867
259c	Beckman & Meyer	1867-1870
259d	Beckman & Schneider	1870-1872
259e	Beckmann & Radeke	1872-1874
259f	F. D. Radeke	1874-1877
259g	F. D. Radeke Brewing Co. (Dearborn Ave. at River St.)	1877-1920
259h	Kankakee Beverage Co. (612/613 S. Dearborn Ave.)	1933-1934
259i	Kankakee Beverage Co. of Kankakee, Ill.	1934-1935
259j	Riverside Brewing Co.	1935-1937
IL 260	Rosenbauer & Hoeffling	1858-1859
IL 261a	John Sigerald	1857-1860
261b	Schumacher & Ziegner	c1862
261c	Adam Hanly	? -1868
261d	John A. Huck	1868-1870
261e	Diehl & Magnus	1870-1873
261f	Geo. Diehl	1873-1877

Kewanee

IL 262	Kewanee Brewing Co. (230 S. Tremont St.)	1905-1920
IL 263	Frederick Lee	1874-1891

Knoxville

IL 264	John Krotter	1874-1884

Lacon

IL 265a	Hochstrasser & Co.	1874-1879
265b	Jacob Hochstrasser	1879-1882
265c	John Eppel	1882-1884
265d	Mast Bros.	1884-1888
265e	Mast & Baumgartner	1888-1890

LaSalle

IL 266a	L. Eliel & Co.	1874-1879
266b	Eliel Brewing Co.	1879-1888
266c	La Salle Brewing Co.	1888-1897
266d	La Salle Malting & Brewing Association	1897-1898
266e	La Salle Brewing Co.	1898-1908

La Salle (cont.)

IL 267 Star Brewing Co. 1893-1893

Lebanon

IL 268 Jacob Hammel 1860-1888

IL 269a Mathias Rithmann 1893-1915
269b Lebanon Brewery (Mathias Rithmann) 1915-1920

Limestone

IL 270 George Keller 1874-1884

Lincoln

IL 271 Peter Mueller & Son 1874-1878

Lyons

IL 272 Mueller Bros. (Ogden Ave. on the Des Plaines River) 1856-1873

Mascoutah

IL 273a (L.) Heiligenstein & (W.) Friedrich 1864-1870
273b Hermann & Eisele 1870-1877
273c Eisele & Koehler 1877-1884
273d Mascoutah Brewing Co. 1884-1920

Mattoon

IL 274 Fred Kinzel 1874-1875

McHenry

IL 275a King & Herber 1875-1877
275b G. Bailey 1877-1884
275c Gottlieb F. Boley 1884-1900
275d McHenry Brewery, Grot & Damgard 1900-1905
275e McHenry Brewery, M. L. Worts 1905-1920
275f McHenry Brewing Co. (Pearl & Green Sts.) 1934-1943

Melrose

IL 276a G. Schanz 1880-1880
276b John Schanz 1880-1882

Mendota

IL 277a Dietrich Volk 1853-1858
277b Volk & (Emil) Haas 1858-1862
277c Volk & Kneip 1862-1866
277d Schlesinger, Volk & Co. 1866-1867
277e Volk & (Christian) Henning 1867-1869
277f Henning & (Frank) Gruber 1869-1875
277g Christian Henning 1875-1890
277h C. Henning & Sons 1890-1895
277i Henning Brewing Co. 1895-1910
277j Mendota Brewing Co. 1910-1912

Metamora

IL 278 Ludwig Siegmann 1898-1908

Millstadt

IL 279a Millstadt Brewing Co. 1902-1902
279b Millstadt Brewery Co. 1902-1920

Mokena

IL 280a C. A. Mitchell & Son, Inc. (Wolfe Rd.) 1933-1937
280b Mitchell Brewing Co. 1937-1940

Moline

IL 281a George Seibel 1874-1874
281b C. M. Lindvall & Co. 1874-1875

IL 282 Swedish Small Beer Brewery, Olaf Soderholm 1905-1906

IL 283a Wetsal-Bergstrom Brewing Co. 1898-1898
283b Wetsell Brewing Co. 1898-1899

Monmouth

IL 284a Fowler & Co. ? -1874
284b Fred. Geyer 1874-1875

Morris

IL 285	Bauman & Wahl	1874-1884
IL 286a	Lewis Gebhardt (W. Washington St.)	1866-1886
286b	William Gebhardt	1886-1920

Mount Carroll

IL 287	Charles Medler	1874-1884

Mount Vernon

IL 288a	Wetzel & Fuchs	1878-1879
288b	John Wetzel	1879-1884

Mundelein, Village of Gilmer

IL 289	Zeman Brewing Co. (Chicago & McHenry Rd.)	1942-1964

Murphysboro

IL 290a	Conrad Broeg	1867-1886
290b	Murphysboro Brewing Co.	1886-1899
290c	Rudolph Stecher Brewing Co.	1899-1920
290d	The Stecher Brewing Co. (1320 Rover St.)	1935-1940

Naperville

IL 291a	Jacob Engelfritz	1848-1848
291b	Peter Stenger Sr. (Franklin Ave. btwn. Main & Webster Sts.)	1848-1851
291c	John Stenger	1851-1892
291d	Chicago and Naperville Brewing and Malt Co.	1892-1893
291e	Chicago and Naperville Brewing Co.	1893-1896
291f	Joseph Schamberger	1896-1897
IL 292	Von Hollen & Kluetsch	1874-1875

Nashville

IL 293	Ewald Lungstras	1874-1875

Nauvoo

IL 294	F. Hausmann	1875- ?
IL 295a	Gottfried T. Schenk	c1849-1880
295b	Schenk & Bro.	1880-1884
295c	Schenk Bros. (Peter & Herman)	1884-1906
295d	H. J. Schenk & Sons	1906-1909

New Athens

IL 296a	Stephen Astor	1874-1875
296b	Jacob Hoos	1875-1877
296c	New Athens Brewery, Jacob Hoos Jr.	1877-1884
296d	New Athens Brewery (Kaskaskia & Benton Sts.)	1884-1904
296e	East St. Louis - New Athens Brewing Co.	1904-1920
296f	Mound City Brewing Co. (100/106 Benton St.)	1933-1951
IL 297	Ambrose Roth	1891-1891

Northville

IL 298a	Richard Reutlinger	1879-1884
298b	Gottlieb Haag	1884-1891
298c	Eliza Haag	1891-1893

Oswego

IL 299	Rudolph Keiff	1874-1875

Ottawa

IL 300	Theodore Giese	1882-1884
IL 301	J. C. Maar	1874-1875
IL 302a	O'Reilly & Hanbury	1855-1856
302b	Hanbury & White	1856-1864
302c	Alfred White	1864-1898
302d	Estate of Alfred White	1898-1902
IL 303a	Ottawa Brewing Association	1906-1920
303b	Ottawa Products Co.	NP 1934-1934
IL 304a	Rabenstein & Bro.	1874-1877
304b	C. Rabenstein	1877-1884

Pecatonia

IL 305a Wm. Berridge 1874-1882
305b Joseph Berridge 1882-1884
305c Charles Hayer 1884-1888
305d Ernst Wenzel 1898-1891

Pekin

IL 306 Seidler & Bender 1874-1875

IL 307 Steger & Reiner 1875- ?

IL 308a Aug. Winkel (100 Caroline St.) 1865-1888
308b August Winkel Brewing Co. 1888-1895
308c Winkel Brewing Co. 1895-1900
308d American Brewing Co. 1900-1920
308e Illinois Brewing Co. NP 1934-1934

Peoria

IL 309a Conrad Bitz (S. Water & Cass Sts.) 1874-1884
309b Joseph Kollmer & Co. 1884-1893
309c S. O. Mittler 1893-1895
309d Columbia Brewery 1895-1898

IL 310a Gipps & Co. (Bridge & Water Sts.) 1874-1882
310b Gipps Brewing Co. 1882-1920
310c Gipps Brewing Co. (500 S. Water St. at Franklin St.) 1934-1954

IL 311 Gipps, Cody & Co. 1874-1875

IL 312a Huber & Rauschkolb, City Brewery 1849- ?
312b J. Huber & Son 1874-1876
312c Jacob Miller (or Mueller) 1876-1880
312d Valentine Ulrich (Irving & Water Sts.) 1880-1884
312e Gustav Leisy & Co. 1884-1888
312f Gus. Leisy Brewing Co. 1888-1894
312g Leisy Brewing Co. (701/733 N. Water St.) 1894-1920

IL 313 Louis Langenberg 1874-1875

IL 314 C. F. Poggensee & Co. 1905-1905

IL 315a Union Brewing Co. (1700/1711 S. Washington St.) 1886-1920
315b Peoria Brewing Co. 1934-1940

IL 316 Aug. Weber 1874-1879

IL 317 John Wichmann 1874-1875

Peoria Heights

IL 318a Premier Pabst Corp. (br. of Milwaukee, WI, 4541 Prospect Rd.) 1934-1938
318b Pabst Brewing Co. (br. of Milwaukee, WI) 1938-1982

Peru

IL 319a Fred Kaiser 1856- ?
319b Anton Hahn 1874-1877
319c Union Beer Co. 1877-1880
319d Union Brewing Co. 1880-1891
319e Star Union Brewing Co. (Jefferson & Brewster Sts.) 1891-1920
319f Star Union Products Co. 1933-1963
319g Star Union Products Co. (br. of Canadian Ace Brewing Co., Chicago, IL) 1963-1966

IL 320a William Rausch (Putnam St. & Chicago, Rock Island & Pacific Railway) 1847-1851
320b Rausch & Behrend 1851-1857
320c Behrend & Kitzinger 1857-1860
320d P. K. Behrend 1860-1868
320e Peru Beer Co. 1868-1872
320f (Andrew) Hebel & (Herman) Brunner 1872-1888
aka Peru Brewing Co. (1874-1879)
320g Charles Herbold 1888-1889
320h Peru Beer Co. (1001 Center St. at Farm St.) 1889-1920
320i Peru Products Co. (9545 Bluff St.) 1933-1943

Petersburg

IL 321 Wolfgang Felner 1875- ?

Princeton

IL 322 Jacob Albrecht 1874-1875

IL 323 John Prafcke 1880-1884

Quincy

IL 324 Anton Delabar 1840- ?

IL 325a Dick & Bros. (Matthew, John & Jacob), Quincy Brewing Co. (9th & York Sts.) 1857-1888
325b Dick & Bros., Quincy Brewery Co. 1888-1920
325c Dick & Bros., Quincy Brewery Co. 1933-1937
325d Dick Brothers Brewing Co. 1937-1951

IL 326a Eber & Hoering 1864-1870
326b Eber Bros. 1870-1879
326c Eber Brewing Co. (6th Ave. & Chestnut St.) 1879-1884
326d Schanz & Wahl Brewing Co. 1884-1891
326e Wahl Brewing Co. 1891-1904

IL 327 Gem City Brewing Co. (9th & Harrison Sts.) 1888-1895

IL 328a M. Koerner 1878-1880
328b J. A. Steinbach & Co. 1880-1882
328c F. X. Schill (Front & Bluff Sts.) 1882-1908
328d F. X. Schill Estate (Theresa Schill) 1908-1909

IL 329a J. Luther & Co. 1874-1877
329b J. Luther 1877-1879
329c Mary Luther 1879-1880
329d Durrstein & Co. 1880-1884
329e L. J. Goerres 1884-1890
329f Gottlieb Schanz, Washington Brewery (600 State St.) 1890-1911

IL 330a Caspar Ruff c1842- ?
330b Ruff & Brinkwirth ? -1850
330c Caspar Ruff 1850-1855
330d Ruff Bros. & Co. (12th & Adams Sts.) 1855-1882
330e Ruff Brewing Co. (1137/1139 S. 12th Sts.) 1882-1920
330f Ruff-Riedel Brewing Co. 1933-1943
330g Ruff Brewing Co. 1943-1948

IL 331 Yeck & Becker 1874-1875

Red Bud

IL 332 Emil Berger 1874-1875

Rochelle

IL 333 Budlong & Miller 1874-1875

IL 334 House & Hall 1875- ?

Rockford

IL 335a J. W. Diamond 1875-1877
335b Aug. Kauffman 1877-1884

IL 336 Fred. Finder 1882-1882

IL 337a Fisher, Wahl & Co. 1874-1877
337b Fisher & Wahl 1877-1891

IL 338a Jonathan Peacock (Foot of Prairie St.) 1849-1884
338b J. Peacock & Son 1884-1897
338c Peacock Brewery 1897-1899
338d Rockford Brewing Co. (200/212 Prairie St.) 1899-1920
338e Rockford Brewing Co. 1933-1937
338f Rock River Brewing Co. 1937-1941

IL 339 Peterson & Davis 1875- ?

IL 340 A. Schlenk 1874-1875

IL 341 Skandia Pop Mfg. Co. 1893-1893

Rock Island

IL 343a	J. A. King & Co.	1874-1880
343b	Raible & Stengel (3rd Ave. & 4th St.)	1880-1891
343c	Raible & Stengel (Rock Island Brewing Co.)	1891-1893
343d	Rock Island Brewing Co.	1893-1902
IL 344a	(August & Peter) Littig & (Joseph) Dormann	1847-1851
344b	Littig & Co.	1851-1854
344c	Ignatz Huber, City Brewery (3rd Ave. & 24th St.)	1854-1893
344d	Rock Island Brewing Co., Ignatz Huber (7th Ave. & 30th St.)	1893-1920
344e	Rock Island Brewing Co. (701 30th St. at 7th Ave.)	1933-1939
IL 345a	Peter Littig, Sr. & Jr. (Moline Ave.)	e1854-1856
345b	Joseph Schmidt	1856-1865
345c	George Wagner, Atlantic Brewery	1865-1893
345d	Rock Island Brewing Co., Atlantic Brewery (3028 5th Ave.)	1893-1897
IL 346	Rock Island Weiss Beer Brewery	1895-1895

Rossville

IL 347	Cornell & Makenthum	1875- ?

Savannah

IL 348	John Bogue	1874-1875
IL 349	Joseph Keller	1874-1884

Sigel

IL 350	D. Wiedmeier & Co.	1874-1879

Silver Creek (see Freeport)

South Chicago (see Chicago)

Spring Bay

IL 351a	Peter Eichhorn, Sr.	1874-1880
351b	Peter Eichhorn, Jr.	1880-1884
IL 352	Mueller Bros.	1891-1891

Springfield

IL 353	Ph. Ackerman	c1865-1877
IL 354a	Franz Sales Reisch (Rutledge St.)	1849-1854
354b	Andrew Kuhn	1854-1857
354c	Franz Sales Reisch	1857-1858
354d	Reisch & (C. A.) Helmle	1858- ?
354e	F. Reisch & Bretz	? -1862
354f	F. Reisch & Son (Frank)	1862-1869
354g	F. Reisch & Sons (Frank, Joseph, George)	1869-1875
354h	F. Reisch & Bros. (George & John) (Herndon & Rutlege Sts.)	1875-1903
354i	Reisch Brewing Co.	1903-1920
354j	Reisch Brewing Co. (801 N. Rutledge St.)	1934-1966
IL 355	Springfield Brewing Co. (1022/1030 Madison St.) aka Southside Brewing Co. (1934)	1933-1948

Sterling

IL 356a	Frank A. Herrmann	1869- ?
356b	Charles Herrmann	1878-1884
356c	Frank Hermann	1884-1891
356d	Helms & Ufken	1891-1893
356e	Ebenbauer & Franke (2nd St. & 2nd Ave.)	1893-1896
356f	Wm. Franke, Excelsior Brewery	1896-1903
356g	Fred Rautert & Son, Excelsior Brewery	1903-1911
IL 357a	David Wolf	1874-1877
357b	J. Decker & Co.	1877-1879
357c	Sterling Brewing Co.	1879-1888

Teutopolis

IL 358	M. Krieg & Son	1874-1875

Streator

IL 359	Streator Brewing and Ice Co.	1907-1907

Thornton		
IL 360a	John S. Bielfeldt	1857-1897
360b	John S. Bielfeldt Brewing Co.	1897-1920
360c	Thornton Brewing Co. (400/416 E. Margaret at Blackstone St.)	1933-1936
360d	Illinois Brewing Co.	1938-1940
360e	Frederick's Brewing Co.	1940-1948
360f	McAvoy Brewing Co.	1948-1950
360g	White Bear Brewing Co., Inc.	1952-1955
Trenton		
IL 361a	Paul Bassler	1874-1900
361b	Bassler Brewing Co.	1900-1920
361c	Trenton Brewing Co. (Clinton County)	1934-1949
Urbana		
IL 362	John A. Soergel	1875- ?
Warsaw		
IL 363a	Rudolph Giller	1860-1861
363b	Martin Popel	1861-1880
363c	Popel & (John H.) Giller	1880-1897
363d	Popel & Giller Brewing Co.	1897-1906
363e	Popel-Giller Co.	1906-1920
363f	Burgemeister Brewing Co.	NP 1934-1934
363g	Warsaw Brewing Corp. (826 Harrison St.)	1936-1950
363h	Warsaw Brewing Corp. (920 N. 6th St.)	1950-1972
IL 364a	Schott & Bros.	1874-1877
364b	Schott & Son	1877-1880
364c	Eyman & Risser	1880-1882
Washington		
IL 365	John Roth	1879-1884
Waterloo		
IL 366	F. H. Borntraeger	1874-1875
IL 367a	Michael Schorr	1884-1902
367b	Waterloo Brewing Co. (N. Main St.)	1902-1920
Watseka		
IL 368	F. Banlow	1874-1879
Waukegan		
IL 369	John L. Hoerber	c1849-1853
IL 370	Carl Kleiner	1874-1875
IL 371a	Sheip	c1840-1853
371b	William Besley	1853-1868
371c	Besley's Waukegan Brewing Co. (306 S. Utica St.)	1868-1913
371d	Waukegan Brewing Co.	1913-1916
West Belleville		
IL 372a	Brandenberger & Co.	1874-1877
372b	Western Brewery Co.	1877-1884
West Hammond (see Calumet City)		
Wheeling		
IL 373	Becker Brewing Co.	1906-1909
IL 374a	Periolat Bros. & Co.	1874-1893
374b	Wheeling Brewing Co.	1893-1895
374c	H. Periolat (Henry)	1895-1898
374d	H. Periolat Brewing Co., aka Periolat Brewing Co.	1898-1903
Wilmington		
IL 375	Markert & Co.	1874-1899
Woodstock		
IL 376a	John Bertchey	1855- ?
376b	Louis Gebhardt	? -1866
376c	A. Zimmer & Co.	1866-1877
376d	Arnold, Zimmer & Co.	1877-1884
376e	Woodstock Brewing and Bottling Co. (Chemung St.)	1884-1902

Anderson

IN	1	Doxey Brewery	? -1866
IN	2a	(Thomas) Norton & (Patrick) Sullivan	1866- ?
	2b	Norton & (Michael) Crowley	? -1882
	2c	Thomas M. Norton	1882-1900
	2d	T. M. Norton Brewing Co. (202/716 Central Ave.at 7th St.)	1900-1918
	2e	T. M. Norton Brewing Co.	1933-1934
	2f	T. M. Norton Brewing Co.	1937-1939

Attica

IN	3	Anna Smith	1874-1875

Aurora

IN	4a	T. W. Gaff & Co.	1874-1877
	4b	Crescent Brewing Co.	1877-1893

Bowling Green

IN	5	Frederick Stucki	1874-1884

Brazil

IN	6	Brazil Brewing, Ice and Power Co. (W. Main St.)	1901-1907

Bremen

IN	7	Hugo Wolff	1875-1884

Brookville

IN	8	John A. Bussald	1874-1875
IN	9	Gottfried Seibel & Son	1874-1875
IN	10	Adam Stock	1874-1875
IN	11	Conrad Wissel	1874-1875

Cambridge City

IN	12a	Henry Ingermann	1874-1891
	12b	Adelheid Ingermann	1891-1893
	12c	Wm. H. Ingermann	1893-1900
	12d	John M. Ingermann	1900-1904
	12e	Ingermann Brewing Co.	1904-1908
IN	13	Cleophas Straub	1874-1882

Cannelton

IN	14a	Eliza Huber	1875-1877
	14b	Jacob Huber	1877-1884

Centre

IN	15	Jacob Weckerle	1874-1878

Columbia City

IN	16	Gabriel Moser	1875- ?
IN	17a	William Walter	1868-1872
	17b	Schaffer & Walter	1872-1875
	17c	H. Schaffer	1875-1879
	17d	(Frederick) Walter & (Benjamin) Raupfer	1879-1893
	17e	Walter-Raupfer Brewing Co. (Whitely & Ellsworth Sts.)	1893-1916

Columbus

IN	18	Aug. Schreiber	1874-1884
IN	19	Elizabeth Seeling	1874-1875

Connersville

IN	20	Valentine Billan	1874-1884

Covington

IN	21a	James Miller	1874-c1877
	21b	Joseph Miller	c1877-1884

Crawfordsville

IL	22a	R. H. Hannan & Co.	1875-c1877
	22b	Jacob Muth	c1877-1879
	22c	Flaiber & Vance	1879-1884

Crown Point

IN 23a Julius Korn 1860- ?
23b Joseph Horst c1875
23c Korn & Suckfield 1878-1880
23d Korn & (John) Berg 1880-1884
23e John Berg 1884-1888
23f Berg Bros. & Co. 1888-1894
23g Crown Brewing Co. 1894-1909

IN 24 Crown Point Brewing Co. 1893-1893

Decatur

IN 25 John Dozenbach 1874-1875

IN 26a Thoedore Rolver 1874-1875
26b Anna Rolver 1875-1879

Evansville (includes Perry)

IN 27a (Frederick) Cook & (Louis) Rice, City Brewery (214 Upper 7th St. at 8th & Sycamore Sts.) 1853-1885
27b F. W. Cook Brewing Co. (11 N.W. 7th St.) 1885-1918
27c F. W. Cook Co. 1933-1942
27d F. W. Cook Co., Inc. 1942-1955

IN 28a Evansville Brewing Co. (1st Ave. & Ingle St.) 1891-1894
28b Evansville Brewing Association, Evansville Brewery 1894-1915

IN 29a John Hartmetz (Clark & Carpenter Sts., Perry) 1877-1890
29b John Hartmetz & Son 1890-1894
29c Evansville Brewing Association, John Hartmetz & Son Brewery 1894-1895

IN 30 Kothe & Co., aka Henry Kothe & Bro. (Perry) c1875

IN 31a (Jacob) Rice & Kroener, Old Brewery 1837-1850
31b F. Kroner & Son, Old Brewery 1874-1875
31c Old Brewery Co. (Fulton Ave. & Indiana St.) 1875-1884

IN 32 M. Stumpf 1874-1875

IN 33a Unknown 1863- ?
33b Ulmer & Hoedt (330/430 Fulton Ave. & 1310 Pennsylvania St.) 1877-1884
33c Reitman & Schulte 1884-1886
33d Fulton Avenue Brewery 1886-1894
33e Evansville Brewery Association, Fulton Avenue Brewery 1894-1918
33f Sterling Products Co. ? -1933
33g Sterling Brewers, Inc. 1933-1964
33h Sterling Brewers, Inc. (br. of Associated Brewing Co., Detroit) 1964-1967
aka Bavarian's Brewing Co. (1966-1972)
aka Cook's Brewing Co. (1966-1972)
33i G. Heileman Brewing Co. of Indiana 1972-1978
33j G. Heileman Brewing Co., Sterling Brewers, Inc. Division 1978-
aka Blitz Weinhard of Evansville

IN 34 William J. Wittekind Brewing Co., Inc. (11 S. Kentucky Ave.) 1937-1940

Ferdinand

IN 35 John Dickman c1891

IN 36a Henry B. Ruhkamp, Jr. 1875-1884
36b Elizabeth Ruhkamp 1884-1891

IN 37a Stallman & Hang 1888-1891
37b Stallmann, Dickmann & Hang 1891-1893
37c Stallman, Kunkler & Hang 1893-1895
37d Stallman & Hang 1895-1896
37e Stallman, Hang & Hang 1896-1897
37f Ferdinand Brewing Co. 1897-1916

IN 38 Herman Wilbers c1875

Fort Wayne			
IN	39a	Herman Berghoff Brewing Co. (Grant Ave.)	1887-1899
	39b	Berghoff Brewing Co.	1899-1908
	39c	Berghoff Brewing Association	1908-1918
	39d	Berghoff Products Co.	? -1933
	39e	Berghoff Brewing Corp. (1019/1051 Grant Ave.)	1933-1954
	39f	Falstaff Brewing Corp. (br. of St. Louis, MO) aka Christian Feigenspan Brewing Co. (1972-1975)	1954-1975
	39g	Falstaff Brewing Corp. (affiliated with General Brewing Co.), aka Great Lakes Brewing Co., Griesedieck Bros. Brewing Co., James Hanley Co.	1975-
IN	40a	Berghoff Bros. Brewery, Inc. (2200/2332 Dwenger Ave. & 801 Glasgow Ave.)	1934-1934
	40b	Hoff-Brau Brewing Corp.	1934-1951
IN	41a	Charles L. Centlivre (Spy Run Ave.)	1862-1893
	41b	C. L. Centlivre Brewing Co.	1893-1918
	41c	Centlivre Brewing Corp. (2501/2538 Spy Run Ave.)	1933-1961
	41d	Old Crown Brewing Corp. aka Renner Co. (1962-1970)	1961-1973
IN	42a	Certia & Rankert	1874-c1877
	42b	Lutz & Co.	c1877-1880
IN	43	L. J. Horning	1879-1879
IN	44	Henry Hubach	1874-1875
IN	45	Fred Kley	c1875
IN	46	Linker, Hey & Co.	1874-1882
IN	47	J. M. Reidmiller	1874-1875
German			
IN	48a	A. & T. Pauli	1874-c1877
	48b	A. Pauli	c1877-1878
Hammond			
IN	49	Continental Brewing Corp.	NP 1934-1934
IN	50	Charles H. Mayer	1898-1910
IN	51	Hammond Brewing Co. (548 W. State St. & Freeland Ave.)	1910-1915
Harmony			
IN	52	John Bauer	1874-1878
Harrison			
IN	53a	Paulus Walser	1874-c1877
	53b	Reinhold Klant	c1877-1880
Haysville P. O. (Harrison)			
IN	54a	J. G. F. Hoffman	1874-1877
	54b	John B. Kroedel	1877-1893
	54c	Barbara Kroedel	1893-1897
IN	55	John Neukam	1890-1890
Huntingburg			
IN	56	Huntingburg Brewing Co.	? -1895
IN	57a	Moenkhaus, Fritch & Co.	1894-1895
	57b	Moenkhaus & Fritch	1895-1897
	57c	Moenkhaus & Seubold, aka Huntingburg Brewing Co.	1897-1918
IN	58	Joseph Schubler	1874-1875
IN	59	J. F. Strickfaden & Co.	1874-1875
Huntington			
IN	60a	Jacob Boos	c1860-1890
	60b	Carl Lang	1890-1901
	60c	Hoch & Knipp	1901-1902
	60d	Huntington Brewing Co.	1902-1918
IN	61	J. A. Herrberg	1874-1884

Indianapolis

IN	62a	American Brewing Co. (315/337 W. Ohio St.)	1897-1910
	62b	American Brewing Co. (332/340 W. Market St.)	1910-1918
IN	63a	Peter Balz	1874-1877
	63b	Balz & Co.	1877-1878
IN	64a	Capital City Brewing Co. (West & Wisconsin Sts.)	1905-1915
	64b	Citizens Brewing Co.	1915-1918
IN	65	Gold Medal Brewing Co. (1300 Madison Ave.)	NP 1934-1934
IN	66a	Harting & Bro.	1874-1877
	66b	Koehler & Co.	1877-1879
IN	67	Albert Hitzelberger	? -1888
IN	68a	Home Brewing Co. (Cruse & Daly Sts.)	1891-1897
	68b	Home Brewing Co. of Indianapolis	1897-1902
	68c	Home Brewing Co.	1902-1918
IN	69a	Gack & Biser	1859-1863
	69b	P. Lieber (512 Madison Ave.)	1863- ?
	69c	(Peter) Lieber & Co. (Herman Lieber & Charles Myer)	1874-1880
	69d	P. Lieber Brewing Co.	1880-1889
	69e	Indianapolis Brewing Co., P. Lieber Brewing Co.	1889-1904
	69f	Indianapolis Brewing Co., P. Lieber Brewery	1904-1918
	69g	Mid-West Brewing Co.	? -1934
	69h	Richard Lieber Brewing Corp.	1934-1935
	69i	Lieber Brewing Corp. (1254 S. West St.)	1935-1937
	69j	Ajax Brewing Corp.	1937-1941
IN	70a	Casper Maus (W. New York St. at Agnes St.)	1868-1889
	70b	Indianapolis Brewing Co., C. Maus Brewery	1889-1903
	70c	Indiana Breweries, Inc. (930/948 W. New York St. at 316 Agnes)	1933-1935
	70d	Indianapolis Brewing Co., Inc.	1935-1948
IN	71	Jacob Metzger & Co.	1896-1897
IN	72	Philip Petri	1874-1875
IN	73a	(Christian F.) Schmidt & Jaeger	c1858-1859
	73b	C. F. Schmidt (S. End Alabama St.) aka Mrs. Caroline Schmidt (1876-1879)	1959-1889
	73c	Indianapolis Brewing Co., C. F. Schmidt Brewery	1889-1918
IN	74	Frank Wright's Ale Brewery (Blake St.)	c1861-1873
IN	75a	(John) Young & (William) Wernberg (Maryland St.)	1834-c1840
	75b	Faux	c1840- ?

Jasper

IN	76a	E. A. Hochgesang	1874-1875
	76b	Mrs. Cecilia Hochgesang	1875-1884
	76c	Habig & Eckstein	1884-1899
	76d	Anton Habig, Excelsior Brewery	1899-1916

Jeffersonville

IN	77a	Henry Lang	1875-1880
	77b	Kirchgessner & Seng	1880-1884
	77c	J. Kirchgessner	1884-1891
	77d	City Brewing Co. (Graham & Maple Sts.)	1891-1899

Kendallville

IN	78	J. Geo. Kratzer	1875- ?
IN	79a	Wm. Seifert & Co.	1875-1877
	79b	H. C. Paul	1877-1884

Lafayette

IN	80a	John H. Newman (111/119 S. 4th St.)	1843-1858
	80b	Newman & Herbert	1858-1872
	80c	Newman & Bohrer	1872-1888
	80d	Geo. A. Bohrer Brewing Co.	1888-1918

Lafayette (cont.)			
IN	82a	(John) Wagner & (C.) Herbert (151 N. 4th St.)	1848-1862
	82b	(Frederick A.) Thieme & Wagner	1862-1889
	82c	Thieme & Wagner Brewing Co. (800/814 4th St.)	1899-1918
	82d	Lafayette Brewery, Inc. (716/814 N. 4th St.)	1933-1952
La Porte			
IN	83a	Nicholas Bader	1865- ?
	83b	John B. Puissant	1875-1879
	83c	Dick & Klaiber	1879-1880
	83d	C. Dick	1880-1884
	83e	(John B.) Puissant & (Clemens) Dick	1884-1887
	83f	John W. Russert	1887-1896
	83g	Guenther Bros. (Tyler & Lake Sts.)	1896-1911
	83h	Guenther & Zerweck	1911-1918
IN	84	Zahn Brewery	c1850
Lawrenceburgh			
IN	85a	Kosmos Frederick	? -1857
	85b	John B. Garnier (closed and built 87)	1857-1866
IN	86	John B. Garnier (closed & bought 85a)	1855-1857
IN	87a	John B. Garnier Brewery	1866-1897
	87b	J. B. Garnier Brewery, Victor Oberting (3rd & Shipping Sts.)	1897-1916
Lawrenceville			
IN	88	Anton Ritze	1874-1884
Lebanon			
IN	89	H. F. Wiesenham & Bro.	1874-1875
Ligonier			
IN	90	Ligonier Brewery	1875- ?
IN	91a	Andrew Walder	1882-1893
	91b	Drachter & Co.	1893-1897
	91c	Charles Franke	1897-1899
Logansport			
IN	92a	August Frost	1866- ?
	92b	John Mutschler	1874-1888
	92c	Logansport Brewing Co.	1888-1893
	92d	Columbia Brewing Co. (424 High St.)	1893-1918
	92e	K. G. Schmidt Brewing Co., Inc. (412/426 High St.)	1934-1951
IN	93	Jacob Klein	1874-1875
Madison			
IN	94	Elizabeth Butz	1874-1875
IN	95a	Mathias Greiner	1852- ?
	95b	M. Greiner & Sons	1874-1877
	95c	John Greiner	1877-1880
	95d	Greiner & Co.	1880-1882
	95e	Madison Brewing Co. (220/224 Park Ave.)	1882-1918
IN	96	Jacob Salmon	1823-1841
IN	97a	Sheik Brewery	1841-1845
	97b	Ross Brewery	?
	97c	Belser & Co.	1874-1878
IN	98a	Peter Weber's Union Brewery aka Adam Weber (1875)	1863-1891
	98b	Peter Weber (Main & Vine Sts.)	1891-1912
Marion			
IN	99a	Indiana Brewing Association (Railroad Ave.)	1897-1912
	99b	Kiley Brewing Co., Inc. (1550 Railroad Ave.)	1934-1942
	99c	Fox DeLuxe Brewing Co. of Indiana, Inc. (br. of Peter Fox Brewing Co., Chicago, IL) (525 Lincoln Blvd.)	1942-1950

Michigan City		
IN 101a	Philip Zorn (9th & York Sts.)	1871-1891
101b	Ph. Zorn Brewing Co.	1891-1918
101c	Zorn Brewing Co., Inc.	1933-1935
101d	Dunes Brewery, Inc.	1935-1938
Mishawaka		
IN 102	Louis H. Van Dinter	1895-1904
IN 103a	John Wagner	1853-1870
103b	C. Dick & Co. (A. Kamm)	1870-1877
103c	A. Kamm	1877-1879
103d	(Adolph) Kamm & (Nicholas) Schellinger	1879-1887
103e	Kamm & Schellinger Brewing Co. (W. 2nd St.)	1887-1918
103f	Kamm & Schellinger Co., Inc. (N. Center St.)	1933-1951
Muncie		
IN 104	Ch. Alvery	1878-1879
IN 105a	Fay & Garst	1875-1877
105b	A. J. Garst	1877-1882
105c	Bartlett & Garst	? -1890
IN 106	Muncie Brewing Co. (Willard & Hoyt Aves.)	1904-1912
Napoleon		
IN 107	Nicholas Morbach	1874-1882
New Albany		
IN 108a	Borchardt & Birk	1898-1898
108b	Edward Birk	1898-1899
108c	Veit Nirmaier, State Street Brewery	1899-1918
IN 109a	Peter Buchheit	1874-1877
109b	Mrs. Barbara Buchheit	1877-1884
109c	Gerhard Brown	1884-1888
109d	Andreas Schlosser	1888-1891
IN 110a	Paul Reising (W. 4th & Spring Sts.)	1847-1884
110b	Paul Reising & Co.	1884-1892
110c	Paul Reising Brewing Co.	1892-1915
110d	Southern Indiana Brewing Co.	1915-1918
110e	Southern Indiana Ice & Beverage Co., Inc. (315 W. 4th St.)	1933-1935
IN 111	Frederick S. Ruoff	1890-1890
IN 112a	Louis Schmidt	1882- ?
112b	Hornung & Atkins	? -1884
112c	Jacob Hornung	1884-1888
112d	Indiana Brewing Co. (West & Main Sts.)	1888-1895
112e	Pank-Weinmann Brewing Co. (merged with 110c)	1895-1899
IN 113a	Louisa Sohn	1874-1877
113b	Frank Nadorff	1877-1884
113c	Threcy Nadorff	1884-1891
113d	Peter Engel (477 Vincennes St.)	1891-1902
113e	Engel & Nardorff Bros.	1902-1907
IN 114	Terstegge & Co.	c1888
New Alsace		
IN 115a	Martin Meyer	1874-1893
115b	Martin Meyer & Co.	1893-1898
IN 116a	Michael Zix	1874-1888
116b	George Zix	1888-1893
Newburgh		
IN 117	Charles Brizins & Co.	1874-1880
New Castle		
IN 118	Patrick Leonard	1874-1875
New Haven		
IN 119	Strasbourg Brewing Co.	1882-1904
Noblesville		
IN 120	Joseph Xafer	1874-1875

North Judson

IN 121a North Judson Brewing Co. 1898-1901
121b Northern Indiana Brewing Co. 1901-1908

North Vernon

IN 122 John Schierling 1874-1884

Oldenburg

IN 123a Balthasar Roell 1878-1879
123b B. Roell & Co. 1879-1882
123c Balthasar Roell 1882-1901

Osgood

IN 124 John Wagner 1874-1875

Perry (see Evansville)

Peru

IN 125a George Rettig & Son 1859-1860
125b Rettig & Cole 1860-1878
125c James O. Cole 1878-1908

Petersburg

IN 126 John Mersenhetter 1874-1875

Plymouth

IN 127 J. Weckerle 1878-1884

Richmond

IN 128a George Buhl 1845-1860s
128b Emil Mink & Co. 1860s-1877
128c Emil Minck 1877-1899
128d Minck Brewing Co. 1899-1918
128e Richmond Brewing Co. NP 1934-1934

IN 129a Joseph Martischang 1874-1879
129b Mrs. Margaret Martischang 1879-1884

Ridgeville

IN 130 J. K. Hammerle 1874-1875

Rochester

IN 131 John B. Metzler 1878-1879

St. Leon

IN 132 L. Bischoff 1878-1880

St. Peters

IN 133 John H. Busold 1878-1884

Seymour

IN 134 Martin Dammrich 1874-1884

IN 135 J. D. Kaufmann 1874-1882

Shelbyville

IN 136 Margaret Stephan 1874-1875

South Bend

IN 137a Christopher Muessel 1852- ?
137b Muessel Bros. 1874-1891
137c W. & W. Muessel 1891-1893
137d Muessel Brewing Co. 1893-1918
137e The Muessel Brewing Co. (1408 Elwood Ave.) 1933-1936
137f Drewrys Ltd., U.S.A., Inc. 1936-1965
137g Drewrys Ltd., U.S.A., Inc. (br. of Associated Brewing Co., Detroit, Michigan) 1966-1972

137f & 137g:
aka Associated Brewing Co. (1967-1972)
aka Atlantic Brewing Co. (1964-1966)
aka Atlas Brewing Co. (1963-1966)
aka Bavarians Brewing Co. (1967-1972)
aka Frankenmuth Brewing Co. (1961-1971)
aka 9 - 0 - 5 Brewing Co. (1966-1970)
aka Old Dutch Brewing Co. (1967-1972)
aka Pfeiffer Brewing Co. (1967-1972)

South Bend (cont.)

IN 138	South Bend Brewing Co. (1622 Michigan Ave.)	1895-1897
IN 139a	South Bend Brewing Association	1905-1918
139b	South Bend Beverage & Ice Association (1622/1702 Lincolnway W. & 739/743 College St.)	1933-1936
139c	South Bend Brewing Co.	1936-1950

Sunman

IN 140	P. Schneider	1879-1882

Tell City

IN 141a	Charles Becker	1872-1884
141b	Alois Becker	1884-1894
141c	Robert E. Huthsteiner	1894-1897
141d	Tell City Brewing Co.	1897-1918
IN 142	Fred Voelke Jr.	1875-1884

Terre Haute

IN 143	Ballard, Seventh Street Brewery	1848- ?
IN 144a	Henry Becker	1898-1905
144b	Estate of Henry Becker	1905-1906
144c	Henry J. Becker	1906-1908
144d	Chas. J. Graf	1908-1908
IN 145a	George & Henry Glick	1850- ?
145b	Moses Easter	1874-1875
IN 146a	George Hager (Outlot 23)	1836-1836
146b	Hoager & Graff	1836-1837
146c	Joseph Graff & Son	1837-1838
146d	John Kittiwill	1838-1843
146e	Demas Fleming	?
146f	Chauncey Warren	c1848
IN 147	Albert Hertwig (8th & Poplar Sts.)	c1851-1860
IN 148	Hermann Imbery	1874-1875
IN 149	Reinhold Klant	1875- ?
IN 150a	Mogger	1855-1868
150b	A. Kaufmann	1868-1868
150c	Kaufmann & Mayer	1868-1869
150d	Anton Mayer (Poplar & 9th St.)	1869-1889
150e	Terre Haute Brewing Co. (901/935 Poplar St. & 9th St.)	1889-1918
150f	Terre Haute Brewing Co. (440 S. 9th St.)	1934-1957
150g	Terre Haute Brewing Corp.	1957-1958
IN 151	Peoples Brewing Co. (1st & Wilson Sts.)	1905-1918
IN 152a	Chris. Stark (200 S. 9th St.)	1900-1906
152b	Estate of Chris. Stark	1906-1910
152c	Chris. Stark Bottling Works	1910-1913
IN 153	N. S. Wheat	1878-1879

Troy

IN 154a	Heinze & Thaney	1874-1877
154b	John Thaney	1877-1884
154c	John S. Winterath	1884-1895
154d	Jacob Kunkler	1895-1905
154e	Troy Model Brewery	1905-1909
154f	Troy Model Brewing Co.	1909-1914

Union City

IN 155	(Thomas) Norton & (Louis) Williams Ale Brewery	c1860-1866

Valparaiso

IN 156a	George Hiller	1874-1880
156b	Korn & Junker	1880-1882
156c	George Hiller	1882-1884

Vera Cruz

IN 157	Samuel Gehring	1874-1875

Vincennes

IN 158a	John Ebner, Eagle Brewery (Indianapolis Ave.)	1859-1875
158b	(Eugene) Hack & (Anton) Simon, Eagle Brewery	1875-1918
158c	Old Vincennes Brewery, Inc.	NP 1934-1934

Wabash

IN 159a	F. A. Rettig	1854-1866
159b	Rettig & (Philip) Alber	1866-1900
159c	Wabash Brewing Co.	1900-1916

Washington

IN 160	Arnold Gubelmann	? -1874
IN 161	Senn & Rekers	1890-1890

Winchester

IN 162	Conrad Meier	1875- ?

IOWA

Ackley

IA 1	Chas. Jacobs	1875-1875

Afton

IA 2	John Heine	1874-1884

Algona

IA 3	F. Pompe & Co.	1880-1882
IA 4	August Zahlton Co.	c1865

Anamosa

IA 5	A. B. Head Co.	c1865
IA 6	M. F. Rick	1878-1880

Arcadia

IA 7	Rudolph Holler	1882-1884

Atlantic

IA 8a	Ernest Fisher	1878-1882
8b	Ernest G. Fisher	1882-1888
IA 9	Philip Young	c1865

Auburn

IA 10a	Ignatz Bilger	1874-1877
10b	Katherine Bilger	1877-1879

Avoca

IA 11	Jacob Kampf	1875-1884

Belle Plaine

IA 12a	Suess & Michel	1875-1875
12b	Mathias Michel	1875-1880

Bellevue

IA 13a	Henry Nienstadt	1878-1903
13b	Herman Ellinghaus	1903-1904
IA 14	Fabion Shirmer	c1865
IA 15	Julius Sineman	c1865

Boone

IA 16	J. M. Hermann	1866-1884

Boonsboro

IA 17a	John Blemen	c1865- ?
17b	John Zimbelman	1874-1877
17c	L. Zimbelman & Co.	1877-1879
17d	L. & A. Zimbelman	1879-1884

Bradford

IA 18a	E. Wimmer	1852- ?
18b	Friderici & Wimmer	1874-1875

Bridgeport

IA	19a	Jaeger & Walz	1874-1877
	19b	Bernhart Walz	1877-1880
	19c	Jaeger & Schwartz	1880-1882

Brown's Station

IA	20a	Staubler & Hemfling	1874-1877
	20b	Henry Brown	1877-1879
	20c	L. Hemfling	1879-1880
	20d	John Hemfling	1880-1882

Buffalo

IA	21a	Frederick & Hoffbauer	c1865- ?
	21b	Hugo Hoffbauer	1874-1888
IA	22	Theo. Kantz	1878-1882
IA	23	John Rathberger	1874-1878

Burlington

IA	24a	George Bosch, Western Steam Brewery (1134 Bosch Road) aka Geo. Bosch & Ch. J. Leonard (1859)	1855-1868
	24b	A. Bosch, Western Steam Brewery aka A. & B. Bosch (1870)	1868-1877
	24c	Bosch Bros., Western Steam Brewery	1877-1882
	24d	Berthold Bosch, Western Steam Brewery aka B. Bosch & Bros. (1884-1885)	1882-1888
IA	25a	Geo. Bosch & Co. (518 S. Main St.)	1852-1877
	25b	John & George Bosch & Co.	1877-1882
	25c	George Bandleon, Lowertown Brewery	1882-1888
IA	26a	Wm. Dambmann & E. Willem (1122 Agency St.)	1856-1859
	26b	Inez Willem	1859-1866
	26c	William Metzger, City Brewery	1866-1874
	26d	Margaret Metzger, City Brewery	1874-1876
	26e	Phil P. Rothenberger, City Brewery	1876-1879
	26f	Bernard Walz & Christ. Mesmer, City Brewery	1879-1882
	26g	Walz & Beck, City Brewery	1882-1884
	26h	Bernard Walz, City Brewery	1884-1885
	26i	Adolph Metzger, City Brewery	1885-1886
	26j	Bosch & Ganz, City Brewery	1886-1888
IA	27a	Eli & Moehn, Hawkeye Brewery (Elm & 2nd Sts.)	1868-1869
	27b	Huber & Moehn, Hawkeye Brewery	1869-1870
	27c	C. L. Huber, Hawkeye Brewery	1870-1871
IA	28a	A. Fensterer, Iowa Brewery (Jefferson & Boundary)	1856-1859
	28b	Alois Fensterer & Frederick Gugel, Iowa Brewery	1859-1860
	28c	Frederick Gugel, Iowa Brewery	1860-1866
	28d	A. Fenster, Iowa Brewery	1866-1870
	28e	Fred Stuckmann, Iowa Brewery	1870-1873
IA	29a	Fisher & Co., City Brewery (Jefferson & 7th Sts.)	1856-1858
	29b	Peter Fisher, City Brewery	1858-1860
IA	30	A. Kammerer	1874-1875
IA	31a	Martin Moehn, Western Brewery (Long St.)	1892-1903
	31b	Moehn Brewing Co.	1903-1911
	31c	Moehn Brewing Co. (Comer, Lucas, Mt. Pleasant & 922 Osborn St.)	1911-1915
IA	32a	Charles Mueller (863/869 Jefferson St.)	1849- ?
	32b	Bauer & Schaffner, Burlington Brewery	1859-1873
	32c	Casper Heil, Burlington Brewery	1874-1889
	32d	Casper Heil, Burlington Brewery aka Heil & Moyer (1900-1901)	1890-1904
	32e	Heil & Son, Burlington Brewery	1904-1905
	32f	Casper Heil Brewing Co.	1904-1915
IA	33	A. Stenger	c1865

Burlington (cont.)

IA	34a	(Alfred V.) Wertmueller & (Charles) Ende Union Brewery (1307 Mt. Pleasant St.)	1865-1889
	34b	Wertmueller & Ende Union Brewery	1892-1902
	34c	Charles Ende aka Ende Brewing Co. (1904-1905)	1902-1905

Camanche

IA	35	August Littig	c1854-1865

Carroll

IA	36a	Henry Daniel	1880- ?
	36b	M. Daniel	? -1884

Cascade

IA	37a	Frank May Co.	c1865- ?
	37b	Francis May	1874-1891
	37c	Clemens, Vogt & Co.	1891-1893
	37d	Clemens Vogt	1893-1895

Cass Township

IA	38	John Kleinlein	1874-1882

Cedar Falls

IA	39a	H. Pfeiffer & Co.	c1865- ?
	39b	H. Pfeiffer & Bro.	1874-1879
	39c	F. Rainer & Co.	1879-1884
IA	40a	Shelley & Wackerott	c1865- ?
	40b	Shelley's Brewery	1874-1875
	40c	Hans N. Lund	1875-1878

Cedar Rapids

IA	41	Sam Lilly & Co.	1874- ?
IA	42a	Jacob Wetzel	1859-1864
	42b	Wetzel & Magnus	1864-1868
	42c	Christian Magnus (8th St. & C. Ave.)	1868-1898
	42d	Magnus Brewing Co. (Dewey Ave. & 8th St.)	1898-1915
IA	43a	M. R. Snyder	1867- ?
	43b	George Williams & Co.	1874-1879
	43c	Geo. Williams	1879-1888

Chariton

IA	44a	Daniel Becker	1850- ?
	44b	W. W. Baker	1853- ?

Charles City

IA	45a	John Andre	1866-1875
	45b	Gertrude Andre	1875-1882
	45c	J. Andre & Co.	1882-1884

Clarinda

IA	46a	Aumer & Peterson	1874-1877
	46b	B. A. Peterson	1877-1884

Clayton

IA	47	Joseph Koevenig	1874-1875

Clermont

IA	48	Francis Hoffer	c1865
IA	49	F. Reof	c1865

Clinton

IA	50	Clinton Ale Brewery	1869-1872
IA	51a	Charles Herman	1869-1870
	51b	Hillberg & Gerard	1870- ?
	51c	Clara Becker	1874-1875
	51d	Lauer & Allen	1875-1884
	51e	Mathis & Lauer	1884-1885
	51f	Jacob Stroh	1885-1888
	51g	Lauer & Co. aka M. Lauer (1890)	1888-1894
	51h	Resen & Co.	1894-1896
	51i	Julius P. Andresen	1896-1900

Clinton (cont.)

IA	52	Hollingworth & Co.	1865- ?
IA	53a	Frank Maxheim & Co. (Ravinet Rd.)	1902-1903
	53b	Clinton Brewing Co.	1903-1908
	53c	Clinton Brewing Co. (1221 N. 2nd & Arnold Sts.)	1908-1915
	53d	Clinton Brewing Co.	1933-1934
	53e	Pointer Brewing Co., Inc. (1301 N. 2nd St. at 13th Ave. N.)	1934-1939
	53f	Gateway Brewing Co.	1939-1941
IA	54a	Seeser & Lauer	1874-1875
	54b	John Seeser aka Seeser & Jansen (1880)	1875-1883
	54c	Mrs. Caroline Seeser aka Chas. Seeser (1884)	1883-1885

Concord

IA	55	A. Sandler Jr.	1878-1878

Council Bluffs

IA	56	Allerman & Bierworth	1874-1875
IA	57	Chas. Bach	1845-1875
IA	58	Conrad Geise (800/812 Broadway)	1858-1888
IA	59	Hagg Brothers	1857- ?
IA	60a	Charles Weymuller	1857-1858
	60b	Stephan Weymuller	1858-1865

Creston

IA	61a	Bolig & Co.	1878-1879
	61b	Albert & Heinike	1879-1880
IA	62a	P. Bolig	1878-1879
	62b	Jacob Bollig	1879-1880
	62c	Mrs. Barbara Bollig	1880-1884

Davenport

IA	63a	Thomas B. Carter, Ale & Porter Brewery (Front & Mississippi)	? -1858
	63b	John Severn, Severn Ale Brewery	1858-1862
	63c	Severn & Son Ale Brewery	1862-1863
	63d	G. & H. Severn	1863-1866
	63e	H. Severn	1866-1873
	63f	William Severn	1873-1875
	63g	Henry Severn	1875-1875
IA	64a	Dr. C. H. Dries, Pacific Brewery (Main & 7th Sts.)	1853-1861
	64b	H. Dries, Pacific Brewery	1861-1869
	64c	George Noth & Sons, Pacific Brewery	1869-1879
	---	Malt House operation	1879-1881
	64d	Baumeier & Herrn	1882-1883
	64e	John G. Baumeier	1883-1884
IA	65a	Mathias Frahm, City Brewery (512/516 Harrison St.)	1850-1884
	65b	M. Frahm & Son, City Brewery	1884-1894
	65c	Davenport Malting Co., M. Frahm & Son	1894-1900
IA	66a	Independent Malting Co. (2nd & Davie Sts.) aka Zoller Brothers (1895)	1894-1906
	66b	Independent Brewing and Malting Co.	1906-1916
	66c	Zoller Brewing Co. (1801 W. 3rd St.)	1935-1944
	66d	Blackhawk Brewing Co.	1944-1952
	66e	Uchtorff Brewing Co., aka Savoy Brewing Co.	1952-1955
IA	67a	Knepper & Scheily, Arsenal Brewery (101 Mound St.)	1858-1862
	67b	Henry Shiley, Arsenal Brewery	1862-1866
	67c	Shiley & Knepper, Arsenal Brewery	1866-1869
	67d	Knepper & (George) Schlapp, Arsenal Brewery	1869-1872
	67e	(Henry) Koehler & (Rudolph) Lange, Arsenal Brewery	1872-1894
	67f	Davenport Malting Co., Koehler & Lange Branch	1894-1900

Davenport (cont.)

IA 68a	Julius Lehrkind & Co., Lehrkind Brewery (2nd & Taylor Sts.)		1869-1878
68b	Julius Lehrkind, Lehrkind Brewery		1878-1894
68c	Davenport Malting Co., Julius Lehrkind Branch		1894-1906
68d	Davenport Brewing Co.		1906-1915
68e	Rock Island Brewing Co. of Iowa (1225 W. 2nd St.)	NP	1934-1934
IA 69a	Julius Lehrkind & Brother, Black Hawk Brewery		1865-1869
69b	A. Zoller & Bro., Black Hawk Brewery		1889-1894
69c	Davenport Malting Co., A. Zoller & Bro. Branch		1894-1895
IA 70a	Peter Littig & Son, Eagle Brewery		1855- ?
70b	Peter Littig & Bro., Eagle Brewery		1874-1876
70c	J. Lage & Co., Eagle Brewery (1235 W. 5th St.)		1876-1890
70d	Mengel & Klindt, Eagle Brewery		1890-1894
70e	Davenport Malting Co., Mengel & Klindt Branch		1894-1900
IA 71	Alfred J. Stege		1884-1884
IA 72	Henning J. Witt (106 Harrison St.)		1890-1890
IA 73a	Henning J. Witt (302/306 W. Front St.)		1899-1905
73b	Rhode & Vollstedt		1905-1915

Decorah

IA 74a	David Addicken		1852-1877
74b	Mrs. G. Addicken		1877-1884
74c	John Addicken & Co.		1884-1890
74d	John Addicken		1890-1891
IA 75	Joseph Klein		1874-1884

Des Moines

IA 76a	A. Aulmann (208/214 W. Elm St.)		1874-1877
76b	Aulmann & Schuster		1877-1893
IA 77	Des Moines Brewing Co. (3rd, Elm & A Sts.)		1908-1915
IA 78	John C. Hierp, City Brewery		c1865
IA 79a	Joseph Kinsley (13th & Mulberry Sts.)		1874-1880
79b	Kindler Bros.		1880-1884
IA 80a	Mattes & Jung (17th & Center Sts.)		1878-1880
80b	Alex. & John Mattes		1880-1884
IA 81a	Alois Mattes (201 E. Locust St.)		1874-1879
81b	Paul Mattes & Bro.		1879-1880
81c	Paul Mattes		1880-1888
IA 82a	G. Muenzenmeier		c1865-1875
82b	Muenzenmeier & Weber		1875-1884
82c	John Weber		1884-1888
82d	Peter Gross		1888-1891
IA 83	Andrew Somer, Union Brewery		c1865

De Witt

IA 84	V. Yegge		1878-1884

Dorchester

IA 85a	Schwartshoff & Peifer Co.		c1865- ?
85b	Jos. Tacke		1878-1880

Douglas

IA 86	Phil. P. Rotherburger		1882-1884

Dubuque

IA 87	W. R. Baird, Excelsior Brewery		1858-1859
IA 88	M. Blumenauer		1856-c1872
IA 89	Dubuque Ale Brewery		1865-1871
IA 90a	Dubuque Malting Co. (27th & Jackson Sts.)		1895-1898
90b	Dubuque Brewing and Malting Co.		1898-1915
90c	Julien Dubuque Brewing Co. (3000 Jackson St.)	NP	1934-1934

Dubuque (cont.)

IA	91a	Adam Glab (Plank Road)	c1850- ?
	91b	Glab & Suess, Northern Brewery (27th & Couler Ave.)	1865-1869
	91c	Adam Glaab, Northern Brewery	1869-1882
	91d	Mrs. Adam Glaab, Northern Brewery	1882-1884
	91e	Glab Bros.	1884-1892
	91f	Dubuque Malting Co., Glab Bros.	1892-1897
	91g	Dubuque Brewing and Malting Co., Glab Bros.	1897-1900
IA	92	Ferdinand Kempf (Southern & Locust Sts.)	1865-1874
IA	93	Key City Brewing Co., Inc. (136 Main St.)	1934-1934
IA	94a	Kohl & Stackere (Union & Victoria Sts.)	1860-1861
	94b	Stackere & Christoph	1861-1865
	94c	Gehringer & Nachtman	1865-1869
	94d	Germania Brewery, Esch & Brother (Nicholas & Peter)	1869-1880
IA	95a	Miners Brewery (W. Dubuque)	1857-1858
	95b	Miners Brewery, G. Boxleiter	1858-1859
	95c	Miners Brewery, G. Boxleiter & S. Stahlmann	1859-1860
IA	96a	(A. H.) Peaslee & Downer (305 White St.)	1866-1870
	96b	A. H. Peaslee (272/290 E. 4th & Iowa Sts.)	1870-1878
	96c	Peaslee & Co.	1878-1888
	96d	Edward C. Peaslee	1888-1902
	96e	Peaslee-Brede Co.	1902-1905
	96f	Peaslee & Co.	1905-1907
IA	97	Herman Schemmel	1862-1880
IA	98a	Titus Schmid & Co. (B. Scherr & F. Beck), Iowa Brewery (2327 Couler Ave.)	1855-1868
	98b	Mrs. B. Scherr	1868-1869
	98c	Keine & Rhomberg Co.	1869-c1872
	98d	M. Blumenauer	c1872-1877
	98e	Meuser & Co.	1877-1884
	98f	Schmid Bros. (Titus & Albert) & Co.(Emil Reh), Iowa Brewery (2327/2329 Couler Ave.)	1884-1892
	98g	Dubuque Malting Co., Schmidt Bros.	1892-1897
	98h	Dubuque Brewing and Malting Co., Schmid Bros.	1897-1900
	98i	Dubuque Weiss Beer Co.	1904-1912
IA	99	John Stahlmann, West Dubuque Lager Brewery	1857-1859
IA	100	Standard Brewing and Malting Co.	1910-1910
IA	101a	Ignatz Seegar, City Brewery	1852-1865
	101b	Ignatz Seegar, Stone Brewery	1865-1869
	101c	Dubuque Joint Stock Beer Brewing Co.	1869-1873
	101d	Ambrose Gleed	1873-1876
	101e	John Pier	1878-1883
IA	102a	Star Brewing Co. (4th & Levee Sts.)	1898- ?
	102b	Dubuque Star Brewing Co.	1904-1915
	102c	Dubuque Star Brewing Co. (E. 4th St. Ext.)	1933-1971
	102d	Pickett Brewing Co., aka Dubuque Star Brewing Co., Joseph S. Pickett & Sons, Inc.	1971-1980
	102e	Pickett Brewing Co., subsidiary of Agri Industries	1980-1982
	102f	Dubuque Star Brewing Co.	1982-1983
IA	103a	Mathias Tschirgi (Main between 6th & 7th Sts.)	1848-1850
	103b	M. Tschirgi & Co. (Julien St.)	1850-1855
	103c	Kurtz & Welder	1855-1880
IA	104a	Tschirgi & Schwind, Western Brewery	1855-1892
	104b	Dubuque Malting Co., Western Brewing Co., aka Estate of Conrad Graf (Julien Ave.)	1892-1897
	104c	Dubuque Brewing and Malting Co., Western Brewing Co.	1897-1900

Dyersville

IA	105a	Esch & Bros.	1874-1888
	105b	Esch Bros.	1888-1896

Eddyville
IA 106 Jaeger & Pfister 1884-1884

Eldora
IA 107 Joseph Rice c1865

Elgin
IA 108 Schori & (John) Lehmann 1857-1884

Elkader
IA 109a J. B. Schmidt & Co. 1874-1875
109b J. B. Schmidt & Bro. 1875-1884

Fairfield
IA 110a John Irmer c1865- ?
110b Toeller & Suess 1875-1879
110c Louis Suess 1879-1888

Fairview
IA 111 M. F. Rick 1874-1875

Farmington
IA 112 William A. Greg c1865

IA 113 Greg Shafer, Farmington Brewery c1865

Festina (Fort Atkinson)
IA 114a Anthony Gaertner Co. c1865
114b A. F. Gaertner 1880-1884

Forest City
IA 115 Jens Paulson 1874-1875

Fort Dodge
IA 116a John Koll 1874-1879
116b Koll Bros. 1879-1880
116c John Koll Jr. 1880-1884

IA 117a Dorothea Schmidt 1874-1879
117b Mrs. Dorothea Murphy 1879-1884

IA 118 F. Wertmire c1865

Fort Madison
IA 119 Henry Brink 1874-1875

IA 120a A. Burster & Co. 1863-1875
120b Anton Burster 1875-1884
120c Burster & Son 1884-1888

IA 121a Garuasius Santo 1844-1855
121b Stephen Girard 1855-1879

IA 122a August Trenschel 1845-1851
122b Henry Koehler 1851-1862
122c Buster & Schlapp 1862-1870
122d G. Schlapp & Bro. 1870-1875
122e Henry Schlapp 1875-1888
122f Hermann Schlapp 1888-1893
122g John G. H. Sterllern (820 2nd St.) 1893-1902

Franklin Center
IA 123 William Best 1875-1879

IA 124 Frederick Haeffer c1865

IA 125 David Riser c1865

Garnaville
IA 126a Henry C. Meyer c1865- ?
126b H. Schumacher 1874-1882
126c Mrs. Margaret Schumacher 1882-1884

German
IA 127 Philip Michel 1874-1875

Glenwood
IA 128 Charles Weymuller 1858-1863

Grand Meadow		
IA 129	Joseph Koering	1878-1884
Guttenberg		
IA 130a	Hosfield & Cruckwith Co.	c1865- ?
130b	Wm. Hosfield	1874-1884
IA 131	Aug. Jungk	1878-1884
IA 132a	Roth & Pink	1874-1875
132b	John Roth	1875-1882
132c	Mrs. Magdalena Roth	1882-1888
IA 133a	Rudolph Wolter	1874-1907
133b	Rudolph Wolter & Co.	1907-1908
133c	Rudolph Wolter	1908-1909
Hamburg		
IA 134a	Phillip Ness & Co.	c1865- ?
134b	P. Neiss & Bro.	1874-1877
134c	Philip Nies	1877-1880
134d	Mrs. Catherine Nies	1880-1882
134e	P. & H. Nies	1882-1884
Harrison		
IA 135	P. Hargelsheimer	1874-1875
Homestead (County of Iowa)		
IA 136	Amana Society	1878-1884
Independence		
IA 137a	Christian Seeland & Co.	c1865- ?
137b	Chris. Seeland	1874-1888
IA 138	John Wengert	1874-1884
Iowa City		
IA 139a	Louis Englert	c1865- ?
139b	Clara Englert	1874-1877
139c	Englert & Rittenmeyer	1877-1882
139d	John J. Englert	1882-1884
139e	George A. Englert	1884-1888
IA 140a	Hotz & Geiger, Union Brewery (Linn & Market Sts.)	1865-1876
140b	Schulze & Graf	1876-1878
140c	Simon Hotz	1878-1881
140d	John Graf	1881-1883
140e	Conrad Graf	1883-1896
140f	Conrad Graf Estate	1896-1903
140g	Graf Brothers (Union Brewing Co.)	1903-1915
IA 141	Frederick Kielmeyer, Atlantic Brewery	c1865
IA 142a	George Rupert, Great Western Brewery	1857-1871
142b	John P. Dostal, Great Western Brewery (Market & Gilbert Sts.)	1871-1882
142c	Dostal Bros. (George A. & John M.), Great Western Brewery	1897-1902
142d	Iowa Brewing Co.	1902-1915
IA 143	John P. Trautmann	1874-1875
Iowa Falls		
IA 144	John Althen	1874-1878
Jefferson		
IA 145	H. Gullick	c1865
IA 146	G. Haberkorn	1874-1875
IA 147a	Roth's Brewery	1875-1875
147b	Peter Roth	1875-1884
Jesup		
IA 148	Daniel Stevenson	c1865

Keokuk

IA 149a	(Jacob) Baehr & (John, Isaac & Rudolph) Leisy Bros., Union Brewery	1862-1866
149b	Leisy & Bro.	1866-1877
149c	Mrs. M. Leisy	1877-1879
149d	Leisy Bros. (13th & 1301 Johnson Sts.)	1879-1884
IA 150	Conrad Begstin	1859-1860
IA 151	City Brewery	1859-1860
IA 152a	Peter Haubert (18/22 N. 14th St.)	1855-1863
152b	(Conard) Pechstein & (John) Nagel, Keokuk Brewery	1863-1905
152c	Pechstein & Nagel Co. (14th, Main & Blondeau Sts.)	1905-1915
IA 153	John Hemrich	1855-1855
IA 154a	Joseph Kurz, Western Brewery (Plank Road & 18th St.)	1865-1873
154b	Reinold & Wedel aka Wedel & Co. (1875)	1873-1876
IA 155	Fred Lederer (16th & Johnson Sts.)	1860-1871
IA 156	George Loudenschlager (Fulton & 8th Sts.)	1857-1857
IA 157a	Mowz & Anschutz (Wolcott's Bluff)	1859-1860
157b	F. W. Anschutz, Mississippi Brewery	1860-1883
IA 158	C. Rheudy, Eagle Brewery (Johnson & 16th Sts.)	1868-1868
IA 159	Johannes Showalter (Main & 12th Sts.)	1857-1857
IA 160	Adolph Vockerodt aka Kennedy & Vockerodt (1873-1874)	1860-1877
IA 161	J. L. Wolff	1882-1883

Kniest

IA 162	A. L. Guam	1875-1875

Lansing

IA 163	Jacob Haas	1869-1886

La Porte City

IA 164	Benedict Sigg	1874-1875

Lemars

IA 165a	Herbert A. Diamond	1878-1878
165b	L. H. Maning & Co.	1879-1879
165c	Marion E. Diamond	1879-1884
165d	Germania Brewing Co.	1884-1888

Leon

IA 166	L. Guiden	1874-1874

Lerne Creek

IA 167	John Weiss	1875-1875

Lockridge

IA 168	John Jacob	c1865

Lucas

IA 169	Clara Baker	1874-1875

Lyons

IA 170a	H. Ellenburger & Co., Western Brewery	1865-1880
170b	Tritschler & Tiesse (merged with 171c)	1880-1881
IA 171a	Ferdinand & Tritschler	c1865
171b	Ph. Tritschler	1866-1874
171c	Tritschler & Tiesse (W. Main St.) aka Western Union Brewery (1883-1893)	1874-1893
171d	Tritschler & Tiesse Malting Co.	1893-1905

Maquoketa		
IA 172a	Scholl Brothers (James & F. D.) aka F. D. Scholl & Co. (1865)	1860-1865
172b	John Dostal	1865-1866
172c	Dostal & (August) Hoffmann	1866-1883
172d	John Dostal	1883-1891
172e	John Dostal Brewing Co. (Decker & Grove Sts.)	1891-1907
172f	Fritz Staemmle	1907-1915
Marengo		
IA 173	T. C. Knepper	1878-1884
Marion		
IA 174a	Ahlers & Woesler, Marion Brewery	c1865
174b	Coenin & Brother	1867-1870
174c	John Coenin	1870-1875
174d	Schneider Bros.	1875-1884
Marshall		
IA 175	Peter Roth	1878-1878
Marshalltown		
IA 176a	Marshall Brewery, George Bowman	1858-1875
176b	Bowman Bros.	1875-1885
IA 177a	Vogel & Collman, Iowa River Brewery	1860-1877
177b	George Vogel	1877-1885
Mason City		
IA 178a	Mason City Brewing Co.	1874-1877
178b	Brohm & McDevitt	1877-1879
178c	M. Brohm	1879-1880
178d	Brohm & Neuhaus	1880-1882
McGregor		
IA 179	Charles L. Centlivre	1855-1862
IA 180	J. L. Hagensick	1845-1886
Missouri Valley, Harrison Co.		
IA 181	Henry Kreter	1875-1875
Monticello		
IA 182	Anton Meyer	1874-1875
IA 183	Henry Poggenklas	1874-1875
Montrose		
IA 184	Martin Spring	1874-1884
Mount Carmel		
IA 185	A. S. Gnam	1879-1882
Mount Pleasant		
IA 186	Mt. Pleasant Brewing Co.	1882-1882
Muscatine		
IA 187	Daniel Bentz	c1865
IA 188a	Sarah Bing	1874-1877
188b	A. Witteman	1877-1882
188c	Chas. Lang (700 Mulberry St.)	1882-1891
IA 189a	John Dold	1865-1867
189b	Jacob Dold	1867-1877
189c	Chas. J. Dold Brewing Co.	1877-1880
189d	Wm. Weidling	1880-1884
189e	Mrs. F. Weidling	1884-1888
IA 190a	Jacob Dorn	1874-1880
190b	Geltz & Weis	1880-1884
IA 191a	Mary Eigenmann	1874-1882
191b	Henry C. Eigenmann (422 E. 7th St.)	1893-1900
191c	Rudolf Gundrum, Muscatine City Brewery	1900-1903
IA 192a	John Schaefer, Western Brewery	1874-1878
192b	G. A. Schaefer	1878-1884

New Hampton		
IA 193	A. A. Gross	1875-1884
New Vienna		
IA 194a	Andreas Baemle	c1865
194b	Baeumle & Ferring	1874-1880
194c	Peter Ferring	1880-1882
194d	Ferring & Mescher	1882-1884
194e	Peter Ferring	1884-1890
194f	New Vienna Brewing Co.	1890-1891
194g	New Vienna Brewing Co.	1901-1907
Nodaway		
IA 195	Auun & Peterson	1878-1878
Nora Springs		
IA 196	Florian Festle	1874-1884
Ohumua		
IA 197	Ketcham & Walker	c1865
Osage		
IA 198	R. H. Pierce	1874-1884
Osceola		
IA 199	Charles Jacob	1878-1882
Oskaloosa		
IA 200a	Blattner & Newbrand	1846-1856
200b	Chas. Blattner	1856- ?
200c	Blattner & Co. (1209 W. C Ave.)	1874-1877
200d	Blattner & Newbrand	1877-1888
Ossian		
IA 201	A. F. Gaertner	1874-1875
Ottumwa		
IA 202a	Kramer & Hausmann	1856-1877
202b	Hausmann & Bauer	1877-1882
202c	John Hausmann	1882-1884
202d	Hausmann's Union Brewery	1884-1888
IA 203a	Schaefer & Hoffmann	1858-1877
203b	B. Hoffmann	1877-1879
IA 204a	The Wm. Kraner Brewing Co.	1878-1879
204b	Kraner, Hoffmann & Co.	1879-1888
IA 205	Ottumwa Brewing and Ice Co.	1905-1911
Pella		
IA 206a	George Blattner & Co.	1864-1865
206b	Blattner & Herbig	1865-1882
206c	G. M. Blattner	1882-1884
Pleasantville		
IA 207	James A. Logan	c1865
Postville		
IA 208a	Joseph Koevenig	1878-1882
208b	William Moll	1882-1884
Red Oak		
IA 209a	Chas. Steinbrecher	1863-1877
209b	Charles Stroh	1877-1882
Rockford		
IA 210	Samuel Marke	1875-1884
Rooca		
IA 211	Peter Weise	1884-1884
Sebastopol		
IA 212a	G. Munzinger	1878-1879
212b	Munzenmaier & Weber	1879-1880
212c	John Weber	1880-1884

Shell Rock

IA 213 James Scully 1874-1880

Sherrill's Mound

IA 214 George Haberkorn 1878-1882

Sioux City

IA 215 John Arensdorf (401 Pearl St.) 1902-1903

IA 216a Simon Hotz 1859- ?
216b J. Franz & Co. (3rd & Elm Sts.) 1874-1882
216c Franz Brewing Co. 1882-1888
216c Sioux City Brewing Co. (Elm & Park Sts.) 1898-1915

IA 217a Inter-State Brewing Co. (N. 1st & Isabella Sts.) 1908-1915
217b Sioux City Brewing Co. (1214/1224 W. 1st & Isabella St.) 1934-1959
217c Kingsbury Sioux City Brewing Co. (br. of Sheboygan, WI) 1959-1960

IA 218 Rudolph Selzer, Steam Brewery (9th & Douglas Sts.) 1853-1888

Spillville

IA 219 Roman Eggspliveler c1865

IA 220a George Lipp & Co. 1851- ?
220b Lipp & Son 1874-1877
220c Schwela & Glasbrenner 1877-1879
220d Frank Schwela 1879-1884
220e P. P. Rothengerber 1884-1888

IA 221 Nisher & Scalusser c1865

IA 222 Frank Nockles 1874-1888

Stacyville

IA 223 J. H. C. Huxhold 1878-1882

Strawberry Point

IA 224 John Kleinlein 1878-1904

Stuart

IA 225 John Eber 1878-1882

Tama City

IA 226a Andrew Matthern & Co. 1877-1879
226b Andrew Matthern 1879-1880
226c A. Matthern, Tama City Brewery 1880-1883

Twin Springs

IA 227a Charles L. Centlivre c1858
227b Meyer & Gartner c1865

Union

IA 228 M. Schroeder 1859-1875

Vail

IA 229a Alois Smutney 1878-1888
229b Alois Smutney 1899-1899

Vinton

IA 230a Joseph Taylor c1865
230b H. Biebesheimer 1874-1879

Washington

IA 231a Wm. Jugenheimer, City Brewery 1851-1877
231b Wm. Jugenheimer & Co. 1877-1882
231c Wm. Jugenheimer 1882-1884

IA 232a F. C. Knepper 1874-1877
232b H. Zahm 1877-1879
232c Lipsius & Zimmerman 1879-1884

IA 233 John P. Spittler 1875-1875

Waterloo

IA 234 Adam Blin 1874-1874

IA 235 B. Meinhofel 1874-1875

Waterloo (cont.)
IA 236a Joseph Taylor c1865-1877
236b Goldstein & Taylor 1877-1880
236c J. Goldstein & Co. 1880-1884

Waukon
IA 237a George Mauch 1874-1880
237b Joseph Greeling 1880-1884

Waverly
IA 238 Ellis & Lashbrook c1865

IA 239 Peter Fosselmann 1874-1884

IA 240 Heiberg Brewing Co. NP 1934-1934

IA 241a E. F. Tabor 1874-1877
241b S. A. Tabor 1877-1882
241c Tabor Bros. 1882-1884

IA 242 Waverly Brewing Co. (W. Water & Ellon Sts.) 1905-1915

Webster City
IA 243 A. Ramharter 1874-1884

West McGregor
IA 244a Van Staden & Klein 1865-1875
244b M. Klein 1880-1884

West Mitchell
IA 245a Frank Coop c1865
245b John Fey 1874-1884

West Point
IA 246a Bernard Lampe 1874-1878
246b B. H. Kempker 1878-1882
246c F. G. Strothmann 1882-1884

IA 247 Fritz Troup 1878-1879

Wilton
IA 248 Philip F. Miller 1874-1884

Winterset
IA 249 Morris Schroeder 1869-1878

KANSAS

Atchison
KS 1a (Hugo) Knecht & (Albert) Weinmann 1860-1864
1b Louis Arras 1864-1867
1c John Stamm 1867-1871
1d Zibold & Haegelin (S. 10th St.) 1871-1909

KS 2 Frank Young c1868-1880

Baxter Springs
KS 3 E. Zelleken 1874-1875

Beloit
KS 4a Pupka & Eberle 1878-1879
4b John Eberle 1879-1884

Carr Creek
KS 5 Peter Marsch, Jr. 1878-1880

Cawker City
KS 6 Joseph Schaaf 1878-1882

Chanute
KS 7 Hartman Bros. 1878-1879

Concordia
KS 8 Williams & Bennett 1874-1875

Ellinwood
KS 9a John Hess 1878-1879
9b Mrs. K. Wolf 1879-1884

Emporia

KS	10a	F. H. Macke	1874-1877
	10b	F. H. Macke & Co.	1877-1882
	10c	F. H. Macke & Son	1882-1884

Eudora

KS	11	Robert Bartusch	1874-1882

Fort Scott

KS	12a	Schultz & Blasch	1874-1877
	12b	Schultz & Co.	1877-1884

Hanover

KS	13	Charles Jockers	1874-1884

Highland

KS	14a	Peter Weidemaier	1874-1879
	14b	Weidemaier & Co.	1879-1880
	14c	Peter Weidemaier	1880-1884

Humboldt

KS	15	Bendecker & Richardson	1874-1875

Hutchinson

KS	16	Bihlmeier & Co.	1874-1875

Independence

KS	17a	Hebrank & Truman	1874-1882
	17b	Hebrank & Freeman	1882-1884

Iola

KS	18	Richard Schindler	1875-1884

Junction City

KS	19	Helmon Cammert	1879-1879
KS	20	L. W. Frzaskowsky	1874-1879

Kansas City

KS	21	Geo. Grubel, Jr. (1100/1106 N. 2nd St.)	1901-1903
KS	22	Prairie Brew Co., Inc. (1519 Minnesota Ave.)	NP 1934-1934

Kinsley

KS	23	J. Kinsler	1878-1879

Kirwin

KS	24	John Strebel	1878-1884

Lawrence

KS	25a	Peter Mugler, Lawrence Brewery	1860s- ?
	25b	John Walruff	1872-1888

Leavenworth

KS	26a	Block & (John) Brandon	1858-1861
	26b	Block, Brandon & Kirmeyer (2nd & Kiowa Sts.)	1861-1863
	26c	Brandon & Kirmeyer	1863-1875
	26d	Brandon & Kirmeyer Brewing Co.	1875-1885
	26e	(John) Brandon & (George) Beal (110 Kickapoo St.)	1893-1899
	26f	(Henry L.) Brandon & (George) Beal	1899-1909
KS	27a	John C. Grund & Co.	1850s- ?
	27b	Gottfried Peipe	1874-1880
KS	28a	Kihm & Werley	1850s- ?
	28b	R. Kihm	1874-1877
	28c	Becker & Link	1877-1884
KS	29a	Joseph Kunz	1850s- ?
	29b	Charles Kunz	1874-1879
	29c	Bornhauser & Aumiller	1879-1880
	29d	F. A. Baurhauser	1880-1884
KS	30	Leeland, Canon Brewery	1850s

KANSAS (cont.)

Le Roy

KS	31a	Le Roy Brewery	1874-1877
	31b	Albert Schmidt	1877-1884

Manhattan

KS	32	Charles Alten	1878-1879

Marysville

KS	33	P. C. Kaltenborn	1874-1884
KS	34	William Meyer	1882-1884

Mitchell County

KS	35	Peter Marsch	1874-1875

Ogden

KS	36	Theo. Weichselbaum	1874-1878

Oswego

KS	37	John Apperger	1875- ?

Paola

KS	38	Conrad Hausman	1874-1880

Salina

KS	39	Gus Behr	1880-1880
KS	40	Peter Mugler	1878-1884

Seneca

KS	41	Minger & Christ	1874-1875

Smoky Hill

KS	42	A. Schwaebel	1874-1875

Topeka

KS	43	A. Herboldsheimer	1874-1884
KS	44	Philip Moser	1874-1884
KS	45a	Olferman & Elsner	1878-1880
	45b	Olferman & Kuehne	1880-1884

Westfield

KS	46	N. G. Collins	1882-1884

Wichita

KS	47	J. W. Brown	1875- ?
KS	48	Cammert & Freelinger	1874-1875
KS	49	Emil Werner & Co.	1874-1875
KS	50a	Adolph Wiegand	1874-1877
	50b	A. Wiegand & Co.	1877-1880
	50c	A. Wiegand	1880-1884

Winfield

KS	51	Jno. Himelspach	1874-1875
KS	52	Frank Manney	1880-1884

Wyandotte

KS	53a	Wehile & Bomhauser	1875-1877
	53b	Anna Hafner	1877-1879

KENTUCKY

Alexandria

KY	1a	August Meister	1874-1882
	1b	Meister & Mueller	1882-1884

Carrollton

KY	2	M. Siersdorfer	1874-1875

Covington (includes Lewisburg)

KY	3a	Brenner & Seiler (601/621 Scott & Pike Sts.)	1880-1886
	3b	John Brenner	1886-1888
	3c	John Brenner Brewing Co.	1888-1910
	3d	Jung Brewing Co.	1910-1913

Covington (cont.)

KY	4a	Deglow, Best & Renner	1861-1872
	4b	Chas. L. Best	1872-1877
	4c	Ruh & Meyer	1877-1879
KY	5a	Chas. Geisbauer	1866-1877
	5b	L. Geisbauer	1877-1879
	5c	John Meyer (367/369 Pike St.)	1879-1882
	5d	Meyer & Riedlin	1882-1889
	5e	Bavarian Brewing Co.	1889-1918
	5f	Bavarian Brewing Co. (533 Pike St., 501/537 Lehrmer St., 528 W. 12th St.)	1935-1959
	5g	International Breweries, Inc. (br. of Detroit, MI) aka Phoenix Brewing Co. (1960-1966)	1959-1966
KY	6	Herzog & Ammann	? -1874
KY	7	J. H. Herzog	? -1874
KY	8a	Chas. Lang & Co., Lewisburgh Brewery	1874-1884
	8b	John Seiler (Baker, Lewis & Cross Sts.)	1884-1893
	8c	C. P. Lang & Co.	1893-1895
	8d	Covington Brewing Co.	1895-1918
	8e	The Heidelberg Brewing Co. (500/520 W. 4th St. at Philadelphia & Bakewell Sts.)	1934-1949
	8f	Bavarian Brewing Co. (Plant 2)	1949-1955
KY	9	H. Niemeyer, Jr.	1874-1875
KY	10	J. H. Steinrude	1878-1879

Frankfort

KY	11a	Sigmund Luscher, Capital Brewery	1874-1884
	11b	Capital Brewing Co.	1884-1888
	11c	Frankfort Brewing Co. (525 Ann St.)	1888-1893
KY	12	Ernest Meyer	1888-1900

Henderson

KY	13a	George Klauder	1866-1872
	13b	Reutlinger & Eisfelder	1872-1887
	13c	Geo. H. Delvin & Co.	1887-1888
	13d	Frank L. Gebhard & Co.	1888-1890
	13e	Holloway & Delvin	1890-1892
	13f	Gerlinger & Reichmann	1892-1894
	13g	Henderson Brewing Co. (8th & Main Sts.)	1894-1900
	13h	Henderson Brewing Co. (5th & Water Sts.)	1900-1918

Jefferson City

KY	14	Antsch & Metzner	1878-1879

Lexington

KY	15a	Lexington Brewing Co. (226/242 E. Main St.)	1897-1918
	15b	Lexington Brewing Co.	NP 1934-1934

Louisville

KY	16a	John Bauer (941/944 Franklin St.)	1874-1877
	16b	Elizabeth Bauer	1877-1888
	16c	Union Brewing Co.	1898-1911
KY	17a	Sebastian Bott (1734 Lexington St. & 18th St.)	1874-1893
	17b	John Bott	1893-1897
	17c	Anna M. Bott	1897-1898
	17d	Lexington Street Brewing Co.	1898-1901
	17e	Lexington Street Brewery, Theo. Menk	1901-1918
KY	18	Brohm & Fehr	1874-1875
KY	19a	Michael Christ (820/834 Baxter Ave.)	1874-1893
	19b	Geo. J. & John M. Christ	1893-1914
	19c	Christ Brewing Co. (318/328 Baxter Ave.)	1914-1918
KY	20	Clay Street Brewery (207 Clay St.)	NP 1934-1934

Louisville (cont.)

KY	21a	J. F. Diersen & Co. (164 Green St.)	1879-1884
	21b	Joseph T. Diersen (500 E. Green St.)	1884-1893
	21c	Catherine A. M. Diersen	1893-1900
	21d	J. T. & H. W. Diersen	1900-1908
	21e	Henry W. Diersen	1908-1910
KY	22a	Falls City Brewing Co. (30th St. & Broadway)	1905-1918
	22b	Falls City Ice & Beverage Co. (3050 W. Broadway)	1933-1933
	22c	Falls City Brewing Co. (3024/3050 W. Broadway) aka Drummond Bros. Brewing Co.	1933-1978
KY	23a	Gebhard & Co., Star Brewery (17th & Harney Sts.)	1874-1877
	23b	Julius Gebhard	1877-1879
	23c	John Kirchgessner & Co.	1879-1882
	23d	John L. Abraham	1882-1884
	23e	Beierle & Schneider	1884-1900
	23f	E. Beierle & Co.	1900-1903
KY	24a	Chas. Hartmetz & Bro. (1400/1404 Story Ave.)	1874-1877
	24b	Charles Hartmetz	1877-1884
	24c	Hartmetz & Oertel	1884-1892
	24d	John F. Oertel	1892-1906
	24e	John F. Oertel Co.	1906-1918
	24f	The Oertel Co., Inc.	1932-1936
	24g	Oertel Brewing Co.	1936-1967
KY	25	Charles Haungs	1876-1877
KY	26a	Huber & Mueller (811 Shelby St.)	1875-1877
	26b	Henry Huber (1953/1955 Shelby & Gosslane)	1877-1896
	26c	Huber & Redle (1963/1969 Shelby St.)	1896-1898
	26d	Otto Redle	1898-1911
KY	27	Jefferson Brewing Co., Inc. (213 S. 5th St.)	NP 1934-1934
KY	28a	Kentucky Brewing Co. (1431/1445 S. 15th St.)	1934-1939
	28b	Frankenmuth-Kentucky Brewing Co. (br. of Frankenmuth, MI)	1939-1942
KY	29a	Knipers, Nadorff & Bro. (Baxter Ave. & Bridge St.)	1874-1877
	29b	Gerhard Knipers	1877-1879
	29c	Knipers & Son	1879-1880
	29d	Gerhard Knipers	1880-1888
KY	30a	Krupp & Schaefer	1882- ?
	30b	Weigel & Ballweg	? -1884
KY	31a	Lauffer & Brands	1878-1880
	31b	Gottlieb Lauffer (34th & Market Sts.)	1880-1903
	31c	Gregory & Stuber	1903-1904
	31d	West Louisville Brewing Co.	1904-1916
KY	32a	Peter Laux (Kentucky St. between 16th & 17th Sts.)	1874-1895
	32b	Ben Laux (W. 17th St.)	1895-1899
	32c	Nicholas Rettner	1899-1903
KY	33a	Adam Loeser (732 E. Walnut St.)	1874-1893
	33b	Carle Bros.	1898-1899
KY	34a	Henry Nadorff (1636 W. Nut St.)	1878-1884
	34b	Nadorff & Bro. (1544/1552 Portland Ave.)	1884-1891
	34c	Nadorff Bros.	1891-1892
	34d	Nadorff Brewing Co.	1892-1902
	34e	Nadorff Brewing Co. (br. Central Consumers Co.)	1902-1903
KY	35	John Nunemann	c1884
KY	36a	Otto Brewery	? -1872
	36b	Otto Brewery, Frank Fehr (430 E. Green St.)	1872-1876
	36c	Frank Fehr, Old Brewery	1876-1890
	36d	Frank Fehr Brewing Co.	1890-1901
	36e	Frank Fehr Brewing Co. (412/425 Fehr Ave.) (br. of Central Consumers Co.)	1901-1918
	36f	Frank Fehr Brewing Co. (412/430 Fehr Ave.)	1933-1964
KY	37	J. Schanzenbecker	1875-1880

Louisville (cont.)

KY	38	John Schneider	c1884
KY	39a	Frank Senn	1874-1876
	39b	Frank Senn & Bros.	1876-1877
	39c	(Frank) Senn & (Philip) Ackermann	1877-1892
	39d	Senn & Ackermann Brewing Co. (1710/1726 W. Main St.)	1892-1901
	39e	Senn & Ackermann Brewing Co. (br. Central Consumers Co.)	1901-1914
KY	40a	M. Senn & Bro. (1906 15th St.)	1878-1888
	40b	Wegenast & Huber	1888-1893
	40c	Geo. F. Huber	1893-1907
KY	41	Alex Stegner Brewing Co. (317/319 Pearl St.)	1938-1940
KY	42a	Stein & Doern, Salvator Brewery (1021/1029 E. Green St.)	1875-1877
	42b	Joseph Stein & Co.	1877-1891
	42c	Joseph Stein Brewing Co.	1891-1900
KY	43	Jacob Steurer (1372 Story Ave.)	1874-1905
KY	44a	Alonzo Templeton (1336 Hamilton Ave.)	1874-1884
	44b	M. Ladenburger	1884-1891
KY	45a	Walter & Kittinger (501/504 E. Kentucky St. at Jackson St.)	1879-1884
	45b	Henry Walter	1884-1895
	45c	Martin Senn	1895-1897
	45d	Wegenast & Berger	1897-1898
	45e	Jackson Brewing Co.	1898-1899
	45f	Joseph Lehmann	1899-1900
KY	46a	Conrad Walter (810/814 Clay St.)	1858- ?
	46b	Mrs. Eva Walter	1874-1890
	46c	John E. & Frank Walter	1890-1912
	46d	Clay Street Brewery, John E. & Frank Walter (512 Clay St.)	1912-1918
KY	47a	Weber & Palmer (Brownsborough Road)	1880-1880
	47b	William Palmer	1880-1895
	47c	William Palmer, Clifton Brewery (2400 Letterle & Ewing Aves.)	1895-1918
KY	48a	Yamm & Christ	1865- ?
	48b	Yamm & Miller	c1870
KY	49a	Philip Zang, Phoenix Brewery	1861-1868
	49b	Vogt & Schillinger, Phoenix Brewery	1868-1869
	49c	Weber & Schillinger (1106 Baxter Ave. & Underhill St.)	1869-1882
	49d	Peter Weber	1882-1883
	49e	Phoenix Brewing Co.	1883-1901
	49f	Phoenix Brewing Co. (br. Central Consumers Co.)	1901-1916
KY	50a	John Zeller, Shelby Street Brewery (1310/1316 Shelby St.)	1860-1881
	50b	Schaefer & Meyer, Shelby Street Brewery	1881-1889
	50c	Schaefer & Meyer Brewing Co. (Logan & Lampton Sts.)	1889-1901
	50d	Schaefer & Meyer Brewing Co. (br. Central Consumers Co.)	1901-1911
	50e	Central Consumers Co., Frank Fehr Brewery, branch No. 2	1911-1918

Maysville

KY	51	Jacob Jaeger	1874-1879

Middlesboro

KY	52a	(Frank) Overbeck Brewing, Cold Storage and Ice Mfg. Co.	1891-1893
	52b	New South Brewing and Ice Co.	1893-1916

Newport

KY	53a	John Butcher (Columbia St.)	? -1870
	53b	Butcher & Wiedemann	1870-1878
	53c	George Wiedemann (151/159 Columbia St.)	1878-1890
	53d	Geo. Wiedemann Brewing Co. (623/637 Columbia St.)	1890-1918
	53e	Wiedemann Brewery Corp.	1933-1934
	53f	Wiedemann Brewing & Distilling Corp. (601 Columbia St.)	1934-1936
	53g	The Geo. Wiedemann Brewing Co.	1936-1967
	53h	The Geo. Wiedemann Brewing Co., div. of G. Heileman Brewing Co., Inc., aka Blatz Brewing Co., Independent Milwaukee Brewing Co., Kingsbury Brewing Co., Oertel Brewing Co. (br. of LaCrosse, WI)	1967-1983

Newport (cont.)

KY	54a	George Butler	?
	54b	Peter Constans	? -1874
	54c	Louis Constans	1874-1876
	54d	Louis & August Constans	1876-1877
	54e	Schussler & Butcher	1877-1879
	54f	G. Artsman	1879-1882
	54g	George Wiedemann	1882-1885
KY	55	Deppe & Co.	? -1878

Owensboro

KY	56a	Emil Breidenbach	1874-1876
	56b	A. Maxmilian Breidenbach	1876-1891
	56c	Schrecker & Snyder	1891-1896
	56d	Winkler & Walk	1896-1899
	56e	Owensboro Brewery	1899-1903

Paducah

KY	57	John Luigs	1876-1877
KY	58	Paducah Brewery Co. (10th & Monroe Sts.)	1900-1916

Winchester

KY	59	Blue Grass Brewery	NP 1934-1934

LOUISIANA

Lafayette

LA	1	Lafayette Brewing Co.	NP 1947-1947

New Iberia

LA	2	Aug. Erath	1878-1884

New Orleans

LA	3a	Algiers Brewery	1889-1892
	3b	Algiers Brewing Co.	1892-1894
	3c	Security Brewing Co. (341/345 N. Diamond St.)	1894-1912
LA	4a	American Brewing Co. (716 Conti & 717/719 Bienville St.)	1892-1918
	4b	American Brewing Co.	1933-1962
LA	5a	J. Armbruster (537 Chartres St.)	1874-1877
	5b	Mrs. W. Armbruster	1877-1880
	5c	Woolrich & Co.	1880-1884
	5d	Xavier Huerstel	1884-1890
LA	6a	Geo. Auer & Co. (540 Tschoupitoulas St.)	1874-1877
	6b	George Auer	1877-1884
LA	7	Henry Bassemeier (1010 New Levee St.)	1874-1884
LA	8a	Peter Blaise	1869-1871
	8b	Peter Blaise, City Brewery (5 Prieur St.)	1871-1884
	8c	M. Hottos & Co.	1884-1890
LA	9	Columbia Brewing Co. (Elysian Fields & Chartres St.)	1899-1918
LA	10	Consumers Brewing Co. (Clio & S. Liberty Sts.)	1905-1918
LA	11a	Crescent City Brewing Co. (Canal & Claiborne Sts.)	1888-1890
	11b	New Orleans Brewing Association, Crescent City Brewery	1890-1891
LA	12a	Dixie Brewing Co. (2537 Tulane Ave. & Tonti St.)	1907-1918
	12b	Merz Products Co., Inc.	1933-1934
	12c	Dixie Brewing Co., Inc. (2401/2537 Tulane Ave.) aka Royal Brewing Co. (1970-1974)	1935-
LA	13	Eugene Erath (282 Villere St.)	1874-1884
LA	14a	Frank Fehr, Louisiana Brewery (Jackson & Tschoupitoulas Sts.)	1884- ?
	14b	Louisiana Brewing Co.	? -1890
	14c	New Orleans Brewing Association, Louisiana Brewery	1890-1899
	14d	New Orleans Brewing Co., Louisiana Brewery	1899-1918
	14e	New Orleans Brewing Co., Inc. (418 Jackson St.)	1934-1949

New Orleans (cont.)

LA	15	Home Brewing Co. (Jeanna & Levee Sts.)	1893-1893
LA	16a	Jackson Brewing Co. (Jefferson & Decatur Sts.)	1890-1918
	16b	Jackson Brewing Co. (620 Decatur St & 411 Wilkinson St.)	1933-1970
	16c	Jackson Brewing Co., aka Premium Brewing Co. (owned by Meisterbrau, Chicago, IL)	1970-1974
LA	17a	Charles Lasse (476-478 Chartres St.)	1874-1877
	17b	Henry Lasse	1877-1879
LA	18a	George Merz (Villere & Toulouse Sts.)	c1850-1882
	18b	Kaiser & Co.	1882-1884
	18c	Southern Brewing Co.	1884-1890
	18d	New Orleans Brewing Association, Southern Brewery	1890-1899
	18e	New Orleans Brewing Co., Southern Brewery	1899-1900
LA	19a	National Brewing Co. (Dorgenois & Gravier Sts.)	1911-1918
	19b	National Brewing Co., Inc. (2600 Gravier St.)	1933-1937
	19c	Falstaff Brewing Corp. (br. of St. Louis, MO)	1937-1975
	19d	Falstaff Brewing Corp. (affiliated with General Brewing Co.) aka Fischer Brewing Co. aka James Hanley Co.	1975-
LA	20a	Pelican Brewing Co. (Peters & Clouet Sts.)	1888-1890
	20b	New Orleans Brewing Association, Pelican Brewery	1890-1900
	20c	New Orleans Brewing Co., Pelican Brewery	1899-1910
LA	21	Pelican Brewing Co. (810 Union St.)	NP 1934-1934
LA	22	Mrs. S. P. Soule (112/113 Peter St.)	1874-1884
LA	23a	Standard Brewing Co. (514/532 S. Johnson St.)	1898-1918
	23b	Standard Brewing Co., Inc.	1934-1947
	23c	American Brewing Co. (Plant 3) (br. of LA 4b)	1947-1951
LA	24	H. F. Sturcken (82/86 Marais St.)	1874-1884
LA	25a	Union Brewing Co. (2829 Robertson & Press St.)	1911-1918
	25b	Union Products Co., Inc. (2809 N. Robertson St.)	1927-1936
	25c	Union Brewing Corp.	1936-1939
LA	26a	J. J. Weckerling (Magazine & Delord Sts.)	1874-1888
	26b	Weckerling Brewing Co.	1888-1890
	26c	New Orleans Brewing Association, Weckerling Brewery	1890 1899
	26d	New Orleans Brewing Co., Weckerling Brewery	1899-1911
	26e	New Orleans Brewing Co., Weckerling Brewery (Magazine St. & Howard St.)	1911-1918

Shreveport

LA	27	Shreveport Ice and Brewing Co., Caddo Brewery (Western Ave. & Culpepper St.)	1905-1915
LA	28	Louisiana Brewery Co. (1105 Spring St.)	NP 1934-1934

MAINE

Lewiston

ME	1	French & Kimball	1874-1875
ME	2	Daniel Sheehan	1875- ?

Portland

ME	3	Louis Matson Co. (420 Fore St.)	1915-1915
ME	4	Patrick McGlinchy	1874-1875
ME	5	Jas. McLaughlin	1874-1875

Annapolis

MD 1 Patrick Creagh (160 Prince George St.) c1749-1759

MD 2 Benjamin Fordham 1703-1716

MD 3 Mark Gibson c1746

MD 4 John Jeudy (near Prince George & East Sts.) 1764-1765

MD 5a James MacKubbin (South River) ? -1772
5b John Broderick 1772- ?

BALTIMORE(including Canton, Carrollton, Georgtown, Highlandtown & Westport)

MD 6 John Albrecht (350 Pennsylvania Ave. nr. Pitcher St.) 1858-1859

MD 7a Johann (Henry) Altvater (44 Wagon Alley - later Clay St. between Park Ave. & Howard St.) 1808-1823
7b Ann Altvater 1823-1827
7c Elbert Michael 1827- ?

MD 8 William Auer (Font Hill Ave. & Frederick Road) 1867-1872

MD 9a Johann (John) Baier (30 Fell St. near Thames St.) 1850-1853
9b Johann Baier (390/392 Canton Ave.) 1853-1866
9c Anna Baier 1866-1869
9d Anna & Frederick Wunder 1869-1871
9e Frederick Wunder (3rd - later Conkling & O'Donnell Sts.) 1872-1880
9f Mrs. Anna M. Wunder 1881-1885
9g Joseph L. Straus & Brother (Wm. L.), National Brewery 1885-1889
9h National Brewing Co. 1889-1899
9i Maryland Brewing Co., National Brewery 1899-1901
9j Gottlieb-Bauernschmidt-Straus Brewing Co., National Brewery 1901-1920
9k The National Brewing Co. (3602 O'Donnell, Conkling, Dillon & 5th Sts.) 1934-1975
9l Carling National Breweries, Inc.(3720 Dillon St.) aka Van Lauter Brewing Co.) 1975-1979
9m G. Heileman Brewing Co. (Br. of LaCrosse, WI) 1979-1980

MD 10a Baltimore Berliner Weiss Beer Brewing Co. (1715 N. Spring St.) 1895-1918
aka August Fenker (1904-1918)
aka Fenker & Michaels (1914-1916)
aka Andrew Gebhardt New York Weiss Beer Brewery (1895-1904)
aka Gebhardt & Wilms (1895-1904)
aka Harker & Gebhardt (1895-1897)
aka Herman F. Wilms (1895-1904)

MD 11a John Leonard Barnitz & Elias Daniel Barnitz (Baltimore & Hanover Sts.) 1748-1749
11b Elias Daniel Barnitz 1749-1780
11c John Hammond & Co. 1780-1794
11d John G. C. Barnitz 1794-1795
11e Thomas Kerr 1796-1809
11f (Captain) Joseph Leonard 1809-1816
11g (Captain) Joseph Leonard & Co. (Hanover, Conway & Perry Sts.) 1816-1822
11h Peter Gloninger, Washington Brewery 1822-1827
11i Gloninger & Johnson, Washington Brewery 1827-1829
11j John Krouse, Washington Brewery 1829-1831
11k (Andrew) Graham & Silvey, Washington Brewery 1831-1832
11l Samuel Lucas, Washington Brewery 1832-1856
11m Francis Dandelet, Baltimore Brewery 1856-1871
11n F. Dandelet & Co. (John Butterfield & Wm. English) 1871-1875
11o English & Co. (Peter Dahme) 1875-1876
11p John Butterfield & Co. (Frederick Gottlieb) 1876-1880
11q Frederick Gottleib & Herman Hobelmann 1880-1881
11r (Frederick) Wehr-Hobelmann-Gottlieb & Co. 1881-1888
11s Wehr-Hobelmann-Gottlieb Brewing & Malting Co., Globe Brewery 1888-1899
11t Maryland Brewing Co., Globe Brewery 1899-1901
11u Gottlieb-Bauernschmidt-Straus Brewing Co., Globe Brewery 1901-1920
11v The Globe Brewing & Mfg. Co. (313/327 S. Hanover St.) 1920-1935
11w The Globe Brewing Co. 1935-1963
aka Hals Brewing Co. (1958-1963)

Baltimore (cont.)

MD	12a	(Gottlieb) Bauer & (Frederick) Buechler (Clinton & Lancaster)	1873-1874
	12b	Sebastian Helldorfer	1874-1893
	12c	S. Helldorfer's Sons (Henry, Nicholas, John & Franz) (Clinton St. & Fait Ave.)	1893-1899
	12d	Maryland Brewing Co., S. Helldorfer's Sons	1899-1899
MD	13a	John Bauerfind (70 S. Wolfe St.)	1864-1880
	13b	A. Dittmann	1880-1882
	13c	Adam Stier	1882-1883
	13d	G. W. Umbach, Empire Brewery	1883-1886
	13e	G. W. Umbach, Empire Brewing Co. (245 S. Wolfe St.)	1886-1891
	13f	Mary Miller	1891-1892
MD	14a	Frederick Bauernschmidt, American Brewery (1104/1128 Hillen)	1900-1920
	14b	Free State Brewery Corp.	1933-1950
	14c	The Wiessner Brewing Co., Inc. (Hillen, Monument, Forest & Ensor Sts.)	1950-1952
MD	15a	George & John Bauernschmidt (281 W. Pratt St.)	1858-1864
	15b	Geo. Bauernschmidt, Greenwood Park Brewery (Belair Ave.)	1864-1887
	15c	Geo. Bauernschmidt Brewing Co. (1505 N. Gay St.)	1887-1899
	15d	Maryland Brewing Co., Geo. Bauernschmidt Brewery	1899-1901
	15e	Gottlieb-Bauernschmidt-Straus Brewing Co., George Bauernschmidt Brewery (Gay & Oliver Sts.)	1901-1915
MD	16a	John Bauernschmidt, Spring Garden Brewery (1540 Ridgley St.)	1864-1879
	16b	Bauernschmidt & Marr	1879-1884
	16c	Bauernschmidt & Marr Brewing Co.	1884-1889
	16d	Baltimore United Breweries, aka Bauernschmidt & Marr Brewing	1889-1899
	16e	Maryland Brewing Co., Spring Garden Brewery	1899-1901
	16f	Gottlieb-Bauerschmidt-Straus Brewing Co., Spring Garden Brewery	1901-1903
	16g	Mount Vernon Brewing Co., aka Consumers Brewery (Ridgeley, Scott & S. Paca Sts.)	1906-1909
MD	17a	John J. Bauernschmidt (71 W. Camden St.)	1856-1857
	17b	George Rossdeutscher	1857-1860
MD	18a	Bayview Brewery, Jacob Keinzle (Eastern Ave. & 16th)	1866-1876
	18b	Hecht, Miller & Co.	1876-1887
	18c	William Miller & Co.	1887-1889
	18d	Baltimore United Breweries, Bay View Brewery	1889-1899
	18e	Maryland Brewing Co., Bay View Brewery	1899-1901
	18f	Gottlieb-Bauernschmidt-Straus Brewing Co., Bay View Brewery	1901-1902
MD	19a	August Beck (Frederick Road)	1865-1884
	19b	August Beck (44/46 Garrison Lane)	1884-1898
	19c	August Beck & Son	1898-1899
	19d	John Marr, Independent Brewery	1899-1900
	19e	Frank Steil Brewing Co.	1900-1920
MD	20	George Beck (360 Pennsylvania Ave.)	1865-1876
MD	21a	Henry Beck, Celebrated Weiss Beer Brewery (153 E. Fayette St.)	1875-1884
	21b	Ernestine Beck (2131 E. Fayette St. & Castle St.) aka Henry C. Beck (1887-1912)	1884-1912
MD	22a	Thomas Beck, Rock Spring Brewery (Calverton Ave. & W. Baltimore St.)	1856-1873
	22b	Thos. Beck & Son, Rock Spring Brewery	1873-1882
	22c	Thos. J. Beck, Rock Spring Brewery	1882-1884
	22d	Thos. M. Dukehart, Maryland Brewery	1884-1891
	22e	Dukehart Brewing Co.	1891-1900
	22f	Dukehart Manufacturing Co.	1900-1913
MD	23	John C. Bergen (836 S. Bond St.)	1888-1890
MD	24a	John Bodenschatz (803 W. Pratt & Mount Sts.)	1860-1873
	24b	John T. Bauernschmidt, Mount Brewery	1873-1889
	24c	Baltimore United Breweries, Mount Brewery (1707 W. Pratt St.)	1889-1899
	24d	Maryland Brewing Co., Mount Brewery	1899-1899
MD	25	John G. Boehn (317 S. Bond St.)	1875-1876

Baltimore (cont.)

MD	26a	(John) Matthias Brandel (W. Saratoga St.)	1851-1858
	26b	(John) Matthias Brandel, Mt. Pleasant Brewery (W. Balt. St.)	1858-1871
	26c	S. & W. Straus	1871-1875
	26d	Joseph Raiber	1875-1876
	26e	(Franz) Thau & (Paul) Mulhauser, Crystal Springs Brewery	1876-1881
	26f	(Elias E.) Adler & (Paul) Mulhauser, Enterprise Brewery (Baltimore St. & Garrison Lane)	1881-1883
	26g	Elias E. Adler	1883-1888
	26h	Elias E. Adler, Trustees of S. & W. Straus	1888-1888
MD	27	Brooklyn Brewing Co., Cloverdale Brewery (2000 Bolton St.)	1934-1934
MD	28a	Viet Butschky (109 Eastern Ave. nr. Central Ave.)	1849-1860
	28b	Viet Butschky (Belair Road)	1867-1869
	28c	Christopher Spengler	1869-1871
	28d	Frank Schlaffer	1872-1881
	28e	Chas. Schlaffer	1881-1882
MD	29a	Carling Brewing Co. (Baltimore Beltway at Hammond's Ferry Rd.) aka Tuborg Brewery Co. (1973-1975)	1961-1975
	29b	Carling National Breweries, Inc. (4501 Hollins Ferry Road)	1975-1979
	29c	G. Heileman Brewing Co. (br. of LaCrosse, WI)	1979-
MD	30	Carrollton Brewery (Carrollton)	1875-1886
MD	31	Columbia Brewing and Ice Co. (Bayard St. & Columbia Ave.)	1899-1899
MD	32a	Theo. Eichhorn (360 S. Caroline St.)	1875-1877
	32b	John M. Berger	1877-1882
	32c	Mrs. Elizabeth Berger	1882-1884
MD	33a	Engel Brewery (Belair Road)	c1850
	33b	Otto J. Engel (59 N. Exeter St.)	1860-1865
	33c	Otto J. Engel (Belair, 2236 E. North Ave.)	1866-1869
	33d	Anna M. Engel	1869-1870
	33e	Joseph Schreier	1870-1884
	33f	(Leo) Ewald & (Henry) Schuchmann	1884- ?
MD	34	J. Ferdinand (Pratt & Exeter Sts.)	1874-1875
MD	35a	Christian Gehl, Bay View Brewery (3rd & O'Donnell Sts., Canton)	1876-1878
	35b	Gunther & Gehl, Bay View Brewery	1878-1880
	35c	George Guenther, Bay View Brewery	1880-1899
	35d	Maryland Brewing Co., Bay View Brewery	1899-1901
	35e	Gottlieb-Bauernschmidt-Straus Brewing Co., Bay View Brewery aka George Guenther Brewery (1901)	1901-1910
MD	36	Francis Gortler (Canton Ave.)	1853-1853
MD	37	Andreas Gransched (Frederick St. near Lexington St.)	175801783
MD	38a	Valentine Grimmer (277 S. Ann & Thames St.)	1860-1863
	38b	Valentine Grimmer (Lancaster & 3rd)	1868-1878
	38c	John G. Beh	1878-1880
	38d	Anton Boehn	1881-1884
	38e	Franz Schlaffer, Oriental Brewery	1884-1888
	38f	Oriental Brewing Co. (702 3rd St.)	1888-1899
	38g	Maryland Brewing Co., Oriental Brewery	1899-1899
MD	39a	George Guenther Jr. Brewing Co. (3rd & Toone Sts.)	1900-1920
	39b	George J. Gunther Mfg. Co.	1920-1932
	39c	Gunther's Breweries, Inc. (1101 S. Conkling St.)	1932-1935
	39d	Gunther Brewing Co., Inc.	1935-1939
	39e	Theo. Hamm Brewing Co., aka Gunther Brewing Co. (br. of St. Paul, MN)	1959-1963
	39f	The F. & M. Schaefer Brewing Co., aka Gunther Brewing Co. (br. of Brooklyn, NY)	1963-1978
MD	40a	John Hager (Belair Road near North Ave.)	1853-1854
	40b	John Hager (191 E. Lombard St.)	1856-1857
MD	41	John Hague (55 Jones between Gay & Hillen Sts.)	1802- ?

Baltimore (cont.)

MD	42a	Conrad Herzog (30 Fell St.)	1851-1853
	42b	Conrad Herzog (Lancaster St. & Burke St.)	1853-1864
	42c	(George F.) Wiessner & (John) Miller	1864-1867
	42d	(George F.) Wiessner	1867-1869
	42e	George Stab (74 Burke St.)	1870-1877
	42f	Lina Stab	1877-1882
	42g	(George) Michael Roesch	1882-1890
MD	43a	Christopher Hitzrodt (22 Thames & Bond Sts.)	1853-1866
	43b	(John M.) Berger Weiss Beer Brewery	1866-1868
	43c	Berger & Co. (Andrew Dittman)	1868-1878
MD	44a	Conrad H. Hoburg (Hampstead Hill nr. Broadway & Fairmount)	1791-1792
	44b	Conrad H. Hoburg, Gorsuch's Brewery (Back St. nr. Griffith's Bridge)	1792-1796
MD	45	Andrew Hoffman (17 Union St. near Pennsylvania Ave.)	1800-1810
MD	46a	Conrad Hoffman (705 W. Mulberry St.)	1847-1848
	46b	Conrad Hoffman (53 Pennsylvania Ave. & Orchard St.)	1849-1860
MD	47	John G. Hoffman, Mt. Royal Brewery (Shirk & Jefferson Pl.)	1860-1877
MD	48	J. H. Hoffmann (Falls Road)	1874-1875
MD	49a	John N. Huebner (4437/4439 Belair Road)	1852-1857
	49b	George Neisendorfer	1857-1859
	49c	Gottfried C. Hertlein	1866-1879
	49d	Otto Woerner	1879-1890
MD	50a	Ferdinand Joh (28/40 Wilkins St.)	1873-1876
	50b	Henry Eigenbrot aka Henry Eigenbrot Brewing Co. (1888-1891)	1876-1892
	50c	Eigenbrot Brewing Co. (10/50 Wilkens St.)	1892-1899
	50d	Maryland Brewing Co., Eigenbrot Brewery	1899-1901
	50e	Gottlieb-Bauernschmidt-Straus Brewing Co., Eigenbrot Brewery	1901-1920
MD	51a	John Kalb (710 Light St. near Wells St.)	1869-1874
	51b	Frank Aberhart	1874-1875
MD	52	Joseph M. Keller (352 Pennsylvania Ave.)	1858-1860
MD	53a	John Kohles (92/94 S. Wolfe St.)	1859-1864
	53b	John Bauerfeind	1864-1875
MD	54a	John Kohles (60 S. Wolfe St.)	1874- ?
	54b	John Kohles (36 S. Wolfe St.)	? -1884
	54c	Elizabeth Kohles	1884-1888
MD	55	John Knecht, Weiss Beer Brewery (Carrolltown)	1878-1879
MD	56a	Michael Krebs (860 Pennsylvania Ave.)	1875- ?
	56b	N. Extel	? -1878
MD	57a	John Laekauf (10 Fell St. nr. Thames St., Fells Pt.)	1847-1848
	57b	Adam Lurz	1851-1852
	57c	Adam Lurz (30 Fell St.)	1855-1856
	57d	Adam Lurz (24 Fell St.)	1856-1857
MD	58a	John Laekauf & John Ludwig (28 E. Pratt St. between E. Fall Ave. & Albemarle St.)	1849-1851
	58b	John Laekauf	1851-1854
MD	59	Liberty Brewing Co., Inc. (Boston & Ponca Sts.)	NP 1934-1934
MD	60	Peter Littig (Wilk St. & Central Ave.)	1779-1789
MD	61	John Loehr (260 E. Pratt St. near Ann St.)	1860-1860
MD	62a	Frederick Ludwig	1848-1858
	62b	Frederick Weber, Albion Brewery	1858-1862
	62c	Jacob Mulhauser, Albion Brewery	1862-1865
	62d	Jacpb Green, Albion Brewery	1865-1872
	62e	Sophia Green (Belvidere Bridge)	1873-1875
	62f	Frederick Schneider Albion Brewery (1422 Belvidere St. & Greenmount Ave.)	1876-1876

cont. page 110...

Baltimore (cont.)

MD	62g	Christian Schneider, Belvidere Brewery	1876-1878
	62h	Bernhard Berger, Albion Brewery	1878-1893
	62i	Berger Brewery, John B. Berger	1893-1899
	62j	Maryland Brewing Co., Berger Brewery	1899-1899
MD	63	John Ludwig (53 N. Frederick St.)	1853-1856
MD	64	Charles Martz (521 N. Conkling St.)	1887-1887
MD	65a	Marcus McCausland & Co. (Holliday, Bath & Hillen Sts.)	1800-1827
	65b	Samuel Lucas	1833-1835
MD	66a	J. & L. Medtart (Joshua & Lewis), Saratoga Brewery (330/340 W. Saratoga St.)	1833-1841
	66b	Jesse L. & Jacob C. Medtart, Saratoga Brewery	1841-1847
	66c	Jacob Medtart, Saratoga Brewery	1847-1857
	66d	Bayley & (Wm.) Blakey	1857-1858
	66e	Wm. Bayley	1858-1859
MD	67	Ambrose Miller (368 Light St. between Cross & West Sts.)	1867-1877
MD	68	George Miller (O'Donnell & 2nd Sts.)	1873-1873
MD	69a	George Miller (Harford Rd. opposite Darley Park)	1868-1870
	69b	Conrad Siegmann	1872-1873
	69c	Straus Bros. (Harford Rd. & North Ave.)	1874-1876
	69d	H. S. Straus Bros. & Bell, Darley Park Brewery	1876-1884
	69e	H. Straus Bro. & Co., Darley Park Brewery	1884-1889
	69f	Baltimore United Breweries, Darley Park Brewery	1889-1899
	69g	Maryland Brewing Co., Darley Park Brewery	1899-1901
	69h	Gottlieb-Bauernschmidt-Straus Brewing Co., Darley Park Brewery	1901-1912
MD	70	R. Miller (373 Biddle St.)	1879-1879
MD	71a	Moller & Paul (1234 Jackson St.)	1890-1890
	71b	Nicholas Moller	1891-1892
MD	72a	Monarch Brewing Co. (9th & Lombard Sts.)	1899-1900
	72b	Monumental Brewing Co. (7th, 8th & Lombard Sts, Highlandtown)	1900-1920
MD	73a	John Mueller (394 Pennsylvania Ave. & Pitcher St.)	1869-1880
	73b	Mrs. John Mueller (Catherine)	1880-1884
	73c	(Catherine) Mueller & (Robert) Handloeser	1884-1890
	73d	Western Maryland Brewery, Robert Handloeser (1552 Pennsylvania Ave.)	1890-1897
MD	74	Valentine Mueller (32/48 Burke St.)	1867-1878
MD	75a	Louis Muth (Belair Ave.)	1867-1880
	75b	Louis Muth & Son	1880-1888
MD	76a	John Nagengast (370 Pennsylvania Ave. bn. Mosher & Pitcher)	1867-1872
	76b	John Nagengast & Bro.	1872-1878
	76c	Werner & Honig	1878-1879
	76d	Henry Werner (1526/1534 Pennsylvania Ave.)	1879-1888
	76e	Phoenix Brewery, John & Franklin Manning	1888-1892
	76f	Chesapeake Brewing Co.	1900-1920
	76g	Theodore Reichhart, Inc. (2208/2210 Harford Road)	1933-1936
	76h	Chesapeake Brewing Corp.	1937-1938
MD	77a	George Neisendorfer (59 S. High St.)	1855-1857
	77b	George Neisendorfer (Belair Ave., Georgetown)	1858-1866
	77c	George Brehm	1866-1899
	77d	Maryland Brewing Co., George Brehm Brewery	1899-1901
	77e	George Brehm & Son	1901-1911
	77f	George Brehm & Son (Brehm's Lane)	1911-1920
	77g	Brehm Beverage Co.	1920-1923
	77h	Baltimore Brewing Co., Inc.	1927-1931
	77i	Baltimore Brewing Co., Inc.	1933-1935
	77j	The Bruton Brewing Co. (3501 Brehms' Lane near Loney's Lane)	1935-1940
MD	78a	Michael Nitzel (Clinton & Elliott Sts.)	1865-1867
	78b	Albert J. Wagner	1867-1868
	78c	Samuel Nitzel	1868-1870

Baltimore (cont.)

MD	79a	(Philip) Odenwald & (Ferdinand) Joh (7 Calverton Rd. between Hollins St. & Frederick Road)	1862-1873
	79b	Sommerfeld & Co.	1873-1875
	79c	John Sommerfeld & Co.	1875-1880
	79d	John Sommerfeld (2215/2225 Calverton Ave.)	1880-1891
	79e	Sommerfeld Brewing Co.	1891-1895
	79f	Lion Brewing Co. (2115/2141 Calverton Ave.)	1895-1901
	79g	Maryland Brewing Co., Lion Brewery	1901-1901
	79h	Gottlieb-Bauernschmidt-Straus Brewing Co., Lion Brewery	1901-1902
MD	80	(Daniel) O'Neill & (John) Fitzgerald (400 S. Chester & Bank)	1902-1903
MD	81a	George Pabst (O'Donnell & 2nd)	1860-1874
	81b	Catherine Pabst	1874-1875
	81c	John Trost	1875-1881
	81d	(William) Kemper & (John) Trost	1881-1883
	81e	William Trost	1883-1883
	81f	William Miller	1883-1883
MD	82a	Louis Pabst, Weiss Beer Brewery (840 S. Bond St.)	1889-1909
	82b	Barbara Pabst	1909-1911
MD	83	John M. Ramming (2706/2708 Harford Road)	1863-1882
MD	84	George Rossdeutscher (27 S. Paca St. btw. Lombard & Pratt Sts.)	1853-1857
MD	85	Christian Rossmarck (239 Aliceanna & 700 S. Ann St.)	1858-1864
MD	86a	George Rossmarck (Liberty & Saratoga Sts.)	1846-1848
	86b	Jacob Wohlleber	1849-1851
	86c	(Frederick) Auer & Lauer	1851-1853
MD	87	George Rossmarck (23 N. Frederick St.)	1852-1862
MD	88a	George Rost (303 S. Bond St. near Lancaster St.)	1849-1853
	88b	Geroge Rost (Belair Ave.)	1853-1871
	88c	Sophia Rost aka John Rost (1881)	1871-1881
	88d	Mrs. M. E. Rost	1881-1884
	88e	Louis Muth	1884-1886
	88f	Standard Brewing Co.	1886-1888
	88g	Standard Brewing Co. (1766 N. Gay St.)	1888-1896
	88h	Standard Brewery, John Marr	1896-1899
	88i	Standard Brewery Co.	1899-1920
	88j	Bis-Mac Co., Inc.	1920-1922
	88k	Bismarck Brewing Corp., subsidiary of Croft Brewing Co., Boston, MA (1808/1838 N. Patterson Park Ave.)	1934-1935
	88l	Bismarck Brewing Corp.	1936-1937
	88m	Imperial Brewing Co. dba Bismarck Brewery	1938-1940
MD	89a	John Rummelmann (326 S. Bond St.)	1867-1869
	89b	John Aummermann	1870-1871
MD	90a	(Balthazar) Salzig & (Louis) Bitter, Weiss Beer Brewery (46 S. Washington St., near Lombard St.)	1873-1873
	90b	Salzig & Bitter, Weiss Beer Brewery (377 E. Lombard St. between Washington & Chester Sts.)	1874-1874
MD	91a	Frank Sandkuhler (2338 McElderrys & Montford Aves.)	1886-1895
	91b	Frank Sandkuhler (101/111 N. Collington Ave.)	1895-1919
MD	92a	J. Henry Saumenig (Brewhouse Alley)	? -1804
	92b	J. Henry Saumenig (129 Camden & Eutaw Sts.)	1804-1804
	92c	J. Henry Saumenig & Co. (Johann Altvater)	1804-1808
	92d	J. Henry Saumenig	1808-1819
	92e	John G. Freinscht	1829-1831
	92f	John G. Freinscht & Peter Gloninger	1831-1835
	92g	John G. Freinscht	1835-1837
	92h	(Capt.) Frederick H. Brandt	1937-1847
	92i	John A. Zwansger & Jesse L. Medtart	1847-1851
	92j	John A. Zwansger	1851-1866

Baltimore (cont.)

MD	93a	George L. Schemm (Light St.)	c1853- ?
	93b	John Schemm	1864-1866
MD	94	Jacob Schierlitz (413 W. Baltimore St.)	1873-1881
MD	95a	Fritz Schneider (249 Aliceanna St. near Broadway)	1864-1866
	95b	Fritz Schneider (502 N. 3rd & Dillon Sts., Canton)	1866-1889
MD	96	John Schriner (42 N. Liberty St. near Lexington St.)	1796-1796
MD	97a	John Schultheis (Frederick Road)	1872-1877
	97b	John Schultheis (Garrison's Lane)	1877-1886
	97c	(John) Schultheis & (Robert) Wiesenfeld, Union Brewing Co.	1886-1886
	97d	(John) Schultheis & (Oscar) Teschner Co.	1886-1889
MD	98a	John Schwingler (20 Shakespeare St.)	1853-1858
	98b	John Schwingler (317 S. Bond & Thames St.)	1858-1874
	98c	Frederick Striebel	1875-1875
	98d	John Beh	1876-1878
	98e	Berger & Co. (Andrew Dittman)	1878-1878
	98f	John M. Berger	1878-1883
	98g	Mrs. Elizabeth Berger	1883-1886
	98h	Mrs. Elizabeth Berger, aka Fells Point Brewing Co. (818 S. Bond & Thames Sts.)	1886-1888
MD	99a	Jacob Seeger (1053 W. Pratt St. & Frederick Ave.)	1854-1888
	99b	Baltimore Brewing Co. (2211 W. Pratt St.)	1888-1899
	99c	Maryland Brewing Co., Baltimore Brewery	1899-1901
MD	100	Theodore Seeger (426 Frederick Road)	1872-1873
MD	101a	Daniel Shettle & Co. (Holliday & Franklin Sts.)	1864-1866
	101b	Jacob Medtart, Maryland Brewery (Holiday St. near Centre St.)	1866-1872
	101c	Medtart & Dukehart	1872-1872
	101d	Thomas Dukehart, Maryland Brewery	1872-1876
	101e	(Thomas) Dukehart & Co., Maryland Brewery	1877-1884
MD	102	Christoph Spengler (382 Eastern Ave.)	1873-1873
MD	103a	James Sterrett (Gay & Water)	1761-1783
	103b	Thomas Peters & Co. (E. Lombard St. & Jones Falls)	1784-1787
	103c	Peters & Co.	1787-1792
	103d	Peters, Johnson & Co.	1792-1796
	103e	Peters & Co.	1796-1807
	103f	Edward Johnson & Co.	1807-1813
	103g	Edward Johnson	1813-1813
	103h	George I. Brown	1913-1918
	103i	Eli Clagett	1818-1848
	103j	William Clagett & Co.	1848-1849
	103k	Clagett & Dannels	1849-1873
	103l	Eleanor Dannels	1874-1877
MD	104	James Sterrett (Lombard & Frederick Sts.)	c1779
MD	105a	(Edward W.) Stiefel & (Thomas) Seeger (Federal Hill)	1854-1856
	105b	Stiefel & Seeger (Frederick Road)	1857-1872
	105c	Edw. W. Stiefel (450/454 Frederick Ave., Carrolton)	1872-1892
	105d	Germania Brewing Co. (848/856 Frederick Ave.)	1892-1899
	105e	Maryland Brewing Co., Germania Brewery	1899-1901
	105f	Gottlieb-Bauernschmidt-Straus Brewing Co., Germania Brewery	1901-1902
MD	106a	Geo. F. Streib	1875-1877
	106b	Schultheis & Bros.	1877-1878
MD	107a	George W. Vogt (Eastern Ave. & 3rd St.)	1876-1880
	107b	William Kemper	1880-1884
	107c	Anna M. Kemper	1884-1885
MD	108a	Von der Horst & Rupprecht (10 Belair Ave.)	1865-1866
	108b	John H. Von der Horst	1866-1880
	108c	John H. Von der Horst & Son	1880-1896
	108d	Von der Horst Brewing Co., aka John Von der Horst Brewery(1897)	1896-1899
	108e	Maryland Brewing Co., Von der Horst Brewery	1899-1901
	108f	Gottlieb-Bauernschmidt-Straus Brewing Co., Von der Horst Brewy.	1901-1912

Baltimore (cont.)

MD	109	Washington Bottling Co., Weiss Beer Brewery (2112 Aliceanna)	1911-1913
MD	110	Fred Weber (Harford Road & Herring Run)	1862-1889
MD	111a	George F. Wiessner, Fort Marshall Brewery (Eastern & Highland Aves., Highlandtown)	1869-1872
	111b	Andrew Hoenervogt, Fort Marshall Brewery	1872-1876
	111c	Mrs. Elizabeth (Wiessner) Hoenervogt, Fort Marshall Brewery (206 Eastern Ave.)	1876-1888
	111d	John F. Wiessner & Bro. Brewing Co.	1888-1899
	111e	Maryland Brewing Co., Wiessner Brewery	1899-1899
MD	112a	John F. Wiessner (1700/1702 N. Gay St.) aka John F. Wiessner & Sons (1888-1891)	1863-1891
	112b	John F. Wiessner & Sons Brewing Co.	1891-1920
	112c	American Brewery, Inc.	1933-1967
	112d	American Brewery aka Fort Pitt Brewing Co. (1956-1965) aka Heibrau Brewing Co. (1966-1971) aka Imperial Brewing Co. (1960-1966)	1967-1973
MD	113	J. F. Wiessner & Son Brewing Co. (1732 N. Chester St.)	NP 1934-1934
MD	114a	Jacob Wohlleber (Cross St. near Federal Hill)	1838-1849
	114b	George & Christopher Rossmarck (Ross & Covington Sts.)	1852- ?
	114c	George Rossmarck	? -1878
	114d	Joseph Claus	1878-1880
MD	115a	John L. Zwansger, Annapolis Beer Brewery (Annapolis Road near Old Fishouse Road, Westport)	1868-1873
	115b	John H. Zwansger	1873-1881
	115c	Adolph Beck	1881-1882

Barton

MD	116a	Henry Creutzberg	c1867-1868
	116b	Geo. Schramm	1874-1877
	116c	Kolberg & Co.	1877-1878

Canton (see Baltimore)

Carrollton (see Baltimore)

Charlestown

MD	117	John Muschett	c1845-1848

Clear Spring

MD	118	William Witzenbacher	1840-1850

Cumberland

MD	119a	Frederick Beck (309 Valley St. near Chestnut St.)	1858-1861
	119b	Mrs. Frederick Beck (Sophia), Common Beer Brewery	1861-1885
	119c	John F. Beck	1885-1886
	119d	Julian Sibley	1886-1888
	119e	George F. Beck	1888-1888
	119f	John D. Beck (57/61 Valley St.)	1888-1911
MD	120	M. S. Beck	1874-1875
MD	121	Beck Brothers (Wm. & Henry) (19/21 Front St.)	1866-1892
MD	122a	Cumberland Brewing Co. (397 N. Centre St.)	1890-1920
	122b	The Cumberland Brewing Co. (711 N. Centre St.)	1933-1958
	122c	Cumberland Brewing Co., div. of The Queen City Brewing Co., aka Sandusky Brewing Co., Globe Brewing Co.	1958-1969
MD	123a	C. Fesenmeier	1877-1879
	123b	Michael Fesenmeier (Baltimore Pike, Lindnersville)	1879-1889
	123c	Geo. F. Beck	1889-1891
MD	124a	German Brewing Co. (208 Market St. & Wills Creek)	1901-1917
	124b	Liberty Brewing Co.	1917-1920
	124c	Queen Co., Inc.	1920-1933
	124d	The German Brewing Co.	1933-1941
	124e	The Queen City Brewing Co. aka American Brewery Co. (1963-1974) aka Cumberland Brewing Co.	1941-1974

Cumberland (cont.)

MD	124e	aka Fischer Brewing Co. aka Globe Brewing Co. (1963-1970) aka Home Brewing Co. (1969-1973)	
MD	125a	Wm. & Michael Gessner (National Pike, Sebastapol)	c1842-1850
	125b	Wm. Gessner, Washington Brewery (32/34 Paca St. near Lee St.)	1859-1863
	125c	George H. Schultz, Washington Brewery	1863-1872
	125d	Paul Ritter	1872-1894
MD	126a	Bartholomew Himmler (Knox & Hays Sts.)	1852-1854
	126b	John H. Zink	1854-1858
	126c	Anna Zink	1858-1859
	126d	Gustav Stucklauser, City Brewery	1859-1872
MD	127	Christ. Hartung & Co.	1875-1875
MD	128a	Batholomew Himmler (836 N. Mechanic St.)	1863-1865
	128b	J. Himmler & Bro. (George)	1865-1877
	128c	George Himmler	1877-1884
	128d	Mrs. George Himmler aka John Himmler (c1888)	1884-1891
	128e	John H. Zink (426 N. Mechanic St.)	1891-1906
	128f	Narrows Brewing Co., aka Jon H. Zink	1906-1909
MD	129a	Nicholas Hodel (N. Centre St. near Valley St.)	1857-1861
	129b	John G. Hodel	1861- ?
	129c	Jos. H. Hodel	1874-1882
MD	130	John A. Kolb	c1880-1882
MD	131	Wm. Leonard (296/298 Mechanic St.)	1878-1879
MD	132	Thomas Martin (Georges St.)	c1880-1882
MD	133a	Gus Stucklauser (416/420 Mechainc St.)	1872-1888
	133b	Wm. Himmler	1888-1891
MD	134	Mrs. Anna Zink (Centre St.)	1859-1860
MD	135	Geo. H. Zink	1875-1875

Emmitsburg

MD	136	John Elour	c1867-1868

Frederick

MD	137	John Grundel (Market & 5th Sts.)	c1859
MD	138	Balser Heck	c1760-1790
MD	139	John Charlton (Patrick & Market Sts.)	1746-1766
MD	140a	John G. Lipps	c1840-1880
	140b	J. Lipps' Sons (W. Patrick St.)	1880-1884
MD	141a	William Small (Brewers Alley)	1846- ?
	141b	Jacob Markell	? -1858
	141c	(John) Pete Baer	1858-1873
	141d	Z. G. Zimmerman	1875-1875
	141e	Paul Hauser	1875-1888
	141f	C. H. Eckstein	1890-1890
	141g	John Kuhn	1891-1901
MD	142	Peoples Service Co., Inc.	1934-1934

Frostburg

MD	143	M. J. Biddington	1875-1875
MD	144	Thos. D. Davis	1875-1875
MD	145	G. H. Eisfelder	1874-1875
MD	146	Frostburg Brewing Co.	1908-1917
MD	147a	John Mayer	1874-1888
	147b	Elizabeth Mayer	1888-1893

Gardenville

MD	148	Otto Werner	1884-1888

Georgetown (see Baltimore)

Hagerstown

MD	149	Margaret Butz, Weiss Beer Brewery (220 S. Potomac St.)	c1840-1867
MD	150a	Conrad Crumbach	1800-1805
	150b	John Coke	1805-1815
MD	151	John Fisher (Franklin St.)	c1867-1868
MD	152	L. S. Fisher (Franklin St. near Potomac St.)	c1867-1868
MD	153	Charles E. Gelwicks	1805-1815
MD	154a	Jonathan Hagar & George Sholl (Franklin & Potomac Sts.)	c1792
	154b	Jacob Rohrer	1800- ?
MD	155a	Hagerstown Brewing Co. (Franklin & Foundry Sts.)	1900-1918
	155b	The Hagerstown Brewing Co. (342/348 W. Franklin St.)	1935-1937
MD	156a	Louis Heist (13/17 Potomac St.)	1862-1874
	156b	Justus Heimel	1874-1893
MD	157a	(Andrew) Leibold & (Louis) Heist (112 S. Potomac St.)	1849-1854
	157b	Andrew Leibold	1854-1862
	157c	Katherine Leibold	1862-1871
	157d	(Justus) Heimel & (John) Spiegel	1871-1874
	157e	Justus Heimel	1874-1877
MD	158a	Peter Middlekauff (Franklin St. near Potomac St.) aka (Peter) Middlekauff & (John) Baer (c1858)	1857-1864
	158b	David M. Good	1864-1867
MD	159	M. Marganstern	c1867-1868
MD	160	Robert Schuster (120 W. Franklin St. near Jonathan St.)	1865-1888
MD	161	William Wagner (52 S. Potomac St.)	1865-1882
MD	162	William Witzenbacher	1874-1884

Highlandtown (see Baltimore)

Lonaconing

MD	163a	Henry Hanekamp & Brothers (Jackson St.)	1861- ?
	163b	Henry Hanekamp	1874-1877
	163c	Fredericks & Hanekamp	1877-1879
	163d	C. F. Fredericks	1879-1880
MD	164a	C. Langlotz & Co. (Detmond St.)	1869-1875
	164b	C. Hohing	1875-1890

Marlborough

MD	165	J. Mercer	c1766

Morgan Creek

MD	166a	(Col.) Isaac Perkins	c1783-1792
	166b	Perkins & Ward	1792- ?

Mount Savage

MD	167a	Peter Henckel	1862-1878
	167b	Henry Henckel	1878-1904
MD	168	James McNulty	1859-1867

Salisbury

MD	169a	The Shore Beverage Co.	1935-1936
	169b	Associated Breweries	1936-1937

Westernport

MD	170	Joseph Benfield	c1871
MD	171	Joseph Erpelt	c1871
MD	172a	Frederick Knorr	c1871
	172b	Margaret Knorr	1874-1875
	172c	Frederick Knorr	1878-1884
	172d	Conrad Nau	1884-1894

Westminster

MD	173	William Leidich (W. Main St.)	c1871

Westport (see Baltimore)

Williamsport

MD	174a	John Gelwicks	1810-1817
	174b	Jacob Weaver	1817- ?

MASSACHUSETTS

Bedford

MA	1	Fred A. Walter	1874-1879

Boston (includes Charleston, East Boston, Highlands, Jamaica Plain, Roxbury, and South Boston)

MA	2	Alley & Nichols	1874-1875
MA	3a	John R. Alley (123 Heath St., Roxbury)	1886-1893
	3b	John R. Alley & Sons	1893-1895
	3c	Alley Brewing Co.	1895-1901
	3d	Massachusetts Breweries Co., Alley Brewery	1901-1918
MA	4a	American Brewing Co. (235 Heath St., Roxbury)	1891-1893
	4b	American Brewing Co. of Boston	1893-1901
	4c	Massachusetts Breweries Co., American Brewery	1901-1918
	4d	Haffenreffer & Co., Inc. (235/249 Heath St.)	1933-1934
MA	5a	Boston Beer Co. (225/249 W. 2nd St. & D. St., South Boston)	1828-1918
	5b	Boston Beer Co.	1936-1956
MA	6	W. L. Broadbent (Bromley Park, Highlands)	c1882
MA	7a	G. F. Burkhardt (Parker & Staion Sts.)	1850-1891
	7b	Burkhardt Brewing Co.	1891-1918
MA	8a	Burton Brewery (907/933 Parker & Heath Sts.)	1870- ?
	8b	Burton Brewing Co.	1878-1880
	8c	J. K. Souther	1880-1884
	8d	J. K. Souther & Sons	1884-1889
	8e	Souther Brewing Co.	1898-1912
MA	9	Isaac Cook & Co. (25 Central St.)	1874-1884
MA	10a	John Cooper & Thomas Gould (Alford St., Charlestown)	1821- ?
	10b	William T. Van Nostrand (40 Alford St., Charlestown)	c1860-1877
	10c	Wm. T. Van Nostrand & Co.	1877-1890
	10d	Bunker Hill Breweries, A. G. Van Nostrand	1890-1918
	10e	Van Nostrand Brewing Co. (60 Alford St.)	NP 1934-1934
MA	11	Conrad Decker (Alna Place, East Boston)	1874-1884
MA	12	Empire Brewing Co. (11/19 Hampden St. & 810 Albany St.)	1888-1891
MA	13a	Franklin Brewing Co. (3175 Washington St.)	1894-1901
	13b	Massachusetts Breweries Co., Franklin Brewery	1901-1902
MA	14a	Frey & King (86/90 Longwood Ave.)	1877-1878
	14b	Lang & King	1878-1883
	14c	Charles A. King	1883-1896
	14d	Continental Brewing Co.	1896-1901
	14e	Massachusetts Breweries Co., Continental Brewery	1901-1902
MA	15a	Edward Habich (171 Cedar St.)	1874-1888
	15b	Habich & Co., Norfolk Brewery	1888-1901
	15c	Massachusetts Breweries Co., Habich Brewery	1901-1902
MA	16a	Haffenreffer & Co. (Bismarck & Germania Sts., Jamaica Plain)	1870-1890
	16b	New England Brewing Co., Haffenreffer & Co.	1890-1918
	16c	Haffenreffer & Co., Inc. (30 Germania St.) aka Boston Brewing Co. (1958-1964) aka Enterprise Brewing Co. (1962-1964) aka Worcester Brewing Co. (1962-1964)	1933-1964
MA	17a	Col. Patrick T. Hanley (104 Ward St.)	c1866- ?
	17b	Hanley & Casey, Cook Brewery	1890-1895
	17c	Hanley & Casey Brewery Co.	1895-1901
	17d	Massachusetts Breweries Co., Hanley & Casey Brewery	1901-1916

Boston (cont.)

MA	18a	Houghton & Co., Ale Brewery	1876-1878
	18b	S. Engle & Co.	1879-1879
MA	19a	A. J. Houghton & Co., Vienna Brewery (37 Station & Hallock Sts)	1870-1892
	19b	A. J. Houghton Co.	1892-1901
	19c	A. J. Houghton Co., Vienna Brewery	1901-1918
MA	20	Hub Brewing Co. (193/197 Norfolk & Shirley Sts.)	1898-1903
MA	21	Wm. P. Hunt, Standard Brewery (24 W. 1st St.)	1879-1880
MA	22	Kenney & Ballou (694 Harrison Ave.)	1878-1880
MA	23a	H. & N. Kenney (Tremont St., Roxbury)	1874-1877
	23b	Neil Kenney (1207 Tremont St.)	1877-1880
	23c	N. & H. F. Kenney	1880-1884
	23d	James W. Kenney	1884-1888
MA	24a	James W. Kenney, Amory Brewery (25 Amory St.)	1877-1880
	24b	A. Robinson & Co.	1884-1893
	24c	Robinson Brewing Co.	1893-1901
	24d	Massachusetts Breweries Co., Robinson Brewery	1901-1902
MA	25	James W. Kenney, Park Brewery (79 Terrace St., Roxbury)	1881-1918
MA	26a	George Lauzendoerfer (Lotus Pl., Jamaica Plain)	1896-1897
	26b	M. H. & G. E. Cobe, Waldberg Brewery	1897-1898
	26c	Waldberg Brewing Co.	1898-1912
MA	27a	James McCormick (95 Central St., Highlands)	1885-1886
	27b	James W. McCormick & Co.	1886-1888
	27c	McCormick Brewing Co. (95 Central St. & 89 Conant St.)	1888-1895
	27d	McCormick Brewery Co.	1895-1915
	27e	Fenway Breweries Co. (89 Conant St.)	1915-1918
MA	28	P. McGlinchy (155 Essex St.)	c1882
MA	29	Otis S. Neale (9 Howard St.)	c1880
MA	30	Parsons & Co.	1878-1879
MA	31a	H. & J. Pfaff (Pynchon & Arch St., Roxbury)	1857-1893
	31b	H. & J. Pfaff Brewing Co.	1893-1901
	31c	Massachusetts Breweries Co., H. & J. Pfaff Brewery (1276 Columbus Ave.)	1901-1918
MA	32a	Puritan Brewing Co. (40/46 Roland St., Charlestown)	1898-1906
	32b	Commercial Brewing Co.	1906-1918
	32c	Commercial Brewing Co.	1933-1940
MA	33a	John Roessle (60 Pynchon St., Roxbury)	1846-1890
	33b	New England Brewing Co., Roessle Brewery	1890-1895
	33c	New England Brewing Co., Roessle Brewery (1250 Columbus Ave.)	1895-1918
	33d	New England Brewing Co. (br. of Haffenreffer & Co.)	? -1933
	33e	Haffenreffer & Co., Inc. (1250 Columbus Ave.)	1933-1951
MA	34	Roxbury Brewing Co. (24/43 Heath & Bromley Sts.)	1898-1904
MA	35a	(Henry H.) Rueter & (John R.) Alley, Highland Spring Brewery (Heath & Parker Sts.)	1867-1885
	35b	Rueter & Co., Inc. (Heath & 165 Terrace Sts.)	1885-1918
	35c	Croft Products Co.	? -1934
	35d	The Croft Brewing Co.	1934-1952
	35e	Narragansett Brewing Co., Croft Branch	1952-1953
MA	36	Captain Sedgwick	1637- ?
MA	37a	J. M. Smith & Co. (44 King St., Roxbury)	1874-1877
	37b	Smith & Engle	1877-1895
	37c	Wm. Smith & Sons Brewing Co., No. 2, Elmwood Spring Brewery	1895-1901
	37d	Massachusetts Breweries Co., Wm. Smith & Sons, Elmwood Spring Brewery	1901-1901
MA	38a	William Smith & Co. (200 Marginal St., East Boston)	1890-1895
	38b	Wm. Smith & Sons Brewing Co., No. 1	1895-1901
	38c	Massachusetts Breweries Co., Wm. Smith & Sons, East Boston Plant	1901-1903

Boston (cont.)

MA	40a	Henry Souther & Co., Bay St. Brewery	c1850-1857
	40b	(Frank) Jones & (J. W.) Johnson & Co., Bay St. Brewery	1857-1877
	40c	Jones, Cook & Co.	1877-1899
	40d	Frank Jones Brewing Co.	1889-1904
MA	41a	Star Brewing Co. (69 Shirley St. near Norfolk Ave., Roxbury)	1896-1918
	41b	Star Brewing Co. (69 Shirley St. & 197 Norfolk Ave.)	1933-1952
MA	42a	Suffolk Brewing Co. (423/443 E. 8th & G St., South Boston)	1861-1890
	42b	New England Brewing Co., Suffolk Brewery	1890-1918
MA	43	Union Brewing Co. (Terrace St.)	1893-1911

Chelsea

MA	44a	Patrick Kiernan	1874-1875
	44b	Rutledge & Gilbert	1875-1875
MA	45	Patrick Shea	1899-1900

Chicopee

MA	46a	Chicopee Brewery	1879- ?
	46b	John Green	1882- ?
	46c	William Ritter	1890-1897
	46d	Consumers Brewing Co.	1897-1899
	46e	Springfield Breweries Co., Consumers Brewery	c1900

Clinton

MA	47	Peter J. Lynsky	1905-1913

Fall River

MA	48a	George E. Arcand	1890-1890
	48b	Finnegan & Fitzsimmons (297 S. Main St.)	1891-1897
	48c	Bristol Brewing Co.	1897-1898
MA	49a	Enterprise Brewing Co. (50 Glasgow St.)	1894-1910
	49b	Old Colony Breweries Co., Enterprise Brewery	1910-1916
MA	50a	Thos. Healey, Jr.	1878-1890
	50b	Mt. Hope Brewing Co.	1890-1891
	50c	Fall River Brewing Co. (255 Columbia St.)	1891-1904
MA	51	George D. Flynn (90 Eagle St.)	1896-1900
MA	52	Jas. H. Hurst	1878-1890
MA	53a	King Philip Brewing Co.	1898-1910
	53b	Old Colony Breweries Co., King Philip Brewery	1910-1911
MA	54	Henry Ogden	1878-1880
MA	55a	Old Colony Brewing Co. (866 Davol St.)	1896-1910
	55b	Old Colony Breweries Co., Old Colony Brewery	1910-1918
	55c	Enterprise Brewing Co. (875/939 Davol St.)	1933-1963

Gloucester

MA	56	Amber Brewing Co.	1898-1902

Haverhill

MA	57a	Linda J. Hale	1902-1902
	57b	George E. Hale	1902-1903
	57c	George E. Hale Brewing Co.	1903-1918
MA	58a	Karl E. Schlosstein	1898-1900
	58b	Geo. W. Smith	1900-1901
	58c	Essex Brewery, Lawrence & Joseph Gardella (168 Merrimac St.)	1901-1918
	58d	Essex Brewing Co., Inc. (Railroad Ave.)	1934-1937
MA	59a	O. A. Smith & Co. (32 Orchard St.)	1890-1893
	59b	O. A. Smith & Co.	1898-1903

Holyoke

MA	60	William Brierly	1874-1875

Lanesboro (Berkshire County)

MA	61	John Hart	c1800

Lawrence

MA	62a	Cold Spring Brewing Co. (609 S. Union St.)	1895-1918
	62b	Cold Spring Brewing Co.	1933-1950
	62c	Hacker Brewing Co.	1950-1952
	62d	Cold Spring Brewing Co.	1952-1952
MA	63a	Evans & Co.	1878-1879
	63b	Thomas Dixon	1879-1882
	63c	Dixon & Co.	1882-1884
	63d	Lawrence Brewing Co.	1884-1886
MA	64a	Holihan Bros., Diamond Spring Brewery (427 Common St.)	1912-1918
	64b	Diamond Spring Brewery, Inc. (50 Diamond St.) aka Blackhorse Brewery Co. (1964-1972) aka Golden Brew Brewery aka Holihan Brewery Co. (1955-1958)	1933-1970
MA	65a	Stanley & Co. (Lowell & Oxford Sts.)	1874-1890
	65b	New England Breweries Co., Stanley Brewery (br. of Boston, MA)	1890-1895

Lowell

MA	66	Alexander Burns	1874-1875
MA	67a	Consumers Brewing Co. (24 Payton St.)	1891-1898
	67b	Harvard Brewing Co.	1898-1918
	67c	Harvard Brewing Co.	1933-1956
MA	68	Hamilton Brewery Co. (Central & Jackson Sts.)	NP 1934-1934

Lynn

MA	69	Clarence B. Coates, Hop Beer Brewery	1909-1909
MA	70	The Waterhill Brewery, M . C. Healt & Co.	1907-1910

Natick

MA	71a	Carling Brewing Co. (1143 Worcester St.) aka Tuborg Breweries Ltd.	1956-1975
	71b	Carling National Breweries, Inc.	1975-1976

New Bedford

MA	72a	Dawson & Son (641/645 Purchase St.)	1899-1909
	72b	Dawson & Son (29/43 Brook St.)	1909-1918
	72c	Dawson's Brewery, Inc.	1933-1967
	72d	Jacob Ruppert, Inc., Forrest Brewing Co. (br. of Rheingold Breweries, Inc., Brooklyn, NY)	1967-1977
MA	73a	Smith Brothers (777 Purchase St.)	1905-1918
	73b	Smith Brothers, Inc. (425 Coggeshall St.)	1933-1951

Newburyport

MA	74	Wm. V. Hewlitt	1905-1910
MA	75a	William Little	1874-1877
	75b	W. H. Whitmore Jr.	1877-1878

North Adams

MA	76a	Albridge Hodskins	1874-1895
	76b	Moore & Murray	1895-1897

Pittsfield

MA	77a	M. Benson	1867-1868
	77b	(Jacob) Gimlich & (John) White (Columbus Ave. & S. John St.)	1868-1878
	77c	Gimlich, White & Co.	1878-1882
	77d	Gimlich & White (Ononta St.)	1882-1891
	77e	Berkshire Brewing Association (352 Columbus Ave.)	1891-1918
MA	78a	Rice Bros. Brewing Assn. (188/190 West St.)	1914-1915
	78b	Rice Bros. Brewing Co.	1915-1915

Salem

MA	79a	F. A. Walter & Co. (60 Union St.)	1878-1879
	79b	J. Oscar Kent	1879-1880
	79c	Edward S. Moody	1880-1882

Springfield

MA	80a	N. C. Johnson	1874-1877
	80b	Springfield Brewery	1877-1880
	80c	G. Gruendler & Co.	1880-1882

Springfield (cont.)

MA	81a	Liberty Brewing Co. (183 Liberty & Charles Sts.)	1902-1910
	81b	Springfield Breweries Co., Liberty Branch	1910-1918
MA	82a	Oscar Rocke	1869-1874
	82b	Susan Rocke	1874-1876
	82c	(Christian) Kalmbach & (Theodore) Geisel (Boston Road)	1876-1894
	82d	Highland Brewing Co.	1894-1899
	82e	Springfield Breweries Co., Highland Branch	1899-1918
MA	83a	Shaw & Co. (41 Water St.)	1860-1877
	83b	Wallace Shaw	1877-1880
	83c	G. Rothfuss	1880-1882
	83d	Max Lutz	1882-1890
	83e	Springfield Brewing Co.	1890-1899
	83f	Springfield Breweries Co., Springfield Branch	1899-1918
	83g	Commonwealth Brewing Corp. (222/226 Chestnut St.)	1933-1945
	83h	Springfield Brewing Corp.	1946-1948

Taunton

MA	84	Rudolf F. Haffenreffer Jr., Cohannet Brewing	c1900

Waltham

MA	85	H. McDonald (Felton & Fountain Sts.)	1893-1893

Watertown

MA	86	John Appleton	1641- ?

Weymouth

MA	87	William Tobin	1899-1901

Willimansett

MA	88a	William Brierly	1878-1878
	88b	(Thomas) McNirney & (John) Coyne	1878-1887
	88c	Holyoke Brewing Co.	1887-1890
	88d	Hampden Brewing Co.	1890-1899
	88e	Springfield Breweries Co., Hampden Branch (br. Springfield, MA)	1899-1918
	88f	Hampden Brewing Co. (45/95 N. Chicopee St.)	1933-1957
	88g	Hampden-Harvard Breweries, Inc.	1957-1961
	88h	Drewrys Ltd., U.S.A, Inc.	1961-1963
	88i	Piel Bros., Inc. (div. of Associated Brewing Co., Detroit, MI) aka Dawson Brewing Co. (1967-1974) aka Fitzgerald Bros. Brewing Co. (1962-1971) aka Hedrick Brewing Co. (1967-1974) aka Hampden Brewing Co. aka Hampden-Harvard Brewing Co. aka Regional Brewing Co. (1964-1968)	1963-1975

Worcester

MA	89a	Bowler Bros., Ltd. (John & Alexander) (Quinsigamond Ave. & Lafayette St.)	1883-1918
	89b	Bowler Brewing Co. (81/87 Lafayette St.)	1934-1935
	89c	Brockert Brewing Co., Inc. (81/87 Lafayette St. & 60 Ellsworth)	1935-1945
	89d	Worcester Brewing Co., Inc.	1945-1962
MA	90	Gindele & Reuther Brewing Co. (Canterbury & Hammond Sts.)	1902-1903
MA	91	N. Hines	1878-1879
MA	92	John McNamara	1878-1882
MA	93a	Geo. Warren Webster	1874-1877
	93b	Esther A. Webster	1877-1878
MA	94a	Worcester Brewing Co. (75 E. Worcester & Plum Sts.)	1896-1899
	94b	Worcester Brewing Corp.	1899-1918

Adrian			
MI	1	Thos. Eason & Son	1874-1879
MI	2a	Jacob Fisher	1874-1877
	2b	Jos. Fischer	1877-1880
	2c	Jacob Fischer	1880-1888
	2d	E. Fischer & Co.	1888-1893
	2e	Catherine Fischer	1893-1898
	2f	Adrian City Brewing Co.	1898-1902
	2g	Adrian City Brewery	1902-1904
MI	3a	William Lehmann (116 N. Main St.)	1859-1882
	3b	R. A. Kaiser	1902-1904
	3c	Springbrook Brewing Co.	1904-1910
MI	4a	Jacob Miller	1874-1877
	4b	Daniel Mulligan	1877-1878
MI	5	Gustave Sauter	c1884
Allegan			
MI	6a	George S. Ellinger	1874-1879
	6b	George S. Ellinger Jr.	1879-1880
	6c	Ellinger Bros.	1880-1884
MI	7a	T. D. Ely	1879- ?
	7b	Mrs. Phebe A. Tierney	c1882
Alpena			
MI	8a	Alpena Brewing Co.	1893- ?
	8b	Pioneer Brewing Co. (Chisholm & 14th Sts.)	? -1897
	8c	Union Brewing Co.	1897-1899
MI	9	Alpena Brewing Co.(Campbell St. at D. &. M. R. R.)	NP 1938-1939
MI	10a	Charles Brand	1884-1885
	10b	John Beck	1885-1888
	10c	John Beck & Co. (Monroe Clark)	1888-1890
	10d	John Beck	1890-1891
	10e	Beck Malting and Brewing Co. (1st Ave.)	1891-1918
MI	11	Dehring Brewing Co.	1905-1914
MI	12	Robert Kaiser	1875- ?
MI	13a	A. Lewis	1874-1877
	13b	Aug. Leins	1877-1891
	13c	Therese Leins	1891-1893
Ann Arbor			
MI	14	Ann Arbor Brewery (State & Fuller - now High St.)	c1868
MI	15	Bavaria Brewery (Fuller)	c1868
MI	16a	Peter Boehm, Western Brewery	1861- ?
	16b	Jacob F. Beck & Bro.	1874-1877
	16c	Franz Ruck	1877-1880
	16d	Martin & Fischer	1880-1902
	16e	Union Brewing Co.	1902-1902
	16f	Michigan Union Brewing Co. (416 S. 4th St.)	1904-1918
	16g	Michigan Beverage Co.	1918-1920
	---	Ice Cream Co. in plant	1920-1933
	16h	A. A. Brewing Co., Inc.	1933-1937
	16i	Ann Arbor Brewing Co.	1937-1949
MI	17	Central Brewery, John Adam Volz (524 N. 5th St. at Summit)	c1865-1875
MI	18	City Brewery, John Reyer (210 S. 1st & Liberty Sts.)	c1868-1886
MI	19	Crystal Brewing Co. (Greene St.)	NP 1934-1934
MI	20a	Northern Brewery, George Krause (Mill St. off Broadway)	1872- ?
	20b	John Frey	1874-1884
	20c	Herman Hardinghaus	1884-1891
	20d	Ann Arbor Brewing Co.	1891-1905
	20e	Ann Arbor City Brewery, Ernest Rehberg	1905-1908
MI	21	Jacob Pfeifle	1874-1875

Bangor			
MI	22	George Kolbs	1874-1875
Battle Creek			
MI	23	Battle Creek Brewing Co.	1901-1915
MI	24a	Food City Brewing Co., Inc. (200 Elm St.)	1933-1936
	24b	Food City Brewing Corp.	1936-1942
MI	25a	Silver Foam Brewing Co., Inc. (66 S. McCamly & Water Sts.)	1938-1940
	25b	Honer Brewing Co.	1946-1948
MI	26	John Stahl	1874-1875
Bay City (includes West Bay City)			
MI	27a	George Kolb Sr., Salzburg Brewery (3 Fitzhugh Ave., West Bay City)	1864-1881
	27b	Kolb & (Morris) Westover, Salzburg Brewery	1881-1887
	27c	Kolb Bros. (George & Adam), Salzburg Brewery	1887-1907
	27d	Kolb Brewing Co. (603 Germania Ave.)	1907-1919
	27e	Kolb Brewing Co.	1933-1939
MI	28a	John Rosa (8th & Water Sts., W. Bay City)	1862- ?
	28b	Thos. Rosa	1878-1879
	28c	Kohler & Jordan	1879-1879
	28d	John Kohler	1879-1880
	28e	B. Fink	1880-1882
	28f	Kohler & Knoblauch	1882-1884
	28g	West Bay City Brewing Co.	1884-1892
	28h	Jacob Knoblauch	1892-1896
	28i	West Bay City Brewing Co.	1896-1898
	28j	Phoenix Brewing Co. (408/410 Arbor Ave.)	1898-1917
	28k	Phoenix Brewing Co.	1933-1952
MI	29	Martin Schramm	1874-1884
MI	30a	A. Van Meter (Water & 22nd Sts.)	1870-1876
	30b	Charles E. Young	1876-1879
	30c	Charles E. Young & Co.	1879-1884
	30d	Bay City Brewing Co.	1884-1919
	30e	Bay City Beverage Co.	? -1933
	30f	Bay City Brewing Co., Inc. (1109 S. Water St.)	1934-1943
MI	31	Waldeman & Co.	1874-1875
Benton Harbor			
MI	32	Benton Harbor Brewing Co., Berrien Brewing Co.	NP 1934-1934
Bessemer			
MI	33a	John Held	1889- ?
	33b	John Held & Co.	? -1893
	33c	Becker & Knapstein	1898-1900
	33d	Bessemer Brewing Co.	1900-1916
Big Rapids			
MI	34a	Erickson & Hoehn	1878-1888
	34b	Fred Hoehn	1888-1893
	34c	Big Rapids Brewing Co.	1896-1899
Blackman			
MI	35	Casper Haehnle & Co.	1874-1879
Boyne Valley			
MI	36	B. W. Ellison & Co.	c1882
Cairo			
MI	37	Volz & Co.	1874-1875
Calumet			
MI	38a	Miswald Bros. & Co.	1898-1899
	38b	Calumet Brewing Co.	1899-1919
Charlotte			
MI	39a	Stallnecker, Light & Bennett	1870- ?
	39b	Crout & Staudacher	1874-1879
	39c	Jos. Crout	1879-1884
	39d	Charlotte Brewing Co.	1900-1909

Cheboygan

MI	40a	C. Hentschel & Bro.		1878-1882
	40b	August Quast		1882-1884
MI	41a	James F. Moloney (Main St.)		1882-1883
	41b	J. F. Moloney & Bro.		1883-1890
	41c	Cheboygan Brewing and Malting Co.		1890-1911

Center Line

MI	42	Walker Brewing Co. (Alex Ave. & Ten Mile Road)		1933-1940

Chelsea

MI	43	The Real Ale Co. (320 North Main St.)		1982-

Clinton

MI	44	William Miller		? -1878

Coldwater

MI	45a	Henning & Schlegel		1874-1877
	45b	Louis Patsch		1877-1879
	45c	Patzsch & Kohl		1879-1880
	45d	G. A. Hayes & Co.		1880-1884
MI	46a	George Kappler		1867-1879
	46b	Geo. Getter		1879-1884
	46c	Frederick Schultz		1884-1891
	46d	Benedict Doll (W. Chicago St.)		1891-1909

Corunna

MI	47	George Storz		1875-1878

Crawford's Quarry (see Rogers City)

Dallas

MI	48	Arens & Drostle		c1882
MI	49	Fred Simon		1874-1875

Dearborn

MI	50	Fort Dearborn Brewing Corp.	NP	1934-1934

Decatur

MI	51	Wm. Griffin		1874-1875

Delray

MI	52a	Exposition Brewing Co.		1890-1901
	52b	American Brewing Co.		1901-1906

Detroit (includes Hamtramack)

MI	53a	Henry Arndt (754/758 Gratiot Ave.)		1874-1884
	53b	Charles Zigave		1884-1890
	53c	Toelle Brewing Co.		1890-1891
	53d	Emil Honer		1891-1897
	53e	Royal Brewing Co.		1897-1897
MI	54a	Auto City Brewing Co. (8213/8221 McDougall Ave., Hamtramack)		1911-1919
	54b	Auto City Brewing Co.		1933-1942
MI	55	P. Beider (189 Gratiot Ave.)		1882-1884
MI	56	Berlin Weiss Beer Brewing Co. (86 Croghan St.)		1890-1893
MI	57a	C. & K. Wagner Brewing Co. (11627/11633 Klinger Ave., Hamt.)		1933-1935
	57b	The Wagner Brewing Co.		1935-1937
MI	58a	City Brewing Co. (425/427 Clinton St.)		? -1887
	58b	Westphalia Brewing Co.		1887-1891
	58c	Ekhardt & Becker Brewing Co. (Plant 2)		1891-1895
	58d	Jefferson Brewing Co. (426 Clinton St.)	NP	1934-1934
MI	59a	John Clemens & Bros. (34/36 Jay St.)		1882- ?
	59b	Joseph F. Clemens		? -1888
	59c	J. F. Clemens & Co.		1888-1893
	59d	East Side Brewing Co.		1893-1904

Detroit (cont.)

MI	60a	Jacob Darmstaetter (412 Howard St.)	1865-1886
	60b	Herman Darmstaetter & Bro. (Gustave)	1886-1893
	60c	West Side Brewery Co.	1893-1902
	60d	West Side Brewery Co., Ltd.	1902-1919
	60e	Mundus Brewing Co., Inc. (1736/1770 Howard St.)	1933-1935
	60f	Albert Brewing Co.	1935-1938
MI	61a	Michael Darmstaetter (227 Catherine St.)	1852-1856
	61b	Jacob & William Darmstaetter	1856-1865
	61c	William Darmstaetter	1865-1885
	---	Operated as Malthouse only	1885-1890
	61d	Columbia Brewing Co.	1890-1919
MI	62a	Davis & Newberry	1874-1877
	62b	East India Brewing Co. (630 Woodridge St.)	1877-1882
	62c	Union Brewing Co.	1882-1884
MI	63a	Dittmer & Co. (230/323 Russell & Sherman Sts.)	1878-1879
	63b	Fred Dittmer	1879-1884
	63c	Fred Dittmer Brewing Co.	1884-1888
	63d	Murzenbach Brewing Co.	1888-1890
	63e	Phoenix Brewing Co.	1890-1897
	63f	Endriss Brewing Co.	1899-1904
MI	64	Dennis Dullea	1874-1875
MI	65	Theo. Elspass (34th St. & Aubin Ave.)	1895-1895
MI	66a	Julius Endriss (350/352 Rivard St.)	1874-1877
	66b	Charles Endriss	1877-1889
	66c	Goebel Brewing Co., Ltd., Charles Endriss Brewery	1889-1894
MI	67	Exposition Brewing Co. (Springwells)	1891-1891
MI	68	Chas. Farrell & Co.	1875- ?
MI	69	D. Fastnacht	1874-1879
MI	70	Germania Brewing Co. (294/296 Sherman St.)	1888-1900
MI	71a	A. Goebel & Co. (54/56 Maple St.)	1874-1889
	71b	Goebel Brewing Co., Ltd., A. Goebel Brewery	1889-1919
	71c	The Goebel Brewing Co., Inc. (2001 Rivard & Maple Sts.)	1934-1936
	71d	Goebel Brewing Co. (acquired by Stroh Brewery Co.)	1936-1964
MI	72	Eliza Grieser	1874-1884
MI	73	Otto Hafele (274 Russell St.)	1901-1901
MI	74	Hammelef Bros. & Scharmong (640 7th St.)	1890-1890
MI	75a	George Hauck (400/408 Wilkins St.)	1873-1873
	75b	George Hauck & Co. (Christian Bauer)	1873-1882
	75c	George Hauck & Co. (Peter Kaiser)	1882-1883
	75d	Hauck Brewing Co.	1883-1892
	75e	Reuter & Kaiser	1892-1895
	75f	(Peter) Kaiser & (Franz) Schmidt, Champion Brewery	1895-1916
	75g	Champion Brewery Co.	1916-1919
	75h	The Schmidt Brewing Co. (1940/1995 Wilkins St.)	1933-1952
MI	76	Joseph Henser (Hamtramack)	1874-1875
MI	77	Independent Brewing Co. (M.C. Railway & Springwells Ave.)	1907-1919
MI	78a	Edward Johnson (6th St. & Michigan Ave.)	1874-1877
	78b	Edw. Johnson Jr.	1877-1888
MI	79a	Phil. Kling & Co. (Michael Martz & Henry Weber), Peninsular Brewery	1856-1884
	79b	Philip Kling Brewing Co. aka Peninsular Brewing Co. (1888-1890)	1884-1919
MI	80a	J. Wm. Koch (129 Sherman St.)	1895-1897
	80b	J. William Koch & Son	1897-1904

Detroit (cont.)

MI	81a	John Koch (244 Russell St.)	1874-1883
	81b	Ekhardt & Becker, Michigan Brewery	1883-1891
	81c	Ekhardt & Becker Brewing Co. (Plant 2) (475/482 Orleans St.)	1891-1919
	81d	Ekhardt & Becker Brewing Co. (Plant 1) (1530/1575 Winder St.)	1935-1944
	81e	E. & B. Brewing Co., Inc. aka Regal Brewing Co. aka Schmidt Brewing Co.	1944-1962
MI	82a	Koppitz-Melchers Brewing Co. (1115/1135 Gratiot Ave.)	1891-1919
	82b	Koppitz-Melchers, Inc. (151 Dubois St.)	1934-1947
	82c	Goebel Brewing Co. (Plant 2)	1947-1958
MI	83	Mrs. A. Kuhl	1874-1884
MI	84	Frederick Langston (242 River St.)	1895-1895
MI	85a	John D. Mackay (74/78 12th & Howard Sts.)	1874-1877
	85b	Moloney, Schneider & Co.	1877-1879
	85c	Wm. E. Moloney	1879-1891
	85d	Vienna Brewing Co.	1891-1896
	85e	Moloney Brewing Co.	1896-1898
	85f	American Brewing Co. (foot of Boyer St.)	1898-1908
	85g	American Brewing Co. (Cary & Medinah Sts.)	1908-1919
	85h	American Beverage Co., Inc. (1000 Cary St.)	? -1934
	85i	American Brewing Co. of Michigan	1934-1939
MI	86a	Christian Mann (2000 Gratiot Ave.)	1874-1880
	86b	Daniel Walz	1880-1882
	86c	Mrs. Daniel Walz	1882-1884
	86d	George Bloss	1884-1897
MI	87a	Jacob Mann (343 Rivard St. at Maple St.)	? -1889
	87b	Jacob Mann Brewery (br. of Goebel Brewing Co., Ltd.)	1889-1890
MI	88a	R. Marsh & Son (115 Chestnut St.)	1874-1877
	88b	George Seeger	1877-1880
	88c	Clemens Bros.	1880-1884
	88d	Naecker & Clemens	1884-1888
	88e	John Clemens	1888-1891
	88f	Kellar & Schultz	1891-1893
	88g	Schultz & Frey	1893-1897
	88h	Frederick W. Frey	1899-1904
MI	89a	Frank Martz & Co., Continental Brewery (Orleans & Bronson)	1868-1874
	89b	F. Martz & Bros.	1874-1875
	89c	Martz Bros. (Frank, John & Michael)	1875-1886
	89d	Detroit Brewing Co. (Orleans & Adelaide Sts.)	1886-1919
	89e	Detroit Brewing Co. (2529/2536 Orleans St.)	1933-1949
MI	90	George Marx	1874-1875
MI	91a	Thomas McGrath (511 7th St.)	1874-1880
	91b	Thomas McGrath (490/500 Grand River Ave.)	1880-1893
	91c	St. Louis Brewing Co., Ltd.	1893-1899
MI	92a	A. Michenfelder (61/71 Sherman St.)	1874-1882
	92b	A. Michenfelder & Co.	1882-1884
	92c	Bavarian Brewing Co.	1884-1889
	92d	Bavarian Brewery (br. of Goebel Brewing Co., Ltd.)	1889-1890
MI	93	Michigan Brewery (1262/1296 Military Ave.)	1913-1919
MI	94	Henry Miller	1874-1879
MI	95a	Phil. Nagel (249/251 Mullett St.)	1888-1891
	95b	Phil. Nagel Estate	1891-1893
	95c	Ph. Nagel Brewing Co.	1893-1899
MI	96a	Fred Nothnagel	1874-1877
	96b	J. A. Kurtz	1877-1884
MI	97	Oakman Brewing Co.	NP 1934-1934

Detroit (cont.)

MI	98a	Adam Ochsenhirt (142/148 Sherman St.)		1874-1877
	98b	French Ochsenhirt		1877-1879
	98c	A. Ochsenhirt		1879-1882
	98d	Ochsenhirt & Co.		1882-1890
	98e	Home Brewing Co.		1890-1897
MI	99	Old Holland Brewing Co. (563/565 E. Larned St.)		1935-1939
MI	100a	Conrad Pfeiffer (908/940 Beaufait Ave.)		1890-1902
	100b	Pfeiffer Brewing Co.		1902-1919
	100c	Pfeiffer Brewing Co. (3700 Beaufait Ave.)		1934-1962
	100d	Associated Brewing Co.		1962-1966
		aka Drewry's Brewing Co.		
		aka Frankenmuth Brewing Co. (1963-1966)		
		aka Old Dutch Brewing Co. (1963-1966)		
		aka Pfeiffer Brewing Co.		
MI	101a	Pros't Brewing Co., Inc. (9920/9937 Knodell Ave.)		1933-1936
	101b	Voight-Prost Brewing Co.		1936-1938
MI	102a	Regal Brewing Co. (3220 Bellevue Ave.)		1935-1937
	102b	Ekhardt & Becker Brewing Co. (Plant 2)		1937-1938
MI	103a	Augustine Ruoff (333/335 Gratiot Ave.)		1874-1884
	103b	A. Ruoff Brewing Co.		1884-1904
MI	104	John Scheu (515 Hastings St.)		1875-1911
MI	105a	John Steiner (327 Marion & Orleans Sts.)		1875-1884
	105b	Fulda & Bommer		1884-1891
MI	106	Peter Stonder		1875- ?
MI	107	Straits Brewing Co. (171 S. Campbell St.)	NP	1934-1934
MI	108a	Julian Strelinger (134 Jay St. & Bates St.)		1880-1891
	108b	Julian Strelinger (247/251 Elliott St.		1891-1893
	108b	Mutual Brewing Co. (625 Hastings St.)		1893-1915
MI	109a	Bernhard Stroh (315/331 Gratiot St.)		1850-1854
	109b	Lion Brewing Co.		1854-1882
	109c	B. Stroh Brewing Co. (253/275 E. Elizabeth St.)		1882-1902
	109d	The Stroh Brewery Co.		1902-1919
	109e	The Stroh Products Co.		? -1933
	109f	The Stroh Brewery Co. (909 E. Elizabeth St.)		1933-1978
		aka Goebel Brewing Co. (1964-1978)		
	109g	The Stroh Brewery Co. (One Stroh Drive)		1978-
		aka Goebel Brewing Co. (1978-)		
MI	110a	Tivoli Brewing Co. (1549/1575 Mack Ave.)		1897-1919
	110b	Tivoli Brewing Co. (10113/10227 Mack Ave.)		1933-1948
	110c	Altes Brewing Co.		1948-1954
	110d	The National Brewing Co. of Michigan		1954-1967
	110e	The National Brewing Co. (3765 Hurlbut Ave.)		1967-1973
		aka Van Lauter Brewing Co.		
MI	111	Union Brewing Co. (631 Fort St., West)		1888-1890
MI	112a	Union Brewing Co. (Mitchell & Gratiot Aves.)		1898-1919
	112b	Cadillac Brewing Co., Inc.		1934-1936
	112c	Union Brewing Co., Inc.		1936-1937
MI	113	Voigt-Pros't Brewing Co. (1 E. 10 Mile at G. T. R. R.) (P.2)	NP	1937-1937
MI	114a	William Voigt, Milwaukee Brewery (203/213 Grand River Ave.)		1866-1871
	114b	E. W. Voigt, Milwaukee Brewery		1871-1888
	114c	Voigt Brewery Co., Ltd.		1888-1919
	114d	E. W. Voigt Brewing Co.	NP	1934-1934
MI	115a	Von Brewing Co., Inc. (1800 E. Forest Ave.)		1933-1935
	115b	Kraft Brewing Co.		1935-1937
MI	116a	Wayne Products & Brewing Co. (3601/3603 Hancock Ave.)		1933-1936
	116b	The Wayne Brewing Co.		1936-1937
MI	117	Anthony Wegener (393 Rioppelle St.)		1888-1897

Detroit (cont.)

MI 118 Williams & Co. (232 Woodbridge St.) 1878-1882

MI 119 Thomas Zoltowski (733 Hastings St.) 1891-1919

MI 120a John Zynda, White Eagle Brewery (25 Macomb & Brush Sts.) 1886-1891
120b John Zynda & Bros., White Eagle Brewery (Canfield & Rioppelle) 1891-1919
120c Zynda Brewing Co. (4232/4268 Rioppelle St.) 1933-1948

Douglas

MI 121 Close & Moulton 1874-1875

Dowagiac

MI 122 Vinzenz Herder 1878-1891

Eagle River

MI 123a Frank Knivel 1855-1878
123b F. Knivel & Bro. 1878-c1880
123c F. Knivel & Sons c1880-1888

East Saginaw (see Saginaw)

Ecorse

MI 124 W. S. Bache Co., Inc., aka Imperial Brewing Co. (240 Salliotte) 1935-1936

Elk Rapids

MI 125a Grammel & Thomson 1875- ?
125b Chas. Grammel 1880-1888
125c Jos. Scurz 1888-1890
125d John Berg 1890-1891
125e Gottlieb Grammel 1891-1895

Elmwood

MI 126a Frank Allgeir 1875- ?
126b C. Simmersbach 1882-1884

Escanaba

MI 127 Richter Brewing Co. 1901-1919

MI 128a Shepley & Nolden 1874-1877
128b Joseph Nolden 1877-1884
128c (Henry) Rahr & Walch Brothers (Nicholas & Peter) 1884-1887
128d Escanaba Brewing Co. 1887-1919
128e Delta Brewing Co. (1601 Ludington St.) 1933-1940

Fenton

MI 129 Nicholas Thiel 1874-1875

MI 130a T. Whittle 1874-1879
130b C. Hux 1879-1884

Flint

MI 131 E. Burrough 1874-1875

MI 132 William Golden 1874-1897

MI 133a Putnam & Henry 1901-1902
133b Putnam & Henry Brewing Co. 1902-1904
133c Putnam & Henry 1904-1906
133d Mortimer H. Putnam 1906-1907

MI 134a Dailey Brewing Co. (1521 St. John St.) 1934-1934
134b Ph. Kling Brewing Co. 1935-1947
134c Pfeiffer Brewing Co. (br. of Detroit, MI) 1947-1958

MI 135 Gorney Brewing Co. (920 Walnut St.) 1934-1936

MI 136a Wildanger & Hux 1874-1877
136b William Lewis 1877-1893
136c Flint Brewing Co. (15th & S. Saginaw Sts.) 1894-1912
136d Flint Hill Brewing Co., Inc. (2001 E. Saginaw St.) 1934-1938
136e King's Tavern Brewing Co. 1938-1939
136f White Seal Brewing Co. 1939-1947
136g Frankenmuth Brewing Co. (br. of Frankenmuth, MI) 1947-1948
136h Valley Brewing Co. 1949-1952
136i Brewery Enterprises, Inc. 1952-1952

Forestville			
MI	137a	C. Leonhardt	1879-1884
	137b	H. Leonhardt & Bro.	1891-1893
Frankenmuth			
MI	138a	Frankenmuth Brewing Co.	1900-1919
	138b	Frankenmuth Brewing Co. (907/926 S. Main St.)	1933-1954
	138c	International Breweries, Inc.	1954-1956
	138d	Carling Brewing Co.	1956-1975
	138e	Carling National Breweries, Inc.	1975-1979
	138f	G. Heileman Brewing Co.	1979-
MI	139a	Heubisch & Knaust, Cass River Brewery (Main St.)	1862-1874
	139b	John G. Geyer	1874-1908
	139c	Geyer Bros., Cass River Brewery	1908-1915
	139d	Geyer Brothers (415/425 S. Main St.)	1933-1949
	139e	Geyer Bros. Brewing Co.	1949-
MI	140a	John Falliers	1857-1864
	140b	Peter Schluckebier	1864-1877
	140c	John Rupprecht	1877-1880
	140d	A. V. Schneider, aka Stahl Brewery	1880-1884
Franklin			
MI	141a	George Rublein	1879-1882
	141b	Mrs. Emma Hofstaetter	1882-1882
Gagetown			
MI	142a	John G. Fehrenbach	1884-1888
	142b	Joseph Weller	1888-1890
	142c	Kastner & Cowmans	1890-1893
	142d	Christopher Kastner	1893-1910
Golden			
MI	143	Wm. Golden Brewing Co.	1897-1899
Grand Haven			
MI	144	Ahrens & Pagels	1874-1875
Grand Rapids			
MI	145a	Adrian & Kantenberger	1874-1877
	145b	Adrian Bros.	1877-1882
	145c	John Adrian	1882-1884
	145d	John Gessler & Co.	1884-1888
MI	146a	George Brandt (87 S. Division St.)	1862-1880
	146b	Brandt & Co.	1880-1884
	146c	George Brandt & Co.	1884-1893
MI	147	Wm. H. Cooper	1895-1897
MI	148a	C. Frey & Bros. (72 Coldbrook St.)	1872-1877
	148b	Frey Bros.	1877-1893
MI	149	Furniture City Brewing Co. (S. Ionia St. & Wealthy Ave.)	1905-1919
MI	150a	A. Goetz (465 Broadway)	1886-1887
	150b	National Brewing Co.	1887-1893
MI	151	Great Lakes Brewing Co. of Michigan (400 Federal Sq. Bldg.) NP	1934-1934
MI	152a	J. C. Kusterer (60 E. Bridge St. & Ionia St.)	1845-1877
	152b	C. Kusterer	1877-1880
	152c	Kusterer Brewing Co.	1880-1893
	152d	Grand Rapids Brewing Co.	1893-1919
	152e	Grand Rapids Brewing Co. NP	1934-1934
MI	153a	Imperial Brewing Co., Inc. (260/270 Leonard St.)	1933-1934
	153b	Old Kent Products Co.	1934-1935
	153c	Valley City Brewing Co., Inc.	1935-1940
MI	154a	The Michigan Brewing Co. (26 Michigan, Ottawa & Ionia Sts.)	1937-1940
	154b	Fox De Luxe Brewing Co.	1941-1951
MI	155a	Smith & Draper	? -1874
	155b	Stiven & Hill	1875-1877
	155c	John Goldsmith	1877-1878

Grand Rapids (cont.)

MI	156	Tusch Bros. (3rd St. & 208 Grandville Ave.)	1878-1893
MI	157a	J. Veit & Co. (Stocking & 1st Sts.)	1876-1879
	157b	Veit & Rathmann	1879-1893
MI	158a	Peter Weirich, Eagle Brewery (296 W. Bridge St.)	1860-1884
	158b	Peter Weirich Brewing Co.	1884-1893
	158c	J. J. Petersen, Eagle Brewery	1893-1895
	158d	Petersen & Willebrand, Eagle Brewery	1895-1898
	158e	Petersen & Damskey, Eagle Brewery	1898-1899
	158f	Julius R. Petersen, Eagle Brewery	1899-1900
	158g	Petersen Brewing Co., Eagle Brewery	1900-1916

Greenville

MI	159	F. Kaupp	1874-1875

Hancock

MI	160a	Park Brewing Co. (Atlantic & Emma Sts.)	1907-1919
	160b	Park Brewing Co.	1934-1940
	160c	A. Haas Brewing Co.	1941-1952
	160d	Copper Country Brewing Co.	1952-1954
MI	161a	Wm. Ault, Union Brewery	1857-1863
	161b	Philip Scheuermann, Frank Mayworth & Adam Youngman, Union Brewery	1863-1875
	161c	Ph. Scheuermann, Union Brewery	1875-1894
	161d	Philip Scheuermann Brewing Co.	1894-1899
	161e	Scheuermann Brewery (br. of Bosch Brewing Co., Lake Linden, MI)	1899-1918
	161f	Bosch Brewing Co. (W. Memorial Road, Houghton)	1934-1973

Highland

MI	162	Jacob Bentler	1874-1884

Hillsdale

MI	163a	Frank Kreiter	1874-1877
	163b	John Haas	1877-1884
	163c	Haas & Co.	1884-1891
	163d	John Haas	1891-1893

Holland

MI	164a	Xavier F. Sutton	1875-1877
	164b	E. F. Sutton	1877-1879
	164c	Anton Seif (153 W. 10th St. & Maple Ave.)	1879-1895
	164d	Geo. Schoenith	1895-1898
	164e	Anton Seif	1898-1899
	164f	Holland City Brewing Co.	1899-1902
	164g	Anton Seif	1902-1904
	164h	Holland City Brewery, Anton Seif & Sons	1904-1911
	164i	Holland City Brewery, Anton Seif Jr.	1911-1916
	164j	Holland Brewery	NP 1934-1934

Houghton (also see Hancock)

MI	165a	Adam Haas (Sheldon & Dodge Sts.)	1859-1877
	165b	Estate of Adam Haas	1877-1879
	165c	Adam Haas Brewing Co.	1879-1919
	165d	A. Haas Brewing Co. (106 Sheldon St.)	1933-1942
	---	Bosch Brewing Co. (see Hancock)	
MI	166a	F. Hahn & Bro.	1874-1875
	166b	Hahn Co., aka Franz Hahn	1875-1882
MI	167	Henry Hofen	1878-1884
MI	168	Park Brewery	NP 1934-1934

Inverness Township

MI	169	C. Hentschell & Bro.	1874-1877
	169b	Charles Hentschell	1877-1882

Ionia

MI	170a	Geo. Summ & Co.	1874-1877
	170b	B. Summ & Co.	1877-1882
	170c	Philip Endres	1882-1891
	170d	Andreas Haberstumpf	1891-1897
	170e	Ionia Brewing and Bottling Co.	1897-1898
	170f	Ionia Brewing Co. (416 N. Dexter St.)	1898-1904
	170g	Grand Valley Brewing Co.	1907-1909
	170h	Grand Valley Brewing Co. (414/420 N. Dexter St.)	1934-1945

Iron Mountain

MI	171a	Iron Mountain Brewing Co.	1891- ?
	171b	Upper Peninsula Brewing Co.	? -1895
	171c	Upper Michigan Brewing Co. (Norway & Grant Sts.)	1895-1899
	171d	Henze-Tollen Brewing Co.	1899-1919

Ironwood

MI	172a	Superior Brewery, Caspar Haehnle	1901-1902
	172b	Ironwood Brewing Co.	1902-1919

Jackson

MI	173a	Elizabeth Frey (Bridge & Water Sts.)	1874-1877
	173b	Gottlieb Frey	1877-1884
	173c	Carl Eberle	1884-1891
	173d	Jackson Brewing and Malting Co.	1891-1897
	173e	Eberle Brewing Co.	1897-1919
	173f	The Eberle Brewing Co., Inc. (901/905 S. Water St.)	1933-1941
MI	174a	Casper Haehnle (1917 Cooper St.)	1864- ?
	174b	Casper Haehnle & Co.	1880-1893
	174c	Haehnle Brewing Co.	1893-1919
	174d	Hill Top Brewing Co., Inc. (1829 Cooper St.)	1933-1933
	174e	Haehnle Brewing Co., Inc.	1933-1937
MI	175a	Thomas Mills	1874-1877
	175b	James H. Mills	1877-1878
MI	176a	Redmond & Free	1874-1877
	176b	John Redmond	1877-1879

Kalamazoo

MI	177	Dorothy Burchnall	1873-1875
MI	178	Hall & Rupello	c1850
MI	179	Jacob Harland	c1850
MI	180a	Peter Heirboldscheimer	c1860-1861
	180b	Bernard Loescher	c1866-1879
	180c	Sarah Loescher	1879-1884
MI	181	James Holmes (Burdick)	c1860-1861
MI	182	Kalamazoo Spring Brewery, George L. Sykes & George Foegele (Asylum Ave. & Oakland Dr.)	c1860-1861
MI	183a	Kalamazoo Steam Brewery, Chas. M. Minard (45 Michigan and Asylum Aves.)	1860-1869
	183b	Kalamazoo Steam Brewery, Nicholas Bauman & Co.	1869-1873
	183c	Kalamazoo Steam Brewery, George Neumaier & Co.	1873-1878
	183d	Kalamazoo Steam Brewery, Leo Kinast	1878-1884
MI	184a	George Neumaier, Cold Stream Brewery (6 Lake)	1881-1883
	184b	George Neumaier, Cold Stream Brewery (818-822 Lake - streets renumbered)	1883-1893
	184c	Alfred G. Neumaier & Leo Wagemann	1893-1896
	184d	Alfred G. Neumaier, City Union Brewery	1896-1904
	184e	Alfred G. Neumaier, Kalamazoo Brewing Co.	1904-1915
MI	185	Henry F. Schoenheit (122 N. Church St.)	1896-1897
MI	186	Henry Schroeder, Frank's Brewery (556 E. Main St. at 77 Kalamazoo Ave.)	1860-1884
MI	187	Gustavus Sepaman	c1860

Kalamazoo (cont.)

MI 188 Frederick W. Seyfferth, Portage Brewery (3/6 Winstead, Portage, and Lovell Roads) 1871-1873

MI 189 Leo Wagemann, Kalamazoo Union Brewery (963 E. Vine St.) 1896-1901

MI 190 Robert Walker (Plank Road) 1878-1878

Lake Linden

MI 191a Joseph Bosch, Torch Lake Brewery 1874-1876
191b Joseph Bosch & Co., Torch Lake Brewery (Centre St.) 1876-1894
191c Bosch Brewing Co. 1894-1918
191d Bosch Brewing Co. (Licensed but did not operate)(see Hancock) 1933-1934

L'Anse

MI 192a Bavarian Brewery, Emil Meisler & Henry Steinback 1873- ?
192b L'Anse Brewing Co., Henry Steinback, John Q. McKernan & T. W. Edwards ? -1878
192c Farley & Meisler 1884- ?
192d Emil Meisler 1890-1893
192e M. Miswald & Bros. 1893-1896

Lansing

MI 193a City Brewery 1874-1877
193b Adam Foerster 1877-1897
193c Lansing Brewing Co. (Turner & Clinton Sts.) 1897-1913
193d Lansing Brewing Co. (1301 Turner St.) 1934-1937

MI 194 Galler & Co. 1875- ?

MI 195a Mary Renz 1878-1878
195b George Schlotter 1878-1879
195c Schlotter & Krieger 1879-1882

MI 196 F. Yeiter & Co. 1874-1880

Lapeer

MI 197a Wm. A. Jackson 1874-1877
197b John A. Buerger 1877-1891
197c Anna M. Buerger 1891-1900
197d John A. Buerger 1900-1901
197e Lapeer City Brewing Co. 1901-1907
197f Lapeer City Brewery Co. 1907-1910

Lexington

MI 198a F. L. Walter 1874-1884
198b Purkiss Bros. 1884-1888

Ludington

MI 199a Albert Vogel 1874-1877
199b Friedman & Stoekle 1877-1879

Manchester

MI 200a Christian Renz 1874-1877
200b Jos. Seckinger 1877-1879
200c Franz Kuck 1879-1884
200d John Koch 1884-1891
200e Charles Adrian & Co. (Monroe St.) 1891-1898
200f Charles Adrian 1898-1906
200g Manchester Brewing Co. 1906-1919

Manistee

MI 201a (Charles) Daniels & (Joseph) Gambs (Jones & 14 Mason Sts.) 1884-1890
201b Manistee Brewing Co., Chas. H. Daniels 1890-1905
201c Manistee Brewing Co., Estate of Chas. H. Daniels 1905-1911
201d Chas. H. Daniels Brewery 1911-1919
201e Manistee Brewing Co. (14/16 Mason St.) 1933-1936
201f Chippewa Brewing Co. 1937-1942

Manistique

MI 202 Willebrand Manistique Brewing Co. aka The Manistique Brewery (1909) 1903-1909

Marine City

MI 203 John Bauman 1878-1882

Marine City (cont.)

MI	204a	Henry Heuser, Jr.	1888-1891
	204b	Henry Heuser Brewing Co.	1896-1899
	204c	Marine City Brewing Co.	1899-1904
	204d	Sicken, Owen & Haug	1904-1911
	204e	Marine City Brewing Co.	1911-1916
MI	205	James Marshall	1874-1882

Marion

MI	206a	Robert A. Miller	1882-1883
	206b	Miller & Co.	1883-1884

Marquette

MI	207	Mrs. Emma Hoffstaedter	1882-1884
MI	208	August Marks	1874-1875
MI	209a	George Rublein	1874-1879
	209b	Meeske & Hoch	1879-1890
	209c	Upper Peninsula Brewing Co. (W. Washington St.)	1890-1919

Marshall

MI	210	Thomas Bolzing	1874-1875
MI	211	Effinger Bros.	1875-1882
MI	212a	Hornberger & Lindner	1880-1881
	212b	Chas. Burgy	1881-1884
MI	213a	Andrew Mayer	1874-1877
	213b	Central Brewery	1877-1879
MI	214a	Nonnemann & Lutz	1878-1882
	214b	Phil. Lutz	1882-1884
	214c	Jos. Gramer Jr.	1884-1888
	214d	Jos. Gramer	1888-1897
	214e	Jos. Gramer Brewing Co.	1897-1912

Menominee

MI	215a	De Heck & Scharmbruch	1870- ?
	215b	George Harter	? -1876
	215c	Leisen & Henes	1876-1891
	215d	Leisin & Henes Brewing Co. (1200 Main St.)	1891-1919
	215e	United Beverage Co.	? -1933
	215f	Menominee-Marinette Brewing Co. (1200 Sheridan Road)	1933-1950
	215g	Menominee-Marinette Brewing Co. (1400 1st St.)	1950-1961
MI	216a	Eichert & Skala	1886-1887
	216b	Skala & (W.) Reindl	1887-1888
	216c	Menominee River Brewing Co. (1612/1614 Ogden Ave.)	1888-1919
MI	217a	Louis Hartung	1870-1872
	217b	Gauch & Berthold	1872-1874
	217c	Adam Gauch	1874-1876
	217d	Leisen & Henes (br. of MI 215c)	1876-1876

Midland

MI	218	Midland Brewing Co., Inc. (144 S. McDonald St.)	1934-1935

Monroe

MI	219a	J. Roeder & Bro.	1874-1877
	219b	Jacob Roeder	1877-1909
MI	220a	John Wahl, aka Wahl's Brewery	1861-1877
	220b	John Wahl Jr.	1877-1897
	220c	Wahl Brewing Co.	1897-1906

Mount Clemens

MI	221a	August Biewer (Court St.)	1874-1912
	221b	August Biewer Jr.	1912-1919
MI	222	William Miller	1874-1884
MI	223a	Mount Clemens Brewing Co. (37 S. Front St.)	1890-1919
	223b	Mt. Clemens Brewing Co. (35/37 S. Broadway)	1933-1937

Muskegon
MI 224a Frederick Neumeister 1867-1874
224b L. A. Johnson 1874-1876
224c Meeske Bros. (Otto & Gustav) 1876-1877
224d Muskegon Brewing Co. (604 Michigan Ave. & Lake St.) 1877-1919
224e Muskegon Brewing Co., Inc. (1159 Michigan Ave.) 1933-1934
224f Grand Rapids Brewing Co. 1934-1946
224g Goebel Brewing Co. (br. of Detroit, MI) 1946-1957

Negaunee
MI 225a F. A. Liebenstein 1878-1879
225b J. J. Kohl & Co. 1879-1880
225c Meeske & Hoch 1880-1890
225d Upper Peninsula Brewing Co. (426 S. Gold St.) 1890-1896

MI 226 George C. Shelden 1874-1875

MI 227a Ferdinand Winter 1878-1890
227b Ferdinand Winter & Son 1890-1897

New Baltimore
MI 228a Henry Heuser 1874-1884
228b Joseph Heuser 1884-1897

Niles
MI 229a John Johnston 1874-1877
229b Aug. Dosch 1877-1880
229c Chas. Hafner 1880-1884
229d Niles City Brewing Co. 1884-1888

MI 230 Four Flags Brewing Co., Inc. 1934-1934

MI 231 J. Pukownik & Son 1874-1875

Ontonagon
MI 232 Miswald Bros. 1895-1897

Owosso
MI 233a John Gute 1874-1877
233b Gute Bros. 1877-1879
233c A. Gute 1879-1880
233d Gute Bros. 1880-1884

MI 234 Owosso Brewing Co. 1895-1898

MI 235a Waterhouse & Burgy ? -1896
235b Mueller Bros. (Louis & Charles) (Main & Water Sts.) 1896-1910
aka Mueller Bros. Brewing Co. (1908)

Oxford
MI 236 William Findon 1878-1880

Pentwater
MI 237 Christ. Fricke 1878-1893

Petoskey
MI 238 Petoskey Brewing Co. 1902-1915

MI 239 Northern Brewing Co. NP 1934-1934

Pontiac
MI 240 Robert Dawson 1874-1884

MI 241a Pontiac Brewing Co. (Patterson St.) 1900-1905
241b Pontiac Brewery 1905-1915
241c Wolverine Brewing Co. (555 Going St.) 1933-1943

Port Huron
MI 242a Charles Samberg (Bard & 601 Michigan Sts.) 1874-1884
242b Charles Samberg Brewing Co. 1884-1897
242c Port Huron Brewing Co. 1901-1919
242d Lakeside Brewing Co. (411 Bard St.) 1936-1937

MI 243a J. Stein 1856- ?
243b J. B. & J. Bellenstein 1874-1875
243c Jacob Densler 1875-1877
243d Chris. Kern 1877-1884
243e C. Kern Brewing Co. (511 River St.) 1884-1891

Port Huron (cont.)

MI	243f	C. Kern Brewing Co.	1933-1946
	243g	The Friars Ale Brewing Co.	1946-1950

Quarry (see Rogers City)

Reed City

MI	244	Reed City Brewing Co.	1888-1888

Rockland

MI	245	Biggi & Kelley	1874-1875

Rogers City

MI	246a	V. Dronsutowicy	1875- ?
	246b	Paul Bittner	? -1880
	246c	Paul Bittner (Crawford's Quarry)	1880-1897
	246d	Paul Bittner (Quarry)	1897-1902
	246e	Paul Bittner (Rogers City)	1902-1906
	246f	Henry Veitel	1906-1909
	246g	Frederick Fisch	1909-1914
	246h	Fred Fisch Brewery (3rd St.)	1914-1919
	246i	Presque Isle Brewing Co.	NP 1934-1934

Saginaw

MI	247a	Banner Brewing Co. (1741 Genesee Ave.)	1902-1919
	247b	Michigan Bud Products Co.	? -1934
	247c	Banner Brewing Co. (1743/1765 E. Genesee St.)	1934-1938
MI	248a	Louis Darmstaetter (1610 S. Washington Ave.)	1874-1880
	248b	Saginaw Brewing Co.	1880-1919
MI	249	John G. Geyer	1874-1875
MI	250	Chas. Hilbig (357 S. 12th St.)	1893-1893
MI	251	Hubinger, Weber & Co.	1893-1893
MI	252	Cris Leonhard	1874-1875
MI	253a	William Mawbray (400/410 Lapeer Ave.)	1874-1883
	253b	Jacob Raquet	1883-1911
	253c	Star Brewing Co.	1911-1913
MI	254a	P. & J. Raquet (Peter & Jacob)	1870-1883
	254b	Peter Raquet, National Brewery	1883-1890
	254c	National Brewing Co. (Genesee Ave. & Walnut St.)	1890-1919
	254d	National Brewing Co. (205 Walnut St.)	1933-1937
	254e	National Brewing Co. (1105 Walnut St.)	1937-1941
MI	255a	John Rosa (729 N. Fayette St.)	1874-1877
	255b	John L. Rosa	1877-1880
	255c	John T. Rosa	1880-1905
	255d	Frederick A. Wiegand	1905-1909
MI	256	Saginaw Premier Brewing Co. (Center & River Sts.)	NP 1934-1934
MI	257a	Schemm & Gruhler (926 N. Hamilton St.)	1866- ?
	257b	Schemm & Schoenheit	1874-1881
	257c	John G. Schemm	1881-1899
	257d	J. G. Schemm Brewing Co., Inc.	1899-1919
	257e	Schemm Brewing Co., Inc.	1934-1938
MI	258	Fred Ziegner	1874-1884

Saint Clair

MI	259	Conrad Ellspas	1882-1895
MI	260a	John Schlinkert	1874-1897
	260b	John Biewer	1897-1904
	260c	John Decker	1907-1909
MI	261a	Jos. Schwabn aka John Schroeder (1878-1879)	1874-1902
	261b	Mary Schwabn	1902-1906

Saint John's

MI	262	Eugene Byra	1874-1875

Saline

MI	263	Lindenschmitt & Co.	1874-1875

Salsburgh

MI 264	Thomas Rosa		1874-1875

Saugatuck

MI 265	Samuel Clipson		1874-1879

Sault Ste. Marie

MI 266a	Arnold Brewing Co. (944/946 Portage Ave.)		1902-1907
266b	Soo Brewing Co.		1907-1919
266c	Soo Beverage Co.		? -1934
266d	Soo Brewing Co. (941/951 E. Portage St.)		1937-1943
MI 267	Rheinbrau Brewing Co.	NP	1934-1934
MI 268a	Spitzig & Vogt		1882-1883
268b	Anton Vogt		1883-1884
268c	A. Vogt & Co.		1884-1888

Sebewaing

MI 269a	Sophia Brandle		1875-1879
269b	Veit & Graf		1879-1880
269c	Henry Graf		1880-1884
269d	Frederick Braendle		1884-1891
269e	Eberlein & Son		1891-1893
269f	Sebewaing Brewing Co.		1893-1896
269g	Braendle & Eberlein		1896-1899
269h	Braendle & Kroll		1899-1903
269i	Frederick Kroll		1903-1905
269j	Huron County Brewing Co.		1905-1919
269k	Sebewaing Brewing Co. (221 E. Main St.)		1934-1964
269l	The Michigan Brewery, Inc.		1964-1966

South Frankfort

MI 270	Hessell & Goenwein		1875- ?

Spring Lake

MI 271	Louis Erhardt		1874-1875

Stevensville

MI 272a	Klier & Schmuhl (Lake Shore Drive)		1900-1904
272b	Anton Klier		1904-1908
272c	Home Brewing Co.		1908-1910

Sturgis

MI 273a	Augustus Esslinger		1875-1877
273b	John Schlegel		1877-1879
273c	Wagner & Schlegel		1879-1884
273d	John Wagner		1884-1893

Three Rivers

MI 274a	Esslinger & Sulliman		1878-1879
274b	Aug. Trockenbrod		1879-1884

Traverse City

MI 275a	Joseph Gambs (710/719 Front St.)		1901-1903
275b	Traverse City Brewing Co.		1903-1919
MI 276	Frank W. Kratockvill		1874-1904
MI 277	John Smith		1878-1879

Utica

MI 278	Nicholas Priemer		1874-1875

Weare

MI 279	Chris. Fricke		1874-1875

West Branch

MI 280a	Brick & Thrasher		1888-1889
280b	Jos. Brick & Co.		1889-1890
280c	Anthony M. Schick & Co.		1890-1893
280d	Anthony M. Schick		1893-1897
280e	Anthony M. Schick & Co.		1897-1901
280f	Anthony M. Schick (E. Houghton Ave.)		1901-1904
280g	Estate of A. M. Schick		1904-1905
280h	Jacob Eck		1905-1910

Westfield

MI	281	H. Kording	1878-1879

Westphalia

MI	282a	Arens & Drostle	1878-1879
	282b	Drostle & Kleiner	1884- ?
	282c	Joseph Drostle	? -1890
	282d	Anthony Drostle	1890-1893
	282e	Fritz & Cook	1893-1895
	282f	Fritz & Koch Brewing Co.	1895-1897
	282g	Peter A. Fritz	1897-1907

Whitefield

MI	283	George Rublein	1878-1879

Wyandotte

MI	284a	Eureka Brewing and Ice Co. (Front & Poplar Sts.)	1891-1892
	284b	Rioppelle & Mehlhose	1892-1893
	284c	Eureka Brewing and Ice Co.	1893-1909
MI	285a	George Marx (Front & Oak Sts.)	1878-1884
	285b	Marx Bros. Brewing Co.	1884-1891
	285c	Marx Bros.	1891-1897
	285d	Wyandotte Brewing Co.	1897-1904
	285e	Frank Marx Brewing Co.	1940-1909
	285f	Marx Brewing Co.	1909-1919
	285g	Marx Brewing Co., Inc. (2907 Van Alstyne Blvd.)	1933-1936
	285h	Wyandotte Brewing Co., Inc.	1936-1937

Ypsilanti

MI	286	Jacob Grob	1874-1915
MI	287a	H. Lee	1866- ?
	287b	H. Lee & Co.	? -1870
	287c	Adam Foerster & Bros.	1870-1875
	287d	L. Z. Foerster & Co.	1875-1884
	287e	Louis Z. Foerster (414 Grove St.)	1884-1893
	287f	L. Z. Foerster Brewing Co.	1893-1914
	287g	Hoch Brewing Co.	1914-1916
	287h	Liberty Brewing Co.	1933-1934
	287i	Ypsilanti Brewing Co.	1934-1935
	287j	Christ Vogt, dba Ypsilanti Brewing Co.	1935-1941
	287k	Dawes Brewing Co.	1941-1943

MINNESOTA

Albert Lea

MN	1a	R. Weile & Co.	1874-1879
	1b	R. Weile	1879-1882
	1c	John Thoreson	1882-1884

Alexandria

MN	2a	Aberle Bros. (Fred & Christian)	1880-1884
	2b	C. Aberle	1884-1895
	2c	Walter R. Towgood	1895-1902
	2d	Kathleen A. Towgood	1902-1904
	2e	Alexandria Brewing Co. (3rd Ave. & 8th St.)	1904-1915
MN	3	Carl Volk	1869-1890
MN	4a	Wegener & Gutheil	1876-1877
	4b	Rudolph Wegener, Alexandria Brewery	1877-1900
	4c	Estate of Rudolph Wegener, Alexandria Brewery	1900-1901
	4d	Rudolph Wegener Brewing Co.	1901-1920
	4e	Alexandria Brewing Co. (201 3rd Ave. W.)	1935-1942

Appleton

MN	5a	Strausch & Ginsberg	1888-1890
	5b	Edward Ginsberg	1890-1893
	5c	Solomon Ginsberg	1893-1901
	5d	Chas. A. Pulkrabek aka Appleton Brewing Co. (1915)	1904-1920

Arlington

MN	6	C. Klinkers	? -1878

City	No.	Brewer	Years
Austin			
MN	7a	C. H. Huxbold	1874-1877
	7b	Jacob Weisel	1877-1880
Beaver Falls			
MN	8	Andreas Betz	1874-1888
Belle Plaine			
MN	9a	Birk & Schmitt	1874-1878
	9b	Christian Schmitt	1878-1904
	9c	Estate of Chr. Schmitt	1904-1906
	9d	Mathias Schmitt	1906-1916
Bemidji			
MN	10	Bemidji Brewing Co.	1905-1915
Beroun			
MN	11	Beroun Bohemian Brewing Co.	1905-1908
Blue Earth City			
MN	12a	Paul Fleckenstein (Harrison St.)	1874-1905
	12b	Theodore Fleckenstein	1905-1906
Brainerd			
MN	13a	Peter Orth	1881-1884
	13b	Brainerd Brewing Co.	1884-1915
Browersville (Hartford)			
MN	14	Albert Minars, Jr.	1891-1920
Brownsville			
MN	15a	V. & J. Fetzner	1874-1895
	15b	Valentine Fetzner	1895-1899
	15c	Fackler & Landkowski	1899-1906
	15d	Aug. Sindermann	1906-1908
	15e	Philip Klenk	1908-1909
Caledonia			
MN	16a	Philip Wagner	1875-1878
	16b	P. Schwebach	1878-1880
	16c	Peter Arnoldy	1880-1884
Canby			
MN	17	J. Schmohl	1878-1880
Cannon Falls			
MN	18	Ferdinand Kowitz	1882-1888
Carver			
MN	19a	Berthold Hertz	1874-1884
	19b	Annie Hertz	1884-1888
Chaska			
MN	20a	Fred Beyrer	1907-1920
	20b	Fred Beyrer (597 Stoughton Ave.)	1934-1955
MN	21	Peter Ittis	1874-1880
MN	22a	George Karcher	1879-1882
	22b	Ottis & Schane	1882-1884
	22c	Gottlieb Beurlen	1884-1893
MN	23a	George Ulmer	1875-1875
	23b	Leman & Liverman	1875-1875
	23c	B. Liverman	1875-1884
	23d	Mrs. B. Liverman	1884-1899
	23e	August Liverman	1899-1905
	23f	August Liverman & Bro.	1905-1920
Cold Spring			
MN	24a	George Sargel	1874-1877
	24b	Michael Sargel	1877-1884
	24c	Jacob Haemen	1884-1888
	24d	Jacob Haemen & Co.	1888-1890
	24e	Haemen & Oester	1890-1895
	24f	Oester & Hilt	1895-1898
	24g	Cold Spring Brewing Co.	1898-1920

Cold Spring (cont.)

MN	24h	Cold Spring Brewing Co. (219 N. Red River St.) aka Cold Spring Brewery Co. (1933-1940) aka Arrowhead Brewing Co. (1957-1968) aka Northern Brewing Co.	1933-

Corunna Falls

MN	25	Ferdinand Kowitz	1878-1880

Crookston

MN	26a	August Molter (Front & 5th Sts.)	1879-1879
	26b	Burkhardt & Co.	1879-1884
	26c	August Walter	1884-1891
	26d	Julia Walter	1891-1893
	26e	Rauch, Schnagl & Riedesel	1893-1899
	26f	Jacob Kiewel Brewing Co., aka J. Kiewel Brewing Co.	1899-1905
	26g	Kiewel Brewing Co.	1905-1920
	26h	Kiewel Products Co.	NP 1934-1934

Detroit

MN	27	Detroit Brewing Co.	1888-1888

Duluth

MN	28	Camahl & Busse	1874-1875
MN	29	Benj. Dickler	1882-1884
MN	30a	Duluth Brewing and Malting Co. (29th Ave. W. & Helm St.)	1896-1920
	30b	Rex Sobriety Co.	1920-1932
	30c	Duluth Brewing and Malting Co. (229/303 S. 29th Ave. W. & 2902/2916 Helm St.)	1934-1966
MN	31a	Michael Fink	1875-1882
	31b	M. Fink & Co.	1882-1884
MN	32a	A. (August) Fitger & Co. (532/600 E. Superior St.)	1883-1903
	32b	Fitger Brewing Co.	1903-1920
	32c	The Fitger Co., Inc.	1933-1937
	32d	Fitger Brewing Co., Inc.	1937-1972
MN	33a	Geyser Bottling Works, E. F. Berg (2234 W. Michigan St.)	1901-1907
	33b	West End Malt Ale Co.	1909-1914
MN	34a	C. J. Johnson	1900-1900
	34b	C. J. Johnson	1905-1906
MN	35	Gustav Kiene	1874-1875
MN	36a	Peoples Brewing Co. (42nd Ave. W. & 4230 Traverse St.)	1907-1920
	36b	Peoples Bottling Co., Inc.	1920-1933
	36c	Peoples' Brewing Co. (4230 W. 2nd St.)	1933-1957

East Grand Forks

MN	37a	Mundigel, Zengel & Co. (Washington Ave.)	1885-1890
	37b	Mundigel & Hoffmann	1890-1892
	37c	Nicholas Hoffmann	1892-1897
	37d	White & Jarvis	1897-1899
	37e	East Grand Forks Brewing Co.	1899-1916

Ellsworth

MN	38a	Frank Romer & Sons	1902-1902
	38b	Roemer Bros.	1902-1903
	38c	Consumers Brewing Co.	1903-1906
	38d	Eagle Brewing Co.	1906-1908

Elysian

MN	39	Theimer & Co.	1874-1875

Evansville

MN	40a	John Schwartz & Co.	1884-1890
	40b	Peter Schwartz	1890-1900
	40c	Albertina Schwartz	1900-1901

Fairmount

MN	41	G. S. Smales	? -1878

Faribault (formerly Fairbault)

MN	42	John Ahles	1875- ?
MN	43a	Brandt & Co.	1874-1877
	43b	S. A. Shefield	1877-1880
	43c	A. W. Mueller & Co.	1880-1882
	43d	George N. Baxter	1882-1884
MN	44a	Ernst Fleckenstein	1872-1901
	44b	Ernst Fleckenstein Brewing Co.	1901-1920
	44c	Ernst Fleckenstein Beverage Co.	1933-1939
	44d	Ernst Fleckenstein Brewing Co.	1939-1964
MN	45a	Fleckenstein Bros. (Ernst & Gottfried)	1857-1872
	45b	Gottfried Fleckenstein	1872-1896
	45c	G. Fleckenstein & Son (E. 3rd St.)	1896-1902
	45d	Louis Fleckenstein	1905-1907

Fergus Falls

MN	46a	Charles Brown & Co.	1878-1879
	46b	Charles Brown	1879-1884
MN	47a	F. Judwitsch	1882-1883
	47b	Kiewel & Haas	1883-1884
	47c	Jacob Kiewel	1884-1895
MN	48a	J. K. O'Brien	1882-1883
	48b	Aberle & Ahrentz	1883-1884
	48c	Andreas Aberle	1884-1891
	48d	C. J. Bender	1891-1896
	48e	Andreas Aberle	1896-1900
	48f	Aberle & Bauer	1900-1902
	48g	John Bauer	1902-1906
	48h	Theo. Hubner	1906-1908
	48i	Fergus Brewing Co.	1908-1920
	48j	Premier Brewing Co., Inc. (121 N. Peck St.)	1933-1935
	48k	Fergus Brewing Co., Inc.	1935-1937
	48l	Fergus Breweries, Inc.	1937-1948
	48m	Falls Breweries	1948-1952
MN	49	Peter Oehlschlager	1879-1884

Frankfort

MN	50a	George E. Weiss	1874-1888
	50b	Dick Bros.	1888-1891

Frazee

MN	51a	John Smraker	1874-1875
	51b	G. Carl	1875-1879

Glencoe

MN	52a	Edward Lammel	1874-1895
	52b	Peter Eickmann	1895-1900
	52c	Glencoe Brewing Co.	1900-1920

Glenwood

MN	53	Miksch Bros.	1884-1884

Granger

MN	54a	Henry Hasse	1874-1884
	54b	R. H. Hasse	1884-1895
	54c	Bina Engelhorn	1895-1897
	54d	Granger Brewing Co.	1897-1901

Hakah

MN	55	John G. Streigel	1878-1882

Hanover

MN	56	Geo. E. Weiss	1888-1888

Hartford (see Browersville)

Hastings			
MN	57a	Frederick Busch	1874-1891
	57b	J. L. Busch & Co. (3rd & Adams Sts.) aka J. L. Busch & Son (1897-1898)	1891-1900
	57c	Laurent & Murphy	1900-1901
	57d	Minnesota Brewing Co.	1901-1902
MN	58a	Ficker & Daffing	1874-1877
	58b	Ficker & Dandelinger	1877-1884
	58c	A. Kehrhoffer	1884-1891
	58d	Hoffmann & Grub	1891-1893
MN	59a	Kehrhoffer & Steffen	1882-1884
	59b	Balthazar Steffen	1884-1902
	59c	Hastings Brewing Co.	1902-1920
MN	60	Samuel Murisch	1874-1875
MN	61a	M. Schaller	1856-1870
	61b	Borser & Yaeger	1870-1870
Helena			
MN	62a	A. Menass Brewing Co.	1888-1890
	62b	Menass & Kokes	1890-1891
	62c	Marieska & Kokes	1891-1895
Henderson			
MN	63a	C. Enes	1879-1882
	63b	Enes & Schuhmacher	1882-1884
	63c	Hans (John) Enes	1884-1920
MN	64	Joseph Ritter	1874-1875
Hibbing			
MN	65	Range Brewing Co. (Howard St. & 1st Ave.)	NP 1934-1934
Hutchinson			
MN	66a	Plotzer & Wetzig	1874-1877
	66b	Englehorn & Co.	1877-1880
	66c	Kleinmann & Bro. (3rd St.)	1880-1896
	66d	Kleinmann Bros.	1896-1905
	66e	Joseph Hajicek	1905-1920
Jackson			
MN	67a	C. J. Gilmore	1891-1892
	67b	Gilmore & Peshek	1892-1893
	67c	William Gilger	1893-1895
MN	68	Evan Owens	1874-1880
MN	69	Mary Winker	1874-1875
Jordan			
MN	70a	Sebastian Gehring	1874-1884
	70b	Schutz & Kaiser	1884-1901
	70c	Schutz & Hilgers	1901-1920
	70d	Schutz & Hilgers Jordan Brewery, Inc.	1933-1946
	70e	Mankato Brewing Co. (br. of Mankato, MN)	1946-1948
MN	71a	Heil & Heiland	1875-1877
	71b	Fred Heiland	1877-1880
	71c	Catherine Heiland	1880-1902
	71d	Koschel & Mesenbrink	1902-1904
	71e	Jordan Brewing Co.	1904-1912
	71f	Jordan Brewing Association	1912-1916
Kensington			
MN	72	Joseph Bisek	1888-1893
Kokah			
MN	73	William Langen	1874-1875
Lake City			
MN	74a	James Fitzsimmons	1874-1877
	74b	Peter Beck & Co.	1877-1884

Lanesboro

MN	75a	M. Frietschel	? -1878
	75b	Radly & Chalupsky	1878-1882
	75c	Frank Radly	1882-1884

Le Sueur

MN	76a	Peter Arbes	1878-1893
	76b	Emil Vollbrecht	1893-1898

Litchfield

MN	77a	Lenhardt & Roetger	1875-1882
	77b	Ehrhardt Lenhardt	1882-1906
	77c	Litchfield Brewing Co.	1906-1916

Little Falls

MN	78a	Leo P. Brick	1882-1884
	78b	Little Falls Brewing Co.	1884-1888
	78c	Marin & Medoed	1888-1891
	78d	Peter Medoed	1891-1893
	78e	Jacob Kiewel	1893-1899
	78f	Jac. Kiewel Brewing Co.	1899-1920
	78g	Kiewel Brewing Co. (512 N.E. 7th St. & 5th Ave.)	1933-1959
	78h	Kiewel Brewing Co. (br. of Minneapolis Brewing Co., Mpls. MN)	1959-1961

Long Prairie

MN	79a	Gebhardt Rohner	c1875
	79b	John Meiner	1882- ?
	79c	Gebhardt Rohner	1890-1901
	79d	Joseph Slaby	1901-1902
	79e	Frederick Beyrer	1902-1905
	79f	Long Prairie Brewing Co.	1905-1920

Loreno

MN	80	G. W. Kramer & Co.	1880-1882

Madelia

MN	81	P. A. Brennes	1878-1897

Mankato

MN	82a	William & Jacob Bierbauer	1856-1863
	82b	William Bierbauer	1863-1893
	82c	William Bierbauer Estate	1893-1903
	82d	Louisa Bierbauer	1903-1904
	82e	Bierbauer Brewery	1904-1905
	82f	Wm. Bierbauer Brewing Co.	1905-1920
	82g	Mankato Brewing Co. (628 E. Rock & 7th Sts.)	1933-1951
	82h	Cold Spring Brewing Co.	1951-1954
	82i	Mankato Brewing Co.	1954-1966
MN	83	Blatt & Boehler	1874-1875
MN	84	Gassler & Co.	1874-1884
MN	85a	Graeber & Son	1880-1882
	85b	Nicholas Graeber	1882-1884
MN	86a	Joseph Ibach	1874-1877
	86b	Joseph Ibach Sr.	1877-1880
	86c	Mrs. Margaret Ibach	1880-1884
MN	87	Nicholas Petersen	1895-1899
MN	88	Rich-Peterson Brewing Co. (708 N. Front St.)	NP 1934-1934
MN	89	Standard Brewing Co.	1900-1908
MN	90	Peter Welch	1874-1875

Mantorville

MN	91a	Charles Ginsberg, Dodge County Brewery	1874-1877
	91b	Henry Naegeli	1877-1879
	91c	Mrs. Anna Ginsberg	1879-1884
	91d	Henry Naegeli	1884-1893
	91e	Henry Naegeli Jr.	1893-1898
	91f	Ferdinand Schnagl	1898-1904
	91g	Frederick Schnagl	1904-1905

Mantorville (cont.)

MN	91h	Estate of Frederick Schnagl	1905-1907
	91i	Anna Schnagl	1907-1911
	91j	John G. Schnagl	1911-1913
	91k	John G. & Ferdinand Schnagl	1913-1916
	91l	Otto's Brewery (6 Bluff St.), Otto Schumann	1933-1937
	91m	Mantorville Brewing Co.	1937-1939

Marine

MN	92a	John Kaufman	1856-1857
	92b	John Jacob Graf	1857-1870
	92c	Wishmann & Garner	1870-1880

Marion

MN	93	John F. Weichmann	1882-1882

Mazeppa

MN	94a	Jos. Trausch	1878-1882
	94b	John Hilger	1882-1884
	94c	Joseph Trausch	1884-1897
	94d	Rother & Manske	1897-1899

Melrose

MN	95a	John P. Schnitz	1882-1883
	95b	Kuhn & Hess	1883-1884
	95c	J. M. Hemmisch	1884-1897
	95d	Melrose Brewery, Wiesner & Wrede	1897-1898
	95e	Melrose Brewery, J. Hermuesch	1898-1901
	95f	Melrose Brewing Co.	1901-1902
	95g	Melrose Brewery, Hilt, Molitor & Rossmeisel	1902-1903
	95h	Melrose Brewery, Hilt & Molitor	1903-1904
	95i	Melrose Brewery, Anton Molitor	1904-1908
	95j	Melrose Brewing Co.	1908-1916
	95k	Schatz-Brau Brewing Co.	NP 1934-1934

Minneapolis

MN	96a	C. Birkhofer Brewing Co. (211 14th Ave. S. & 2nd St.)	1894-1906
	96b	Purity Brewing Co.	1906-1920
MN	97	Patrick J. Gilbridge	1882-1884
MN	98a	Gottlieb Gluek, Mississippi Brewery (2000 Marshall St. & 20th)	1857-1880
	98b	G. Gluek & Sons	1880-1894
	98c	Gluek Brewing Co.	1894-1920
	98d	Gluek Brewing Co. (2021 Marshall St., N.E.	1933-1965
MN	99	Hiawatha Brewing Co. (31st & Hiawatha Ave. S.)	NP 1934-1934
MN	100	Imperial Brewing Co. (23 21st Ave. S.)	1901-1905
MN	101a	Karlson & Lundquist (2014 Central Ave. N.E.)	1900- ?
	101b	John E. Tjerneld	1904-1905
	101c	Youngstrom Bros.	1905-1906
MN	102a	(John G.) Kranzlein & (John B.) Mueller (S. 4th St.)	1866-1870
	102b	Mueller & Heinrich	1870-1884
	102c	Heinrich Brewing Association	1884-1890
	102d	Minneapolis Brewing and Malting Co., No. 1, Heinrich Brewing Assn. Branch	1890-1893
	102e	Minneapolis Brewing Co., No. 1., Heinrich Brewing Assn. Branch (4th St. & 22nd Ave.)	1893-1897
MN	103a	Lauritzen Malt Co. (1900 3rd St. N.E.)	1903-1910
	103b	Hennepin Brewing Co.	1910-1920
MN	104a	Andrew Liden (210 Sverdrap St.)	1895-1910
	104b	Arvid Sundbeck	1910-1911
MN	105	Wm. Massolt Bottling Co. (126/128 Plymouth Ave.)	1895-1897
MN	106	Monahan Mfg. & Bottling Co.	1890-1890
MN	107	Olsen & Andersen (4215 Tyndale Ave.)	1896-1896

Minneapolis (cont.)

MN	108a	John Orth's Brewery (1228 Marshall St. & 13th Ave. N.E.)	1850- ?
	108b	John Orth & Co.	1874-1875
	108c	John Orth	1875-1883
	108d	John Orth Brewing Co.	1883-1890
	108e	Minneapolis Brewing and Malting Co., No. 2, John Orth Brewing Co. Branch	1890-1893
	108f	Minneapolis Brewing Co. aka John Orth Brewing Co. Branch (1893-1896)	1893-1920
	108g	Minneapolis Brewing Co.	1933-1967
	108h	Grain Belt Breweries, Inc. aka John Hauenstein Co. (1970-1975)	1967-1975
	108i	I. J. Enterprises, dba Grain Belt Breweries	1975-1975
MN	109a	(Herman A.) Westphal & (John B.) Mueller	1884-1885
	109b	H. A. Westphal	1885-1888
	109c	Germania Brewing Association	1888-1890
	109d	Minneapolis Brewing and Malting Co., Germania Branch	1890-1890
MN	110a	Anton Zahler (Bluff St. & 20th Ave., S.)	1870-1877
	110b	Zahler & Nohrenberg	1877-1879
	110c	F. D. Nohrenberg	1879-1890
	110d	Minneapolis Brewing and Malting Co.	1890-1890

Minneiska

MN	111a	H. W. Mead	1874-1875
	111b	Parker & Mead	1875-1875

Minnesota City

MN	112a	Otto Vill (Lake St.)	1869-1915
	112b	Otto Vill Brewery	1915-1920

Montgomery

MN	113a	Mathias Chalapsky	1881-1884
	113b	John Chalapsky	1884-1888
	113c	Montgomery Brewing Co.	1888-1891
	113d	Soulek Bros.	1891-1893
	113e	Bazel & Perchal	1893-1897
MN	114a	Handschuh & Pexa	1893-1898
	114b	Joseph Handschuh (merged with 116c)	1898-1905
MN	115	Pepin Lake Brewery	1910-1910
MN	116a	Richter Bros. & Hug	1900-1901
	116b	Richter Bros.	1901-1901
	116c	Richter-Washa Brewing Co. (merged with 114b)	1901-1905
	116d	Handschuh & Richter, City Brewery	1905-1907
	116e	Handschuh-Richter Brewing Co.	1907-1912
	116f	Montgomery Brewing Co.	1912-1920
	116g	Montgomery Brewing Co. (201 2nd St. & Boulevard Ave. W.)	1933-1942

Moorhead

MN	117a	Larkin Brothers	1874-1875
	117b	John Erickson	1875-1897
	117c	Ole Aslesen	1898-1901

New Munich

MN	118a	John Froehler	1874-1877
	118b	N. Schmidt	1877-1879
	118c	Schmidt & Co.	1879-1882
MN	119a	J. Froehler & Son	1874-1875
	119b	Froehler Bros.	1882-1883
	119c	Wimmer & Froehler	1883-1884
	119d	Victoria Froehler	1884-1888
	119e	Mathias Pitzel	1888-1905
	119f	Pitzel & Schweibers	1905-1908
	119g	Math. Pitzel Brewing Co.	1908-1920

New Prague

MN	120a	Menars Brewing Co.	1888- ?
	120b	Menars & Kokes	1893- ?
	120c	Thomas Kokes, aka Kokes & Piemeisl	1896-1898
	120d	(John) Piemeisl & (Mathias) Rybok, "O.K. Brewery"	1898-1904

New Prague (cont.)

MN	121a	Frank Raddy	1888-1891
	121b	Schulz & Kaiser	1891-1893
	121c	New Prague Brewing Co.	1893-1895
	121d	Frank Roemer	1895-1899
	121e	Roemer & Kodedek	1899-1900
	121f	Chas. Mickus	1900-1904
	121g	New Prague Brewing Co.	1904-1920
	121h	New Prague Brewing Co.	NP 1934-1934

New Ulm

MN	122a	Jacob Bender (Front St.)	1866-1888
	122b	New Ulm Brewing Co.	1888-1891
	122c	Jacob Bender	1891-1911
MN	123	August Friton, Andrew Batz Brewery	c1862
MN	124a	(John) Hauenstein & Betz (Franklin St.)	1864-1867
	124b	Hauenstein & (John) Toberer	1867-1869
	124c	John Hauenstein	1869-1897
	124d	John Hauenstein Brewing Co. (Jefferson & 16th Sts. S.)	1897-1920
	124e	John Hauenstein Co. (1601 S. Jefferson St.)	1934-1969
MN	125a	Aug. Holl	1878-1879
	125b	John Piemeisle	1879-1884
MN	126a	August Schell	1860-1902
	126b	August Schell Brewing Co.	1902-1920
	126c	August Schell Brewing Co. (S. Payne St.) aka Augie's Brewing Co. aka Steinhaus Brewing Co.	1933-
MN	127a	Joseph Schmucker (German St.)	1870-1904
	127b	New Ulm Brewing & Malting Co. aka Joseph Schmucker Brewing Co. (1904-1907)	1904-1916

Northfield

MN	128a	Moes & Grafmueller	1874-1877
	128b	Adolph Grafmueller	1877-1896
	128c	Grafmueller Brothers	1896-1897
	128d	Hermann Wenner, Northfield Brewery, aka Hermann Wenner Brewery (Greenville Ave.)	1897-1920

Ortonville

MN	129a	Geiger & Ebermann	1884- ?
	129b	John Fey	? -1890
	129c	John Fey & Son	1890-1893
	129d	Ortonville Brewing Co. (Main St.)	1893-1897
	129e	Edward Lammel	1897-1904
	129f	Lakeside Brewing Co.	1904-1911

Oshawa

MN	130a	Frederick Veith	1874-1877
	130b	Fred A. Veith	1877-1880

Owatonna (formerly Owatumwa)

MN	131a	Louis Bion	1875-1884
	131b	Marie Bion	1884-1888
	131c	C. Bion & Son	1888-1891
MN	132a	Knobloch & Mannheim	1863-1865
	132b	Peter Ganser, City Brewery	1865-1893
	132c	Chas. Fuermann Brewing Co.	1893-1900
	132d	Peter Ganser	1900-1920

Perham

MN	133a	Peter Schroeder	1876-1904
	133b	Northern Pacific Brewing Co.	1904-1909
	133c	Peter Schroeder Brewing Co. (54/60 S. Oak St.)	1909-1915

City	No.	Brewery	Years
Pine City	MN 134a	Rud. Buselmeyer	1882-1884
	134b	Amalie Buselmeier, aka Buselmeier Brewery	1885-1910
	134c	John P. Blass	1910-1913
	134d	Amalie Buselmeier, aka Buselmeier Brewery	1913-1915
Pine Island	MN 135	John Ferber	1875-1893
Preston	MN 136a	Yager & Luhmann	1888-1900
	136b	Geo. Riedel	1900-1909
	136c	Preiss & Eickmann	1909-1911
	136d	Preston Brewing Co.	1911-1913
	136e	Preston Brewery, Aug.. F. Knapp	1913-1915
	136f	Preston Brewery, George Riedel	1915-1915
Princeton	MN 137	Roos Bros.	1888-1890
Red Lake Falls	MN 138a	Red Lake Falls Brewing Co.	1884- ?
	138b	August Walters	? -1888
	138c	August Walters & Co.	1888-1890
Red Wing	MN 139	John Hartmann	1874-1880
	MN 140a	William Heising (5th & Bush Sts.)	1864-1875
	140b	A. Remmler	1875-1897
	140c	Remmler's Brewery	1897-1920
	140d	Remmler Brewing Co., Inc. (405 W. 5th St.)	1934-1943
	140e	The Remmler Brewing Co.	1943-1948
	140f	Goodhue County Brewing Co.	1948-1951
	MN 141	Lorenz Hoffmann	1874-1882
	MN 142a	John Melander	1874-1877
	142b	Jacob Christ (1602/1636 Main St.)	1877-1890
	142c	Christina Christ	1890-1891
	142d	Red Wing Brewing Co.	1891-1904
	142e	Zimmermann & Featherston	1904-1908
	142f	Red Wing Brewing Co.	1908-1920
	142g	Red Wing Brewing Co.	1934-1935
	142h	Mid West Brewing Co., Inc.	1935-1937
Redwood	MN 143	Jacob Schmohl	1874-1875
Redwood Falls	MN 144a	John Weiss	1874-1880
	144b	Dietrich & Drischel	1880-1888
Reeds	MN 145a	Ruckhaber & Grams	1875-1877
	145b	J. Voelke	1877-1880
Reed's Landing	MN 146a	G. Burkhardt & Co.	1874-1877
	146b	Samuel Burkhardt	1877-1880
	146c	Gottfried Burkhardt	1880-1884
	146d	Burkhardt Bros.	1884-1893
	146e	Gottlieb Burkhardt	1893-1909
Richmond	MN 147	Claudius Weber	1874-1884
Rochester	MN 148a	Joseph Bang	1874-1880
	148b	Wm. Schindler	1880-1882
	148c	Louis Schroeder	1882-1884

Rochester (cont.)

MN	149a	Adam Drescher (Main & College Sts.)	1858-1864
	149b	Henry Schuster	1864-1885
	149c	Estate of Henry Schuster	1885-1897
	149d	Schuster Brewing Co.	1897-1920
	149e	Rochester Brewing Co.	NP 1934-1934
MN	150a	Adam Stenger	1874-1875
	150b	Adam Stenger	1882-1884

Rolling Stone

MN	151	Otto Vill	1874-1896

Rush City

MN	152a	Gustav Victor	1874-1879
	152b	Louis Fahrenholz	1879-1884
	152c	Fred Schnagl	1884-1893
	152d	Rush City Brewing Co.	1898-1904

Rushford

MN	153a	Larsen	1865-1874
	153b	Oechsle & Schaupp	1874-1877
	153c	Jacob Pfeiffer	1877-1900
	153d	John Pfeiffer	1900-1904
	153e	Estate of John Pfeiffer	1904-1906

St. Charles

MN	154a	F. William Mueller	1875-1879
	154b	Henius & Co.	1879-1880
	154c	John Waltham & Co.	1880-1882
	154d	John Waltham	1882-1884
	154e	Pfester & Waller	1884-1890

St. Cloud

MN	155a	Lorenz Enderle	1874-1882
	155b	Schindler & Co.	1882-1891
	155c	Wendelin Merz	1891-1893
	155d	Caroline Merz	1893-1895
	155e	Fred W. Zertler	1895-1897
MN	156a	Fritz Herberger	1857- ?
	156b	Herberger & Schmitt	? -1874
	156c	Herberger Brothers	1874-1877
	156d	John Brick	1877-1882
	156e	Brick & Legler	1882-1884
	156f	Preiss & Wimmer (9th Ave. & 6th St.)	1884-1900
	156g	Preiss & Wimmer Brewing Co.	1900-1911
	156h	Preiss Brewing Co.	1911-1920
	156i	St. Cloud Brewing Co., Inc. (601 8th Ave. N. & 6th St.)	1933-1939
MN	157a	Remely & Thierry	1874-1877
	157b	Thierse & Balder	1877-1880
	157c	Balder & Weber	1880-1884
	157d	Frank Balder	1884-1895
MN	158a	Valentine Udermann (409 6th Ave. N & 4th St.)	1896-1908
	158b	Val. Udermann Brewing Co.	1909-1916

St. Michaels

MN	159a	Frey & Zahler	1884- ?
	159b	Dick Bros.	1893-1897

St. Paul

MN	160	J. L. Bausch & Son	1895-1895
MN	161	Benzberg Brewery	c1850
MN	162a	Martin Bruggeman (Channel St. btwn Edward & Walter Sts.)	1853-1897
	162b	Martin Bruggeman Estate	1897-1900
	162c	Aiple Brewing Co.	1900-1904
MN	163	E. & G. Fleckenstein	1855-1857

St. Paul (cont.)

MN	164a	Melchior Funk Company (Colborne & Palace)	1865-1891
	164b	M. Funk Brewing Co.	1891-1903
MN	165a	William Gilger & Co.	1874-1877
	165b	R. Koch & Co.	1877-1884
MN	166	Joseph Hamm & John Reimer (Joy Ave. near Lilydale Road)	1885-1887
MN	167	Frank Hornung (124 S. Washington St.)	1876-1883
MN	168a	Andrew F. Keller, Pittsburgh Brewery	1860-1864
	168b	Theodore Hamm (Minnehaha St. & Greenbrier Ave.)	1864-1896
	168c	Theodore Hamm Brewing Co.	1896-1920
	168d	Theo. Hamm Brewing Co. (681/707 E. Minnehaha Ave.)	1933-1937
	168e	Theo. Hamm Brewing Co. (720 Payne Ave.) aka Buckhorn Brewing Co. (1955-1964) aka Burgie Brewing Co. aka Theodore Hamm Co.	1937-1975
	168f	Olympia Brewing Co., aka Theo. Hamm Brewing Co. (br. of Olympia, WA)	1975-1983
	168g	Olympia Brewing Co., subsidiary of Pabst Brewing Co., Milwaukee, WI	1983-1983
	168h	Stroh Brewing Co. (br. of Detroit, MI)	1983-
MN	169	Minnesota Weiss Beer Co.	1884- ?
MN	170a	North Mississippi Co., Mr. Rowe	1853-1859
	170b	North Mississippi Co., Charles Rausch	1859-1865
	170c	North Mississippi Co., F. A. Rinz	1865-1865
	170d	Frederick & William Banholzer	1871-1879
	170e	Wm. Banholzer	1879-1897
	170f	Wm. Banholzer Estate	1897-1898
MN	171a	North Star Brewery, Drewry & Scotten (702/710 Payne Ave.)	1855-1866
	171b	L. B. & C. Graig	1866-1872
	171c	William Constans	1872-1879
	171d	Koch and Company	1879-1884
	171e	Jacob Schmidt	1884-1899
	171f	Jacob Schmidt Brewing Co.	1899-1900
MN	172a	Putnam & Dexter	1861-1862
	172b	Edward Drewry	1862-1866
MN	173	H. W. Reichow (off Lilydale Road)	1885-1886
MN	174	Roelke Brothers	1874-1875
MN	175a	Chr. Stahlmann (882 W. 7th St.)	1854-1882
	175b	Ch. Stahlmann Brewing Co.	1882-1897
	175c	St. Paul Brewing Co.	1897-1900
	175d	Jacob Schmidt Brewing Co.	1900-1920
	175e	Jacob Schmidt Brewing Co.	1933-1954
	175f	Pfeiffer Brewing Co., dba Jacob Schmidt Brewing Co. (br. of Detroit, MI)	1954-1962
	175g	Associated Brewing Co. aka Pfeiffer Brewing Co. (1962-1972) aka Jacob Schmidt Brewing Co. (1962-1972)	1962-1972
	175h	G. Heileman Brewing Co., Inc. (br. of LaCrosse, WI)	1972-
MN	176a	Dominick Troyner, aka City Brewery (Eagle & Exchange Sts.)	1855-1860
	176b	(William) Funk & (Ullrich) Schweizer	1860-1866
	176c	(Frederick) Emmert & Schweizer	1866-1871
	176d	Frederick Emmert (187 S. Exchange St.)	1871-1889
	176e	Fred. Emmert Brewing Co. (168/170 Exchange St.) 1901- purchased by 168c for storage facility	1889-1901
MN	177a	A. L. Upham	1874-1877
	177b	Frank Horning	1877-1880
MN	178a	Conrad Wurm (Jefferson and Grace)	1863-1877
	178b	Johanna Wurm	1877-1889
MN	179a	Anthony Yoerg (S. Washington St. btwn. Chestnut & Eagle)	1848-1871
	179b	Anthony Yoerg (Ohio & Ethel Sts.)	1871-1884
	179c	Anthony Yoerg Brewing Co.	1884-1897
	179d	Yoerg Brewing Co.	1897-1920
	179e	Yoerg Brewing Co. (229 Ohio St.)	1933-1952

St. Peter

MN	180a	Matthew Engesser	1856-1880
	180b	Matthew Engesser & Sons	1880-1888
	180c	Engesser Brewing Co.	1888-1920
	180d	Engesser Brewing Co. (1202/1212 S. Front St.)	1933-1942
MN	181	Hohmann & Young	1880-1880
MN	182a	Jacob Steizer	1874-1888
	182b	George Steizer	1888-1891

Sauk Center

MN	183a	George Gruber	1874-1884
	183b	Henry Diehl	1884-1888
	183c	Ahrentz & Co.	1888-1890
	183d	Antonette I. Minette	1890-1893

Sauk Rapids

MN	184	Sauk Rapids Brewing Co.	1888-1895

Shakopee

MN	185a	A. T. Husmann	1874-1882
	185b	J. B. Husmann	1882-1884
	185c	Husmann Bros.	1884-1888
	185d	H. Husmann	1888-1890
	185e	H. H. Heller	1890-1901
	185f	J. M. Engelhorn, Union Brewery	1901-1906
MN	186a	Herman H. Strunk	? -1863
	186b	Andrew Winker	c1860-1870
	186c	A. Winker's Estate	c1870
	186d	Hubert Nyssen, Shakopee Brewery	1878-1920
	186e	Shakopee Breweries, Inc. (92 Arthur Ave., S.E.)	NP 1934-1934

Silver Lake

MN	187a	Wenzel Chalupsky	1888-1904
	187b	Frank Chalupsky	1904-1912
	187c	Silver Lake Brewing Co.	1912-1920

Sleepy Eye

MN	188a	George W. Kramer	1874-1877
	188b	G. W. Kramer & Co.	1877-1880
	188c	Frank Burginger	1880-1888
	188d	Anton Steffen	1888-1912
	188e	Steffen Brewing Co.	1912-1914
	188f	Bernard Schueller	1915-1920

Stillwater

MN	189	A. Haase & Hermann	1875- ?
MN	190a	Norbert Kimmick	1851-1852
	190b	Francis X. Aiple	1852-1869
	190c	Hermann Tepass	1869-1887
	190d	(Frank J.) Aiple & (Carl) Piper	1887-1889
	190e	Frank J. R. Aiple (734/802 S. Main St.)	1889-1896
MN	191	Gerhard Knips	1874-1875
MN	192a	Martin Wolf	c1850
	192b	Wolf, Tanner & Co.	1872-1875
	192c	Joseph Wolf & Co.	1875-1879
	192d	Joseph Wolf (402/414 S. Main St.)	1879-1896
	192e	Joseph Wolf Co.	1896-1920
	192f	Wolf's Brewery	NP 1934-1934

Taylor's Falls

MN	193a	J. Beyer & Brother	1874-1877
	193b	J. Schottmuller	1877-1884
	193c	Geo. Zigner	1884-1888
	193d	Schottmuller Bros.	1888-1890

Tower

MN	194a	Fink	1892-1893
	194b	Iron Range Brewing Co., aka Iron Range Brewery	1893-1897
	194c	Iron Range Brewing Association	1897-1920

Virginia			
MN	195	Virginia Brewing Co. (Spruce & Ohio Sts.)	1906-1920
Wabasha			
MN	196a	Charles Leslin	1872-1874
	196b	Mrs. Mary Leslin	1874-1884
	196c	John T. Ginthner	1884-1890
	196d	Robert Anderson	1890-1893
	196e	Christ. Grass, Wabasha Brewery	1893-1920
MN	197	Eugene Zahler	1884- ?
Waconia			
MN	198	Michael Zahler	1874-1884
Wadena			
MN	199a	Carl & Roller	1882-1883
	199b	George Carl	1883-1884
	199c	Annie E. Ebner	1884-1891
	199d	Henry Ebner	1891-1895
	199e	Wadena Brewing Co.	1895-1916
Waseca			
MN	200a	John Bierwalter	1878-1880
	200b	Jos. Ramsdale	1880-1884
	200c	Anthony Guyer	1884-1888
	200d	Hermann Wenner	1888-1897
	200e	Robert Reichel	1897-1900
	200f	Adam & Ringer	1902-1905
	200g	Waseca Brewing Co.	1905-1912
MN	201a	Ginsberg & Bro.	1874-1877
	201b	Simon Kraft	1877-1880
Watertown			
MN	202a	Catherine Becker	1874-1877
	202b	Fritz Lueders	1877-1884
Wesely			
MN	203a	Joseph Pavek aka Joseph Pavek Brewing Co. (1898)	1890-1898
	203b	Joseph Pavek	1901-1907
Willmar			
MN	204	William Gilger	1878-1898
Winona			
MN	205a	Becker & Neifert	1865- ?
	205b	John S. Becker	1874-1882
	205c	Becker & Schellhas	1882-1891
	205d	Schellhas Brewing Co.	1891-1895
	205e	William Schellhas	1895-1906
	205f	Wm. Schellhas Brewing Co.	1906-1920
MN	206	C. C. Boeck	1874-1875
MN	207	Brentle, Scherer & Rath, Gilmore Valley Brewery	1855- ?
MN	208	Park Brewing Co. (Front & Walnut Sts.)	1905-1920
MN	209a	Jacob Weisbrod	1856-1870
	209b	Peter Bub, Sugar Loaf Brewery	1870-1911
	209c	Sugar Loaf Brewery, Peter Bub Estate	1911-1920
	209d	Peter Bub Estate (Sugar Loaf & Mankato Aves.)	1933-1935
	209e	Peter Bub Brewery, Inc.	1935-1969
Young America			
MN	210	A. Schmasse & Co.	1874-1880

MISSISSIPPI

Mississippi never had a brewery

Appleton (see Old Appleton)

Augusta

MO	1	Theodore Rungle	1874-1875

Bellefontaine

MO	2	St.Vrain & Hab	1810-1812

Bonne Terre

MO	3	P. A. Wigger & Son	1882-1884

Boonville

MO	4	Griessmaier & Roeschel	1874-1878
MO	5	Klein & Muehlschuster	1875-1875

Brunswick

MO	6	J. S. Quer	1874-1875

Cape Girardeau

MO	7a	Cape Brewery and Ice Co. (Morgan & Oak Sts.)	1891-1919
	7b	Cape Brewing Co. (400 S. Middle St.)	1934-1939
MO	8a	Ferdinand Hanney	1874-1884
	8b	Julius Hanney	1884-1888
MO	9	Frederick Henninger	1874-1888
MO	10	Edward Ortel	1875-1875
MO	11a	C. Uhl & Co.	1874-1877
	11b	Casper Uhl	1877-1891

Carrollton

MO	12	H. Rhomburg	1874-1884

Carthage

MO	13a	James C. Beamer	1878-1879
	13b	John Apperger & Co.	1880-1882
	13c	John Apperger	1882-1884
MO	14	John Hillyer	1882-1882

Chillicothe

MO	15a	Joseph Pierson	1874-1877
	15b	Peter Pierson	1877-1879
	15c	Frank Pierson	1879-1880
	15d	Frank Pierson & Co.	1880-1882
	15e	Butcher & Pierson	1882-1884
	15f	Pierson & Krick	1884-1888

Clinton

MO	16	George Hormann	1874-1875

Columbia

MO	17	Robert Hartung	1874-1875

Deep Water

MO	18	C. H. Trueman	1890-1891

Edina

MO	19a	Staeblin & Geisman	1874-1877
	19b	F. G. Strohman	1877-1879

Festus

MO	20	Julius Sekrit	1895-1895

Forrest City

MO	21	Jacob Schweinfurth	1882-1884

Frederickstown

MO	22a	Gamma & Offer	1874-1877
	22b	Jacob Gamma	1877-1880

Fulton

MO	23a	Sarton & Lorenz	1875-1878
	23b	Edward Lorenz	1878-1890
	23c	Ignatz Maderer	1890-1891

Glasgow

MO	24	John Siebel	1874-1878

Glenwood			
MO	25	John Storm	1874-1875
Hannibal			
MO	26	Frederick Gugel	1874-1875
MO	27a	H. C. Kleine	1880-1891
	27b	Herl & Rendlen Brewing Co., South Side Brewery	1895-1896
MO	28a	Reidel & Co. (Grand Ave.)	1863-1877
	28b	George Reidel	1877-1891
	28c	Elizabeth Reidel	1891-1902
	28d	J. M. Friederich	1902-1903
	28e	William Heil, City Brewery	1903-1905
	28f	Albert S. Schorr, City Brewery	1905-1910
MO	29a	W. F. Schaubacker	1878-1890
	29b	John Herl	1890-1891
	29c	Herl & Rendlen (117 Lindell Ave.)	1891-1893
	29d	Herl-Rendlen Brewing and Ice Co.	1893-1896
	29e	Herl-Rendlen Brewing Co.	1896-1902
	29f	Hannibal Brewing Co.	1904-1919
Hermann			
MO	30	Geo. Baumeister	1875-1875
MO	31a	Jacob Strobel (E. Front St.)	1869- ?
	31b	Charles C. Kropp	1875-1877
	31c	Hugo Kropp, aka Hugo Kropp's Brewery	1877-1905
	31d	Kropp Brewing Co.	1905-1907
	31e	Hermann Brewing Co.	1907-1910
	31f	J. M. Danzer's Brewery & Ice Co. aka Home Brewing and Ice Manufacturing Co. (1912)	1910-1916
Jefferson City			
MO	32	L. Franz & Bro. (Bolivar & Miller Sts.)	1874-1891
MO	33a	George Wagner & Son	1874-1880
	33b	George Wagner & Sons	1880-1884
	33c	C. & L. Wagner	1884-1891
	33d	Capitol Brewing Co. (118 W. Dunklin St.)	1891-1897
	33e	Capitol Brewery Co.	1897-1919
	33f	Capitol Brewery, Inc.	1933-1947
Joplin			
MO	34	Crescent Brewing Co. (br. of Marionville, MO)	NP 1934-1934
MO	35a	(George) Muennig & (Nicholas) Zentner (507 Main St.)	1881-1888
	35b	Nicholas Zentner	1888-1893
	35c	Joplin Brewing Co.	1893-1904
	35d	Middle West Brewing Co.	1904-1905
	35e	Middle West Brewery Co.	1905-1907
	35f	Home Brewing and Ice Co.	1907-1919
MO	36	Abner Pierson	1875-1875
Kansas City			
MO	37	Barrett & Barrett Brewing Co.	1902-1902
MO	38a	Bremer & Thoma (20 E. 24th St.)	1898-1900
	38b	Leo Thoma	1900-1911
	38c	Leo Thoma (1308 W. 28th St.)	1911-1919
MO	39a	Guttenberg Ale Brewing Co. (2924 Fairmount Ave.)	1901-1902
	39b	Butler Ale Brewing Co.	1902-1903
MO	40	M. K. Goetz Brewing Co. (3406/3412 E. 17th St. & Indiana Ave.)	1936-1956
MO	41a	Ferd. Heim Brewing Co. (1400/1402 Main St.	1888- ?
	41b	Bavarian Brewing Co.	? -1893
MO	42a	John Hurt	1864-1870
	42b	G. Muehlebach & Bro.	1870-1875
	42c	John Muehlebach	1875-1879
	42d	John & George Muehlebach (18th & Main Sts.)	1879-1888
	42e	George & John G. Muehlebach	1888-1890
	42f	Geo. Muehlebach (1734 Main St.)	1890-1904

Kansas City (cont.)

MO	42g	George Muehlebach Brewing Co.	1904-1919
	42h	Geo. Muehlebach Brewing Co. (316 Oak St.) aka Griesedieck Western Brewery (1949)	1934-1956
	42i	Jos. Schlitz Brewing Co. (br. of Milwaukee, WI)	1956-1973
MO	43a	(J. D.) Iler & (1.) Burgweger, Rochester Brewery (Washington St. between 20th & 21st Sts.)	1888-1892
	43b	J. D. Iler, Rochester Brewery	1892-1895
	43c	J. D. Iler Brewing Co., Rochester Brewery	1895-1901
	43d	Rochester Brewing Co.	1901-1905
	43e	Rochester Brewery, "A" Plant (br. of Kansas City Breweries)	1905-1919
MO	44a	Imperial Brewing Co. (2825 S.W. Blvd.)	1901-1905
	44b	Imperial Brewery (br. of Kansas City Breweries Co.)	1905-1906
	44c	Rochester Brewery, "B" Plant (br. of Kansas City Breweries)	1906-1915
	44d	Imperial Brewing Co. (122/124 Southwest Blvd.)	1933-1938
MO	45a	Kansas City Brewing Co.	1875- ?
	45b	Kansas City Brewing Co. (24th & Walnut Sts.)	? -1891
MO	46	John H. Kump (Main & 14th Sts.)	1875-1875
MO	47a	Frank H. Kump	1874-1884
	47b	Heim Brewing Co.	1884-1887
	47c	Ferdinand Heim Brewing Co. (Agnes & Guinotte Aves.)	1887-1905
	47d	Ferdinand Heim Brewery (br. of Kansas City Breweries Co.)	1905-1919
MO	48	Midwest Brewing Co. (3028 E. 18th & Agnes Sts.)	1934-1938
MO	49	M. Schandler Bottling Co. (12 E. 3rd St.)	1890-1891
MO	50a	Walter L. Schmidt (1701 Holmes St.)	1898-1913
	50b	Frank J. Quigg (1700 Madison St.)	1913-1915
MO	51	P. Setzler & Sons	1898-1899
MO	52	Stulz Bros. (618 Southwest Blvd.)	1915-1916
MO	53	Swedish Ale Mfg. Co. (2928 Fairmount Ave.)	1902-1902

Kimswick

MO	54	Charles G. Gehre	1875-1875

Kirksville

MO	55	A. D. Maloney & Co.	1878-1878
MO	56	Henry Sloan	1878-1878

Lexington

MO	57a	Ernst Hoffmann	1875-1893
	57b	Lexington Brewing Co.	1901-1919
	57c	Lexington Brewing Co. (212 S. 11th St.)	1935-1935

Louisiana

MO	58a	Lissette Wahl	1875-1875
	58b	William Winkler	1875-1882
	58c	George Wahl	1882-1888

Macon

MO	59a	Dorner & Steinbrecher	1874-1877
	59b	George Steinbrecher	1877-1884
	59c	Macon Brewing Co.	1884-1890

Manchester

MO	60	Ferdinand Heim	1857-1859

Marionville

MO	61a	Crescent Brewing Co. (Elm & Logan Sts.)	1934-1935
	61b	Pride of Missouri Brewing Co.	1935-1938
	61c	McGovern Brewery Co.	1938-1940

Marshall

MO	62	J. G. Steinemann	1882-1882

Maryville

MO	63a	William Sutter	1874-1877
	63b	Weissendorfer & Co.	1877-1884

Middlebrook

MO	64a	Thomas Seitz	1874-1877
	64b	Edward Seitz	1877-1880

Moberly

MO	65	G. F. Hochberger	1874-1884

Neosho

MO	66a	Fred. W. Mertins	1874-1875
	66b	Charles Hamm	1875-1884

Old Appleton (formerly Appleton)

MO	67a	Casper Ludwig	1874-1904
	67b	Appleton Brewing Co.	1906-1908
	67c	Appleton Brewing and Ice Co., aka Appleton Brewery and Ice Co.	1908-1919
	67d	Appleton Brewery and Ice Co.	1933-1934
	67e	McGovern Brewery Co.	1934-1938
	67f	Appleton Brewery Co.	1940-1947

Palmyra

MO	68a	A. Hiner & Co.	1874-1877
	68b	A. Hiner	1877-1879
	68c	A. Hiner & Co.	1879-1888
MO	69	Christopher Menge	1874-1880

Perryville

MO	70	F. Strobel & Co.	1874-1880

Princeton

MO	71a	F. Aufricht	1874-1877
	71b	Ferd. Antricht & Co.	1877-1879
	71c	Stroh Bros.	1879-1882
	71d	Hulka & Stocklasa	1882-1884

Rock Port

MO	72a	R. Sommerhaeuser	1874-1877
	72b	William Hartman	1877-1884
	72c	Wm. Sutter	1884-1891

St. Charles

MO	73a	(Thomas) Ruenzi & (Bernard) Fetter	1849-1852
	73b	Deobold Schaefer	1852-1860
	73c	Stachlen & Stewart	1860-1870
	73d	Ernestine Schaefer (Clay St.)	1870-1889
	73e	Charles Schibi	1889-1907
	73f	Schibi Brewing Co.	1907-1908
	73g	Fischbach Brewing Co. (Benton Ave. & Clay St.)	1908-1919
MO	74a	Theo. Runge	1878-1884
	74b	Jacob Moerschel (3rd & Water Sts.)	1884-1900
	74c	Moerschel Spring Brewing Co.	1900-1912
	74d	Schibi Spring Brewing Co.	1912-1919
	74e	The Fischbach Brewing Co. (300 Water & 3rd Sts.) aka Grand Lager Brewing Co. (1953-1965) aka Kol Brewing Co. (1957-1959) aka Skooner Brewing Co. (1961-1964)	1933-1966
	74f	Van Dyke Brewing Co. aka Cardinal Brewing Co.	1967-1970

St. Genevieve

MO	75a	Valentine Rottler (3rd St.)	1874-1893
	75b	St. Genevieve Brewing and Lighting Association	1893-1919

St. Joseph

MO	76	Aniser & Co. (Frederick Ave. between 12th & 13th Sts.)	1861- ?
MO	77	Dietrich	c1864
MO	78	Fetzner & Co.	1867-1872
MO	79a	M. K. Goetz & Co., City Brewery (6th & Albemarle Sts.)	1859-1882
	79b	M. K. Goetz	1882-1895
	79c	M. K. Goetz Brewing Co.	1895-1919
	79d	M. K. Goetz Brewing Co. (603 Albemarle St.)	1933-1961
	79e	M. K. Goetz div. Pearl Brewing Co., aka Pearl Brewing Co. (br. of San Antonio, TX)	1961-1976

St. Joseph (cont.)

MO	80	William Hoffman	1868-1872
MO	81	Home Brewing Co.	1900-1900
MO	82	Frederick Islaub & Co. (near Levee & Franklin Sts.)	1858- ?
MO	83	John Jester (1308 Sacramento St.)	1879-1899
MO	84	Louis Koerner	c1864-1875
MO	85a	Joseph Kuechle (Charles & 7th Sts.)	1853-1875
	85b	E. J. Kuechle	1875-1880
	85c	Kuechle & Greiner	1880-1882
	85d	John B. Huber & Co.	1882-1888
	85e	St. Joseph Brewing Co.	1888-1895
MO	86	William Liebig	1867-1872
MO	87	Lowenstein	c1864
MO	88a	Henry Nunning (Frederick Ave. & Faraon St.)	1855-1877
	88b	Henry Nunning & Son (August)	1877-1884
	88c	August Nunning	1884-1886
	88d	August Nunning Brewing Co.	1886-1890
	88e	St. Joseph Brewing Co. (15th & Faraon Sts.)	1895-1919
MO	89a	Ohnesorg & Eger	1862-1877
	89b	Ohnesorg & Co.	1877-1879
	89c	Shaefer & Rosenmund (717 Felix St.)	1879-1882
MO	90a	Star Brewing Co. (10th & 108 Jackson Sts.)	1901-1907
	90b	Peter J. Schenk	1907-1919
MO	91	Peter Walter (4th & Edmond Sts.)	c1858

St. Louis

MO	92a	American Weiss Beer Co. (1940/1942 N. Broadway)	1888-1890
	92b	American Weiss Beer Brewery (1904/1906 N. Broadway), August Hauschild	1890-1893
	92c	American Weiss Beer Brewery, Lohmueller & Beuber	1894-1899
	92d	American Weiss Beer Brewery, Charles E. Lohmueller	1899-1900
MO	93a	W. F. Bartalls, Rocky Branch Brewery (9th & Tyler Sts.)	1844-1851
	93b	Zoller & Blome, Rocky Branch Brewery (Bellefontaine St.)	1851-1853
	93c	Charles Zoller, Rocky Branch Brewery (9th & Tyler Sts.)	1853-1860
	93d	Charles Zoller, Rocky Branch Brewery (Bellefontaine Road)	1860-1860
	93e	Peter Haxel, Rocky Branch Brewery	1860-1864
	93f	Windeck & Co.	1866-1868
MO	94a	Charles F. Becker, Liberty Brewery (21st & Dodier Sts.)	1865-1866
	94b	Becker & Kuester, Liberty Brewery	1866-1868
	94c	John H. Kuester, Liberty Brewery	1868-1869
	94d	Heidbreder & Co., Liberty Brewery	1869-1870
	94e	John F. Heidbreder & Co.	1870-1872
	94f	Heidbreder & Neimann, Liberty Brewery	1872-1874
	94g	John F. Heidbreder, Liberty Brewery	1874-1882
	94h	Liberty Brewing Co. (2534 Dodier St.)	1883-1890
	94i	St. Louis Brewing Association, Liberty Brewery	1890-1893
	94j	Burton Ale & Porter Brewing Co.	1899-1902
MO	95a	Thomas Biddle, Phoenix Brewery	c1825
	95b	Fleischbein & Ketterer, Phoenix Brewery (44 S. Front St.)	1835-1839
	95c	Gronenbold & Ketterer, Phoenix Brewery (Front & Myrtle Sts.)	1839-1841
	95d	Staehlin & Ketterer, Phoenix Brewery (Lafayette & 2nd Carondelet Aves.)	1841-1852
	95e	Christian Staehlin, Phoenix Brewery	1852-1859
	95f	Staehlin & Halm, Phoenix Brewery	1859-1864
	95g	Staehlin & Breidenbach, Phoenix Brewery	1864-1866
	95h	Christian Staehlin, Phoenix Brewery aka Phoenix Brewery Co. (1874)	1866-1875
	95i	St. Louis Brewery Co.	1875-1881
	95j	Anton Griesedieck Brewing Co.	1883-1889
	95k	St. Louis Brewing Association, Griesedieck Brewery	1889-1891
	95l	St. Louis Brewing Association, Phoenix Brewery	1891-1912
	95m	Marth Brewing Corp.	NP 1934-1934

St. Louis (cont.)

MO	96a	Leon Block (6th & Market Sts.)	? -1851
	96b	Leon Block & Bros.	1851-1854
MO	97	Blowser (98 2nd St.)	c1852
MO	98	Jacob Brandenberger, City Brewery (214 Cherry St.)	1867-1868
MO	99a	Charles & Richard Brewer, Franklin Brewery (Market & 17th Sts.)	1848-1851
	99b	Brewer & Son, Franklin Brewery	1851-1852
	99c	Rich. Brewer, Franklin Brewery	1852-1854
	99d	Tinker Brothers & Co., Franklin Brewery (17th & Clark Ave.)	1854-1866
	99e	John B. Fleming, Franklin Brewery (255 S. 17th St.)	1866-1873
	99f	Fleming & Co. (212 N. 3rd St.)	1874-1875
	99g	Fleming Ale Brewery (210 N. 2nd St.)	1875-1878
MO	100	Rudolph Brisselbach	c1855
MO	101a	George Busch, Busch's Brewery (134 S. 3rd & Plum Sts.)	1848-1854
	101b	Buena Vista Brewery	1854-1855
MO	102a	J. G. Buttner, Jackson Brewery (Easton St. near Victor St.)	1857-1859
	102b	Jacob Steuber, Jackson Brewery	1859-1865
	102c	Jacob Decker, Jackson Brewery	1865-1868
MO	103	Brandon Cairns & Co. (11th St. near Market St.)	c1866
MO	104	Carondelet Brewing Co., aka Greentrees Breweries, Inc. (2025 Gravois Ave.)	1933-1940
MO	105a	Columbia Brewing Co. (20th & Madison Sts.)	1892-1906
	105b	Independent Breweries Co., Columbia Brewery	1906-1919
	105c	Columbia Brewing Co. (2000 Madison St.)	1934-1948
	105d	Falstaff Brewing Co.	1948-1967
MO	106a	Columbia Weiss Beer Brewery, Samuel King (2543/2545 Dodier St.)	1898-1901
	106b	Columbia Weiss Beer Brewery, H. Leonard Gross	1901-1909
	106c	Missouri Weiss Beer Brewing Co., Columbia Weiss Beer Brewery	1909-1919
MO	107	John Coons	1809-1811
MO	108a	Coste, Krochling & Co., Pittsburgh Brewery (439/441 Carondelet Ave. between Sidney & Victor Sts.)	1857-1859
	108b	Coste & Leusler, Pittsburgh Brewery	1859-1869
	108c	A. Leussler & Co., Pittsburgh Brewery (2506 Carondelet Ave.)	1869-1876
MO	109a	Empire Brewing Co. (Sarah St. & Wabash Ry.)	1901-1906
	109b	Independent Breweries Co., Empire Brewery	1906-1919
	109c	Empire Brewing Co. (Sarah St. & Duncan Ave.)	1934-1934
MO	110a	E. O. English, Jr. (241 S. 4th St.)	1864-1866
	110b	E. O. English, Jr. (Chouteau Ave. & Convent, 13th & 14th Sts.)	1867-1868
MO	111a	James & William Finney, City Brewery	1834-1849
	111b	Stifel & Co., City Brewery (217 Broadway)	1849-1851
	111c	C. & J. Stifel, City Brewery (62/63 Cherry St. between 2nd St. & Broadway)	1851-1852
	111d	Charles G. Stifel, City Brewery (38/40 Cherry St.)	1852-1859
	111e	Charles G. Stifel, City Brewery (1911 N. 14th)	1859-1880
	111f	Charles G. Stifel's Brewing Co.	1880-1889
	111g	St. Louis Brewing Association, Charles G. Stifel's Brewery	1889-1904
	111h	St. Louis Brewing Association, City Brewery (1402 Chambers St.)	1904-1919
MO	112a	Joseph L. Fischgens, Laurel Brewery (Hickory btw. 7th & 8th)	1845-1852
	112b	Jaeger & Neff, Laurel Brewery	1853-1855
	112c	Fred Groeninger, Laurel Brewery	1856-1857
	112d	Conrad Elliot, Hickory Brewery	1858-1860
	112e	P. R. Alexander & Co.	1860-1861
MO	113a	Forest Park Brewing Co. (3662/3884 Forest Park Blvd. & Spring)	1910-1917
	113b	Griesedieck Beverage Co.	1917-1920
	113c	The Falstaff Corp.	1920-1933
	113d	Falstaff Brewing Corp. (Plant 2)	1933-1958
MO	114	C. W. Fries (806 S. 2nd St.)	1888-1891

St. Louis (cont.)

MO	115a	Jacob Fritz, Carondelet Brewery (2nd btwn. Market & Grundy)	c1859
	115b	Ferdinand Gsell	1873-1874
	115c	Alfonse Gsell	1874-1875
MO	116	John Gankman	c1860
MO	117	John Gast (Carondelet Ave.)	1844-1851
MO	118a	Gast Brewing Co. (8500 N. Broadway & Hornsby Ave.)	1900-1906
	118b	Gast Brewery, Inc.	1906-1908
	118c	Independent Breweries, Gast Brewery	1908-1919
	118d	Gast Brewery, Inc. (851 Hornsby Ave.)	1934-1946
	118e	Gast St. Louis Brewing Co.	1946-1948
MO	119a	Adolph Gebhard & Meyer, Iron Mountain Brewery (704 Jackson)	1856-1858
	119b	Adolph Gebhard, Iron Mountain Brewery	1858-1873
	119c	John Kuepfert, Iron Mountain Brewery	1873-1875
MO	120a	Great Western Weiss Beer Co. (3107/3113 N. 11th St.)	1887-1888
	120b	Saint Louis Weiss Beer Brewing Co.	1888-1906
MO	121a	Henry Grone & Co., Clark Ave. Brewery (2211/2219 Clark Ave.) aka Grone & Whelan (1878-1879) aka Grone, Whelan & Link (1880)	1861-1882
	121b	H. Grone Brewery Co.	1882-1889
	121c	St. Louis Brewing Assn., H. Grone Brewery	1889-1919
	121d	Grone Brewing Co. (2217 Clark Ave.)	NP 1934-1934
MO	122	Joseph Guggemos (3027 N. 11th St.)	1890-1891
MO	123a	Joseph Halm (2nd Carondelet Ave. bn. Geyer & Lafayette Ave.)	1865-1868
	123b	Henry Mick (1627 S. Carondelet Ave.)	1868-1871
MO	124a	F. R. S. Hama, Jefferson Brewery (Franklin bn. 17th & 18th)	1851-1854
	124b	Bruenning & Wettekamp, Jefferson Brewery (381 Franklin Ave.)	1854-1860
	124c	Bruning & Linze (Morgan St. bn. 25th & 26th Sts.)	c1864
MO	125a	John J. Hamm, Washington St. Brewery (15th & Washington St.)	1853-1858
	125b	Hamm & Hoppe, Washington St. Brewery	1858-1864
	125c	John J. Hamm	1864-1866
	125d	Robert Lungstras	1866-1867
MO	126a	Carl Hannemann (Hebert & Plank Sts.)	1857- ?
	126b	Mrs. Lina Hannemann (20th & Hebert Sts.)	1865- ?
	126c	Hannemann & Deuber, Weiss Beer Brewery, aka George Deuber (20th & Dodier Sts.)	1873-1883
	126d	Lena W. Hannemann (25th & Dodier Sts.)	1888-1888
MO	127a	Hay & Wagner, National Brewery (153/155 S. 2nd St. between Plum & Atwood Sts.)	1848-1857
	127b	Fred Wagner, National Brewery	1857-1860
MO	128	Charles Heitz, Schricker & Co. (Alley near Hazel St.)	c1859
MO	129a	(Fred) Herold & (George) Loebs, Cherokee Brewery (Cherokee St. & Iowa Ave.)	1867-1876
	129b	Cherokee Brewery Co.	1876-1889
	129c	St. Louis Brewing Assn., Cherokee Brewery (2726 Cherokee St.)	1889-1902
MO	130a	Herschfeld & Co., Philadelphia Brewery (670 Morgan St.)	1856-1859
	130b	Adolphus Deutschmoser, Philadelphia Brewery	1859-1860
	130c	William Oberschelp (Morgan St. between 25th & 26th)	? -1866
	130d	Oberschelp & Anthony, Philadelphia Brewery (2620 Morgan St.)	1866-1868
	130e	Henry Anthony & Francis Kuhn, Philadelphia Brewery	1868-1869
MO	131a	Charles Hoelzle, Excelsior Brewery (2814/2824 7th near Lynch)	1857-1859
	131b	Casper Koehler & Co., Excelsior Brewery	1859-1863
	131c	Henry Koehler & Brother (Casper)	1863-1868
	131d	H. Koehler & Co. (Philip Hehner)	1868-1870
	131e	H. Koehler & Co. (Jacob Heimenz)	1868-1872
	131f	C. Koehler & Co. (Jacob Heimenz)	1872-1876
	131g	Excelsior Brewery Co.	1876-1880
	131h	Henry Koehler Brewing Association	1880-1882
	131i	American Brewing Co. (S. 7th & 2814/2825 S. Broadway)	1890-1906
	131j	Independent Breweries Co., American Brewery	1906-1919

St. Louis (cont.)

MO	131k	A. B. C. Brewing Corp.	1934-1936
	131l	A. B. C. Brewing Corp. (Br. of Champagne Velvet Brewery, Terre Haute, IN)	1936-1938
	131m	A. B. C. Brewing Co.	1939-1940
MO	132	Sam Jackson (159 S. 2nd St.)	c1836
MO	133a	Anton Jaeger, Gambrinus Brewery (Menard St. bn. Sidney & Victor Sts.)	1857-1863
	133b	Crone & Co.	1864-1864
	133c	Charles A. Huber, Jaeger's Brewery	1865-1866
	133d	(Charles A.) Huber & (Herman) Apel, Jaeger's Brewery	1866-1868
	133e	Charles A. Huber, Jaeger's Brewery	1868-1870
	133f	(Henry) Anthony & (Francis) Kuhn (Sidney, Buel & Menard Sts.)	1870-1884
	133g	Anthony & Kuhn Brewing Co.	1884-1889
	133h	St. Louis Brewing Co., Anthony & Kuhn Brewery (11th between Victor & Sdiney Sts.)	1889-1899
MO	134	Jeffery Jefferson (98 S. 14th St.)	c1860
MO	135	Ideal Brewery (1629 S. 13th St.)	1898-1899
MO	136a	F. Kertzinger, Mound Brewery (Broadway & Webster)	1852-1854
	136b	F. Kertzinger, Kertzinger's Cave Brewery	1854-1858
MO	137a	Louis Koch, Schlop Brewery (816/822 Sidney & Buel Sts.)	1860-1874
	137b	Koch & Feldkamp	1874-1875
	137c	Koch & Schilling Brewing Co.	1875-1882
	137d	Schilling & Schneider Brewing Co.	1882-1889
	137e	St. Louis Brewing Assn., Schilling & Schneider Brewery (10th & Sidney Sts.)	1889-1891
MO	138a	Kuntz & Hoffmeister, Pacific Brewery (16th & Singleton)	1860-1871
	138b	Henry Kuntz, Pacific Brewery	1871-1872
MO	139a	Michael Kuntz, Lafayette Brewery (68/70 Car St.)	1843-1849
	139b	Berges & Brinkwirth, Lafayette Brewery	1849-1858
	139c	Theodore Brinkwirth, Lafayette Brewery	1858-1864
	139d	(T.) Brinkwirth & (Frank) Griesedieck, Lafayette Brewery (1820 Cass Ave. & 19th St.)	1864-1874
	139e	Brinkwirth, Griesedieck & Nolker, Lafayette Brewery	1874-1879
	139f	Brinkwirth & (Wm.) Nolker	1879-1883
	139g	Brinkwirth-Nolker Brewing Co.	1883-1889
	139h	St. Louis Brewing Assn., Brinkwirth-Nolker Brewery (1714 Cass)	1889-1907
	139i	St. Louis Brewing Assn., Lafayette Brewery	1907-1910
MO	140a	Andrew A. LeBeau & Co., St. Louis Steam Brewery	1856-1858
	140b	J. F. Boyd & Co., Steam Brewery (263/265 Main St.)	1858-1860
MO	141	Ch. Longuemare, Stern Brewery (148 Carondelet Ave.)	1858-1860
MO	142a	Louis Loos (65 S. 7th St.)	c1864
	142b	Stamm & Co., Weiss Beer Brewery	c1866
MO	143	Lungstras & Co.	c1860
MO	144a	James C. Lynch, New St. Louis Brewery	1826-1835
	144b	James C. Lynch & Son, Jefferson Brewery	1838-1839
MO	145	William Metcalfe & Son (Church St. bn. Plum & Cedar Sts.)	1838-1840
MO	146	Missouri Brewing Co. (120 Iron St.)	1934-1937
MO	147a	William Moran, Emmet Brewery (Salisbury & 16th St.)	1862-1876
	147b	Robert Jacob & Co., Hyde Park Brewery	1876-1878
	147c	Hyde Park Brewery Co. aka Marquard Foster, Hyde Park Brewery	1878-1889
	147d	St. Louis Brewing Assn., Hyde Park Brewery (Florissant Ave. & Salisbury St.)	1889-1919
	147e	Hyde Park Breweries Assn., Inc.	1933-1948
	147f	Griesedieck Western Brewery Co.	1948-1954
	147g	Carling Brewing Co.	1954-1957
MO	148	Mutual Brewing Co. (224/236 S. Boyle Ave.)	1912-1916
MO	149a	National Brewery Co. (18th & Gratiot Sts.)	1888-1906
	149b	Independent Breweries Co., National Brewery	1906-1919

St. Louis (cont.)

MO	150a	C. Niemann, Steam Brewery (146 Carondelet Ave.)	1857-1859
	150b	George Rothweiler, Star Brewery aka Rothweiler & Christopher Sutter (1866)	1863-1868
MO	151a	Pearson, Smith & Co., Bellefontaine Brewery (49 N. Commercial)	1856-1860
	151b	John Williamson & Co. (77 Commercial St.)	? -1864
	151c	John Williamson, Bellefontaine Brewery (17 Locust St.)	1864-1865
	151d	English & Quinlivan, Southern Ale Brewery (17 Locust & 251 Biddle Sts.)	1865-1866
MO	152a	Robert Peyinghaus & Co., Missouri Brewery	c1852
	152b	G. Bautenstrauch, Missouri Brewery (18th & Morgan Sts.)	c1860
MO	153a	Fred Pfund (155 Carondelet Ave.)	1857-1859
	153b	Eckerle & Weiss, German Brewery	1859-1865
	153c	(Theodore) Eckerle & (Ferdinand) Siemon aka Eckerle & Co. (1866)	1865-1867
	153d	Theodore Eckerle, German Brewery (1710/1712 Carondelet Ave. & Miami St.)	1867-1870
	153e	Theodore Eckerle, German Brewery (Miami St. & Capitol Ave.)	1870-1871
	153f	E. Anheuser & Co., Bavarian Brewery Branch	1873-1875
	153g	E. Anheuser & Co's Brewing Association	1875-1879
	153h	Home Brewing Co. (Main & Salena Sts.)	1892-1901
	153i	Independent Breweries Co., Home Brewery	1907-1909
MO	154a	Joseph Philipson, St. Louis Brewery (Main & Carr)	1817-1820
	154b	Matthew Murphy, Nagle & Philipson, St. Louis Brewery	1820-1821
	154c	Joseph Philipson	1821-1821
	154d	Simon Philipson	1821-1824
	154e	John Mullanphy	1824-1829
MO	155a	Pilsener Weiss Beer Brewery Co. (1877 S. 13th St.)	1896-1897
	155b	Pilsener Weiss Beer Brewery Co. (811 S. 17th St.)	1897-1898
MO	156	Reid & Co., Calledonian Brewery (24th & Morgan)	c1852
MO	157	Reising & Chambers (1503 S. 7th St.)	1867-1868
MO	158	Royal Breweries, Inc. (1030/1040 Victor)	1934-1934
MO	159a	F. Schaeffer & Co., Salvator Brewery (Carondelet Ave. btwn. Marion & Carroll Sts.)	1853-1859
	159b	Schaeffer, Boernstein & Co. (82 Carondelet)	1858-1859
MO	160	N. Schaeffer (2nd Carondelet Ave.)	1874-1875
MO	161a	John Schmidt (Soulard St. & Carondelet Ave.)	c1845
	161b	Constantine Schnerr, Schnerr's Brewery	1854-1858
	161c	Constantine Schnerr (1206 Park Ave. btwn. 12th & 13th Sts.)	1858-1868
MO	162a	Joseph Schmitt & Co., Lowell Brewery (Bryan Ave. & Broadway)	1866-1867
	162b	Schmitt & Leonori, Lowell Brewery	1867-1868
	162c	Joseph Schmitt, Lowell Brewery	1868-1869
MO	163a	Jos. Schnaider, Choteau Av. Brewery (Choteau Ave. between Mississippi & Armstrong Aves.) aka Schnaider & Breidenbach (1867-1868)	1865-1879
	163b	Jos. Schnaider Brewing Co., aka Joseph Schnaider's Brewing Co. (2000 Choteau Ave.)	1879-1889
	163c	St. Louis Brewing Assn., Jos. Schnaider's Choteau Ave. Brewery	1889-1893
MO	164a	J. Schnaider (Wood & Miller Sts.)	1853-1855
	164b	Jos. Schnaider, Green Tree Brewery (135/137 S. 2nd St.)	1855-1858
	164c	Jos. Schnaider & Co., Green Tree Brewery, aka Schnaider & Feuerbacher, Green Tree Brewery	1858-1865
	164d	Feuerbacher & Schlosstein, Green Tree Brewery (906 Sidney)	1865-1880
	164e	Green Tree Brewery Co.	1889-1889
	164f	St. Louis Brewing Assn., Green Tree Brewery	1889-1919
MO	165a	George Schneider (Carondelet Ave. btwn. Lynch & Dorcas Sts.)	1852-1856
	165b	George Schneider, Bavarian Brewery (8th St. between Pestalozzi & Crittenden Sts.)	1856-1857
	165c	Philip Carl Hammer & Co., (Adam Hammer), Bavarian Brewery	1857-1858
	165d	Adam Hammer & Dominic Urban, Bavarian Brewery	1858-1860
	165e	Eberhard Anheuser & Co. (Wm. D'Oench), Bavarian Brewery	1860-1875
	165f	E. Anheuser & Co.'s Brewing Association	1875-1879

St. Louis (cont.)

MO 165g Anheuser-Busch Brewing Association 1879-1919
165h Anheuser-Busch, Inc. (721 Pestalozzi St.) 1933-

MO 166a George Schneider, Washington Brewery (545 3rd & Elm Sts.) 1844-1853
166b John Ruedy, Washington Brewery 1853-1854
166c Charles Schneider, Washington Brewery (Carondelet Ave. between Harper & Anna Sts.) 1858-1861

MO 167a Constantine Schnerr, Star Brewery (Rosatti St. & Park Ave.) 1851-1853
167b (Johann) Gaul & Reinhardt, Star Brewery 1853-1854
167c Reinhardt & Vager, Star Brewery 1854-1855
167d John Gaul (13th & Park Ave.) c1865

MO 168a Schorr Brewing Co. (Natural Bridge Road & Farrar Sts.) 1901-1902
168b Schorr-Kolkschneider Brewing Co. (2537 Natural Bridge Road & Parnell St.) 1902-1919
168c Schorr-Kolkschneider Brewing Co. 1933-1939

MO 169a J. Schroeder (834 Chouteau Ave.) 1888-1890
169b Schroeder's Berliner Weiss Beer Co. (1013 Paul St.) 1890-1917

MO 170 Fred. Schultz, aka Berlin Weiss Beer Brewing Co. (1108 S. 11th) 1888-1891

MO 171a Ch. Schumann, Schumann's Brewery 1860-1860

MO 172 Scotch Hop Ale Co. (729 Clark Ave.) 1915-1916

MO 173 Small & Rohr, Missouri Brewery 1837-1841

MO 174 Charles Smith (146 Washington St.) c1845

MO 175 S. D. Smith & Co. (Washington Ave. & 7th St.) c1845

MO 176a Louis Spori, aka L. Sperri & Co., New Bremen Brewery (Broadway & Maguire St. near Bremen St.) 1842-1859
176b Tobias Spengler, New Bremen Brewery 1859-1871
aka Spengler & Smith (1860)
176c Tobias Spengler & Son, Bremen Brewery (3823 Broadway) 1871-1879
176d T. Spengler & Co., Bremen Brewery 1879-1886
176e Bremen Brewery Co. (3905/3913 S. Broadway) 1886-1889
176f St. Louis Brewing Assn., Bremen Brewery 1889-1905

MO 177 August Spitzbarth (3905 Kossuth St.) 1890-1893

MO 178a A. & G. Steinkauler, Arsenal Brewery (Carondelet between Sidney & Lynch Sts.) 1853-1859
178b Guido Steinkauler, Arsenal Brewery 1859-1863
178c Weiss & Hehner, Arsenal Brewery 1863-1866
178d Mathias Weiss, Arsenal Brewery (2701/2705 Carondelet Ave.) 1866-1874
178e Wahl & Leiss, Arsenal Brewery (Lynch & State Sts.) 1874-1876
178f M. Weiss & Obert, Arsenal Brewery 1876-1881
178g Louis Obert, Arsenal Brewery (Lynch & 12th Sts.) 1881-1900
178h Louis Obert Brewing Co. (2700 S. 12th St.) 1900-1919
178i Louis Obert Brewing Co. 1933-1936

MO 179a (Fred) Stifel & (Julius) Winkelmeyer, Union Brewery (352 S. 2nd St. between Convent & Rutger Sts.) 1843-1847
179b Stifel & Winkelmeyer, Union Brewery (Market St. bn. 17th & 18th) 1847-1848
179c Jul. Winkelmeyer, Union Brewery 1848-1857
179d Winkelmeyer & (George) Schiffer, Union Brewery 1857-1864
179e Julius Winkelmeyer, Union Brewery 1864-1869
179f J. Winkelmeyer & Co., Union Brewery (1700/1714 Market St.) 1869-1879
179g Julius Winkelmeyer Brewing Association 1879-1889
179h St. Louis Brewing Assn., Jul. Winkelmeyer Brewery 1889-1892

MO 180a Stephen Stock Oregon Brewery (412/414 S. 7th St. between Barry & Main Sts.) 1843-1864
aka Stock Brothers (1860)
180b Windecke & Heitcamp 1864-1865
180c John Neff, Mississippi Valley Brewery 1865-1866

MO 181a Ch. Stolzh, Laclede Brewery c1860
181b August Wetekamp & Co., Laclede Brewery (Estelle & Naomi Sts.) 1863-1868
181c August Wetekamp, Laclede Brewery (22nd & Walnut Sts.) 1868-1870
181d Ausust Wetekamp & Co., Laclede Brewery 1870-1877

St. Louis (cont.)

MO	182a	Wm. Stumpf (Ann Ave. & Decatur St.)	1850-1857
	182b	Stumpf, Hoppe & Krug	1857-1857
	182c	Stumpf, Hazen & Krug, Stumpf's Brewery	1857-1858
	182d	William Stumpf, Stumpf's Brewery	1858-1860
	182e	Stumpf & Lemp	1860-1866
	182f	Wm. Stumpf (Buena Vista St & Shenandoah Ave.)	1866-1875
	182g	Wm. Stumpf & Co.	1875-1877
	182h	Thamer Brewing Co.	1877-1879
	182i	Anton Griesedieck & Co.	1879-1882
	182j	Miller & Wagenhaeuser	1882-1884
	182k	Miller Bros. Brewery Co. (2301 Buena Vista St.)	1884-1889
	182l	St. Louis Brewing Assn., Miller Bros. Brewery	1889-1890
	182m	Consumers Brewing Co. (1900 Shenandoah Ave.)	1896-1906
	182n	Independent Breweries Co., Consumers' Brewery	1906-1911
	182o	Griesedieck Bros. Brewing Co.	1911-1919
	182p	Griesedieck Bros. Brewery Co., aka Lami Brewing Co.	1933-1957
	182q	Falstaff Brewing Corp., aka Griesedieck Bros., James Hanley Co.	1957-1975
	182r	Falstaff Brewing Corp., affiliated with General Brewing Co., San Francisco, CA	1975-1977
MO	183a	Tener & Fischer (Park Ave. & Hamptramack)	1865-1866
	183b	Fischer & (Christian) Zeiner, Atlantic Brewery (1804 Park Ave.)	1866-1868
MO	184a	Julius Thomas (Mallinckrodt below Broadway)	c1859
	184b	Frederick Angelbeck (Bellefontaine & Mallinckrodt)	1864-1866
MO	185a	William C. Trumbour, St. Louis Ale Brewery (75 Commercial St.)	c1864
	185b	Cooper & Conger	1864-1864
	185c	B. F. Young & Co., St. Louis Ale Brewery	1864-1866
	185d	B. F. Young & Co., Young's Premium Ale Brewery (313 N. Commericial St.)	1866-1868
MO	186a	Ignatz Uhrig (Pratt Ave. btwn. Locust St. & Washington Ave.)	c1857
	186b	Herman Apfel	c1864
MO	187a	(Joseph) Uhrig & (Wm.) Kraut, Camp Spring Brewery (1800 Market & 18th Sts.)	1847-1849
	187b	Joseph Uhrig, Camp Spring Brewery	1849-1874
	187c	Joseph Uhrig & Co., Camp Spring Brewery	1874-1876
	187d	Jos. Uhrig Brewing Co.	1876-1880
	187e	Mrs. Walsburga Uhrig	1880-1880
	187f	Excelsior Brewery Co.	1880-1889
	187g	St. Louis Brewing Assn., Excelsior Brewery	1889-1891
	187h	St. Louis Brewing Assn., Excelsior Brewery (5 S. 17th & Market Sts.)	1891-1916
MO	188a	Union Brewing Co. (Gravois & Michigan Aves.)	1898-1906
	188b	Otto F. Stifel's Union Brewing Co.	1906-1919
	188c	Falstaff Brewing Corp. (318 Michigan & Gravois Aves.)	1933-1951
MO	189a	Samuel Wainwright	1848- ?
	189b	(Chas. A.) Fritz & (Samuel) Wainwright	1857-1870
	189c	Samuel Wainwright (727 S. 9th St.)	1870-1883
	189d	Wainwright Brewery Co. (1015 Papin, 10th & 11th Sts.)	1883-1889
	189e	St. Louis Brewing Assn., Wainwright Brewery	1889-1919
MO	190a	Wainwright & Coutts, Fulton Brewery (21 Almond St.)	1831-1839
	190b	Wainwright & Coutts & Co., Fulton Brewery (1st & Almond Sts.)	1839-1841
	190c	Wainwright & Withnell, Fulton Brewery	1841-1846
	190d	Ellis Wainwright, Fulton Brewery (29 Almond St.)	1846-1848
	190e	Ellis & Samuel Wainwright, Fulton Brewery	1848-1850
	190f	Samuel Wainwright & Co., Fulton Brewery	1850-1851
	190g	Samuel Wainwright, Fulton Brewery (Almond btwn. Main & 2nd)	1851-1857
MO	191a	John M. Weyand, Lion Brewery (2840 Carondelet Ave. & Dorcas)	1865-1868
	191b	Martin, Weygand, Lion Brewery	1868-1869
MO	192a	Wittemann, Rost & Co. (211/213 Anna St.)	1888-1895
	192b	Wittemann-Rost Brewing Co. (1809 Arsenal St. & Lemp Ave.)	1895-1908
MO	193a	Zepp & Hartmann, National Brewery (Carondelet Ave. & Cherokee)	1869-1870
	193b	C. Wagner, National Brewery	1870-1870

St. Louis (cont.)

MO	194a	John G. Zoller, Broadway Brewery (55 Palm St.)	1857-1858
	194b	John G. Zoller & Co., Broadway Brewery	1858-1866
	194c	Bernard F. Young & Co., St. Louis Ale Brewery	1866-1875
	194d	B. F. Young, Chaddick Ale Brewery (508 Chestnut St.)	1875-1876
	194e	B. F. Young (121 N. 2nd St.) aka B. F. Young & Co. (1880-1884)	1878-1884

Salt River

MO	195	Amesbury & Walker	1875-1879

Sedalia

MO	196	Moerschel Brewing Co. (Main St. & Missouri Ave.)	1897-1919
MO	197a	Schell & Helm	1875-1877
	197b	Siebel & Helm	1877-1882
	197c	Sedalia Brewing Co.	1882-1893
	197d	Henry Weigand	1893-1897
	197e	Henry Weigand	1899-1919

Shelbina

MO	198a	Amesbury & Walker	1880-1882
	198b	Ray & Savage	1882-1884

Springfield

MO	199a	Philip Finkmann	1874-1877
	199b	Sebastian Dingeldein	1877-1893
	199c	Springfield Brewing Co. (1055 College St.)	1898-1911
	199d	Ozark Brewing Co.	1911-1913

Stockton

MO	200	M. Gast	1879-1879

Trenton

MO	201	Otto Schaub	1874-1875

Union

MO	202a	William Loemer	1875-1877
	202b	Richenmacher & Gory	1877-1880

Warrensburg

MO	203a	Philip Gross	1874-1891
	203b	Elizabeth Gross	1891-1896
	203c	Charles P. Anton	1896-1897
	203d	Franz Murche	1897-1906
	203e	Peter J. Schenk	1906-1907

Washington

MO	204a	John B. Busch (S. Jefferson St.)	1854-1893
	204b	John B. Busch Brewing Co.	1893-1919
MO	205	Peerless Brewing Co. (18 E. Front St.)	1934-1939

Weston

MO	206a	John Georgian (Hickory & 15th Sts.)	1842-1857
	206b	Joseph Kunz	1857-1864
	206c	August Kunz	1864-1872
	206d	Luther Teegarden	1875- ?
	206e	Weston Brewery	? -1885
	206f	Brandon & Mack	1885-1886
	206g	John Wahlruff	1886-1887
	206h	Weston Brewing Co. (Hickory & 15th Sts.)	1887-1901
	206i	Royal Brewing Co.	1901-1919

Wittenburg

MO	207a	Frank A. Brenner	1850-1877
	207b	C. D. Milster	1877-1879

MONTANA

Anaconda

MT	1a	Joseph Faul	1890-1895
	1b	Anaconda Brewing Co.	1895-1918
	1b	Anaconda Brewing Co. (1200 E. Park Ave.)	1933-1958
MT	2	Washoe Brewing Co.	1905- ?

Bannack

MT	3	James Harby	1874-1884

Barker

MT	4	Jos. Winkler	1893-1893

Basin

MT	5a	Basin Brewing Co.	1905-1908
	5b	State Brewing Co.	1908-1910

Beartown

MT	6	Charles Kroger	1874-1875

Billings

MT	7	Ash & Boots	1884-1884
MT	8a	Billings Brewing Co.	1899-1918
	8b	Billings Brewing Co. (2319 Montana Ave. & N. 24th St.)	1933-1952
MT	9a	Grampp & Co.	1884- ?
	9b	Rammchuger & Seelig	? -1888

Blackfoot

MT	10	George Schuster	1874-1875

Blackford City

MT	11	E. Beirzel	1874-1875

Bozeman

MT	12a	Spieth & Krug	1874-1888
	12b	Hellinger & Hansen	1888-1897
	12c	Julius Lehrkind	1897-1918
	12d	Gallatin Brewing Co., Inc. (805 N. Wallace Ave.)	1933-1939

Butte

MT	13	Beecher & Co.	1884-1884
MT	14	Louis P. Bowman	1890-1891
MT	15	Hugo J. Hoppe	1884-1884
MT	16a	Henry Muntzer (220 N. Wyoming St.)	1885-1899
	16b	Butte Brewing Co.	1899-1918
	16c	Butte Brewing Co.	1933-1960
	16d	Butte Brewing Corp.	1960-1963
MT	17	Olympia Brewing Co.	1899-1911
MT	18	Buol Saile	1879-1879
MT	19a	Leopold F. Schmidt	1876-1877
	19b	Schmidt & Garner, Centennial Brewery	1877-1884
	19c	Centennial Brewing Co. (112 N. Hamilton St.)	1884-1897
	19d	Centennial Brewery Co.	1897-1918
MT	20a	Tivoli Brewery, Huber & Co.	1900-1902
	20b	Tivoli Brewing Co.	1902-1918

Clendenin

MT	21	Joseph Winkler	1890-1891

Coulson

MT	22	Ash Bros.	1884-1884

Deer Lodge

MT	23a	Fenner & Co.	1874-1879
	23b	Fenner & Van Gundy	1879-1880
	23c	Jacob E. Van Gundy	1880-1884
	23d	J. E. Van Gundy & Co.	1884-1890
	23e	Van Gundy & Miller	1890-1891
	23f	J. E. Van Gundy & Co.	1891-1899
	23g	Gerstacker & Richards	1899-1901
	23h	Gerstacker & Doelker	1901-1902

Deer Lodge (cont.)

MT	23i	John Gerstacker & Co.	1902-1916
	23j	Western Brewery	1916-1918
MT	24a	Peter Valiton	1874-1877
	24b	Contancier & Fish	1877-1879
	24c	N. Contancier	1879-1884

Diamond City

MT	25	H. J. Ramspeck	1874-1880

Dillon

MT	26a	J. Trimborn	1888-1891
	26b	Burfeind Bros.	1891-1899
	26c	Dillon Brewery, James L. Weiser	1899-1906
	26d	Beaverhead Brewery, Ritz & Bechtold	1908-1909
	26e	Beaverhead Brewing Co.	1909-1918

Egan

MT	27	Lang & Lideman	1891-1891

Fort Benton

MT	28a	M. Longevine & Co.	1875-1877
	28b	Moersberger & Co.	1877-1882
	28c	J. H. Evans & Co.	1882-1884
	28d	Walstadt & Benz	1884-1888

Glendale

MT	29a	John Mannheim	1874-1877
	29b	Frank Gilg	1877-1879
	29c	Gilg & Hemrich	1879-1880
	29d	Louis Heinbockel & Co.	1880-1884

Great Falls

MT	30a	American Brewing and Malting Co. aka American Brewing Co. (1916-1918)	1895-1918
	30b	Great Falls Breweries, Inc. (410 14th St. S.W.)	1933-1944
	30c	Sicks' Great Falls Breweries, Inc.	1944-1949
	30d	Great Falls Breweries, Inc.	1949-1966
	30e	Great Falls Breweries, Inc. (br. of Blitz-Weinhard Co., Portland, OR)	1966-1968
MT	31a	Andrew Johnson	1891-1893
	31b	Montana Brewing Co. (Central Ave.)	1893-1918
	31c	Volk Brewery (324/326 3rd Ave. S.)	1935-1948
	31d	National Brewers, Inc. (310 4th St. S.)	1948-1950
MT	32	Volk Bros.	1891-1897

Havre

MT	33a	Havre Brewing Co.	1905-1906
	33b	Havre Brewing and Malting Co.	1911-1918

Helena (formerly Last Chance Gulch)

MT	34a	Charles Beehrer	1864-1865
	34b	Beehrer & Kessler	1865-1866
	34c	Nicholas Kessler	1866-1900
	34d	Kessler Brewing Co. (51 S. Main St.)	1900-1918
	34e	Kessler Brewing Co.	1934-1958
MT	35a	August Foller	1875-1888
	35b	Jacob Doerr	1888-1893
MT	36a	A. Gerhauser & Co.	1875-1877
	36b	B. Binzel	1877-1879
	36c	Weimar & Co.	1879-1882
	36d	M. Jakobi	1882-1884
MT	37a	Horsky & Butz	1865-1870
	37b	Horsky & (Jacob) King aka Horsky & Kuech (1874-1879)	1870-1884
	37c	Horsky, Miller & Co.	1884-1892
	37d	Miller & Co.	1892-1899
	37e	Helena Brewing Co.	1899-1901
	37f	Capital Brewing and Malting Co. (W. Main St.)	1901-1908
	37g	Capital City Brewing Co.	1908-1911

Helena (cont.)			
MT	38	Benjamin Schlegel	1890-1890
MT	39	Union Brewing Co.	1900-1900
Kalispell			
MT	40a	(Henry & Charles) Lindlahr & (Gust.) Garner	1893-1894
	40b	Kalispell Malting and Brewing Co.	1894-1918
	40c	Kalispell Malting and Brewing Co. (22 5th Ave. W.)	1933-1953
Last Chance Gulch (see Helena)			
Lewistown			
MT	41a	Lewistown Brewery, (Frank) Haas & (Philip) Laux	1894-1896
	41b	Lewistown Brewing Co. aka Bernard McDonnell (1903)	1901-1918
	41c	Lewistown Brewing Co., Inc.	1934-1935
	41d	Lewistown Brewery, Inc.	1935-1938
Livingston			
MT	42	Julius Lehrkind	1905-1918
Maiden			
MT	43	Landt & Co.	1888-1891
MT	44a	Schneider & Fleiner	1900-1901
	44b	Maiden Brewing Co.	1901-1901
Marysville			
MT	45a	Lorenz Zembsch	1882-1883
	45b	Zembsch & Co.	1883-1884
	45c	Henry Lindlahr aka Pafendorf & Lindlahr (1890)	1884-1898
	45d	Laier & Parisel	1898-1899
	45e	Marysville Brewery, Geo. Held	1899-1900
Miles			
MT	46a	Buch & Rodener	1879-1879
	46b	Lansing & McClane	1879-1880
	46c	W. H. Bullard	1880-1884
	46d	Fritz & Leonard	1884-1888
MT	47	Eastern Brewing Co.	1914-1916
Missoula			
MT	48a	George Gerber	1874-1877
	48b	John Hayes	1877-1879
	48c	Chas. Otto	1879-1884
	48d	Wagner & Pelikan	1884-1888
	48e	Joseph Wagner	1888-1891
	48f	Benz & Co.	1891-1893
	48g	Lang & Martin (Madison St.)	1896-1897
	48h	Garden City Brewery	1897-1898
	48i	Steiger & Co.	1898-1899
	48j	Garden City Brewing Co.	1899-1918
	48k	Missoula Brewing Co.	1933-1944
	48l	Sicks' Missoula Brewing Co.	1944-1949
	48m	Missoula Brewing Co., aka Highlander Brewing Co.	1949-1964
Philipsburg			
MT	49a	Christian Guth	1878-1879
	49b	Jacob Stortz	1879-1888
MT	50a	Charles Kroger	1875-1897
	50b	Estate of Charles Kroger, aka Kroger's Brewery	1897-1915
	50c	Philipsburg Brewing Co.	1915-1918
Pioneer			
MT	51	Peter Hauck	1874-1875
Radersburg			
MT	52a	John William Hamper	1874-1877
	52b	Thomas Dixon	1877-1884
Red Lodge			
MT	53	Red Lodge Brewing Co.	1911-1918

Rock Vale

MT 54 Walter Lehrkind 1900-1900

Salmon City

MT 55 Stadtmiller & Deck 1884-1884

Silesia

MT 56a Carbon County Brewery, Walter Lehrkind 1899-1906
56b Carbon Brewing Co. 1906-1908

Silverbow

MT 57a Nissler & Rapp 1869-1871
57b Christian Nissler 1871-1901
57c Christian Nissler's Estate 1901-1902
57d Silverbow Brewing Co. 1902-1905
57e Capital Brewing Co. 1905-1906
57f Crystal Brewery (131 W. Broadway) 1906-1911

Silver Star

MT 58a Lewis Fullhart 1875-1882
58b Frederick Sipfle 1882-1884

Sun River

MT 59a John Devine 1874-1875
59b G. W. Weigand 1875-1879
59c John Rohner 1879-1879

Townsend

MT 60a Thomas Dixon 1883-1912
60b Dixon Brewery 1912-1918

Twin Bridges

MT 61a Leybold Bros. 1898-1899
61b Twin Bridges Brewing Co. 1899-1900
61c Frederick Feilke 1900-1906

Virginia City

MT 62a Thomas Smith 1863- ?
62b Henry S. Gilbert (Coover & Hamilton Sts.) 1874-1903
62c Estate of Henry S. Gilbert 1903-1904
62d Gilbert Brewing Co. 1904-1918

NEBRASKA

Atkinson

NE 1a Mary Krajicek 1890-1891
1b Frank Wosterchill 1891-1901

Beatrice

NE 2a Coffin & Sonderegger 1879-1879
2b Wiswell & Sonderegger 1879-1880
2c Wiswell & Hochstrasser 1880-1882
2d Getzloff & Nass 1882-1884
2e Carl Mallon 1884-1886

Bloomington

NE 3 Ernst Arnold 1882-1901

Brownsville

NE 4 C. Schreiner 1882-1891

Buell

NE 5 August Boerner 1874-1875

Colfax

NE 6 Martin Jetter 1878-1884

Columbus

NE 7a Charles Brenner 1866-1875
7b Kersenbrock & Hengeler 1875-1880
7c Hengeler & Wandel 1880-1882
7d Joseph Hengeler 1882-1888
7e Kersenbrock & Mack 1888-1895
7f J. H. Kersenbrock (7th & Douglas Sts.) 1895-1905
7g Columbus Brewing Co. 1905-1917
7h The Columbus Brewing Co. (670/672 15th Ave.) 1933-1954

City	State	No.	Brewery	Notes	Dates
Crete					
	NE	8a	Melchior Neher		1872-1882
		8b	John H. Kersenbrock		1882-1884
		8c	Muff & Co.		1884-1888
		8d	William Muchow		1888-1902
		8e	Frank J. Kobes		1902-1903
		8f	Josephine Kobes		1903-1905
		8g	Western Brewing Assn.		1905-1906
		8h	Dr. (George R.) Miller Co., Crete Brewery (414 W. 13th St.)		1934-1942
Fairmount					
	NE	9	C. Rock		1878-1882
Falls City					
	NE	10a	Brackhahn & Fricke		1879-1879
		10b	Brackhahn Bros.		1879-1900
	NE	11	Falls City Brewing Co.		1910-1910
	NE	12a	Huber & Gehring		1882-1883
		12b	Michael Gehring & Son		1883-1884
		12c	Michael Gehring		1884-1895
		12d	Creszentia Gehling		1895-1907
		12e	Gehling Brewing Co.		1907-1916
		12f	Gehling Brewery		1916-1917
Franklin					
	NE	13	Ernst Arnold		1878-1884
Fremont					
	NE	14a	Fremont Brewing Co.		1891-1917
		14b	Fremont Brewing Co.	NP	1934-1934
	NE	15a	Magenan & Co.		1874-1877
		15b	E. Magenan		1877-1879
		15c	Oswald Miller		1879-1884
Grand Island					
	NE	16a	George Boehm		1873-1882
		16b	Mrs. Catherine Boehm		1882-1885
		16c	Andrew Ott		1885-1888
		16d	Catherine Ott		1888-1892
		16e	Lange Bros.		1892-1893
		16f	Lange Bros. Brewing Co.		1893-1897
		16g	Grand Island Brewing Co. (1100 Block W. Front)		1902-1907
		16h	Grand Island Brewing Co.		1913-1917
Grant					
	NE	17	F. W. Platz		1893-1893
Hastings					
	NE	18	Theo. Bauersachs		1888-1888
	NE	19	Alfred Calvert		? -1878
	NE	20	Hastings Brewing Co. (2nd & Minnesota Sts.)		1908-1917
Indianola					
	NE	21a	Schneider & Schmidt		1888-1889
		21b	Balthasar Lehn		1890-1893
Kearney					
	NE	22	Charles Harinz		1893-1893
Lead City					
	NE	23	M. Selig		1890-1890
Lincoln					
	NE	24a	J. Fitzgerald, Antelope Brewery		1878-1880
		24b	Fitzgerald & Co.		1880-1884
Nebraska City					
	NE	25a	Frederick Beyschlag		1859-1886
		25b	John Mattes		1886-1887
		25c	The Mattes Brewery		1887-1893
		25d	Mattes Brewing Co., aka Mattes Brewery Co.		1893-1906
		25e	Otoe Brewing Co.		1906-1917
	NE	26	Andrew Roos		1878-1897

Niobrara

NE	27a	Adam Foerster	1879-1880
	27b	Foerster & Leuger	1880-1884
	27c	Foerster & Gail	1884-1890
	27d	Adam Foerster	1890-1897
	27e	John Foerster	1897-1899
	27f	Anna Foerster	1899-1906

North Platte

NE	28a	Distel, Erickson & Co.	1878-1879
	28b	Distel & Erickson	1879-1884

Omaha (includes South Omaha)

NE	29a	P. B. Ballon	1874-1877
	29b	Albert Bacon	1877-1878
	29c	Richard Siemon	1882-1884
NE	30	The Brewer & Bemis Brewing Co.	1870-1878
NE	31	Cronemeyer & Windspear	1862-1872
NE	32a	Ebenezer Dallow	1863-1865
	32b	Joseph Baumann	1865-1876
	32c	Mrs. W. Baumann (Grace & 16th Sts.)	1876-1884
	32d	(Gottlieb) Storz & (Joseph D.) Iler	1884-1891
	32e	Omaha Brewing Association (N. 16th, 17th, Clark Sts. & 1819 Sherman Ave.)	1891-1901
	32f	Storz Brewing Co.	1901-1917
	32g	Storz Brewing Co. (1807/1819 N. 16th St.)	1933-1967
	32h	Grain Belt Breweries, Inc. (br. of Minneapolis, MN)	1967-1972
NE	33	Downer, Willow Springs Brewery	1862-1865
NE	34a	Ephraim Engler (1106/1110 N. 18th St. & Canton St.)	1874-1896
	34b	Frederick Boye	1896-1901
	34c	Boye Brewing Co.	1901-1902
	34d	Henry Sachs	1902-1903
	34e	Peter Brunner (1419 Canton St.)	1903-1904
NE	35a	Joseph Guggenmos (3rd & Hickory Sts.)	1896-1898
	35b	Nebraska Brewing Co.	1898-1901
	35c	Willow Springs Brewing Co.	1901-1917
	35d	Fontenelle Brewing Co., Inc. (210 Hickory St.)	1933-1938
	35e	Metz Brewing Co. (br. of George Muehlebach & Co., Kansas City, MO)	1938-1950
	35f	Metz Brewing Co. aka My Brewing Co. (1959-1961)	1950-1961
NE	36a	Joseph Guggenmos (1st St. & Boulevard)	1898- ?
	36b	Caroline Guggenmos	?-1907
	36c	Joseph Guggenmos (3709/3711 S. 14th St.)	1907-1917
NE	37a	Hartmann	? -1861
	37b	(Philip) Metz & Baumann	1861-1864
	37c	Metz & Bro. (Philip & Frederick), Nebraska Brewery (6th & Leavenworth Sts.)	1864-1879
	37d	Metz Bros. Brewing Co.	1879-1885
	37e	Frederick Metz & Sons (Charles & Frederick Jr.)	1885-1894
	37f	Metz Bros. Brewing Co. (Charles & Frederick Jr.)	1894-1917
NE	38	John Fallon (South Omaha)	1895-1895
NE	39a	Jetter & Young (952/964 30th St & Y St., South Omaha)	1887-1888
	39b	B. Jetter	1888-1891
	39c	South Omaha Brewing Co.	1891-1902
	39d	Jetter Brewing Co.	1902-1917
	39e	Jetter Brewing Co. (6016 S. 30th St. at Upland Pkwy.)	1933-1934
NE	40a	(Fred) Krug & (Rudolph) Selzer (11th St.)	1859-1861
	40b	Fred Krug (Farnham between 10th & 11th Sts.)	1861-1891
	40c	Fred Krug Brewing Co. (1007 Jackson St.)	1891-1912
	40d	Fred Krug Brewing Co. (Krug Ave. & Deer Park Blvd.)	1912-1917
	40e	Fred Krug Brewing Co., Inc.	1933-1935
	40f	Falstaff Brewing Corp. (25th St. & Deer Park Blvd.)	1935-1975
	40g	Falstaff Brewing Corp., affiliated with General Brewing Co., CA	1975-

Omaha (cont.)

NE	41	Poggensee & Saggan	1891-1891
NE	42	Sterling Ale and Porter Co.	1893-1893
NE	43	Union Brewery	1871-1873
NE	44a	(Charles) Weymuller	1863-1876
	44b	Weymuller & Co. (1714 Burt St.)	1883-1897
	44c	Charles Weymuller	1903-1904

Plattsmouth

NE	45	Heisel & Rippele	1878-1880

Red Cloud

NE	46a	J. Bernzen & Co.	1874-1877
	46b	J. Bernzen	1877-1880

Rulo

NE	47	Aug. Boerner	1878-1891
NE	48	Ephraim Elshire	1882-1884

St. Helena

NE	49a	(Carl) Lamm & (Adolph) Schrempp	1870- ?
	49b	Carl Lamm	? -1881
	49c	Peter J. Fielke & Co.	1881-1884
	49d	Anton Fielke	1884-1892
	49e	Anton Fielke & Co.	1892-1895
	49f	Anton Fielke	1895-1903
	49g	Joseph Wrede	1903-1910

Saratoga

NE	50	A. Saltzmann	1880-1880

Schuyler

NE	51a	Fritz Lommert	1873-1875
	51b	Berkin & Seibert	1884- ?
	51c	Platz & Kurth	? -1888
	51d	F. W. Platz	1888-1900
	51e	William Platz	1900-1902
	51f	Paul P. Platz	1902-1904
	51g	George Rambour	1904-1905

South Sioux City

NE	52	Kruger Brewing Co.	1912-1913

Stromsburgh

NE	53	Palm & Johnson	1888-1888

Wahoo

NE	54a	A. Jansa	1882-1884
	54b	R. Safranek	1884-1888
	54c	Max A. Jaensch	1888-1891
	54d	Caley & Jaensch	1891-1893
	54e	M. C. Caley, City Brewery	1893-1895

Wahpeton

NE	55	Lambert & Heippele	1884-1884

West Point

NE	56a	Frank Wala	1868- ?
	56b	Jos. Wala	? -1882
	56c	J. Vostoupal	1882-1884
	56d	Ernest Kadish	1884-1891
	56e	West Point Brewing Co.	1891-1893
	56f	West Point Brewing Association	1893-1917

Wilber

NE	57a	John Kobes	1878-1879
	57b	Robert Shary	1879-1882
	57c	Shary & Hokuf	1882-1884
	57d	F. J. Kobes & Co.	1884-1899
	57e	F. J. Hayek	1899-1901
	57f	Wilber Brewery Co.	1901-1917

Aurora

NV	1a	Esmeralda Brewery	1875-1877
	1b	F. Staehler	1877-1888

Austin

NV	2	Ploshke & Betz	1863- ?
NV	3a	B. Wehrfritz & Co.	? -1874
	3b	G. A. Bauer	1874-1884
	3c	A. Hoffman	1884-1890

Battle Mountain

NV	4a	Union Brewery	1874-1877
	4b	John Amfahr	1877-1880
	4c	M. J. Stahl	1880-1884

Belleville

NV	5a	Belleville Brewery	1879-1880
	5b	A. Glasser	1880-1884

Belmont

NV	6a	J. C. Bauer	1875- ?
	6b	Wm. Faber	1880-1882
	6c	Bohle & Bick	1882-1888

Bristol

NV	7a	C. Goldicke	1882-1883
	7b	Riepe & Kieseler	1883-1884

Buell

NV	8	Adolph Finck	1875- ?

Carson City

NV	9a	R. C. Berryman	1878- ?
	9b	T. C. Taylor	1890-1891
NV	10a	Carson City Brewery	? -1860
	10b	(Jacob) Klein, (August) Gerhauser and (John) Wagner (West 2nd St. between S. Minnesota & S. Division Sts.)	1860-1864
	10c	Wagner & Klein (South Division & West King Sts.)	1864-1879
	10d	Jacob Klein	1879-1888
	10e	James A. Raycraft	1888-1900
	10f	Carson Brewing Co.	1900-1948

Cherry Creek

NV	11a	Peter Newman	1874-1875
	11b	M. H. Cochran	1875-1884

Cornucopia

NV	12	McAvin & Rogers	1874-1875

Crystal Peak

NV	13	Grazer & Weissig	1874-1875

Elko

NV	14a	Antonie Bixel	1874-1884
	14b	A. J. Hybschman	1884-1888
	14c	N. P. Guldager	1888-1891
NV	15	Ilawley & Curieux	? -1878

Ely

NV	16a	George Mezger	1888-1889
	16b	Max Schaefer	1889-1890
	16c	Leo Welti	1890-1891
	16d	Ely Brewing Co.	1891-1906
	16e	Consumers Brewing and Malting Co.	1909-1913

Eureka

NV	17a	T. J. Bremenkampf (Lower Main St.)	1875-1877
	17b	F. J. Bremenkampf & Co.	1877-1880
	17c	Bremenkampf & Regli	1880-1884
	17d	F. J. Bremenkampf & Co.	1884-1891
NV	18a	Charles Lautenschlager	1874-1903
	18b	Estate of Charles Lautenschlager	1903-1904
	18c	Paul Yost	1904-1909

Eureka (cont.)

NV	19a	Joseph Oberer	1875-1877
	19b	H. Mann & Co. (Main & Gold Sts.)	1877-1880
	19c	Mann & (Fred) Hetiman	1880-1884
	19d	H. Mann & Co.	1884-1891
NV	20a	Smith & Mendes	1879-1880
	20b	Jos. Mendes	1880-1882
NV	21	Henry Vosberg	1878-1880

Goldfield

NV	22a	Goldfield Brewing Co.	1905-1908
	22b	Consumers Brewing Association	1908-1911

Gold Hill

NV	23a	Sylvester Schweiss	1874-1895
	23b	Carrie C. Schweiss	1895-1897

Grantsville

NV	24	William Koch	1878-1884

Halleck

NV	25a	F. F. Gruenberg	1875-1877
	25b	Chr. Gruenberg	1877-1879

Hamilton

NV	26	Davison & Wagner, Philadelphia Brewery	1869- ?
NV	27a	St. Louis Brewery	1874-1877
	27b	Casper Schmidt	1877-1878

Highland

NV	28	Louis Klein	1882-1882

Ione

NV	29	R. R. Brown	1882-1884

Jefferson

NV	30	F. Goodbook & Co.	1875- ?

Lewis

NV	31	Fuchs & Cozzens	1882-1882

Paradise Valley

NV	32a	Kirchner & Co.	1879- ?
	32b	Wm. Kirchner	? -1884
	32c	Mrs. Wm. Kirchner	1884-1888

Pioche

NV	33a	Charles Goedricke	1875-1877
	33b	J. W. Staler	1877-1879
NV	34a	Schustrich & Klein	1874-1880
	34b	Louis Klein	1880-1884
	34c	Pioche Brewing Co.	1884-1891
	34d	Max Schaefer	1891-1893
	34e	John Jochimsen	1893-1895

Reno

NV	35a	John George Becker and Charles Knust, Washoe Brewery	1870-1882
	35b	George Becker	1882-1888
	35c	Casper Becker	1888-1895
	35d	Becker Brewing Co. (6th & Sierra Sts.)	1895-1899
	35e	Henry Riter	1902-1905
NV	36	John George Becker, Pacific Brewery	c1881
NV	37a	Frederick Hertlein, Reno Brewery (Commercial Row)	1868-1873
	37b	William Hoffman	1873-1888
	37c	John George Kerth	1888-1891
NV	38a	Reno Brewing Co. (990 East 4th St.)	1903-1918
	38b	Reno Brewing Co., Inc.	1933-1956

Silver City

NV	39	Philip Geyer	1875-1880

Taylor

NV	40	Max Schaefer	1888-1888

Tuscarora

NV	41a	F. Curiaux	1878-1882
	41b	Mrs. F. Curieux	1882-1884
	41c	Brinkman & Smith	1884-1888
	41d	Tuscarora Brewing Co.	1888-1890
	41e	Mrs. F. Curieux	1890-1893
	41f	A. H. Smith	1893-1904
NV	42a	Iwan & Trilling	1878-1879
	42b	Otto Trilling	1879-1882

Tybo

NV	43	Henry Bohle	1878-1884

Unionville

NV	44	Humboldt Brewery	1874-1875

Virginia City

NV	45a	John P. Deininger	1874-1882
	45b	John H. Deininger	1882-1888
	45c	Richard Schweiss	1888-1908
	45d	Wm. Klaus & Co.	1908-1909
NV	46	J. F. Erb	1880-1880
NV	47a	Franklin & Schroeder	1874-1882
	47b	Henry Arend	1882-1884
NV	48a	Langan & Co.	1880-1882
	48b	P. J. Langan	1882-1884
	48c	Langan & Co.	1884-1888
	48d	John S. Werrin	1888-1891
NV	49	Geo. Muck	1874-1875
NV	50a	J. & H. Rapp	1874-1875
	50b	Rapp & Langan	1875-1879
	50c	Wm. Rapp	1879-1884
		Reich/Schnitzer Brewery - office only in Virginia City - Brewery located in Six Mile Canyon, CA	

Ward

NV	51	Geo. Mezger	1880-1884

Wells

NV	52	Adolph Finck	1882-1884
NV	53	L. T. Greenburg	1882-1884

White Pine

NV	54	Metzger Bros.	1878-1879

Winnemucca

NV	55a	John Jurgens	1875-1877
	55b	Fink & Hinkey	1877-1879
	55c	Reid & Hinkey	1879-1880
	55d	John Diehl	1880-1891
NV	56a	Charles Kessler, Empire Brewery (Bridge St.)	1869-1874
	56b	Charles Kessler	1874-1879
	56c	Estate of Charles Kessler	1879-1884
	56d	Gies & Rehfuss	1884-1886
NV	57	Winnemucca City Brewery, Head & Krinkle (Bridge St.)	c1869

NEW HAMPSHIRE

Cold River (see Walpole)

Dover

NH	1	A. Pathe & Co.	1875- ?

Manchester

NH	2	Harris Dunn & Co.	1875- ?

Manchester (cont.)

NH	3a	Captain Tucker Brewrey	1865- ?
	3b	A. C. Wallace	1874-1877
	3c	Carney, Lynch & Conner (Bakersville)	1879-1888
	3d	New Hampshire Brewing Co.	1888-1891
	3e	True W. Jones Brewing Co. (Hancock St.)	1891-1918

Merrimack

NH	4	Anheuser-Busch, Inc. (1000 Daniel Webster Hwy.) (br. of St. Louis, MO)	1970-

Portsmouth

NH	5a	H. Fisher & Marcellus Eldredge	1858-1870
	5b	Herman Eldredge & Son	1870-1874
	5c	Eldredge Brewing Co. (24/26 Bow St.)	1874-1916
NH	6	Asa Hamm	c1771
NH	7a	(Arthur) Harris & Co. (62/64 Bow St.)	1870-1875
	7b	Portsmouth Brewing Co.	1875-1918
NH	8	Michael Martin	c1820
NH	9a	Portsmouth Brewing and Bottling Co.	1893-1894
	9b	Belfast Brewing Co.	1894-1895
NH	10a	John Swindell (19 Bridge St.)	1856-1858
	10b	Swindell & Jones (Market St.)	1858-1859
	10c	Frank Jones (85/87 Market St.)	1859-1888
	10d	Frank Jones Brewing Co., Ltd. (87 Market St.)	1888-1918
	10e	Eldredge Brewing Co., Inc. (1 Cate St.)	1933-1937
	10f	Eldredge Brewing Co., Inc., dba Frank Jones Brewing Co., Inc. (1 Cate St. & 698 Islington St.)	1937-1943
	10g	Frank Jones Brewing Co., Inc.	1943-1950
NH	11	John Swindell (near the Creek)	1858-1864
NH	12	Henry Sherburne	c1640
NH	13	Samuel Wentworth	c1670

Walpole (including Cold River)

NH	14a	Walker, Blake & Co.	1876-1879
	14b	Walker, Dewey, Blake & Co., aka Falls Mountain Lager Co., Cold River	1879-1889
	14c	Bellows Falls Brewing Co.	1886-1893
	14d	Mountain Spring Brewing Co.	1893-1895
	14e	New Mountain Spring Brewing Co.	1895-1900
	14f	Crescent Brewing Co.	1900-1902
	14g	New Mountain Spring Brewing Co.	1902-1904
	14h	Manila Brewing Co. of New Hampshire	1904-1907

NEW JERSEY

Atlantic City

NJ	1a	Home Brewing Co.	1899-1900
	1b	Atlantic City Brewing Co. (107 W. Missouri & Arctic Aves.)	1900-1920
	1c	Atlantic City Brewing & Ice Co. (105 N. Missouri Ave.)	NP 1934-1934

Bergen

NJ	2	J. H. Meierdierck	1890-1895

Camden

NJ	3a	Camden City Brewery (Filmore, Bulson & 6th Sts.)	1905-1909
	3b	F. A. Poth & Sons, Inc.	1909-1920
	3c	Camden County Beverage Co.	1933-1963
NJ	4a	Jacob Morgenthaler	1895- ?
	4b	Benjamin Roeshman	1899- ?
	4c	William Molt	1904-1909
	4d	Julius Belz	1909-1910
NJ	5	Xavier Schnurr (3rd & Spruce Sts.)	1896-1904
NJ	6	Gustav Schwoeri (705 Chestnut St.)	1890-1907

Belleville

NJ	7	Garden State Brewery Co.	1934-1934

Clinton

NJ	8	J. G. Krack	1878-1880

Cramer's Hill

NJ	9	Dora Andrews	1895-1895

Egg Harbor City

NJ	10	August Arnoldt	1890-1890
NJ	11a	Lena Atz	1888-1897
	11b	Christian Atz	1897-1920
	11c	Egg Harbor Brewery (459 Philadelphia Ave.)	1933-1935
	11d	Zerbey Brewing Co.	1935-1937
NJ	12	Thomas Metzner	? -1874
NJ	13a	Phil. A. Scheufele (Hamburg Ave.)	1884- ?
	13b	Catherine M. Scheufele	? -1888
	13c	Joseph Kopf	1888-1893
NJ	14	Henry Schmitz	1878-1888

Elizabeth

NJ	15	P. J. Eckert	1878-1884
NJ	16a	Eller & Beyer (600/616 Pearl St.)	1865-1882
	16b	Laible & Breidt	1882-1885
	16c	Peter Breidt City Brewery Co.	1885-1920
	16d	City Products Co.	1920-1933
	16e	Elizabeth Brewing Corp.	1933-1935
	16f	Peter Breidt Brewing Co.	1935-1951
NJ	17a	John F. Wagner (7th & Marshall Sts.)	1865-1884
	17b	Benjamin Widder Brewing Co.	1884-1887
	17c	Rising Sun Brewing Co.	1887-1920
	17d	Rising Sun Brewing Co.	1933-1933
	17e	Seeber Brewing Co.	1933-1937

Gloucester City

NJ	18	Gloucester Brewing Co. (9th & Charles Sts.)	1896-1896
NJ	19	Menge Bros.	1897-1897
NJ	20a	Moritz Wiedmaier	1888-1890
	20b	Jacob Grun	1890-1890
	20c	Jacob Lutz & Co.	1890-1891
	20d	Zwoyer Bros.	1891-1893
	20e	Moritz Wiedmaier	1893-1895
	20f	Max Garschutz & Co.	1895-1896

Guttenberg

NJ	21a	Otto Koehler & Andrew Finck, White Brewery	1855-1862
	21b	Koehler & (Woltze) Kamena	1862-1877
	21c	Koehler & Son	1877-1880
	21d	Hauenstein & Weiss	1880-1884
	21e	Alois Kremer	1880-1884
	21f	A. Kremer Brewing Co.	1890-1891
	21g	August Hammersen	1891-1896
NJ	22	M. Lederer & Co.	1875- ?
NJ	23a	Adolph Meckert, Standard Brewery (Park Ave. btwn. 69th & 70th)	1874-1877
	23b	Biela & Eypper	1877-1880
NJ	24a	John H. Meierdierck (New Blvd. near Herman Ave.)	1896-1904
	24b	Meierdierck Brewing Co.	1904-1905
	24c	O. K. Brewing Co.	1905-1908
NJ	25a	Standard Malt and Hop Brewing Co. (Herman Ave. & Bulls Ferry)	1898-1905
	25b	Consumers Park Brewing Co.	1905-1906
	25c	Standard Malt and Hop Brewing Co.	1906-1908
	25d	Standard Brewing and Refrigerating Co., aka Standard Brewing and Refining Co.	1908-1910

Hamilton
NJ 26a Jacob Hetzel 1878-1879
26b S. Schloetterer 1879-1880
26c Mrs. Barbara Schloetterer 1880-1884

Harrison (see Newark)

Hammonton
NJ 27a Eastern Beverage Corp. (13th & Railroad Ave.) 1933-1943
27b Eastern Beverage Corp. (334 N. Washington St.) 1943-
aka Canadian Ace Brewing Co. (1970-1973)
aka Circle Brewing Co. (1956-1969)
aka Colonial Brewing Co. (1953-)
aka Colony House Brewing Co. (1954-1966)
aka Dawson Brewing Co.
aka Fischer Brewing Co. (1973-)
aka Fox Head Brewing Co. (1974-1976)
aka Garden State Brewing Co. (1963-)
aka Hampden Brewing Co. (1974-)
aka Hedrick Brewing Co. (1974-)
aka Polar Brewing Co. (1973-1976)
aka San Juan Cerveceria (1966-1975)
aka Tube City Brewing Co. (1955-1958)
aka Waukee Brewing Co. (1958-)
aka Commodities & Technology, Inc.

Hoboken (includes West Hoboken)
NJ 28a John Axtmann 1875-1893
28b Mary Axtmann 1893-1895

NJ 29 Alexander Fehy 1875- ?

NJ 30 Fox Hill Brewing Co. NP 1927-1934

NJ 31 Franz Hackenberg (2nd & Jefferson Sts.) 1875-1884

NJ 32 Hoboken Brewing Co. (3rd & Clinton Sts.) 1898-1902

NJ 33a Hudson County Consumers Brewing Co. (45/47 Newark St.) 1900-1910
33b Hudson County Consumers Brewing Co. (481/517 Summit Ave. & Dodd St., West Hoboken) 1910-1920

NJ 34 Mears & Freed, aka Freed, Mears & Co. 1875- ?

NJ 35 Aert Teunison c1648

NJ 36a John H. Wittig (W. Hoboken) 1874-1877
36b Catherine Wittig 1877-1879

Hopewell
NJ 37 Deutsche Brewing Co. NP 1934-1934

Hudson City (see Jersey City)

Jersey City (formerly Hudson City)
NJ 38a John J. Bundschuh 1875-1877
38b H. Newman 1877-1879
38c Newman Bros. 1879-1882

NJ 39 Carling Breweries (15 Exchange Place) NP 1934-1934

NJ 40 Central Brewing Co. (309 Grand St.) NP 1934-1934

NJ 41a Henry F. Cox 1874-1877
41b Hudson City Brewery 1877-1880
41c Jersey City Heights Brewing Co. 1880-1882

NJ 42 Joseph Endres (204 Griffith St.) 1896-1898

NJ 43a (Charles) Ferger, (Adolph) Becker & (Daniel) Kohl, Bavarian Brewery (foot of Girard Ave.) 1890-1895
43b Greenville Brewing Co. 1895-1905
43c Columbia Brewing Co. (225 Bartholdi Ave.) 1905-1915
43d Columbia Brewing Co., Inc. 1933-1934

NJ 44 General Breweries Corp. NP 1934-1934

NJ 45a Wm. Hirschberg 1875-1877
45b H. C. Freund (783/785 W. Newark Ave.) 1877-1902

Jersey City (cont.)

NJ 46a (Henry) Lembeck & (John) Betz (164/182 9th St. between Grove & Henderson Sts.) 1869-1890
46b Lembeck & Betz Eagle Brewing Co. 1890-1920

NJ 47 Muehlig's Brown Beer Brewery 1902-1902

NJ 48 Wm. Paulson 1874-1875

NJ 49 (John) Roemmelt & (Andrew) Leicht 1857-1879

NJ 50a Schmale & Frohwitter 1874-1877
50b Marion Brewery 1877-1882

NJ 51 Henry P. Simon (230 Baldwin Ave.) 1875-1902

NJ 52 Louis Steinberger (496 Pavonia Ave.) 1916-1916

Keansburg

NJ 53 Jersey Brewing Corp. (Palmer Ave.) 1933-1934

Kearney

NJ 54 Gilbert & Son (1075 Harrison Ave.) 1890-1890

Lindenhurst

NJ 55 Lindenhurst Brewery, Inc. NP 1934-1934

Little Ferry

NJ 56a D. Ehlers 1874-1874
56b George Ehlers & Co. 1874-1875

Manville

NJ 57 Great Eastern Breweries, Inc. (92 Main St.) NP 1934-1934

Maywood

NJ 58a Bergen Brewers, Inc. 1934-1936
58b Maywood Brewing Corp. (foot of E. Hunter Ave.) 1936-1937

Midland

NJ 59a Ed. J. Keeley 1875-1877
59b James Keeley 1877-1878

Newark (including Harrison)

NJ 60 Abendschoen & Bro. (64 Belmont Ave.) 1875-1888

NJ 61 Adam & Koch (Ave. L. & Magazine St.) 1905-1916

NJ 62a Aurnhammer & Schelling 1874-1877
62b F. A. Traudt 1877-1880
62c Morgan & O'Reilly (2nd St.) 1880-1882

NJ 63a John Baier (333 Springfield Ave.) 1860- ?
63b Baier & Hill 1874-1877
63c Hill & Piez 1877-1884
63d William Hill 1884-1889
63e Hill's Union Brewery Co., Ltd. 1889-1899
63f Union Brewing Co. of Newark 1899-1920
63g United Brewing Co. 1933-1938

NJ 64 Anheuser-Busch, Inc. (200 U.S. Hwy. 1) (br. of St. Louis, MO) 1951-

NJ 65 Wm. Bohler & Co. 1874-1875

NJ 66a Braun & Laible 1852- ?
66b Laible & Adam ? -1858
66c Louis Adam 1858-1865
66d (Gottlieb) Hill & (Gottfried) Krueger (75/101 Belmont Ave.) 1865-1875
66e Gottfried Krueger 1875-1889
66f Gottfried Krueger Brewery Co. (br. of U.S. Brewing Co., New York, NY) 1889-1896
66g Gottfried Krueger Brewing Co. (br. of United States Brewing Co., New York, NY) 1896-1920
66h Gottfried Krueger Brewing Co., Inc. 1933-1934
66i G. Krueger Brewing Co. 1934-1961

NJ 67 John Callahan 1875- ?

Newark (cont.)

NJ	68a	(General) John N. Cumming	1805-1832
	68b	Morton Brothers	1832-1838
	68c	Tain & Collins	1838-1840
	68d	Peter Ballantine & Erastus Patterson	1840-1847
	68e	Peter Ballantine (Front, Fulton & Rector Sts.)	1847-1857
	68f	P. Ballantine & Sons (78/110 Front St.)	1857-1920
NJ	69a	(Franz) Ehehalt & (Carl) Seidel	1866-1869
	69b	Christopher Trefz (28 Beacon St.)	1869-1877
	69c	Christiana Trefz	1877-1884
	69d	C. Trefz	1884-1889
	69e	C. Trefz Brewery (br. of United States Brewing Co., NY, NY)	1889-1920
NJ	70	A. Fehleisen	1859-1879
NJ	71	Gustave L. Freche	1875-1879
NJ	72a	George Froescher	1875-1879
	72b	Max Stadelhofer	1879-1882
	72c	Thoe. Schulz (171 Belmont Ave.)	1882-1888
NJ	73	Fred Haas	1874-1875
NJ	74a	Fred Hartdorn	1875-1876
	74b	M. Laderer (48 Nesbitt St.)	1876-1880
	74c	Laderer & Weber	1880-1882
	74d	Moritz Laderer	1882-1888
NJ	75a	Joseph Harth (194/202 S. Orange St.)	1868-1882
	75b	Balthasar Huemmer	1882-1884
	75c	Huemmer & Hotz	1884-1885
	75d	B. Huemmer	1885-1892
	75e	Philip Bunn	1892-1894
	75f	Birkenhauer & Baumann, Old Fashioned Brewery	1894-1905
	75g	Birkenhauer & Berger, Old Fashioned Brewery Co. (258 Morris Ave.)	1905-1909
	75h	Birkenhauer Brewing Co.	1909-1916
NJ	76a	Joseph Harth (38 Hayes St.)	1860-1880
	76b	Gustav Schmid, Jumbo Brewery	1880-1888
	76c	Fred Liesiewski, Jumbo Brewery	1888-1892
	76d	Eagle Brewery of Newark, Fred Liesiewski	1892-1895
	76e	Eagle Brewing Co., of Newark (20/40 Hayes St.)	1895-1920
NJ	77a	John Hartmann	1862-1872
	77b	Stegmueller & Wehr	1872-1873
	77c	Stegmueller	1873-1874
	77d	Elizabeth Ziehr, aka Ferdinand Ziehr	1879-1891
	77e	Essex County Brewing Co.	1891-1920
NJ	78a	John Haster (530/535 Harrison Ave., Harrison)	1888-1890
	78b	Caroline Haster	1890-1891
	78c	Fritz & Wiedemann	1891-1901
	78d	Fritz & Wiedemann Brewing Co.	1901-1904
NJ	79a	Peter Hauck (505 Harrison Ave., Harrison)	1859-1882
	79b	Peter Hauck & Co.	1882-1891
	79c	United States Brewing Co., Ltd., New York City, Peter Hauck & Co. (500/520 Harrison Ave.)	1891-1920
	79d	Harrison Beverage Co.	1933-1933
	79e	West Hudson Brewery, Inc.	1933-1934
	79f	Harrison Brewing Co., Inc.	1934-1934
	79g	Peter Doelger Brewing Corp.	1936-1948
	79h	Camden County Beverage Co.	1949-1949
NJ	80a	John Heinickel	1874-1882
	80b	Heinickel & Co. (396 15th St.)	1882-1890
NJ	81a	C. W. Helm	1874-1877
	81b	Jac. Mander	1877-1879
	81c	Weiss & Mander (15th & Morris Aves.)	1879-1884
NJ	83a	Jas. R. Hensler Ale Brewing Co. (192/204 Murray St.)	1910-1913
	83b	Joseph Hensler Brewing Co.	1913-1915

Newark (cont.)

NJ	84a	Hoffman Beverage Co. (391/400 Grove St.)		1934-1946
	84b	Pabst Brewing Co. (br. of Milwaukee, WI)		1946-
		aka Hoffman Beverage Co.		
		aka Blatz Brewing Co.		
		aka Blitz-Weinhard		
NJ	85a	Franz J. Kastner, Phoenix Brewery (3/27 Lewis St.)		1874-1889
	85b	Emerald and Phoenix Brewing Co. of New York City, Franz J. Kastner Brewery		1889-1902
	85c	F. J. Kastner Co.		1902-1911
	85d	Schalk Brewing Co.		1911-1915
	85e	Schalk Brewery, Inc.		1915-1920
NJ	86a	Charles Kolb		1866- ?
	86b	C. Feigenspan & Co. (2/50 Freeman St.)		1875-1879
	86c	Christian Feigenspan, Inc.		1879-1920
	86d	Christian Feigenspan Brewing Co.		1933-1943
	86e	Ballantine Brewing Co. (Plant 2)		1943-1945
	86f	P. Ballantine & Sons (Plant 2)		1945-1948
NJ	87a	Frederick Kolb		1854-1879
	87b	Albert Fehleisen (315 Orange St.)		1879-1884
	87c	Fehleisen & Co.		1884-1905
NJ	88	C. Kurzenberger (419 High St.)		1890-1891
NJ	89a	Lorenz & Jacquillard		1855-1860
	89b	Lorenz & Hensler		1860-1866
	89c	Joseph Hensler (73 Hamburg Pl.)		1866-1889
	89d	Joseph Hensler Brewing Co.		1889-1920
	89e	The Joseph Hensler Brewing Co. (71/83 Wilson Ave. & 60/72 Alyea St.)		1933-1958
NJ	90a	D. M. Lyon & Son (95/97 S. Canal St.)		1874-1882
	90b	D. M. Lyon & Sons		1882-1888
	90c	D. M. Lyon & Sons Brewing Co.		1888-1897
	90d	Lyon & Sons Brewing Co.		1897-1920
NJ	91a	Morton Bros. (235/239 High St.)		1874-1875
	91b	Morton & Bro.		1875-1884
	91c	Morton Brewing Co.		1884-1890
	91d	Wilkens & Kupfer		1890-1891
NJ	92	National Brewing Co. (Springfield Ave. & S. 13th St.)		1906-1907
NJ	93a	Charles Neitzer (472 S. 10th ST.)		1874-1884
	93b	John Gehri		1884-1888
NJ	94a	John Neu (99/103 Springfield Ave.)		1874-1888
	94b	Citizens Brewing Co.		1888-1893
	94c	John Fergg		1893-1895
	94d	John Fergg's Brewery		1895-1910
		aka John Fergg Brewing Co. (1909)		
NJ	95a	Newark Enterprise Brewing Co. (320/332 Orange St.)		1886-1888
	95b	Geyer's Enterprise Brewing Co.		1888-1890
	95c	Home Brewing Co.		1890-1920
NJ	96	Old Fashion Brewing Co. (43 Kormorn St.)		1933-1933
NJ	97	People's Brewing Co. (10 Magnolia St.)		1884-1884
NJ	98	F. Pflitschinger (396 Court St.)		1888-1888
NJ	99a	Jacob Piez (457/461 Springfield Ave.)		1884-1886
	99b	Jacob Piez's Sons		1886-1888
NJ	100a	Fred W. Roesser		1875-1877
	100b	Catharina Roesser		1877-1879
NJ	101	Roosevelt Breweries, Inc. (60 Park Pl.)	NP	1934-1934
NJ	102	Edward Saub (10 Bowery St.)		1888-1888

Newark (cont.)

NJ	103a	Schalk Bros.	1852-1879
	103b	Ballantine & Co. (Freeman, Christie, Ferry & Bowery Sts.)	1879-1911
	103c	P. Ballantine & Sons	1911-1933
	103d	P. Ballantine & Sons (57 Freeman St.)	1933-1971
		aka Blitz-Weinhard Brewing Co. (1968-1971)	
		aka Christian Feigenspan (1968-1971)	
		aka Lexington Brewing Co. (1966-1971)	
		aka Richards Brewing Co. (1968-1971)	
NJ	104	U. Scheiner	1874-1875
NJ	105a	Shaffery & Farley (23 Polk St.)	1893-1897
	105b	Bernard Farley	1897-1900
NJ	106a	Srandt & Krack	1874-1875
	106b	John Griffith & Co.	1875-1878
NJ	107	Superior Manufacturing Co.	1933-1933
NJ	108a	Tivoli Brewing Co. (310 Springfield Ave.)	1899-1900
	108b	Heitzmann & Reiser	1900-1901
	108c	Adolph Heitzmann	1901-1903
	108d	Consumers Brewing Co.	1903-1909
NJ	109a	Adam Wackenhuth & Co.	1874-1877
	109b	F. C. Wackenhuth	1877-1879
NJ	110	Chas. Weiland (21 Jay St.)	1890-1890
NJ	111	Weiss & Birkenhaeuser	1874-1880
NJ	112	Christopher W. Wiedenmayer	1858-1880
NJ	113a	George W. Wiedenmayer (588/602 Market St.)	1878-1896
	113b	George W. Wiedenmayer, Inc.	1896-1920
NJ	114	Geo. C. Wiedenmayer (50/56 Commercial St.)	1916-1916

New Brunswick

NJ	115a	Martin Klein	1857- ?
	115b	Thomas Teneson	1874-1875
	115c	Joseph Schneider	1884- ?
	115d	John W. Russert, Rock Spring Brewery (Highland Park)	1898-1905
	115e	Rock Spring Brewery	1905-1907
	115f	New Brunswick Brewing Co.	1907-1910
	115g	Berger & Fischer	1910-1912
NJ	116a	New Brunswick Brewing Co. (339/345 Sanford St.)	1935-1938
	116b	The Butler Co.	1938-1938
NJ	117	Geo. W. Wiedenmayer	1877-1878

North Bergen

NJ	118a	Roland Brewing Co. (Hamilton Ave.)	1896-1900
	118b	North Bergen Brewing Co.	1900-1900
	118c	Philip Adler	1900-1901
	118d	Robert Rother Brewing Co.	1901-1903

Orange

NJ	119a	The Orange Brewing Co. (Hill & Prince Sts.)	1901-1902
	119b	Orange Brewery, Michael Winter	1902-1920
	119c	John F. Trommer, Inc. of New Jersey (119 Hill St.)	1934-1946
	119d	John F. Trommer, Inc.	1946-1950
	119e	Liebmann Breweries, Inc. (br. of Brooklyn, NY)	1950-1964
	119f	Rheingold Breweries, Inc.	1964-1977
		aka Forest Brewing Co. (1972-1977)	
		aka Jacob Ruppert (1966-1977)	

Passaic

NJ	120a	Hygeia Brewing Co. (21/27 Central Ave.)	1901-1920
	120b	Vanderveer Ice & Cereal Products Co.	NP 1934-1934
NJ	121	Teodozia Nectar of Honey Mfg. Co.	1906-1906

Paterson			
NJ 122a	Christian Braun (Marshall & Braun Sts.)		1855-1870
122b	Sprattler & Mennel		1870-1876
122c	Christian Braun		1876-1879
122d	Braun Brewing Co., aka Braun Brothers (Christian & Louis)		1879-1890
122e	Paterson Consolidated Brewing Co., Braun Bros.		1890-1898
122f	Paterson Brewing and Malting Co., Braun Bros. (293 Marshall)		1898-1920
NJ 123a	Graham & Post (Hamburg & Matlock Sts.)		1874-1877
123b	Graham & Co., Passaic Springs Brewery		1877-1893
123c	Paterson Consolidated Brewing Co., Graham Brewing Co.		1893-1898
123d	Paterson Brewing and Malting Co., Graham Brewing Co.		1898-1899
NJ 124a	Jas. A. Graham & Co. (Straight & Cedar Sts.)		1887-1890
124b	Paterson Consolidated Brewing Co., Jas. A. Graham Brewing Co.		1890-1898
124c	Paterson Brewing and Malting Co., James A. Graham Brewing Co.		1898-1920
124d	Burton Products Co., Inc. (69/83 Straight St.)		1933-1934
124e	Burton Products, Inc.		1934-1940
124f	Burton Brewing Co.		1940-1949
NJ 125a	Katz Bros., Red Star Brewery (65 Godwin & Bridge Sts.)		1877-1882
125b	Katz Bros., Burton Brewing Co. (Straight & Governor Sts.)		1882-1890
125c	Paterson Consolidated Brewing Co., Katz Bros. Burton Brewing Co.		1890-1898
125d	Paterson Brewing and Malting Co., Katz Bros. Burton Brewery		1898-1915
125e	Kelly Brewing Co. (422 Straight St.)	NP	1934-1934
NJ 126	Ph. Pfannebecker (21 Bridge St.)		1878-1888
NJ 127a	Eagle Brewery		1861-1861
127b	Hinchcliffe & Co.		1861-1867
127c	Shaw, Hinchcliffe & Penrose (Governor & Ann Sts.)		1867-1878
127d	Shaw & Hinchcliffe		1878-1882
127e	John Hinchcliffe		1882-1886
127f	Hinchcliffe Bros.		1886-1890
127g	Hinchcliffe Bros. Brewing and Malting Co.		1890-1899
127h	Paterson Brewing and Malting Co., Hinchcliffe Brewery		1899-1920
NJ 128a	(Gustave) Sprattler & (Christian) Mennel (Marshall & Van Winckle Sts.)		1876-1890
128b	Paterson Consolidated Brewing Co., Sprattler & Mennel Brewing Co.		1890-1898
128c	Paterson Brewing and Malting Co., Sprattler & Mennel Brewing		1898-1920
128d	Sprattler & Mennel Brewing Co. (236/248 Marshall St.)		1939-1941
NJ 129	Wohlieb & Scheffels, Inc.		1915-1915
Perth Amboy			
NJ 130	Home Brewing Co.		1912-1914
NJ 131	Peterson Bros. (John U. & Niels C.) (254 New Brunswick Ave.)		1896-1902
Philipsburg			
NJ 132	Murray & McFadden		c1874
NJ 133	Paulus & Gluck		c1874
Plainfield, North			
NJ 134	Wm. M. Linnett		1895-1895
Rahway			
NJ 135	Edw. L. Adams		1898-1899
NJ 136a	Geyer Bros. (George's Ave.)		1878-1882
136b	Adam Geyer		1882-1884
Raritan			
NJ 137a	Kunster & Smith		1875-1877
137b	Joseph Schneider		1877-1891
Stockton			
NJ 138a	Otto & Layer		1882-1884
138b	Dora Andrews		1890-1891
138c	Jos. R. Diehm Co. (424 Main St.)		1897-1898
138d	Max Garschutz & Co.		1898-1904

Trenton

NJ 139a Capital City Brewing Co. 1899-1920
139b J. J. Murphy Brewing Co. (Perrine Ave.) 1933-1934

NJ 140a Consumers Brewing Co. 1898-1899
140b Peoples Brewing Co., Consumers Brewing Co. 1899-1900

NJ 141 F. Haas Son's 1878-1882

NJ 142a Jacob Hetzel 1874-1875
142b (Jacob) Hetzel & (John) Fisher 1875-1891
142c Franz Hill Brewery 1891-1899
142d Peoples Brewing Co., Franz Hill Brewery 1899-1920

NJ 143a Catherine John 1874-1877
143b S. Schlotterer 1877-1879

NJ 144 F. W. Kemp 1874-1875

NJ 145a (Col.) A. R. Kuser (Lalor & 1053 Lamberton Sts.) 1891-1892
145b Trenton Brewing Co. 1892-1899
145c Peoples Brewing Co., Trenton Brewing Co. 1899-1932
145d Peoples Brewing Co. of Trenton 1932-1950
145e Metropolis Brewery of New Jersey, Inc. 1950-1967
aka Banner Brewing Co. (1956-1957)
aka Class A Brewing Co. (1961-1965)
aka Gilt Edge Brewing Co. (1961-1967)
aka Hornell Brewing Co. (1961-1966)
aka Old Bohemian Brewing Co.
aka P. B. Brewing Co. (1962-1964)
aka Rialto Brewing Co. (1955-1963)
aka Tudor Brewery
145f Champale, Inc. 1967-
aka Black Horse Brewing Co. (1973-)
aka Colony House Brewing Co. (1967-1972)
aka Wilco Brewing Co.

Union (see Union City)

Union City (formerly Weehawken in Town of Union and Union Hill)

NJ 146a Daniel Bermes, Boulevard Brewery (Boulevard & Columbia Sts.) 1853-1898
146b Daniel Bermes Boulevard Brewery, Inc. (Park Ave., Fulton & Columbia Sts.) 1898-1920

NJ 147a Otto Brueck 1875-1877
147b Aug. Boemecke (Bulls Ferry Ave.) 1877-1884

NJ 148 Arnold & Gottfried Gaertner 1874-1875

NJ 149a Fred. H. Icke 1875-1875
149b Charles Wegenburg 1875-1880

NJ 150a Louis Linnewerth (Jefferson & Bloome Sts.) 1874-1882
150b Union Brewing Co. 1882-1897
150c Sahner & Hauenstein, Union Brewery (Boulevard & Blum St.) 1897-1900
150d A. Marshall & Co., Union Brewery 1900-1902
150e United States Brewing Co., Ltd. of NYC, Union Brewery 1902-1903

NJ 151a William Peter (Hudson Ave. & Weehawken St.) 1859-1888
151b William Peter Brewing Co. 1888-1920
151c The William Peter Brewing Corp. (651/653 Hudson Ave.) 1933-1940
151d The William Peter Brewing Corp. (3315/3317 Hudson Ave.) 1940-1949
151e George Ehret Brewery, Inc. (Peter St. bn. Hudson & Park Aves.) 1949-1950

NJ 152a Union City Brewing Co. 1933-1934
152b Schultz Brewing Co., Inc. (106 44 St. & Park Ave.) 1934-1938

NJ 153 Diedrich Wahlers 1895-1895

Union Hill (see Union City)

Weehawken (see Union City)

West Hoboken (see Hoboken)

West New York

NJ 154 Wm. C. Beutel (15th & Hudson Ave.) 1916-1920

Albuquerque			
NM	1	Albuquerque Brewing and Ice Co.	1908-1908
NM	2a	Ferdinand Selva	1883-1884
	2b	DeMars & Koenig	1884-1885
	2c	George Lail	1885-1887
	2d	Southwestern Brewery	1887-1891
	2e	Southwestern Brewery and Ice Co.	1891-1915
	2f	Western Brewery and Ice Co.	1915-1918
	2g	Rio Grande Brewing Corp. (502 N. 2nd St.)	1937-1939
Bland			
NM	3	F. Kleiner	1900-1900
Deming			
NM	4a	Deckert & Ehrmann	1884-1888
	4b	Deckert & Raithel	1888-1890
Elizabethtown			
NM	5	Schwenk & Will	1874-1875
Fort Stanton			
NM	6	Rufley & Co.	1888-1888
Fort Union			
NM	7	Thomas Lahey	1874-1875
Georgetown			
NM	8a	Deckert & Bodmer	1882-1883
	8b	George Bodmer	1883-1884
Golondrinas			
NM	9	Frank Weber	1874-1882
Kingston			
NM	10	Frank Kleiner	1888-1890
Las Vegas			
NM	11a	Leininger & Rothgeb	1884-1886
	11b	G. A. Rothgeb	1886-1888
	11c	Las Vegas Brewing Co.	1888-1895
NM	12a	Montezuma Brewing Co.	1899-1900
	12b	Emil Tschann, Montezuma Brewery	1900-1903
NM	13	(A. H.) Reingruber Brewing Co.	1909-1910
Lincoln			
NM	14	John Copeland & Co.	1874-1875
Mogollon			
NM	15	John Croenne & Son	1896-1897
Santa Fe			
NM	16a	Wm. Carl & Co.	1874-1875
	16b	Fischer Brewing Co.	1882-1891
	16c	Santa Fe Brewing Co.	1891-1896
NM	17a	Probst & Kirchner	1874-1875
	17b	C. C. Probst	1880-1882
	17c	Adam Grohe	1882-1884
Silver City			
NM	18a	Thomas Smith	1874-1877
	18b	John L. May & Co.	1877-1882
	18c	Tallant & Hauswald	1882-1884
	18d	Chas. Hauswald	1884-1888
	18e	Hauswald & Weigt	1888-1890
Socorro			
NM	19a	Hammel Bros. (John & Wm. G.)	1883-1884
	19b	Hammel Bros. & Co.	1884-1887
	19c	Illinois Brewing Co.	1887-1918
	19d	Illinois Brewing Co.	NP 1934-1934

Addison

NY	1a	John Schmid	1893-1894
	1b	Addison Brewing Co.	1894-1896

Albany (formerly Fort Orange and earlier Beaverwyck)

NY	2a	Amsdell Bros. (George I. & Theodore M.) (Jay, Dove, and Lancaster Sts.)	1854-1892
	2b	Geo. I. Amsdell	1892-1897
	2c	Amsdell Brewing and Malting Co.	1897-1911
	2d	Amsdell Brewing Co.	1911-1912
	2e	Amsdell-Kirchner Brewing Co.	1912-1916
	2f	Citizens' Brewing Corp.	1916-1920
NY	3	Hendrick Andriessen (Fort Orange)	c1650
NY	4a	Beverwyck Brewing Co. (24/28 N. Ferry St.)	1867-1888
	4b	Quinn & Nolan Beverwyck Brewing Co. (30/52 N. Ferry St.)	1888-1893
	4c	Beverwyck Brewing Co.	1893-1916
	4d	Beverwyck Breweries, Inc.	1933-1950
	4e	The F. & M. Schaefer Brewing Co. (br. of Brooklyn, NY)	1950-1972
NY	5a	James Boyd (Arch & Green Sts.)	1796-1800
	5b	Robert Boyd	1800-1808
	5c	(Robert) Boyd & (Hawthorn) McCulloch	?
	5d	Robert Boyd & Son	? -1850
	5e	Boyd & Brother	1850-1854
	5f	Boyd Bros. & Co.	1854-1863
	5g	Coolidge, Pratt & Co.	1863-1872
	5h	Albany Brewing Co. (60 S. Ferry St.)	1872-1896
	5i	United States Brewing Co., Ltd., of New York City, Albany Brewing Co. (Arch, Ferry, Franklin & Green Sts.)	1896-1904
	5j	Consumers' Albany Brewing Co.	1904-1915
	5k	Albany Brewing Corp.	1915-1916
NY	6	William Brouwer (Fort Orange)	c1650
NY	7a	Uri Burt	1819-1836
	7b	Uri Burt & Son (Charles A.)	1836-1847
	7c	Burt & Son (Montgomery, Lumber, Centre & Colonie Sts.)	1847-1865
NY	8	Uri Burt (Bleecker & Quay Sts.)	1890-1893
NY	9a	S. D. Coleman & Bros. (138/154 Chestnut St.)	1874-1877
	9b	Coleman Bros.	1877-1880
	9c	T. D. Coleman & Bros.	1880-1893
NY	10a	Patrick Cuddy	1880-1882
	10b	Cook & Mantsch	1882-1884
NY	11	Fred Dietz	1874-1875
NY	12a	Robert Dunlop	1806-1810
	12b	Robert Dunlop (Broadway above Quackenbusch St.)	1810-1834
	12c	Peter Ballantine & Co. (N. Market St.)	1834-1839
	12d	Peter Ballantine & Co. (14 Lansing St.)	1839-1840
NY	13	M. H. Farren	1878-1880
NY	14a	(Lancelot) Fiddler & (John) Taylor	1822-1832
	14b	John Taylor	1832-1844
	14c	John Taylor & Sons (John R. & Joseph B.)	1844-1851
	14d	John Taylor & Sons (133 Broadway & Arch St.)	1851-1863
	14e	John Taylor's Sons	1863-1873
	14f	Taylor & Son	1873-1887
	14g	Taylor Brewing and Malting Co.	1887-1905
NY	15	Alex. Gregory (Central Ave.)	1874-1882
NY	16a	John F. Hedrick (396/422 Central Ave.)	1856-1891
	16b	Hedrick Brewing Co.	1891-1920
	16c	Hedrick Brewing Co., Inc.	1933-1965
NY	17	Hoerl & Frank	1878-1879
NY	18	Howard & Ryckman	c1850

Albany (cont.)

NY	19a	Kirchner & Co. (9 Central Ave.)	1874-1877
	19b	J. Kirchner	1877-1882
	19c	J. Kirchner (8 Sherman St.)	1882-1884
	19d	Estate of Jacob Kirchner	1884-1905
	19e	Kirchner Brewing Co.	1905-1912
NY	20a	Andrew Kirk (Broadway North of Van Woert St.)	1832-1857
	20b	James McQuade	1860-1861
	20c	Wilson & Co.	1865-1870
	20d	Smyth & Walker	1870-1877
	20e	James Walker	1877-1879
NY	21	Jean Labadie	c1647
NY	22a	John McKnight (W. Broadway above Orange St.)	1840- ?
	22b	John McKnight (Canal St.)	? -1860
	22c	William G. McKnight	1860-1875
NY	23a	McNamara & McLaughlin	1874-1877
	23b	A. S. Long	1877-1880
	23c	Fleming & Paris	1880-1882
	23d	George F. Granger (Broadway & 4th Ave.)	1882-1884
	23e	Granger & Story	1884-1891
	23f	Geo. F. Story	1891-1900
NY	24a	Marshall & Rapp	1874-1875
	24b	Wm. Fullgraff	1875-1877
	24c	Estate of Wm. Fullgraff	1877-1882
	24d	Fort Orange Brewing Co., Ltd. (900/910 Broadway)	1882-1888
	24e	Municipal Brewing Co.	1888-1891
	24f	Capital Brewing Co.	1891-1898
	24g	Consumers' Brewing Co.	1903-1904
NY	25	Frans Barentse Pastoor (Fort Orange)	c1650
NY	26a	James Quinn, Ale Brewery (26/30 N. Ferry St.)	1845-1866
	26b	(T. J.) Quinn & (Michael N.) Nolan, Ale Brewery	1866-1884
	26c	Quinn & Nolan Ale Brewing Co.	1884-1920
	26d	Quinn & Nolan Ale Brewing Co.	NP 1934-1934
NY	27a	William Schindler (397 S. Pearl St.)	1874-1879
	27b	Mrs. Minna Schindler	1879-1882
NY	28a	Schinnerer & Hinckel	1852- ?
	28b	Fred Hinckel (Swan St., Myrtle & Park Aves.)	? -1884
	28c	Hinckel Brewing Co.	1884-1903
	28d	Hinckel Brewery Co.	1903-1920
NY	29a	J. G. Schneider (133 4th Ave.)	1874-1880
	29b	Mrs. Margaret B. Schneider	1880-1884
NY	30a	Julius Szomaski	1878-1882
	30b	McQuade & Clemishire (137 Canal St.)	1882-1884
	30c	Anthony McQuade	1884-1893
NY	31	Jeremiah Van Rensselaer	1600s
NY	32	Rutgers Hendrickson Van Soest	c1633
NY	33a	George Weber (42/48 3rd Ave.)	1858-1877
	33b	G. Weber & Son	1877-1879
	33c	George Weber	1879-1906
	33d	A. C. & G. F. Weber	1906-1915
	33e	Weber Star Bottling Works, aka Weber Brewing & Bottling Works	1915-1920
NY	34a	Darius S. Wood (Myrtle Ave., Swan & Elm Sts.)	1860s
	34b	John Dobler	1874-1885
	34c	A. F. Dobler	1885-1891
	34d	Theo. M. Amsdell	1891-1893
	34e	Dobler Brewing Co. (Theo M.) Amsdell & (George C.) Hawley	1893-1908
	34f	Dobler Brewing Co.	1908-1920
	34g	Dobler Brewing Co., Inc. (187 S. Swan & Elm Sts.) (owned by Christian Feigenspan Brewing Co.)	1933-1943
	34h	Dobler Brewing Co.	1943-1959
NY	35	Cornelis Wyncoop (Fort Orange)	c1650

Albany (cont.)

NY	36	William Newman (32 Learned St.)	1981-

Allegany

NY	37	W. F. Zink	1878-1879

Amherst (see Williamsville)

Amsterdam

NY	38a	Harry F. Bowler (Main, Ann & Carmichael Sts.)	1889-1916
	38b	Estate of Harry F. Bowler	1916-1920
	38c	Amsterdam Brewing Co., Inc. (399 W. Main St.) aka Emerald Brewing Co. (1940)	1933-1940
NY	39	John Brewer	c1875
NY	40	Charles Moat	1874-1884
NY	41a	John Windbiel	1874-1875
	41b	John F. Pabst	1875-1879
	41c	Anna S. Pabst	1879-1880
	41d	Charles Mattmann	1880-1884

Attica

NY	42a	C. S. Thompson, assignee of R. H. Farnham	1879-1879
	42b	Hodecker & Brecheisen	1879-1880
	42c	B. Brecheisen	1880-1882
	42d	Charles Briem (138 Main St.)	1882-1903

Auburn

NY	43a	Burtis, Cary & Son	1874-1877
	43b	Burtis & Son	1877-1888
	43c	E. C. Burtis	1888-1899
	43d	Underwood, Bartels, & Clifford	1899-1899
NY	44	G. S. Fanning (10 Garden St.)	1874-1898
NY	45a	William Koenig (corner Grant & State Sts.)	1868-1891
	45b	C. Aug. Koenig	1891-1898
	45c	C. A. Koenig & Co.	1898-1916
	45d	Independent-Koenig Brewing Co.	1916-1920
	45e	Koenig Brewing Corp. (245 State St.)	1934-1935
NY	46	Lucas Bros. (41 Moravia St.)	1907-1920
NY	47a	William Sutcliffe (117 Clark St.)	1858-1891
	47b	Sutcliffe Brewing Co.	1891-1895
	47c	Auburn Brewing Co.	1895-1898
	47d	Ehrmann Brewing Co.	1898-1902
	47e	Independent Brewing Co.	1902-1916
NY	48a	William Sutcliffe (132 York St.)	1880-1895
	48b	William Wildner, Cold Spring Brewery	1895-1899
	48c	Estate of William Wildner	1899-1904
	48d	Wildner & Co.	1904-1920
	48e	Cold Springs Beverage Co., Inc.	1933-1934

Augusta

NY	49	Risley & Smith	1874-1875

Baldwinsville

NY	50a	Jos. Schlitz Brewing Co. (2885 Belgium Road) (br. of Milwaukee, WI)	1977-1979
	50b	Anheuser-Busch, Inc. (br. of St. Louis, MO)	1983-

Batavia

NY	51a	Eli H. Fish, Batavia Brewery	c1845
	51b	Eagar & Co., Genesee Brewery	1874-1887
	51c	Batavia Brewing Co.	1890-1891
	51d	William Gamble	1891-1901
	51e	Estate of William Gamble	1901-1904
	51f	William Gamble Brewery, E. H. Gamble	1904-1920
	51g	William Gamble Brewery	NP 1934-1934
NY	52a	Jos. Winling & Co.	1874-1875
	52b	L. Millschauer	1875-1878
	52c	Wm. Gamble	1880-1884

Bedford

NY	53	W. N. Besant	1898-1898

Binghamton

NY	54	Binghamton Brewing Co.	1882-1884
NY	55	John Ehresman & Co. (Laurel Ave.)	1882-1920
NY	56	Hait Bros. & Co. (12 Wall St.)	1882-1882
NY	57a	Laurer Brewing Co. (Laurel Ave.)	1892-1894
	57b	Joseph Laurer Brewing Co.	1894-1920
	57c	Laurer Beverage Corp. (137/143 Laurel Ave.)	1933-1936
	57d	Evans Brewery, Inc.	1936-1937
NY	58a	West & Kress	? -1875
	58b	Lewis West	1875-1884
NY	59a	White & Fuller (19/31 Collier St.)	1848-1884
	59b	S. T. & F. L. White	1884-1888
	59c	F. L. White	1888-1890
	59d	Columbia Brewery, O'Brien & Roberts	1890-1891
	59e	Columbia Brewing Co.	1891-1905

Bleeker

NY	60a	Reinhold Swartz	1874-1875
	60b	Gotthard Lechner	1875-1876
	60c	Roman Ernst	1876-1878

Booneville

NY	61	Chas. Kilkenny	1890-1890

Breslau

NY	62a	Feller & Speiler	1874-1877
	62b	John Feller	1877-1891

Brooklyn (includes Evergreen, Fort Hamilton, Newtown & Williamsburg)

NY	63a	Robert Allen (22 Talmon St.)	1834-1835
	63b	Robert Allen (Neutra Alley)	1936-1937
NY	64a	A. Altenbrand & Co. (96 Kent Ave.)	1888-1890
	64b	A. Altenbrand	1890-1891
NY	65a	John Atkinson (John St. near Jackson)	1840-1841
	65b	T. Haskins (Marshall St. near Jackson)	1846-1847
NY	66	Black Malt Beer Co. (672 Rockaway Ave.)	1907-1907
NY	67	Joseph Blankly (11 Talmon St.)	c1850
NY	68	Farmer Branch & Co. (411 Fulton St.)	1840-1841
NY	69	John Brooks (117 Gold St.)	1824-1826
NY	70a	Joseph Burger (68/84 Meserole & Leonard Sts.)	1861- ?
	70b	Mary A. Brown	1874-1877
	70c	Joseph Burger	1877-1886
	70d	Joseph Burger's Estate	1886-1887
	70e	Burger & Hower Brewing Co., Ltd.	1887-1892
	70f	Burger Brewing Co., Ltd.	1892-1904
NY	71a	Henry Claus (493 Bushwick Ave. & Forrest St.)	1865-1870
	71b	Catherine Lipsius	1870-1876
	71c	Claus-Lipsius aka Rudolph Lipsius (1879-1882)	1876-1889
	71d	Claus-Lipsius Brewing Co.	1889-1904
	71e	Henry Claus Brewing Co. (br. of S. Liebmann's Sons)	1904-1906
NY	72a	Consumers Park Brewery Co. (946/978 Franklin Ave. & Montgomery)	1897-1899
	72b	Consumers Park Brewing Co.	1899-1913
	72c	Interboro Brewing Co.	1913-1920
NY	73a	Dahlbender & Greener (174 Ewen St.)	1875-1880
	73b	Peter Greiner	1880-1882
NY	74	Charles Delavon (Wyckoff & Smith)	c1850
NY	75	Griswold Denison (N. 2nd)	c1870
NY	76	J. V. Devell (16 Osmond Pl.)	1878-1882

Brooklyn (cont.)

NY	77a	Henry Deventhal (30 Webster Pl.)	1874-1888
	77b	Deventhal & Schalk (217/219 21st St.)	1888-1904
NY	78a	Diogenes Brewing Co. (Wyckoff Ave. & Decatur St., Evergreen)	1898-1920
	78b	Malt-Diastase Co.	1920-1932
NY	79	Peter Doelger Brewing Corp. (by Forrest St.)	1929-1935
NY	80a	Samuel Duell, Long Island Brewery (83 3rd Ave. nr Flatbush)	1854-1872
	80b	Arthur Brown, Long Island Brewery, aka A. Brown Brewing Co.	1872-1877
	80c	Long Island Brewing Co. (81/83 3rd Ave., Dean & Bergen)	1877-1896
	80d	Long Island Brewery	1896-1902
	80e	Federal Brewing Co.	1902-1907
NY	81	Empire City Brewing Co., Inc. (583/587 Johnson Ave.)	1933-1937
NY	82a	(Joseph) Eppig & (Frank) Ibert (176 Grove St. & 535 Central)	1888-1889
	82b	Joseph Eppig	1889-1907
	82c	Joseph Eppig Estate	1907-1915
NY	83a	Joseph Fallert (52/66 Meserole St.)	1878-1884
	83b	Joseph Fallert Brewing Co.	1884-1920
NY	84	Farrell & Co.	1874-1875
NY	85a	(Hubert) Fischer & (Leonhard) Eppig (22/32 George St. near Evergreen)	1866-1876
	85b	Leonard Eppig, Germania Brewery	1876-1884
	85c	Leonard Eppig & Sons	1884-1888
	85d	Leonard Eppig	1888-1893
	85e	Estate of Leonard Eppig (193 Melrose St.)	1893-1904
	85f	Leonard Eppig Brewing Co., Germania Brewery	1904-1920
	85g	Interboro Cereal Beverage Co. (198 Melrose & 24 George Sts.)	1920-1932
	85h	Interboro Beverage Corp., aka Brooklyn Bottling & Distributing Co., Inc.	1932-1935
	85i	George Ehret Brewery, Inc.	1935-1949
	85j	Jos. Schlitz Brewing Co. (br. of Milwaukee, WI)	1949-1973
NY	86a	William Forster (1089 Myrtle Ave.)	1870-1874
	86b	Wm. Behr	1874-1875
	86c	William Raether	1875-1880
	86d	John Reimers (Myrtle Ave. & Jay St., Ridgewood)	1890-1897
NY	87a	F. Fries (2 Meserole St.)	c1870
	87b	Lukas Marquardt	1874-1884
	87c	J. Marquardt (42 Union Ave.)	1884-1891
NY	88a	Junius A. Fuller	1835-1854
	88b	(William) Howard & (Junius A.) Fuller (Bridge & Plymouth Sts.)	1854-1888
	88c	Howard & Fuller Brewing Co.	1888-1914
NY	89	Garser & Steinhauser (156 Ewen St.)	c1870
NY	90	Balthasar Gehrhardt (Marion St.)	1870-1875
NY	91a	Geo. Gillig	c1844
	91b	Hamm	c1850
NY	92a	(Charles) Gluck & (Hermann B.) Scharmann (172 Bushwick Ave.)	1873-1882
	92b	H. B. Scharmann (355/375 Pulaski St.)	1882-1888
	92c	H. B. Scharmann & Sons	1888-1920
NY	93a	(Charles) Gluck & (Herman B.) Scharmann (Bushwick Ave., Meserole, and Scholes St.)	1869-1873
	93b	Henry A. Urban	1873-1879
	93c	Urban & Abbott	1879-1880
	93d	Warren G. Abbott	1880-1882
	93e	W. G. Abbott Brewing Co.	1882-1893
	93f	Abbott-Katz Brewing Co.	1893-1896
	93g	Eastern Brewing Co.	1896-1915
NY	94a	John George Grauer, Ridgewood Park Brewery (Cypress Ave., Willow, and Green Sts., Evergreen)	1891-1907
	94b	John George Grauer Estate	1907-1910
NY	95	James J. Gray	1874-1875
NY	96	William Guenther (436 S. 5th St.)	1874-1893

Brooklyn (cont.)

NY	97	Thomas Harkins (38 Stanton)	c1850
NY	98	Albert H. Harris (241 Adams St.)	1895-1895
NY	99	Henry Hecht (Washington St. near Jefferson)	c1870
NY	100a	Henry Herrmann (14 N. 9th St.)	1874-1880
	100b	Herrmann & Mannell (174 N. 9th St.)	1880-1882
	100c	Anton Mannell	1882-1901
	100d	George Ehret's Weiss Beer Brewery	1901-1902
	100e	Anton Mannell	1902-1911
	100f	Strasser & Schwing	191101916
NY	101	Hower & Urban Brewing Co. (Newtown)	1898-1899
NY	102a	Fred'k Hower Brewing Co. (239/269 Pulaski St.)	1890-1896
	102b	Excelsior Brewing Co.	1896-1932
	102c	Kings Brewery, Inc. (225/279 Pulaski St.)	1932-1938
NY	103a	Hughes & Grass (361 1st St.)	1870- ?
	103b	Henry Grass	? -1877
	103c	Grass & Co. (435 1st St.)	1877-1884
NY	104a	Frank Ibert (405 Evergreen Ave. & Linden & Grove Sts.)	1891-1894
	104b	Frank Ibert Brewing Co.	1894-1914
NY	105	Illig & Kraus (Williamsburg)	c1857
NY	106a	Casper Illig (60 Scholes St.)	1870-1877
	106b	John Raber	1877-1882
	106c	New York and Brooklyn Brewing Co. (48/60 Scholes & Lorimer Sts. & Bushwick Ave.)	1882-1915
NY	107a	Henry Immen (46 Commercial St.)	1874-1888
	107b	Henry Immen's Sons	1888-1895
	107c	Christopher Immen	1895-1901
	107d	Henry Immen's Son	1901-1912
NY	108a	India Wharf Brewing Co. (48/60 Hamilton Ave.)	1889-1920
	108b	India Wharf Brewery, Inc.	1933-1934
NY	109a	John Joerger (Graham Ave. & Meserole St.)	? -1866
	109b	Otto Huber	1866-1868
	109c	Otto Huber (242 Meserole St. & Bushwick Ave.)	1868-1889
	109d	Otto Huber Brewery (1/3 Bushwick Place)	1889-1920
	109e	Edward B. Hittleman Brewery, Inc.	1920-1934
	109f	Hittleman-Goldenrod Brewery, Inc.	1934-1937
	109g	Edelbrau Brewery, Inc.	1937-1945
	109h	Edelbrew Brewery, Inc.	1945-1951
NY	110a	John Johnson (Jay & Front Sts.)	1830-1870
	110b	Leavy & Keany	1870-1872
	110c	Leavy & Keany Brewing Co.	1872-1877
	110d	Leavy & Britton Brewing Co.	1877-1911
NY	111a	William Johnson (49 Front St.)	1820-1823
	111b	William Johnson & Son (John)	1823-1825
	111c	William Johnson & Son (56 Front St.)	1825-1830
	111d	William Johnson (8 Hicks St.)	1830-1834
NY	112a	Thomas Kiefer (132/140 Scholes St.)	1875-1876
	112b	Henry Kiefer	1876-1884
	112c	Metropolitan Brewing Co.	1884-1890
NY	113	John Keenan (103 Bridge St.)	1845-1846
NY	114a	Kings County Brewing Co. (3rd Ave. & 96th St., Fort Hamilton)	1893-1897
	114b	George Apfel	1897-1898
	114c	Apfel-Klueg Golden Horn Brewing Co.	1898-1903
	114d	Golden Horn Brewing Co.	1903-1906
	114e	(Conrad) Eurich's Fort Hamilton Brewery	1906-1907
NY	115a	John Kissel & Son (169 Harrison Ave. & Wallabout St.)	1893-1904
	115b	John Kissel & Son	1912-1913
NY	116a	Jacob Klein	1875-1875
	116b	Goliath & Klein	1875-1876
	116c	Daniel McGoldrich (55 Atlantic St.)	1876-1879

Brooklyn (cont.)

NY	117a	Charles Kolb (283 Witherspool St. & Yates Ave.)	1870-1880
	117b	Ferdinand Muench (277/299 Vernon Ave.)	1880-1888
	117c	Ferd. Muench Brewery, Inc.	1888-1920
NY	118a	(Philip) Leibinger & (Henry) Oehm Brewing Co. (Wyckoff Ave. & Halsey St., Newtown)	1887-1895
	118b	Leibinger Brewing Co. (Wyckoff Ave. & Fairfield St.)	1895-1899
	118c	Conrad Eurich's Brewery	1899-1903
	118d	Elm Brewing Co.	1903-1907
NY	119a	Samuel Liebmann (Meserole St., Williamsburg)	1854-1855
	119b	S. Liebmann (36 Forrest & Bremen Sts.)	1855-1870
	119c	S. Liebmann's Sons	1870-1884
	119d	S. Liebmann's Sons Brewing Co.	1884-1920
	119e	Liebmann Breweries, Inc.	1920-1964
	119f	Rheingold Breweries, Inc., aka Forrest Brewing Co., Jacob Ruppert	1964-1976
NY	120a	Limburger & Walter (1040/1042 Dean & Bergen Sts.)	1849-1866
	120b	Goetz & Muench	1866-1876
	120c	Christian A. Goetz, Bedford Brewery	1876-1884
	120d	Budweiser Brewing Co.	1884-1898
	120e	Nassau Brewing Co.	1898-1916
NY	121	H. H. Linnerman (150 Ewen St.)	c1870
NY	122	Henry Lott (Dean St.)	c1840
NY	123	Nicholas Ludewig (190 Union Ave.)	c1870
NY	124a	George Malcolm's Wallabaut Brewery (394/414 Flushing Ave. & Skillman St.)	1869-1891
	124b	Malcolm Brewing Co.	1891-1903
	124c	Franklin Brewing Co.	1903-1917
NY	125a	J. G. & F. Mark (26 Bremen St.)	1874-1877
	125b	John G. Mark	1877-1879
NY	126a	Louise Markgraf (182 Graham St.)	1874-1877
	126b	Weber & Amthor	1877-1880
NY	127	Klaus Martens (23 Union St.)	c1870
NY	128	Edward L. Martin (24 Kent Ave.)	c1870
NY	129	William Maupai (168 Ewen St.)	1878-1884
NY	130a	John Meninger (162/183 Cook St.)	1879-1884
	130b	Robert Schleicher	1884-1897
	130c	John Meninger	1897-1902
NY	131a	Meltzer Bros. (John & Gottfried) (60 Meserole St.)	1865-1873
	131b	Meltzer Bros. (185 Suydam & 170 Myrtle Sts.)	1873-1901
	131c	Meltzer Bros. Brewing Co.	1901-1917
NY	132a	Leonard Michel Brewing Co. (122 3rd, Bond & 4th Sts.)	1907-1920
	132b	Rubel Ice Co.	1920-1927
	132c	The Ebling Brewing Co., Inc. (122/140 3rd & Bond Sts.)	1927-1937
NY	133a	F. Moesmer, Washington Brewery (Washington & Franklin Aves.)	1898-1900
	133b	F. Moesmer's Brewery, Inc.	1900-1902
	133c	Consumers Star Brewing Co.	1902-1904
	133d	Geisler & Kramm	1904-1905
	133e	Benjamin Bros., Muenchner Brewery	1905-1907
	133f	Park Brewery	1907-1908
	133g	Beck Bros. Brewing Co.	1908-1911
NY	134a	Joseph Nickel	1874-1877
	134b	L. Schmidt (36 Broadway)	1877-1879
NY	135a	North American Brewing Co. (1306 Greene, Hamburg & Myrtle Ave.)	1892-1933
	135b	North American Brewing Co. (1306/1336 Greene Ave.)	1933-1946
	135c	Chas. Schaefer Corp.	1946-1948
NY	136a	(David) Obermeyer & (Joseph) Liebmann, Havana Brewery (59/71 Bremen & Noll Sts.)	1868-1924
	136b	S. Liebmann's Sons, Obermeyer & Liebmann Dept.	1924-1933

Brooklyn (cont.)

NY	137	Old Dutch Brewers, Inc. (761/797 E. 42nd St. & Glenwood Road)	1934-1948
NY	138	John A. Oxley & Co. (25 Union St.)	c1870
NY	139a	Landzer (Liberty Ave.)	? -1883
	139b	Piel Bros. (Gottfried, Michael & Wilhelm) (Liberty & Sheffield Aves.)	1883-1933
	139c	Piel Bros., Inc. (315 Liberty Ave.)	1933-1962
	139d	Piel Bros., Inc. (br. of Associated Brewing Co., Detroit, MI)	1962-1973
	139e	Piel Bros., Inc.	1973-1973
NY	140a	Prospect Park Brewing Co. (Coney Island Ave.)	1898-1900
	140b	Park Circle Brewing Co.	1900-1905
NY	141a	Runge & Seidler (51st St. between 3rd & 4th Aves.)	1874-1877
	141b	A. Seidler	1877-1879
NY	142	Elizabeth Sander	1875- ?
NY	143	John Saunders (Clasin near Myrtle)	1845-1850
NY	144a	Peter Scharnagle	1865- ?
	144b	Scharnagle & Reitzner	?
	144c	Edward Reitzner (Bushwick Ave. near Wall)	c1870
	144d	Reitzner & Lutz	c1870-1875
	144e	J. J. Jones, Boulevard Garden Brewery (31/35 Bremen St.)	1875-1880
	144f	David Jones, Boulevard Garden Brewery	1880-1884
	144g	(Isaac) Dannenberg & (Thomas) Coles, Boulevard Garden Brewery (Bushwick Ave. & Bremen St.)	1884-1902
NY	145	The F. & M. Schaefer Brewing Co. (430 Kent Ave. & 2 S. 9th St.)	1916-1976
NY	146	Schnaderbeck & Co. (30/32 Remsen St.)	1862-1870
NY	147a	John Schneider (Ewen St.)	1855-1856
	147b	John Schneider (197 Humboldt & Meserole & Scholes St.)	1856-1876
	147c	Jacob Bossert	1876-1876
	147d	Williamsburg Brewing Co.	1876-1894
	147e	Congress Brewing Co., Ltd.	1894-1917
NY	148a	J. P. Schoenewald (96 Ewen St.)	c1870
	148b	J. P. Schoenewald (Forrest & Bremen Sts., Williamsburg)	1874-1878
NY	149	Charles Scofield	1840-1842
NY	150a	Nicholas Seitz (13th St.)	1846-1847
	150b	Nicholas Seitz (Remsen St. opposite Lafayette)	1847-1871
	150c	(Michael & Joseph) Seitz & (Francis X.) Bill	1871-1873
	150d	N. Seitz & Sons (256/266 Maujer St.)	1873-1878
	150e	N. Seitz's Son (Michael)	1878-1909
	150f	Seitz Brewing Co.	1909-1911
NY	151a	Robert Selg (238/252 Scholes St. near Southwick Ave.)	1860-1870
	151b	Margaretha Selg	1870-1875
	151c	(Hubert) Fischer & (Charles) Frese	? -1884
	151d	Chas. Frese	1884-1893
	151e	Estate of Chas. Frese	1893-1901
	151f	Frese's Consumers Brewery	1901-1904
	151g	Frese & Urff Brewery	1904-1907
NY	152	Thomas H. Smith (250/252 Marshall St.)	1837-1841
NY	153	Smith & Fuller	c1850
NY	154a	Staats Bros.	1855-1875
	154b	William Markgraf	1875-1876
	154c	Ernest Ochs	1876-1877
	154d	Ochs & Lehnert (193 Bushwick Ave. & Scholes St.)	1878-1884
	154e	Ernest Ochs	1884-1893
	154f	Ernest Ochs, Inc.	1893-1905
	154g	New York and Brooklyn Brewery, Ochs Brewery	1905-1906
NY	155a	Star Excelsior Brewing Co. (33 Cranberry St.)	1875-1877
	155b	H. C. Foster, Jr.	1877-1878

Brooklyn (cont.)

NY	156a	Joseph Breitkopf	1899- ?
	156b	Joseph Breitkopf Brewing	? -1903
	156c	Adolf Schmidt's Kloster Brewrey (Jamaica & Pennsylvania Aves.)	1903-1908
	156d	Bushwick Brewery (129 Bradford St.)	1908-1909
NY	157	Stilwell & Co. (Columbia St. near Atlantic St.)	1870-1875
NY	158a	William Stratton (13 State St.)	1846-1847
	158b	William Stratton (Boerum St.)	1847-1847
NY	159a	Streeter & Denison (84 N. 2nd St.)	1870-1899
	159b	Streeter & Denison (241 Wythe Ave.)	1899-1920
NY	160a	(Joseph) Stehlin & (Joseph) Breitkopf (1632 Bushwick Ave. & Conway St.) aka Breitkopf & Trommer (1897)	1895-1897
	160b	J. F. Trommer's Evergreen Brewery	1897-1902
	160c	John F. Trommer, Evergreen Brewery	1902-1920
	160d	John F. Trommer, Inc.	1920-1951
	160e	Piel Bros.	1951-1955
NY	161	Twenty-Sixth Ward Brewing Co. (Osborne St. & Eastern Pkwy.)	1899-1899
NY	162a	(Anton) Vigelius & (Wm.) Ulmer (Beaver & 29/31 Belvidere St.)	1871-1877
	162b	William Ulmer	1877-1899
	162c	William Ulmer Brewery, Inc.	1899-1920
NY	163	Anton Von Fricken	1874-1875
NY	164	Jacob Weber (Lafayette Ave. near Throop Ave.)	c1870
NY	165a	Paul Weidmann (1st & Berry Sts.)	1890-1892
	165b	Paul Weidmann Brewing Co.	1892-1906
NY	166a	John Welz (Scholes St.)	1857-1861
	166b	John Welz (Myrtle & Wyckoff Aves.)	1861-1883
	166c	(John) Welz (Jr.) & (Charles) Zerweck, High Ground Brewery	1883-1920
NY	167a	Frederick W. Witte (59 Commerce St.)	1874-1877
	167b	Fred. W. Witte, White Beer Brewery (96/102 Luqueer St.)	1877-1903
NY	168a	Woodside Brewing Co. (Newtown)	c1891
	168b	Rheinhold Grunberg (Summerfield St. & Rathjen Ave., Evergreen)	1896-1900
	168c	R. & A. Gruenberg (60 Summerfield St.)	1900-1903
	168d	Adolph Gruenberg	1903-1904
NY	169	Saunders Worthschaft (Classen Ave.)	c1850
NY	170	Frederick Wunchenmeyer (Walworth St. near Myrtle Ave.)	c1850

Buffalo

NY	171a	Albert Albrecht (815 Broadway)	1852-1880
	171b	Julius Binz	1880-1887
	171c	Broadway Brewing and Malting Co. (797/815 Broadway)	1887-1920
	171d	Broadway Brewing Co., Inc.	1933-1934
	171e	George F. Stein Brewery, Inc.	1935-1958
NY	172a	Phillip Born (Genesee & Jefferson Sts.)	1840-1862
	172b	(Mrs. Phillip) Born & (Gerhard) Lang	1862-1876
	172c	Gerhard Lang, Park Brewery (Jefferson & Best Sts.)	1876-1897
	172d	Gerhard Lang Brewery (Jefferson, Best, Berlin & Dodge Sts.)	1897-1933
	172e	Gerhard Lang Brewery (400 Best St.)	1933-1949
NY	173a	Buffalo Co-operative Brewing Co. (160 High, Goodrich and Michigan Sts.)	1880-1920
	173b	Mohawk Products Co., Inc. (146/160 High St.)	1933-1934
	173c	Iroquois Beverage Corp.	1934-1937
NY	174	Buffalo Weiss Beer Brewing Co. (90 Raze St.)	1891-1891
NY	175	Channsley's Cold Springs Brewery	1840-1855
NY	176a	Christian Dier	1874-1877
	176b	John Karn	1877-1879
NY	177a	Mrs. Fred. Driskel (Burton Alley)	1874-1880
	177b	Burton Co-operative Brewing Co.	1880-1882
	177c	Andrew Driskel	1882-1884

Buffalo (cont.)

NY	178a	Joseph Friedmann (Oak St. near Tupper)	1840-1855
	178b	Beck & Baumgartner	1855-1860
	178c	Magnus Beck	1860-1865
	178d	Magnus Beck (407 N. Division St.)	1865-1883
	178e	Magnus Beck's Estate	1883-1886
	178f	Magnus Beck Brewing Co. (466/468 N. Division & Spring Sts.)	1886-1920
	178g	Magnus Beck Brewing Co., Inc. (461/475 N. Division St.)	1933-1955
NY	179a	Gecman & Schroeter	1879-1880
	179b	Anna Gecman	1880-1880
NY	180a	Charles Gerber (821 Main St.)	1874-1884
	180b	Empire Brewing Co.	1884-1891
	180c	Busch Brewing Co.	1891-1893
NY	181	Great Lakes Brewery, Inc.	1933-1934
NY	182a	David Haas, Star Brewery (642/644 Spring St.)	1873-1884
	182b	Star Brewery	1884-1901
NY	183a	Conrad Hammer (1615/1621 Broadway)	1893-1894
	183b	Germania Brewing Co.	1894-1912
NY	184	M. Heinold (637 Exchange St.)	1879-1882
NY	185a	Heiser Bros. (Seneca St. near Michigan)	1845-1850
	185b	Gottfried Heiser	1850-1870
NY	186a	Nicholas Hiemenz	1874-1877
	186b	George Reis	1877-1879
NY	187	Hydraulic Weiss Beer Brewing Co. (736 Exchange St.)	1890-1890
NY	188a	Francis J. Jost Jr. (419 Broadway)	1874-1877
	188b	Jost Brewing Co.	1877-1882
NY	189a	Kaltenbach, Hofflin & Costello (Lutheran Alley)	1850-1874
	189b	F. X. Kaltenbach	1874-1876
	189c	F. X. Kaltenbach (Pratt St. near Eagle)	1876-1886
	189d	Excelsior Brewing Co.	1886-1887
	189e	Kaltenbach Brewing Co., Excelsior Brewery (1571/1575 Clinton & Pratt Sts.)	1887-1906
	189f	Buffalo Brewing Co.	1910-1920
NY	190a	Jacob F. Kuhn (644/652 Broadway)	1874-1884
	190b	Jacob F. Kuhn & Sons	1884-1891
	190c	Gambrinus Brewing Co.	1891-1904
NY	191	George F. Lang	1874-1875
NY	192a	(J. M.) Luippold & (Wm.) Voetsch (298/300 Emslie St.)	1869- ?
	192b	John M. Luippold	1874-1887
	192c	East Buffalo Brewing Co.	1887-1920
	192d	Phoenix Brewery Corp.	1934-1957
	192e	Phoenix Brewery Corp., br. of International Breweries, Inc.	1957-1959
NY	193	August Moeller	1874-1879
NY	194a	James Moffat (Mohawk & Morgan Sts.)	1860- ?
	194b	Moffat & Service	1878-1890
	194c	Henry C. Moffat (143 W. Mohawk St.)	1890-1920
	194d	Moffats Ale Brewery	NP 1934-1934
NY	195a	Muehlbauer & Co. (118 Puerner Ave.)	1893- ?
	195b	Berliner White Beer Brewing Co.	1897-1905
NY	196	Alois Muehlbauer, Jr. (868 N. Hampton St.)	1910-1912
NY	197	People's Brewing Co. (Broadway & Belt Line Crossing)	1899-1899
NY	198a	Fred. Phillipbar	1875- ?
	198b	F. W. Phillipbar (1859 Niagara St.)	? -1888
NY	199a	George Rochevot, Lion Brewery (1033 Jefferson St.)	1856-1892
	199b	Lion Brewing Co., aka Lion Brewery (993/1041 Jefferson St.)	1892-1904
	199c	Consumers' Brewery	1904-1920

Buffalo (cont.)

NY	200a	John G. Rohrer	1874-1877
	200b	Margaret Rohrer	1877-1879
NY	201a	Jacob Roos (Broadway between Church & York Sts.)	1830- ?
	201b	George Roos (95 Roos & 230 Pratt St.)	1874-1887
	201c	Roos Co-operative Brewing Co.	1887-1892
	201d	Iroquois Brewing Co. (210/256 Pratt St.)	1892-1920
	201e	Iroquois Beverage Corp.	1933-1955
	201f	International Breweries, Inc.	1955-1967
	201g	Iroquois Brewing Co., div. of Iroquois Industries, Inc.	1967-1971
NY	202a	Alois Schaeffer (128/132 Lake View & Porter Aves.)	1860-1885
	202b	Lake View Brewing Co.	1885-1920
NY	203a	(J. F.) Schanzlin & Hoffman (Main & St. Paul Sts.)	1840-1842
	203b	Hoffman	1842- ?
NY	204	Jacob F. Schanzlin (1857 Main St.)	1842-1882
NY	205a	Jacob Scheu (644 Spring St.)	1885- ?
	205b	Columbia Brewing Co.	1888-1890
	205c	Queen City Brewing Co.	1890-1891
NY	206a	Jacob Scheu (1088 Niagara St. & Albany St.)	1874-1884
	206b	International Brewing Co.	1884-1920
NY	207a	Philip Scheu	1849-1859
	207b	Joseph L. Haberstroh (11/13 High St. aka Haberstroh & Scheu (1875)	1859-1885
	207c	German-American Brewing Co.	1885-1920
	207d	German-American Brewing Co. (525 Humboldt Parkway) NP	1934-1934
NY	208a	Conrad Schleucher (167 Cherry St.)	1874-1875
	208b	Mrs. Eva Schleucher	1875-1884
NY	209a	A. Schreiber Brewing Co. (662/686 Fillmore Ave. nr. Broadway)	1899-1920
	209b	Schreiber Brewing Co., Inc.	1933-1950
NY	210a	John Schusler (143/147 Emslie St.)	1859-1889
	210b	John Schusler Brewing Co.	1889-1900
	210c	William Simon Brewery (127/161 Emslie St.)	1900-1920
	210d	The William Simon Brewery	1933-1972
NY	211	Francis X. Schwab Brewing Corp.	1933-1933
NY	212a	Shoemaker & Noble	1875-1877
	212b	E. D. Shoemaker	1877-1879
NY	213	W. W. Sloan	1874-1880
NY	214a	Louis Torge	1874-1875
	214b	George Torge	1875-1877
	214c	Scobell & Schub	1877-1879
NY	215a	Frederick & Mary Voetsch	1874-1877
	215b	Scheufele & Co.	1877-1878
NY	216a	William Voetsch (10/24 W. Bennett St.)	1874-1881
	216b	Clinton Co-operative Brewing Co.	1881-1902
	216c	Clinton-Star Brewery	1902-1909
	216d	John L. Schwartz Brewing Co.	1909-1920
	216e	Downs Brewing Co.	1939-1940
	216f	Van Buren Products, Inc.	1940-1947
	216g	Iroquois Beverage Corp.	1947-1950
NY	217a	Margaret Welte	1874-1877
	217b	Philip Schneider	1877-1880
	217c	Fredk. Wilting	1880-1882
	217d	George Zeiler (1147 Main St.)	1882-1884
NY	218a	Christian Weyand (785/795 Main St.)	1866-1890
	218b	Chr. Weyand Brewing Co. (785/795 Main St. & Goodell St.)	1890-1920
NY	219a	Albert Ziegele (Genesee St.)	1850-1855
	219b	Albert Ziegele (831 Main St.)	1855-1880
	219c	Z. Ziegele & Co.	1880-1887
	219d	Ziegele Brewing Co., Phoenix Brewery (Washington & Virginia)	1887-1920

Caledonia

NY 220	H. M. Mather	1875-1875

Canaan

NY 221a	Patrick Losty	1856-1891
221b	John B. Losty	1891-1899
221c	John B. Losty & Co.	1899-1903

Canajoharie

NY 222a	Louis Bierbauer	1860-1904
222b	Bierbauer Brewing Co.	1904-1920
222c	Canajoharie Brewing Co.	1933-1934

Canandaigua

NY 223a	James & Alexander McKechnie, Canandaigua Brewery	1843-1888
223b	McKechnie Brewing Co.	1888-1895
223c	J. & A. McKechnie Brewing Co.	1895-1913
223d	Canandaigua Brewery, Inc., aka Canandaigua Brewing Co.	1913-1916
223e	J. & A. McKechnie Brewing Co., Inc.	NP 1934-1934

Cape Vincent

NY 224a	George Scobell	1872-1874
224b	Scobell & Kinghorn	1874-1877
224c	R. S. Scobell	1877-1891
224d	Henry Steinmann	1891-1893
224e	Theo Aubertine	1893-1895
224f	S. S. Bloch	1895-1900

Carthage

NY 225a	Joseph Smith	1874-1875
225b	C. Clifford	1877-1884
225c	Cold Spring Brewery Co.	1884-1888

Castleton

NY 226	William Kirk (15 Downing St.)	1874-1875

Catskill

NY 227a	Catherine Heiselmann	1898-1898
227b	Mountain Dew Brewing Co.	1898-1899
NY 228	S. C. Pullman	1888-1888

Chautauqua

NY 229	George Himelien	1874-1875

Clarkstown

NY 230	J. G. C. Schmersahl	1874-1879

Cohoes

NY 231a	Cohoes Brewing Co.	1887-1890
231b	Cohoes Brewing Co., Inc.	1890-1891
231c	(Edward) Penrose & (Martin) McEniry (Lansing & Newark Sts.)	1891-1920

Colden

NY 232a	Charles Miller & Co.	1874-1877
232b	Mrs. E. Miller	1877-1884
232c	Benj. Witter	1884-1888
232d	Colden Brewing Co.	1888-1891

College Point (L. I.)

NY 233a	Herman Weber	1874-1877
233b	Joseph Ochs	1877-1880
233c	Hirsch & Herman	1880-1884
233d	Fitzgerald Brewing Co.	1884-1890
233e	Mutual Brewing Co. (1st St. & 2nd Ave.)	1890-1895
233f	Geo. Karsch	1895-1896
233g	Karsch Brewing Co.	1896-1910

Collins

NY 234	Henry Kehrer	1874-1875
NY 235	Charles Trunk	1874-1875

Concord

NY 236	Joseph Lutz	1878-1880

Constableville

NY 237a Jos. Siegel 1878-1882
237b Doyle Bros. & Roser 1882-1884
237c A. J. Steinbrenner 1884-1886
237d Conrad Ament 1886-1906

Corning

NY 238 Fred Haischer 1874-1902

NY 239 John C. Weller 1874-1875

Cuba

NY 240a Edward Agate (Spring St.) 1874-1890
240b W. & J. Agate 1890-1891

Dansville

NH 241a John Klink 1860-1880
241b Robert Dotterweich 1880-1888
241c Dansville Brewing Co. (Liberty St.) 1888-1903
241d Philip Keppeler 1903-1909

Dobbs Ferry

NY 242a Peter M. Biegen 1852-1881
242b Hudson River Brewing Co. 1881-1886
242c Anchor Brewing Co. 1886-1900
242d Manilla Anchor Brewing Co. 1900-1920

Dunkirk

NY 243a George Dotterweich, City Brewery (537 Dove & 6th Sts.) 1855-1884
243b Andrew Dotterweich 1884-1900
243c A. Dotterweich Brewing Co., City Brewery 1900-1920

NY 244a Metz Brewery c1870
244b Finck ? -1888
244c (Frank) Wehrle & (Fred) Koch (13/15 W. Courtney St.) 1888-1896
244d Fred. Koch, Lake City Brewery 1896-1911
244e Fred Koch Brewery, Inc. 1911-1920
244f Fred Koch Brewery (25 W. Courtney St.) 1933-
aka Blackhorse Brewery (1973-)
aka Iroquois Brewing Co. (1976-)

NY 245 Henry Smith 1879-1879

NY 246a Andrew Unschuld 1865-1869
246b Henry Finck 1869-1889
246c Henry Finck, Jr. 1889-1902

Eden

NY 247 Daniel Schweikhart 1874-1884

Edgewater (Staten Island)

NY 248 Charles Buschoff 1874-1875

Ellenville

NY 249a John Kuhlmann (2 Market St.) 1880-1884
249b Catherine Kuhlmann 1884-1895
249c John Kuhlmann Brewing Co. 1895-1920
249d John Kuhlmann Brewing Co., Inc. (Berme Road) 1933-1935

Elmira

NY 250a Thomas Briggs (116/121 E. 2nd St.) 1866-1870
250b T. Briggs & Co. 1870-1920

NY 251a Chemung Consumers Brewing Co. (735 Baldwin St.) 1902-1907
251b Record Brewing Co. 1907-1920

NY 252 Edward P. Gardner 1884-1884

NY 253a Kolb & Baldwin 1869- ?
253b P. Pfohl & Co. 1874-1877
253c Arnold, Kolb & Co. 1877-1879
253d Charles Gerber Jr. 1879-1893
253e Elmira Brewing Co. (River Road) 1893-1902
253f Krantz-Laurer Brewery 1902-1902
253g Elmira Brewing Co. 1902-1903

Elmira (cont.)

NY 254a Adam Mander 1856-1884
254b Gertrude Mander 1884-1895
254c C. A. & F. Mander 1895-1900
254d C. & A. Mander 1900-1920

NY 255 Nectar Brewing Corp. (302 Tuttle Ave.) 1933-1939

Esopus

NY 256 Fred Staudacher 1879-1880

Evans' Mills

NY 257 Carleton Clifford 1875-1882

Evergreen (see Brooklyn)

Fayetteville

NY 258 Globe Brewing Co. 1888-1888

NY 259 Jones & Kingsley 1874-1875

Fishkill

NY 260 J. V. Walshe 1878-1880

Flushing

NY 261 Levinger & Co. 1874-1875

Fort Edward

NY 262 J. M. Blaisdell 1874-1875

NY 263a A. Wing & Co. 1859- ?
263b Durkee & Co. 1874-1888
263c Fort Edward Brewing Co. 1888-1927

Fort Hamilton (see Brooklyn)

Fort Plain

NY 264a John Beck 1878-1897
264b Pelican Brewery 1897-1900
264c Berthold Matt, Pelican Brewery 1900-1904

Four Corners (see West New Brighton)

Freedom

NY 265 Barbara Hofreiter 1875- ?

Fremont

NY 266 Joseph Kille 1874-1884

NY 267 J. Schneider 1879-1879

Fulton (see South Valley)

Geddes (see Syracuse)

Geneva

NY 268a Lyon & Thwaites 1888-1889
268b James Thwaites 1889-1897
268c Geneva Brewing Co. 1897-1898
268d Geneva Brewing Co. 1902-1906
268e Seneca Brewing Co. 1906-1908
268f Geneva Brewing Co. 1910-1915

NY 269 George Spink 1890-1890

NY 270 Thomas J. Stone 1901-1902

Glens Falls

NY 271a Coney & Hicks 1874-1877
271b Coney & Sheldon 1877-1880
271c John W. Knight 1880-1884
271d Glens Falls Ale Co. (South St.) 1884-1920
271e Glens Falls Ale Co. NP 1934-1934

Gloversville

NY 272 Adirondack Brewing Co. (432 N. Main St.) 1898-1913

Gowanda

NY 273a Frank Garcis 1875- ?
273b Fischer & Garber 1879-1880
273c Fischer & Co. 1880-1884
273d A. Fischer 1884-1888

Great Valley
NY 274a J. Sprecher & Co. 1875-1877
274b L. Forge 1877-1884

Greenfield
NY 275 Granite Lake Brewery 1891-1891

Half Moon
NY 276a Reinhold Wenner 1874-1879
276b R. Wenner & Son 1879-1882

Halls Corners (Seneca)
NY 277a Wesley P. Stokes 1878-1884
277b Edward Wyand 1884- ?
277c Wesley P. Stokes 1888-1904
277d Nichols Bros. 1905- ?
277e Murray Bros. 1908-1910

Hamburg
NY 278 Frank J. Fink 1874-1884

Haverstraw
NY 279a Thomas Finegan (W. Broad St. & Clove Ave.) 1896-1904
279b Jas. E. Finegan 1904-1906

Herkimer
NY 280a Ph. Hellmick 1874-1877
280b Anna M. Goldsmith 1877-1891
280c Peter Yanner 1891-1893
280d Mohawk Valley Brewing Co. (22 Canal St.) 1893-1896

Hicksville (Long Island)
NY 281a William Becker (Broadway & 4th St.) 1874-1903
281b Staehle Bros. 1903-1905

Hoosick Falls
NY 282a Hoosick Falls Brewing Co. 1895-1898
282b Hoosick Falls Brewing Co. 1903-1904

Hornell (Hornellsville until 1906)
NY 283a Leach & Kennedy (River & Front Sts.) 1874-1882
283b Horace D. Leach 1882-1890
283c Louis Eydt 1890-1893

NY 284 John Sauter 1874-1884

NY 285a Schwarzenbach Brewing Co. (Erie R. R. & Franklin St.) 1895-1920
285b Hornell Brewing Co., Inc. (1/13 Franklin St.) 1934-1960
285c Hornell Brewing Co., aka Consumers Brewing Co. (br. of Metropolis Brewery of New Jersey, Inc.) 1960-1964

Hudson
NY 286a (Benjamin) Millard & (Stephen B.) Barnard 1858-1864
286b Millard & Waterbury 1864-1872
286c Waterbury & Peabody 1872-1877
286d Ezra Waterbury 1877-1881
286e (Wm.) Granger & (Henry L.) Gregg 1881-1886
286f Granger & Gregg Brewing Co. (2nd & State Sts.) 1886-1897
286g Granger Brewing Co. 1897-1903
286h Yuengling's Hudson-New York Breweries 1903-1904
286i Philip Schauble 1904-1905
286j Hudson City Brewing Co. 1905-1908

NY 287a Benjamin Faulkins (Prospect Hill formerly Windmill Hill) 1786-1835
287b George Robinson 1836-1840
287c Robinson & Phipps 1840-1856
287d Jas. L. Phipps 1856-1865
287e Phipps & Evans 1865-1873
287f C. H. Evans & Co. 1873-1878
287g C. H. Evans 1878-1888
287h C. H. Evans & Sons (Hill & N. 2nd Sts.) 1888-1928
287i C. H. Evans & Sons NP 1934-1934

Ilion
NY 288a Spedding & Sayert 1874-1877
288b S. Spedding 1877-1884
288c Mohawk Valley Brewing Co. (22 Canal St.) 1884-1897

Jamestown			
NY	289a	Hardinghaus & Smith	1874-1877
	289b	Charles Smith	1877-1882
NY	290a	Jamestown Brewing Co.	1897-1920
	290b	Kuhn's Beer, Inc.	1933-1937
		aka Chautauqua Brewing Co., Inc. (1933)	
	290c	Chautauqua Brewing Co., Inc.	1939-1941
Johnson City (see Seitz Brewing Co., Easton, PA)			
Johnstown			
NY	291	Fulton County Brewing Co. (Charles St.)	1898-1916
Kingston (Rondout)			
NY	292a	Geo. Dressell & Co. (Wurts & McEntee Sts., Rondout)	1864-1884
	292b	George Hauck	1884-1890
	292c	George Hauck Brewing Co.	1890-1902
	292d	Geo. Hauck & Sons Brewing Co.	1902-1916
	292e	Frank D. Brady (54/62 & 77/81 McEntee St.)	1933-1934
	292f	Peter Doelger Brewing Corp.	1935-1937
	292g	Hauck Brewing Co., Inc.	1937-1938
NY	293a	James Hargraves	1874-1877
	293b	Valentine Thiele	1877-1879
NY	294a	Heiselmann & Spinner Brewing Co. (Pine St. & Green Hill Ave.)	1897-1899
	294b	William Bush	1899-1900
	294c	Roman Spinner	1903-1904
NY	295a	Philip Hoffmann (46 Hone St., Rondout)	1882-1884
	295b	Jacob Hoffmann Brewing Co.	1884-1900
	295c	Hoffmann & Jacob, Hard Rock Cellar Brewery	1900-1910
	295d	Kingston Brewing Corp. (Hone & German Sts.)	NP 1934-1934
NY	296a	Theo Kiernan	1875-1877
	296b	Catherine Cummings	1877-1890
	296c	Mary Kiernan (Lucas & Washington Aves.)	1890-1895
	296d	James Cummings	1895-1897
NY	297	C. Schieck	1879-1884
NY	298a	B. Schwalbach	1852- ?
	298b	Elizabeth Schwalbach	1874-1878
	298c	Peter Barmann (Fort Clinton Ave.)	1879-1901
	298d	Peter Barmann (24 Barman Ave., formerly Fort Clinton Ave.)	1901-1908
	298e	Peter Barmann Estate	1908-1920
	298f	Peter Barmann Brewing Co. (30 Barmann Ave.)	1920-1934
	298g	Peter Barmann Brewery, Inc.	1936-1939
	298h	Peter Barmann Brewery, Inc. (owned by Jacob Ruppert, N.Y.C.)	1939-1941
NY	299	Chas. Staudaucher	1874-1875
NY	300a	F. Stephan & Co.	c1868-1877
	300b	G. F. Stephan	1877-1878
NY	301	Gustave Teichler	c1880
NY	302	Frank Weber (Rondout)	1882-1884
Lancaster			
NY	303a	John Demaugeot	1874-1879
	303b	Demaugeot & Nuner	1879-1884
	303c	Lancaster Brewing Co.	1884-1895
	303d	Lancaster Brewery	1895-1897
	303e	Lancaster Ale Co.	1897-1902
	303f	Mohawk Brewing Co. (Aurora St.)	1902-1904
NY	304a	Sylvester Hilbert	1874-1897
	304b	Joseph Hilbert	1897-1899
NY	305a	Charles I. Soemann	1874-1890
	305b	Margaretha Soemann	1890-1893
	305c	Peter J. Soemann	1893-1897
Langford			
NY	306a	Henry Kehrer	1878-1882
	306b	Frederick Kehrer	1882-1884

Lansingburg (see Troy)

LeRoy

NY	307a	Linxweiler & Sailer	1874-1877
	307b	J. D. Linxweiler	1877-1884
NY	308	Lorenz Sellinger	1874-1882

Lindenhurst (Long Island)

NY	309a	John Feller (Humboldt Place)	1893-1907
	309b	Jos. Hastreiter	1907-1908
	309c	Henry Heddendorf	1910-1911
	309d	Otto F. Eichhammer	1916-1920
	309e	Linden Brewery, Inc. (80/90 E. Montauk Highway)	1934-1948
NY	310	Val. Thiele	1902-1902

Little Falls

NY	311a	W. & J. Beattie	1874-1884
	311b	Patrick Grace	1884-1888
	311c	James J. Grace	1897-1904
NY	312	Nicholas Gerhard	1874-1878

Lockport

NY	313	Benjamin Draper	1874-1875
NY	314	Dunville Brewery	1908-1912
NY	315	John Gibson	1874-1875
NY	316a	Niagara Ale Brewing Co. (Van Buren St.)	1888-1914
	316b	F. J. Mumm Brewery, Inc.	1933-1934
	316c	Van Buren Products Co., Inc.	1939-1939
NY	317	J. G. & W. L. Norman	1874-1875
NY	318a	James Reden	1842-1845
	318b	William Pie	1845-1848
	318c	William Draper (Malthouse)	1848-1853
	318d	Joseph Dumville	1853-1888
	318e	John Hawkes (153 Van Buren St.)	1888-1898
	318f	Geo. H. Downs (133/181 Van Buren St.)	1898-1920
NY	319a	George Stainthorpe	1845-1860
	319b	Anton Ulrich	1860-1882
	319c	Mrs. Cecilia Ulrich	1882-1885
	319d	Lockport Brewing Co.	1885-1896
	319e	Union Brewing Co. (198 Chestnut St.)	1896-1898
	319f	Lock City Brewing Co.	1898-1920

Long Island City

NY	320a	Edward & John Burke, Ltd. (2701/2719 47th Ave. & 4624/4658 28th St.)	1934-1934
	320b	Burke Brewery, Inc.	1934-1949
	320c	Arthur Guinness & Son, Inc.	1949-1954
NY	321	Consumers Brewing Co. (2908 N. Blvd.)	NP 1934-1934

Lowville

NY	322a	John Siegel & Co.	1874-1877
	322b	Joseph Siegel	1877-1878
	322c	John Siegel	1878-1890
	322d	Margaret Siegel	1890-1891
	322e	Charles W. Sharp & Co.	1891-1895

Lyons

NY	323a	Geo. Brock & Co.	1878-1890
	323b	Geo. Brock	1890-1893

Maspeth, Queens (New York City)

NY	324a	Fred Licht (Williamsburg)	1862-1880
	324b	Safarik & Cerowski (Maspeth, Queens)	1880-1888
	324c	G. Feigenspan	1888-1888
	324d	First Bohemian Brewing Co.	1888-1891
	324e	Queens County Brewing Co.	1891-1893
	324f	Mariano Brewery (Metropolitan & Forest Ave., Metro., L.I.)	1893-1897
	324g	Milwaukee Brewing Co.	1897-1900
	324h	Montauk Brewing Co. (1522 Metropolitan Ave.)	1900-1906

Mattawan

NY	325a	Jos. W. Walsh	1874-1880
	325b	A. Clifford	1880-1882

McKownville

NY	326	William Amsdell	1842-1854

Mechanicsville

NY	327a	Werner Brewing Co. (Viall Ave.)	1891-1895
	327b	Saratoga Brewing Co.	1895-1903

Medina

NY	328a	William Remde	1868-1897
	328b	William Remde Estate	1897-1902
	328c	Heumann & Luksch	1902-1902
	328d	Henry Heumann	1902-1903
	328e	Pius Luksch	1903-1904
	328f	Medina Brewery	1904-1920

Middletown

NY	329a	Annie Burke	1874-1877
	329b	T. Cohalan	1877-1880
NY	330	Monroe Eckstein	1874-1875
NY	331	George Ludwig Herbert	1878-1884
NY	332a	Orange County Brewery, Schamble & Reinecke, aka Orange County Brewing Co. (Lake St.)	1897-1911
	332b	Orange County Brewery, Charles C. Young (133 Lake Ave.)	1911-1920
	332c	Orange County Brewery, Inc.	1933-1934

Minden

NY	333	John Beck	1874-1875

Morrisania (see New York City)

Mount Morris

NY	334a	Meyer & Settel	? -1874
	334b	J. E. White & Bro.	1878-1884
	334c	Lina De Crizinus	1895-1895

Mount Vernon

Office for brewery located in Pelham - see Pelham for brewery info. Office located at 14/20 S. West St.

Muitzeskill

NY	335	Huss Bros.	1888-1890

Nesconset (Long Island)

NY	336	Suffolk County Breweries, Inc.	NP 1934-1934

New Bremen

NY	337a	Peter Beller	1874-1875
	337b	John G. Sauter	1880-1884
	337c	Andrew Zehr	1884-1888
NY	338a	Croghan Brewery	1874-1877
	338b	John Zimmerman	1877-1880
	338c	Amery & Co.	1880-1882
	338d	George Jarger	1882-1888

Newburgh

NY	339a	John Beveridge	c1830- ?
	339b	T. Beveridge & Co. (Front & 5th Sts.)	1874-1884
	339c	Beveridge Brewing Co.	1884-1895
NY	340	Grant, Mabbett & Co.	1875- ?
NY	341a	Newburgh Lager Beer Co.	1874-1877
	341b	Newburgh Brewing Co.	1877-1879
	341c	Leicht Bros. (North St.)	1879-1890
	341d	Chas. K. Leicht, Highland Brewery (North Road)	1890-1920
	341e	Highland Brewery	1933-1934
NY	342	F. Wallace & Co.	c1857

New Lots

NY	343	Christian Gardine	1874-1875
NY	344	Joseph Henry	1874-1875

New Rochelle

NY	345a	Andrew Luckhardt & Co.	1850-1875
	345b	David Jones	1875-1880
	345c	John J. Jones	1880-1882
	345d	Estate of David Jones	1882-1884

Newtown (see Brooklyn)

New York City (includes East New York, Greenwich, Morrisania, New Amsterdam)

NY	346a	Jacob Ahles (Ave. A. near 11th St.)	1850-1853
	346b	(John) Kress & (Christian) Schaefer	1853-1855
	346c	Kress & Schaefer (54th St.)	1855-1863
	346d	John Kress (207/213 E. 54th St.)	1863-1879
	346e	Mrs. Susanna Kress	1879-1884
	346f	John Kress Brewing Co.	1884-1904
	346g	Jetter Brewing Co. (207/224 E. 54th St.)	1904-1911
NY	347a	Jacob Ahles (149/155 E. 54th St.)	1854-1887
	347b	Jacob Ahles Brewing Co.	1887-1899
NY	348a	Jacob & Peter Ahles (Houston St.)	1850-1850
	348b	Peter Ahles	1850- ?
	348c	Peter Ahles (888 2nd Ave.)	1874-1875
	348d	Peter Ahles, Jr.	1875-1878
NY	349a	Aktien Brauerei	? -1850
	349b	Turtle Bay Brewery, Franz Ruppert	1850-1869
	349c	Turtle Bay Brewery, Jacob Robinson	1869- ?
NY	350	Peter Anderson (Stone St., New Amsterdam)	c1645-1670
NY	351a	Atlantic Brewery (East New York)	1878-1879
	351b	John Scheufele (541 1st Ave.)	1879-1880
	351c	John Scheufele (258 Ave. B)	1880-1884
	351d	John Scheufele (719 E. 11th St.)	1884-1906
NY	352	Richard Auldrick	c1762
NY	353	T. Barry & Bro. (319 E. 40th St.)	1875-1882
NY	354	Nicholas Bayard (High St., New Amsterdam)	c1665
NY	355	R. & W. Bender (169 Spring St.)	1874-1884
NY	356a	Charles Bentle (403 E. 76th St. btwn. Ave. A & 1st Ave.)	1874-1880
	356b	Charles Beutel	1880-1888
NY	357a	(Emanuel) Bernheimer & (August) Schmid, Constanz Brewery (E. 4th St. near Ave. B)	1850-1856
	357b	August Schmid, Constanz Brewery	1856-1860
NY	358	(Emanuel) Bernheimer & (August) Schmid, Melrose Brewery	c1860
NY	359	(Emanuel) Bernheimer & (August) Schmid, South Rondout Brewery	c1860
NY	360a	Bertina Weiss Beer Co. (235/237 5th St.)	1884- ?
	360b	Frank Martens (232 5th St.)	1898-1900
NY	361a	John F. Betz, Eagle Brewery (347/355 W. 44th St.)	1853-1880
	361b	L. H. Roemer & Co., Eagle Brewery	1880-1888
	361c	Roemer Brewing Co.	1888-1890
	361d	Eagle Brewing Co.	1890-1892
NY	362	Gustav Boemer	1874-1875
NY	363	Jacobus Bomper	c1727- ?
NY	364	Philip Brecher (437 5th St.)	1875-1884
NY	365	Jaxsen Calder (Stone St., New Amsterdam)	c1645-1670
NY	366	Albert Camack (Stone St., New Amsterdam)	c1645-1670
NY	367	Central Brewing Co. (68th St. & East River)	1899-1920

New York City (cont.)

NY	368a	Clausen & Bauer (11th Ave. & 59th St.)	1871-1874
	368b	Charles C. Clausen	1874-1877
	368c	Clausen & (Walter J.) Price	1877-1884
	368d	Clausen & Price Brewing Co.	1884-1899
	368e	Clausen & Price Brewing Co. (59th St. & West End Ave.)	1899-1910
NY	369a	Henry Clausen (309/313 E. 47th St.)	1855-1866
	369b	H. Clausen & Son	1866-1882
	369c	H. Clausen & Son Brewing Co.	1882-1888
	369d	New York Breweries Co., H. Clausen & Son Brewing Co.	1888-1909
	369e	Clausen-Flanagan Brewery, Clausen Branch	1909-1910
NY	370a	Coleman Brewing Co. (455/457 W. 14th St.)	1890-1893
	370b	Globe Brewing Co.	1893-1895
NY	371a	Consumers Brewing Co. (Ave. A between 54th & 55th Sts.)	1889-1893
	371b	Consumers' Brewing Co. of New York, Ltd.	1893-1928
NY	372	Consumers Brewing Co. of Brooklyn (Betts Ave., Woodside, Quns.)	1893-1912
NY	373	Thomas Conville	1885-1892
NY	374	Coulter's Old Brewery (Fire Point)	1792-1837
NY	375	Richard Davis	c1702
NY	376a	Philip Decker	1875-1877
	376b	Henry Loehr (428 W. 55th St.)	1877-1884
NY	377a	Isaac De Forest (Stone St., New Amsterdam)	c1645-1675
	377b	John De Forest	c1675- ?
NY	378	William DePue	c1758
NY	379	Catherine Diehl (Morrisania)	1874-1878
NY	380a	Peter Doelger (101 Ave. A)	c1858-1863
	380b	Peter Doelger, New York Brewery (407/417 E. 55th St. between Ave. A & 1st St.)	1863-1912
	380c	Peter Doelger Brewing Co.	1912-1920
	380d	Peter Doelger Brewing Co.(501/505 W. 125th St.)	1933-1937
NY	381	Doemich & Schnell (291 Broome St.)	1874-1884
NY	382	J. H. Doerrbecker (188 William St.)	1874-1884
NY	383	William R. Dunton (84 Cherry St.)	1874-1880
NY	384a	Philip Ebling & Bro. (William) (156th St. & 760 St. Anns Ave., Morrisania)	1868-1874
	384b	Philip & William Ebling	1874-1889
	384c	Ph. & Wm. Ebling Brewing Co.	1889-1901
	384d	Ebling Brewing Co.	1901-1920
	384e	The Ebling Brewing Co., Inc. (756 St. Anns Ave.)	1933-1950
NY	385a	Eckert & Winter (218/221 E. 55th St.)	c1868-1880
	385b	George Winter	1880-1882
	385c	George Winter Brewing Co.	1882-1888
NY	386a	George Ehret, Hell Gate Brewery (E. 217/235 92nd St. between 2nd & 3rd Aves.)	1866-1927
	386b	Estate of George Ehret	1934-1934
NY	387a	(John) Eichler & (M.) Solmon	1861-1861
	387b	John Eichler	1861-1865
NY	388a	Henry Elias (W. 39th St.)	c1853-1855
	388b	Henry Elias (near 15th St. & Broadway)	1855-1865
	388c	(Henry) Elias & (George) Schmitt, Central Park Brewery (163 E. 59th St. between 3rd & Lexington Aves.)	1865-1868
	388d	Schmitt & (Christian) Koehne, Central Park Brewery	1868-1881
	388e	Schmitt & (Louis Von) Schwanenfluegel, Central Park Brewery	1885-1892
	388f	Schmitt & Schwanenfluegel (1065 Ave. A between 56th & 57th) aka Consumers Park Brewing Co. (1906)	1892-1906
NY	389a	(Henry) Elias & Betz (403/405 E. 54th St.)	1874-1880
	389b	Henry Elias	1880-1884
	389c	Henry Elias Brewing Co.	1884-1920

New York City (cont.)

NY	390a	Henry Elias (E. 92nd St. btn. 2nd & 3rd Aves.)	1868-1872
	390b	(George) Ringler & (Christian) Hagemeister	1872-1874
	390c	Geo. Ringler & Co. (1643 3rd Ave. & 203 E. 92nd St.)	1874-1920
NY	391a	Jacob Engelhardt (537 W. 54th St.)	1875-1884
	391b	Louis Frieman	1884-1888
	391c	Wellmann & Holste	1888-1891
	391d	Stapff Bros.	1891-1893
NY	392	Ernst & Reimsland	1874-1875
NY	393a	James Everard (12 E. 133rd St. & 3rd Ave.)	1885-1893
	393b	James Everard's Breweries, aka James Everard	1893-1926
NY	394a	James Everard (3 E. 134th St.)	1904-1912
	394b	James Everard's Breweries	1912-1920
	394c	Eberhart Brewing Co., Inc. (7 E. 134th St.)	1934-1934
NY	395a	H. Evers & Co. (49 Monroe St.)	1874-1877
	395b	Henry Evers	1877-1901
NY	396	Wessel & Cornelius Evertsen (Stone St., New Amsterdam)	c1645-1670
NY	397	Nicholas Eyre	c1721
NY	398	Charles Fassert (Morrisania)	1874-1875
NY	399a	H. Ferris & Sons (249/251 10th Ave.)	1874-1884
	399b	Henry Ferris' Son	1884-1901
NY	400	Adrian Feyh (266 William St.)	1874-1893
NY	401	Edward Fossdick (120 E. 78th St.)	1874-1875
NY	402	Peter Frasier	c1760
NY	403	Junius A. Fuller (Hudson St.)	c1835
NY	404	Peter Gardner (Stone St., New Amsterdam)	c1645-1670
NY	405a	George Gillig (5th Ave. btn. 50th & 51st Sts.)	1840-1842
	405b	George Gillig (30th St. & Lexington Ave.)	1842-1843
	405c	George Gillig (3rd St. btn. Aves. A & B)	1843-1853
	405d	Joseph Doelger	1853-1870
	405e	Joseph Doelger (227/234 E. 54th St.)	1870-1882
	405f	Joseph Doelger's Sons (Jacob & Anthony)	1882-1913
NY	406a	George Gillig (320/346 E. 46th St.)	1853-1862
	406b	George Gillig's Estate	1862-1865
	406c	(John G.) Gillig & (Frederick) Oppermann	1865-1873
	406d	Gillig, Oppermann & Co.	1873-1875
	406e	Oppermann & Mueller	1875-1884
	406f	Frederick Oppermann, Jr.	1884-1886
	406g	Thomas Conville Brewing Co.	1892-1911
NY	407	J. George Gottsberger (52 New Bowery)	1874-1875
NY	408a	Xavier Gnant (161st St. & 3rd Ave., Morrisania)	1857-1863
	408b	Anton Hupfel	1863-1873
	408c	A. Hupfel's Sons	1873-1883
	408d	A. Hupfel's Son	1883-1889
	408e	United States Brewing Co., A. Hupfel's Son (161st St. & St. Ann's Ave.)	1889-1904
	408f	A. Hupfel's Sons	1904-1920
	408g	Allied Brewing and Distilling Co., Inc. (586 E. 161st St.)	1933-1934
	408h	Pilser Brewing Co., Inc.	1934-1947
NY	409	William Grinding	c1786
NY	410a	Michael Groh (9th Ave. & 60th St.)	1874-1875
	410b	John J. Betz	1875-1880
	410c	Mrs. Julia Groh	1880-1882
	410d	Peter L. Biegen	1882-1884
NY	411a	Haddock, Langdon, Read & Co. (410/414 E. 14th St.)	1875-1877
	411b	Haddock & Langdon	1877-1884
	411c	Langdon & Granger Brewing Co.	1884-1893

New York City (cont.)

NY	412a	Mathias Haffen (632/644 152nd St. & Melrose Ave., Morrisania)	1856-1871
	412b	J. & M. Haffen	1871-1899
	412c	J. & M. Haffen Brewing Co.	1899-1908
	412d	J. & M. Haffen Brewing Co. (386/398 E. 152nd St.)	1908-1913
NY	413	Andrew Hafner	1874-1875
NY	414a	Thomas Hall (Beekman & Williams St., New Amsterdam)	c1654-1670
	414b	William Beekman	1670-1707
NY	415a	Charles P. Hawkins (345 W. 41st St.)	1874-1880
	415b	C. P. Hawkins & Co.	1880-1882
	415c	C. P. Hawkins' Sons	1882-1893
	415d	C. P. Hawkins' Sons Brewing Co.	1893-1895
NY	416a	Casper Heindel, Manhattan Brewery (10th Ave. & 128th St.)	1865-1870
	416b	William Maack, Manhattan Brewery	1870-1875
	416c	Yuengling & Co., Manhattan Brewery	1875-1880
	416d	D. G. Yuengling, Jr., Manhattan Brewery	1880-1884
	416e	D. G. Yuengling Brewing Co.	1884-1897
	416f	John F. Betz, Manhattan Brewery (Amsterdam Ave. & 128th St.)	1897-1901
	416g	Betz & Sons Brewing Co. of New York, Manhattan Brewery	1901-1903
	416h	Bernheimer & Schwartz, Pilsener Brewing Co.	1903-1920
	416i	Horton Pilsener Brewing Co., Inc. (450 W. 128th St.)	1933-1941
NY	417	Richard Heins (237 6th St.)	1901-1901
NY	418a	Gus C. Hertel (134 Elm St.)	1874-1893
	418b	John Scheufele	1893-1895
NY	419a	Hoffmann, Merkel & Co. (210 E. 55th St.)	1867- ?
	419b	Hoffmann & Merkel	? -1876
	419c	Jacob Hoffmann, Oriental Brewery	1876-1884
	419d	Jacob Hoffman Brewing Co. (204/218 E. 55th St.)	1884-1920
NY	420	Thomas Horsfield	c1769
NY	421a	Jessup & Cole	1860- ?
	421b	(James) Flanagan & (F.) Wallace (262 10th Ave. & 450 26th St.)	1874-1881
	421c	Flanagan, (James) Nay & Co.	1881-1888
	421d	New York Breweries Co., Flanagan, Nay & Co.	1888-1908
	421e	Clausen-Flanagan Brewery, Flanagan Branch	1908-1915
	421f	Flanagan-Nay Brewing Co.	1933-1937
NY	422a	David Jones (638 6th St.)	1874-1880
	422b	John J. Jones	1880-1882
	422c	Estate of David Jones	1882-1884
	422d	David Jones Co. (325 E. 44th St.)	1884-1898
NY	423a	Kerr & Parr (133/143 W. 18th St.)	1874-1875
	423b	H. R. Kerr	1875-1877
	423c	Kerr & Smith	1877-1882
	423d	Germania Brewing Co.	1882-1884
	423e	Empire State Brewing Co.	1884-1893
NY	424	Jacobus Kip (East River btn. 33rd & 37th Sts., New Amsterdam)	c1655
NY	425	Frederick Kleinschroth (89 Sheriff St.)	1874-1880
NY	426a	Andrew Koch (455 1st Ave.)	1874-1891
	426b	Andrew Koch & Sons	1891-1897
	426c	Andrew Koch's Son	1897-1903
NY	427a	Hermann Koehler (Sheriff St.)	1852- ?
	427b	Hermann Koehler (503 1st Ave. & 341/345 29th St.)	1866-1883
	427c	Hermann Koehler & Co.	1883-1902
	427d	H. Koehler & Co., Inc.	1902-1917
	427e	Fidelio Brewing Co., Inc.	1917-1920
	427f	Fidelio Brewery, Inc. (501 1st Ave.)	1933-1940
	427g	The Greater New York Brewery, Inc.	1940-1942
	427h	Metropolis Brewery, Inc.	1945-1950
NY	428	Koenig & Heindl	c1860-1868

New York City (cont.)

NY	429a	Kolb's Brewery (3582 3rd Ave. & 169th St., Morrisania)	1862-1865
	429b	John Eichler	1865-1888
	429c	John Eichler Brewing Co.	1888-1920
	429d	The John Eichler Brewing Co. of New York (3544/3582 3rd Ave.)	1933-1938
	429e	The John Eichler Brewing Co.	1938-1947
	429f	Liebmann Breweries, Inc.	1947-1961
NY	430a	J. & L. F. Kuntz (168th St. & 3rd Ave., Morrisania)	1874-1884
	430b	Joseph Kuntz	1884-1888
	430c	Joseph Kuntz Brewing Co.	1888-1893
	430d	American Brewing Co.	1893-1903
	430e	North Side Brewing Co.	1903-1906
	430f	National Brewing Co.	1909-1910
NY	431	Matthew Lawrence	c1761
NY	432	Leonard Lispenard (Greenwich St.)	c1804
NY	433a	Valentine Loewer (W. 51st St. near 11th ST.)	1868-1870
	433b	Val. Loewer (529 W. 41st St. btn. 10th & 11th Aves.)	1870-1884
	433c	V. Loewer's Gambrinus Brewery Co.	1883-1920
	433d	V. Loewer's Gambrinus Brewery Co.	1933-1943
	433e	Brewery Management Corp.	1943-1943
	433f	Loewer's Brewery Co. (W. 40th, 41st & 42nd Sts.)	1944-1948
NY	434a	T. C. Lyman & Co. (528/532 W. 33rd St.)	1874-1880
	434b	Henry Howard & Co. (518/538 W. 33rd St.)	1882-1884
	434c	Howard & Childs	1884-1907
	434d	Howard & Childs Co.	1907-1910
NY	435a	T. C. Lyman & Co., Emerald Brewery (414/430 W. 38th St.)	1880-1889
	435b	Emerald and Phoenix Brewing Co., aka T.C. Lyman Co.	1889-1902
NY	436	Charles Mansfield	c1702
NY	437a	Mrs. S. M. McKnight (159 Sullivan St.)	1878-1882
	437b	W. G. McKnight	1882-1884
NY	438a	William G. McKnight (13/17 Downing St.)	1875-1877
	438b	William Kirk	1877-1884
	438c	Kirk & Kelly	1884-1888
	438d	Champion Brewing Co.	1888-1890
NY	439	Cornelius Melyn (Stone St., New Amsterdam)	c1645-1670
NY	440a	J. J. Mentges (4th Ave. & 68 E. 87th St.)	1874-1877
	440b	Wheatcroft & Rintoul	1877-1880
	440c	John Rintoul	1880-1884
NY	441	Peter Mesier	c1724
NY	442a	Miles & Bacon, Croton Brewery	1823-1827
	442b	William B. Miles, Miles' Croton Brewery	1827-1835
	442c	Wm. B. & A. Miles, Miles' Croton Brewery	1835-1855
	442d	Wm. B. Miles, Miles' Croton Brewery	1855-1870
	442e	Wm. A. Miles & Co., Croton Brewery (57/59 Chrystie St.)	1870-1909
NY	443a	Millbank Brothers (68/70 Madison st.)	1874-1876
	443b	James Wallace	1876-1886
	443c	James Wallace & Son (390/400 Cherry st.)	1886-1899
	443d	Salvator Brewing Co.	1899-1907
	443e	Wm. A. Miles & Co.	1909-1920
NY	444	Peter Minuit (Market Field, New Amsterdam)	1633-1638
NY	445	Henry Moll	1874-1875
NY	446a	Moore & Vincent (225 E. 21st St.)	1874-1877
	446b	Michael E. Moore	1877-1897
NY	447	Francis Munch (143 W. 30th St.)	1874-1884

New York City (cont.)

NY	448a	Jacob Marquardt (403 Leonard St.)	1865-1870
	448b	Marquardt Bros.	1870-1879
	448c	G. Marquardt	1879-1888
	448d	Feigenspan Brewing Co. (912 Cypress Ave., Willow & Greene Sts.)	1888-1892
	448e	William H. Frank Brewing Co.	1892-1898
	448f	The Frank Brewery	1898-1916
	448g	Enterprise Brewery, Inc.	1916-1920
	448h	City Brewing Corp.	1933-1941
	448i	The Greater New York Brewery, Inc.	1941-1945
	448j	The Greater New York Industries, Inc.	1945-1946
	448k	The Greater New York Brewery, Inc.	1946-1950
NY	449	Harman Myndartsen (Stone St., New Amsterdam)	c1645-1670
NY	450	Rynier Nack	c1733
NY	451a	(Abraham) Nash, (Ebenezer) Beadleston & Co., Empire Brewery (291/295 W. 10th, Washington & Charles Sts.)	1846-1856
	451b	Beadleston & Nash, Empire Brewery	1856-1860
	451c	Beadleston & (W. W.) Price, Empire Brewery	1860-1865
	451d	Beadleston, Price & (E.G.W.) Woerz, Empire Brewery	1865-1877
	451e	Beadleston & Woerz, Empire Brewery	1877-1920
NY	452a	F. A. Neuman (233/237 E. 47th St. btn. 2nd & 3rd Aves.)	1874-1880
	452b	Hermann Schalk	1880-1882
	452c	New York Brewing Co.	1882-1884
NY	453a	John Noller (168th St. & 3rd Ave., Morrisania)	1848- ?
	453b	Charles Rivinius	1874-1882
	453c	David Mayer (3650 3rd Ave. & 168th St.)	1882-1891
	453d	David Mayer Brewing Co.	1891-1920
NY	454	John Oothout	c1732
NY	455	Gysbert Opdyke (Stone St., New Amsterdam)	c1645-1670
NY	456a	Frederick Oppermann, Jr. (330/336 E. 45th St.)	1878-1896
	456b	Estate of Frederick Oppermann, Jr.	1896-1897
	456c	Frederick Oppermann, Jr. Brewing Co.	1897-1910
NY	457a	O'Reilly, Skelly & Fogarty, Centennial Brewery (409 W. 14th)	1876-1890
	457b	O'Reilly, Skelly & Fogarty Co., Centennial Brewery	1890-1899
NY	458a	Franz Otto (58 E. 4th St.)	1875-1890
	458b	H. M. Otto (83 E. 4th & 19 Stuyvesant Sts.)	1890-1905
NY	459	Jacob Peters	1875- ?
NY	460	Matthew P. Read	1858-1866
NY	461	Valentine Rehberger (101 Broome St.)	1874-1884
NY	462	Abret Rittenhouse (Stone St., New Amsterdam)	c1645-1670
NY	463	William Robertson	c1700
NY	464	John Roe	c1761
NY	465a	John Roemmelt & Co. (223/229 E. 38th St.)	1854-1858
	465b	Andrew Leicht & Anton Hupfel	1858- ?
	465c	Anton Hupfel	? -1873
	465d	A. Hupfel's Sons	1873-1883
	465e	J. Chr. G. Hupfel	1883-1887
	465f	J. Chr. G. Hupfel Brewing Co.	1887-1920
	465g	J. Chr. G. Hupfel Brewing Corp.	1934-1938
NY	466a	Rottman & Eckhoff (315/317 W. 47th St.)	? -1873
	466b	John F. Rottmann	1874-1879
	466c	John F. Rottman (549/557 W. 46th St. & 630/636 11th Ave.)	1879-1884
	466d	John F. Rottman & Sons	1884-1901
NY	467a	Jacob Ruppert (1639 3rd Ave. btn. 91st & 92nd Sts.)	1867-1910
	467b	Jacob Ruppert, Inc. (1601/1639 3rd Ave.)	1933-1940
	467c	Jacob Ruppert	1940-1965
NY	468	John Russel	c1698
NY	469	Anthony Rugers (Stone St. between William & Nassau)	1717-1732

New York City (cont.)

NY	470	Jean Rutgers	c1653
NY	471a	Harman Rutgers II (Maiden Lane & Rugers St.)	? -1753
	471b	Mrs. Harman Rutgers III	1753-1755
	471c	Robert Rutgers	1755- ?
NY	472	Peter Rutgers (Maiden Lane)	c1740
NY	473	Petrus Rutgers	c1724
NY	474	Rutgers Brothers (Brewers Hill)	c1783
NY	475	Harman Rutgerson	c1695
NY	476a	Philip Schaefer (530/540 W. 57th St.)	1860-1880
	476b	F. Foehrenbach	1880-1884
	476c	Philip Schaefer & Son	1884-1897
	476d	Mount Vernon Consumers Brewing Co.	1897-1900
	476e	Manhattan Consumers' Brewing Co.	1900-1904
NY	477a	Adolph H. Schmedtje (418 E. 115th St.)	1933-1936
	477b	York Brewery, Inc.	1936-1937
NY	478	Schoenberger & Light	1874-1875
NY	479a	Julius J. Schumann (140/150 E. 58th St. btn Lexington & 3rd)	1874-1876
	479b	Baur & Betz	1876-1882
	479c	John F. Betz	1882-1884
	479d	Peter Buckel	1884-1891
NY	480	Schwaner & Amend (514 W. 57th St.)	1874-1880
NY	481a	Michael C. Schweyer	1857-1870
	481b	A. Finck & Son (324/326 W. 39th St.)	1870-1911
NY	482a	Charles Seitz (240/242 W. 28th St.)	1878-1883
	482b	Mrs. Julia A. Groh	1883-1884
	482c	Michael Groh's Sons (Michael Jr. & John)	1884-1897
	482d	M. Groh's Sons, Inc.	1897-1916
NY	483	Patrick Sexton	1875- ?
NY	484	Julius Seyfert	1874-1875
NY	485	Morris Shieman (1903 Mulford Ave.)	1910-1911
NY	486a	Patrick Skelly (646/652 1st Ave. & 37th & 38th Sts.)	1894-1895
	486b	Kips Bay Brewing Co.	1895-1903
	486c	Kips Bay Brewing and Malting Co.	1904-1910
	486d	Kips Bay Brewing Co.	1910-1913
	486e	Kips Bay Brewing and Malting Co.	1913-1920
	486f	Kips Bay Brewing Co., Inc.	1934-1947
NY	487a	Smith Brothers, Colonial Brewery (232/242 W. 18th St.)	1852- ?
	487b	McPherson & Smith	1874-1876
	487c	Smith, McPherson & Donald	1876-1880
	487d	M. & D. Smith	1880-1884
	487e	Knickerbocker Brewing Co.	1884-1891
	487f	Bavarian Star Brewing Co.	1891-1897
	487g	The Colonial Brewery	1897-1901
	487h	Eastern Brewing Co., Colonial Brewery	1901-1902
NY	488	George W. Smith	1825-1835
NY	489a	S. Sommer, Jr. (221/227 W. 18th St.)	1874-1876
	489b	De LaVergne & Burr	1876-1882
	489c	Burr, Son & Co.	1882-1884
	489d	Burr Brewing Co.	1884-1891
NY	490a	Sebastian Sommers (Broadway between 18th & 19th Sts.)	1838-1842
	490b	F. & M. Schaefer	1842-1845
	490c	F. & M. Schaefer (7th Ave. between 16th & 17th Sts.)	1845-1849
	490d	F. & M. Schaefer (4th Ave. between 50th & 51st Sts.)	1849-1878
	490e	F. & M. Schaefer Brewing Co.	1878-1880
	490f	F. & M. Schaefer Brewing Co. (112/114 E. 51st St.)	1880-1911
	490g	F. & M. Schaefer Brewing Co. (Park Ave. & 50th, 51st & 52nd)	1911-1916
NY	491	George Sorg (647 11th Ave.)	1875-1879

New York City (cont.)

NY	492a	Speyers Brothers	1852-1860
	492b	(James) Speyers & (Emanuel) Bernheimer	1860-1862
	492c	Bernheimer & (August) Schmid, Lion Brewery (9th Ave., 107th & 108th Sts.)	1862-1890
	492d	Bernheimer & Schmid (Columbia Ave. & W. 108th St.)	1890-1903
	492e	Lion Brewery of New York City	1903-1920
	492f	Lion Brewery of New York City (104 W. 108th St.)	1933-1941
	492g	The Greater New York Brewery, Inc.	1941-1942
NY	493	A. Spiegel	1874-1875
NY	494a	H. Spoehrer (75 Norfolk St.)	1875-1884
	494b	Herman Spoehrer (472 2nd Ave.)	1884-1898
	494c	Chas. L. Spoehrer	1898-1901
	494d	Herman Spoehrer	1901-1905
	494e	Frances Spoehrer	1905-1908
	494f	Franz Otto Brewing Co.	1908-1909
	494g	Berliner Weiss Beer Brewing Co.	1909-1911
NY	495a	E. Springmeyer (106 E. 88th St.)	1878-1884
	495b	E. Springmeyer & Co. (518 E. 119th St.)	1884-1890
	495c	Edw. Springmeyer (522 E. 119th St.)	1890-1899
	495d	Mrs. E. Springmeyer	1899-1901
	495e	Julian Horowitz	1901-1901
	495f	Elizabeth Urbach	1901-1903
NY	496	Staeheli & Freimann (428 W. 42nd St.)	1882-1882
NY	497a	(Conrad) Stein & (Philip) Schaefer (Broadway & 50th St.)	1864-1866
	497b	Brown & Esselborn	1875-1877
	497c	Geo. Esselborn	1877-1879
	497d	George Esselborn (613/617 W. 47th St.)	1879-1884
	497e	George Esselborn's Sons	1884-1900
	497f	George Esselborn	1900-1907
NY	498a	Stein & Schaefer (520/528 57th St.)	1866-1867
	498b	Conrad Stein	1867-1900
	498c	Conrad Stein's Sons	1900-1903
NY	499	Fred. Stengel (48 Ludlow St.)	1874-1880
NY	500a	David Stevenson (519/521 10th Ave. & 501/503 W. 39th St.)	1851- ?
	500b	David Stevenson, Jr.	1874-1884
	500c	David Stevenson	1884-1891
	500d	Estate of David Stevenson	1891-1894
	500e	David Stevenson Brewing Co.	1894-1920
NY	501	John Townsend	c1759
NY	502a	(Edward) Tracy & (James) Russell (61/71 Greenwich Ave.)	1864-1891
	502b	Russell & Rees, Continental Brewery	1891-1903
NY	503a	Olaff Stevensen Van Cortlandt (Stone St., New Amsterdam)	1648-1684
	503b	Anthony Lispenard	1684- ?
NY	504a	Peter Van Couwenhoven (Stone St., New Amsterdam)	c1645-1670
	504b	Isaac Van Vleck	c1670-1695
NY	505a	Jacob Van Couwenhoven (Stone St., New Amsterdam)	c1645-1670
	505b	John Van Couwenhoven	c1670- ?
NY	506	Jan Jansen Van Steenwyck (Stone St., New Amsterdam)	c1645-1670
NY	507	Jean Vigne (Brower Straat, New Amsterdam)	c1633
NY	508	Anthony Wear	c1761
NY	509	Adam Werner (526 E. 12th St.)	1875-1882
NY	510a	George Werner (344 E. 105th St.)	1874-1882
	510b	A. G. Werner	1882-1884
	510c	A. G. Werner (709 E. 164th St.)	1884-1904
NY	511	Jacob Wernz (50/51 Norfolk St.)	1874-1884
NY	512	West India Co. (New Amsterdam)	c1633

New York City (cont.)

NY	513a	Thomas B. Whitney (667/675 Washington St.)	1874-1876
	513b	Shook & Everard	1876-1891
	513c	James Everard	1891-1893
NY	514	O. Wieland (212 W. 30th St.)	1875-1890
NY	515	Winderberger & Hartman (354 E. 91st St.)	1891-1891
NY	516a	Yuengling & Co. (4th Ave. & 128th St.)	1871-1873
	516b	Ryerson & Yuengling	1873-1877
	516c	Yuengling & Co.	1877-1880
	516d	D. G. Yuengling, Jr.	1880-1882
NY	517a	Henry Zeltner (3rd Ave. & 170th St., Morrisania)	1860-1891
	517b	Henry Zeltner Brewing Co.	1891-1904
	517c	Zeltner Brewing Co.	1904-1909
	517d	Liberty Brewing Co.	1909-1911
NY	518a	Zinser & Friedrich (165 E. 87th St.)	1912-1915
	518b	Eugene Zinser (201 E. 88th St.)	1915-1920

Niagara Falls

NY	519a	Cataract Brewing Co.	1900-1905
	519b	Cataract Consumers Brewery	1905-1913
	519c	Cataract Brewing Co., Inc.	1913-1920
	519d	Canavan-Leggett Brewery, Inc. (227 10th St.)	1933-1938
	519e	Power City Brewery, Inc.	1938-1940
NY	520a	Niagara Falls Brewing Co.	1882-1920
	520b	Riverview Products, Inc. (732 3rd St.)	1933-1939
NY	521	Whirlpool Co-operative Brewing Co.	1893-1893

Normansville

NY	522	Frederick Hinckel	1904-1904

North Bergen

NY	523	Jac. Winkler Co.	1915-1915

Norwich

NY	524a	A. C. Scott & Son	1874-1877
	524b	M. A. Scott	1877-1893
	524c	Thos. D. Scott	1893-1900
	524d	John H. White	1900-1904
	524e	Norwich Brewing Co.	1904-1915

Nunda

NY	525	George E. Boulton	1878-1879

Oakland

NY	526	Jonathan Gould	1882-1882
NY	527	Mount Morris Ale Brewery	1896-1896

Obernburg

NY	528a	Joseph Kille	1888-1893
	528b	Margaret Schwab	1893-1895
	528c	Ferl & Co.	1895-1897
	528d	John G. Landeck	1899-1901
	528e	Geo. J. Landeck	1901-1902
	528f	Joseph Mueller	1904-1905
	528g	Obernburg Brewery	1905-1906

Ogden

NY	529	Henry Mann	1880-1880

Ogdensburg

NY	530	Cornnell & Co.	1905-1906
NY	531a	Hoard, Seymour & Co.	1859-1861
	531b	Morgan, Arnold & Co.	1861-1863
	531c	Arnold & Co. (50 Main St.)	1863-1877
	531d	J. F. Arnold	1877-1883
	531e	Arnold & Co.	1883-1920

Olean

NY	532	Bear & Hanauer (187 8th St.)		1893-1893
NY	533a	Charles Dotterweich (301 Henley & 2nd Sts.)		1854-1884
	533b	Estate of Charles Dotterweich		1884-1891
	533c	Dotterweich Brewing Co.		1891-1920
	533d	Dotterwyck Brewing Co.		1920-1933
	533e	Empire State Brewery Corp.		1933-1940
NY	534	Dotterweich Brewing Co. (209 S. 3rd St.)	NP	1934-1934
NY	535a	Olean Brewing Co. (Barry & Green Sts.)		1907-1920
	535b	Flower City Brewing Co., Inc. (202/210 E. Green St.)		1933-1934
	535c	Seneca Brewing Co., Inc.		1937-1941

Oneonta

NY	536	Oneonta Consumers' Brewing Co.		1910-1911

Orangetown

NY	537	Dorsch & Herterich		1874-1875

Oriskany Falls

NY	538a	Thomas Hinds		1810-1837
	538b	E. Smith		1878-1882
	538c	H. Morgan & Co.		1882-1893
	538d	Oriskany Falls Brewing Co.		1893-1901

Oswego

NY	539a	Alexander Brewery		? -1855
	539b	Lewis Brosemer, Old Brewery (472/474 W. 1st St. between Murray & Ellen Sts.)		1855-1895
	539c	L. Brosemer Brewing Co.		1895-1915
NY	540a	McGowan Brewing Co. (62/64 E. 1st St.)		1899-1903
	540b	Oswego Brewery, Patrick J. Doyle		1905-1906
NY	541a	Nacey & Flanigan (14 E. Cayuga St.)		1896-1898
	541b	Ontario Brewing Co. (E. Cayuga & 2nd Sts.)		1898-1916
NY	542a	Oswego German Brewing Co. (193/195 E. 1st St.)		1878-1882
	542b	Wiegand Brewing Co.		1882-1884
	542c	Lewis Wiegand		1884-1893
	542d	Louis Wiegand Brewing Co.		1893-1896
	542e	Louis Wiegand & Son		1896-1916
NY	543a	Waful & Millot (458/460 W. 1st St.)		1875-1877
	543b	John B. Millot		1877-1903
	543c	McGowan City Brewery		1903-1904
	543d	Mary A. McGowan dba Greenway		1915-1915
	543e	McGowan City Brewery	NP	1934-1934
	543f	Oswego Brewing Co.		1936-1938

Owego

NY	544a	Henry P. Lauer		1874-1877
	544b	Caroline Burrows		1877-1882

Palmyra

NY	545	Downing Bros.		1874-1878

Peekskill

NY	546a	Jos. C. Wharton (Hudson St.)		1874-1875
	546b	Robert McCord		1875-1878
	546c	Meyer & Amott		1878-1879

Pelham (see note under Mount Vernon)

NY	547a	The Bronx Co. (14/20 S. West St.)		1898-1905
	547b	Westchester County Brewery		1905-1909
	547c	Westchester County Brewing Co.		1910-1920
	547d	Temperance Beverage Co.		1920- ?

Penn Yan

NY	548a	Oliver Ainsworth		1878-1882
	548b	Herman Ainsworth		1882-1884
NY	549a	Thomas S. Burns		1896-1897
	549b	"T. S. B." Wine and Brewing Co.		1898-1901

Perkinsville

NY 550 N. Didas & Co. 1874-1882

Plattsburgh

NY 551a Guindon Brewing Co. 1891-1892
551b Champlain Brewing Co. 1892-1893

NY 552 Payette, Mendelsohn & Co. (37 Bridge St.) 1895-1906

NY 553a Woerner & Parker 1879- ?
553b E. T. Delaney & Co. ? -1884
553c Plattsburgh Brewing Co. 1884-1891
553d J. Scheyer Brewery 1891-1894

Portage

NY 554 William C. Bates 1884-1884

NY 555 Jonathan L. Gould 1891-1891

Port Jervis

NY 556 Jos. & Patrick Byrne 1888-1890

NY 557a Deer Park Brew Co. 1899-1922
557b Deerpark Breweries, Inc. (71 Reservoir Ave.) 1933-1935
557c Deerpark Beverages, Inc. 1936-1942

NY 558 Port Jervis Brewing Co. 1893-1893

NY 559 Fred Redeker 1874-1875

Poughkeepsie

NY 560a Leonard Biegel 1874-1879
560b M. Biegel 1879-1882

NY 561a Frank & Klady 1874-1875
561b Valentine Frank 1875-1878
561c V. Frank's Sons (11/21 Tulip St.) 1878-1920

NY 562 John Gass 1874-1884

NY 563a Frederick Gillmann (7/17 Front St.) 1874-1884
563b Frederick Gillman & Sons 1884-1896
563c F. R. Gillmann & Sons 1896-1904

NY 564a Lorenz Ramstetter 1874-1875
564b Wm. Gotthard 1875- ?

NY 565a James Vassar (50 Mill St.) 1797-1810
565b Matthew Vassar, Eagle Brewery 1810-1867
565c M. Vassar & Co. (Water St.) 1867-1896

NY 566a Wolf & Zimmer 1874-1877
566b M. Klein 1877-1879
566c Buffalo Brewery 1879-1880

Rensselaerwyck (see Troy)

Ridgewood (see New York City)

Rochester

NY 567 Bartholomay & Englehart (140 N. Clinton & Kelly Sts.) 1857-1861

NY 568a Louis Bauer (Lyell Ave.) 1849-1871
568b G. B. Switehard & Louis Bauer 1871-1872
568c George B. Switehard (104 Lyell Ave.) 1872-1875
568d Rochester Ale Co. 1877-1879

NY 569a Wm. H. Burtis (S. Water St.) 1857-1864
569b Samuel N. Oothout & W. H. Burtis (13 S. Water St.) 1864-1870
569c Henry Oothout 1871-1873
569d Samuel N. Oothout 1873-1874

NY 570a Caldwell & Ball (143½ South Ave.) 1871-1871
570b T. E. Caldwell 1872-1872

NY 571 Frank Clay 1871-1871

NY 572a Jacob Englert (117 N. St. Paul St.) 1866-1870
572b Catherine Englert 1871-1873

Rochester (cont.)

	No.	Name		Years
NY	573a	Patrick Enright (149 Mill & Factory Sts.)		1861-1875
	573b	Patrick Enright & Son		1875-1885
	573c	Thomas J. Enright (336/338 State St.)		1885-1887
	573d	T. J. & M. P. Enright		1887-1888
	573e	M. P. Enright		1888-1891
	573f	Estate of P. Enright		1891-1893
	573g	Enright Brewing Co.		1893-1907
NY	574a	Fable & White (23 Hudson Ave.)		1871-1871
	574b	Louis Bauer		1872-1872
NY	575	Flower City Brewing Co., Inc. (56 Orleans St.)	NP	1934-1934
NY	576	E. M. Higgins Co.	NP	1934-1934
NY	577	Louis Hof (160/168 Brown St. near Buffalo Road)		1851-1870
NY	578	George House (178 N. Clinton)		1872-1872
NY	579	House Bros.		1896-1896
NY	580	Volney Hyde		1864-1865
NY	581a	N. Karasinski (Andrews & N. Water Sts.)		1866-1871
	581b	N. Karasinski (76 N. St. Paul St.)		1871-1872
NY	582	Hendry Kondolf (Jay & Child Sts.)		1847-1852
NY	583	F. F. L. Leppens (20 Brisbane St.)		1872-1872
NY	584a	Caspar Listman (Smith St.)		1857- ?
	584b	Caspar Listman (Wilder & Orchard Sts.)		1859-1867
	584c	P. R. & J. Grentzinger (Jay St.)		1867-1870
	584d	Soss, Thon, Huber & Co. (Jay & Saxton Sts.)		1870-1872
	584e	Soss & Huber		1872-1872
	584f	Christian Soss		1873-1874
NY	585a	John & Gabriel Longmuir (80/93 Water St.)		1834-1850
	585b	Alex Longmuir		1851-1857
	585c	Charles Gordon		1864-1865
	585d	Gordon & Bevier		1865-1870
	585e	H. H. Bevier & Co.		1870-1871
	585f	(H. B.) Hathaway & (Charles) Gordon		1871-1912
NY	586a	Nathan Lyman (Near Central Ave. & St. Paul St.)		1819-1844
	586b	Samuel Warren, City Springs Brewery (67 N. St. Paul St.)		1844-1845
	586c	Samuel Warren & Son, City Springs Brewery		1845-1849
	586d	E. K. Warren & Bros.		1849-1856
	586e	E. K. Warren, City Springs Brewery (Atwater & N. St. Paul Sts.)		1857-1882
	586f	E. K. Warrn & Son, City Springs Brewery (115 Central Ave.)		1882-1891
	586g	E. K. Warren Brewing Co.		1891-1904
NY	587a	John Lynch (West & Bowery Sts.)		1861- ?
	587b	John Lynch (South Ave. & Munger St.)		1864-1865
NY	588	Malt Brew Co. (1486 St. Paul St.)	NP	1934-1934
NY	589a	George Marburger (106 N. Clinton St.)		1845-1850
	589b	Marburger Bros. (George, Jacob, Louis)		1850-1852
	589c	Jacob Marburger (80 N. Clinton St.)		1853-1877
	589d	Marburger & Spies		1877-1882
NY	590	Meyer Martin (168 Brown St.)		1871-1871
NY	591a	(Christian) Meyers & (Frederick) Loebs (110 Hudson Ave.)		1855-1859
	591b	Frederick Loebs		1859-1861
	591c	(Geo.) Meyers & (Frederick) Loebs & Co.		1861-1879
	591d	Meyers, Loebs & Co. (250/254 Hudson Ave.)		1879-1885
	591e	Loebs Bros., Lion Brewery		1885-1889
	591f	American Brewing Co. (420/440 Hudson Ave.)		1889-1920
	591g	American Brewing Co. of Rochester, N.Y., Inc.		1933-1950
NY	592a	Frederick Miller (106 Lake Ave. & Brown St.)		1851-1881
	592b	Miller Brewing Co. (190 Lake Ave.)		1881-1902
	592c	Flower City Brewing Co. (440/448 Lake Ave.)		1902-1920
	592d	Standard Brewing Co., Inc.		1933-1956
	592e	Standard Rochester Brewing Co., Inc.		1956-1958

Rochester (cont.)

NY	593	Frederick J. Miller (North & Main Sts.)	1876-1876
NY	594	William Miller (58 North Ave. & German St.)	1865-1878
NY	595a	Moerlbach Brewing Co. (770 Emerson St.)	1908-1920
	595b	Rochester Brewing Co., Inc.	1934-1956
	595c	Standard Rochester Brewing Co., Inc.	1956-1970
NY	596a	Joseph Nunn (Brown & 23 Wentworth Sts.)	1863-1890
	596b	Straub & Angele (347 Wentworth St.)	1890-1891
	596c	Emich & Mueller	1891-1896
	596d	Geo. Emich & Co.	1896-1897
	596e	Burton Brewing Co.	1897-1905
NY	597a	Jacob Rau (111 N. St. Paul St.)	1855-1856
	597b	Charles Rau	1857-1868
	597c	Rauber & Meyers	1868-1872
	597d	Jacob Rauber	1873-1873
	597e	Rau & Reisky	1874-1874
	597f	(Emil) Reisky & (Henry) Spies	1874-1878
	597g	Genesee Brewing Co.	1878-1883
	597h	Genesee Brewing Co. (345 N. St. Paul St.)	1883-1889
	597i	Bartholomay Brewing Co., Genesee Brewery	1889-1896
	597j	Bartholomay Brewing Co., Genesee Brewing Co.	1896-1911
	597k	Bartholomay Brewing Co., Genesee Brewery	1911-1915
	597l	Genesee Brewing Co. (421 St. Paul St.)	1915-1920
	597m	Genesee Brewing Co., Inc. (419/445 St. Paul St. & 14/33 Cataract St.)	1933-
NY	598a	John Ripsam (247 Exchange near Clarissa St.)	1853-1865
	598b	Geck & Rau	1866-1867
	598c	John Ripsam	1867-1870
NY	599a	Rochester Brewing Co. (38 Cliff St. near Lake Ave.)	1875-1889
	599b	Bartholomay Brewing Co., Rochester Brewing Co.	1889-1902
NY	600a	Schroth & Olarich	1853-1854
	600b	Jacob Baetzel (N. Clinton near Clifford St.)	1857-1865
	600c	J. G. Baetzel & Bro. (855 N. Clinton Ave.)	1871-1886
	600d	J. G. Baetzel	1886-1889
	600e	Union Brewing Co.	1889-1899
	600f	Monroe Brewing Co.	1899-1920
NY	601a	Schrudd & Brother (St. Joseph near R.R.)	1857- ?
	601b	Jacob Schroth (106 St. Joseph St.)	1866-1872
	601c	Matthias Kirst	1873-1878
NY	602a	John Seiler (N. Clinton St.)	1859-1861
	602b	Seiler & Long (Cottage St.)	1869-1870
	602c	Charles J. Seiler	1870-1872
	602d	George Mayer	1873-1875
	602e	Mayer & Suiler	1876-1877
NY	603	Amos Sparks (S. St. Paul near Marshall St.)	c1830
NY	604a	Standard Brewing Co. (13 Cataract & Platt Sts.)	1889-1927
	604b	Cataract Brewing Co., Inc. of Rochester, N.Y.	1928-1940
NY	605	Stichel & Co.	1857-1857
NY	606a	Joseph Straubel (50 Ontario St.)	1859- ?
	606b	Strobel & Gleich Auf (46 Ontario St.)	1864-1865
	606c	Joseph Strobel	1866-1877
NY	607a	Frank Weinmann (165 Jay St.)	1858-1876
	607b	Margaret Weinmann	1876-1889
	607c	Charles G. Weinmann (351 Jay St.)	1889-1904
	607d	Charles G. Weinmann (635 Jay St.)	1904-1916
NY	608a	(Phillip) Will & (Henry) Bartholomay	1852-1857
	608b	Henry Bartholomay (139 N. St. Paul St. & Vincent Pl.)	1857-1874
	608c	Bartholomay Brewing Co.	1874-1889
	608d	Bartholomay Brewing Co., Bartholomay Brewery	1889-1912
	608e	Bartholomay Brewing Co., Bartholomay Brewery (555 St. Paul St.)	1912-1933
	608f	Bartholomay Brewing Co.	NP 1934-1934

Rochester (cont.)

NY	609a	Robert Wilson (218 Alexander St.)	1855-1861
	609b	Andrew Wilson	1861-1869
	609c	Robert Syme	1869-1870
	609d	Foulds & Wilson	1870- ?
NY	610a	William Wilson (Fish St.)	1849-1850
	610b	William Wilson (1 Hill St.)	1851- ?
	610c	William Wilson (State St. & Lyell Ave.)	1857- ?
	610d	William Wilson (Lake Ave. near Lorimer St.)	1861-1864
NY	611a	John Wolf (103/104 High St. & Canal)	1851-1864
	611b	John Wolf (130 Caledonia Ave.)	1864-1865
NY	612a	Joseph Yaman (247 Exchange St.)	1861- ?
	612b	Joseph Yaman (120 Jay St. & Saxton St.)	1864-1872
	612c	Yawman & Aab	1873-1873
	612d	Joseph Yaman	1874-1875
	612e	Yaman & Nase	1875-1881
	612f	Catherine Yaman	1882-1882
	612g	Joseph Yaman	1883-1888
NY	613a	Zimmermann & Boehm (Colvin & W. Maple Sts.)	1874-1875
	613b	John Boehm	1875-1877
NY	614a	George Zimmermann (Colvin & Syke Sts.)	1875-1881
	614b	Kase & Sprang	1881-1882
	614c	John Kase	1882-1901

Rome

NY	615a	Edward Evans (572/529 W. Dominick St.)	1875-1884
	615b	(Edward) Evans & (John) Giehl	1884-1913
	615c	Evans & Giehl, Inc.	1913-1920
	615d	Rome Brewery, Inc. (527/601 W. Dominick St.)	1933-1935
	615e	Fort Stanwix Brewing Co., Inc.	1937-1940
NY	616a	(John) Kelley & (Lawrence) Gaheen (101/107 Depuyster St.)	1858-1901
	616b	S. P. Gaheen & Co., Oneida Central Brewery	1901-1902
	616c	Independent Brewing Co.	1902-1902
NY	617a	Julius Smith (513/514 W. Court St.)	1873-1882
	617b	Rome Brewing Co.	1882-1884
	617c	Julius Smith & Co.	1888-1897
	617d	Philippina Smith	1897-1898
	617e	P. Amtmann & Co. (514 W. Liberty St.)	1898-1901
	617f	Amtmann Brewing Co.	1901-1909

Rondout (see Kingston)

Rosebank (Staten Island)

NY	618a	Garibaldi & Mucci (Clifton)	1852-1853
	618b	Antonio Mucci	1853- ?
	618c	Gabriel Mayer	? - ?
	618d	Mayer & Bachman (Edgewater)	1874-1881
	618e	Fred. Bachmann	1881-1884
	618f	Bachmann Brewing Co., Clifton Brewery (Forest St., Maple & Willow Aves.)	1884-1900
	618g	Bachmann Consumers Brewing Co., Clifton Brewery	1900-1901
	618h	Bachmann Brewing Co., Clifton Brewery	1901-1907
	618i	Bachmann-Bechtel Brewing Co. (78 Bachmann St.)	1907-1911
NY	619a	R. Werner & Son (Clifton)	1884- ?
	619b	R. Werner's Sons (Clifton Park)	? -1890
	619c	Werner Brewing Co.	1890-1891
	619d	John Kaltenmeir	1891-1897

Rye

NY	620	H. Henry Rush	1890-1891

Sag Harbor

NY	621	Alan O. Dalzell	1893-1897

Salina

NY	622	Edwin Austin	1882-1884
NY	623	Tetzner & Ziegler	1882-1882

Saratoga Springs

NY 624 George H. Ehemann 1874-1884

Saugerties

NY 625 John Hiller 1874-1875

NY 626a L. Loerzel 1874-1875
626b M. Loerzel 1875-1882
626c Estate of M. Loerzel 1882-1888
626d Loerzel Bros. 1888-1893

Schenectady

NY 627 Virginia Dickson 1878-1884

NY 628a John Dunn & Co. (235 Dock St.) 1893-1897
628b Dunn Brewing Co. 1897-1905
628c Mohawk Valley Brewing Co. 1905-1913
628d Mohawk Valley Brewing Corp. (Foster Ave.) 1913-1916

NY 629a Peter Engel, Nutt Terrace Brewery 1874-1891
629b Schenectady Brewing Co. (161 Nott Terrace) 1891-1895
629c White & Fabricius 1895-1901

NY 630a Jos. S. Meyers 1878-1880
630b Edwards Ijoni 1880-1882

NY 631 Powers & Draper 1895-1895

NY 632 Charles E. Scott 1899-1901

Seneca (see Halls Corners)

Seneca Falls

NY 633a Wm. A. Booth 1875-1877
633b Weiss Bros. 1877-1879

Sheldon

NY 634 Thomas Bettendorf 1874-1884

Southfield

NY 635 Jos. Kaltenmeir 1874-1880

NY 636a Joseph Lutz 1874-1875
636b H. Freimann 1875-1880

South Volney

NY 637 Miller Brewing Co. (Owens Rd.) (br. of Milwaukee, WI) 1976-

Springville

NY 638 Joseph L. Lutz 1882-1882

Stapleton (Staten Island)

NY 639a John Bechtel 1853-1865
639b (George) Bechtel & Rubsam 1865-1870
639c George Bechtel 1870-1888
639d Estate of Geo. Bechtel 1888-1891
639e George Bechtel's Brewery 1891-1894
639f George Bechtel Brewing Co. 1894-1907

NY 640 Henry Freimann 1882-1891

NY 641a George Gillig 1845-1854
641b Charles Bischoff 1854-1882
641c Estate of Chas. Bischoff 1882-1884
641d Wm. Horrmann 1884-1890
641e New York and Staten Island Brewing Co. 1890-1891

NY 642 Geo. L Herbert 1888-1893

NY 643a Joseph Kaltenmeir 1882-1891
643b Estate of Joseph Kaltenmeir 1891-1893
643c John H. Grieme 1893-1900
643d Rebecca Grieme 1900-1903
643e Bahr & Krasman 1903-1908

NY 644 Gottlieb Korner ? -1878

Stapleton (cont.)

NY	645a	Krug & Bach	1865-1870
	645b	(Joseph) Rubsam & (August) Horrmann	1870-1888
	645c	Rubsam & Horrmann Brewing Co.	1888-1920
	645d	Rubsam & Horrmann Brewing Co. (191/193 Canal St.)	1933-1953
	645e	Piel's Inc., Rubsam & Horrmann Branch	1953-1955
	645f	Piel Bros.	1955-1963
NY	646	Fred. Menken (New Dorp, Edgewater)	1874-1893
NY	647a	Mueller & Kramer	1888-1890
	647b	Martin Mueller	1890-1891
NY	648	Reinhardt, Muller & Hower	1875- ?

Strykersville

NY	649a	John Demongo	1840- ?
	649b	George & Peter Metzger	? - ?
	649c	Margaret Metzger	? -1875
	649d	Frank Glaser	1875-1910
	649e	Albert Glaser, Jr.	1910-1920

Suspension Bridge

NY	650	Theo. Hager	1878-1882

Syracuse (includes Geddes)

NY	651a	Herman Ackermann (Laurel & Union Sts.)	1874-1877
	651b	Ackermann & Stuber	1877-1882
	651c	Ackermann & Sons	1882-1884
	651d	Syracuse Brewing Co. (Prospect & Laurel Sts.)	1884-1893
	651e	Ackermann & Pfohl	c1900
NY	652	Paul Alpert	1910-1911
NY	653a	Jacob Becker	1879-1880
	653b	Frank Klasi (204 Gifford St.)	1880-1895
NY	654a	Brewster Brothers (Catherine St. & Hawley Ave.)	? -1853
	654b	Greenway Brothers (John & George)	1853-1867
	654c	John Greenway (67/107 W. Water St.)	1867-1877
	654d	Greenway Brewing Co.	1877-1888
	654e	Greenway Brewing Co. (308/358 W. Water St.)	1888-1906
	654f	Greenway Brewery	1906-1916
	654g	Greenway Brewery (1925 Park St. & Hiawatha Ave.)	1916-1920
	654h	Greenway Brewery Co., Inc.	1933-1939
	654i	Greenway's, Inc.	1939-1952
NY	655a	Crystal Spring Brewing Co. (Burnet Ave. & Vine St.)	1887-1900
	655b	Haberle-Crystal Spring Brewing Co., Crystal Spring Brewery	1900-1904
	655c	Haberle-Crystal Spring Brewing Co., National Brewery (1001 Burnet Ave.)	1904-1920
NY	656	Dalton & Fleming	1874-1875
NY	657	Easterly Brewery (1234 Wolf St.)	c1850
NY	658	Great Northern Brewing Co.	1905-1905
NY	659a	John Greenway	1878-1884
	659b	Mantel & Haas	1884-1886
	659c	Germania Brewing Co.(9 N. West St.)	1886-1893
	659d	Bartels Brewing Co. (100/200 N. West St.)	1893-1920
	659e	Bartels Brewing Co. (104 N. West St.)	1933-1942
NY	660a	Benedict Haberle (Butternut & McBride Sts - N.E. Corner)	1857-1880
	660b	Haberle, Holweck & Co.	1880-1882
	660c	Haberle & Hoffmann, Onondaga Brewery	1882-1883
	660d	Ryan, Hoffmann & Co.	1883-1885
	660e	Ryan & Hoffmann	1885-1887
	660f	Thomas Ryan	1887-1900
	660g	Thomas Ryan's Consumers Brewing Co.	1900-1924
NY	661a	Benedict Haberle (Butternut & McBride Sts. - S.W. Corner)	1865-1875
	661b	B. Haberle & Son	1875-1881
	661c	Haberle Brewing Co.	1881-1892
	661d	Haberle-Crystal Spring Brewing Co., Haberle Brewery	1892-1920

Syracuse (cont.)

NY 661e Haberle Beverage & Products Co., Inc. 1920-1933
661f Haberle Congress Brewing Co., Inc. (500 Butternut St.) 1933-1962

NY 662a Henry Hartmann 1884-1886
662b Lewis House (518/522 Lock St.) 1886-1893
662c Lewis House & Sons 1893-1900
662d Lewis House & Sons (713/715 N. State St.) 1900-1913
662e L. House & Sons Co. 1913-1920

NY 663 Michael Heitz, Prospect Hill Brewery c1870

NY 664a William Kearney (N. Salina & Wolf Sts.) 1869-1895
664b William Kearney's Sons 1895-1900
664c Haberle-Crystal Spring Brewing Co., Kearney Brewery 1900-1904

NY 665 Johann Mang (N. Salina St. near Wolf St.) 1804-1810

NY 666a Jacob Mantel, Rock Spring Brewery (Split Rock Road, Geddes) 1875-1879
666b Rosina Mantel, Rock Spring Brewery (Grand & Avery Aves. Geddes) 1879-1888
666c Rock Spring Brewing Co. 1888-1898

NY 667a (Frank) Moore, (Wm.) Quinn & Co. (Chestnut & E. Water Sts.) 1881-1888
667b Moore, Quinn & Co. (102/110 S. Crouse Ave.) 1888-1901
667c Moore & Quinn 1901-1920
667d Moore & Quinn, Inc. 1933-1950

NY 668a Murphy Bros. (121 Avery St.) 1895-1896
668b Murphy Bros. (110 Grand Ave.) 1897-1904
668c John Murphy 1904-1907
668d Flanigan & Murphy 1907-1910
668e Cornelius Murphy 1910-1915
668f Cornelius Murphy (656 S. Geddes St.) 1915-1916

NY 669a National Brewing Co. (921/923 Lock & Division Sts.) 1888-1900
669b Haberle-Crystal Spring Brewing Co., National Brewery (921 State St. between N. Division & Ash Sts.) 1900-1904

NY 670a Jacob Pfohl (Pond & Park Sts.) 1874-1884
670b John F. Scanlan 1893-1900

NY 671a Xavier Zett (407 Lodi & Court Sts.) 1858-1877
671b Xavier Zett & Son 1879-1882
aka Zett & Kohles (1880)
671c George Zett 1882-1895
671d George Zett (2314 Lodi St.) 1895-1898
671e George Zett Brewing Co. 1898-1902
671f George Zett Brewery 1902-1920
671g George Zett Brewing Co., Inc. (2318 Lodi St.) 1933-1934
671h Syracuse Brewery, Inc. (affiliated with Genesee, Rochester) 1934-1937

Tappan

NY 672 Edward Tracy 1905-1906

Tonawanda

NY 673a George Zent 1874-1882
673b Niagara River Brewing Co. 1882-1893
673c Busch Brewing Co. 1893-1898
673d Niagara River Brewing Co. 1898-1899
673e Tonawanda Brewing Co. (533 Niagara St.) 1899-1920
673f Tonawanda Brewing Corp. 1933-1935
673g Frontier Brewery, Inc. 1935-1948

NY 674 Best Brewing Corp. NP 1934-1934

Troy (includes Lansingburg, Rensselaerswyck, West Troy)

NY 675a Samuel Bolton (327/333 State St., Lansingburg) 1865-1877
675b Samuel Bolton & Sons 1877-1888
675c S. Bolton's Sons (331 2nd Ave. & 7th St.) 1888-1920

NY 676a D. P. Chesborough & Son (Head of Richard St., Lansingburg) 1884-1888
676b Cold Spring Brewing Co. 1888-1890

NY 677a Philip Conners (2nd St.) 1878-1880
677b James Daly 1880-1884
677c Donohue Bros. (229 2nd St.) 1884-1891

Troy (cont.)

NY	678a	Daly & Stanton (194/198 5th St.)	1874-1880
	678b	John Stanton	1880-1895
	678c	John Stanton Brewing and Malting Co. (1428/1450 5th Ave.)	1895-1920
	678d	The Stanton Brewery, Inc.	1933-1950
NY	679a	Wm. J. Dickson (West Troy)	1875-1877
	679b	Reilly & McGrath	1877-1879
	679c	T. H. McGrath	1879-1880
	679d	Winslow & Co.	1880-1882
	679e	Mathew A. McGrath (Ohio & Auburn Sts.)	1882-1888
NY	680a	Robert Dunlop (West Troy)	1834- ?
	680b	Peter Ballantine	? -1839
NY	681	Evans & Booke (Lansingburg)	1875-1875
NY	682a	Fitzgerald Bros. (Edmund, Michael, John) (495/511 River St.)	1866-1899
	682b	Fitzgerald Bros. Brewing Co.	1899-1920
	682c	Fitzgerald Bros. Brewing Co.	1933-1962
NY	683a	Gaffigan & Myers	1875-1877
	683b	Julia Gaffigan	1877-1884
	683c	Dennis J. Whelan (104 Jefferson St.)	1884-1908
	683d	Dennis J. Whelan Estate	1908-1916
NY	684a	(Charles) Hurstfield & (Thomas) Trenor (124 Ferry St. & 6th)	1809-1823
	684b	Read & Armstrong	1823-1832
	684c	Read, Armstrong & Co.	1832-1837
	684d	Read & Son	1837-1841
	684e	M. P. Read & Brothers	1841-1847
	684f	Read & Brothers	1847-1856
	684g	Arba Read	1856-1857
	684h	Read Brothers	1857-1867
	684i	Dunn & Kennedy	1867-1867
	684j	Kennedy & Murphy	1867-1895
	684k	Kennedy & Murphy Brewing and Malting Co.	1895-1916
NY	685a	Christian Isengart (Hoosick & 10th Sts.)	1865-1870
	685b	Isengart & Voigt	1870-1887
	685c	(Wm.) Donohue, Tierney & Gross	1887-1888
	685d	Donohue-Tierney-Isengart Brewing Co.	1888-1901
	685e	Isengart Brewing Co.	1901-1915
NY	686a	Leo Kirchner (846/852 River St.)	1859-1877
	686b	Andrew & Adam Quandt	1877-1884
	686c	Quandt Brewing Co.	1884-1920
	686d	Quandt Brewing Co., Inc. (846/869 River St.)	1933-1942
NY	687a	Abraham Nash	1825-1830
	687b	Nash & Co.	1830-1840
	687c	Nash, Beadleston & Co.	1840- ?
NY	688a	Evert Pels (Rensselaerswyck)	1642-1647
	688b	Rutgers Jacobsen Van Schoenderwoerdt & Goosen Gerritsen Van Schakk	1649-1660
NY	689	Evert Pels (Rensselaerswyck)	1647- ?
NY	690a	A. Louis Ruscher (474/484 4th & Trenton Sts.)	1852-1882
	690b	Ruscher & Co.	1882-1903
	690c	Ruscher Brewing Co.	1903-1905
	690d	The Ruscher Co.	1905-1912
NY	691a	Sands Star Brewery	1850- ?
	691b	Sands & Potter (146 N. 4th St.)	? -1878
	691c	William H. Potter	1878-1880
	691d	Mrs. Margaret A. Potter	1880-1883
	691e	Conway Bros. (N. T. & Daniel E.) & Kane (Henry A.)	1883-1897
	691f	Conway Bros. & Kane (2312/2332 7th Ave.)	1897-1903
	691g	Conway Bros. Brewing and Malting Co.	1903-1916
NY	692	(Jacob) Stoll & (A. L.) Ruscher	1855-1864

Troy (cont.)

NY	693a	Jacob F. Stoll (35/41 Spring Ave.)		1864-1888
	693b	The Jacob Stoll Brewery		1888-1895
	693c	Stoll Brewing Co.		1895-1920
	693d	Stoll Brewing Co., Inc. (41 Spring Ave.)	NP	1934-1934
NY	694	Wm. H. Walter (River & Hoosick Sts., Lansingburg)		1882-1884
NY	695a	Adam Weinbender (West Troy)		1882-1883
	695b	Adam Weinbender & Son		1883-1884
	695c	Adam Weinbender		1884-1890
	695d	Estate of Adam Weinbender		1890-1895

Utica

NY	696a	Charles Bierbauer (9/21 Edward St.)		1853-1885
	696b	Columbia Brewing Co.		1885-1887
	696c	West End Brewing Co. (9/21 Edward St.)		1888-1920
	696d	West End Brewing Co., Inc. (811 Edward St.) aka West End Brewing Co. of Utica, N.Y.		1933-1981
	696e	West End Brewing Co., dba F.X. Matt Brewing Co.		1981-
NY	697a	Brown, Failey & Co. (96/102 Catherine St.)		1885-1886
	697b	Failey, Joyce & Co., Old Fort Schuyler Brewery		1886-1891
	697c	Fort Schuyler Brewing Co.		1891-1901
	697d	Callahan Brewery		1901-1903
	697e	Fort Schuyler Brewing Co.		1903-1920
	697f	Utica Brewing Co., Inc. (434 Catherine St.)		1933-1934
	697g	The Utica Brewing Co., Inc., of Utica, N.Y.		1935-1937
NY	698a	Eagle Brewing Co. (31/43 3rd Ave.)		1888-1913
	698b	Eagle Brewing Co. (313/315 3rd Ave.)		1913-1920
	698c	The Eagle Brewing Co.		1933-1943
NY	699a	Michael McQuade, Gulf Brewery (Jay St. & 3rd Ave.)		1830-1877
	699b	Gulf Brewery		1877-1882
	699c	Gulf Brewing Co.		1882-1920
	699d	Globe Brewing Co., Inc. (610/615 Jay St.)		1933-1937
	699e	The Utica Brewing Co., Inc. of Utica, N.Y.		1937-1959
NY	700	John Myers & Co. (Mohawk & Jay St.)		1875-1901
NY	701a	George Ralph (42 Court & State Sts.)		1832-1855
	701b	George Ralph, Jr. & Co.		1855-1884
	701c	Oneida Brewing Co.		1884-1920
	701d	Oneida Brewing Co., Inc. (915 Lincoln Ave.)		1933-1942
NY	702	Chas. W. Sharp & Co. (Kossuth Ave.)		1893-1893
NY	703a	Strom		1848-1850
	703b	Charles Bierbauer		1850-1853
	703c	Charles Hutton (92/105 3rd St.)		1853-1890
	703d	Barnes & Metzger		1890-1895
	703e	Barnes, Metzger & Doll		1895-1896
	703f	LaFayette Brewing Co.		1896-1896
	703g	Consumers Brewing Co.		1896-1897
	703h	August Mueller		1897-1899
	703i	Consumers Brewing Co. of Utica		1899-1900
	703j	Consumers Brewery		1900-1902
NY	704a	Utica Brewing Co. (193/203 South & Vincent Sts.)		1884-1890
	704b	National Brewing Co.		1890-1892
	704c	Utica National Brewing Co.		1892-1899
NY	705a	Winslow, Moore & Co.		1880- ?
	705b	People's Brewing Co. (2nd & Catherine Sts.)		1890-1899

Vienna

NY	706	Mrs. Mary C. Herder		1884-1884

Wappinger's Falls

NY	707	Thomas Mather		1874-1875

Waterloo

NY	708	Geneva Brewing Co.		1910-1910

Watertown

NY 709a Henry M. Hind 1874-1877
709b Alonzo Kellogg 1877-1878

NY 710 Peter Seibert 1874-1878

NY 711a Watertown Brewing Co. (457 Poplar St.) 1893-1901
711b Watertown Consumers Brewing Co. 1901-1920
711c The Northern Brewing Co., Inc. 1933-1943

Waterville

NY 712 E. S. Peck 1874-1882

Watervliet

NY 713 Adam Weinbender 1874-1880

Watkins Glen

NY 714a Ben Record Brewery, Inc. (210 Madison Ave.) 1934-1937
714b Glen Brewing Co. 1937-1940

Wawarsing

NY 715 John Kuhlmann 1874-1879

Weedsport

NY 716a A. L. Chatfield 1874-1875
716b Brewster & Becker 1875-1884
716c Weedsport Brewing Co. 1884-1893

Westfield

NY 717 August Rorig 1874-1880

Westmoreland

NY 718a G. A. Brockett & Son 1874-1877
718b J. A. Brockett 1877-1882
718c A. G. Brockett 1882-1884

West New Brighton (Staten Island)

NY 719a Bernheimer & Schmid, Constanz Brewery (Four Corners) 1852-1850
719b August Schmid 1856-1862
719c Bernheimer & Schmid 1862-1865
719d Fenzel & Decker 1865-1867
719e Joseph Setz 1874-1875
719f Monroe Eckstein 1875-1890
719g Mornoe Eckstein Brewing Co. 1890-1920
719h Monroe Eckstein Brewery (owned by Edward B. Hittleman Brewing Co., Brooklyn, N.Y.) NP 1934-1934

West Seneca

NY 720a Gottlieb Haas 1874-1875
720b J. L. Uebelhoer 1875-1882

NY 721a Anthony Messner 1874-1877
721b Mrs. A. Messner 1877-1884

West Troy (see Troy)

Williamsburg (see Brooklyn)

Williamsville

NY 722a J. Batt & Co. 1874-1884
722b Williamsville Brewing Co. 1884-1891
722c Williamsville Co-operative Brewing Co. 1891-1892
722d Fisher & Durlam 1895-1896
722e W. J. Fisher (Main & Grove Sts.) 1896-1897
722f Erie County Brewing Co. 1897-1899
722g Erie County Brewery 1899-1900
722h Eugene Irr 1900-1901

Woodside (see New York City)

Yonkers

NY 723a Charles Kraft (S. Broadway) 1878-1895
723b John F. McMahon (21 Morgan St.) 1895-1897
723c David H. Smith (James & John Sts.) 1897-1899

Yonkers (cont.)

NY	724a	Henry & Co., Edward Underhill Sr. (Chicken Island)		1857- ?
	724b	E. Underhill & Co.		? -1874
	724c	E. Underhill & Son		1874-1877
	724d	E. Underhill's Sons		1877-1880
	724e	Underhill, Jackson & Co., aka Underhill & Jackson		1880-1891
	724f	Jackson & Co.		1891-1897
	724g	Yonkers Brewery		1897-1920
	724h	State Cereal Beverage Co.		1920-1930
	724i	The Penar Corp. (18 Ann St.)		1930-1934
	724j	Yonkers Colonial Corp.		1935-1938

NORTH CAROLINA

Charlotte				
NC	1a	Atlantic Ice and Coal Co. (br. of Atlanta, Ga.) (300 S. Graham St.)		1936-1937
	1b	Atlantic Co. (br. of Atlanta, Ga.)		1937-1956
NC	Note:	Southern Breweries, Inc. - see Seitz Brewing Co., Easton, Pa.		
Durham				
NC	2	North State Breweries, Inc.	NP	1934-1934
Eden				
NC	3	Miller Brewing Co. (br. of Milwaukee, WI) (863 E. Meadow Road)		1978-
Elizabeth City				
NC	4	Thomas M. Jenkins (Road St.)		1884-1884
Fayetteville				
NC	5	J. W. Lancashire		1879-1882
Statesville				
NC	6	C. S. Colyer		1884-1884
NC	7	Old South Brewing Co.	NP	1934-1934
Winston-Salem				
NC	8a	Jos. Schlitz Brewing Co. (br. of Milwaukee, WI) (4791 Schlitz Ave.)		1970-1982
	8b	Jos. Schlitz Brewing Co. (br. of Detroit, MI)		1982-

NORTH DAKOTA

Bismarck				
ND	1	Dakota Brewing and Malting Co. (Main Ave. at 26th St., Mandan)		1961-1965
ND	2a	Gerard & Co.		1875-1877
	2b	J. E. Walker		1877-1880
	2c	Otto Setzer		1880-1884
ND	3a	Walter & Fischer		1880- ?
	3b	Fischer & Gegen		? -1884
	3c	Milwaukee Brewing Co.		1884-1889
ND	4	Walters & Kalberer		1878-1884
Dunseith				
ND	5	Carl Stofft		1889-1889
East Grand Forks				
ND	6	East Grand Forks Brewing Co.		1910-1910
Fargo				
ND	7a	Ole Aslesen		1882- ?
	7b	Aslesen & Hult		? -1889
ND	8	Jos. W. Brokorsch		1879-1879
ND	9a	John G. Kraenzlein		1882 - ?
	9b	Kraenzlein & Klinkert		? -1884
	9c	Red River Valley Brewing Co.		1884-1889
Fort Totten				
ND	10a	Brenner & Terry		1874-1877
	10b	E. W. Brenner		1877-1880
	10c	Wm. G. Peck & Co.		1880-1884

Grand Forks

ND	11a	J. Gahr & Co.	1882- ?
	11b	Jacob Dobmeier (826 S. 3rd St.)	1890-1899

Jamestown

ND	12	Philip Bauer	1889-1889
ND	13a	Henry Danne	1882-1884
	13b	Jamestown Brewing Co.	1884-1889
ND	14	Gasa Bros.	1889-1889

Minot

ND	15	Wentz & Kocher	1888-1889

Pembina

ND	16	Myrick's Brewery	1875- ?
ND	17	Pembina Brewing Co.	1888-1889
ND	18	A. W. Stiles (Fort Pembina)	1874-1875

Wahpeton

ND	19a	Stofft & Hoppe	1882-1883
	19b	Stofft & Huppeler	1883-1884
	19c	Michael Schmitt	1884-1889

OHIO

Akron

OH	1a	Akron Brewing Co. (S. High & E. Voris Sts.)	1905-1919
	1b	Akron Brewing Co. (260 S. Forge & Hill Sts.)	1934-1943
OH	2a	Jacob Fornecker	c1863
	2b	Frederick Gassler	1874-1877
	2c	Gassler & Burkhardt	1877-1879
	2d	William Burkhardt	1879-1882
	2e	Mrs. Margaret Burkhardt (152/156 Sherman St.)	1882-1903
	2f	M. Burkhardt Brewing Co. (513/529 Grant St.)	1903-1919
	2g	The Burkhardt Brewing Co.	1933-1956
	2h	The Burger Brewing Co.	1956-1964
OH	3a	Oberholz	1862- ?
	3b	Kempel	?
	3c	Good	?
	3d	Fred Horix (247/313 N. Forge St.)	1874-1888
	3e	Geo. J. Renner	1888-1900
	3f	George J. Renner Brewing Co.	1900-1919
	3g	The Renner Products Co.	1919-1933
	3h	The Geo. J. Renner Brewing Co.	1933-1953
OH	4	White Rock Brewing Co.	NP 1934-1934

Alliance

OH	5	Alliance Brewing Co. (Summit St. & C & P R.R.)	1905-1919
OH	6a	Florian Knam	1874-1879
	6b	Mary Knam	1879-1880

Amherst

OH	7	William Braun	1874-1884

Anderson (Hamilton County)

OH	8	Philip Hirsch	1874-1875

Archbold

OH	9a	A. Walder	1878-1884
	9b	Casper Herrmann	1884-1893
	9c	Andrew Walder	1893-1904
	9d	Andrew Walder & Son	1904-1909

Arnheim

OH	10a	Conrad Katlein	1874-1877
	10b	Katlein & Co. (Franklin)	1877-1879
	10c	L. Kattine	1879-1884

Arnwell			
OH	11a	Peter Rich	1878-1879
	11b	Rich & Son	1879-1882
Ashtabula			
OH	12	Consumers Brewing Co.	1905-1910
Barberton			
OH	13a	Chas. W. Specht	1896-1898
	13b	Christina Specht	1898-1901
Bellaire			
OH	14a	Bellaire Brewing Co. (32nd & Hamilton Sts.)	1905-1919
	14b	Matz Brewing Co.	1937-1953
OH	15	John E. Vogel	1875- ?
Blackfield			
OH	16	Rudolph Kapizky	1874-1875
Bluffton			
OH	17a	Hubelheimer & Bender	1855-1867
	17b	Bowers & Zehrbach	1867-1875
	17c	Adam Bowers	1875-1878
	17d	Maltz & Yearbaugh	1878-1879
	17e	Manger & Schancie	1879-1880
	17f	Kraft & Schlap	1880-1881
	17g	John Schlap	1881-1883
	17h	Konrad N. Kraft	1883-1897
	17i	Casper Herrmann	1897-1919
Brighton			
OH	18	Martin Frank & Co.	1874-1875
Brookville			
OH	19	Louis Feuer	1882-1884
Bryan			
OH	20a	George Weiss	1856- ?
	20b	Henry Arnold	? -1865
	20c	Jacob Halm (Beech & Center Sts.)	1865-1884
	20d	Halm's Fountain City Brewery	1884-1888
	20e	Halm Brewing Co. (Beach & Centre Sts.)	1888-1908
Bucyrus			
OH	21a	(George) Donnenwirth & (Henry) Anthony	1857- ?
	21b	Geo. Donnenwirth & Son	1874-1875
	21c	G. Donnenwirth & Bro.	1875-1889
	21d	Frank Dick (538/568 N. Railroad St.)	1889-1902
	21e	Dostal Brothers	1902-1912
	21f	Bucyrus Brewing Co.	1912-1919
	21g	Dostal Products Co. (500 Norton Way & George St.)	1919-1934
	21h	Bucyrus Products, Inc.	1934-1937
Cambridge			
OH	22	Hermann Berne	1874-1875
OH	23	Cambridge Brewing Co. (145 Steubenville Ave.)	1901-1909
Canal Dover			
OH	24a	Andy Dangleisen	1862- ?
	24b	F. Bernhardt & Bro.	1875-1877
	24c	Fred. Bernhardt	1877-1896
	24d	Dover Brewing Co.	1896-1902
	24e	Christian Bernhardt	1902-1904
	24f	Stark-Tuscarawas Breweries Co., Dover Branch	1904-1907
OH	25a	Tuscarawas Valley Brewing Co.	1905-1910
	25b	Martin Brewery	1910-1912
	25c	Consumers Brewing and Ice Co.	1912-1914
Canal Fulton			
OH	26a	Ruch & Moore	1874-1877
	26b	Christian Ruch	1877-1893
OH	27	Ernest Schneider	1890-1890

Canton				
OH	28a	Charles Freeze		1870- ?
	28b	Giessen & Bohn		1875-1877
	28c	Otto Giessen		1877-1887
	28d	William Roemmel		1887-1888
	28e	Canton Brewing Co. (216/230 N. Cherry St.)		1888-1904
	28f	Stark-Tuscarawas Breweries Co., Canton Brewery		1904-1919
OH	29	Groeber Brewing Co.		1933-1933
OH	30a	Home Brewing Co. (1200 E. 40th St.)		1906-1919
	30b	Home Brewing Co. (108 3rd St. S.E.)	NP	1934-1934
OH	31	Jos. Klopfenstein		1875- ?
OH	32a	Knobloch & Hermann		1875-1880
	32b	Adam Knobloch		1880-1888
	32c	Union Brewing Co.		1888-1894
OH	33a	C. Kropf & Co.		1884-1904
	33b	Kropf Cream Ale Co.		1904-1909
OH	34a	T. C. Nightman		1830-1865
	34b	Kasper Balser		1865-1876
	34c	Mrs. Louisa Balser		1876-1890
OH	35a	Stark Brewing Co. (624/630 N. Cherry St.)		1904- ?
	35b	Stark-Tuscarawas Breweries Co., Stark Branch		1908-1919
	35c	The Canton Brewing Co. (1216/1218 High St., S.W.) aka Tuscara Brewing Co. (N.P. 1934)		1933-1941
Celina				
OH	36a	Ph. Schmitt & Bro.		1874-1875
	36b	A. Ott		1875-1880
Chagrin Falls				
OH	37a	Goodwin & Sheffield		1875-1877
	37b	A. A. Goodwin		1877-1880
Chasetown				
OH	38	Nicklaus Gines		1875-1878
Chillicothe				
OH	39a	P. J. Loepel		1874-1877
	39b	Knecht & Muehling		1877-1883
	39c	Jacob Knecht (45/51 E. Water St.)		1883-1886
	39d	Jacob Knecht & Son, Scioto Brewery		1886-1919
	39e	Old Capitol Brewery, Inc.		1934-1944
	39f	Old Capitol Brewery, Inc.		1946-1947
	39g	August Wagner Breweries, Inc. (br. of Columbus, OH)		1947-1951
OH	40a	Reinhard Wissler (2nd St. & Western Ave.)		1856-1882
	40b	R. Wissler & Sons		1882-1884
	40c	Otto Wissler & Co.		1884-1919
Cincinnati				
OH •	41a	Henry Adam, Camp Washington Brewery (Miami Canal & Straight St)		1881-1907
	41b	Camp Washington Brewing Co.		1907-1910
	41c	Adam Brewing Co.		1910-1912
	41d	Bowman-Harman Brewing Co.		1912-1916
OH	42a	Wm. Attee (4th St. between Smith & John)		1825-1829
	42b	Wm. Lofthouse & Wm. Attee, Western Brewery		1829-1836
	42c	Wm. Lofthouse (572 W. Row)		1836-1844
OH	43a	Banner Brewing Co. (Walnut, Clay & Canal Sts.)		1888-1897
	43b	Cincinnati Consumers Brewing Co.		1897-1898
	43c	F. Bartels Brewing Co.		1898-1900
	43d	Ralston-Neurich Brewing Co.		1900-1902
OH	44	F. Beck		c1861
OH	45	Beltz & (Adam) Noelp (436 Vine St.)		1866-1868
OH	46	Berlina Weiss Beer Import Co. (Reading Rd. & June St.)		1888-1888

Cincinnati (cont.)

OH	47a	Fred & Thomas Billiod, Lafayette Brewery (184 Hamilton Rd.)	1836-1863
	47b	Wm. Fey & Co.	1864-1868
	47c	H. Darusmont	1869-1880
OH	48a	Frederick Bruckmann, Cumminsville Brewery	1856-1858
	48b	Bruckmann Bros., Cumminsville Brewery	1858- ?
	48c	John C. Bruckmann, Cumminsville Brewery (Ludlow Ave.)	1872-1891
	48d	John C. Bruckmann Brewing Co., Cumminsville Brewery (Dodsworth Ave. & Canal)	1891-1901
	48e	Bruckmann Brewing Co., Cumminsville Brewery	1901-1919
	48f	The Bruckmann Co. (Plant 1 - Ludlow Ave.)	1933-1949
	48g	The Herschel Condon Brewing Co.	1849-1850
OH	49a	Louisa Brueck (62 13th St.)	1865-1865
	49b	Siebert & Koegel	1865-1866
OH	50	Cincinnati Weiss Beer Import Co. (16/18 Ellen St.), aka Berliner Weiss	1888-1891
OH	51a	City Brewery	? -1855
	51b	(Herman) Lackman & (J. H.) Sandman, City Brewery	1855-1868
	51c	Herman Lackman (443/445 W. 6th St.)	1868-1890
	51d	Herman Lackman Brewing Co. (801/825 W. 6th St.)	1890-1919
	51e	Sohn Brewing Co.	NP 1934-1934
	51f	The Hudepohl Brewing Co. (5th, Gest, & 809/833 W. 6th Sts.)	1934-
OH	52a	Craney & (Thomas) Drum (51/53 Smith & 2nd Sts.)	1848-1859
	52b	Wm. Walker	1859-1860
	52c	Thomas Drum	1860-1863
	52d	John Draper	1863-1865
	52e	J. F. Frohmeyer & Sons	1865-1866
OH	53a	Frank Eichenlaub	?
	53b	Eichenlaub & Kaufmann (Vine St.)	?
	53c	(John) Kaufmann & (Rudolph) Rheinboldt	1856- ?
	53d	John Kauffman & Co. (596/606 Vine St.)	1871-1876
	53e	John Kauffman	1876-1882
	53f	John Kauffman Brewing Co.	1882-1893
	53g	John Kauffman Brewing Co. (1622/1628 Vine St.)	1893-1919
OH	54	Elsas, Strauss & Co. (119 W. Pearl St.)	1867-1868
OH	55	Davis Embree (75 Water St.)	1811-1825
OH	56	Fleischman	1844- ?
OH	57	William Floyd	1813-1817
OH	58	Fortmann & Muenzenberger, aka Fortmann & Co. (Main nr. 12th)	1846-1848
OH	59a	Fuchs & Sommer (45/47 Hamilton Road)	1850- ?
	59b	John Bauer & G. Glass	?
	59c	Leonard Bauer & M. Beck	? -1871
	59d	(Leonard) Bauer & (George) Bach	1871-1875
	59e	Schmidt & Adam	1875-1875
	59f	(Henry) Schmidt & (Fred) Prell	1875-1876
	59g	Schmidt & Bro. (45/51 McMicken Ave.)	1876-1891
	59h	Schmidt Bros. Brewing Co. (125/140 E. McMicken Ave.)	1891-1904
	59i	Crown Brewing Co.	1904-1919
OH	60a	Germania Brewing Co. (947/951 Central Ave.)	1885-1891
	60b	Germania Brewing Co. (2125 Central Ave.)	1891-1902
	60c	Wetterer Brewing Co.	1902-1919
OH	61	Charles Glossner & George Daniel (436 Main St.)	1856-1863
OH	62a	John Hare (Lebanon Park & Corp. Line)	1857-1861
	62b	John Burkholtz	1861-1865
OH	63a	Harris & Co. (Sycamore between 3rd & 4th Sts.)	1850-1852
	63b	David Harris	1853-1866
	63c	S. S. Ashcraft & Co. (100 Sycamore St.)	1866-1867
	63d	Dyett & Thatcher	1867-1872

Cincinnati (cont.)

OH	64a	(John) Hauck & (John) Windisch (1/39 Dayton St.)	1863-1879
	64b	John Hauck	1879-1881
	64c	John Hauck Brewing Co.	1881-1896
	64d	John Hauck Brewing Co. (400/435 Dayton St.)	1896-1919
	64e	Red Top Brewing Co. (421 Dayton St. & 1747 Central Ave.) aka Wunderbrau Brewing Co. (1955)	1933-1956
OH	65a	Geo. M. Herancourt, City Brewery (Harrison Ave.)	1836-1880
	65b	Herancourt Brewing Co. (1400 Harrison Ave.)	1880-1919
OH	66a	Peter Herancourt (Denman & Hamilton)	1857-1861
	66b	Rothert & Groene (Denman, Bank & Central)	1862-1864
OH	67a	Jos. Hochenlutner (83/87 Harrison & Division Sts.)	1856-1859
	67b	Louis Bruck, Brighton Brewery	1859-1861
	67c	Jos. Hochenluther & Jos. Renner, Brighton Brewery	1861-1862
	67d	Jos. Renner & Co.	1865-1870
OH	68a	Jos. Hofflein (487 Vine St.)	1853-1854
	68b	(Ludwig) Ziegler & Conradi (490 Vine St.)	1857-1863
OH	69	Charles Holler & Co. (126 Cutter)	1861-1861
OH	70a	Andrew Jackson	1832-1855
	70b	Kleiner Brothers (282 Hamilton Road)	1855-1874
	70c	George Weber	1874-1877
	70d	George Weber (284 McMicken Ave. & Elm St.)	1877-1880
	70e	Leo. A. Brigel	1880-1882
	70f	George Weber Brewing Co.	1882-1889
	70g	Jackson Brewing Co.	1889-1919
	70h	Squibb-Pattison Breweries, Inc.	1934-1934
	70i	Jackson Brewing Corp. (200/220 W. McMicken Ave. & Elm St.)	1937-1941
OH	71a	Peter Jonte	1832-1855
	71b	(Christian) Boss & (David) Ray	1855-1858
	71c	Christian Boss	1858-1867
	71d	Christian Boss & Co. (400 Sycamore, Abigail & Elliott Sts.)	1867-1876
	71e	Gambrinus Stock Co. (400 Sycamore, E. 12th & Elliott Sts.)	1876-1919
	71f	The Vienna Brewing Co. (312 Elliott St. & 322 Reading Road)	1933-1940
OH	72a	George & Louis Klotter (Browne St.)	1870- ?
	72b	Klotter Sons	1874-1877
	72c	C. Kinsinger, assignee for Klotter's Sons	1877-1888
	72d	Bellevue Brewing Co. (601/615 W. McMicken & Freeman Aves.)	1888-1919
OH	73a	Gottfried Koehler	1852- ?
	73b	Koehler Bros. (Buckeye St.)	? -1885
	73c	(Louis) Hudepohl & (George H.) Kotte, Buckeye Brewery (34/48 E. McMicken Ave. & 77/97 Clifton Ave.)	1885-1899
	73d	Hudepohl Brewing Co. (38/48 E. McMicken Ave. & 105/125 E. Clifton Ave.)	1899-1919
	73e	The Hudepohl Brewing Co. (Plant 1)	1933-1953
OH	74	Marhofer & Webben (Providence between Everett & Mason)	1855-1856
OH	75a	George Middlewood (4th & N. Row Sts.)	1836- ?
	75b	Matthew & Wood & Bros.	? -1861
OH	76a	(Christian) Moerlein & (Adam) Dillmann, Elm Street Brewery (711/712 Elm St.)	1853-1854
	76b	Moerlein & (Conrad) Windisch, Elm Street Brewery	1854-1866
	76c	Christian Moerlein	1866-1881
	76d	Christian Moerlein Brewing Co. (2019 Elm St.)	1881-1919
	76e	The Old Munich Brewing Co., Inc.	1933-1937
OH	77	Peter Noll (Vine St. between 13th & 14th Sts.)	1849-1853
OH	78a	Ohio Union Brewing Co. (Spring Grove & Garrard Aves.)	1905-1915
	78b	Cincinnati Home Brewing Co.	1915-1919
	78c	The Bruckmann Beverage & Products Co.	1919-1933
	78d	The Bruckmann Co. (Plant 2 - 2960/2974 Spring Grove Ave.)	1933-1949
OH	79a	Arnold Ordeng (220 Clark St.)	1871- ?
	79b	Walker Bros. (Clark & Harriet Sts.) aka Cincinnati Ale & Porter Brewery (1879-1881)	1879-1884

Cincinnati (cont.)

OH	80a	Charles Rebstock, Park Brewery (13th & Race Sts.)	1859-1859
	80b	Matthias Hauser	1859-1861
	80c	Dieterle & Frick	1861-1861
	80d	Niehaus & Klinckhammer, aka Joseph Niehaus & Co.	1862-1884
	80e	H. Klinckhammer & Son	1884-1888
	80f	John Klinckhammer & Co.	1888-1890
	80g	Klinckhammer Brewing Co.	1890-1895
OH	81a	Patrick Reily (Congress & Pike)	1819-1825
	81b	Perry & Reily	1825-1836
	81c	(Francis) Fortmann & Co. (Conrad Muenzenberger) (1846/1848 Agniel, Main & 12th St.)	1836-1862
	81d	Mueller & Gogreve	1862- ?
OH	82	Sarah Rolls & Co. (Corp. Line & Clifton)	1859-1862
OH	83a	Schaller & Schiff, Eagle Brewery	1854-1866
	83b	Schaller & (John) Gerke, Eagle Brewery (Plum & 233/235 Canal)	1866-1882
	83c	Gerke Brewing Co.	1882-1912
OH	84a	Schneider & Mueller	1855- ?
	84b	Michael Mueller (652/658 Main St.)	1875-1879
	84c	Mueller & Froelking	1879-1880
	84d	Schaller Bros.	1880-1896
	84e	Schaller Brewing Co. (1622/1632 Main St.)	1896-1919
	84f	Schaller Brewery Co. NP	1934-1934
OH	85a	Louis Schneider (Augusta St. between John & Smith Sts.)	1849-1867
	85b	Schneider & Foss	1867-1867
	85c	(John) Foss, (Peter) Schneider & (John) Brenner (259 Freeman & Fillmore Sts.)	1867-1877
	85d	Foss & Schneider	1877-1884
	85e	Foss-Schneider Brewing Co. (279/297 Freeman St.)	1884-1893
	85f	Foss-Schneider Brewing Co. (943/1005 Freeman St.)	1893-1919
	85g	The Foss-Schneider Co.	1933-1939
OH	86a	The Schoenling Brewing and Malting Co., Inc. (1625 Central Parkway & Oliver St.)	1934-1934
	86b	The Schoenling Brewing and Ice Co.	1934-1937
	86c	The Schoenling Brewing Co., aka Frank Fehr Brewing Co. & Top Hat Brewing Co.	1937-
OH	87a	Adam Schultz Brewing Co. (Thinnis St. & S. Branch Road)	1888-1891
	87b	Becker Brewing Co. (Thinnis St. & Quebec Ave.)	1891-1899
	87c	Bartels Bros. Brewing Co. (Westwood Ave.)	1899-1902
	87d	Fairmount Brewing Co. (Westwood & Quebec Aves.)	1902-1919
	87e	Fairmount Brewing Co. (1921 Westwood Ave.) NP	1934-1934
OH	88	W. J. & C. J. Schultz, Washington Brewery (483 E. Front & Main)	1831-1867
OH	89a	John G. Sohn & Co. (George Klotter) (330 Hamilton Road) aka Conradi & Co. (1858-1860)	1846-1867
	89b	Sohn, (Edward) Kistner & Co.	1867-1870
	89c	J. G. Sohn & Co. (244/252 McMicken Ave.)	1870-1900
	89d	Wm. S. Sohn Brewing Co.	1900-1910
	89e	Mohawk Brewing Co.	1910-1925
	89f	The Clyffside Brewing Co.	1933-1945
	89g	Red Top Brewing Co. (Plant 2) aka Wunderbrau Brewing Co. (1955)	1945-1958
OH	90	Matt. Spinner & Jos. Scott (Browne between Central Parkway & Hamilton)	1853-1854
OH	91	A. Tiemann & Co. (Montgomery Park)	1857-1857
OH	92	Walker Bros. (Clark & Harriet Sts.)	1880-1884
OH	93a	P. Walker (Woodward & Broadway)	1828-1834
	93b	John & Blake Walker	1834-1836
	93c	John & Blake Walker (391 Sycamore St. btwn. 12th & Abigail)	1836-1836
	93d	J. Walker & Co. (385/393 Sycamore St.)	1836-1882
	93e	Schultz & Andrews	1882-1884
	93f	J. Walker Brewing Co. (1125/1135 Sycamore St.)	1884-1911

Cincinnati (cont.)

OH	94a	Weyand & Jung (771 Freeman St.)	1857-1879
	94b	Weyand, Jung & Hellmann	1879-1885
	94c	Jung Brewing Co. (2011/2025 Freeman St.)	1885-1899
	94d	Cincinnati Breweries Co., Jung Brewing Co.	1899-1908
	94e	Jung Brewing Co.	1908-1919
OH	95a	(Conrad) Windisch & (Gottlieb) Muhlhauser & Bro. (Henry), Lion Brewery (Miami Canal between Wade & Liberty Sts.)	1866-1882
	95b	Windisch-Muhlhauser Brewing Co., (Plum, Liberty, 15th & Providence Sts.)	1882-1919
	95c	Lion Brewery, Inc. (Central Parkway & Liberty St.)	1933-1934
	95d	The Burger Brewing Co. aka Red Lion Brewing Co. (1966-1971)	1934-1973
OH	96a	Thomas Wood (5th & Vine St.)	1819-1825
	96b	Wood & (Wm.) Metcalf (Water & Race Sts.)	1825-1829
	96c	Wood & (Wm.) Price	1829-1830s
OH	97	A. & G. Yarold, Stone Jug Brewery (Wearman Ave.)	1868-1868

Circleville

OH	98	Frank, Ebert & Co.	1874-1875
OH	99a	Kruemmel & Hoover	1874-1882
	99b	Kruemmel & Mueller	1882-1884

Cleveland

OH	100a	Aenis & Fenelich (557 Columbus St.)	1878-1879
	100b	William Aenis & Co.	1879-1880
OH	101	A. L. Allen (127 Vermont St.)	1878-1879
OH	102a	Jacob Baehr (225 Pearl St.)	1866-1873
	102b	Mrs. Magdalena Baehr (325 Pearl St.)	1873-1898
	102c	Cleveland and Sandusky Brewing Co., Jacob Baehr Brewery	1898-1900
OH	103	M. Basil	1874-1875
OH	104a	Beltz & Mueller (59 Cyprus St.)	1876-1882
	104b	Joseph Beltz (223/225 Outhwaite Ave. & 80 Slater St.)	1882-1897
	104c	Jos. Beltz & Sons	1897-1901
	104d	Beltz Brewing Co.	1901-1905
	104e	Beltz Brewing Co. (2501/2515 61st St. & Outhwaite Ave., S.E.)	1905-1906
	104f	Cleveland Home Brewing Co.	1906-1919
	104g	The Cleveland Home Brewing Co.	1933-1952
OH	105a	J. A. Bishop (371 Broadway)	1874-1879
	105b	W. Bishop	1879-1882
	105c	Lexius & Kanzig	1882-1882
	105d	Christian Kanzig	1882-1884
	105e	Mrs. E. Kanzig	1884-1888
	105f	Louis Lexius (522 Broadway)	1888-1890
OH	106a	Bohemian Brewery	1854- ?
	106b	Aenis & Haller (1031/1033 Pearl St.)	? -1882
	106c	Wenzl Medlin Bohemian Brewery	1886-1889
	106d	Bohemian Brewing Co.	1889-1898
	106e	Cleveland and Sandusky Brewing Co., Bohemian Brewing Co.	1898-1904
	106f	Cleveland and Sandusky Brewing Co., Bohemian Brewery (1530 Riverbed Road, N.W.)	1904-1911
OH	107a	Brown & Schneider (2 Ash & Train Sts.)	1874-1877
	107b	C. Schneider	1877-1880
	107c	C. Schneider & Son	1880-1888
	107d	J. H. Schneider	1888-1893
	107e	Union Brewing Co. (W. 47th St. & Train Ave., S.W.)	1893-1898
	107f	Cleveland and Sandusky Brewing Co., Union Brewing Co.	1898-1899
OH	108a	Brewing Corp. of America (9400 Quincy Ave., S.E.)	1934-1953
	108b	Carling Brewing Co.	1953-1971
	108c	C. Schmidt & Sons, Inc. (br. of Philadelphia, PA) aka Duquesne Brewing Co. aka Valley Forge Brewing Co.	1971-1981
	108d	Christian Schmidt Brewing Co.	1981-

Cleveland (cont.)

OH 109 Buckeye Weiss Beer Brewing Co. (396 Dennison Ave.) 1899-1899

OH 110 Crump, Porter & Bro. 1874-1875

OH 111a Excelsior Brewing Co. (Sackett Ave., S.W. & 3333 W. 32nd St.) 1905-1919
111b Eilert Beverage Co. 1919-1933
111c The Eilert Brewing Co.(3131/3135 Sackett Ave.) 1933-1940
111d Kings Brewery, Inc. 1940-1941

OH 112a Fishel Brewing Co. (2764/2776 55th St.) 1905-1907
112b Cleveland and Sandusky Brewing Co., Fishel Brewery 1907-1919
112c Cleveland-Sandusky Co., Inc. 1934-1937
112d Cleveland-Sandusky Brewing Corp. 1937-1962

OH 113a Forest City Brewing Co. (6900/6922 Union Ave., S.E.) 1905-1919
113b Forest City Brewery, Inc. 1933-1944
113c Carling's, Inc. (br. of Brewing Corp. of America) 1944-1946
113d Brewing Corp. of America (Plant 2) 1946-1948

OH 114a Daniel Fovargue (30/36 Irving St.) 1874-1879
114b Fovargue & Newman 1879-1882

OH 115a Charles E. Gehring (11/19 Brainard St.) 1857-1891
115b C. E. Gehring Brewing Co. 1891-1898
115c Cleveland and Sandusky Brewing Co., C.E. Gehring Brewing Co. 1898-1904
115d Cleveland and Sandusky Brewing Co., C.E. Gehring Brewery (W. 25th St. & Freeman Ave., N.W.) 1904-1919

OH 116 Francis Geib 1874-1875

OH 117a Philip Griebel (529 Columbus St.) 1874-1879
117b Mrs. M. Griebel 1879-1879
117c J. Griebel (1005 Pearl St.) 1879-1882

OH 118a Fred Halthnorth 1858-1873
118b Isaac Leisy & Co. (135/139 Vega St. & Fulton Road, S.W.) 1873-1882
118c Isaac Leisy (282/290 Vega Ave.) 1882-1893
118d Isaac Leisy Brewing Co. 1893-1919
118e The Leisy Brewing Co. (3400 Vega Ave.) 1934-1960

OH 119a V. D. Hammond 1874-1877
119b Rudolph Mueller (483 Pearl St.) 1877-1879
119c Jacob Mueller 1879-1884

OH 120a Hoffmann & Co. (153/155 Walton Ave.) 1874-1877
120b Henry Hoffmann 1877-1880
120c Henry Hoffmann & Co. (789 Walton Ave.) 1880-1882

OH 121a John M. Hughes (15/21 West St.) 1874-1880
121b Mrs. Cornelia A. Bowlsby 1880-1884
121c Hughes Brewing Co. 1884-1895
121d Spencer Brewing Co. 1899-1900

OH 122 H. H. Imberg (947 Pearl St.) 1888-1888

OH 123a Kindsvater & Mall, Lion Brewery (Wilson St.) 1860- ?
123b Jacob Mall 1874-1877
123c Jacob Mall (5/15 Davenport St.) 1877-1889
123d Jacob Mall Brewing Co. 1889-1899
123e Gund Brewing Co. (147/1476 Davenport St., N.E.) 1899-1919
123f The Sunrise Brewing Co. 1933-1939
123g The Tip Top Brewing Co. 1939-1944

OH 124a James Koestle (38 Freeman St.) 1874-1877
124b Mrs. J. Koestle 1877-1879

OH 125 Kress Weiss Beer Co. (Louis & Sackett Sts.) 1904-1904

OH 126a (Henry) Lloyd & (Daniel H.) Keys (19/25 St. Clair St.) 1860-1895
126b Daniel H. Keys (39/47 St. Clair St.) 1895-1905
126c Daniel H. Keys (954 St. Clair St.) 1905-1908

OH 127a Mack Brothers (239 Broadway) 1874-1877
127b J. M. Mack 1877-1882

Cleveland (cont.)

OH 128a Medlin Pilsener Brewing Co. (Clark & Gordon Aves. & W. 65th) 1893-1894
128b Pilsener Brewing Co. 1894-1919
128c Pilsener Ice, Fuel & Beverage Co. 1919-1933
128d The Pilsener Brewing Co., Inc., aka City Ice and Fuel Co. (6605 Clark Ave. & 3110 W. 65th st.) 1933-1949
128e The Pilsener Brewing Co. 1949-1959
128f The Pilsener Brewing Co. (City Products Corp., Chicago) 1959-1962

OH 129 Wenzl Medlin Weiss Beer Brewery (1417/1419 Pearl St.) 1899-1904

OH 130 John Miller (107 Irving St.) 1880-1880

OH 131 M. Mueller (44 Cypress St.) 1882-1882

OH 132a George Muth & Son (8/10 Buckley St.) 1869-1882
132b Geo. V. Muth, Star Brewery 1882-1896
132c The Star Brewing Co. 1896-1898
132d Cleveland and Sandusky Brewing Co., Star Brewing Co. 1898-1904
132e Cleveland and Sandusky Brewing Co., Star Brewery (4125 Buckley Ave.) 1904-1913

OH 133a Oppmann & Lehr (285 Columbus & Willey Sts.) 1870-1877
133b A. W. Oppmann 1877-1882
133c Oppmann Brewing Co. 1882-1890
133d Phoenix Brewing Co. 1890-1898
133e Cleveland and Sandusky Brewing Co., Phoenix Brewing Co. 1898-1900
133f Cleveland and Sandusky Brewing Co., Baehr-Phoenix Brewery (2240 Columbus St.) 1900-1908

OH 134 The Real Brewery, Inc. (1109/1111 Central Ave., S.E.) 1935-1935

OH 135a Rogers & Hughes (Seneca & Canal Sts.) 1874-1877
135b J. P. Haley 1877-1880
135c Carling & Co. 1880-1884
135d Carling & Co. (393 W. River St.) 1884-1890
135e Carling Brewing Co. 1890-1891
135f Barrett Brewing Co. 1891-1898
135g Cleveland and Sundusky Brewing Co., Barrett Brewing Co. 1898-1904

OH 136a Edward A. Ruble 1860- ?
136b Louis Chormann (37/39 Pittsburgh St. & 27th St.) 1880-1884
136c Diebolt & Uehlein 1884-1888
136d (Anthony J.) Diebolt & (Edward A.) Ruble 1888-1891
136e Diebolt Brewing Co. 1891-1919

OH 137a Leonard Schlather (52 York, Carroll & Bridge Sts.) 1857-1884
137b Leonard Schlather Brewing Co. 1884-1902
137c Cleveland and Sandusky Brewing Co., Leonard Schlather Brewing Co.) 1902-1904
137d Cleveland and Sandusky Brewing Co., Leonard Schlather Brewery (1903 W. 28th St.) 1904-1919

OH 138 Joseph Schlitz Brewing Co. (br. of Milwaukee) (1954 E. 55th) 1908-1910

OH 139a Schmidt & Hoffmann (Hough & Ansel Aves.) 1852-1884
139b Cleveland Brewing Co. 1884-1898
139c Cleveland and Sandusky Brewing Co., Cleveland Brewing Co. 1898-1904
139d Cleveland and Sandusky Brewing Co., Cleveland Brewery (9907 Hough Ave., N.E.) 1904-1919

OH 140 Wm. Schneider & Co. (Pearl & Monroe Sts.) 1878-1882

OH 141a Carl Seyler (39 Broadway) 1874-1877
141b L. Schauermann 1877-1879

OH 142a Standard Brewing Co. (5801/5812 Train Ave.) 1905-1919
142b The Standard Brewing Co. (5708/5936 Train Ave.) 1933-1961
142c Schaefer Brewing Co. of Ohio, Inc. 1961-1964
142d C. Schmidt & Sons, Inc. (br. of Philadelphia, PA) 1964-1972
aka Duquesne Brewing Co.
aka Erie Brewery
aka Pilsner Brewing Co.
aka Rheingold Brewing Co.

Cleveland (cont.)

OH	143a	Stoppel Brewery (Ohio & Canal Sts.)		1860- ?
	143b	J. Kraus & Co.		1874-1877
	143c	Joseph Stoppel		1877-1882
	143d	Stoppel's Sons & Co.		1882-1884
	143e	Stoppel's Sons		1884-1888
	143f	Stoppel Co-operative Brewing Co. (37/51 Commercial St.)		1888-1891
	143g	Columbia Brewing Co.		1891-1898
	143h	Cleveland and Sandusky Brewing Co., Columbia Brewing Co.		1898-1904
	143i	Cleveland and Sandusky Brewing Co., Columbia Brewery (2740/2742 E. 6th St.)		1904-1919
OH	144	Jacob Strieberger (Seneca & Canal Sts.)		? -1878
OH	145a	Stumpf		1860-1866
	145b	John Davis (7/11 Briggs St.)		1866-1876
	145c	Clark R. Hodge		1876-1879
	145d	Gavagan, Sterling & Co.		1879-1880
	145e	Gavagan & Sterling		1880-1881
	145f	Patrick Gavagan		1881-1896
	145g	Patrick Gavagan (184 Davenport St. & 57 Briggs St.)		1896-1911
	145h	Patrick Gavagan (1181 E. 22nd St.)		1911-1914
	145i	Segal & Oppmann (1181 E. 22nd St. & 57 Briggs St.)		1914-1915
OH	146a	M. Stumpf (240 Lake St.)		1874-1879
	146b	Wm. H. Stumpf		1879-1884
OH	147a	Mrs. Jacob Voelker (Howe St.)		1888-1895
	147b	C. Voelker's Brewery		1895-1897

Cobrain

OH	148	George M. Bauer		1874-1875

Columbus

OH	149	Anheuser-Busch, Inc. (br. of St. Louis, MO) (700 E. Schrock Rd)		1968-
OH	150	Bavarian Brewing Co. (Yuster Bldg., 150 E. Broad St.)	NP	1934-1934
OH	151a	Henry Biehl & Co. (Front & Schiller Sts.)		1878-1879
	151b	Henry Biehl		1879-1880
OH	152a	Conrad Born		1859-1860
	152b	Born & Silbernagel		1860-1864
	152c	Conrad Born & Son, Capital Brewery (449 S. Front St.)		1864-1870
	152d	Born & Co., Capital Brewery (579 S. Front & College Sts.)		1870-1904
	152e	Hoster-Columbus Associated Breweries Co., Born Brewery		1904-1907
OH	153a	Columbus Brewing Co. (Frankfort & Bank Sts.)		1898-1904
	153b	Hoster-Columbus Associated Breweries Co., Columbus Brewery Br.		1904-1919
OH	154a	Franklin Brewing Co. (585 N. Cleveland Ave.)		1905-1919
	154b	Riverside Brewing Co. (699 River St.)		1933-1934
	154c	The Franklin Brewing Co. (117 N. Sandusky St.)		1934-1952
	154d	The Pilsener Brewing Co.		1952-1954
OH	155	Hannah Frieman		1874-1875
OH	156a	Gambrinus Brewing Co. (S. Front & College Sts.)		1906-1919
	156b	The August Wagner & Sons Product Co., Inc.		? -1933
	156c	The August Wagner & Son Brewing Co. (631 S. Front St.)		1933-1939
	156d	August Wagner Breweries, Inc. aka Iroquois Brewing Co. (1971-1974)		1939-1974
OH	157a	Home Brewing Co. (581 S. High St.)		1907-1908
	157b	Ohio Brewing Co. (1775 S. High St. & Reeb Ave.)		1908-1919
	157c	Ohio Brewery, Inc.		1941-1948
OH	158a	(Louis) Hoster, (Jacob) Silbernagel & (G. M.) Herancourt		1836-1840
	158b	Louis Hoster		1840-1870
	158c	L. Hoster & Sons		1870-1876
	158d	L. Hoster, Sons & Co. (371 S. Front St.)		1876-1884
	158e	L. Hoster Brewing Co. (435 S. Front St. & Livingstone Ave.)		1884-1904
	158f	Hoster-Columbus Associated Breweries Co., Hoster Brewery		1904-1915
	158g	Hoster-Columbus Co., Hoster Branch		1915-1919
OH	159	Hoster Brewing Co. (Mound & Furnace Sts.)	NP	1934-1934

Columbus (cont.)

OH	160a	Charles Say (50 E. 3rd Ave.)	1875-1877
	160b	Joseph Say	1877-1879
OH	161a	Nicholas Schlee, Bavarian Brewery (667 S. Front St.)	1870-1888
	161b	Nicholas Schlee & Son, Bavarian Brewery (526/544 S. Front)	1888-1904
	161c	Hoster-Columbus Associated Breweries Co., Schlee Brewery	1904-1915
OH	162a	Schlegel & Co. (404 S. Front St.)	1875-1877
	162b	Geo. Schlegel & Bro.	1877-1878
OH	163	Erhard Stoker	1874-1875
OH	164a	Washington Brewing Co. (W. 2nd Ave. & Perry St.)	1906-1919
	164b	Washington Breweries, Inc.	1933-1953

Coshocton

OH	165	Charles Boes	1874-1875

Crestline

OH	166a	C. Blocher & Bro.	1875- ?
	166b	B. Wesnitzer	1879-1884

Cuyahoga Falls

OH	167	Joseph Clarkson, Cuyahoga Falls Brewery	1856-1873

Dayton

OH	168a	John Bergman	1874-1877
	168b	Bergmann & Tettman	1877-1879
	168c	John Bergman	1879-1882
OH	169	August Bescher	1874-1875
OH	170	A. & F. Buscherr (45 Broome St.)	1879-1884
OH	171a	Fred. Euchenhofer (3495 3rd St.)	1874-1888
	171b	Otto Euchenhofer (1519/1523 E. 3rd St.)	1888-1895
	171c	Pruden & Altherr	1895-1897
	171d	Kern & Altherr	1897-1899
	171e	Peter J. Altherr	1899-1902
OH	172	Chas. Harries	1874-1875
OH	173	George Hecker (751 Van Cleve St.)	1874-1884
OH	174a	(Theodore) Hollencamp & (John) Aleschleger, Dayton Ale Brewery (Hickory & Brown Sts.)	1885-1887
	174b	Hollencamp & Kramer, Dayton Ale Brewery	1887-1895
	174c	Theodore Hollencamp, Dayton Ale Brewery	1895-1901
	174d	Hollencamp Ale Brewing Co.	1901-1904
	174e	Hollencamp Ale Brewery	1904-1905
	174f	Hollencamp Brewing Co.	1905-1919
	174g	The Hollencamp Products Co. (800/816 S. Brown St.)	1933-1940
	174h	Airline Brewing Co.	1942-1943
	174i	The "Ol-Fashun" Brewing Co.	1943-1949
	174j	Dayton Brewing Corp.	1949-1954
OH	175a	Metz & Braun (1st & Beckel Sts.)	1874-1877
	175b	Anton Braun	1877-1880
	175c	John Wager	1880-1880
	175d	N. Thomas & Co.	1880-1893
	175e	N. Thomas, Hydraulic Brewery	1893-1900
	175f	N. Thomas Brewing Co., Hydraulic Brewery	1900-1906
	175g	Dayton Breweries Co., N. Thomas Brewery	1906-1907
	175h	Dayton Breweries Co., Schantz-Thomas Brewery	1907-1919
	175i	The Miami Valley Brewing Co.	1933-1950
OH	176a	Olt Brewing Co. (20/34 N. McGee St.)	1907-1911
	176b	Olt Bros. Brewing Co.	1911-1919
	176c	The Olt Bros. Brewing Co. aka The Olt Bros. Brewery Co. (1938-1939)	1933-1941
OH	177a	Sachs-Pruden Ale Brewing Co. (Wyandotte St.)	1888-1890
	177b	Sachs-Pruden Ale Co.	1890-1891
	177c	Sachs-Pruden Brewing Co.	1891-1895
	177d	Dayton Brewing Co.	1895-1904
	177e	Dayton Breweries Co., Dayton Brewery	1904-1907

Dayton (cont.)

OH 178a (George) Schantz & (Louis) Schwind, Gem City Brewery (Perry & Bayard Sts.) 1888-1895
178b Schantz & Schwind Brewing Co. 1895-1904
178c Dayton Breweries Co., Schantz & Schwind Brewery 1904-1919

OH 179a Schantz Bros. (George & Adam), Riverside Brewery 1877-1882
179b Geo. Schantz & Co., Riverside Brewery (114/128 W. River St.) 1882-1884
179c Adam Schantz 1884-1903
179d Estate of Adam Schantz 1903-1904
179e Dayton Breweries Co., Adam Schantz Brewery 1904-1906

OH 180a John & Michael Schiml 1852-1858
180b Michael Schiml (Wayne & Hickory Sts.) 1858-1889
180c (Aloys) Schiml & (Frank J.) Bucher 1889-1891
180d Frank J. Bucher (739 Wayne St.) 1891-1900
180e Wehner Brewing Co. 1900-1901
180f Pioneer Brewing Co. 1901-1901
180g Pioneer Brewery, M. Schiml's Estate 1901-1902

OH 181 Mrs. Agnes Schwind (345 S. Main St.) 1874-1882

OH 182a Coelestin Schwind (212/224 River St.) 1874-1893
182b Schwind Brewing Co. 1893-1899
182c Schwind Brewery Co. 1899-1904
182d Dayton Breweries Co., Schwind Brewery 1904-1919

OH 183a Walker & Butz 1856- ?
183b Jacob Stickle, City Brewery (713 Warren & Brown Sts.) 1874-1904
183c Dayton Breweries Co., Stickle Brewery 1904-1905

OH 184a (Louis L.) Wehner Brewing Co. (Concord & Scovil Sts.) 1901-1904
184b Dayton Breweries Co., Wehner Brewery 1904-1907

OH 185a Wilke & Seubert 1878-1879
185b Poock & Seubert 1879-1879
185c A. Seubert 1879-1882

Defiance

OH 186a Jacob Karst 1867-1870
186b Karst & (Joseph) Bauer 1870-1871
186c Bauer & (Christian) Diehl 1871-1873
186d (Joseph) Bauer & Co. 1873-1885
186e Christian Diehl 1885-1891
186f Christ. Diehl Brewing Co. (Water & N. Clinton Sts.) 1891-1919
186g The Christ. Diehl Brewing Co. (24 N. Clinton St. & W. River) 1933-1955

Delaware

OH 187a F. Anthony 1874-1879
187b F. Anthony & Sons 1879-1888
187c F. Anthony 1888-1891

OH 188a Wm. Kurley 1874-1877
188b C. H. Wittlinger 1877-1891
188c Delaware Brewing and Ice Co. 1891-1893

Delphos

OH 189a C. A. Eysenbach 1858- ?
189b Delphos Brewery Co. 1875-1884
189c Steinle & Co. 1884-1901
189d Felix Steinle Brewing Co. (2nd & Douglas Sts.) 1901-1906
189e Steinle Brewing and Ice Co. 1906-1927
189f Steinle Brewing Co. (533 E. 2nd St.) NP 1934-1934

East Liverpool

OH 190a Crockery City Brewing and Ice Co. (Franklin Ave. & Ravine St.) 1900-1919
190b Crockery City Ice and Products Co. (242 W. 8th St.) 1933-1946
190c The Webb Corp. 1946-1952

OH 191a Greenwood Bros.(Sheridan Ave.) 1888-1890
191b Henry Greenwood 1890-1904
191c Greenwood Bros. 1904-1912
191d Greenwood Brewery 1912-1915

East Palestine			
OH	192a	J. Anderton & Co.	1880-1884
	192b	William Arnold	1895-1900
	192c	John Schilpp	1902- ?
Eaton			
OH	193	Fassnacht & Rau	1874-1884
Elyria			
OH	194a	John Bishop	1875-1877
	194b	Andrew Plocher	1877-1879
Findlay			
OH	195a	Brilliant City Brewing Co. (Jefferson St. & Clinton Court)	1890-1898
	195b	Krantz Brewing Co.	1898-1919
	195c	The Krantz Products Co., Inc.	? -1933
	195d	The Krantz Brewing Co., Inc.	1933-1936
	195e	Krantz Brewing Corp.	1936-1957
	195f	International Breweries, Inc., Old Dutch-Frankenmuth Div.	1957-1966
OH	196	Frank Zeller	1875- ?
Franklin (see Arnheim)			
Fremont			
OH	197	C. F. Geisin	1874-1875
OH	198a	J. M. Paulus	c1870-1877
	198b	Fremont Brewing Co. (432 Oak & Knapp Sts.)	1877-1919
Galion			
OH	199a	J. G. Kraft	1851-1880
	199b	H. Altstaetter	1880-1901
	199c	Galion Brewing Co.	1901-1919
Gallipolis			
OH	200a	Xavier Brandstetter	1874-1877
	200b	F. Henkel	1877-1888
Germantown			
OH	201	C. J. Rohrer	1874-1875
Green			
OH	202	J. S. Burkholder	1874-1875
Greenville			
OH	203a	Reinhard & Co.	1875-1877
	203b	J. Wagner	1877-1884
Hamilton			
OH	204a	Schalk & Stahl	1856-1868
	204b	Henry Eger	1868-1875
	204c	John F. Neilan	1875-1877
	204d	Casper Engert	1877-1880
	204e	A. Haberstumpf & Bro.	1880-1882
	204f	Kamm & Haberstumpf	1882-1884
	204g	Eagle Stock Brewing Co.	1884-1884
	204h	H. P. Deuscher	1884-1886
	204i	Eagle Brewing Co.	1886-1890
	204j	Martin Mason	1890-1896
	204k	Martin Mason Brewing Co. (350/365 S. "C" St.)	1896-1919
	204l	The Hamilton Brewing Co.	1933-1940
OH	205a	John W. Sohn	1858-1867
	205b	Vanderveer & Reutti	1867-1874
	205c	Peter Schwab & Co.	1874-1882
	205d	Cincinnati Brewing Co. (Front, Sycamore & Monument Ave.)	1882-1919
Hanover			
OH	206	Fred Krause, Sr.	1874-1875
Harrison			
OH	207a	Schneider & Stephany (Hill & Harrison Sts.)	1874-1877
	207b	J. Schneider & Bro.	1877-1879
	207c	J. Schneider	1879-1882
	207d	Hansen Brewing Co.	1882-1884
	207e	Geo. Kacher	1884-1890
	207f	Rodenberg & Babrink	1890-1891

Ironton

OH 208a	Leo Ebert		1861-1880
208b	Leo Ebert & Co. (13 N. 7th & Railroad Sts.)		1880-1897
208c	Leo Ebert Brewing Co.		1897-1901
208d	Ebert Brewing Co.		1910-1919
OH 209a	Joseph Hochgesang		1875-1877
209b	Jacob Mayer		1877-1880

Jackson Township

OH 210a	Christian Kropf		1878-1879
210b	H. C. Kropf		1879-1882

Jefferson

OH 211	Jacob Gerhart		1874-1875

Kenton

OH 212	Anton Kayser		1878-1884
OH 213a	John Ruffer		1878-1880
213b	Knox & Shirtz		1880-1882
OH 214	Peter Waldeck, Kenton Brewery (Detroit & Letson Sts.) aka Kenton Brewery Co. (1906-1909)		1892-1916

Lakewood

OH 215	Schuster Brewing Co.	NP	1934-1934

Lancaster

OH 216a	(Christian & George) Ochs & Co.		1867-1868
216b	Becker, Ochs & Co.		1868-1877
216c	Becker & Co.		1877-1884
216d	E. Becker Brewing Co. (Forest Rose Ave. & Union St.)		1884-1916
216e	The Lancaster Brewing Co.		1934-1942

Lawrence

OH 217	Homig & Schneider		? -1878

Leetonia (formerly Laetonia)

OH 218a	Gerlach & Seeger		1873-1874
218b	Haller & Seeger		1874-1877
218c	Benjamin F. Haller & Bro.		1877-1881
218d	D. Zanini		1881-1882
218e	D. Zanini & Co.		1882-1884
218f	Zanini & Siegle		1884-1887
218g	Louis T. Siegle & Co.		1887-1888
218h	Louis F. Siegle		1888-1906
218i	Leetonia Brewing Co.		1906-1913

Lima

OH 219a	F. Roast		1874-1877
219b	Charles Duvel		1877-1884
OH 220a	Zimmermann & Duvel		1875-1877
220b	Zimmermann Bros.		1877-1884
220c	A. & L. Zimmermann		1884-1890
220d	Dietrich Brewing Co.		1890-1891
220e	Lima Brewing Co.		1891-1893
220f	Fruch & Wilhelmy		1893-1895
220g	Quilna Brewery (E. Pittsburgh St.)		1895-1900
220h	Lima Brewing Co.		1900-1919
220i	Lima Brewing Co.	NP	1934-1934

London

OH 221	Peter Weber		1874-1878

Lorain

OH 222	Cleveland and Sandusky Brewing Co., Lorain Brewery (12th St. & 5th Ave.)		1905-1919

Louisville

OH 223a	Roth & Graber		1874-1877
223b	Dilger & Mengay		1877-1882
223c	Geo. Dilger		1882-1897
223d	Knopf Ale Co.		1897-1898
223e	Louisville Brewing Co.		1898-1900
223f	Louisville Brewing Co.		1904-1906

McConnellsville

OH 224a T. D. Young 1874-1877
224b Burckhalter & Reed 1877-1879

Mansfield

OH 225a (Martin) Frank & (Henry) Weber 1865-1878
225b Martin Frank (110/112 N. Diamond St.) 1878-1899
225c Martin Frank & Son 1899-1919
225d M. Frank & Son (121/123 N. Franklin Ave.) 1933-1940

OH 226a Harvey & Long 1855-1860
226b Long & Aberle 1860-1863
226c (Martin) Frank & (Theodore) Aberle 1863-1865
226d Reiman & Aberle 1865-1883
226e (Andrew) Reiman & (Henry) Weber 1883-1884
226f (Geo. J.) Renner & Weber (75/85 E. 4th St.) 1884-1900
226g Renner & Weber Brewing Co. 1900-1919
226h The Renner & Weber Brewing Co. (75 E. Temple Court) 1934-1951

OH 227a (Joseph) Leuthner & Schmutzler 1864-1866
227b Schmutzler & Co. 1874-1875
227c Frank & Weber, Union Brewery 1875-1883
227d M. Frank & Son, Union Brewery 1883-1883

Marietta

OH 228a William Feller & Co., Union Brewery (St. Clair & 2nd Sts.) 1899-1903
228b Marietta Brewing Co., Union Brewery 1903-1919
228c Marietta Brewing Co. NP 1934-1934

OH 229a F. & W. Rapp 1874-1877
229b John Schneider 1877-1884
229c Elizabeth Schneider 1884-1890

Marion

OH 230a Frederick Walter 1895-1895
230b Marion Brewing Co. (22 Bellefontaine Ave.) 1895-1896
230c Marion Brewing and Bottling Co. 1896-1919

Martins Ferry

OH 231a Belmont Brewing Co. 1890-1919
231b Belmont Products Co. 1919-1933
231c Belmont Brewing Co. (208 Jefferson St.) 1933-1940

Marysville

OH 232a Paul Schlegel 1875-1880
232b George Schlegel 1880-1888

Massilon

OH 233a Bammerlin & Ruch 1874-1877
233b L. Bammerlin 1877-1882
233c Martin Huss & Co. 1882-1884

OH 234a Massilon Brewing Co. (J. H.) McLain & Co. 1883-1887
234b Erhardt & Schimke 1887-1893
234c Paulina C. Schimke 1893-1894
234d Anton Kopp (26 Exchange St.) 1894-1898
234e John W. Schuster 1898-1900
234f Schuster Brewing Co. 1900-1904
234g Stark-Tuscarawas Breweries Co., Schuster Brewery (36 N. West) 1904-1919

OH 235a Stoolmiller & Supple 1875-1877
235b Emma Halbysan 1877-1879
235c Jul. Wittmann & Co. 1879-1884

Miamisburg

OH 236a William Nuss 1874-1882
236b Aug. Kuehn 1882-1888
236c Miamisburg Brewing Co. 1888-1899

Middleburg

OH 237a Edward Davis 1874-1877
237b E. Davis & Son 1877-1879
237c E. Davis, Jr. 1879-1884

Middletown

OH 238a	Schwitzgable & Helwig		1852-1860
238b	George Weibold		1860-1864
238c	Wm. & Louis Sebald (3rd & Canal Sts.)		1864-1886
238d	William Sebald Brewing Co.		1886-1919
238e	Premier Beverage Co.	NP	1934-1934

Milan

OH 239a	Anton Herb	1874-1893
239b	Mary Herb	1893-1897
239c	Herb Bros.	1897-1899
239d	Joseph Herb	1899-1904
239e	Joseph Herb Brewing Co.	1904-1919
239f	The Milan Brewing Corp. aka Milan Brewing Co., Inc. (1934)	1934-1951

Millersburg

OH 240	Peter Moyers	1874-1875

Milton

OH 241	Peter Rich	1874-1875

Minster

OH 242a	Frank Lange	1869-1882
242b	Steinemann & Bro. (Ohio St.)	1882-1890
242c	Star Brewing Co.	1890-1919
242d	The Star Beverage Co. (137 S. Ohio St.)	1933-1939
242e	The Wooden Shoe Brewing Co.	1939-1954

Monroeville

OH 243a	C. P. Prentiss	1874-1877
243b	Urban, Rapp & Co.	1877-1884

Morrow

OH 244a	Scheer, Thompson & Co.	1874-1890
244b	Morrow Brewing Co.	1890-1904
244c	Morrow Ale Brewing Co.	1904-1907
244d	Morrow Ale Co.	1907-1908

Mount Vernon

OH 245	Geo. F. Keller	1874-1875

Napoleon

OH 246a	John Herbolsheimer	1874-1877
246b	F. Roessing	1877-1891
246c	J. W. Tietjens & Co.	1891-1895
246d	John W. Tietjens (Front St.)	1895-1912
246e	Tietjens Brewing Co.	1912-1919

Navarre

OH 247	Edward J. Hug	1874-1875

Nelsonville

OH 248a	Hocking Valley Brewing Co.	1905-1919
248b	Hocking Valley Brewery, Inc. (693 Jackson St.)	1948-1950

Newark

OH 249a	Bentlich Bros. & Eichhorn	1874-1879
249b	Bentlich & Eichhorn	1879-1884
OH 250a	Bingmann & Korzenborn	? -1874
250b	Charles Korzenborn	1874-1891
250c	Korzenborn Brewery, Charles Bingmann	1891-1897
250d	Charles Korzenborn Brewing Co. (42 E. Walnut St.)	1897-1915
250e	Home Brewery	1915-1916
OH 251a	Consumers Brewing Co.	1897-1919
251b	The Consumers Brewing Co. (75 E. Locust & 1st Sts.)	1933-1954
OH 252a	Rickrich & Bro.	1874-1877
252b	Philip Rickrich	1877-1879
252c	Rickrich & Senger	1879-1880
252d	Philip Rickrich	1880-1884

New Berlin
OH 253a Christ. Kropf 1874-1875
253b H. C. Kropf 1875-1884

New Bremen
OH 254a Michael Vossler 1874-1877
254b Meyer & Schwers 1877-1879

New Philadelphia
OH 255a Michael Berger 1860- ?
255b M. Hafenbrank & Seibold 1876-1884
255c New Philadelphia Brewing Co. (S. Broadway) 1884-1904
255d Stark-Tuscarawas Breweries Co., New Philadelphia Brewery 1904-1919
255e New Philadelphia Brewery, Inc. (646 S. Braodway) 1933-1945
aka Seibold Products Co. (1934)
255f The New Philadelphia Brewery Co. 1945-1949

New Richmond
OH 256 Charles Baumann 1874-1878

New Springfield
OH 257 John Seeger 1874-1879

Newtown
OH 258 Jacob Christman 1874-1875

North Georgetown
OH 259 Neuwirth & Kickenbaugh 1875- ?

North Robinson
OH 260 Jacob Gerhard 1878-1884

Norwalk
OH 261a Anthony Lais, Star Brewery 1874-1884
261b Estate of Anthony Lais 1884-1889
261c Henry Lais (S. Pleasant St.) 1889-1905
261d Lais Brewing Co. 1905-1912

OH 262a Peter Ott & Bro. 1874-1877
262b Fletcher & Ott 1877-1879
262c Ott & Miller 1879-1880
262d Mrs. Theresa Ott 1880-1905

Ottawa
OH 263 Joseph Drerupp 1874-1875

Painesville
OH 264a Garfield & Warner 1874-1879
264b H. Carroll 1879-1888

Perry
OH 265a Christian Sommers 1874-1877
265b J. Sommers & Co. 1877-1878
265c C. Kropf & Co. 1878-1882

Piqua
OH 266a Hartman Ploch (Spring St.) 1850s- ?
266b Franz & Ploch 1874-1877
266c Butcher & Mittler 1877-1879
266d Butcher & Freyer 1879-1880
266e Butcher & Schneider 1880-1882
266f Henry Schneider (430 Green St.) 1882-1902
266g Carl H. Schnell 1902-1914

OH 267a Schmidlapp & Bro. 1874-1877
267b L. Kiefer 1877-1879
267c Schmidlapp & Kaiser 1879-1880
267d L. Kaiser 1880-1882
267e Karl Kaiser 1882-1904

OH 268a Louis Schneyer (Spring & Water Sts.) 1869- ?
268b J. L. Schneyer & Son 1874-1875
268c J. L. Schneyer 1875-1882
268d Mrs. Catherine Schneyer, aka J. L. Schneyer (1897) 1882-1897
268e Lange Brewing Co. 1897-1919
268f The Lange Products Co. 1933-1939

Pleasant			
OH	269	John Bechtel	1874-1875
Polk			
OH	270	Daniel Roth	1879-1882
Pomeroy			
OH	271a	Frederick Schaefer	1847-1870s
	271b	Gottleib Wildermuth (Condor St.)	1874-1898
	271c	Gottlieb Wildermuth Brewing Co.	1898-1919
Portsmouth			
OH	272a	Schiele & Muhlhauser	1843-1845
	272b	Muhlhauser	1845-1858
	272c	Muhlhauser & (Felix) Geiger	1858-1865
	272d	Frank Huffner	1865-1872
	272e	Huffner & Maier	1872-1878
	272f	Kleffner & Maier	1878-1880
	272g	Roettcher & Maier (W. 2nd St.)	1880-1884
	272h	Conrad Gerlach	1884-1889
	272i	Julius G. Esselborn	1889-1891
	272j	Portsmouth Brewing Co.	1891-1892
	272k	Portsmouth Brewing and Ice Co.	1892-1919
Ravenna			
OH	273	Philip Balser	1874-1875
Reading			
OH	274a	The Delatron Brewing Co. (Reading & Amity Road)	1934-1946
	274b	Cincinnati Brewing Co.	1946-1951
OH	275a	J. B. Kroger & Co.	1874-1882
	275b	Vardman & Lehrter	1882-1884
	275c	Klaiber & Lehrter	1884-1888
	275d	Klaiber & Bothe	1888-1890
OH	276	Wettermann & Aherns	1874-1875
Ripley			
OH	277	August Mischler	1874-1875
Rome			
OH	278	C. Kropf & Co.	1874-1884
Roscoe			
OH	279a	Conrad Mayer	1874-1880
	279b	Frederick Bohn	1880-1884
Salem			
OH	280a	William Muff	1874-1884
	280b	Gust. Zelle	1884-1890
Sandusky			
OH	281a	Philip Dauch	1850-1862
	281b	Windisch, Bricht & Cable	1862-1868
	281c	Fox & Windisch	1868-1872
	281d	John Bender	1872-1873
	281e	Bender & Co.	1873-1877
	281f	Lena Bender	1877-1880
	281g	Franz Stang	1880-1892
	281h	Stang Brewing Co. (Madison St. between King St. & Broadway)	1892-1895
	281i	Kuebeler-Stang Brewing and Malting Co., Stang Plant	1895-1898
	281j	Cleveland and Sandusky Brewing Co., Kuebeler-Stang Brewing and Malting Co., Stang Plant	1898-1919
	281k	The Cleveland and Sandusky Brewing Co. (508 King St.) aka Crystal Rock Products Co. (1934)	1933-1935
OH	282	V. Fox	1862-1863
OH	283a	Jacob Kuebeler	1867-1870
	283b	Jacob Kuebeler & Co. (W. Tiffin Ave.)	1870-1892
	283c	Jacob Kuebeler Brewing and Malting Co.	1892-1895
	283d	Kuebeler-Stang Brewing and Malting Co., Kuebeler Plant.	1895-1898
	283e	Cleveland and Sandusky Brewing Co., Kuebeler-Stang Brewing and Malting Co., Kuebeler Plant	1898-1919

Sandusky (cont.)

OH	284a	Strobel & Ilg	1874-1877
	284b	Anthony & Ilg	1877-1879
	284c	A. Ilg	1879-1884
	284d	A. Ilg & Co.	1884-1888
	284e	Ilg & Co.	1888-1890

Sedamsville

OH	285	Beuter & Betting	1871-1874

Sidney

OH	286a	Joseph F. Wagner (Poplar St.)	1854-1859
	286b	John Wagner & Bro.	1859-1876
	286c	John Wagner	1876-1881
	286d	John Wagner's Sons	1881-1896
	286e	John Wagner Sons Brewing Co.	1896-1919
	286f	Wagner Brewery	NP 1934-1934
	286g	The John Wagner Co. (326 E. Poplar St.)	1936-1939

Springfield

OH	287a	Baker & Brown, City Brewery	1860-1863
	287b	Engert & Dinkel, City Brewery	1863-1880
	287c	Stephen Dinkel, City Brewery	1880-1884
	287d	Schneider Bros., City Brewery	1884-1890
	287e	Springfield Breweries Ltd., City Brewery (Penn & Section Sts.)	1890-1916
OH	288a	Home City Brewing Co. (500 W. Main St. & Bell Ave.)	1906-1919
	288b	Springfield Brewers, Inc.	NP 1934-1934
OH	289a	S. A. Vorce, Springfield Brewery	1856-1866
	289b	Zittler, Evans & Edgar, Springfield Brewery	1866-1869
	289c	Vorce & Blee, Springfield Brewery	1869-1890
	289d	Springfield Breweries Ltd., Springfield Plant	1890-1916

Sterling

OH	290a	Christian P. Rich	1884- ?
	290b	Peter Rich	? -1888

Steubenville

OH	291a	M. J. Basler	1874-1882
	291b	Mrs. C. Basler	1882-1884
OH	292a	John C. Butte, City Brewery	1861-1882
	292b	Chas. Rail & Klein, City Brewery	1882-1886
	292c	Charles L. Rail, City Brewery	1886-1893
	292d	Mrs. Lucy E. Rail, City Brewery	1893-1896
	292e	John Buehler, City Brewery	1896-1906
	292f	City Brewery, Minnie Buehler (head of Adams St.)	1906-1910
	292g	Steuben Brewing Co. (904 Adams St.)	1912-1919
OH	293	Bernhard Miller	1874-1875
OH	294a	E. H. Schaeffer	1874-1877
	294b	J. Basler, Jr.	1877-1879
OH	295	M. Weishaar	1874-1875

Strasburg

OH	296a	Harberdier & Klopfenstein	1875-1877
	296b	Jacob Seikel	1877-1890

Tiffin

OH	297a	(Ch.) Mueller & (Valentine) Schmidt	1854- ?
	297b	Christ. Mueller (River St.)	1874-1884
	297c	Philip Grummel	1884-1884
	297d	Schumann & Co.	1884-1888
	297e	Tiffin Brewing Co.	1888-1919
OH	298a	Siegrist	c1855-1860
	298b	Franz J. Wagner	c1860-1877
	298c	Henry Hubach	1877-1906
	298d	Hubach's Brewery Co.	1906-1919

Toledo

OH	299	Andrew Bellner (South Toledo)	c1875
OH	300	City Brewing Co.	1896-1896
OH	301a	William J. Finlay	1853-1876
	301b	Finlay & Zahn	1876-1880
	301c	Wm. J. Finlay (Summit & Cedar Sts.)	1880-1884
	301d	Finlay Brewing Co.	1884-1904
	301e	Huebner-Toldeo Breweries Co., Finlay Brewery (1024 Summit St.)	1904-1919
OH	302	John H. George	1874-1875
OH	303a	(Joseph) Grasser & (Henry) Brand (S. St. Clair & Williams Sts.)	1863-1877
	303b	Grasser & Brand Brewing Co.	1877-1904
	303c	Huebner-Toledo Breweries Co., Grasser & Brand Brewery	1904-1910
OH	304a	Home Brewing Co. (2 Oak & Front Sts.)	1904-1919
	304b	The Koerber Brewing Co.	1933-1949
OH	305a	Lehmann & Eckhardt Bros.	? -1873
	305b	Eliz. Stephan & Co.	1873-1877
	305c	Jacobi, Coghlin & Co. (Bush, Champlain & Michigan Sts.)	1877-1886
	305d	Buckeye Brewing Co. (1501 Michigan St.)	1886-1919
	305e	The Buckeye Brewing Co.	1933-1966
	305f	Meister Brau, Inc. (br. of Chicago, IL) aka Buckeye Brewing Co. (1968-1971) aka Cleveland-Sandusky Brewing Co. (1968-1971) aka Iroquois Brewing Co.	1966-1972
OH	306a	Maumee Brewing Co. (22/40 Superior St.)	1897-1901
	306b	Toledo Brewing and Malting Co., Maumee Brewery	1901-1902
	306c	Gambrinus Brewing and Bottling Co.	1902-1904
	306d	Bavarian Brewing Co.	1907-1911
	306e	City Brewing Co.	1911-1919
	306f	Lubeck Brewing Co., Inc.	1933-1935
	306g	Lubeck Brewing Co.	1937-1939
OH	307a	A. Stephan	1852-1853
	307b	Stephan & Co.	1853-1856
	307c	Peter Lenk	1856-1876
	307d	Toledo Brewing Co. (Hamilton & Division Sts.)	1876-1882
	307e	Toledo Brewing and Malting Co.	1882-1902
	307f	Huebner Brewing Co., Ltd.	1902-1904
	307g	Huebner-Toledo Breweries Co., Huebner Brewery	1904-1933
	307h	Huebner-Toledo Breweries Co.	NP 1934-1934
OH	308a	John Vogelsang	1838-1844
	308b	Philip Koehler	1844-1850
	308c	(Ernest) Greiner & (Joseph) Grasser	1850-1855
	308d	Grasser & (Joseph) Welzhofer	1855-1856
	308e	Grasser & (John) Villhauer	1856-1859
	308f	Grasser & (Henry) Brand	1859-1865
	308g	F. Lang, Sr.	1865-1866
	308h	Lang & Co.	1866-1874
	308i	F. Lang & Son (Michigan St. near Cherry St.)	1882-1884
	308j	Eagle Brewing Co.	1884-1899
	308k	Schmitt Brewing Co.	1899-1902
	308l	Toledo Brewing and Malting Co., Schmitt Brewery	1902-1903

Trenton

OH	309	Miller Brewing Co. (br. of Milwaukee, WI)	1982-

Troy

OH	310a	Tittus Schwind	1860-1874
	310b	(Joseph) Henne & (George) Mayer	1874-1877
	310c	Joseph Henne	1877-1885
	310d	Joseph Henne & Son (Water St.)	1885-1908

Tuscarawas

OH	311	M. Weber	1880-1882

Tuscarora

OH	312	Louis Heim	1878-1879

Union City			
OH 313a	Louis Guillaume		1874-1875
313b	Hauck & Dersil		1875-1875
Upper Sandusky			
OH 314a	Altstaetter & Bechler		1849-1882
314b	Severin Bechler		1882-1884
314c	Severin Bechler Estate		1884-1891
314d	Upper Sandusky Brewing Co.		1891-1900
314e	Upper Sandusky Brewing Co., Albert H. Martens		1900-1919
314f	Upper Sandusky Beverage & Ice Plant		1919-1933
314g	Freimann Beverage & Ice Co. (121 N. 4th St.)		1933-1947
314h	The Imperial Brewing Co.		1947-1947
Van Buren			
OH 315	Mrs. M. Becherer		1882-1882
Van Wert			
OH 316	Van Wert Brewery		1882-1884
Versailles			
OH 317	Herman Seibt		1874-1875
Wapakoneta			
OH 318a	C. Kolter & Bro.		1874-1879
318b	C. Kolter		1879-1884
318c	Kolter & Koch		1884-1893
318d	City Brewing Co. (206/210 N. Water St.)		1893-1919
318e	The Koch Beverage and Ice Co.		1933-1951
OH 319a	Schuman & Bro.		1874-1877
319b	Schuman Bros.		1877-1880
Warren			
OH 320	George Clement, Jr.		1874-1880
OH 321	Jacob Waldeck		1874-1875
OH 322	Western Reserve Brewing Co.	NP	1934-1934
Waynesburg			
OH 323a	Henry Gruber		1874-1877
323b	C. Gruber		1877-1884
Waynesville			
OH 324	Arbogast Amann		1875- ?
Wellington			
OH 325	John M. Crabtree		1874-1875
Wellston			
OH 326	Holzappel Brothers	NP	1934-1934
OH 327	Wellston Brewing and Ice Co.		1905-1910
Williamsburg			
OH 328	John Bools		1878-1884
Willoughby			
OH 329	Oscar F. White		1879-1884
Winesburg			
OH 330	Leo Wiegand		1874-1884
Woodville			
OH 331a	Jonas Keil		1874-1888
331b	Elizabeth Keil		1888-1890
OH 332a	Michael Lang		1874-1882
332b	John H. Lang		1882-1884

Wooster

OH	333a	Joseph Ramsey	1860-1870
	333b	(Martin) Rich & (Jacob) Roth	1870-1874
	333c	Rich & (Jacob) Mongey	1874-1879
	333d	Mongey & (John) Graber	1879-1882
	333e	Graber & (Geo. J.) Renner	1882-1884
	333f	John Graber	1884-1886
	333g	Frederick Weis	1886-1890
	333h	Wooster Brewing Co.	1890-1904
	333i	Wooster Artificial Ice and Brewing Co.	1904-1916
OH	334	Wendel Young	1874-1875

Xenia

OH	335a	(B.) Hollencamp & (Henry) Ferneding	1852- ?
	335b	Hollencamp Bros. (Columbus & Water Sts.)	1874-1877
	335c	Farrell & Co.	1877-1884
	335d	Hollencamp & Co.	1884-1886
	335e	The Hollencamp Co.	1886-1891
	335f	Hollencamp & Weddle (Columbus & 3rd Sts.)	1891-1897
	335g	Hollencamp Brewing and Bottling Co.	1897-1898
	335h	Xenia Brewing and Ice Co.	1898-1899
	335i	Hollencamp & Co.	1899-1901
	335j	Hollencamp Xenia Ale Brewing Co.	1901-1903
	335k	Brinkle & Reading Co. (Columbus & Water Sts.)	1903-1904
OH	336	Jacob Klein	1874-1875

Youngstown

OH	337a	Mary Haid	1874-1877
	337b	Knott & Klas	1877-1880
	337c	John Bayer	1880-1882
	337d	Jacob Knott (Henrietta St.)	1882-1891
OH	338a	Mathias Seeger	1861-1885
	338b	Geo. J. Renner, Jr. (203/209 Pike St.)	1885-1913
	338c	Renner Brewing Co.	1913-1919
	338d	Renner Realty Co.	1919-1933
	338e	The Renner Co.	1933-1962
OH	339a	John Smith (532 W. Federal St.)	1845-1874
	339b	John Smith & Son	1874-1875
	339c	John Smith's Sons	1875-1901
	339d	John Smith's Sons Brewing Co.	1901-1904
	339e	Smith Brewing Co.	1904-1919
	339f	Youngstown Brewing Co. (305 North Ave. & Rayen St.)	1936-1947
	339g	Crystal Top Brewery, Inc.	1947-1948

Zanesville

OH	340a	Christian F. Achauer (350 E. Main St.)	1846-1880
	340b	Herman Achauer	1880-1884
	340c	Zinsmeister & Linser	1884-1891
	340d	Simon Linser, Washington Brewery	1891-1901
	340e	Simon Linser Brewing Co., Washington Brewery	1901-1919
	340f	Simon Linser Brewing Co. (976 Main St.)	NP 1934-1934
OH	341a	Sebastian Bohn (144 Marietta St.)	1860-1892
	341b	August Bohn	1892-1914
	341c	August Bohn (1016 Marietta St.)	1914-1919
OH	342a	John A. Brenner & Co. (Spring & High Sts.)	1874-1890
	342b	Brenner & Horn	1890-1891
	342c	Frank L. Normann	1898-1900
OH	343a	Conrad Fisher, aka Phoebe Fisher (29/31 Monroe St.)	1874-1875
	343b	Fisher Bros.	1875-1883
	343c	Star Brewing Co.	1893-1893
	343d	Armbruster Bros. & Schmitt, Star Brewery	1893-1895
	343e	Armbruster & Schmitt, Star Brewery	1895-1900
	343f	Simon Linser Brewing Co., Star Brewery	1900-1902
OH	344a	Merkle Bros.	1874-1880
	344b	Adolph Merkle	1880-1891

Zanesville (cont.)

OH	345a	Riverside Brewing Co. (162 Main St.)		1893-1899
	345b	Bavarian Brewing Co.		1899-1914

Zoar

OH	364a	The Zoar Community Brewery, aka Zoar Society		1819-1898
	364b	Zoar Brewery	NP	1934-1934

OKLAHOMA

Alva

OK	1	Gerhard Willers		1895-1895

Bartlesville

OK	2	Bartlesville Brewing Co.	NP	1934-1934

Oklahoma City

OK	3a	Broder B. Moss		1900-1902
	3b	Moss Brewing Co.		1902-1907
OK	4a	Oklahoma Brewing and Malting Co.		1901-1905
	4b	New State Brewing Association		1905-1907
OK	5a	Progress Brewing Co., Inc. (501 N. Douglas Ave.)		1934-1960
	5b	Lone Star Brewing Co. (br. of San Antonio, TX)		1960-1971
OK	6a	Southwestern Brewing Corp. (2 W. 3rd St.)		1934-1946
	6b	Peter Fox Brewing Co. (affiliated w/ Fox, Chicago, IL)		1946-1948

Tulsa

OK	7	Ahrens Brewing Co. (515 S. Troost Ave.)		1934-1940

OREGON

Albany

OR	1a	Edward Bellanger		1874-1880
	1b	E. I. Bellanger		1880-1884
OR	2a	Farber Bros.		1884-1887
	2b	William Farber		1887-1892
	2c	Albany Brewing Co. (9th & Lyons Sts.)		1892-1906
	2d	Salem Brewery Association, Albany Brewery		1906-1907
OR	3a	Charles Kiefer		1874-1886
	3b	Adam Luchsinger		1886-1888
	3c	Geo. Pfau		1888-1890
	3d	Geo. Pfau & Co.		1890-1891

Ashland

OR	4	Charles Wurz		1884-1884

Astoria

OR	5	Astoria Brewing Co. (Commercial St.)	NP	1934-1934
OR	6a	John Kopp, North Pacific Brewery		1884-1902
	6b	North Pacific Brewing Co. (Franklin Ave. & 30th St.)		1902-1916
OR	7	Michael Meyer		1874-1884
OR	8	Mrs. T. O'Brien		1886-1887
OR	9a	Papmahl & Block		1874-1875
	9b	Papmahl & Co.		1875-1875
	9c	John Hahn		1875-1884
	9d	St. Louis Brewing Co.		1884-1895

Baker City

OR	10a	Kastner & Lachner		1874-1877
	10b	N. Kastner		1877-1879
	10c	Mrs. F. Kastner		1879-1880
	10d	John Stack		1880-1882
	10e	Kastner & Schlickeisen		1882-1884
	10f	Julius Lachs		1884-1887
	10g	Wm. Widman		1887-1888
	10h	Lachs & Widman		1884-1887

Baker City (cont.)

OR	11a	Henry Rust	1874-1901
	11b	Pacific Brewery, Henry Rust	1901-1903
	11c	American Brewing and Crystal Ice Co., (Dewey Ave.)	1903-1916
OR	12	Carl Stofft	1904-1916

Bandon

OR	13a	Mary A. Mehl	1893- ?
	13b	Joseph Walser (Iris St.)	1896-1900
	13c	George Gehring	1904-1910
	13d	Bruno & Anselmo	1910-1910

Brookville

OR	14	L. Feurer	1880-1880

Brownsville

OR	15	B. Cloner	1878-1879

Burns

OR	16a	Paul Lochner (3rd St.)	1888-1895
	16b	John Rohrman	1895-1896
	16c	Paul Lochner	1900-1902
	16d	Lochner & Berg	1902-1903
	16e	Paul Lochner	1903-1905
OR	17a	Woldenberg & Berg, Harney Valley Brewery	1898-1901
	17b	Louis Woldenberg, Sr., Harney Valley Brewery	1901-1904
	17c	Harney Valley Brewing Co.	1904-1912

Canyon City

OR	18a	Stahl & Solaro	1863- ?
	18b	F. C. Sels	1874-1886
	18c	John Kuhl	1886-1888
	18d	Henry Breyer	1888-1890
	18e	F. C. Sels, City Brewery (Washington St.)	1890-1911

Canyonville

OR	19	Leonard Stenger	1874-1884

Clarksville

OR	20	Henry Rust	1874-1875

Coaleda

OR	21	Henry Tolle	1874-1875

Coquette City (see Coquille)

Coquille

OR	22	G. Mehl	1878-1891

Corvallis

OR	23a	Fischer & Riley	1882-1884
	23b	John Riley	1884-1890
OR	24a	Hunt & Pfleiderer	1874-1875
	24b	Henry Hughes	1875-1879
	24c	Ignatz Furst	1879-1880
	24d	John Zeis, U.S. Brewery	1880-1890

Cottonwood

OR	25	Anton Melzer	1884-1884

East Portland (see Portland)

Enterprise

OR	26a	Frank Ott	1898-1905
	26b	Enterprise Brewing Co.	1905-1906

Eugene

OR	27a	Henry Hageman	1874-1875
	27b	Mathias Miller	1875-1880
	27c	Michael Vogl	1880-1886
	27d	Joseph Vogl	1886-1891
OR	28	Eugene Weideman	1886-1891

Gardner

OR	29a	B. M. Akerblad & Co.	1874- ?
	29b	Frank Varrelmann	1886-1905

Gervais

OR	30	Glaser & Kern	1879-1890

Grants Pass

OR	31	Eagle Brewing Co.	1905-1905
OR	32a	William Neurath	1888-1891
	32b	Eugene Kienlen	1891-1904
	32c	Marie T. Kienlen	1904-1911
OR	33	Geo. Walter	1891-1897

Heppner

OR	34a	A. J. Stevenson	1880-1881
	34b	Wm. Roesch	1881-1882
	34c	J. B. Natter	1882-1890

Island City

OR	35	Ott Bros.	1889-1891

Jacksonville

OR	36a	Veitz Schutz aka Val. Schutz (1878-1879)	1874-1891
	36b	Frank Theising	1891-1893
OR	37a	Joseph Wetterer	1874-1879
	37b	Mrs. Frederica Wetterer	1879-1884
	37c	William Heeley	1884-1889

Joseph

OR	38a	Hulery & Binswange	1889-1890
	38b	G. W. Hulery	1890-1890
OR	39	John Rohrman (Main St.)	1902-1906

Junction City

OR	40a	Braun & Seeger	1878-1879
	40b	H. R. Linke	1879-1882
	40c	Adolph Jaissle	1882-1884
	40d	Eugene Weidmann	1884-1888

Klamath Falls

OR	41	A. Castel (Main St.)	1904-1912
OR	42	Klamath Falls Brewing Co. (11th & Walnut Sts.)	NP 1934-1934

La Grande

OR	43a	Roesch & Arnold	1885-1887
	43b	Julius Roesch, La Grande Brewery	1887-1916

Lake Park

OR	44	Klaus & Umbricht	1893-1893

Lakeview

OR	45	N. A. Clark	1889-1890
OR	46a	W. M. Goos	1886-1887
	46b	A. W. Goos	1888-1890
	46c	Geo. Jammerthal	? -1896
	46d	Ayers & Tonningsen, Lakeview Brewery	1896-1900
	46e	Ayers & Schlegel, Lakeview Brewery	1900-1912
OR	47	O. L. Stanley	1889-1890

Linkville

OR	48	John Uerlings (Main St.)	1886-1893

McMinnville

OR	49a	Anton Ahrens	1878-1879
	49b	W. R. Bachman	1879-1879
	49c	Hermann Rehfuss	1879-1882
	49d	Isidore Ertie	1882-1886

Marshfield

OR	50a	Reichert & Stauff	1868- ?
	50b	William Reichert	1874-1882
	50c	Clemmensen & Co.	1882-1884
	50d	Clemmensen & Evanoff	1884-1888
	50e	Lars Clemmensen	1888-1901
	50f	Marshfield Brewing Co.	1901-1902
	50g	Robert Marsden	1902-1904
	50h	Marshfield Brewing Co.	1904-1907
	50i	Coos Bay Eagle Brewing Co.	1910-1912
OR	51	Peters & Kling	1904-1904
OR	52	Schaufel & Youngmayr	1910-1910

Medford

OR	53a	Southern Oregon Brewing, Ice and Cold Storage Co.	1893-1896
	53b	G. W. Blasford	1896-1897
	53c	Medford Brewing Co.	1897-1900
	53d	Southern Oregon Brewing Co., Inc. (301 N. 1st St.)	1933-1938
	53e	A-One Brewing Co.	1938-1945
	53f	Chrystal Brewing and Dist. Co.	1945-1947

Merganser

OR	54	Paul Breistenstein	1884-1884

Monument

OR	55	Mary C. Allen & Co.	1900-1900

Newport

OR	56a	Blattner & Brandt	1884-1886
	56b	Robert Schaibold	1886-1893
	56c	Yaquina Bay Brewery	1893-1897

North Bend

OR	57a	North Bend Brewing Co.	1907-1908
	57b	Coos Bay Brewing Co.	1908-1916

Oakland

OR	58a	Gottlieb Mehl	1874-1877
	58b	A. D. Robinson	1877-1878
	58c	McGregor & Freyer	1878-1879
	58d	J. A. Freyer	1879-1884

Oregon City

OR	59a	Henry Hubel	1862-1877
	59b	H. Rehfuss	1877-1879
	59c	J. Mader & Co.	1879-1880
	59d	Jacob Mader, Oregon City Brewery	1880-1890
	59e	Listman & Co.	1890-1891
	59f	Geo. Hartmann & Co., Oregon City Brewery	1891-1894

Pasco

OR	60	Vasco De Lay	1893-1893

Pendleton

OR	61a	Adolph Lang & Co.	1878-1884
	61b	Arnold & Schmeer	1884-1888
	61c	Frank Arnold	1888-1890
	61d	R. Lambrecht & Co.	1890-1891
	61e	Adam Nolte	1891-1895
	61f	Anton Nolte	1895-1896
	61g	Polydore Moens	1901-1902
OR	62a	William Roesch, City Brewery	1882-1916
	62b	William Roesch Bottling Works (400/406 S.E. Court St.)	? -1934
	62c	Wm. Roesch Brewing Co. (300/320 S.E. Court St.)	1934-1947
OR	63	Schull & Co.	1884-1884
OR	64a	Schultz & Ricke	1897-1897
	64b	Schultz Brewing Co.	1897-1902
	64c	Schultz & Stricker	1905-1910

Pendleton (cont.)

OR	65a	Adam Stang		1878-1879
	65b	Matter & Stang		1879-1880
	65c	J. B. Matter & Co.		1880-1884
OR	66	Umatilla Brewery		1889-1890

Portland

OR	67	Cartwright Brewing Co.		1980-1982
OR	68a	Louis Feurer		1877-1889
	68b	Gambrinus Brewing Co. (22nd & B Sts.)		1889-1895
	68c	Gambrinus Brewing Co. (Washington & 24th Sts.)		1895-1916
	68d	Rose City Brewing Co., Inc. (817 N.E. Madrona St.)		1933-1940
OR	69	A. Jubitz		1874-1875
OR	70a	Henry Ludwig (East Portland)		1874-1875
	70b	Henall & Kroetz		1875-1880
	70c	Kroetz & Humbel		1880-1881
	70d	John Kroetz & Co.		1881-1882
	70e	Lambert Kratz		1882-1884
OR	71a	Molson & Sons		1879-1882
	71b	Diesing & Neunert		1882-1884
OR	72a	Mount Hood Brewing Co. (Hawthorne Ave. & E. Water St.)		1905-1911
	72b	Mount Hood Brewing Co. (E. 9th St. & Marion Ave.)		1911-1913
OR	73	Northwest Brewing Co.	NP	1934-1934
OR	74	Oregon Breweries & Hop Farms Affiliated	NP	1934-1934
OR	75	Pilsener Brewing Co. (N.W. 2nd & Couch Sts.)	NP	1934-1934
OR	76a	Portland Brewing Co. (20th & Upshur Sts.)		1905-1928
	76b	Blitz-Weinhard Co., Inc. (Plant 2 - 1991 N.W. Upshur St.)		1928-1940
OR	77a	Portland Weiss Beer Brewing and Bottling Co. (537 Milwaukee)		1902-1904
	77b	Deter & Co.		1904-1907
OR	78	Schaefer & Burelbach		1886-1887
OR	79	Scheland & Co.		1874-1875
OR	80a	United States Brewing Co. (Water & Harrison Sts.)		1878-1880
	80b	Herrall & Zimmermann		1880-1884
	80c	United States Brewing Co.		1884-1895
OR	81	Jos. Weber (S. 1st & Gibson Sts.)		1882-1884
OR	82a	City Brewery (founded by Henry Saxer)		1852-1862
	82b	(Henry) Weinhard & (George) Bottler, City Brewery		1862-1866
	82c	Henry Weinhard, City Brewery (12th & B Sts.)		1866-1891
	82d	Henry Weinhard, City Brewery (475 Burnside & 13th Sts.)		1891-1904
	82e	Henry Weinhard Brewery		1904-1928
	82f	Blitz-Weinhard Co. (1133 W. Burnside St.)		1928-1979
	82g	Pabst Brewing Co., aka Blitz-Weinhard Co. (br. of Milwaukee)		1979-1983
	82h	G. Heileman Brewing Co., aka Blitz-Weinhard Co. (br. of LaCrosse, WI)		1983-

Prairie City

OR	83	Paul Fairnan		1889-1890
OR	84	Otto Mahl		1880-1880

Prineville

OR	85a	Locker & Solomon		1882-1883
	85b	Frank Locker		1883-1884
	85c	Evans & Miles		1884-1886
	85d	Asa Miles		1886-1890
OR	86a	S. W. Woods		1893- ?
	86b	O'Neil & Geiger		? -1897
	86c	O'Neil Bros.		1897-1902
	86d	O'Neil & Geiger		1902-1904
	86e	O'Neil Bros.		1904-1906

Randolph			
OR	87	Joseph Walser	1884-1891
Roseburg			
OR	88	Th. F. Kreuztscher	1878-1879
OR	89a	David Meyer	1895-1896
	89b	Leonard Schmitt	1896-1896
OR	90a	John Rast	1874-1879
	90b	Criterer & Rast	1879-1880
	90c	John Rast	1880-1893
	90d	Delaney & Meyer	1893-1896
	90e	Oregon Brewing and Ice Co.	1899-1902
	90f	Max Weiss	1902-1904
	90g	Roseburg Brewing and Ice Co.	1904-1916
St. Paul			
OR	91	Anton Ahrens	1875-1879
Salem			
OR	92a	Samuel Adolph	1874-1877
	92b	S. Adolph & Co.	1877-1886
	92c	Klinger & Beck	1886-1900
	92d	Mrs. Margarite Beck (174 Commercial St.)	1900-1903
	92e	Salem Brewery Association	1903-1916
	92f	Salem Brewery Association (268 S. Commercial St.)	1934-1943
	92g	Sicks' Brewing Co., affiliated with Sicks' Seattle Brewing and Malting Co.	1943-1953
OR	93a	L. Westacott	1874-1879
	93b	L. Westacott & Son	1879-1880
	93c	L. Westacott	1880-1884
Scottsburg			
OR	94	L. H. Rumelhort	1878-1879
Sellwood			
OR	95a	John G. Wilhelm	1889-1901
	95b	Mary A. Wilhelm	1901-1904
Summerville			
OR	96	George Ott	1886-1910
Sumpter			
OR	97a	John Rohrman	1899-1900
	97b	Columbia Brewing and Malting Co.	1900-1902
	97c	Ellis & Zizelman	1902-1903
	97d	A. W. Ellis	1903-1905
The Dalles			
OR	98	Columbia Brewery	1886-1887
OR	99a	Emil Schanno	1874-1875
	99b	R. O. Porak	1880-1882
	99c	R. O. Porak & Co.	1882-1884
OR	100a	Weinhard & Buchler	1876-1878
	100b	August Buchler	1878-1904
	100c	Eastern Oregon Brewing Co.	1904-1916
Union			
OR	101a	S. N. Washburn & Co.	1878-1879
	101b	Stickler & Zuber	1879-1882
	101c	Henry Stickler	1882-1884
Utter City			
OR	102	Stauf	1874-1875
Weston			
OR	103	Thomas Berry	1882-1884
Wilderville			
OR	104	David Closner	1879-1880

Aliquippa

PA	1	Mutual Union Brewing Co.	1907-1920

Allentown

PA	2a	Allentown Brewing Co. (3rd & 311/323 Gordon Sts.)	1897-1902
	2b	Horlacher Brewing Co.	1902-1921
	2c	The Horlacher Co.	1921-1933
	2d	Horlacher Brewing Co. (311 Gordon St.) aka Hofbrau Brewing Co. (1960-1964 & 1967-1972) aka Old Dutch Brewing Co. (1960-1976)	1933-1978
PA	3	Dan Deily (E. Hamilton & N. Water)	c1860
PA	4a	Leopold Kern (819 Lawrence St. between 7th & 8th Sts.)	1860-1879
	4b	G. Muehlberger & Bro.	1879-1880
	4c	Leopold Kern	1880-1884
	4d	Andreas Hoag & Co.	1885-1885
	4e	Charles Ritter	1886-1887
	4f	Christian Franklin	1887-1888
PA	5a	Henry Koenig & Co. (16 S. 8th St.)	1869-1876
	5b	H. Koenig & Co. (Lawrence & Jefferson Sts.)	1876-1877
	5c	Jacob Daeufer	1877-1890
	5d	Daeufer & Co.	1890-1911
	5e	Daeufer Brewing Co.	1911-1915
	5f	Daeufer-Lieberman Brewing Co.	1915-1933
	5g	Daeufer-Lieberman Brewing Co., aka Allen W. Buffington (1247 Lawrence St.)	1933-1935
	5h	Daeufer-Lieberman Brewing Co,, aka Daeufer-Lieberman Brewery	1935-1948
PA	6	Hiram McHose (145 Hamilton St.)	c1873-1874
PA	7a	Benedict Nuding, Germania Brewery (114/122 S. 7th St.)	1875-1891
	7b	Nuding Brewing Co.	1891-1905
	7c	Louis F. Neuweiler & Son	1905-1913
	7d	Louis F. Neuweiler & Sons (Charles & Louis, Jr.) (401/431 N. Front. St.)	1913-1925
	7e	Louis F. Neuweiler's Sons	1925-1968
PA	8a	William Oberly (6th & Union Sts.)	1845-1864
	8b	Lieberman & Co., Eagle Brewery	1864-1879
	8c	Joseph Lieberman & Co., Eagle Brewery	1879-1888
	8d	Joseph Lieberman, Eagle Brewery	1888-1890
	8e	John Birkenstock, Sunrise & Sunset Brewery	1890-1897
	8f	Joseph Lieberman	1897-1900
	8g	Jos. Lieberman's Sons	1900-1910
	8h	Lieberman Brewing Co.	1910-1915
PA	9a	The F. & M. Schaefer Brewing Co., aka Piel Bros.	1972-1980
	9b	The F. & M. Schaefer Brewing Co., subsidiary of Stroh Brewery Co., Detroit, MI	1980-
PA	10a	James Wise (4th & Hamilton Sts.)	1866-1875
	10b	Knauss & Lichtenwalner	1875-1876
	10c	M. D. Lichtenwalner	1876- ?
	10d	J. J. Hottenstein	? -1882

Altoona

PA	11	James Anderton	1890-1890
PA	12	Wm. H. Bender (1419 4th Ave.)	1896-1897
PA	13a	George Enzbrenner (13th Ave. between 14th & 15th Sts.)	1852-1880
	13b	Conrad Enzbrenner	1880-1882
	13c	John Enzbrenner, Empire Brewery	1882-1893
	13d	John M. Enzbrenner, Empire Brewery (1808/1812 9th Ave.)	1893-1896
	13e	Jon Kazmaier, Germania Brewery	1896-1919
	13f	City Ice and Beverage Co., aka George Frye (1718/1734 9th)	1933-1936
	13g	Altoona Brewing Co.	1936-1974
PA	14a	Charles Haid	1874-1884
	14b	Mary Haid	1884-1888
	14c	Daniel Rittman	1888-1890
	14d	Frederick Haller	1890-1891
	14e	Mary Rittman	1891-1893
	14f	Chas. Rabenschlag	1893-1896

Altoona (cont.)

PA	15a	Gustav Klemmert (1226 4th Ave. & 13th St.)	1874-1891
	15b	Geo. A. W. Arnholt	1891-1895
	15c	American Brewing Co.	1895-1900
	15d	V. A. Oswald, American Brewery	1900-1920
	15e	Oswald Brewing Co.	1933-1936
PA	16	Peter Mayor	1884-1884
PA	17a	Joseph Stehle	1874-1877
	17b	John B. Stehle (3rd Ave. & 7th St.)	1877-1884
PA	18a	Christ. Wahl	1874-1884
	18b	L. P. Stick	1884-1890
	18c	Kimmel & Werner	1890-1891
PA	19a	George Wilhelm	1855-1870
	19b	Martin Hoelle, Old Hickory Brewery	1870-1895
	19c	Schimminger & Wilhelm	1895-1895
	19d	(George J.) Wilhelm, (George) Schimminger & (William R.) Ramsey, Altoona Brewery (15th Ave. & 1410 13th St.)	1895-1920

Ambridge

PA	20a	Ambridge-Economy Brewing Co.	1908-1911
	20b	Arnold Schonegg Harmony Brewery	1911-1915
	20c	Arnold Schonegg Harmony Brewing Co.	1915-1916

Armstrong

PA	21	A. Koch & Bros.	1874-1875

Ashland

PA	22a	Schuylkill Home Brewing Co.	1911- ?
	22b	Ashland Brewing Co.	1915-1920
	22c	Ashland Brewing Co.	1934-1935
	22d	Thomas V. Melley, dba Ashland Brewery	1935-1940

Athens

PA	23	N. J. Knasesboro	1874-1875

Beatty or Beatty Station (see Latrobe)

Beaver Falls

PA	24a	James Anderton (24th St.)	1869-1891
	24b	Anderton Brewing Co.	1891-1904
	24c	Independent Brewing Co., Anderton Brewery (br. of Pittsburgh)	1904-1920
	24d	Anderton Brewery (owned by Duquesne Brewery, Pittsburgh) NP	1934-1934
PA	25	John L. Greenham	1882-1884
PA	26a	Holmes & Timmings	1878-1879
	26b	Beaver Falls Brewing Co.	1879-1884
PA	27	George Tyler	1890-1890
PA	28a	Volk & Falk	1874-1875
	28b	John Volk	1875-1884
	28c	Francis Volk	1884-1886
	28d	Volk's Brewery	1886-1891
	28e	Bernard Rengers	1891-1893
PA	29a	Henry Wagner	1882-1884
	29b	Lewis J. Wagner	1884-1890
	29c	Yochum & Zimmermann	1890-1891

Bellefonte

PA	30a	Louis Doll	1896-1897
	30b	Peter Jacobs	1897-1898
	30c	Robert L. Haas	1898-1899
	30d	Matthew Volk	1899-1901
PA	31a	Louis Haas	1878-1882
	31b	Catherine Haas	1882-1888

Benner

PA	32	Louis Haas	1874-1875

Bennett or Bennett's Station (see Pittsburgh)

Bentleyville

PA	33a	Acme Brewing Co.	1907-1920
	33b	Bentleyville Brewing Co., Inc.	1933-1934

Benzinger

PA	34a	B. Wenitzer	1874-1877
	34b	Peter Straub	1877-1884

Bernharts (see Reading)

Berwick

PA	35	Berwick Brewing Co.	1907-1908

Bethlehem

PA	36a	(Edward) Benz & (Francis) Fenner (South Bethlehem)	1880-1883
	36b	Edward Benz (Old York Road)	1883-1884
	36c	Carl Eckert	1884-1888
	36d	Jacob Widman & Co., Monocacy Brewery (2 Old York Road)	1888-1920
	36e	J. Widman Brewing Co., Inc.	1933-1934
	36f	Widman Brewing Co. (1 Old York Road)	1934-1938
PA	37	Wm. Fritsche	1874-1875
PA	38	Labor Products Co. (South Bethlehem)	NP 1934-1934
PA	39a	Moravian Brewery (Lehigh River Bank)	1783-1803
	39b	John Sebastian Goundie	1803-1811
	39c	John Sebastian Goundie (Monocacy Creekbank behind Main St.)	1814- ?
PA	40a	John Schilling (Union & Monocacy Sts.)	1856-1870
	40b	Mathias Uhl	1870-1887
	40c	Anna Uhl	1887-1893
	40d	Uhl's Brewery	1893-1895
	40e	Uhl's Estate	1895-1896
	40f	Bertha Uhl, aka Uhl's Brewery	1896-1904
	40g	Uhl's Brewery, aka Uhl's Estate	1904-1920
	40h	Beth-Uhl Brewing Co. (128 W. Union Blvd.)	1933-1941
	40i	Arlington Brewing Co.	NP 1942-1942
PA	41a	South Bethlehem Brewing Co. (Elm & 4th Sts.)	1901-1920
	41b	South Bethlehem Brewing Co. (325/329 Webster St.)	1933-1954

Bloomsburg

PA	42a	Bloomsburg Brewing Co.	1910-1911
	42b	Exchange Brewery	1911-1913
	42c	Eagle Brewing Co.	1913-1913

Blossburg

PA	43a	Charlotte House	1874-1877
	43b	Elijah Plummer	1877-1879
	43c	Joseph Brooks	1879-1884
	43d	Thos. Brooks & Sons	1884-1891

Boswell

PA	44a	Idlewild Brewing Co. (Jenner Township)	1912-1913
	44b	Jenner Brewing Co.	1913-1915
	44c	Jenner Brewing Co.	1918-1920
	44d	Jenner Springs Brewing Co., Inc. (Boswell Road)	

Boyertown

PA	45a	Boyertown Brewing Co. (128 E. Philadelphia Ave.)	1934-1948
	45b	Boyertown Brewing Corp.	1948-1953

Brackenridge

PA	46	Brackenridge Brewing Co., Inc. (849 6th Ave.)	1933-1940

Braddock

PA	47a	Braddock Brewing Co.	1898-1901
	47b	Home Brewing Co. (804 Halket Ave.)	1901-1904
	47c	Independent Brewing Co., Home Brewery (br. of Pittsburgh, PA)	1904-1920
	47d	Home Beverage Co.	? -1933
	47e	General Braddock Brewing Co.	1933-1937
PA	48a	Gustav Schulz	1874-1884
PA	49a	Peter C. Seewald & Co.	1874-1877
	49b	Nick Schafer	1877-1890

Bradford

PA	50	Bacher & Co.	1880-1884
PA	51a	Bradford Brewing Co. (10 4th St.)	1899-1920
	51b	Bradford Beer Corp.	1933-1934

Bridgewater

PA	52	Cooper Bros.	1882-1884
PA	53	Herman Millstine	1884-1884
PA	54	Conrad C. Weisgerber (West Bridgewater)	1874-1888

Brisbin

PA	55a	Chas. Selbitz	1888-1893
	55b	Schmitt & Schwab	1893-1895
	55c	William Schwab	1895-1897

Brookville

PA	56a	Magnus Allgeier, Spring Brewery	1874-1912
	56b	M. Allgeier Sons, Spring Brewery	1912-1916
PA	57a	Sebastian C. Christ (Mill & Water Sts.)	1862-1896
	57b	Brookville Brewing Co.	1896-1916

Brownsville

PA	58a	Brownsville Brewing Co.	1905-1920
	58b	Brownsville Brewing Co. (15 Bolivar St.)	1933-1935

Butler

PA	59a	Butler Brewing Co.	1902-1904
	59b	Independent Brewing Co., Butler Brewery (br. of Pittsburgh)	1904-1912
	59c	Independent Brewing Co., Butler Brewery (br. of Pittsburgh)	1918-1920
PA	60	Jordan Eyth	1874-1875
PA	61	Gabriel Kohler	1874-1875
PA	62a	Andrew Miller	1874-1875
	62b	John P. Miller	1875-1875
PA	63	Daniel Walters	1882-1882

Cadwallader (see Elco)

Cambria

PA	64	Jacob Goenner	1874-1884

Canonsburg

PA	65	Empire Brewing Co.	1907-1907

Carbondale (see Simpson)

Carlisle

PA	66	Cumberland Valley Brewing Co.	1906-1906
PA	67	C. C. Faber	1878-1879
PA	68a	E. J. Krause	1874-1879
	68b	Frey & Hoelzle	1879-1884
	68c	Jacob Marks	1884-1888
	68d	R. F. J. Weber	1888-1891

Carnegie

PA	69a	Chartier Valley Brewing Co. (Chestnut & Jane Sts.)	1901-1904
	69b	Independent Brewing Co., Chartiers Valley Brewery (br. of Pittsburgh, PA)	1904-1920
	69c	Duquesne Brewing Co. of Pittsburgh, Chartiers Valley Brewery	1933-1952

Carrolltown

PA	70	Wm. Booth	1880-1884
PA	71a	Henry Blum	1874-1884
	71b	Barbara A. Blum	1884-1899
PA	72a	F. & C. Eger	1878-1879
	72b	F. Eger & Co.	1879-1882
	72c	Fredk. Eger	1882-1884
	72d	C. A. Farabaugh	1884-1897
	72e	Mrs. Celeste A. Farabaugh	1897-1899
	72f	Henry Swope	1899-1900

Carrolltown (cont.)

PA	73	Henry C. Schrotte	1890-1891
PA	74	Julius Stich	1874-1884

Catasauqua

PA	75a	Catasauqua Brewery, Kirsch & Rice	1901-1902
	75b	Henry C. Rice	1902-1904
	75c	Chas. L. Lehnert, Catasauqua Brewery (115 Railroad St.)	1904-1920
	75d	Viking Brewery, Nathan L. Edelstein (117 Railroad St.)	1933-1934
	75e	Viking Brewery, (Nathan L.) Edelstein & (Francis E.) Walter	1934-1935
PA	76	Henry P. Geisel	1890-1890
PA	77	Abraham Knaus (S. 2nd St.)	1893-1893
PA	78a	Schaefer & Kostenbader, Eagle Brewery	1867-1872
	78b	(John) Kreutzer & Kostenbader, Eagle Brewery	1872-1876
	78c	Herman Kostenbader, Eagle Brewery (2nd St.)	1876-1902
	78d	Herman Kostenbader & Sons, Eagle Brewery	1902-1920
	78e	Walter K. Miller (Railroad & Mulberry Sts.)	1933-1934
	78f	Eagle Brewing Co.	1934-1964
PA	79a	Christ. Stockberger	1874-1877
	79b	M. J. Stockberger	1877-1880
	79c	Christ. Stockberger	1880-1884
	79d	M. J. Stockberger	1884-1888

Centreville

PA	80a	Andrew Hau	1874-1877
	80b	John Dluzer	1877-1879
	80c	Hermann Hert	1879-1884

Chambersburg

PA	81a	Henry A. Klenzing	1879-1893
	81b	Samuel L. Fortney (N. Franklin St.)	1893-1897
PA	82	L. B. Kurtz	1874-1884
PA	83	Charles Ludwig (Water St.)	1874-1891
PA	84	Martin Ludwig	1874-1875
PA	85	Henry Richter	1874-1884

Charleroi

PA	86a	Charleroi Brewing Co.	1899-1904
	86b	Independent Brewing Co., Charleroi Brewery (br. of Pittsburgh)	1904-1920

Chartiers (see Pittsburgh)

Cherry Township

PA	87	Benj. Helbert	1882-1882

Chester

PA	88a	Franx X. Haser (2nd & West Sts., South Chester)	1888-1895
	88b	Fossberger & Killinger	1895-1896
	88c	John Frostburg	1896-1897
	88d	Chester Brewing Co. (2400 W. 2nd & Palmer Sts.)	1898-1920
	88e	Thomas G. Berry, aka Chester Brewery Co.	1933-1934
	88f	Chester Brewery, Inc.	1934-1951
	88g	Chester Brewing Co.	1951-1953

Chewton

PA	89	Chewton Brewing Co.	1884-1884
PA	90a	Frederick Roth	1893-1894
	90b	Matilda Roth	1894-1895
	90c	Geo. S. Jordan	1895-1900
	90d	Michael Fisher	1900-1901
	90e	Spring Brewing Co.	1901-1908
PA	91	Peter Schmidt	1895-1895

Christian Springs

PA	92	Moravian Brewery	1749- ?

Clairton

PA	93	Monongahela Valley Brewing Co.	1902-1916

Clarion

PA	94a	F. J. Elschlager	1874-1877
	94b	H. J. Sandt	1877-1879
PA	95a	George Hartle	1874-1880
	95b	P. & W. Miller	1880-1882
	95c	Peter Miller	1882-1891

Clearfield

PA	96	W. Endres & Co.	1874-1875
PA	97	Casper Leipoldt	1874-1884
PA	98a	Charles Shafer	1872- ?
	98b	Th. Sell	1878-1880
	98c	Hiram Schafer	1880-1884
	98d	Theodore Ries	1884-1888
	98e	Rosa Ries	1888-1895
	98f	M. Wagner	1895-1895
	98g	J. W. & Charles Roessner	1895-1896
	98h	Clearfield Brewing Co. (295 Bigler Ave.)	1896-1920

Coal Township

PA	99a	M. Markle & Co.	1874-1877
	99b	M. Markle	1877-1882

Coalport

PA	100a	Peter G. Niebauer (Spruce St.)	1882-1897
	100b	J. Kutruff	1897-1898
	100c	Coalport Brewery, L. X. Lickert	1901-1902
	100d	N. X. Lickert	1902-1904

Columbia

PA	101a	Anthony Brink	1874-1877
	101b	A. H. Brink & Co.	1877-1879
PA	102	Joseph Desch	1874-1879
PA	103	F. Shillof & Co.	1874-1875
PA	104	Jacob F. Wisler	1874-1875
PA	105a	Gottlieb Young	1874-1890
	105b	Loder & Kazmaier, Columbia Brewery (251 S. 4th St.)	1890-1895
	105c	Joseph Loder, Columbia Brewery	1895-1897
	105d	Loder Brewing Co.	1897-1901
	105e	Columbia Brewing Co.	1901-1904
	105f	Rieker Brewing Co.	1904-1905
	105g	Rieker's Columbia Brewing Co.	1905-1906
	105h	Columbia Brewing Co. aka Rieker Brewing Co. (1910)	1906-1912
	105i	Columbia Brewing Co.	1912-1920
	105k	Columbia Brewing Co.	1933-1934
	105l	Chas. Kloidt Brewery (233/235 S. 4th St.)	1934-1941
PA	106	Hillory Zepfel	c1873

Condersport

PA	107	C. Zimmermann	1878-1880

Conemaugh

PA	108a	Lawrence Kost	1874-1904
	108b	Conemaugh Brewing Co. (Railroad St.)	1906-1920
PA	109	Lambert & Kress	1874-1879

Connellsville

PA	110a	Connellsville Brewing Co. (8th & Pulaski Sts.)	1892-1899
	110b	Pittsburgh Brewing Co., Connellsville Brewery aka Connellsville Brewing Co. (1899-1900)	1899-1920
PA	111	Henry P. Snyder	1874-1875
PA	112a	Tippmann & Bleimer	1888-1895
	112b	Joseph Tippmann	1895-1899
	112c	Yough Brewing Co.	1899-1920
	112d	Yough Brewing Co. (1050 S. Arch St.)	1933-1940
	112e	Yough Brewing Corp.	1940-1941

Connewango

PA 113 Ph. Gisselbrecht 1874-1875

PA 114 Philip Leonhart 1874-1875

Conshohocken

PA 115a Gulf Brewing Co. 1896-1897
115b Conshohocken Brewing Co. 1897-1898
115c Crystal Spring Brewing Co. 1898-1902

PA 116a Frank X. Rieger (Hector & Jones Sts.) 1893- ?
116b Louisa Rieger ? -1896
116c Albert Loeble 1896-1897
116d McGrath & Barrett 1897-1898

Coopersburg

PA 117 Thomas Cooper 1884-1884

Corry

PA 118a Louisa Bissontza 1874-1877
118b Gustav Spreter 1877-1884

PA 119 Julius Hohler c1870

PA 120 Hiram Morris (Smith & N. Wayne Sts.) 1870-1879

PA 121 Michael Whitman (Spring St.) c1870

Covington

PA 122 William Hockenberger, Jr. 1875- ?

Cresson

PA 123a Cresson Springs Brewery 1905-1915
123b Cresson Springs Brewery Co. 1915-1920

Danville

PA 124a John Bausch 1874-1877
124b G. Fraudenberger & Co. 1877-1880
124c J. & C. Bausch 1880-1882
124d Charles Bausch 1882-1884
124e J. & C. Bausch 1884-1891
124f J. Bausch & Co. 1891-1893
124g J. & C. Bausch 1893-1897
124h Germania Brewing Co., aka Germania Brewery, Emil Gaertner (E. Front & Ferry Sts.) 1897-1920
124i Danville Brewing Co., Inc. 1933-1934

PA 125a John F. Gerstner 1874-1877
125b Maria A. Gerstner 1877-1890
125c Steeb & Faber (16/34 Spring St.) 1890-1895
125d Polish-Lithuanian Brewing Co. 1895-1905
125e Hanover Brewing Co. 1905-1915

Decatur

PA 126 Wm. Pritchard 1882-1884

Dickson City

PA 127a Elizabeth S. Bryden 1893- ?
127b J. A. Gutknecht & Co. ? -1897
127c Dickson Brewing Co., Dept. Penna. Central Brewing Co., Scranton 1897-1899

Donora

PA 128 Donora Brewing Co. (1st St. & Meldon Ave.) 1905-1920

Drifton

PA 129 Daniel Walters 1884-1884

Dubois

PA 130a Dubois Brewing Co. (S. Main St.) 1897-1920
130b Dubois Brewing Co., aka The DuBois Brewing Co. 1933-1973

Dunmore (see Scranton)

Dunstable

PA 131 Chas. P. Fahel 1874-1875

Duquesne

PA	132a	Eagle Brewing Co.	1906-1910
	132b	People's Brewing Co.	1910-1915
	132c	Duquesne Brewing Co. (br. of Crescent Brewing Co., Irwin, PA) (118 E. Duquesne Ave.)	1915-1920

Dushore

PA	133	Erb & Billion	1875-1875
PA	134a	Benjamin Hilbert	1884- ?
	134b	C. Specht	? -1888
	134c	Leonard Hilbert, Sullivan County Brewery	1896-1900

East Bethlehem

PA	135	George Siddell	1884-1888

East Economy (see Economy)

East Mauch Chunk (see Mauch Chunk)

Easton

PA	136a	(Charles) Glanz & (Willibald) Kuebler (Church & Bank Sts.)	c1850-1853
	136b	Glanz & Kuebler (Route 611)	c1853-1875
	136c	Bormann & Kuebler	1875-1878
	136d	Willibald Kuebler (foot of Lehigh St.)	1878-1898
	136e	W. Kuebler's Sons	1898-1920
	136f	Kuebler Brewing Co., Inc. (S. Delaware Drive)	1933-1953
PA	137a	(Frederick) Seitz & (John) Goundie	1821-1823
	137b	Frederick Seitz	1823-1867
	137c	John A. Seitz & Bros.	1867-1877
	137d	Seitz Bros. (Bushkill & Front Sts.)	1877-1897
	137e	Seitz Brewing Co.	1897-1928
	137f	Judd Brewing Co.	1928- ?
	137g	Harry J. Osterstock	1933-1934
	137h	Seitz Brewing Co., Inc. aka Johnson Bottling Works of Johnson City, NY aka Southern Breweries, Inc. of Charlotte, NC	1934-1938
PA	138a	Xavier Veile	1848-1884
	138b	Charles H. Seip	1884-1888
	138c	Veile & Seip (675 Northampton St.)	1888-1893
	138d	Isabella R. Seip (Spring Garden & Locust Sts.)	1893-1913
	138e	Xavier Veile Brewery, Inc.	1913-1916
	138f	Bushkill Products Co. (58/72 Locust & Pearl Sts.)	1933-1941

East Stroudsburg

PA	139a	John Burt	1874-1884
	139b	Burt Bros.	1884-1888

Economy

PA	140a	Economy Brewing Co. (East Economy)	1904-1906
	140b	Ambridge-Economy Brewing Co.	1910-1913

Edwardsville (see Wilkes-Barre)

Elco

PA	141a	Mann & Schrieder	1874- ?
	141b	W. A. Thistlethwaite	1896-1897
	141c	Elco Brewing Co.	1897-1904

Emaus

PA	142a	Fred Kling	1878-1879
	142b	Diller & Weaver	1879-1882
	142c	Weaver & Leister	1882-1884

Emlenton

PA	143	Sebastian Kreis	1874-1884

Emporium

PA	144	F. X. Blumle	1878-1890

Ephrata

PA	145	Geo. S. Keller	1875- ?

Erie

PA	146a	Blass & Vogt (State St. & S. Cityline)	1873-1877
	146b	Hopedale Brewery	1877-1888
	146c	Frank Vogt, Hopedale Brewery	1888-1911
	146d	Vogt Brewing Co., aka Frank X. Vogt Brewery	1911-1913
	146e	Perry Brewing Co. (30th & State Sts.)	1914-1920
PA	147	James Carnagie Ale Brewery (Myrtle St. between 2nd & 3rd Sts.)	1837- ?
PA	148a	Jacob Diefenthaler (French St. between 3rd & 4th Sts.)	1836-1845
	148b	John Knobloch	c1853
PA	149a	Adam Dietz (17th & Parade Sts.)	1840-1853
	149b	Frederick Dietz	1853-1860
	149c	Charles Koehler Lager Beer Brewery	1860-1864
	149d	Alfred King, Erie Ale Brewery	1865-1870
	149e	Keystone Brewery	1870-1871
	149f	Michael Wittman	1871-1872
	149g	(Truman) Downer & (Ervin J.) Howard Ale Brewery	1872-1896
	149h	Ervin J. Howard	1897-1899
	149i	Consumers Brewing Co.	1899-1907
	149j	Wayne Brewing Co.	1907-1922
	149k	Wayne Brewing Co.	1934-1951
PA	150a	George Frey (26th & Poplar St.)	1862-1863
	150b	Alfred King, Erie City Lager Brewery	1863-1870
	150c	Joseph F. Seelinger, Erie City Brewery	1870-1872
PA	151a	Jacob Fuess	1848-1850
	151b	Jacob Fuess, National Brewery (6th & Parade Sts.)	1852-1863
	151c	Charles M. Conrad, National Brewery	1863-1895
	151d	Charles M. Conrad, National Brewery (5th & Parade Sts.)	1895-1899
	151e	Erie Brewing Co., C. M. Conrad Branch, National Brewery	1899-1920
PA	152a	Gabel & Mauer (27th St. between Peach & State St.)	1868-1875
	152b	Gabel & Vogt	1875-1876
	152c	Jacob Gabel	1876-1877
PA	153a	Glover (Myrtle St. near 10th)	? -1843
	153b	Peter Fischer (Myrtle St. between 9th & 10th)	1843-1853
	153c	Jacob Weschler	1854-1859
	153d	George Frey	1859-1862
	153e	Jacob Weschler	1862-1865
	153f	Jacob Weschler (9th & Walnut Sts.)	1866-1870
PA	154a	J. Heilmann (French St. between 3rd & 4th Sts.)	c1853
	154b	William Jacobi	1860-1873
	154c	George L. Baker Co.	1874-1874
PA	155a	William Jacobi, Jr. (4th St. between Cherry & Poplar Sts.)	1868-1870
	155b	Mrs. Wm. E. Jacobi, Jr.	1870-1872
	155c	F. Schott	1873-1876
	155d	Anton Fogt	1877-1896
	155e	Christian A. Kraus (634 W. 4th St.)	1896-1899
PA	156a	Henry Kalvelage, Eagle Brewery (22nd & State Sts.)	1855-1862
	156b	Schraf & Kalvelage	1862-1865
	156c	J. Henry Kalvelage, Eagle Brewery	1865-1883
	156d	Jackson Koehler, Eagle Brewery	1883-1899
	156e	Erie Brewing Co., Jackson Koehler Branch, Eagle Brewery	1899-1922
	156f	Imperial Beverages	1922-1933
	156g	The Erie Brewing Co., aka Iroquois Brewing Co. (2124/2212 State St.)	1933-1978
PA	157a	Henry Knibe (Parade St. near 11th St.)	1854-1859
	157b	Jacob & Henry Knibe	1859-1860
	157c	Jacob Knibe	1860-1862
PA	158a	Charles Koehler (26th & Holland Sts.)	1864-1869
	158b	Mrs. Rosina Koehler	1864-1869
	158c	Fred Koehler	1869-1875
	158d	Fred Koehler & Bro. (Jackson), aka Koehler Bros.	1875-1883
	158e	Fred Koehler	1883-1887
	158f	Fred Koehler & Co. (Adolph Curtze)	1887-1899
	158g	Erie Brewing Co., Fred Koehler & Co. Branch	1899-1910

Erie (cont.)

PA	159	(Major) David McNair (Turnpike N. of L.S. & M.S. R.R.)	1815- ?
PA	160	St. Boniface Parish Brewery	c1860-1887
PA	161a	Peter Schaaf (10th & Ash Lane)	1857-1860
	161b	Schaaf & Kalvelage	1861-1862
PA	162	Chas. Strick & Bro. (Mill Creek Township)	1874-1875
PA	163a	(Brand) Vogt & (Joseph) Platz (Mill Creek Township)	1874-1879
	163b	Frank Voigt	1879-1884
PA	164	Fred J. Welde	1895-1895
PA	165	Henry Weschler (4th & Chestnut Sts.)	1859-1861
PA	166a	West End Brewery, C. E. Ball (W. 8th St. & Delaware Ave.)	1893-1894
	166b	West End Brewery, Clark M. Cole	1895-1897
	166c	Cascade Brewing Co.	1897-1899
	166c	Erie Brewing Co., Cascade Brewery Branch	1899-1901

Etna

PA	167	Michael Metzger	1874-1893

Exeter

PA	168a	A. A. M. Burschel, Forest Castle Brewery	1873-1874
	168b	John A. Burschel	1874-1878
	168c	H. R. Hughes & Co.	1878-1887
	168d	Hughes & Glennon	1887-1891

Fairbanks (see Masontown)

Fair Oaks

PA	169	Old Economy Brewing Co.	1907-1916

Farmer's Valley

PA	170	Erwin Schott	1879-1888

Farrell

PA	171a	Mercer County Brewing Co. (South Sharon)	1911-1913
	171b	Mercer County Brewing Co. (Staunton St.)	1914-1920

Fernwood (see Lansdowne)

Finleyville

PA	172a	Thomas Morrison	1888-1902
	172b	Finleyville Brewing Co.	1902-1905
	172c	Washington County Brewing Co.	1905-1906

Fountain Springs

PA	173a	(Wm. E., C. M., & Henry R.) Engel & Schmidt Brewing Co.	1897-1909
	173b	Fountain Springs Brewing Co.	1909-1920
	173c	Pure Springs Brewing Co., Inc.	1933-1934

Fox Township

PA	174	Peter Connor	1882-1882

Frackville

PA	175	Frackville Brewing Co. (Chestnut & Middle Sts.)	1933-1934

Frankford (see Philadelphia)

Franklin

PA	176a	Bowman & Rollo	1865- ?
	176b	Henry Giesel	1874-1875
	176c	Philip Worst	1880- ?
	176d	Christian Brecht	1888-1908
	176e	Christian Brecht Brewery	1908-1911
	176f	Christian Brecht Brewing Co. (29 Rocky Grove Ave.)	1911-1916
PA	177	Philip Grossman (Otter & S. Park Sts.)	1874-1897

Freeland

PA	178a	Freeland Brewing Co. (500/524 Fern & South Sts.)	1900-1920
	178b	New Freeland Brewing Co.	1933-1934
	178c	Freeland Brewing Co.	1934-1939
	178d	Kehoe-Tilinski Brewing Corp.	1941-1942

Galeton
PA 179a Schwarzenbach Brewing Co. (25 Bridge St.) 1902-1920
179b Galeton Brewing Co. (Bridge & Sherman Sts.) 1933-1937
aka Schwarzenbach Brewing Co. (1934)

Gallitzin
PA 180a Ankenbauer & Gaegler 1879-1888
180b Geo. Ankenbauer 1888-1897

Germania
PA 181a Frank Meixner 1874-1880
181b John Schmid 1888-1891

PA 182a J. Schwarzenbach 1857-1884
182b Jos. Schwarzenbach & Sons (Roland, Herman & James) 1884-1892
182c Schwarzenbach Brewing Co. (Broadway) (moved to Galeton) 1892-1902

PA 183 Michael Schwarzenbach 1860-1864

Germantown (see Philadelphia)

Gettysburg
PA 184 John F. Bartel 1874-1879

PA 185 John Henning 1874-1879

Green Lane
PA 186a James O. Hendricks 1893-1904
186b Samuel Jerzy 1904-1905
186c Perkiomen Valley Brewing Co. 1905-1907
186d Perkiomen Valley Brewery, Samuel Jerzy 1907-1910
186e Perkiomen Valley Brewing Co. 1910-1915
186f Perkiomen Valley Brewery, Robert Rother 1915-1916

Greensburg
PA 187a John Hagl 1874-1888
187b Greensburg Brewing Co. 1888-1920
187c Greensburg Brewing Co. (305 Alwine Ave.) 1933-1936
187d Victor Brewing Co. 1936-1938
187e Old Reliable Brewing Co. 1941-1942

PA 188a Star Brewing Co. 1905-1920
188b Club Brewing Co. (801 S. Main St.) 1933-1934

Greentown
PA 189 J. L. Schnell & Bro. 1878-1880

Gulf Mills
PA 190 Gulf Brewery 1893-1895

Hamburg
PA 191a George Ulmer 1874-1875
191b Christian Maier 1875-1877
191c Jacob Bruckman 1877-1880

Hancock (see Hemlock)

Hanover
PA 192 John Neiderhofer 1874-1884

PA 193 John M. Wolf 1874-1875

Harrisburg
PA 194a Barnitz Brewery c1854
194b (Henry) Fink & (Christian) Boyer (312-320 Forster & James St.) 1862-1875
194c Henry Fink, Keystone Brewery 1875-1898
194d Henry Fink's Sons, Keystone Brewery 1898-1909
194e Fink Brewing Co. 1909-1920
194f Fink Brewing Co. 1933-1934

PA 195 Geo. Biester 1875- ?

PA 196a George Doehne (322 Chestnut & 29 S. Dewberry Sts.) 1865-1910
196b George Doehne Brewery 1910-1920
196c George Doehne Brewery, George & Charles A. Doehne 1933-1939

PA 197 Charles Engel 1844-1844

Harrisburg (cont.)

PA	198a	Koenig & Bro. (Edward & John), Centennial Brewery	1875-1877
	198b	Christian A. Dressel, Centennial Brewery (207 Chesnut St.)	1877-1893
	198c	Graupner & Bauer	1893-1893
	198d	Robert H. Graupner, Centennial Brewery (261 S. 11th St.)	1893-1895
	198e	Harrisburg Consumers Brewing and Bottling Co.	1895-1903
	198f	Robert H. Graupner Brewery	1903-1905
	198g	Estate of Robert H. Graupner	1905-1910
	198h	Robert H. Graupner's Brewery (829/841 Market & 10th Sts.)	1910-1911
	198i	Graupner's Brewery, M. Graupner	1911-1920
	198j	Mary L. Graupner Estate, trading as Rob't H. Graupner Mfg.	? -1933
	198k	Robert H. Graupner, aka Robert H. Graupner's Brewery	1933-1935
	198l	Robert H. Graupner, Inc.	1935-1951
PA	199	E. F. Leimbach (213 Chestnut St.)	1882-1882
PA	200	National Brewing Co.	1915-1915
PA	201a	John Walford	1874-1877
	201b	Byrne & Ogden	1877-1879
	201c	Philip Elbett	1879-1884

Harrison City

PA	202a	John Brewer	1874-1882
	202b	Peter Schmitt	1893- ?
	202c	G. W. Luther	1900- ?

Harrisonville

PA	203	C. A. Brown	1888-1888

Hawley

PA	204	Samuel Case	1874-1875
PA	205	Hans Distler	1896-1897

Hazleton

PA	206a	(Henry) Bach & (Severin) Teufel	1849-1856
	206b	Bach & (Gottfried) Ulmer	1856- ?
	206c	Henry Bach	1874-1879
	206d	(John) Arnold & (John) Krell	1879-1893
	206e	Hazleton Lion Brewery, John Arnold (Mine & Mill Sts.)	1893-1897
	206f	Pennsylvania Central Brewing Co. of Scranton, John Arnold Dept.	1897-1931
PA	207	Hazleton Brewing Co.	1897-1910
PA	208a	Pilsener Brewing Co. (Seybert St. & Diamond Ave.)	1906-1920
	208b	Pilsener Brewing Co. (N. Cedar St. & E. Diamond Ave.)	1933-1954

Heidelberg

PA	209	Ambrose Schmidt	1874-1879

Hemlock

PA	210	Theodore Sell	1888-1890

Hollidaysburg

PA	211	George Ankenbauer	1874-1875
PA	212a	A. Buckberger	1879- ?
	212b	Ferdinand Bender	? -1888
	212c	Gebhard Bender	1888-1890
PA	213a	John B. Haid	1880-1882
	213b	Mrs. Mathilda Haid	1882-1884
	213c	Chas. J. Sprenger	1884-1890
PA	214a	F. W. Rauch	1874-1877
	214b	J. J. Springer	1877-1879

Homestead

PA	215a	Chas. A. Schulz	1890-1891
	215b	Homestead Brewing Co. (6th & West Sts.)	1893-1895
	215c	Homestead Brewing Co.	1899-1904
	215d	Independent Brewing Co., Homestead Brewery (br. of Pittsburgh)	1904-1920
	215e	Homestead Ice Co., aka Homestead Ice & Brewing Co. (602/614 Hayes St. & 207 7th Ave.)	1937-1953

Honesdale

PA 216a	Kessler & Burkhardt		1852-1868
216b	(August) Hartung & (Peter) Kranz		1868-1890
216c	August Hartung (Brewery St.)		1890-1897
216d	Pennsylvania Central Brewing Co., A. Hartung Dept.		1897-1910
PA 217a	Jacob Lauer		1882- ?
217b	John Guckenberger		? -1890
217c	M. B. Guckenberger		1890-1896
217d	Schimpff Brewing Co.		1896-1897

Huntingdon

PA 218	Schneider & Zilius		? -1874

Hyde Park

PA 219a	Hyde Park Brewing and Ice Mfg. Co.		1905-1920
219b	Hyde Park Brewing Co.		1933-1934
219c	A. Kim, Victor Brewing Co.		1936-1937
219d	Hyde Park Brewing Corp.		1937-1938

Indiana

PA 220a	Indian Brewing Co. (Oak & 11th Sts.)		1905-1915
220b	Indian Brewing Co.		1918-1920
220c	Indiana Breweries, Inc. (1079 Oak St.)		1933-1934
220d	Penn-Indiana Brewing Co.		1934-1937
220e	Old Indian Brewing Co.		1937-1939
PA 221	John Rogner		1874-1875
PA 222a	J. C. Stadtmiller		1874-1877
222b	George Stadtmiller		1877-1884
222c	F. M. Doberneck		1884-1891

Irwin

PA 223a	Crescent Brewing Co.		1904-1920
223b	Friara, Inc., Crescent Brewery	NP	1934-1934
PA 224	Mutual Union Brewing Co.		1905-1905

Jackson

PA 225	Alex Schilling		1874-1875

Jeannette

PA 226a	National Brewing Co. (Gaskill Ave.)		1896-1899
226b	Pittsburgh Brewing Co., National Brewery		1899-1904
226c	Pittsburgh Brewing Co., Jeannette Brewery		1904-1920
PA 227a	Victor Brewing Co. (11th St. & Penn Ave.)		1908-1920
227b	Victor Brewing Co. (1100 Penn Ave.)		1933-1941
227c	Fort Pitt Brewing Co. (br. of Sharpsburg)		1941-1955

Jefferson

PA 228	John Werner		1874-1890

Jenner Township (see Boswell)

Jersey Shore

PA 229a	Andrew Kempf		1874-1877
229b	Charles Hauser		1877-1893

Johnstown

PA 230	Jacob Albrecht		1890-1890
PA 231a	Cambria Brewing Co. (Broad St. & 4th Ave.)		1897-1920
231b	Cambria Brewing Corp.(401/407 Broad St. & 4th Ave.)		1933-1937
231c	Cambria Brewing Co.		1937-1939
PA 232a	John Emmerling (102/110 Horner St.)		1878-1904
232b	Emmerling Brewing Co.		1904-1920
PA 233a	Zack Entress		1850- ?
233b	Seeger & Wehn		1874-1877
233c	Charles Wehn		1877-1880
233d	J. Widmann		1880-1884
233e	John Goenner		1884-1888
233f	Margaretha Goenner		1888-1892
233g	Goenner & Co. (3rd Ave. & Power St.)		1892-1920
233h	Goenner & Co.		1933-1954

Johnstown (cont.)

PA	234	Germania Brewing Co. (6th Ave.)	1907-1920
PA	235	Oscar Grafe	1874-1875
PA	236a	Henry Hausman	1874-1877
	236b	W. H. Beamly	1877-1878
PA	237a	Max Heubach	1874-1879
	237b	Lambert & Kress (173 Washington St.)	1880-1893
PA	238	Lawrence Kost	1895-1906
PA	239a	Jacob Meier & Bro.	1884-1886
	239b	Jacob Meier	1886-1888

Kersey's

PA	240	Alois Uhrman	1888-1897

Kingston

PA	241	Anthracite Beer Co.	1899-1899

Lancaster

PA	242	John Arnold (Mifflin St. between S. Duke & S. Christian Sts.)	c1842
PA	243	Andrew Eberly (N. Charlotte & Lemon Sts.)	c1863-1864
PA	244a	Jacob Effinger (28 S. Queen St.)	c1863
	244b	Effinger, Schut & Kegel (Locust & Rockland Sts.)	c1869-1877
	244c	James Effinger	1877-1880
PA	245a	G. H. Erisman (329 Church St.)	c1871
	245b	Michael Bastendorff, Lion Brewery	1874-1877
	245c	D. B. Landis	1877-1882
PA	246	Jacob Fisher (133 N. Queen St.)	c1863-1864
PA	247	John Franciscus (104 S. Queen St.)	c1863-1864
PA	248	Phillip Frank (S. Lime & Locust Sts.)	c1872
PA	249a	Henry Franke (230 N. Prince St.)	1863-1878
	249b	Koehler & Casper (328 Middle St.)	1878-1889
	249c	Adeline Sprenger, Lyon Brewery	1889-1891
PA	250	Bernard & John Haag (43 W. King St. & S. Water St.)	1853-1860
PA	251	Jacob Kieffer (W. Strawberry & W. Vine Sts.)	c1863-1868
PA	252	Charles Knapp (54 N. Queen St.)	c1863-1868
PA	253a	Lawrence Knapp (62 E. King St.)	1859-1870
	253b	Lawrence Knapp (135 Locust St.)	1870-1886
	253c	Jos. Haefner	1886-1907
	253d	Joseph Haefner Estate	1907-1911
	253e	Joseph Haefner, Empire Brewery	1911-1914
	253f	Empire Brewery	1914-1920
	253g	Haefner Brewing Co. (123/143 Locust St.)	1933-1946
	253h	Lancaster Brewery, Inc.	1946-1949
PA	254	Barnett Kuhlman (Strasburg Road)	c1863-1868
PA	255	Christian Maier (Middle & Rockland Sts.)	c1869
PA	256	G. E. Richman	1878-1879
PA	257	Frank A. Rieker & Co., Lion Brewery	1873-1873
PA	258a	Schoenberger & (John) Miller (Locust & Rockland Sts.)	1855-1863
	258b	Augustus Schoenberger	1863-1873
	258c	W. A. Schoenberger	1874-1884
PA	259a	Elizabeth Sprenger, Eagle Brewery	1859-1863
	259b	Joseph Wacker	1865-1877
	259c	S. V. S. Wacker Bros.	1877-1879
	259d	C. C. Wacker & Bro.	1879-1884
	259e	Chas. V. Wacker & Bro. (203 W. Walnut & Water Sts.)	1884-1920
	259f	Old Lancaster Brewing Co. (201/223 W. Walnut St.)	1933-1938
	259g	Wacker Brewing Co.	1939-1956

Lancaster (cont.)

PA	260a	John A. Sprenger (407 E. Orange St.)	1842-1857
	260b	J. A. Sprenger (125/127 E. King & Duke Sts.)	1857-1870
	260c	J. A. Sprenger (205 Locust & Lime Sts.)	1870-1883
	260d	Mrs. Adeline Sprenger, Excelsior Brewery	1883-1891
	260e	J. A. Sprenger	1891-1895
	260f	Sprenger Brewing Co.	1895-1920
	260g	Sprenger Brewing Co. (205/217 Loucst St.)	1933-1951
PA	261	Teufel & Wisemann	1890-1890
PA	262a	John Wittlinger (W. King St. & Columbia Pk.)	1847-1870
	262b	Felix Senn	1870-1874
	262c	H. Strobel & Co. (F. A. Rieker)	1874-1876
	262d	Frank A. Rieker, Star Brewery (602/606 W. King St.)	1876-1907
	262e	Frank A. Rieker Estate	1907-1912
	262f	F. A. Rieker Brewing Co.	1912-1920
	262g	Penn State Brewery (W. Rieker & 1st Sts. & Brewery Ave.)	1933-1935
	262h	Penn-Star Brewery Co. (554 W. King St.)	1935-1938
PA	263	Hilaire Zaeppel (3 N. Duke St.)	c1860
PA	264	Charles Zech (707 W. Orange St. & Columbia Ave.)	1886-1897

Lansdowne

PA	265	Fernwood Brewing Co. (Baltimore Pike & Melrose Ave.)	1934-1941

Latrobe

PA	266	Benedictine Society (of St. Vincent's Abbey) aka St. Vincent Brewing Co., Beatty (1884-1888)	1856-1898
PA	267a	Latrobe Brewing Co. (N. Ligonier Ave.)	1893-1899
	267b	Pittsburgh Brewing Co., Latrobe Brewery aka Latrobe Brewing Co. (1899-1900)	1899-1920
	267c	Latrobe Brewing Co. (119 Ligonier & Maple Sts.)	1934-
PA	268a	Loyalhanna Brewing Co. (Jefferson St.)	1901-1906
	268b	Independent Brewing Co., Loyalhanna Brewery (br. of Pittsburgh)	1906-1920
	268c	Loyalhanna Brewery (owned by Duquesne Brewing Co., Pitts.) NP	1934-1934
PA	269	Union Brewing Co.	1899-1899

Lawrence

PA	270	Charles Schafer	1875- ?

Lebanon

PA	271a	Joseph Hoelzle	1874-1884
	271b	John A. Goerner	1884-1888
	271c	John Goerner & Co.	1888-1890
PA	272a	Lebanon Brewing Co.	1884-1893
	272b	New Lebanon Brewing Co.	1893-1920
	272c	Lebanon Valley Brewing Co. (840 N. 7th St.)	1934-1959
PA	273a	Iron City Brewing Co.	1889-1920
	273b	P. & H. Brewing Co.	1933-1934
PA	274a	Union Brewing Co. (216/220 N. 12th St.)	1891-1898
	274b	Gustav Schneider	1898-1900
	274c	Chas. F. Schneider, Union Brewery	1900-1906
	274d	Schneider Brewing Co.	1906-1910
PA	275a	John Yost, Jr.	1874-1877
	275b	F. A. Leubert	1877-1879
	275c	D. Behney	1879-1880
	275d	Schick & Tice	1880-1882

Lewistown

PA	276a	Henry Bossinger	1874-1884
	276b	Fredericka Bossinger	1884-1895
PA	277a	Theo. Haeben	1874-1880
	277b	Mrs. W. Haeben	1880-1884

Liberty

PA	278a	Miller, Zeifle & Co.	1875- ?
	278b	John Zeifle	? -1884

Ligonier

PA 279a Ligonier Brewing Co. 1908-1910
279b Idlewild Brewing Co. 1910-1911

Lilly

PA 280 Francis Bradly 1896-1897

Lititz

PA 281 Zartman & Scheef 1884-1884

Lock Haven

PA 282a (Joseph) Bacher & (Joseph) Garger 1860-1862
282b Joseph Bacher 1862-1865
282c (Jacob) Widmann & (Fidel) Pfeffer 1865-1866
282d Jacob Widmann 1866-1873
282e (Rudolph) Widmann & (David) Dubler 1873-1874
282f Rudolph Widmann 1874-1915
282g Mountain Spring Brewery 1915-1920

PA 283a Philip Fable 1863- ?
283b Charles P. Fable ? -1883
283c Fred C. Lucas, Castania Brewery 1883-1920

PA 284a Flaig & Gackle 1874-1877
284b Matthew Flaig 1877-1884
284c Geo. W. Luther 1884-1888

PA 285 Gans & Hippe 1874-1875

PA 286 Lockport Brewing Co. 1933-1942

PA 287a Valentine Shomer 1874-1875
287b Mary Pfeffer 1875-1880
287c C. Morgenthau 1880-1884

Loretto

PA 288 Jos. Bengele 1878-1879

Lower Saucon

PA 289a Peter Hilknie 1874-1877
289b Edward Benz 1877-1884

Loyalsock

PA 290a Smith & Moeschlin 1884- ?
290b Welker & Goodbrod 1890-1897
290c John Welker 1903-1904

Lucyville (see Roscoe)

Lykens

PA 291a Hiram Bueck (South St.) 1860-1884
291b Estate of H. Bueck 1884-1891
291c Mrs. Barbara A. Bueck 1891-1895
291d Lykens Brewing Co. 1895-1917
291e Katherine Wentzler 1933-1936
291f Wentzler Brewery 1936-1940

Madera

PA 292a Edward Kraft 1890-1891
292b John & Andrew Vesser ? -1909
292c John Vesser 1909-1911
292d Edward L. Binder 1911-1916
292e Amos C. Hensel 1916-1920

Mahanoy City

PA 293a Chas. D. Kaier 1880-1882
293b Chas. D. Kaier & Co. 1882-1884
293c Francis X. Kaier 1884-1891
293d Chas. D. Kaier Brewing Co. 1891-1894
293e Chas. D. Kaier Co., Ltd. (67/79 N. Main & W. Laurel Sts.) 1894-1920
293f Charles D. Kaier Co. (Oak & Laurel Sts. & 67/79 N. Main St.) 1933-1966
293g Charles D. Kaier Co. (br. of Henry F. Ortlieb Brewing Co., Philadelphia) 1866-1868

Manheim			
PA	294a	David B. Landis	1874-1877
	294b	Frederick Loehrer	1877-1884
	294c	Baumler & Hefft	1884-1888
	294d	Louis J. Hefft	1888-1890
Manor Station			
PA	295	W. J. Snyder	1888-1888
Marietta			
PA	296	Henry R. Haeffner	1874-1875
PA	297a	Fred Manlick	1874-1884
	297b	Ernest Manlick	1884-1897
PA	298	Geo. Vogel	1880-1880
Masontown			
PA	299a	Masontown Brewing Co.	1905-1920
	299b	Masontown Brewery, Palo Bros. (Fairbanks)	NP 1934-1934
	299c	West Masontown Brewery Co.	1937-1940
Matamoras			
PA	300	Robert Koenig	1874-1875
Mauch Chunk			
PA	301	Mathilde Gerster (East Mauch Chunk)	1874-1882
PA	302a	John Schaefer	1860- ?
	302b	Simon Meister	1874-1877
	302c	Weysser & Zinser	1877-1879
	302d	John R. G. Weysser, West End Brewery (301 Broadway)	1879-1910
	302e	Hugo Ortlieb	1910-1912
	302f	Ortlieb Brewing Co.	1912-1915
PA	303a	P. & P. Schweibinz (2nd & North Sts.)	1880-1882
	303b	P. Schweibinz	1882-1884
	303c	L. Schweibinz	1884-1888
	303d	Pius Schweibinz aka Estate of Pius Schweibinz (1894-1895)	1888-1912
	303e	Ortlieb Brewing Co.	1912-1920
	303f	Sterling Brewing Co., Inc. (20/22 N. 2nd St.)	1933-1934
	303g	Mauch Chunk Brewing Co.	1934-1941
McKees Rock (Stone Township)			
PA	304a	First National Brewing Co.	1901-1904
	304b	Independent Brewing Co., First National Brewery (br. Pitts.)	1904-1920
	304c	Duquesne Brewing Co., First National Brewery (Plant 2) (Thomas St. at Nat Alley & McKees Ave.)	1933-1951
McKeesport			
PA	305a	McKeesport Brewing Co.	1897-1899
	305b	Pittsburgh Brewing Co., McKeesport Brewery (Jerome & Ryan Sts.) aka McKeesport Brewing Co. (1899-1900)	1899-1920
PA	306	Ernest Reichenbach	1874-1884
PA	307a	Tube City Brewing Co. (12th & Walnut Sts.)	1903-1920
	307b	Tube City Brewing Co. (1200 Walnut St.)	1933-1955
Mead			
PA	308a	S. S. Thurston	1874-1875
	308b	Fred Moessner	1875-1877
	308c	E. A. Smith	1877-1879
	308d	Dippold & Miller	1879-1882
Meadville			
PA	309a	N. Dudenhoeffer	1888-1897
	309b	Geo. Dudenhoeffer	1897-1899
PA	310	Jacob Fuess	1850-1852
PA	311a	Hetherington & Downer	1884-1886
	311b	Robert Hetherington	1886-1888
	311b	Young & Co.	1888-1891

Meadville (cont.)

PA	312a	Frank Schwab (French Creek Road)	1888-1903
	312b	Meadville Brewing Co.	1903-1905
	312c	Union Brewing Co.	1905-1906
	312d	Meadville Brewing Co.	1906-1916
PA	313a	Walster, Echnoz & Curty (Terrace St. & Oak Ave.)	1891-1895
	313b	Walster & Echnoz	1895-1906
	313c	Valentine Hofmann	1906-1907
	313d	Julius F. Echnoz	1907-1910
	313e	City Ale Brewery Co. aka City Brewery (1910)	1910-1913
	313f	French Creek Valley Brewing Co.	1913-1916
	313g	Valley Mead Brewing Co. (Terrace St. Ext.) NP	1934-1934

Meyersdale

PA	314	Henry Eisfeller	1875- ?
PA	315	Meyersdale Brewing Co.	1901-1920

Middletown

PA	316	G. E. Reichmann	1874-1875

Mill Creek Township (see Erie)

Millerstown

PA	317	Gottlob Hoch	1874-1875

Millvale (see Pittsburgh)

Minersville

PA	318	Daniel Freiler	1874-1875
PA	319a	F. J. Kear & Co.	1879-1879
	319b	F. G. Kear	1879-1880
PA	320a	Charles Zapf & Co. (E. Sunbury St.)	1875-1901
	320b	Charles Zapf	1901-1904
	320c	Charles Zapf & Co.	1904-1909
	320d	Charles Zapf	1909-1920
PA	321a	Miners Brewing Co.	1890-1890
	321b	Miners Brewing Co.	1904-1906
	321c	Union Brewing Co.	1906-1907

Monessen

PA	322a	Monessen Brewing Co.	1902- ?
	322b	Independent Brewing Co., Monessen Brewery (br. of Pittsburgh)	1905-1920
	322c	Monessen Brewery (owned by Duquesne Brewing, Pitts.) NP	1934-1934

Monongahela

PA	323a	Anton Brewing Co. (Railroad St.)	1899-1904
	323b	Independent Brewing Co., Globe Brewery (br. of Pittsburgh)	1904-1920
	323c	Stag Brewing Co. (West Alley & Railroad St.)	1933-1937
PA	324	William Booth (Carroll Township)	1888-1902
PA	325a	Henry Harrison	1888-1891
	325b	William Harrison (Carroll Township)	1891-1902
PA	326a	Wm. J. Markel	1888-1890
	326b	M. J. Markel	1890-1891
	326c	Wm. Tyrrell	1891-1893
	326d	Monongahela Brewing Co.	1896-1897
PA	327	Thomas Morrison	1898-1901
PA	328	Riverview Brewing Co.	1905-1910
PA	329a	Andreas Roth	1895-1898
	329b	Helena Roth (Carroll Township)	1898-1910
	329c	Jos. S. Roth	1910-1920
	329d	Roth Brewing Co.	1933-1935
PA	330	John Sax	1875- ?

Morrellville

PA	331	Jacob Albrecht	1888-1888

Morrisville

PA 332 F. Haas & Son 1884-1884

Mount Carbon (see Pottsville)

Mount Carmel

PA 333a Anthracite Brewing Co. 1897-1920
333b John P. Muldowney (Lehigh Ave. & Turnpike St.) 1933-1936
333c Mt. Carmel Brewery (Lehigh Ave. & Poplar St.) 1936-1951

Mount Joy

PA 334a Frank Lenhard 1874-1877
334b Alois Bube 1877-1884
334c Charles Bube 1884-1891
334d Alois Bube 1891-1907
334e Alois Bube Estate 1907-1915
334f Mount Joy Brewery, John Hallgren 1915-1920

Mount Oliver

PA 335a Hill Top Brewing Co. (132 Southern Ave.) 1902-1904
335b Independent Brewing Co., Hill Top Brewery (br. of Pittsburgh) 1904-1920

Mount Pleasant

PA 336a Mt. Pleasant Brewing Co. 1894-1899
336b Pittsburgh Brewing Co., Mt. Pleasant Brewery 1899-1920
aka Mt. Pleasant Brewing Co. (1899-1900)

Muhlenberg (see Reading)

Muncy

PA 337a Godfrey Harp 1874-1877
337b William Harp 1877-1880

Nanticoke

PA 338a George W. Flock Brewing Co. 1895-1897
338b Susquehanna Brewing Co. (controlled by Stegmaier Brewing Co., Wilkes-Barre, PA) (Alden Road & Main St.) 1897-1920

Natrona

PA 339 John Brewer 1884-1884

New Bethlehem

PA 340 Ludwig Freuger 1890-1890

PA 341a New Bethlehem Brewing Co. 1908-1915
341b B. B. B. B. Brewing Co. 1915-1920

New Castle

PA 342a C. Koch 1878-1884
342b F. L. Genkinger 1884-1891
342c Wm. F. Carthans (South St.) 1891-1896
342d New Castle Brewing Co. 1896-1911

PA 343 Fred Roth 1890-1890

PA 344a Adam Treser 1858-1880
344b Treser & Bollinger 1880-1882
344c Adam Treser & Son 1882-1888
344d John Treser 1888-1891
344e Carl Kirst (124 S. Railroad St.) 1891-1893
344f John Kirst 1893-1895
344g E. C. Pagenstecker 1895-1897
344h Standard Brewing Co. (510 Sampson St.) 1897-1910
344i Jacobson Bros. 1910-1911
344j Standard Brewing Co. 1911-1920
344k Union Brewing Co. (506/528 Sampson St.) 1933-1948

New Kensington

PA 345a Gambrinus Brewing Co. 1897-1900
345b Gambrinus Brewing Co. 1900-1904

PA 346a New Kensington Brewing Co. (9th St. & 1st Ave.) 1897-1904
346b Independent Brewing Co., New Kensington Brewery (br. Pitts.) 1904-1920

New Salem

PA 347a Johnson Brewery 1906-1908
347b Johnson Brewing Co. 1908-1920

Norristown

PA 348a A. R. Cox (257 W. Main St.) 1874-1891
348b Adam Scheidt Brewing Co., Plant 2 1891-1896

PA 349a Moeschlin Bros. 1870-1873
349b Charles Scheidt (Marshall & Barbadoes Sts.) 1873-1882
349c C. & A. Scheidt 1882-1884
349d Adam Scheidt 1884-1890
349e Adam Scheidt Brewing Co., Plant 1 1890-1920
349f Adam Scheidt Brewing Co. (151 W. Marshall St.) 1933-1954
349g Adam Scheidt Brewing Co. (br. of C. Schmidt & Sons, Phila.) 1954-1960
349h Valley Forge Brewing Co. (br. of C. Schmidt & Sons, Phila.) 1960-1963
349i C. Schmidt & Sons, Inc., aka Prior Brewery (Norristown branch of Philadelphia, PA) 1963-1975

Northampton

PA 350a Northampton Brewing Co. 1898-1920
350b Northampton Brewing Corp. (1247/1267 Newport Ave.) 1933-1950

North East

PA 351 James Bannister 1874-1884

North Huntington

PA 352 Conrad Hufnagel 1874-1884

North Manheim

PA 353 Hillside Brewery 1875- ?

Oakland

PA 354 Frank Neinau 1884-1884

Oil City

PA 355a John J. Saltzmann 1881-1882
355b John J. Saltzmann & Sons 1882-1888
355c John J. Saltzmann, Jr. 1888-1890
355d Saltzmann Bros. (Palace Hill) 1890-1920
355e Oil City Brewing Co., Inc. (4 Union St.) 1933-1936

PA 356a Charles Wurster 1875-1880
356b Geo. & Philip Wurster 1880-1882
356c Wurster & Snyder 1882-1884

Osceola

PA 357a August Muller 1884- ?
357b James Taylor 1893- ?

Patton

PA 358 Patton Brewing Co. (4th & Herriman Ave.) 1905-1916

Penn Township

PA 359 Chas. Cunliffe 1874-1875

Pennsbury

PA 360 William Penn c1683

Philadelphia

PA 361a Samuel Allen (57/59 N. 4th St.) c1790-1791
361b Samuel Allen (24 Wood St.) c1792-1793

PA 362 Adam Ambron (338 Dillwyn St.) 1875-1885

PA 363a Lorenz Amrhein, aka L. Amrhein & Son (3036 N. 6th & Clearfield) 1850-1890
363b (Lorenz) Amrhein & (Albert) Hoch (3036 N. 6th & Indiana Sts.) 1890-1893
363c Amrhein Bros. (George & Joseph) 1893-1898
363d Independent Brewing Co. 1898-1913

PA 364a Lawrence Amrhein (514 N. Front St.) 1868-1873
364b Eliza F. Leimbach (1749/1751 Brodine & 514 N. Front St.) 1873-1880
364c Frederick Goelze 1880-1884

PA 365a Jacob & Peter Baltz (3rd St.) 1851-1862
365b J. & P. Baltz (31st & Thompson Sts.) 1862-1881
365c J. & P. Baltz Brewing Co. 1881-1920

PA 366 Jacob Bauder (400 Lynd & 616 N. 4th Sts.) 1879-1891

PA 367 Emil Baumner (921 N. 29th St.) 1878-1880

Philadelphia (cont.)

PA	368a	Francis Beckler (also Ignatz & Xavier Beckler)	1859-1869
	368b	Wm. & Louis Beckler (11th, Oxford & Mervine Sts.)	1873-1877
	368c	Charles Wolters	1877-1886
	368d	Prospect Brewing Co.	1886-1920
PA	369	(Xavier) Beckler & (Louis J.) Wolf (Edgemont & Ann Sts.)	1869-1873
PA	370	John Benk (320 Poplar St.)	1859-1860
PA	371a	Jacob Bentz (508 N. 3rd St.)	1864-1865
	371b	(Jacob) Bentz & (Jacob) Reyle (31st between Jefferson & Master Sts.)	1866-1869
	371c	Fred A. Poth (31st & Jefferson Sts.)	1870-1887
	371d	F. A. Poth Brewing Co.	1887-1893
	371e	F. A. Poth & Sons	1893-1920
	371f	Poth Brewing Co., Inc.	1933-1936
PA	372a	Bergdoll & Psotta (3365 Ridge Ave.)	1853-1857
	372b	Hilderbrand & Stein	1857-1859
	372c	John Stein	1860-1885
	372d	Henry Stein	1885-1890
PA	373a	Bergdoll & (Peter) Schemm (508 Vine St.)	1859-1850
	373b	Bergdoll & Psotta	1851-1857
	373c	Bergdoll & Psotta (29th & Parrish Sts.)	1857-1876
	373d	Louis Bergdoll	1876-1881
	373e	Louis Bergdoll Brewing Co.	1881-1920
	373f	Louis Bergdoll Brewing Co., aka City Park Brewing Co.	1933-1934
PA	374	Charles W. Bergner (476 N. 7th St.)	1854-1857
PA	375a	Gustavus Bergner (586 N. 7th St.)	1854-1857
	375b	Gustavus Bergner (32nd, 33rd, Thompson & Master Sts.)	1857-1869
	375c	Bergner & Engel	1869-1879
	375d	Bergner & Engel Brewing Co., Plant 1	1879-1920
PA	376	Bergner & Engel Brewing Co., Plant 3 (33rd, Thompson & Pennsylvania Ave.)	1894-1920
PA	377a	(Philip) Bless & (Henry) Bergmann (181 St. John St.)	1855-1858
	377b	Philip Bless (612 St. John St.)	1859-1863
PA	378	William Boefflins (436 St. John St.)	1857-1862
PA	379	John Borden (1609 Pine St.)	1860-1860
PA	380	H. Bower (1236 Hutchinson)	1863-1865
PA	381a	John Bower (33rd & Master Sts.)	1874-1877
	381b	Estate of John Bower	1877-1884
	381c	Burg & Pfaender	1885-1896
	381d	John M. Pfaender	1896-1900
	381e	John G. F. Pfaender	1900-1901
	381f	Miller & Pfaender	1901-1903
	381g	Emma C. Bergdoll (33rd & Master Sts.)	1903-1913
	381h	Bergdoll Brewing Co., Inc.	1913-1915
PA	382a	Chas. L. Braunwarth (919 N. 28th & 2734 Cambridge Sts.)	1888-1898
	382b	Charles Pra, Crown Brewery	1898-1898
	382c	Pra, Kuebeler & Kayser, Crown Brewery	1898-1898
	382d	Commonwealth Brewing Co.	1898-1916
PA	383a	Francis L. Brehm (129 Coates St.)	1843-1858
	383b	Francis L. Brehm (323 Coates St.)	1858-1870
PA	384a	Charles Bremer, Jr. (3246 Germantown Ave.)	1888-1891
	384b	Rising Sun Brewing Co.	1891-1915
	384c	Rising Sun Brewing Co. (1729 Marvine St.)	1915-1920
PA	385	Jacob Burd (285 Callowhill St.)	1815-1816
PA	386	George Burkhardt (56 New Market above Callowhill St.)	1850-1857
PA	387	George Butz (10th & Callowhill Sts.)	1863-1866
PA	388a	Charles Christmann (1605 Cabot & 1604 Thompson Sts.)	1878-1889
	388b	Charles Christmann (27th & Huntingdon Sts.)	1889-1896

Philadelphia (cont.)

PA	389a	Alois Christoph (117/125 W. Thompson St.)	1882-1884
	389b	Henry Hauser	1884-1886
PA	390a	Class & Nachod Brewing Co. (1801/1823 N. 10th & Montgomery)	1913-1920
	390b	Class & Nachod Breiwng Co.	1933-1936
	390c	Poth Brewing Co.	1936-1941
PA	391	Thos. Clements (292 Queen St.)	1884-1884
PA	392	James Connor (819 Carpenter St.)	1879-1888
PA	393a	Jacob Conrad, Keystone State Brewery (27th & Parrish Sts.)	1873-1907
	393b	Jacob Conrad Brewing Co., Keystone State Brewery	1907-1910
PA	394	John Cooper (2nd & Huntington Sts.)	1872-1877
PA	395	Corporation Brewery	c1849
PA	396a	Robert Coutrenny (113 Edward St.)	1859-1860
	396b	Borden & Brother	1860-1861
	396c	Borden & Brother (113 Edward St.) & Christian Schmidt (117 Edward St.) (in same building)	1861-1863
	396d	Christian Schmidt	1863-1892
	396e	C. Schmidt & Sons (Henry Co., Edward A. & Frederick W.)	1892-1902
	396f	C. Schmidt & Sons Brewing Co.	1902-1920
	396g	C. Schmidt & Sons, Inc. (113/127 Edward St.) aka Bergheim Brewing Co. (1976+) aka Pilsener Brewing Co. (1973+) aka Reading Brewing Co. (1976+) aka Rheingold Brewing Co. (1977+) aka Ruppert Brewery (1977+) aka Valley Forge Brewing Co.	1933-1981
	396h	Christian Schmidt Brewing Co., aka Ortlieb Brewing Co.	1981-
PA	397a	George Croskey (21 Sansom St.)	1809-1910
	397b	(George) Croskey & (Benj.) Say (110 New & 116 Vine Sts.)	1810-1817
PA	398a	Dawson & Spowden (134 Water St.)	1784-1790
	398b	William Dawson (79/81 Chestnut St.)	1790-1807
	398c	(William) Dawson & (William) Morrison	1808-1828
	398d	M. L. Dawson & Co. (10th & Filbert Sts.)	1829-1849
	398e	(Charles) Poultney, (Frederick) Collins & (Wm.) Massey	1849-1854
	398f	Poultney & Massey	1854-1857
	398g	(Wm.) Massey, (Fred) Collins & Co. (Samuel Houston)	1857-1866
	398h	Massey, Houston & Co.	1866-1869
	398i	William Massey & Co.	1869-1882
	398j	William Massey Brewing Co.	1882-1892
PA	399	Simon Delbert (23rd & Sansom Sts.)	1860-1866
PA	400	Diehm Bros. (900 N. Front St.)	1885-1888
PA	401a	Frederick L. Dithmar (520 N. 3rd St.)	1835-1843
	401b	(Fred) Dithmar & (George) Butz	1843-1858
	401c	Dithmar & Butz (934/942 N. 3rd St.)	1858-1865
	401d	Thomas O'Neill & Co.	1866-1866
	401e	(Mary A.) Gaul & (George) Carey	1867-1870
	401f	(George) Carey & (George) Riehl	1871-1877
	401g	George Carey & Co. (Robert Conway & Julia Carey)	1877-1892
PA	402	(Fred) Dithmar & (George) Butz (32nd & Thompson Sts.)	1859-1860
PA	403a	William Dyer & John Dorey (2nd & Noble Sts.)	1804-1808
	403b	William Dyer (121 Green St.)	1809-1828
	403c	William C. Rudman's Eagle Brewery (309/321 Green St.)	1829-1864
	403d	Robert Gray	1865-1875
	403e	(Charles) Ashby, (William) McLean & Co. (Wm. B. Taylor)	1876-1880
PA	404	(Max) Eble & (Christian) Herter (32nd, 33rd & Thompson Sts.)	1873-1891
PA	405a	Charles Ehinger (438 Dauphin St.)	1881-1892
	405b	Lehmann & Miller	1892-1895
PA	406	Charles Ehinger (1150 Germantown Ave.)	1900-1912
PA	407	Eich & White (2312 Ridge Ave.)	1888-1888

Philadelphia (cont.)

PA	408a	Franz Eisele (2630 Girard Ave.)	1878-1880
	408b	Franz Eisele (2205 Richmond Ave.)	1880-1881
PA	409a	Franz Eisele & Co., aka Eiselle & Elsasser (31st & Thompson)	1859-1868
	409b	Franz Eisele	1868-1872
	409c	(Charles) Goldbeck & (Francis) Eisele	1873-1874
	409d	Goldbeck & (Charles) Boehmer	1874-1876
	409e	Franz Eisele	1876-1879
	409f	Arnholt & (Henry) Schaefer	1884-1887
	409g	Arnholt & Schaefer Brewing Co.	1887-1920
	409h	Arnholt & Schaefer Brewing Co.	NP 1934-1934
PA	410a	Zachariah Endrifs (Brewers Alley between 2nd & 3rd Sts.)	c1784-1789
	410b	Samuel Allen	c1794-1803
PA	411a	Charles C. Engel (26/28 Dillwyn St.)	1844-1847
	411b	(Charles) Engel & (Charles) Wolf, Plant 1	1847-1858
	411c	Engel & Wolf (352/354 Dillwyn St.)	1858-1870
PA	412	(Charles) Engel & (Charles) Wolf, Plant 2 (Pennsylvania Ave. near Columbia Bridge-Fountain Green)	1849-1870
PA	413	Mathias Engelke (835 St. John St.)	1873-1890
PA	414a	George Enser (1831 Frankford Ave. & Vienna St.)	? -1874
	414b	(George) Enser & (Christian) Theurer (2nd & Ontario Sts.)	1874-1879
	414c	Louisa Enser	1879-1880
	414d	John Spaeth	1880-1886
	414e	Spaeth, Krautter & Hess	1886-1888
	414f	Joseph Redford (2nd & Ontario Sts.)	1889-1891
	414g	Joseph Redford (411 Cherry St.)	1891-1891
PA	415a	Andrew Erdrich, Bridesburg Brewery (142/144 Ash & Brown Sts.)	1866-1886
	415b	Andrew Erdrich, Bridesburg Brewery (Bridge & Walker Sts.)	1886-1891
	415c	Andrew Erdrich & Son	1891-1920
PA	416	Casper Erwin (6 Elbow Lane)	1813-1816
PA	417a	George Esslinger (1012 Jefferson St.)	1868-1879
	417b	Louis Geiger	1879-1884
PA	418a	George Esslinger (412/422 Rugan St.)	1879-1893
	418b	George Esslinger & Son	1893-1906
	418c	George Esslinger & Son Brewing Co.	1906-1920
	418d	Esslinger's Inc., Plant 1 (911/913 Callowhill & 417 N. 10th)	1933-1964
PA	419a	Frederick Feil (2200/2204 Fairhill St.)	1878-1888
	419b	Frederick Feil (2207 N. 6th)	1888-1906
	419c	Fred Feil Brewing Co.	1906-1920
	419d	Fred Feil Brewing Co.	NP 1934-1934
PA	420	E. & L. Fielmeyer (2427 Ontario St.)	1890-1891
PA	421a	Joseph Fielmeyer (2423/2425 N. Broad St.)	1874-1879
	421b	Edward Fielmeyer	1878-1887
PA	422a	Frederick Fink (518 W. York St.)	1882-1882
	422b	John Enisslen	1882-1884
PA	423	Theo. Finkenauer, Plant 2 (31st above Master St.)	1878-1879
PA	424a	Charles Fischer (341 N. 4th St.)	1872-1875
	424b	Henry Dauterich	1875-1882
	424c	Henry Dauterich (2778 Kensington Ave.)	1882-1888
	424d	Mathias Lehmann (2776 Kensington Ave.)	1890-1891
PA	425a	Albert Fischer (2900 Frankford Road)	1872-1884
	425b	Fischer & Kauffmann	1884-1884
	425c	Fischer & Kauffmann (3037 Salmon St.)	1884-1888
PA	426	William Frampton (Front St. between Walnut & Spruce)	1685-1700
PA	427	John Franks (253 High(Market)St.)	1804-1805
PA	428	Conrad Frey (1124 N. 3rd St.)	1858-1865

Philadelphia (cont.)

PA	429a	John Fritsch (7th & Coates Sts.)	1856-1864
	429b	John Fritsch (4224 Edward St.)	1865-1898
	429c	John Fritsch & Sons (4224 Penn St.)	1898-1907
PA	430a	John Gentner (4th St. below Cherry)	1853-1857
	430b	John Gentner (4th & Montgomery Sts.)	1858-1863
PA	431	John Gentner (3100 N. 6th St. & Clearfield Ave.)	1873-1876
PA	432	David Gerstlauer (2211 N. 15th St.)	1889-1890
PA	433	George Gilligan (10 Elbow Lane)	c1796-1815
PA	434a	George Gindele (1024/1030 W. Girard St.)	1867-1888
	434b	George Gindele Estate	1889-1890
PA	435a	Frederick C. Goos (150 Brown St.) aka Frederick C. Goos & Brother (1888)	1887-1890
	435b	Jacob Goos	1890-1891
	435c	Hugo Schumann	1891-1891
PA	436a	John Grausch (7th & Germantown)	1862-1864
	436b	John Grausch, Fairhill Brewery (2318 Marshall & 2319 N. 7th)	1865-1871
	436c	John Grauch (4228/4234 Edward St.)	1874-1887
	436d	Estate of John Grauch (4228/4240 Penn St.)	1887-1888
	436e	Catherine Grauch	1888-1891
	436f	Grauch Brewing Co.	1891-1899
PA	437a	Andrew Graus (227 Brown St.)	1861-1862
	437b	John Salber (227 Brown St.)	1868-1875
	437c	John Salber (520/522 Richmond St.)	1875-1879
	437d	John Narr	1881-1891
PA	438	Joseph Gray (61 N. 6th St.)	c1784-1793
PA	439a	William Gray (22/30 S. 6th St.)	1772-1784
	439b	Thomas Gray	1784-1789
	439c	Gray & Kennedy	1807-1811
	439d	Robert E. Gray	1811-1841
	439e	Robert E. & George Gray	1841-1845
	439f	(George) Gray & (Samuel) White	1845-1850
	439g	George Gray	1850-1855
	439h	Gray & Staley	1855-1859
	439i	George W. Gray	1859-1866
	439j	(Elisha A.) Whitney & Son (William)	1866-1869
PA	440a	Louis Gross (2421 N. Broad St.)	1874-1877
	440b	Estate of Louis Gross	1877-1882
	440c	Louis Gross Brewing Co.	1884-1892
	440d	F. Schwamb	1884-1892
PA	441a	(John) Grundler & (Charles) Schwarz (1538 Germantown Ave.)	1871-1872
	441b	John Grundler	1873-1876
	441c	Leonard & Frank Rieger (1536 Germantown & 404/408 Oxford St.)	1881-1881
	441d	Rieger & Gretz	1881-1909
	441e	Rieger & Gretz Brewing Co.	1909-1920
	441f	William Gretz Brewing Co. (1536 Germantown Ave., Oxford & Lawrence Sts.)	1933-1960
PA	442	Philip Guckes (School Lane)	1873-1880
PA	443a	Philip Guckes (822/834 St. John St.) aka Guckes, Riehl & Co. (1878-1879)	1853-1884
	443b	Philip Guckes' Sons	1884-1895
	443c	International Brewing Co.	1895-1899
PA	444a	Charles Gutmann (943 N. 5th St.)	1882-1884
	444b	Charles Gutmann (2322 Gaul St.)	1885-1887
PA	445a	Frank Haas, Jr. (10 N. 7th St.)	1872-1874
	445b	Frank Haas, Jr. (415 N. 10th St.)	1875-1876
PA	446	Haas & Pfeiffer	1874-1875

Philadelphia (cont.)

PA	447a	Charles Haeberle	1855-1862
	447b	Charles Kasper (606/608 St. John St.)	1862-1882
	447c	Vollmer & Binder	1882-1883
	447d	Gottfried Binder	1883-1897
	447e	B. B. S. Brewery, G. Binder, C. Biederbeck & H. Schmidheiser (606/612 N. American St.)	1897-1905
	447f	B. B. & S. Brewing Co.	1905-1916
PA	448	Valentine Haeffner (Pennsylvania above Thompson)	1859-1860
PA	449a	Reuben & Casper Haines (201 Market St.)	1785-1791
	449b	Reuben Haines (145 High St.)	1791-1794
	449c	Godfrey Twells	1794-1801
	449d	Twells, Morris & Co.	1801-1804
	449e	Casper Morris & Frederick Gaul	1804-1818
	449f	Frederick Gaul & Sons, Plant 1	1819-1843
PA	450a	Robert Hare, Porter Brewery (35 Callowhill St.)	1790-1799
	450b	Robert Hare & Son (155 Chestnut St.)	1800-1804
PA	451a	Robert Hare	1780- ?
	451b	Robert Hare & Son (401/421 New Market & Callowhill Sts.)	1805-1817
	451c	Jacob Smith	1817-1823
	451d	Frederick Gaul & Sons, Plant 2	1824-1860
	451e	Gaul & Austin	1860-1861
	451f	William Gaul	1861-1869
	451g	John F. Betz	1869-1880
	451h	John F. Betz & Son (415 Callowhill, 5th & Lawrence Sts.)	1880-1889
	451i	John F. Betz & Son, Ltd.	1889-1918
	451j	John F. Betz & Son, Inc.	1933-1939
PA	452a	H. Louis Hauser & Co. (920 W. College, 25th, Poplar & N. Stillman Sts.)	1855-1858
	452b	(Louis) Hauser & (Peter) Schemm	1858-1868
	452c	Peter Schemm	1868-1887
	452d	Peter Schemm & Son	1887-1908
	452e	Peter Schemm & Son (br. of the Robert Smith Ale Brewing Co.)	1908-1920
PA	453a	(John) Henzler & (Henry) Flach (32nd & Thompson Sts.)	1873-1880
	453b	Henzler & Flach (1400 N. 31st & Master Sts.)	1880-1884
	453c	Henry Flach	1884-1888
	453d	Henry Flach & Sons	1888-1897
	453e	American Brewing Co.	1897-1920
PA	454	(John) Henzler & (Henry) Flach, Plant 2 (705 Girard Ave.)	1880-1881
PA	455a	Frederick Herrmann (2500 Frankford Ave.)	1887-1888
	455b	Frederick Herrmann (1841 Passyunk Ave.)	1888-1889
PA	456a	Hobyberger & Naudascher (1630 N. 11th St.)	1859-1860
	456b	Ferdinand Naudauscher	1860-1864
	456c	Frank Haas	1864-1873
	456d	Caroline Haas	1874-1875
PA	457	Jacob Hohenadel (311 Brown St.)	1858-1872
PA	458a	John Hohenadel (29th St. & Pennsylvania Ave.)	1875-1875
	458b	John Hohenadel (35th & Queen Sts.)	1875-1920
	458c	John Hohenadel, trading as John Hohenadel Falls Brewery (35th St. & Indian Queen Lane)	1933-1935
	458d	John Hohenadel Brewery, Inc. (Conrad St. & Indian Queen Lane)	1935-1953
PA	459a	Jacob Hornung, Tioga Brewery (3111 N. 22nd & 2123/2125 Clearfield Sts.)	1885-1920
	459b	Jacob Hornung Brewing Co. (3107/3123 N. 22nd & 212 Clearfield)	1933-1953
PA	460	Jacob Hortman (286 N. 8th St.)	1804-1806
PA	461	Howard & Porter (9 Moravian Alley)	1804-1807
PA	462a	William Innis (357/365 S. Front St.)	c1790-1799
	462b	George Rehn	1800-1815
PA	463	William Innis & Co. (129/131 N. Water St.)	1799-1812
PA	464	Otto Jacobi (913 N. 4th St.)	1875-1883

Philadelphia (cont.)

PA	465a	George Jaeckel (Thorp's Lane)	1878-1880
	465b	Peter Hill	1880-1884
PA	466	C. Jans (410 N. 3rd St.)	1854-1855
PA	467	John Jones (390 Front St.)	c1785
PA	468	Kapp & Fizaine (311 S. 6th St.)	1884-1884
PA	469	George Kappel (206 Frankford Road)	1856-1857
PA	470a	Charles Kasper (1703/1707 N. 12th & 1706/1710 Mervine Sts.)	1884-1891
	470b	Theo. C. Nichterlein	1891-1893
	470c	Caroline Nichterlein	1893-1898
	470d	Columbia Brewing Co.	1898-1902
	470e	Arnholt Brewing Co.	1902-1904
PA	471a	George Keller (139 New St.)	1862-1862
	471b	George Keller (1025 N. 3rd St.)	1862-1869
	471c	George Keller (31st & Master Sts.)	1869-1882
	471d	George Keller (33rd & Master Sts.)	1882-1891
	471e	George Keller Brewing Co.	1891-1912
PA	472	Andrew Keppler (3819 N. 5th St.)	1887-1890
PA	473	Christian Keppley (134 Callowhill St.)	1815-1816
PA	474a	Charles Kerner (3301 Richmond St., Torpin & Westmoreland)	1888-1891
	474b	Adolph Mischler, Jr.	1891-1895
PA	475	Thomas Kerr (38 Meade Alley)	1813-1816
PA	476a	Philip Klein, Sr. (2310 Fairmount Ave. & 2309/2311 Wallace St.)	1863- ?
	476b	Philip Klein & Son	1888-1896
	476c	Philip Klein, Jr.	1896-1916
PA	477	A. Klenk (Bodine near Montgomery)	1864-1866
PA	478a	Christian Klopfer (2427/2433 N. Braod St.)	1875-1884
	478b	Broad Street Park Brewing Co.	1884-1888
	478c	Charles H. Schwerdfeger, aka Golden Eagle Brewing Co.	1892-1903
	478d	John Roehm Brewing Co. (2438 N. Broad & Cumberland Sts.)	1903-1920
PA	479a	John Klumpp (86 Callowhill St.)	1854-1858
	479b	John Klumpp (270 Callowhill St.)	1858-1860
	479c	John Klumpp (1746/1748 Mervine St.)	1861-1872
	479d	Eva Mary Klumpp & Co., aka Klumpp & Schuebel	1873-1876
	479e	Christian Haisch	1877-1882
	479f	Mrs. Mary Haisch	1882-1884
	479g	(Edward) Nichterlein & (John) Kellermann	1884-1891
	479h	Excelsior Brewing Co.	1891-1897
	479i	Consumers Brewing Co., Excelsior Brewery	1897-1904
PA	480a	Koehnle & Gerken (315/323 Fairmount Ave.)	1874-1875
	480b	Koehnle & Son	1875-1877
	480c	Joseph Koehnle	1877-1880
	480d	Peter Wolters aka Enterprise Brewery (1883-1884)	1880-1884
PA	481a	Carl Kramer (1700/1722 Germantown Ave. & 1713/1717 N. 5th St.)	1868-1873
	481b	Anton Walz	1873-1876
	481c	Theodore Finkenauer	1876-1908
	481d	Theodore Finkenauer Brewing Co.	1908-1920
PA	482	Casper Kraus (140 Coates & 4th Sts.)	1842-1857
PA	483	Daniel Kraus (629 N. 35th St.)	1874-1877
PA	484a	Frederick Kraus (1709/1713 S. 4th St.)	1886-1887
	484b	Gottlieb Lutz	1888-1888
	484c	Frederick Kraus	1888-1891
PA	485	John Krause (169 N. 4th St.)	1847-1855
PA	486a	Melchior Larer (50 N. 6th St.)	1805-1814
	486b	Melchior Larer & Son (John)	1815-1824
	486c	John Larer	1825-1838
	486d	John Larer (113 Wood St.)	1839-1843

Philadelphia (cont.)

PA	487a	Philip J. Lauber (1716 N. Braod St. above Columbia Ave.)	1875-1887
	487b	Germania Brewing Co.	1887-1901
	487c	Henry Hess Brewing Co.	1901-1911
PA	488	Ferdinand Lauckhardt	1874-1875
PA	489a	Leeds & Gray	1857-1865
	489b	Robert Gray (727/735 Vine St.)	1865-1875
	489c	Richard Magee	1875-1884
	489d	Small & Magee	1884-1888
PA	490	James Leigh	1874-1875
PA	491a	Lorenz Leiling (Queen & Baird Sts.)	1888-1891
	491b	Germantown Brewing Co.	1893-1893
	491c	Mutual Brewing Co. of Philadelphia	1893-1897
	491d	Consumers Brewing Co., Mutual Brewery (245 Queen Lane)	1897-1899
PA	492a	Ferdinand Leimbach (1752 N. American & 1751 Bodine Sts.)	1875-1878
	492b	Eliza F. Leimbach	1878-1879
	492c	Christian Stengel	1880-1885
	492d	Frederick Goelz	1885-1890
PA	493a	(P.) Liebert & (Herman) Obert (156/160 Oak St.)	1873-1901
	493b	Liebert & Obert (173/203 Carson St.)	1901-1907
	493c	Liebert & Obert Brewing Co.	1907-1920
	493d	Liebert & Obert aka Cooper Brewing Co. (1938-1946)	1933-1946
	493e	Cooper Brewing Co., Inc., aka Liebert & Obert	1946-1948
PA	494	John Lips (1101 N. 2nd & Germantown)	1843-1860
PA	495a	(Henry) Loesch & (Louis) Zickler (12th & Montgomery Sts.)	1860-1863
	495b	Henry Loesch	1864-1866
PA	496	John Loescher (1735 Walter St.)	1879-1882
PA	497a	Christian Lutz (130 Vine St.)	1806-1807
	497b	Christian Lutz (121 N. 4th St.)	1808-1812
PA	498	Gottlieb Lutz (2232/2234 Callowhill St.)	1882-1888
PA	499a	Charles Maass (1204/1214 Germantown Ave.)	1874-1880
	499b	Charles Maass (1203 N. 3rd St.)	1880-1886
	499c	Charles Maass & Son (1320 N. 5th St.)	1886-1890
	499d	Charles Maass	1890-1892
PA	500a	Anton Maier (1441 N. 10th St.)	1886-1886
	500b	Anton Maier (2401/2403 N. 10th St.)	1887-1891
PA	501a	Gottfried Manz (1200 Frankford St.)	1864-1864
	501b	Gottfried Manz (3037 6th & Clearfield Sts.)	1873-1887
	501c	Gottlieb Manz Brewing Co.	1887-1893
	501d	Philadelphia Brewing Co.	1893-1920
	501e	Philadelphia Brewing Co.	1933-1949
PA	502	John Marbacker (119 N. 4th St.)	1815-1820
PA	503a	Miller & Teufel (13 Ashmead & Wakefield Sts.)	1866-1869
	503b	John C. Miller	1873-1886
	503c	Geo. J. Miller	1886-1891
	503d	John C. Miller Brewing Co.	1891-1897
	503e	Consumers Brewing Co., John C. Miller Brewery	1897-1901
PA	504a	James L. Moore (1314 Fitzwater St.)	1874-1884
	504b	(John) Welde & (John) Thomas (1200/1316 Fitzwater & Juniper)	1887-1891
	504c	Welde & Thomas Brewing Co.	1891-1897
	504d	Consumers Brewing Co., Welde & Thomas Brewery	1897-1904
	504e	Consumers Brewing Co., The South Plant	1904-1920
	504f	Trainer Brewing Co., Plant 2 (1306/1330 Fitzwater, Juniper & Clarion Sts.)	1934-1934

Philadelphia (cont.)

State	No.	Brewery	Dates
PA	505a	Anthony Morris (Front St.)	1687-1706
	505b	Anthony Morris, Sr. & Jr.	1706-1721
	505c	Anthony Morris, Jr.	1721- ?
	505d	Anthony Morris, III	? -1745
	505e	Anthony Morris, III (2/4 Dock St. & 1 Pear Sts.)	1745- ?
	505f	Luke Morris & Co.	c1790-1799
	505g	W. Isaac Morris & Co.	1800-1804
	505h	(William) Abbott & (Caleb) Sherwood	1805-1811
	505i	William Abbott	1812-1814
	505j	William & James Abbott	1815-1833
	505k	Abbott & Newlin	1834-1834
	505l	William Abbott	1835-1842
PA	506a	Thomas Morris (86 N. 2nd St.)	c1790-1812
	506b	Thomas Morris & Co. (Thos. Jr. & Joseph)	1813-1829
	506c	Thomas Morris & Sons	1830-1834
	506d	(James) Abbott & (Robert) Newlin	1835-1846
	506e	Robert Newlin	1846-1858
	506f	Robert Newlin (136 N. 2nd St.)	1858-1859
	506g	Robert Newlin & Co.	1859-1859
	506h	Newlin, Thompson & Co.	1860-1860
	506i	Newlin, Abbott & Zell	1861-1862
	506j	Wilson Abbott & Co.	1862-1865
	506k	J. Henry Abbott	1866-1867
PA	507	W. Isaac Morris & Co. (98 S. Front St.)	1805-1813
PA	508a	Charles Mueller (715 Belgrade Ave.)	1874-1875
	508b	Charles Mueller (2107 Germantown Ave.)	1878-1880
	508c	Weisbrod & Hess	1880-1884
	508d	Albert Hoch	1884-1890
PA	509a	Henry Mueller (31st & Jefferson Sts.)	1873-1881
	509b	Estate of Henry Mueller	1881-1892
	509c	Bergner & Engel Brewing Co., Plant 2	1892-1900
PA	510a	Henry Mueller (1220/1222 Mascher St.)	1864-1873
	510b	Charles Wolters	1875-1877
	510c	W. & L. Beckler	1877-1878
	510d	Ferdinand Schaefer	1878-1882
	510e	Ferdinand Schaefer, aka Frederick Schaefer (338/340 Brown St.)	1882-1892
PA	511a	Christian Muellerschoen (495/497 N. 3rd St.)	1878-1882
	511b	(A.) Mary Muellerschoen	1882-1891
	511c	Muellerschoen's Weiss Beer Brewery, Andrew Rudolph	1891-1902
	511d	Muellerschoen's Weiss Beer Brewery, John C. Muellerschoen	1902-1920
PA	512	Sebastian Nagel (Springfield near Ridge Ave., Roxborough)	1874-1880
PA	513	Christian Narr (1011 Norris St.)	1888-1888
PA	514a	John Narr (2551 N. 2nd St.)	1872-1873
	514b	Fred Schauffele	1874-1876
	514c	Jacob F. Schauffele	1876-1879
	514d	Jacob F. Schauffele (2401 N. 2nd St.)	1880-1889
PA	515a	John Narr (262 E. Girard Ave.)	1873-1876
	515b	John Narr (242/244 N. 4th St.) aka Mrs. Minnie Narr (1878-1879)	1876-1881
	515c	Andrew Sonnenmaier	1881-1885
	515d	Andrew Sonnenmaier (312 S. 4th St.)	1885-1888
PA	516a	Ferdinand Naudascher (1441 N. 10th St.)	1872-1875
	516b	Joseph Straubmiller	1878-1880
	516c	Ferdinand Seemann	1880-1882
	516d	Fleisch & Mayer	1882-1884
	516e	August Hess aka Anton Maier (1886)	1884-1890
PA	517	Nentzel & Hensel (1001 N. 3rd & Beaver Sts.)	1856-1860
PA	518	Frederick Nentzel, Jr. (1012 N. 3rd St.) aka Robert Ortlieb (1861)	1845-1865

Philadelphia (cont.)

PA	519	Henry Ohse (1423 Germantown Ave.)	1867-1884
PA	520	Francis Orth (33rd St. below Master St.)	1878-1882
PA	521a	Leonard Otterbach	1877-1882
	521b	Elizabeth Otterbach	1882-1883
	521c	August Vollmer	1883-1889
	521d	Elizabeth Vollmer (1417/1449 Randolph & Jefferson Sts.)	1889-1920
	521e	Vollmer Brewing Corp. (1420/1430 N. Randolph St.)	1933-1934
	521f	Schaffhauser Brewing Corp.	1934-1939
	521g	Schiller Brewing Co.	1940-1941
	521h	Jaeger Brewing Co.	NP 1942-1943
PA	522a	Otto & Layer (518/520 2nd St.)	1874-1875
	522b	Otto & Layer (518/520 Locust St.)	1876-1882
	522c	Geo. W. Otto (226 Bainbridge St.)	1882-1884
PA	523a	Peerless Brewing Co. (2205/2219 N. American St.)	1934-1934
	523b	Gruenewald Brewery, Inc.	1934-1935
	523c	Esslinger's Inc, Plant 2	1937-1947
PA	524	Samuel Pemberton (60 Dock St.)	c1790-1793
PA	525	George Pepper (176 High St.)	1804-1807
PA	526a	Francis Perot (2nd, Cherry & Broad Sts.)	1818-1823
	526b	Francis & Wm. S. Perot (120 Vine & New Sts.)	1824-1854
PA	527a	Frederick Pfahler (931 St. John St.)	1869-1877
	527b	Mrs. Mary Pfahler	1878-1885
PA	528	Fred Pfahler (1425 N. Broad St.)	1874-1875
PA	529	(Christian) Pfeiffer & (Frederick) Schauffele (4021 Germantown)	1872-1873
PA	530	Philadelphia Brewing Co. (315 Fairmount Ave.)	1888-1888
PA	531a	(George) Planck & (Valentine) Haeffner (10/12 Pegg St.)	1853-1855
	531b	George Planck	1855-1858
	531c	George Planck (124 Pegg St.)	1858-1863
PA	532	Gottlieb Pframmer (Cedar St. below 10th St.)	1843-1857
PA	533	F. A. Poth (3rd & Green Sts.)	1865-1870
PA	534a	Joseph Potts (2/4 S. 5th & Minor Sts.)	c1774-1785
	534b	Henry Pepper & Sons	1786-1807
	534c	George Pepper	1807-1836
	534d	David Pepper aka Pepper & Seckel (1836-1837)	1836-1840
	534e	Robert Smith	1840-1843
	534f	(Robert) Smith & (Frederick) Seckel	1843-1850
	534g	Robert Smith	1850-1858
	534h	Robert Smith (20 S. 5th & Minor Sts.)	1858-1880
	534i	Robert Smith, aka Robert Smith & Co. (owned by Christian Schmidt)	1880-1882
	534j	Robert Smith's Son (William D.)	1882-1887
	534k	Robert Smith India Pale Ale Brewing Co.	1887-1888
	534l	Robert Smith India Pale Ale Brewing Co. (38th St. & Girard)	1888-1896
	534m	Robert Smith Ale Brewing Co.	1896-1920
PA	535a	Presser & Lubbermann (35th & Aspen Sts.)	1860-1865
	535b	Charles Presser	1868-1875
	535c	Charles Presser, Jr.	1875-1884
PA	536	William Pudey (351 Chestnut St.)	c1785
PA	537	(George) Reges & (John) Hoffman (808 S. 6th St.)	1888-1888
PA	538a	George Rehn (60/68 New St.)	1792-1793
	538b	George & John Rehn	1894-1899
	538c	John Rehn	1800-1806
	538d	George & John Rehn	1816-1827

Philadelphia (cont.)

PA	539a	Albert Reiser	1874- ?
	539b	Albert Reiser (1226 N. Front St.)	1881-1882
	539c	Albert Reiser (816 N. 2nd St.)	1862-1883
	539d	Albert Reiser (705 N. 2nd St.)	1883-1884
PA	540a	Gottlieb Reitter (933 N. Broad St.)	1888-1889
	540b	G. H. Reitter (Broad & Cumberland Sts.)	1890-1891
PA	541a	Rentschler & Legle (240 Girard Ave.)	1857-1858
	541b	Christian Rentschler (1214 N. 5th St.)	1858-1859
PA	542a	Jos. Rieger (1708/1714 Cadwallader & 4th Sts.)	1874-1893
	542b	Joseph Rieger & Sons	1893-1906
	542c	Joseph Rieger	1906-1910
	542d	Louise Rieger	1910-1914
PA	543a	Rittmaier & Weihmann, Bushkill Brewery (1715/1733 Buttonwood)	1866-1871
	543b	Joseph Kohnle	1882-1891
	543c	Joseph Kohnle Brewing Co.	1891-1900
PA	544a	Phillip J. Roemmich (851 N. 4th St.)	1859-1860
	544b	John Scheurer	1860-1861
PA	545a	Henry Rothacker (1919 Market St.)	1876-1877
	545b	Henry Rothacker (1912/1914 N. 20th St.)	1877-1882
PA	546	Andrew Rudolph (241 E. Girard Ave.)	1883-1885
PA	547a	Moritz Ruoff (1224/1236 Frankford Road)	1874-1882
	547b	William Heimgaertner	1882-1895
	547c	William A. Heimgaertner aka Kensington Brewery (1906-1907)	1895-1907
	547d	William A. Heimgaertner Estate aka Kensington Brewery (1907-1909) aka Frankford Ave. Brewery (1909-1910)	1907-1910
	547e	Proto Brewing Co.	1910-1917
PA	548a	August Rustenbach (420/422 Diamond & Lawrence Sts.)	1874-1876
	548b	Fritz Zierfuss	1876-1879
	548c	William Wurster	1879-1885
	548d	Mathias Lehmann	1885-1887
PA	549a	J. Salomon (1514 N. Front St.)	1878-1879
	549b	Joseph Salomon (999 N. 2nd St.)	1880-1883
PA	550	Jacob Salter (18 S. 4th St.)	1802-1810
PA	551a	Mrs. E. N. Schaefer (723 N. 4th St.)	1888-1891
	551b	The Gallivan Co.	1895-1896
	551c	Baltic Brewing Co. (403 Brown & 4th Sts.)	1896-1902
PA	552a	Charles Schaufler (2610 Frankford Ave.)	1875-1876
	552b	William Kumpf & Nicholas Hernig	1876-1880
	552c	William Kumpf & Co.	1880-1881
	552d	Kumpf & Hernig	1881-1883
	552e	John N. Hernig	1884-1887
	552f	Estate of John N. Hernig, aka Sophia Hernig	1887-1887
	552g	William Kumpf (2812 Frankford Ave. & Hartland St.)	1888-1890
PA	553a	Charles Schaufler (1742 N. 2nd St.)	1876-1878
	553b	Charles Schaufler (1742 N. 4th St.)	1878-1879
	553c	Peter Wolters	1879-1880
	553d	William Gretz	1880-1884
PA	554a	Chas. Schaufler (816/818 N. 12th St. & 1205 Ely Ave.)	1881-1882
	554b	Catherine Schaufler	1882-1890
	554c	Chas. Schaufler	1890-1900
	554d	Christopher Stollsteimer	1900-1906
PA	555a	Jacob Schick (2201 N. 15th St. above Susquehanna Ave.)	1880-1883
	555b	Funk & Krein Brewing Co.	1883-1884
PA	556a	George Schittinger (1020 E. Cumberland St.)	1879-1879
	556b	George Schittinger (601 W. Lehigh Ave. & 6th St.)	1879-1882
	556c	Geo. Schittinger (810 Fairmount Ave.)	1882-1888

Philadelphia (cont.)

PA	557a	John Schlecht (1325 Germantown Ave.)	1874-1876
	557b	William Wurster	1878-1882
	557c	Matthias Lehmann	1882-1884
	557d	George Frank	1885-1889
PA	558a	August Schlemmer (2112 Ridge Ave.)	1884-1887
	558b	August Schlemmer (2701 Columbia Ave. & 27th St.)	1888-1893
	558c	Park Brewing Co.	1893-1896
PA	559a	S. Schloetterer (118 Master St.)	1869-1878
	559b	Jacob Schick	1878-1879
	559c	Gottlieb Reitter	1879-1882
	559d	Jacob Schick	1882-1884
PA	560	F. Schmidt (1751 N. 4th St.)	1863-1865
PA	561a	Gottlieb Schmid (715 S. 7th St.)	1878-1882
	561b	Raphael Fisher	1882-1884
	561c	Julius Schraishuhn	1886-1892
PA	562	(John) Schneider & (Conrad) Breining (2107 Germantown Ave.)	1875-1875
PA	563a	Christian Schnitzel (31st St. below Master St.)	1855-1864
	563b	Harry Rothacker	1864-1870
	563c	G. F. Rothacker	1870-1880
	563d	G. F. Rothacker & Sons (31st & Master Sts.)	1880-1893
	563e	G. F. Rothacker Brewing Co.	1893-1912
PA	564	Charles Schnitzer (629/631 Girard Ave.)	1866-1867
PA	565	John G. Schoch (747 S. Front St.)	1859-1861
PA	566	John Schoenheiter (431 Moore & 430 Pierce Sts.)	1887-1891
PA	567a	William Schultz (209 St. John St.)	1805-1807
	567b	Mrs. William Schultz	1808-1810
PA	568a	Louis Schweitzer (837 N. 3rd St.)	1859-1860
	568b	Schweitzer & Grim	1860-1861
PA	569a	Louis Schweitzer (715 N. 3rd St.)	1859-1860
	569b	Schweitzer & Grim	1860-1861
	569c	Caroline Kuhn	1874-1875
	569d	(John) Grundler & Co. (Fred Vetter)	1877-1884
	569e	John P. Schoettle	1884-1890
PA	570a	Schweitzer & Grim (11th & Columbia Sts.)	1862-1867
	570b	Louis Schweitzer (1700 N. 11th St.)	1872-1875
PA	571	Gustave Schwoeri (712 Passyunk Ave.)	1885-1888
PA	572	Frederick Seckel (164 S. 9th St.)	1836-1837
PA	573	Ferdinand Seemann (312 New Market St.)	1880-1880
PA	574	Ferdinand Seemann (561 E. Cumberland St.)	1882-1882
PA	575	George Seitz (2327 N. 7th St.)	1875-1884
PA	576	William Sharswood & Co. (4th St. above Vine St.)	1808-1810
PA	577a	Joseph Shurr (136 Brown St.)	1856-1858
	577b	Joseph Shurr (982 N. 7th St.)	1858-1859
	577c	Christian Rentschler	1860-1862
PA	578	Christian Siebolt (4340 Lancaster Ave. & N. 44th St.)	1874-1877
PA	579	John M. Simon (1949 S. 2nd St.)	1858-1862
PA	580	Robert Smith (St. John & Noble Sts.)	1836-1840
PA	581a	Samuel Smith (373 Mulberry St.)	1804-1805
	581b	Samuel Smith (24 N. 7th St.)	1805-1806
PA	582a	James Smyth (21st & Washington Sts.)	1866-1874
	582b	John Gardiner & Co.	1874-1883
	582c	Continental Brewing Co.	1883-1920

Philadelphia (cont.)

PA	583a	Daniel Snowden (130 N. Front St.)	1791-1792
	583b	Leonard Snowden	1793-1800
	583c	Snowden & Fisher (107 New St.)	1801-1810
	583d	John Coleman	1811-1817
	583e	John Coleman (23 Powell St.)	1817-1828
PA	584a	Spaeth, Krautter & Hess (2703 Germantown Ave. & Lehigh Ave.)	1888-1897
	584b	Consumers Brewing Co., Spaeth, Krautter & Hess Brewery	1897-1904
PA	585a	C. Frederick Specht (96/102 Shippen St.)	1844-1858
	585b	C. Frederick Specht (230/236 Shippen St.)	1858-1861
	585c	Catherine Specht	1861-1868
	585d	Catherien Specht (230/236 Bainbridge St.)	1868-1871
PA	586a	Louis Specht (1033/1035 W. Girard Ave.) aka Karl Specht (1875)	1871-1877
	586b	C. L. Specht	1878-1884
PA	587a	Christopher Steger (1801/1805 S. 4th St.)	1868-1884
	587b	Gottliebe Schmid	1884-1884
	587c	Franz Hill	1885-1888
	587d	Jacob Steiger	1888-1891
	587e	Charles Reppe	1891-1897
PA	588a	Ferdinand Steinbach	1853-1862
	588b	Charles Class	1862-1868
	588c	Charles Class, Jr. (1720/1738 Mervine St.)	1868-1890
	588d	(Charles) Class & (Julius) Nachod	1890-1896
	588e	Class & Nachod Brewing Co.	1896-1915
PA	589a	Chas. Stengel (2310/2312 N. 2nd St.)	1880-1884
	589b	Otto Ruoff	1884-1889
	589c	Christiana Ruoff aka Mrs. Otto Ruoff (1893)	1889-1893
	589d	F. Mott's Brewing Co.	1894-1895
PA	590a	Christian Stengel (2400/2404 Germantown Ave.)	1888-1890
	590b	Alois Kopp, Fairhill Brewery	1890-1891
	590c	Christian Stengel	1891-1893
	590d	Thomas L. Ordish, Fairhill Brewery	1898-1904
	590e	Gottlieb Schmidt, Fairhill Brewery	1905-1906
PA	591a	Steppacher & (Henry) Becker (Dutch Hollow at foot of Arnold St)	1857-1870
	591b	Jacob Hohenadel, Falls Park Brewery	1870-1878
	591c	George Arnholt aka Philadelphia Brewing Co. (1878-1879)	1878-1883
PA	592a	(Abraham) Steppacher & Brother (Joseph) (686 N. 10th St.)	1850-1858
	592b	Steppacher & Brother (1310/1312 N. 10th St.)	1858-1866
PA	593	Henry Steyert (405 Hackley St.)	1885-1887
PA	594a	Michael Stiefel (408 Coates St.)	1871-1874
	594b	McCaffrey & O'Reilley (408 Fairmount St. & 407 Lynd St.)	1879-1880
PA	595	Michael Stiefel (2203/2205 N. 6th St.)	1874-1878
PA	596a	Joseph Straubmiller (York St. & 2411 Trenton & Boston Aves.)	1882-1905
	596b	Joseph Straubmiller & Son	1905-1920
	596c	Quaker City Brg. Corp. (controlled by Geo. Ehret Brewing Co.)	1933-1934
PA	597a	Martin Strauss (1148 N. 3rd St.)	1869-1876
	597b	Joanna Schnitzer (1150 Canal St. & 1148 N. 3rd St.)	1878-1888
PA	598a	Anton Stroebele (849 N. 4th & 856 N. Charlotte St.)	1870-1888
	598b	John Roehm	1888-1897
	598c	Consumers Brewing Co., John Roehm Brewery	1897-1903
	598d	Consumers Brewing Co., Roehm & Spaeth	1903-1904
	598e	Consumers Brewing Co., North Plant	1904-1909
	598f	Henry Hess Brewing Co.	1909-1912
	598g	Premier Brewing Co.	1912-1920
	598h	Trainer Brewing Co. (844/854 N. Orianna St.)	1933-1937
	598i	Otto Erlanger Brewing Co.	1937-1951
PA	599	Stumph & Zimmerman (317 Callowhill St.)	1853-1855

Philadelphia (cont.)

PA	600a	V. Clement Sweatman (120 Vine St.)	1855-1858
	600b	V. Clement Sweatman (314 Vine St.)	1858-1862
	600c	V. Clement Sweatman (112 Callowhill St.)	1863-1867
PA	601	Lewis Talmon (Vine & Callowhill Sts.)	1853-1867
PA	602	Lewis Talmon (31st above Thompson St.)	1859-1861
PA	603	William Bankson Taylor (Vine near 8th St.)	1848-1860
PA	604	Frederick Tedele (5th St. above Columbia	1859-1860
PA	605a	Charles Theis (St. John near Callowhill)	1846-1869
	605b	Charles Theis & Co. (Ladner & Weger) (532 N. 3rd & Buttonwood)	1870-1874
	605c	Charles Theis & Co. (32nd & Master Sts.)	1874-1877
	605d	(Chas.) Theis & (Frank) Weger aka C. Theis-Weger (1888-1892)	1877-1892
	605e	Weger Bros.	1892-1920
PA	606	George Twitchell (13th & Buttonwood Sts.)	1855-1859
PA	607	Union Brewing Co. (403 N. 10th St.)	1898-1901
PA	608	(Reinhold) Volmer & (August) Born (341/343 N. 3rd St.)	1860-1864
PA	609	John Wagner (455 St. John St. near Poplar) (First lager beer brewed in America)	1840-1859
PA	610a	B. Waldsauer (514 Franklin St.)	1857-1859
	610b	B. Waldsauer (514 Girard St.)	1859-1861
PA	611	Conrad Walter (392 St. John St.)	1804-1812
PA	612a	Henry J. Walter (33rd & Thompson Sts.)	1872-1875
	612b	Jos. Straubmueller	1875-1879
	612c	H. J. Walter	1879-1880
PA	613	John Weihmann (815 Callowhill & 10th Sts.)	1871-1897
PA	614a	(George) Weisbrod & (Christian) Hess (Frankford Ave., Adams & Holman Sts.)	1882-1910
	614b	Weisbrod & Hess Brewing Co.	1910-1920
	614c	Weisbrod & Hess Brewing Co., Inc. (Frankford Ave. & E. Hagert St.)	1933-1934
	614d	Weisbrod & Hess Corp.	1934-1938
PA	615	C. Ferdinand Weisgerber (Tioga & Cooper Sts.)	1868-1875
PA	616	Paul Wetzel	1874-1876
PA	617	Daniel Wiedemann (2611 Gray Ferry Road & Washington)	1882-1889
PA	618a	Daniel Wiedemann (805/809 S. 11th St.)	1879-1880
	618b	Margaret Wiedemann	1880-1884
	618c	Hermann Rose	1884-1905
PA	619a	John Whitesides & Co. (10 St. George St.)	1805-1806
	619b	Richard Croskey	1807-1810
PA	620a	Wile & McArthur (9 Bread St.)	1812-1815
	620b	John Wile	1815-1816
	620c	Wile & Partenheimer	1816-1817
	620d	Adam Partenheimer & Co.	1818-1830
PA	621a	August Winnig (25th & Coates St.)	1860-1862
	621b	(Otto) Winnig (620 N. 3rd St.)	1863-1873
	621c	Philip Zaun	1873-1885
	621d	Philip Zaun (1425/1429 Germantown Ave.)	1885-1897
	621e	Zaun & Newman	1897-1908
	621f	Zaun's Brewery	1908-1910
	621g	Zaun's Weiss Beer Brewery	1910-1912
PA	622a	Andrew Wirth (1534 Germantown Ave. & 4th St.)	1851-1863
	622b	C. Lewis Wirth	1863-1876
	622c	Fritz Zierfuss	1879-1884
	622d	Mrs. Margaret Zierfuss	1884-1885
	622e	John A. Lengel	1885-1888
PA	623	Frederick Wolf (3514 Germantown Ave. & 1321/1325 Tioga St.)	1907-1916

Philadelphia (cont.)

PA	624a	Albert Wolf, White Bear Brewery (3702 N. 6th St. & 603 Erie)	1898-1901
	624b	Philip Hildenbrand, White Bear Brewery	1901-1910
	624c	F. J. P. Hildenbrand, White Bear Brewery	1910-1911
PA	625a	Fred Wolf	1874-1877
	625b	Christian Wolf (238 Beaver St.)	1877-1880
	625c	Christian Wolf (210/212 N. 3rd St.)	1881-1884
	625d	Albert Wolf	1884-1901
PA	626a	William Wurster (1929 N. 2nd St.)	1887-1887
	626b	Henry Stengert	1888-1891
PA	627a	W. H. Zimmermann & Co., Star Brewery (421 Leiper St.)	1908-1915
	627b	Lila M. Zimmermann	1915-1916
PA	628a	Gehring & Spunger (31st & Haverford)	1858-1859
	628b	Gehring & Spunger (434 Poplar St.)	1859-1861
PA	629a	Manger & Psotta (2nd & New Sts.)	1848-1850
	629b	George Manger	1850-1851
	629c	(George) Manger & (Peter) Schemm	1851-1855
	629d	George Manger	1855-1867
PA	630a	Trupert Ortlieb, Weiss Beer Brewery (1312 Germantown Ave.)	1866-1870
	630b	Trupert Ortlieb, Weiss Beer Brewery (1248 N. 3rd.)	1871-1879
	630c	August Weiler	1880-1884
PA	631a	Jacob Oswald (102 Coates St.)	1853-1858
	631b	Jacob Oswald (232 Coates St.)	1858-1861
PA	632	Godfrey Twells (18 Margaretta St.)	1784-1790

Philipsburg

PA	633a	Philipsburg Brewing Co. (N. Front St.)	1905-1920
	633b	The Philipsburg Brewing Co. (401 N. Front & Locust Sts.)	1933-1941
PA	634	Peter Schmidt	1874-1875

Pittsburgh (including Allegheny, Bennett, Bennett's Station, Birmingham, Hazelwood, Millvale, Millvale Station, Shaler Township)

PA	635	Allegheny Brewing Co. (Bismarck & Woods Run Aves.)	1902-1911
PA	636	Allegheny County Brewing Co. (River Ave. & Walnut Sts.)	1906-1910
PA	637a	American Brewing Co. (E. Ohio St., Millvale Station)	1902-1905
	637b	Independent Brewing Co., American Brewery	1905-1920
PA	638	Atlas Brewing Co. (88/90 S. 13th St.)	1901-1903
PA	639a	Peter Auen (Manor St.)	1874-1877
	639b	Philip Auen (1100 Manor & 1210 Bingham Sts.)	1877-1879
	639c	Peter J. Auen	1879-1890
	639d	Frank J. Walker	1890-1891
PA	640a	Adam Baeuerlein (5th Ward)	1845- ?
	640b	Adam Baeuerlein (Bennett)	? -1867
	640c	A. Baeuerlein & Sons (Christian & Adam A.)	1867-1868
	640d	C. Baeuerlein Bro. & Co., Star Brewery (Bennett's Station)	1868-1888
	640e	C. Baeuerlein Brewing Co. (Butler & Evergreen Aves., Bennett)	1888-1898
	640f	Pittsburgh Pure Beer Brewing Co. (Evergreen Ave. & Ohio St.)	1898-1899
	640g	Pittsburgh Brewing Co., Baeuerlein Brewery	1899-1920
	640h	Keystone Mfg. & Sales Co., aka Baeuerlein Brewery	1933-1934
PA	641	Bohemian Brewing Co. (308 Grant St.)	1916-1916
PA	642	Joseph Braen (Shaler Township)	1874-1875
PA	643a	Brown & Verner	c1843
	643b	Brown, Verner & Smith	c1844
	643c	George W. Smith	c1844-1845
PA	644a	Darlington & Co. (110 1st Ave.)	1874-1890
	644b	Pittsburgh Brewing Co.	1890-1891
	644c	DeWald, Wuesthoff & Co. (206/210 1st Ave.)	1891-1896
	644d	DeWald & Co.	1896-1898
PA	645	Darlington & Co. (Rebecca St.)	1882-1884

Pittsburgh (cont.)

PA	646a	J. & H. Dippel (153 Market St.)	1874-1877
	646b	Henry Dippel	1877-1884
PA	647a	H. Dippel (63 Juniata St.)	1882- ?
	647b	John L. Straub	1888-1890
	647c	B. H. Gangwisch	1890-1891
PA	648a	Duquesne Brewing Co. (S. 21st, 22nd & Mary Sts.)	1899-1905
	648b	Independent Brewing Co., Duquesne Brewery	1905-1933
	648c	Duquesne Brewing Co., Duquesne Brewery	1933-1937
	648d	Duquesne Brewing Co. of Pittsburgh, Duquesne Brewery	1937-1972
PA	649a	Eberhardt & Ober, Eagle Brewery (1/9 Troy Hill Road & Vinial)	1852-1883
	649b	Eberhardt & Ober Brewing and Malting Co.	1883-1885
	649c	Eberhardt & Ober Brewing Co.	1885-1899
	649d	Pittsburgh Brewing Co., Eberhardt & Ober Brewery aka Eberhardt & Ober Brewing Co. (1899-1900)	1899-1920
	649e	Pittsburgh Brewing Co., Eberhardt & Ober Plant (1100/1124 Troy Hill Road & 800/825 Vinial St.)	1933-1952
PA	650	Eberhardt & Ober Brewing Co., Ale Brewery (152/155 S. Canal)	c1885
PA	651	August Erbrich (5th Ave. & Robinson St.)	1882-1882
PA	652	Erikson Bros.	1893-1893
PA	653	First National Brewing Co.	1899-1899
PA	654a	(Edward) Frauenheim & (August) Hoevler (17th St.)	1861-1866
	654b	Frauenheim & Hoevler (34th St. & Liberty Ave.)	1866-1869
	654c	Frauenheim, Miller & Co.	1869-1874
	654d	Frauenheim & (Leopold) Vilsack (32nd & Liberty Sts.)	1874-1888
	654e	Iron City Brewing Co. (Liberty Ave., 33rd & 34th Sts.)	1888-1899
	654f	Pittsburgh Brewing Co., Iron City Brewery aka Iron City Brewing Co. (1899-1900)	1899-1920
	654g	Pittsburgh Brewing Co., Iron City Brewery (3340 Liberty Ave. & Sassafrass St.)	1933-1955
	654h	Pittsburgh Brewing Co. aka DuBois Brewing Co. aka Magna Carta Brewing Co. aka Pilsener Brewing Co.	1955-
PA	655a	Henry Friedel (1700 Josephine St.)	1874-1884
	655b	Ch. Meussner	1884-1888
PA	656a	John Gangwisch (46th St. & A. V. RR)	1878-1880
	656b	Gangwisch, O'Reilly & Co.	1880-1882
	656c	Hopf, Roth & Co.	1882-1884
PA	657a	Gast & Bro., Willow Grove Brewery (Butler Plant Road, Bennett)	1866-1882
	657b	Val. Gast, Willow Grove Brewery	1882-1885
	657c	Enz & Schaefer, Willow Grove Brewery	1885-1889
	657d	Michael Enz, Willow Grove Brewery	1889-1893
	657e	Michael Enz Brewing Co.	1893-1898
	657f	American Brewing Co.	1898-1904
PA	658a	Philip Gast (314 Spring Garden Ave.)	1859- ?
	658b	Gast & Bro.	? - ?
	658c	John M. Mueller	1874-1883
	658d	Hopf, Roth & Co., Enterprise Brewery	1883-1884
	658e	(Isaac) Hippely & Hopf, Enterprise Brewery	1884-1888
	658f	Hippely & Son, Enterprise Brewery	1888-1899
	658g	Pittsburgh Brewing Co., Hippely & Son	1899-1899
PA	659a	Ernest Hauch	1849-1853
	659b	Ernst Hauch (26th & 2601 Sarah Sts.)	1853-1888
	659c	Ernst Hauch's Sons	1888-1899
	659d	Pittsburgh Brewing Co., Ernst Hauch's Sons aka Hauch Brewery (1899-1900)	1899-1904
PA	660a	Hazelwood Brewing Co. (5007/5011 Lytle & Tecumseh Sts.)	1905-1920
	660b	Hazelwood Beverage Co.	1933-1934
	660c	Derby Brewing Co.	1934-1938

Pittsburgh (cont.)

PA	661a	Hechelmann & Co., Lion Brewery (Villa & Vinial Sts.)	1858-1872
	661b	Lutz & Walz, Lion Brewery aka Lion Brewing Co. (1874-1879)	1872-1879
	661c	D. Lutz & Son, Lion Brewery	1879-1900
PA	662a	Henry Herdt	1874-1877
	662b	Mrs. D. Herdt	1877-1879
PA	663	Geo. Hoefling (Wylie St.)	1874-1875
PA	664a	Henry Hoehl (Bennett)	1863-1884
	664b	Henry Hoehl, Jr.	1884-1888
	664c	Hoehl Brewing Co. (Stanton Ave. & Black Alley) aka H. & S. Hoehl (Millvale, 1893)	1888-1904
PA	665	John Huckenstein	1874-1875
PA	666	Val. Kaltenhaeuser (5th Ave. & Robinson St.)	1874-1884
PA	667a	Keystone Brewing Co. (33rd & 3301 Carson Sts.)	1887-1899
	667b	Pittsburgh Brewing Co., Keystone Brewery aka Keystone Brewing Co . (1899-1900)	1899-1920
PA	668	Margaret Lang	1874-1875
PA	669a	Philip Lauer (head of 18th St.)	1874-1884
	669b	Henry Lauer & Bros.	1884-1891
	669c	Philip Lauer	1891-1899
	669d	Pittsburgh Brewing Co., Philip Lauer	1899-1899
PA	670a	Leonhard, Schlaffner & Weissert, Amber Brewery (12/18 Vinial)	1858-1860
	670b	Ober & Koenig, Amber Brewery	1860-1864
	670c	George Ober, Amber Brewery	1864-1878
	670d	Frank L. Ober	1878-1879
	670e	Frank L. Ober & Bro. (Chas.)	1879-1888
	670f	Frank L. Ober & Bro. Brewing Co.	1888-1890
	670g	Ober Bros. Brewing Co. (63/75 Vinial St.)	1897-1899
	670h	Pittsburgh Brewing Co., Ober Bros. Brewery aka Ober Bros. Brewing Co. (1899-1900)	1899-1904
PA	671	Liberty Brewing Co. (Julius St. & Penn RR)	1905-1920
PA	672a	D. Lutz & Son, Allegheny Brewery (11 Spring Garden Ave. & Chestnut St.)	1878-1897
	672b	D. Lutz & Son Brewing Co., Allegheny Brewery	1897-1904
	672c	Independent Brewing Co., Lutz & Son Brewery	1904-1909
PA	673	Jac. Muth, Jr. & Co. (5th Ave. & Gist St.)	1884-1884
PA	674a	John Nusser (Manor St., Birmingham)	1852-1883
	674b	John H. Nusser, National Brewery (Birmingham Ave. head of S. 12th St.)	1883-1899
	674c	Pittsburgh Brewing Co., John H. Nusser	1899-1900
PA	675a	Pier, Dannels & Co. (Stevenson St. & Forbes Ave.)	1874-1880
	675b	Pier & Dannels, Oregon Brewery	1880-1895
PA	676a	John N. Reichenbach (Blackberry Alley)	1874-1883
	676b	Michael Winter & Bros. (Wolfgang & Alois) (21st & Josephine)	1883-1893
	676c	M. Winter Bros. Brewing Co.	1893-1899
	676d	Pittsburgh Brewing Co., Winter Brewery aka M. Winter Bros. Brewing Co. (1899-1900)	1899-1920
PA	677	Joshua Rhodes (Duquesne St. & Barker Alley)	1874-1880
PA	678	Wm. Rueckeisen (34 6th St.)	1882-1882
PA	679	John Schaler	1874-1882
PA	680	Henry Schmelz, West End Brewery (Steuben & Chartiers Aves.)	1874-1890
PA	681a	G. W. Schminella	1875-1877
	681b	H. T. Wood & Bro. (Laurel Ave. & Juniper St.)	1877-1879
	681c	Wood Bros.	1879-1882
	681d	Wood Brewing Co.	1882-1884
PA	682	George Shiras (at the Point)	c1795

Pittsburgh (cont.)

PA	683	John G. Stirm (Butler St.)	1874-1884
PA	684a	John N. Straub (152 S. Canal St.)	1840-1863
	684b	Gilmore, Straub & Co.	1867-1870
	684c	John N. Straub & Co.	1870-1883
PA	685a	John N. Straub (Main St. & Liberty Ave.)	1831-1840
	685b	John Gangwisch	1840- ?
	685c	Gangwisch & Straub	? -1875
	685d	Straub & Son (Theodore)	1875-1877
	685e	Straub & Son (Herman)	1877-1880
	685f	Union Brewing Co.	1880-1885
	685g	Herman Straub & Co.	1885-1890
	685h	Straub Brewing Co.	1890-1899
	685i	Pittsburgh Brewing Co., Straub Brewery aka Straub Brewing Co. (1899-1900)	1899-1920
PA	686a	Joseph Wainwright (36th & Charlotte Sts.)	1818-1852
	686b	Wainwright Bros. (Jarvis & Zachariah)	1852- ?
	686c	Z. Wainwright & Co.	1874-1893
	686d	Wainwright Brewing Co. (56th & Butler Sts.)	1893-1899
	686e	Pittsburgh Brewing Co., Wainwright Brewery (3615 Butler St.) aka Wainwright Brewing Co. (1899-1900)	1899-1920
PA	687a	Frank Weber	1878-1879
	687b	F. Weber & Co.	1879-1880
PA	688	Joseph Weis	1874-1875
PA	689	Henry Weising	1880-1882
PA	690a	Henry L. Wilhelm (2600/2604 Josephine & 26th Sts.)	1865-1882
	690b	Mrs. Caroline Wilhelm, Washington Brewery	1882-1890
	690c	Edel & Seiferth	1890-1890
	690d	Washington Brewing Co.	1890-1895
	690e	John Seiferth & Bros.	1895-1899
	690f	Pittsburgh Brewing Co., J. Seiferth & Bros.	1899-1899
PA	691	Anton Wolf (Collings Ave.)	1874-1875
PA	692a	Wood & Hughes (24th & Smallman Sts.)	1845-1862
	692b	(Joseph) Spencer & (James) McKay	1862-1870
	692c	Spencer, McKay & Co.	1870-1886
	692d	Spencer & (Robert) Liddell	1886-1890
	692e	Wm. Tann, Phoenix Brewery	1890-1890
	692f	Wm. Tann Brewing Co.	1890-1891
	692g	Phoenix Brewing Co.	1891-1899
	692h	Pittsburgh Brewing Co., Phoenix Brewery aka Phoenix Brewing Co. (1899-1900)	1899-1920
PA	693a	Young & Booth	1874-1877
	693b	Thomas Booth	1877-1880

Pittston

PA	694	James E. Clark	1873- ?
PA	695	Coggins & McNally	1890-1890
PA	696	Thos. J. Corcoran	1891-1891
PA	697a	Peter Daily	1873-1875
	697b	A. Burschell	1875-1878
	697c	H. R. Hughes & Co.	1878-1884
	697d	H. R. Hughes	1884-1887
	697e	Estate of H. R. Hughes	1887-1896
	697f	Pennsylvania Central Brewing Co. of Scranton, Hughes Ale Brewery Dept.	1896-1906
	697g	Jos. H. Glennon's Brewery (Main St.)	1907-1920
	697h	Liberty Brewing Corp. (N. Main & New Sts.)	1933-1934
	697i	Pittston Brewing Corp. (N. Main & Esther Sts.)	1934-1942
	697j	Yankee Brewing Co. (4/14 Esther & 5/15 New Sts.)	1942-1946
	697k	Champ Brewing Co.	1946-1948
PA	698	Jacob Dentler	1890-1890

Pittston (cont.)

PA 699 Joseph Fellows 1789- ?

PA 700a Howarth & Law (Dock St.) 1848-1860
700b H. R. & M. Hughes 1860-1887
700c Hughes & Glennon 1887-1897
700d Pennsylvania Central Brewing Co. of Scranton, Hughes & Glennon Dept. 1897-1912

PA 701 Mohawk Brewing Co. NP 1934-1934

PA 702a Union Brewery c1860
702b Howell & King 1874-1875
702c George Bishop 1875-1884
702d E. B. Long, receiver for estate of Howell & King 1884-1888
702e Howell & King Co. 1888-1920
702f Howell & King Co. (7 Thomas St.) 1933-1935
702g Howell & King Co., Inc. 1935-1939

Plumer

PA 703 Christian Brecht 1878-1879

Porter

PA 704 Geo. W. Keilman 1888-1888

Pottstown

PA 705a Joseph M. Sellinger 1884- ?
705b A. H. Kretz & Bro. ? -1891
aka A. H. Kretz & Co. (1890)
705c Froelich & Pfaender 1891-1897
705d Pottstown Brewing Co. 1897-1912
705e Froelich Brewing Co. 1912-1920

Pottsville

PA 706a George Lauer c1845-1860
706b Frederick Lauer ? -1877
706c Lorenz Schmidt 1877-1893
706d Estate of Lorenz Schmidt (Main St., Mount Carbon) 1893-1906
706e Schmidt Estate Brewing Co. 1906-1908
706f Mellett & Nichter Brewing Co. 1908-1920
706g Matthew Keeley, trading as Mt. Carbon Brewery (716 S. Centre) 1933-1935
706h Mount Carbon Brewery 1935-1976
aka Mt. Carbon Mfg. & Supply Co. (1936-1942)

PA 707 Ludwig Raeder 1882-1884

PA 708a (Charles) Rettig & (John) Liebner 1865-1877
708b Charles Rettig 1877-1892
708c Estate of Charles Rettig (820 W. Market St.) 1892-1893
708d Charles Rettig & Son 1893-1901
708e Rettig Brewing Co. (818/900 W. Market & 9th Sts.) 1901-1920
708f Rettig Brewing Co. NP 1934-1934

PA 709a David G. Yuengling (N. Centre St.) 1829-1831
709b David G. Yuengling (501 Mahantonga St.) 1831-1873
709c D. G. Yuengling & Son 1873-1914
709d D. G. Yuengling & Son, Inc. 1914-1920
709e D. G. Yuengling & Son, Inc. (5th & Mahantonga Sts.) 1933-

Punxsutawney

PA 710 Elk Run Brewing Co. 1902-1916

PA 711 Christian Haag 1884-1884

PA 712a Kraus & Baumgartner 1893- ?
712b Joseph Baumgartner ? -1897
712c Baumgartner & Schneider 1897-1900
712d Joseph Baumgartner 1900-1904
712e Punxsutawney Brewing Co. 1904-1920

PA 713a Nicholas Phillips 1890-1893
713b Peter Phillips & Co. 1893-1894
713c Peter Phillips 1894-1895
713d Otto Phillips 1895-1897

Railroad P.O., York County (see Shrewsbury)

Reading

PA	714a	(Peter) Barbey & (Abraham) Paeltzer	1859-1861
	714b	Peter Barbey (435 Penn St.)	1861-1869
	714c	Peter Barbey (Hockley & N. River Sts.)	1869-1880
	714d	Peter Barbey & Son, aka P. Barbey & Son (430 Court, Hockley, W. Elm & Gordon Sts.)	1880-1920
	714e	Barbey's, Inc.	1933-1951
	714f	Sunshine Brewing Co. aka Bavarian Brewing Co. (1968-1970) aka Esslinger, Inc. (1967-1970) aka Falcon Brewing Co. (1961-1963) aka Hatfield-McCoy Brewing Co. (1963-1965) aka Jamaica Brewing Co. (1964-1966) aka Muhlheim Brewing Co. (1962-1968) aka Playmate Brewing Co. (1967-1968) aka Ruppert Brewing Co.	1951-1970
PA	715a	John Borell (Penn above 7th St. near Cherry)	1843-1857
	715b	Mrs. John Borell	1857-1861
	715c	Henry Seidel	1861-1863
	715d	Levi L. Bertolet	1863-1865
	715e	Henry Seidel	1865-1870
PA	716	George Brobst (bank of Schuylkill River)	1814-1832
PA	717a	Henry Eckert (4th St. between Franklin & Chestnut)	1763-1766
	717b	John Spohn	1766-1775
	717c	Jacob Bright	1775-1815
	717d	Jacob Bright Estate	1815-1826
PA	718a	Herman Floto	c1884
	718b	Reading Brewing Co. (S. 9th & Little Laurel Sts.)	1886-1920
	718c	Health Beverage Co.	1920-1933
	718d	The Old Reading Brewery, Inc. aka Dutch Country Brewing Co. (1961-1965)	1933-1965
	718e	Reading Brewing Co. aka Bergheim Brewing Co. aka Mein Brewing Co. (1973-1976)	1965-1976
PA	719	Heidelberg Brewery (131 S. 2nd St.)	1934-1934
PA	720a	Joseph S. Hoyer, Keystone Brewery	1871-1874
	720b	Wm. Reiser & Rudolph Heintz	1874-1874
	720c	Abraham Peltzer (38 S. 7th St.)	1875-1882
	720d	Peltzer & Flaig	1882-1884
	720e	Abraham Peltzer	1884-1890
	720f	Roehrich & Raab (purchased by Deppen Brewing Co. & closed)	1890-1903
PA	721a	David C. Keller (242 Ash St.)	1875-1877
	721b	Samuel C. Keller	1877-1880
	721c	Keller & Schaeffer	1880-1884
	721d	Keller & Eyring	1884-1888
	721e	Otto Eyring	1888-1893
	721f	Edward H. Gaul	1893-1895
	721g	Rich. C. Osterhaut	1895-1900
PA	722a	Frederick Lauer, Plant 2 (3rd & Walnut Sts.)	1874-1882
	722b	Lauer Brewing Co., Plant 2	1882-1920
PA	723a	George Lauer (3rd & Chestnut Sts.)	1826-1847
	723b	Frederick Lauer, Plant 1	1847-1882
	723c	Lauer Brewing Co., Plant 1	1882-1902
PA	724a	Muhlenberg Brewing Co. (Kutztown Road, Bernharts)	1895-1920
	724b	Munich Brewery	1934-1934
PA	725a	Peter Nagel	1828-1845
	725b	Nicholas A. Felix (935 Chestnut St.)	1845-1875
	725c	Estate of N. A. Felix	1875-1879
	725d	Wm. P. Deppen	1879-1901
	725e	Deppen Brewing Co.	1901-1908
	725f	Deppen Brewing Co., Spring Garden Brewery (341 N. 3rd St.)	1908-1920
	725g	Deppen Manufacturing Co.	1933-1937
PA	726	Sebastian Schmitt	1884-1888

Reading (cont.)

PA	727a	John Spohn (Penn St. below 6th)	c1780-1798
	727b	Joseph Hoch	1798-1867
PA	728a	(John C.) Stocker & (John) Roehrich (1700 N. 11th St.)	1891-1897
	728b	John C. Stocker	1897-1904
	728c	Estate of John C. Stocker	1904-1906
	728d	Fairview Brewery, August Schneider	1906-1912
	728e	Mt. Penn Brewing Co.	1912-1920
	728f	Fisher Brewing Co., Inc., aka Fisher Brewery	1928-1934
	728g	Woerner Brewery (N. 11th St.)	1937-1938
	728h	Adam C. Jaeger Brewing Co. (2000 N. 11th St.)	NP 1942-1943

Red Bank

PA	729	Henry & Lace	1884-1884

Renovo

PA	730a	Luke Binder	1874-1897
	730b	Edward L. Binder	1897-1910
	730c	Binder's Brewery	1910-1920
	730d	Joseph H. Velott, trading as Binder's Brewery (Hwy. Rt. 120)	1935-1938

Republic

PA	731	Republic Brewing Co.	1910-1920

Reyburn

PA	732	Elk Brewing Co.	1895-1895

Reynoldsville

PA	733	Kingsley & Co.	1878-1879

Riverview

PA	734	Riverview Brewing Co.	1904-1904

Rochester

PA	735a	Beaver Valley Brewing Co.	1905-1910
	735b	Beaver Brewing Co.	1911-1911

Rockwood

PA	736a	Rockwood Brewing Co.	1908-1920
	736b	Rockwood Brewing Corp. (204 W. Main St.)	1933-1934
	736c	Belmont Ale Brewery Corp.	1934-1935

Roopsburg

PA	737	Mrs. Catherine Haas	1884-1884

Roscoe (Lucyville)

PA	738a	Moose Brewing Co.	1903-1920
	738b	Moose Brewing Co. (Good St., Hickory Alley & Monongahela River)	1933-1949
	738c	Penn Brewing Co., aka Moose Brewing Co. of Lucyville	1949-1950

Roxborough

PA	739	Sebastian Nagle	c1878

Ruffsdale

PA	740a	Xenius Snyder	1893-1894
	740b	Union Brewing Co.	1894-1895

Saint Marys

PA	741a	Burgess & Wesnitzer	1884-1885
	741b	Francis J. Roeder	1885-1886
	741c	Karl Wacker	1886-1890
PA	742	William Geier	1874-1884
PA	743a	St. Mary's Brewing Co. (441 Hall Ave.)	1900-1909
	743b	Elk County Brewing Co., aka Elk Brewing Co.	1909-1920
	743b	St. Mary's Beverage Co.	1933-1940
PA	744	Lorenz Vogel	1874-1879
PA	745a	Chas. Volk	1872-1876
	745b	Peter Straub (Brussel St.)	1876-1911
	745c	Benzinger Spring Brewery	1911-1913
	745d	Peter Straub Sons	1913-1920
	745e	Straub Brewery (303 Sorg St.)	1933-1947
	745f	Straub Brewery, Inc.	1947-

Saint Marys (cont.)

PA	746a	Jos. Windfelder	1845-1877
	746b	Chas. Luhr & Co.	1877-1891
	746c	Henry Luhr	1891-1908

Saint Vincent's

PA	747a	Wimmer & Null	1874-1875
	747b	St. Vincent's Brewing Co.	1875-1888

Salisbury

PA	748	W. G. Staehle	1888-1888

Saucon

PA	749	George Rennig	1874-1878

Saxonburg

PA	750	F. Laube & Son	1874-1875

Sayre

PA	751a	Sayre Brewing Co., Ltd. (Thomas Ave.)	1905-1920
	751b	Sayre Brewing Co. (317 S. Thomas Ave.)	1933-1935

Scottdale

PA	752a	Scottdale Brewing Co. (Broadway)	1891-1899
	752b	Pittsburgh Brewing Co., Scottdale Brewing Co.	1899-1899
PA	753	Union Brewing Co.	1896-1896

Scranton (includes Dunmore)

PA	754	P. Burschell & Son (Dunmore)	1875- ?
PA	755a	Casey & Kelly Brewing Co. (Remington Ave. & Locust St.)	1892-1897
	755b	Pennsylvania Central Brewing Co., Casey & Kelly Brewing Co. Dept.	1897-1920
	755c	Pennsylvania Central Brewing Co. (431 N. Central Ave.)	1933-1934
PA	756a	Consumers Beer Co. (420 Nay Aug. Ave.)	1899-1899
	756b	Anthracite Beer Co.	1899-1920
	756c	A. B. Company	1934-1937
PA	757	Walter Gorman	1874-1875
PA	758	M. M. Kearney	1874-1875
PA	759a	Lackawanna Brewing Co. (Poplar St. & Monsey Ave.)	1896-1897
	759b	Pennsylvania Central Brewing Co., Lackawanna Brewery Dept.	1897-1920
	759c	Lackawanna Beer and Ale Corp. (1101/1121 Monsey Ave.)	1933-1943
PA	760a	McQuade & Son (340 Blakely St., Dunmore)	1890-1894
	760b	McQuade's Son & Wills	1894-1896
	760c	Keystone Brewing Co.	1896-1920
	760d	Intercoast Brewing Co.	1933-1935
	760e	Keystone Brewing Co.	1935-1936
	760f	Union Brewing Co. of Scranton	1936-1939
PA	761	Meadowbrook Brewing Co.	1891-1891
PA	762a	Morton & Briggs	1874-1884
	762b	Scranton Brewing Co. (1216 Cedar Ave. & Brick St.)	1884-1897
	762c	Pennsylvania Central Brewing Co., Scranton Brewing Co. Dept.	1897-1910
PA	763a	Mrs. Mina Robinson (Cedar Ave. & Alder St.)	1882-1897
	763b	Pennsylvania Central Brewing Co., Mina Robinson Dept.	1897-1901
PA	764a	P. Robinson, Jr.	1862-1875
	764b	Elizabeth Robinson (Cedar Ave.)	1875-1891
	764c	E. Robinson's Sons (433/455 N. 7th St.)	1891-1897
	764d	Pennsylvania Central Brewing Co., E. Robinson's Sons Dept.	1897-1920
PA	765	Reinheit Brewing Co. (Genet St.)	1934-1936
PA	766a	Standard Brewing Co. (Penn Ave. & Walnut St.)	1904-1920
	766b	Standard Brewing Co. of Scranton	1933-1953
	766c	Standard Industries, Inc.	1953-1954
PA	767	Henry Weissenrieder	1882-1882
PA	768a	Wenzel & Pfuhl	1882-1884
	768b	Conrad Wenzel (Dunmore)	1884-1884

Sewickly

PA 769 Paul Deutsch 1874-1875

Shaler Township (see Pittsburgh)

Shamokin

PA 770a Gottlieb Fritz, Eagle Run Brewery 1854- ?
770b John Geywitz, Eagle Run Brewery ?
770c Swenk & Lehner, Eagle Run Brewery ?
770d John Douty, Eagle Run Brewery ?
770e Marke & Schweibenz, Eagle Run Brewery ? -1871
770f Martin Markel 1871-1893
770g Philip H. Fuhrmann 1893-1896
770h Fuhrmann & Schmidt, Eagle Run Brewery (Commerce & Washington) 1896-1906
770i Fuhrmann & Schmidt Brewing Co., Eagle Run Brewery 1906-1920

PA 771a Shamokin Brewing Co. 1905-1911
771b Fuhrmann & Schmidt Brewing Co., Shamokin Brewery (Harrison St.) 1911-1920
771c Fuhrmann & Schmidt Brewing Co. (235/249 S. Harrison St.) 1933-1966
771d Fuhrmann & Schmidt Brewing Co. (owned by Ortlieb Brewing Co., Philadelphia) 1966-1975

Sharon

PA 772 F. M. Derr 1882-1884

PA 773 August Huck 1874-1875

PA 774 Mrs. Maria Robinson 1882-1882

PA 775 Union Brewing Co. 1901-1920

Sharpsburg

PA 776a Fort Pitt Brewing Co. (16th & S. Canal) 1906-1920
776b Fort Pitt Brewing Co. (16th & Mary Sts.) 1933-1957
776c Fort Pitt Brewing Co., div. of Fort Pitt Industries, Inc. 1957-1957

Shenandoah

PA 777a Columbia Brewing Co. (110/114 S. Main St.) 1894-1920
777b Columbia Brewing Co. (101/115 S. Ferguson St.) 1933-1968

PA 778a Home Brewing Co. (234 N. Main St.) 1899-1920
778b The Home Brewing Co., aka Muhlheim Brewing Co. 1933-1934

PA 779 J. Tunnah 1878-1880

Shickshinny

PA 780 Freeland Brewery NP 1934-1934

Shireoaks

PA 781a E. W. Townsend 1890-1891
781b Oliver Gregg 1891-1891
781c Shireoaks Brewing Co. 1891-1903

Simpson (formerly Carbondale)

PA 782a Fell Brewing Co. (Belmont St.) 1901-1920
782b Fell Brewing Co. (404 Belmont St. & 15 Railroad St.) 1933-1951

PA 783a John Nealon 1856-1883
783b Loftus & Nealon 1883-1889
783c Peter Krantz (86 S. Church St.) 1889-1897
783d Pennsylvania Central Brewing Co., Peter Krantz Brewery 1897-1920

Smithton

PA 784a Eureka Brewing Co. 1907-1920
784b Pure Aqua Products & Ice Co. 1920-1933
784c Jones Brewing Co. (2nd St. & B&O R.R.) aka Fort Pitt Brewing Co. (1965-) 1933-

South Fork

PA 785a South Fork Brewing Co. 1907-1920
785b South Fork Brewing Co. (301 River St.) 1933-1940

South Sharon (see Farrell)

Spangler

PA 786a Spangler Brewing Co. 1905-1916
786b Rex Brewing Co. 1916-1920

Spring, Centre County

PA 787 J. Gassner 1874-1875

Spring Garden

PA 788 Abraham Pfeiffer 1874-1880

Steelton

PA 789a National Brewing Co. 1905-1920
789b Penn Brewing Co. (317/319 Frederick & Conestoga Sts.) 1933-1934
789c Imperial Brewing Co. 1937-1938
789d National Brewing Co. 1938-1939

Stroudsburg

PA 790a Stroudsburg Brewing Co., (Lincoln Ave. & 1st Ave.) 1899-1913
790b Stroudsburg Brewery Co. 1913-1916
790c Neustadtl Brewing Corp. 1933-1935
790d Stroudsburg Brewing Co. 1935-1937

Stone Township (see McKees Rocks)

Sugar Creek

PA 791a Philip Worst 1874-1875
791b Alex. Schnell 1882- ?
791c Christian Brecht 1888-1893

Summit

PA 792a Charles E. Schwaderer 1888- ?
792b Robert J. McNally ? -1899
792c Lickert & Querin 1899-1901

Sunbury

PA 793a Joseph Bacher 1865-1873
793b J. & A. Moeschlin, Cold Spring Brewery 1873-1920
793c Melvin G. Fahringer, Sunbury Brewery (7th & Packer Sts.) 1933-1934
793d Sunbury Brewing Co., Inc. 1934-1937

Susquehanna

PA 794 M. J. Prendergast 1882-1882

Sutersville

PA 795 Westmoreland Brewing Co. 1899-1920

Tamaqua

PA 796a Joseph Adam 1874-1891
796b Redig ?
796c John F. McGinty's Brewery 1898-1909
796d Liberty Brewing Co. 1909-1920
796e Lehigh Valley Brewing Co., Inc. 1933-1934
796f Rahn Brewing Co., Inc. 1934-1934

PA 797a Henry M. Kalb 1874-1877
797b Jos. Haefner 1877-1884
797c George Sinzer 1884-1886

Tarentum

PA 798a Adolph Richter 1884- ?
798b Geo. W. Luther 1891- ?
798c Schmidt & Willinger 1896-1897
798d J. C. Willinger (Humes St.) 1897-1897
798e Anchor Brewing Co. 1897-1920

Tarrs (Tarr)

PA 799a Union Brewery 1896-1899
799b Union Brewing Co. 1899-1905
799c Crescent Brewing Co., Union Brewery 1905-1913
799d Union Brewery, aka Union Brewing Co. 1913-1920
799e Tarr Brewing Co. 1933-1939

Texas

PA 800 Hartung & Krantz 1874-1880

PA 801 Jacob Lauer 1874-1880

Tioga

PA 802 Frederick Hofer 1890-1891

PA 803 G. F. Ochs 1878-1897

Titusville (includes Pithole City)

PA	804a	Hoenig & Theobald	c1872-1877
	804b	John Theobald	1877-1884
	804c	Francis Theobald aka Theobald Bros. (1890)	1884-1897
	804d	George W. Theobald (11 South & Franklin Sts.)	1897-1898
	804e	Frances Theobald, City Brewery	1898-1910
	804f	City Brewery, Chas. Roesner	1911-1920
PA	805a	Charles Schwartz	1874-1899
	805b	Katharina Schwartz	1899-1901
	805c	Edward Benke	1901-1904
PA	806	D. Steadman (Duncan St. between 1st & 2nd, Pithole City)	1865-1867

Towanda

PA	807a	Anton Loder	1878-1891
	807b	Loder & Walbridge	1891-1893

Tremont

PA	808	Krebs & Keller	1874-1875
PA	809a	Stocker & Roehrich	1888-1890
	809b	Hewel & Son	1890-1891
	809c	John J. Hewel	1891-1895
	809d	Miller & Michel (Clay St.)	1895-1897
	809e	Tremont Brewing Co.	1899-1908
	809f	Ferd. Petruschak	1908-1910
	809g	Sievers' Tremont Brewery	1910-1911

Tyrone

PA	810a	C. Gratten	1850-1877
	810b	Jos. Hewel	1877-1890
	810c	Bavarian Brewing Co.	1890-1897
	810d	Tyrone Brewing Co.	1897-1902
	810e	Royal Brewing Co.	1902-1903

Union City

PA	811	West E. French	1874-1875
PA	812	Christian Koch	1874-1875
PA	813	A. Saltsman (Main St.)	c1870
PA	814	Treser & Siegle	1874-1875
PA	815a	Protosius Wager	1874-1877
	815b	Theresa Wager	1877-1884
	815c	John Wager	1884-1891

Uniontown

PA	816	Fayette Brewing Co. (30 E. Fayette St.)	1900-1920
PA	817	Highhouse Brewing Co.	1907-1910
PA	818	Labor Brewing Co.	1905-1920
PA	819a	Uniontown Brewing Co.	1898-1899
	819b	Pittsburgh Brewing Co., Uniontown Brewing Co. (33/34 N. Beeson) aka Uniontown Brewery (1899-1900)	1899-1920
	819c	Pittsburgh Brewing Co., Uniontown Brewery	1933-1948

Unity

PA	820	Benedictine Society	1878-1880

Upper Augusta (see Sunbury)

Vernon

PA	821	N. Dudenhoeffer	1875-1884
PA	822	Frank Schwab	1874-1884

Walker

PA	823	George Hagle	1874-1884

Warren

PA	824a	Philip Leonhart, Jr.	1878-1884
	824b	David Ridelsperger	1884-1890
	824c	Philip Leonhart, Jr.	1890-1891
PA	825	Warren Brewing Co.	1906-1920

Washington

PA 826a C. P. Corlett 1896-1897
826b Crescent Brewing Co. (Wheeling & Oregon Sts.) 1897-1920

PA 827 Andrew Ditz 1874-1884

PA 828 G. J. Schnarderer 1874-1884

PA 829 Theodore Sell 1884-1888

PA 830 Star Brewing Co. (Chartiers & Star Sts.) 1902-1911

PA 831a Louis Zelt & Bro. (Wheeling & Oregon Sts.) 1874-1884
831b Louis Zelt 1884-1891
831c Jacob Zelt 1891-1895
831d Henry Zelt 1895-1900
831e Zelt & Bros., Washington Brewery 1900-1920
831f Washington Brewing Co. (740/748 Jefferson Ave.) 1933-1940

Waynesboro

PA 832 Elias B. Wilson 1884-1884

Waynesburg

PA 833 Waynesburg Brewing Co. 1901-1911

Weissport

PA 834 Catherine Geisel ? -1878

Wellsboro

PA 835 John Ochs 1874-1888

PA 836 Mrs. Christina Scheffer 1874-1890

PA 837 Michael Schwarzenbach 1865- ?

West Bridgewater (see Bridgewater)

West Elizabeth

PA 838 John Werner 1891-1891

Westfall

PA 839 Henry Geiger 1874-1875

West Homestead (see Homestead)

West Millcreek

PA 840 C. E. Ball 1893-1893

West Salem

PA 841 Peter Saal 1874-1875

Wilkes-Barre (includes Edwardsville, Kingston Station)

PA 842a (George C.) Baer & (Charles) Stegmaier (S. Canal St.) 1857-1863
842b Baer & Stegmaier (E. Market St.) 1863-1873
842c C. Stegmaier & Son (230/246 E. Market St.) 1880-1897
842d Stegmaier Brewing Co. 1897-1920
842e Stegmaier Brewing Co., aka Gold Medal Brewing Co. (152 Market & Baltimore Sts.) 1933-1974

PA 843a Bartels Brewing Co. (Edwardsville) 1898-1906
843b Bartels Brewing Co. (Kingston Station) 1907-1920
843c Bartels Brewing Co. (Plymouth St. & Toby's Creek, Edwardsville) 1933-1968

PA 844 Martin Baur & Co. 1874-1875

PA 845a Joel Bowkley Brewery (N. River St. & The Canal) 1854-1867
845b James E. Clarke 1867- ?
845c C. E. Stegmaier 1875-1877
845d Charles Stegmaier & Son 1877-1880

PA 846 Andrew M. Bryden 1888-1893

PA 847a Franklin Brewery, Emil Malinowski (River Road, St. Marys Road, Hanover Township) 1911-1927
847b Hanover Co. 1937-1933
847c Wyoming Brewing Co., Inc. (St. Marys Road near River Road) 1933-1934
847d The Franklin Brewing Co. 1934-1956

Wilkes-Barre (cont.)

PA	848a	Thomas Ingham (N. River & Union St.)	1823-1823
	848b	Thomas Ingham (N. River & W. Union St.)	1823-1824
	848c	Christian Reichard	1824- ?
	848d	John Reichard	? -1850
	848e	Reichard & Stegmaier	1850-1857
	848f	Reichard & Stauff (85/87 Water St.)	1857-1877
	848g	Reichard & Son	1877-1884
	848h	Reichard's Sons	1884-1888
	848i	Reichards & Co.	1888-1891
	848j	Reichard, Weaver & Katz	1891-1893
	848k	Reichard & Weaver	1891-1893
	848l	Pennsylvania Central Brewing Co., Reichard & Weaver Dept. (121/135 Water St.)	1897-1920
PA	849a	Luzerne County Brewing Co. (N. Pennsylvania Ave.)	1905-1910
	849b	Lion Brewing Co.	1910-1920
	849c	The Lion, Inc. (5/6 Hart St. & 700 N. Pennsylvania Ave.) aka Gibbons Brewery (1943-1974) aka Gibbons/Stegmaier Brewery (1974-) aka Pocono Brewing Co. (1973-)	1933-
PA	850	Williams & Norris	1874-1875

Williamsport

PA	851a	City Brewery, Jacob Hoffman	1854-1854
	851b	City Brewery, Frederick Buehler	1855-1865
	851c	Henry Jacob Flock	1865-1874
	851d	Jacob Flock (601/625 Franklin St.)	1874-1884
	851e	Mrs. Jacob Flock	1884-1901
	851f	Flock Brewing Co.	1901-1920
	851g	Flock Brewing Co. (252 E. Edwin & 601/625 Franklin)	1933-1951
PA	852a	Bennann & Kuebler	1878-1882
	852b	James Smith	1882-1884
PA	853a	August Koch, Sr.	1850- ?
	853b	A. Koch & Bro.	1878-1893
	853c	Koch Brewing Co.	1893-1920
	853d	Kochs, Inc. (535 Main St.)	1933-1937
	853e	Kochs Brewery, Joseph H. Velott	1937-1943
	853f	Kochs Brewery, branch of Flock Brewing Co.	1943-1943
PA	854a	Chris. Schroeder & Bros.	1874-1877
	854b	William Schroeder	1877-1880
PA	855a	Welker & Goodbrod	1898-1899
	855b	John Welker	1899-1902
	855c	Star Brewing Co. (1500 Market St.)	1907-1920

Windber

PA	856a	Windber Brewing Co.	1905-1911
	856b	Windber Brewing Co., No. 2	1914-1920
	856c	Windber Brewing Co. (1700 Graham Ave.)	1934-1940

Womelsdorf

PA	857	George Lauer	1824-1826

Wood's Run

PA	858	Mann & Shider	1888-1888

Woodward

PA	859	Rudolph Widmann	1874-1880

York

PA	860	John W. Free	1874-1875
PA	861a	Kurtz, Nes & Son	1875-1877
	861b	F. W. Ulrich	1877-1884
PA	862	A. Pfeiffer	1882-1884
PA	863a	Andrew Schlegel	1863-1873
	863b	Theodore R. Helb, Keystone Brewery (King & Queen Sts.)	1873-1920
	863c	Helb's Keystone Brewery (50 S. Queen St.)	1933-1950

York (cont.)

PA 864a York Brewing Co. (West & Company Sts. & Pa. R.R.) 1893-1920
864b York Brewing Co. (380 West Norway St.) 1934-1935
864c Cooper Brewing Co. 1935-1936

Young

PA 865 Christian Haag 1874-1882

RHODE ISLAND

Arlington (see Providence)

Cranston (see Providence)

Hillsgrove (see Warwick)

Lonsdale

RI 1 Geo. W. Hogue 1905-1912

Newport

RI 2a Alfred W. Hill & Son 1874-1877
2b W. S. Cooper 1877-1882

Pawtucket

RI 3a John H. Gregory 1905-1906
3b Emily Rodney 1908-1908

RI 4a Hand Brewing Co. (Mendon Ave. & Freeman St.) 1898-1920
4b Rhode Island Brewing Co. (20 Freeman St.) 1933-1939

Providence (includes Arlington & Cranston)

RI 5a American Brewing Co. (Harris Ave. & Eagle St.) 1892-1896
5b Providence Brewing Co. 1896-1920

RI 6 Sergeant Baulston 1639- ?

RI 7a Albert Dinter 1875-1877
7b Nauman & Gauch 1877-1878
7c Charles Gauch 1878-1879

RI 8 Pelatiah Fletcher 1875- ?

RI 9 Herman Gartner 1878-1879

RI 10 Hebe Co. NP 1934-1934

RI 11 Henry Herrman 1878-1879

RI 12a Otis Holmes (Jackson & Fountain Sts.) 1835-1862
12b John Blight 1867-1875
12c (John P.) Cooney & (James) Hanley 1875-1879
12d James Hanley & Co. 1879-1885
12e Rhode Island Brewing Co. 1885-1896
12f James Hanley Brewing Co. (35 Jackson St.) 1896-1920
12g The James Hanley Co. 1934-1957

PA 13a Keiley & Sullivan 1873-1877
13b Keiley Bros., Eagle Brewery (450/455 W. Exchange St.) 1877-1888
13c Bartholomew Keiley, Eagle Brewery 1888-1899
13d Eagle Brewing Co. 1899-1920

RI 14a Narragansett Brewing Co. (Depot Ave.) 1890-1915
14b Narragansett Brewing Co. (New Depot Ave., Arlington) 1915-1920
14c Narragansett Brewing Co. (New Depot & Coombs Aves., Cranston) 1933-1951
14d Narragansett Brewing Co. (Cranston & Garfield Ave.) 1951-1965
aka Croft Brewing Co. (1957-1965)
aka Haffenreffer Brewing Co. (1964-1965)
aka James Hanley Co. (1957-1965)
aka G. Krueger Brewing Co. (1960-1965)
14e Falstaff Brewing Corp., dba Narragansett Brewing Co. 1965-1975
aka Chr. Feiganspan
aka Krueger Brewing Co. (1965-1975)
aka Richards Brewing Co. (1971-1974)
14f Falstaff Brewing Corp., dba Narragansett Brewing Co., affiliated with General Brewing Co., California 1975-1981
aka P. Ballantine
aka Krueger Brewing Co. (1975-1981)
14g Falstaff Brewing Corp., dba Narragansett Brewing Co. 1983-

Providence (cont.)

RI	15	Park Brew Co. (1100 Elmwood Ave.)	1899-1913
RI	16	H. Perpente	1880-1880
RI	17	Roger Williams Brewing Corp. (61/65 Troy St.)	1934-1940
RI	18	Union Brewing Co.	1910-1910
RI	19	What Cheer Brewing Co.	1910-1910
RI	20a	(A.) Woelfel & (Nicholas) Molter (14/20 Potter St.)	1868-1876
	20b	Nicholas Molter	1876-1877
	20c	Molter & Oehm	1877-1877
	20d	Nicholas Molter	1877-1885
	20e	N. Molter's Sons	1885-1895
	20f	Molter Bros. (Henry T. & John W.)	1895-1897
	20g	Henry T. Molter (14/20 Garnet St.)	1897-1911
	20h	Consumers Brewing Co. (Cranston Station)	1911-1920

Tiverton

RI	21	Tiverton Brewing Co.	1914-1915

Warwick

RI	22	Canadian Brewing Co.	NP 1934-1934
RI	23a	Consumer's Brewing Co. (Jefferson Ave.)	1933-1935
	23b	Hollen Brewing Co., Inc.	1936-1938
RI	24	Lombardi Brewing Co. (Eastern Ave.)	NP 1934-1934
RI	25a	Warwick Brewing Co. (27 East Ave.)	1933-1935
	25b	Bond Brewing Co.	1935-1937

West Warwick

RI	26	Kent Brewing Co. (2 Bridal Ave.)	1933-1934

SOUTH CAROLINA

Charleston

SC	1a	Claussen Brewery, J. C. H. Claussen	1880-1882
	1b	Claussen Brewing Co.	1882-1884
	1c	Cramer & Kersten	1884-1888
	1d	Palmetto Brewing Co. (Hayne & Anson Sts.)	1888-1896
	1e	Germania Brewing Co.	1896-1918

Columbia

SC	2	Carolina Brewing Co.	NP 1934-1934
SC	3a	John C. Seegers	1874-1884
	3b	John C. Seegers	1895-1899

Walhalla

SC	4	A. Brennecke	? -1874
SC	5a	Chr. Bush	1878-1880
	5b	Christopher Burns	1880-1881
	5c	Wanner & Weldon	1881-1882
	5d	John G. Gutekunst	1882-1884
SC	6	John Kaufman	1874-1875

SOUTH DAKOTA

Athol

SD	1	Jacob Nikolas	1888-1889

Big Stone

SD	2	Peter F. Carlton	1882-1882

Canton

SD	3	Andreas Handschigl	1882-1888

Central City			
SD	4a	Rosenkranz & Werner	1878- ?
	4b	Henry Rosenkranz	? -1889
	4c	Black Hills Brewing and Malting Co.	1896-1897
	4d	Faulkner & Conner	1897-1898
	4e	Black Hills Brewing and Malting Co.	1898-1900
	4f	Black Hills Brewing Co.	1900-1917
Custer City			
SD	5a	Robert Parks	1878-1879
	5b	Chas. Bissinger	1879-1880
Deadwood			
SD	6	C. E. Downer & Co.	1878-1884
SD	7	Wm. Nishwitz	1878-1879
SD	8a	Rodebank & Nielson	1878-1879
	8b	Parkhurst & Co.	1879-1882
SD	9	A. Schuchardt	1878-1879
Eureka			
SD	10	Eureka Brewing Co.	1899-1904
Galena City			
SD	11	Charles Weymuller	1877-1878
Gayville			
SD	12	John H. Heckmann	1882-1884
SD	13a	Hein & Silkinson	1882-1884
	13b	John Lang	1884-1889
Huron			
SD	14a	(Frank) Blume & (Anton) Osten	1884-1884
	14b	Mrs. Helene Blume	1884-1895
	14c	Blume Brewing Co.	1895-1900
	14d	Prairie Queen Brewing Co.	1900-1901
	14e	Blume Brewing Co.	1901-1910
	14f	Huron Brewing Co.	1910-1912
	14g	Blume Brewing Co.	1912-1917
	14h	Huron Beverage Co.	1917-1932
	14i	Dakota Brewing Co. (255 Columbia Ave.)	1934-1942
Lead City			
SD	15a	Hall Jentes	1878- ?
	15b	Seelig, Lang & Co.	1882-1883
	15c	Lang & Walter	1883-1884
	15d	Michael Seelig	1884-1891
	15e	John Lang	1891-1893
	15f	Michael Seelig	1893-1897
SD	16	Sidonie Thomas	1890-1890
Pierre			
SD	17	H. J. E. Meyer	1882-1884
Rapid City			
SD	18	Briggs & Bliss	1884-1884
SD	19	Parkhurst & Brown	1882-1884
Sioux Falls			
SD	20a	G. A. Knott & Co.	1875-1883
	20b	Sioux Falls Brewing Co.	1883-1898
	20c	Sioux Falls Brewing and Malting Co.	1898-1912
	20d	Sioux Falls Brewing Co.	1912-1917
	20e	Sioux Brewing Co.	NP 1934-1934
SD	21	Minnehaha Brewing and Malting Co.	NP 1934-1934
SD	22	Tri-State Brewing Co. (419 N. Phillips Ave.)	NP 1934-1934
Spearfish			
SD	23	Frank Geis	1882-1884

Sturgis

SD	24	Weller & Otto	1888-1889

Yankton

SD	25a	John Foerster	c1860-1882
	25b	Mrs. Eliza Foerster	1882-1889
	25c	Foerster's Brewery	1890- ?
	25d	Paul Keller	1896-1897
	25e	Eureka Brewing Co.	1898-1899
SD	26a	C. F. Roptenscher & Co.	1875-1884
	26b	Martin Blume	1884-1886
	26c	Blume & Hameister	1886-1889
	26d	Brodre B. Moss, Yankton Brewing Association (2nd St.)	1894-1898
	26e	Louis Moritz, Yankton Brewing Association	1898-1901
	26f	Louis Moritz Brewing Co.	1901-1901
	26g	Schwenk-Barth Brewing Co. (2nd & Walnut Sts.)	1901-1917
	26h	Schwenk-Barth Brewing Co.	NP 1934-1934
	26i	F.W. Schwenk Brewing and Malting Co. (114 Walnut St.)	NP 1939-1939

TENNESSEE

Chattanooga

TN	1	Charles A. Bohr	1874-1875
TN	2a	(Conrad) Geise & (E. D.) Kohn (2nd & Broad Sts.) aka Conrad Geise & Co. (1890)	1888-1890
	2b	Chattanooga Brewing Co.	1890-1915
	2c	Purity Extract & Tonic Co.	? -1934
	2d	Atlantic Ice and Coal Co. (37 W. 13th St.) aka Southeastern Brewery Co. (1934)	1934-1936
	2e	Atlantic Co.	1936-1941

Jackson

TN	3a	King & O'Fallon	1874-1877
	3b	Kunz & Co.	1877-1879

Knoxville

TN	4	Lucas Graf	1869-1869
TN	5a	Knoxville Brewing Co., aka Martin Shea, Knoxville Brewery	1878-1879
	5b	East Tennessee Brewery, Charles Kohlkase	? -1885
	5c	Knoxville Brewing Association aka E. Tennessee Brewing Co. (1886-1888)	1886-1889
	5d	Knoxville Brewing Co.	1889-1893
	5e	New Knoxville Brewing Co. (613 McGhee & Chamberlain Sts.)	1893-1902
	5f	East Tennessee Brewing Co.	1902-1915
TN	6	Paul Sturm, Union Brewery	1869-1869

Memphis

TN	7a	P. Brady & Co. (Orleans & Court)	1870-1870
	7b	P. Brady & Co. (80 Desoto)	1871-1871
TN	8	Patrick Gatens (63 Causey)	1870-1870
TN	9a	Sebastian Kaufman (70 Bradford)	1870-1873
	9b	City Brewery, Sebastian Kaufman	1873-1874
TN	10	Legler Bros. (Huppert Alley & Poplar)	1871-1871
TN	11	Memphis Ale Brewrey, Lyman Parkhurst (Court & Lauderdale Sts.)	1866-1866
TN	12a	Memphis Brewing Co.	1877- ?
	12b	Memphis Brewing Co. (Butler & Tennessee Sts.)	? -1884
	12c	Tennessee Brewing Co.	1885-1916
	12d	Tennessee Brewing Co.	1933-1955
TN	13a	Memphis Brewing and Malting Co.	1906-1908
	13b	Memphis Brewing Co.	1908-1910
TN	14	Ruser & Hundhausen, City Brewery (72 Hill St.)	1866-1868
TN	15	(Joseph) Salls & Co. (3rd & Hill St.)	1864-1871

Memphis (cont.)

TN	16a	Jos. Schlitz Brewing Co. (5151 E. Raines Rd.) (br. of Milw.)	1971-1982
	16b	Jos. Schlitz Brewing Co., subsidiary of Stroh Brewery Co., Detroit, MI	1982-
TN	17a	Louis Schnepel (411 Front St.)	1866-1867
	17b	Shelby Lager Beer Brewery, Louis Schnepel	1867-1868
	17c	Louis Schnepel (3rd & Webster Sts.)	1869-1871
	17d	Louis Schnepel & Co.	1872-1874
TN	18	Francis Schulz	1874-1875
TN	19	Star Brewery, Henry A. Cordes (Exchange btwn. Front & Water)	1866-1866
TN	20	Patrick Twohig (202 Vance)	1872-1873
TN	21a	Wachter & Zweifel (371/373 Front St.)	1866-1867
	21b	Wachter & Zweifel, Eagle Brewery	1867-1868
TN	22	Washington Brewery	1860-1860

Nashville

TN	23	W. Beaty (7 Front St.)	1868-1875
TN	24a	Crossman & Drucker, Tennessee Brewery (14 Market St.)	1859-1861
	24b	M. J. Drucker (41 Broad St.)	1865-1865
	24c	M. J. Drucker, Spring Water Brewery (between Murfreesboro & Chicken Pikes)	1865-1875
TN	25	C. Holshuh & Co., City Brewery (16/18 Market & Front Sts.)	1859-1859
TN	26	F. Laitenberger, City Brewery (near 4th & Church Sts.)	1866-1866
TN	27	Henry Metz	1874-1875
TN	28a	J. Stiefel Co., Nashville Brewery	1859-1863
	28b	Stiefel & Pfeifer, South Nashville Brewery (Mulberry & S. High)	1863- ?
	28c	Jacob Stiefel	1874-1876
	28d	J. B. Kuhn, South Nashville Brewery	1876-1878
	28e	C. A. Maus & Bros., Nashville Brewery	1878-1880
	28f	Nashville Brewing Co., (John) Burkhardt & Herschel	1880-1882
	28g	Nashville Brewing Co., Burkhardt, Walker & Bros. (819/837 S. High & Mulberry Sts.)	1882-1890
	28h	(Christian) Moerlein-(Wm.) Gerst Brewing Co. aka Nashville Brewing and Bottling Co. (1890)	1890-1893
	28i	Wm. Gerst Brewing Co.	1893-1915
	28j	The William Gerst Brewing Co., Inc. (821 6th Avenue S.)	1933-1954
TN	29	Union Brewery (S. High St. & Grove Ave.)	1868-1875

TEXAS

Austin

TX	1	Capitol Brewing and Bottling Co.	1907-1907
TX	2a	Paul Pressler	1874-1878
	2b	H. Samuelsohn	1882-1882
TX	3	W. J. Sutor	1874-1875

Bastrop

TX	4	Anton Jung	1875-1875

Belleville

TX	5a	Fred Frank	1872-1877
	5b	F. J. Frank & Bro.	1877-1879
	5c	F. Frank, Jr.	1879-1880
	5d	Henry Frank	1880-1882
	5e	Herman Frank, Home Brewery	1882-1918

Ben Ficklin

TX	6	H. Wolters & Co.	1878-1879

Beaumont

TX	7	Beaumont Brewing Co.	NP 1934-1934

Boerne				
TX	8a	Martin Stricht		1874-1877
	8b	Hammer & Buelle		1877-1882
Brackett				
TX	9a	Fred Weidlich		1875-1877
	9b	Weidlich Bros.		1877-1879
	9c	Fred Weidlich		1879-1884
Brenham				
TX	10	G. F. Giesecke & Bro.		1874-1880
TX	11	Lorenz Zeiss		1874-1884
Castroville				
TX	12a	Blaise Kieffer		1875-1880
	12b	Mrs. Louise Kieffer		1880-1884
Cleburne				
TX	13	John Guffee		1875-1878
TX	14	Fritz Wulfert		1875- ?
Columbus				
TX	15	Hugo Walter		1874-1875
TX	16	T. Zangg		1874-1875
Corpus Christi				
TX	17	Schwartz Brewing Co.	NP	1934-1934
Cuero				
TX	18	Hugo Buschick		1874-1884
TX	19	F. F. Leber		1874-1875
TX	20	Henry Schoenfeld		1896-1897
Cypress Creek				
TX	21a	T. & M. Jugenhutt		1878-1879
	21b	T. Jugenhutt & Bro.		1879-1882
	21c	Thos. Jugenhutt		1882-1884
Dallas				
TX	22	Excelsior Weiss Beer Brewery		1901-1901
TX	23a	Klein & Wolff		1875-1877
	23b	E. Arnoldi		1877-1878
TX	24a	Simon Mayer		1895-1900
	24b	Mayer & Bruce		1900-1901
TX	25a	Schepps Brewing Corp. (1026 Young St.)		1934-1939
	25b	Time Brewing, Inc.		1939-1940
	25c	Dallas-Fort Worth Brewing Co. aka Schepps Brewery (1945)		1940-1951
TX	26	Anton Wagenhauser		1891-1897
TX	27a	Wagenhauser Brewing Association		1880-1887
	27b	Dallas Brewing Association		1887-1889
	27c	Dallas Brewing Co. (Cochran & Houston Sts.)		1889-1893
	27d	Dallas Brewery		1893-1901
	27e	Dallas Brewery, Inc. (1817 Houston St.)		1901-1918
	27f	Dallas Brewery, Inc. (311 Duncan St.)		1934-1939
El Paso				
TX	28a	El Paso Brewing Association		1905-1918
	28b	Harry Mitchell Brewing Co. (3801 Frutas & Latta Sts.)		1935-1955
	28c	Falstaff Brewing Corp. (br. of St. Louis, MO)		1955-1967
Fayetteville				
TX	29	Jos. Janak		1878-1884
Flatonia				
TX	30	Amsler & Co.		1879-1879
TX	31	Vincent Richter		1878-1880

Fort Concho

TX	32a	Walter Hubert		1879-1879
	32b	Henry Wolters		1879-1884

Fort Worth

TX	33a	Carling Brewing Co., Inc. (7001 S. Freeway)		1964-1966
	33b	Miller Brewing Co. (br. of Milwaukee, WI)		1969-
TX	34	Milwaukee Brewing Co. (814 9th Ave.)	NP	1934-1934
TX	35a	Texas Brewing Co. (9th & Jones Sts.)		1890-1918
	35b	Superior Brewing Co. (1001/1003 Jones St.)		1933-1940

Fredericksburg

TX	36	Fredk. Probst		1874-1895
TX	37a	Henry Warner		1875-1877
	37b	John Mauer		1877-1884

Galveston

TX	38a	J. A. Brockman		1906-1908
	38b	Weiss & Son		1908-1909
TX	39a	Galveston Brewing Co. (33rd & Church Sts.)		1895-1918
	39b	Galveston-Houston Breweries, Inc.		1934-1955
	39c	Falstaff Brewing Corp.		1956-1975
	39d	Falstaff Brewing Corp. affiliated with General Brewing Co., CA		1975-1981
		aka Christian Feigenspan		
		aka Fischer Brewing Co.		
		aka General Brewing Co.		
		aka James Hanley Co.		

Giddings

TX	40	Theo. Umlang		1878-1880

High Hill

TX	41a	Adolph Richter		1874-1877
	41b	Richter & Kiushel		1877-1879
	41c	A. Richter		1879-1882
	41d	August Richter		1882-1884

Houston

TX	42a	American Brewing Association (Railroad & 2nd Sts.)		1893-1918
	42b	Houston American Brewery (Railroad & Girard Sts.)	NP	1934-1934
TX	43	Anheuser-Busch, Inc. (775 Gellhorn Drive) (br. of St. Louis)		1966-
TX	44a	Gulf Brewing Co. (5301/5303 Polk Ave.)		1933-1963
	44b	Theo. Hamm Brewing Co. (br. of St. Paul, MN)		1963-1967
TX	45	Fritz Hahn		1874-1875
TX	46a	Houston Ice and Brewing Co. (4th & Washington Sts.)		1893-1915
	46b	Houston Ice and Brewing Association		1915-1918
	46c	Houston Ice and Brewing Co. (2510 Calumet Dr.)	NP	1934-1934
TX	47	G. Schulte		1874-1875
TX	48	Southern Brewing Co. (110 Buffalo & 707 N. Drennan Sts.)		1933-1939
TX	49	Wagner & Hermann		1874-1879

Industry

TX	50a	Shilburne & Walter		1875-1877
	50b	J. W. Walter		1877-1879

La Grange

TX	51a	H. L. Kreisch		1874-1882
	51b	Mrs. Josephine Kreisch		1882-1884
TX	52	Wilhelm Rack		1874-1875
TX	53	G. Zuhlecke		1874-1875

Lando

TX	54	J. J. Knott		1878-1879

Longview

TX	55a	Jos. Schlitz Brewing Co. (1400 W. Cotton St.) (br. of Milw.)		1966-1982
	55b	Jos. Schlitz Brewing Co., subs. of Stroh Brewery, Detroit		1982-

Mercedes			
TX	56	Valley Brewing Co. (1501 Hildago)	1961-1962
Meyersville			
TX	57	Gustave Franke	1884-1903
Millheim			
TX	58	Hubert Galler	1874-1884
Mingus			
TX	59	Mingus Brewing Co.	1908-1909
New Braunfels			
TX	60a	Karl H. Guenther	1860-1868
	60b	Margarethe Guenther	1868-1870
TX	61	New Braunfels Brewing Co. (Katy Track)	1914-1918
TX	62	Julius Rennert	1874-1879
TX	63a	H. K. Schumaker	1874-1875
	63b	C. L. Schumaker	1882-1884
New Ulm			
TX	64a	A. & W. Hagemann	1874-1877
	64b	W. Hagemann	1877-1879
Paris			
TX	65	T. H. Freeze	1874-1875
Port Arthur			
TX	66	Frederick Miller	1907-1918
Round Top			
TX	67	H. E. Schulze	1874-1875
San Antonio			
TX	68	Felix Bachrach	1890-1890
TX	69a	J. B. Behloradsky	1881-1883
	69b	San Antonio Brewing Co.	1883-1888
	69c	San Antonio Brewing Association (312 James St. & Ave. A)	1888-1918
	69d	San Antonio Brewing Association (312 Pearl Parkway)	1933-1952
	69e	Pearl Brewing Co.	1952-1978
	69f	Pearl Brewing Co., subs. of General Brewing Co., Calif.	1978-
TX	70a	Bongo & Weiss Beer Bottling Works and Mfg. Co. (309 3rd St.)	1902-1903
	70b	Brown Beer Brewing Co.	1903-1905
	70c	Albert Drankowski	1905-1906
	70d	Bergmann & Walz	1906-1907
	70e	Beck's Muenchener Weiss Beer Co.	1907-1908
TX	71	F. Buelle & Co.	? -1874
TX	72a	Charles Degen (237/239 Blum St.)	1879-1911
	72b	Louis W. Degen, aka Degen's Brewery	1911-1915
TX	73a	Wm. Esser & Co.	1874-1875
	73b	William Esser	1875-1884
	73c	Alamo Ice and Brewing Co. (31 Cameron St.)	1884-1888
	73d	Alamo Brewery aka Alamo Brewing Association (1890)	1888-1893
TX	74	Joseph Hutzler	1874-1878
TX	75	Lareoda & Beau	1878-1879
TX	76a	Lone Star Brewing Co. (120 Jones Ave.)	1884-1918
	76b	Sabinas Brewing Co. (600 Simpson St.)	193 -1939
	76c	Champion Brewing Co.	1939-1940
	76d	Lone Star Brewing Co. (owned by Geo. Muehlebach, K.C., MO)	1940-1949
	76e	Lone Star Brewing Co.	1949-1976
	76f	Lone Star Brewing Co., subs. of Olympia Brewing Co., Olympia, WA	1976-1983
	76g	Lone Star Brewing Co., subs. of G. Heileman Brewing Co., LaCrosse, WI	1983-

San Antonio (cont.)

TX	77a	William A. Menger, Western Brewery	1855-1878
	77b	Mrs. W. A. Menger, Western Brewery	1878-1878
TX	78a	(Lorenz) Ochs & (George) Aschbacher (530 Oakland Ave.)	1890-1904
	78b	Geo. Aschbacher	1904-1915
TX	79	Peter Bros. Brewery	1905-1910
TX	80	Pfeiffer & Nuhn	1906-1908
TX	81	Schober Ice and Brewing Co. (101 River St.)	1905-1918
TX	82	Joseph Wesp	1906-1908

Sequin

TX	83	C. P. Krause	1878-1879
TX	84a	C. A. Schmidt	1874-1877
	84b	F. F. Weber	1877-1884

Serbin

TX	85	Theodore Umlang	1874-1875

Shiner

TX	86a	Shiner Brewing Association	1909-1914
	86b	Home Brewing Co.	1914-1915
	86c	Petzold & Spoetzl	1915-1918
	86d	Spoetzl Brewery and Ice Factory (606 E. Brewery St.)	1933-1934
	86e	Spoetzl Brewery	1934-1966
	86f	Spoetzl Brewery, Inc.	1966-

Tyler

TX	87	Wm. C. Scott & Bro.	1875- ?

Victoria

TX	88	Glock & Zahn	1874-1875
TX	89	L. F. Mack	1875-1884
TX	90	Neumayer & Mack	1874-1875
TX	91	H. A. Newmayer	1874-1875
TX	92	M. Weber	1874-1884

Waco

TX	93	Charles Koehler	c1874

Weatherford

TX	94	W. F. Both & Co.	c1878

Yorktown

TX	95	Michael Cellmer	1878-1891

Town unknown

TX	96	Fritz Riedel	1875-1875

UTAH

Alta City

UT	1a	Wm. Nichnitz	1874-1877
	1b	P. Schmidt	1877-1884
	1c	Charles Thied	1884-1888

Beaver

UT	2a	Geo. Buchner	1874-1877
	2b	A. A. Fischer	1877-1880
	2c	Jas. Vallentine	1880-1884

Bingham

UT	3a	Albert Uebel	1875-1877
	3b	B. Wehrsitz	1877-1878

Corinne City

UT	4a	N. Amsler	1874-1880
	4b	Baier & Dehler	1880-1884

Emigration Canyon

UT	5	Henry Wagener	1874-1875

Frisco

UT	6a	John Savior & Co.	1879-1880
	6b	John C. Reher	1880-1884

Hot Springs

UT	7a	Crossley & Co.	1874-1877
	7b	James Crossley	1877-1879

Logan

UT	8a	Jacob Theurer	1886-1887
	8b	Theurer & Bloom	1887-1888
	8c	Cache Valley Brewing Co. aka Barbara Theurer (1893-1897)	1888-1912
UT	9a	Henry Worley	1879-1884
	9b	Hermann Vogel	1884-1893
	9c	Logan City Brewing Co., aka Logan City Brewery, Hermann Vogel	1893-1901

Milford

UT	10	M. Ormound	1882-1884

Minersville

UT	11a	Dupax & Keisler	1874-1877
	11b	G. Kiesche	1877-1878

Murray

UT	12a	South Cottonwood Brewery	1888- ?
	12b	Mayfield & Co.	1893- ?

Nephi City

UT	13	Samuel Coulson	1878-1884

Ogden

UT	14a	Becker Brewing and Malting Co. (19th St. & Lincoln Ave.)	1892-1918
	14b	Beckers Products Co. (1900 Lincoln Ave.)	1934-1962
	14c	Becker Brewing Co.	1962-1965
UT	15a	Brickmiller & Wells	1874-1879
	15b	Ransom A. Wells (5th St.)	1879-1882
	15c	Ransom A. Wells & Co. aka Moritz Richter (1896)	1882-1897
UT	16	M. Brickmiller	1874-1875
UT	17a	Richter & Frey	1874-1882
	17b	John J. Frey	1882-1884
	17c	Richter & McCarthy	1884-1886
	17d	L. Schmidt & Co.	1886-1890
UT	18	Schellhas Brewing Co.	1891-1891

Ophir City

UT	19	J. B. Benedict	1874-1875
UT	20	Hall & Beyer	1874-1875

Provo

UT	21	Henry Horning	1875- ?
UT	22	Nestler Brewing Co. (395 N. 6th West St.)	1904-1904

Salt Lake City

UT	23	James Burns	? -1878
UT	24	Joseph Dudler	1874-1875
UT	25a	A. Fisher Brewing Co. (2nd S. & 10th W. Sts.)	1884-1918
	25b	Fisher Brewing Co. (160 S. 10th West St.)	1934-1960
	25c	Lucky Lager Brewing Co.	1960-1964
	25d	General Brewing Corp. (br. of San Francisco, CA)	1964-1967
UT	26	William Fuller	1874-1875
UT	27	Fred Heime	1875- ?

Salt Lake City (cont.)

UT	28a	Richard B. Margetts (317 North & 2nd West Sts.)	1878-1881
	28b	Richard B. Margetts' Estate	1881-1895
	28c	A. B. & S. H. Margetts	1895-1900
	28d	Utah Brewery, Buller & Springman	1900-1901
	28e	Utah Brewery, Peter Buller	1901-1902
	28f	Peter Buller & Co.	1902-1904
	28g	P. Buller Brewing Co., Utah Brewery	1904-1913
	28h	Utah Brewing Co.	1913-1918
UT	29	Mayetto & Donse	1874-1875
UT	30a	Jacob Moritz	1871-1874
	30b	Moritz & Co.	1874-1877
	30c	Keyser & Moritz	1877-1882
	30d	Keyser & Cullen	1882-1884
	30e	Salt Lake City Brewing Co. (10th E. & 5th S. Sts.)	1884-1918
UT	31	Moritz & Johnson	1874-1875
UT	32	Nestler & Co. (323 N. 1st W. St.)	1903-1904
UT	33	Pfaudler & Co.	1874-1875
UT	34a	Henry Wagener	1864-1894
	34b	Wagener Brewing Co., Inc. (17 2nd St. S.)	1894-1897
	34c	Henry Wagener Brewing Co. (74 E. 1st St. S.)	1897-1915

Sandy

UT	35a	Joseph Schueler	1874-1877
	35b	Maria Schueler	1877-1882
	35c	Geo. Martin & Co.	1882-1884
	35d	John Hardcastle	1884-1886
	35e	Riley H. Graves	1886-1888

Silver Reef

UT	36	B. Noebling	1879-1879
UT	37a	P. Welte	1878-1884
	37b	Leo Welte	1884-1888

South Cottonwood

UT	38a	R. Winkler	1878-1879
	38b	John Arnold	1879-1884

Springville

UT	39a	Geo. Dallin	1875-1877
	39b	John Dallin	1877-1884

Vernal

UT	40	Joseph Dudler	1890-1891

VERMONT

Barre

VT	1	Henry Frenier	1893-1893

Morrisville

VT	2	Samuel B. Doty	1893-1893

Rockingham

VT	3	Chalres M. Blake	1875-1879

Waterbury

VT	4	George J. Burnham	1893-1893

Bellows Falls (see Walpole, NH)

Alexandria

VA	1	H. Engelhardt	1878-1890
VA	2	Klein's Lager Beer Brewery	c1862-1864
VA	3	Martin's Ale Brewery	c1862-1864
VA	4a	Portner & Co.	1862-1865
	4b	Robert Portner (St. Asaph, Whyte & Washington Sts.)	1865-1883
	4c	Robert Portner Brewing Co.	1883-1918

Newport News

VA	5a	Leo Schulz Brewing Co.	1900-1902
	5b	Haven View Brewery	1902-1902
	5c	W. H. Davis & Co. (1111 25th St.)	1902-1903
	5d	Old Dominion Brewing and Ice Co.	1905-1910

Norfolk

VA	6a	Atlantic Ice and Coal Co. (219 Boush St. & Brooke Ave.)	1936-1937
	6b	Atlantic Co.	1937-1949
	6c	Glasgow Brewing Co., Inc.	1949-1951
VA	7a	Consumers Brewing Co. (Church St. & Washington Ave.)	1896-1918
	7b	Southern Breweries, Inc. (710 Washington Ave.)	1934-1942
	7c	Jacob Ruppert-Virginia, Inc., dba Jacob Ruppert	1942-1953
	7d	Century Brewery Corp.	1953-1967
		aka Banner Brewing Co. (1957-1967)	
		aka Embassy Club Brewing Co. (1956-1960)	
		aka Grenay Brewing Co. (1959-1967)	
		aka Monticello Brewing Co. (1955-1963)	
		aka Red Fox Brewing Co. (1954-1960)	
		aka Spearman Brewing Co. (1964-1967)	
		aka Tudor Brewing Co. (1961-1966)	
		aka Tuxedo Brewing Co.	
	7e	Champale Products Corp.	1967-1980
VA	8	Mohawk Brewing Co.	NP 1934-1934
VA	9	Old Dominion Brewing Co.	1900-1900

Petersburg

VA	10	Miller Brewing Co.	1910-1910
VA	11a	Newberry & Raulston, Cockade City Brewery	1865-1868
	11b	Cockade City Brewery and Milling Co.	1868-1873

Richmond

VA	12	Euker's Brewery	c1865
VA	13a	(Emil) Kersten & (Alfred Von N.) Rosenegk, Richmond Brewery (head of Leigh St., Hermitage Road)	1891-1897
	13b	Rosenegk Brewing Co., Richmond Brewery	1897-1918
VA	14	Norfolk Brewing Co.	1896-1896
VA	15	Radford Brewing Co.	NP 1934-1934
VA	16a	Richmond (Virginia) Brewing Co.	1891-1895
	16b	Peter Stumpf Brewing Co. (Harrison & Clay Sts.)	1895-1897
	16c	Home Brewing Co.	1897-1918
	16d	Home Brewing Co., Inc.	1934-1969
VA	17	G. W. Robson	1878-1881
VA	18	P. H. Wells, Inc. (208 S. 6th St.)	NP 1934-1934
VA	19	D. G. Yuengling, Jr.	1874-1875

Roanoke

VA	20a	Virginia Brewing Co. (1218 Wise Ave., S.E.)	1890-1918
	20b	Virginia Brewing Co., Inc.	1934-1957
	20c	Mountain Brewing Co., Inc.	1957-1959

Rosslyn

VA	21a	Consumers Brewing Co.	1890-1902
	21b	Arlington Brewing Co.	1902-1918
	21c	Dixie Brewing Corp. (Lee Hwy.)	NP 1934-1934

Virginia Beach

VA	22	Chesapeake Brewing, Inc.	1983-

West End

VA 23 H. Engelhardt 1874-1875

Williamsburg

VA 24 Anheuser-Busch, Inc. (br. of St. Louis, MO) (2000 Pocahontas Trail) 1972-

Winchester

VA 25 Ed. Hoffman 1875- ?

Wytheville

VA 26 Victoria Brewery 1875- ?

WASHINGTON

Aberdeen

WA 1a L. Blum 1889-1890
1b H. E. Anderson 1890-1890

WA 2a Gray's Harbor Brewing Co. (River & Lincoln Sts.) 1901-1901
2b Aberdeen Brewing Co. 1901-1915
2c Pioneer Brewing Co., Inc. (408 S. Lincoln St.) 1934-1944
aka Aberdeen Brewing Co. (1934)

WA 3 Quinaults Prdoucts Co. 1935-1935

Auburn (Slaughter until 1893)

WA 4 Friend-Degginger Import Co. 1893-1897

WA 5a Slaughter Brewing and Malting Co. 1891-1893
5b Slaughter Malt and Brewing Co. 1893-1896

Bellingham (see Whatcom)

Chelan Falls

WA 6a Schindler & Son 1902-1905
aka Schindler & Son Brewing and Malting Co. (1905)
6b Chelan Falls Brewing and Malting Co. 1907-1910

Cheney

WA 7 Frank Loacker & Charles Jensen, City Brewery (Railroad St.) 1884-1887

WA 8a Josef Weber, Bavaria Brewery ? -1888
8b Weber & Forster 1884-1888
8c Joseph Weber 1888-1904
8d Fannie Weber 1904-1907
8e Alois Schmidt 1907-1910

Chesaw

WA 9 Krause, Clerff & Wilkstrom 1900-1900

Chewelah

WA 10a Loaker & Delva 1886-1887
10b Joseph Fox 1890-1890
10c Leible & Wrage 1893- ?
10d Otto Mengert 1897-1898
10e Engelbert Leible 1898-1904
10f Frank Ernst 1904-1906
10g Ernst & Ernst 1906-1907
10h Pohle & Ernst 1907-1912

Colfax

WA 11a Erford & Palmtag 1879-1882
11b Werford & Woolford 1882-1888
11c Michaelson Bros. & Co. 1888-1890
11d M. E. Bourgardes 1890-1892
11e Alvin Schmidt 1892-1902
11f Schultz Brewing Co. 1902-1904
11g Colfax Brewing and Malting Co. 1904-1915

Colville (Colville Valley, Port Colville; Pinkney City unitl 1867)

WA 12a John V. Hofstetter, Colville Brewery 1861-1890
12b Oscar Runnels 1890-1890
12c Andrew Schips 1890-1892
12d Joseph Pohle & Co. 1892-1902
12e Arnold Krueger 1904-1906
12f Colville Brewing and Bottling Co. 1906-1908

Davenport

WA	13a	A. Miltzer	1886-1887
	13b	Robert Tischner aka Tischner & Schultheis (1896)	1893-1897
	13c	W. A. Crawford	1897-1899

Dayton

WA	14a	Rumpf & Dunkel	1878-1879
	14b	Rumpf & Weinhard, Dayton Brewery	1879-1884
	14c	Jacob Weinhard, Dayton Brewery	1884-1900
WA	15a	Scott & Hohlberg	1880- ?
	15b	Scott & Schmidt	? -1884
	15c	Benjamin Scott & Julius G. Mary, City Brewery	1884-1885
	15d	Scott & Godde	1885-1887

Douglas

WA	16	Frank Thompson	1890-1890

East Kittias (see Ellensburg)

Ellensburg

WA	17	John Blomquist (East Kittias-1884)	1884-1888
WA	18	Chang & Becker	1886-1887
WA	19	James Dickson	1886-1887
WA	20a	Theo Heft	1880-1884
	20b	Theodore Hess	1884-1887
	20c	Hoscheid & Dewiscourt	1887-1888
	20d	M. Dewiscourt	1888-1890
	20e	Dewiscourt & Shuller	1890-1891
	20f	M. Dewiscourt	1891-1900
	20g	George Taylor (2nd & Sampson Sts.)	1904- ?
	20h	Adolph Krulish, City Brewery	1908-1911
	20i	Richter & Broese Brewing Co.	1911-1914
	20j	Frederick E. Broese (505 E. 2nd St.)	1914-1915
WA	21a	St. Louis Brewing Co.	1895-1896
	21b	St. Louis Brewing and Malting Co.	1896-1906
	21c	Ellensburg Brewing and Malting Co.	1906-1915
	21d	Ellensburg Brewing Co., Inc. (414 W. 5th St.)	1934-1937
	21e	Mutual Brewing Co., Inc.	1937-1943

Everett

WA	22a	Washington Brewing Co.	1899-1904
	22b	Everett Brewing Co.	1904-1915

Fairhaven

WA	23	Richard Asbeck	1889-1890

Farmington

WA	24	Andrew Christ	1884-1893

Fort Vancouver (see Vancouver)

Granite Falls

WA	25	Henry Kern	1893-1893

Kalama

WA	26a	John Schauble & Bro.	1874-1877
	26b	J. Schauble	1877-1880

Lacamas

WA	27	John Nager	1886-1887

Loomis

WA	28a	Langendorf & Anderson	1900-1901
	28b	(Charles) Langendorf & Garrett (R. A.)	1901-1903
	28c	Frank Lintz	1904-1915

Medical Lake

WA	29	Thomas Robinette	1882-1882
WA	30	Geo. E. Staples	1882-1882

Methow

WA	31	Michael Schuster	1895-1895

Miles

WA	32	Bernhard Bockemuehl, Fort Spokane Brewery	1888-1906

Mukilteo

WA	33a	Geo. Cantrini & Co.	1878-1879
	33b	S. N. Snyder & Co.	1879-1884

Northport

WA	34	Northport Brewing Co.	1897-1905

North Yakima (see Yakima)

Ocosta

WA	35	Richard E. Sandbach	1893-1893

Olympia

WA	36a	Capital Brewing Co. (Tumwater)	1896-1902
	36b	Olympia Brewing Co.	1902-1915
	36c	Olympia Brewing Co.	1934-1983
	36d	Olympia Brewing Co., subs. of Pabst Brewing Co., Milwaukee, WI	1983-
WA	37a	J. C. & J. R. Wood	1874-1880
	37b	Xavier Hosneder	1880-1888

Oroville

WA	38	Oroville Brewing Co.	1906-1912

Orting

WA	39	G. Koller & Co.	1891-1898

Palouse

WA	40a	Choate & Pelkes	1884-1887
	40b	Dimmick & Schmidt	1887-1888
	40c	Schmidt & Parker	1888-1890
	40d	John Schmidt	1890-1890
	40e	Schmidt & Smith	1890-1891
	40f	Schmidt & Saunder	1891-1898
	40g	Saunders & Choat	1898-1900
	40h	Saunders & McGraw	1900-1904
	40i	Palouse Brewing Co.	1904-1912

Pasco

WA	41a	Northern Pacific Brewing and Malting Co.	? -1890
	41b	Milwaukee Brewing and Ice Mfg. Co.	1890-1892

Pataha City

WA	42a	Jacob Bihlmaier	1882-1887
	42b	E. J. Wolf	1887-1889
	42c	Jacob Bihlmaier	1889-1890
	42d	Thos. W. Shannon	1890-1892

Pomeroy

WA	43	Garfield	1889-1890
WA	44a	Scholl Bros., Columbia Brewery	1879-1884
	44b	John Rehorn	1884-1891

Poncers

WA	45	Ernest Scholl	1886-1887

Port Angeles

WA	46a	Angeles Brewing Co.	1901-1901
	46b	Port Angeles Brewing Co.	1901-1902
	46c	Angeles Brewing and Malting Co. (3rd & Tumwater Sts.)	1904-1914
	46d	Angeles Brewing Co.	1914-1915

Port Colville (see Colville)

Port Orchard

WA	47a	Kitsap Brewing Co., Inc. (1209 Bay St.)	1934-1935
	47b	Silver Springs Brewing Co.	1935-1950

Port Townsend

WA	48a	William Goelert	1874-1877
	48b	W. Roesch	1877-1879
	48c	Charles Eisenbeis	1879-1888
WA	49a	Port Townsend Brewing Co.	1906-1915
	49b	Peninsula Brewery, Inc. (Monroe & Washington Sts.)	1934-1934

Republic

WA	50a	(George) Falligan & (Joseph) Winkler		1898-1899
	50b	Republic Brewing Co.		1899-1915

Roslyn

WA	51a	(Wm.) Dewitt & (Frank) Groger		1891-1892
	51b	Rachor & Durrwachter		1892-1894
	51c	Kuhl, Durrwachter & Co.		1894-1896
	51d	Schlotfeldt Bros.		1896-1901
	51e	Roslyn Brewing Co.		1901-1915

Ruby

WA	52a	L. Rachenberger		1888-1891
	52c	John Wise & Co.		1891-1893

Seattle

WA	53a	Albert Braun Brewing Association		1890-1892
	53b	Seattle Brewing and Malting co., Albert Braun Brewing Assoc.		1892-1893
WA	54	George Cantierri		1874-1875
WA	55a	Stuart Crichton		1874-1877
	55b	Aug. Mehlhorn		1877-1884
	55c	Ernest Romey		1884-1888
	55d	Chas. A. Saake, Pacific Brewery (Lincoln St.)		1891-1897
WA	56	Gilmak Brewing and Distilling Co.	NP	1934-1934
WA	57a	Hemrich Investment Corp., aka Western Brewing Co. (5225 E. Marginal Way)		1934-1934
	57b	Hemrich Brewing Co.		1934-1940
WA	58a	George F. Horluck (606/610 Westlake Ave. & Mercer)		1934-1934
	58b	Horluck Brewing Co., Inc.		1934-1939
	58c	Seattle Brewing and Malting Co., dba Century Brewery		1939-1944
	58d	Sicks' Century Brewery		1944-1957
WA	59	Independent Brewing Co., Loeb & Moyses (8th & Pacific Aves.)		1902-1915
WA	60a	Andrew Hemrich		1878-1883
	60b	(J.) Kopp & (A.) Hemrich (9th Ave., S.)		1883-1885
	60c	Hemrich & Co.		1885-1889
	60d	Bay View Brewing Co.		1889-1892
	60e	Seattle Brewing and Malting Co., Bay View Brewery		1892-1912
WA	61	Northwest Brewing Co., Inc.	NP	1934-1934
WA	62	Pilsener Brewing Co., Inc. (548 1st Ave. S.)		1934-1934
WA	63	The Red Hook Ale Brewery (4620 Leary Way N.W.)		1982-
WA	64a	Rule & Sweeney		1884-1886
	64b	E. F. Sweeney		1886-1887
	64c	(E. F.) Sweeney & Co.		1887-1888
	64d	(H. J.) Claussen- (E. F.) Sweeney Brewing Co.		1888-1892
	64e	Seattle Brewing and Malting Co., Claussen- Sweeney Brewery		1892-1904
	64f	Seattle Brewing and Malting Co., Sweeney Brewery		1904-1906
	64g	Seattle Brewing and Malting Co., Rainier Brewery (6004 Duwamish Ave.)		1906-1915
WA	65a	Martin Schmieg		1874-1877
	65b	Slorah & Co.		1877-1880
	65c	Andrew Slorah		1880-1888
	65d	Hemrich Bros. Brewing Co. (515 Howard Ave. N.& Republican St.) aka Alvin Hemrich Brewing Co. (1898)		1897-1915
	65e	Hemrich Brewing Co., Inc., aka Hemrich Investment Corp. (2918 Airport Way)		1934-1934
	65f	Apex Brewing Co., Inc.		1934-1937
WA	66a	Spellmire-West Brewing Co. (1320 Almy St. & 1019 E. Lake Ave.)		1905-1908
	66b	Spellmire Brewing Co.		1908-1913
	66c	Washington Brewing Co.		1913-1915
WA	67a	Standard Brewing Co.		1901-1901
	67b	Claussen Brewing Association, Tannhaeuser Brewery (3255 21st Ave. W.)		1901-1915
WA	68a	Tsuji, Sakae, dba Asahi Wine Mfg. Co. (719/721 Dearborn St.)		1935-1936
	68b	Asahi Wine Mfg. Co.		1936-1940

Seattle (cont.)

WA 69 Julius Weigert & Co. 1889-1890

WA 70a (J. H.) West & Co. (Westlake Ave. & Galer St.) 1899-1900
70b W. H. Armstrong 1900-1900
70c Seattle Ale and Porter Co. 1900-1901
70d American Brewing Co. 1901-1903

WA 71a Century Brewing Association, Inc. (3100 Airport Way) 1934-1935
71b Seattle Brewing and Malting Co. 1935-1944
71c Sicks' Seattle Brewing and Malting Co. 1944-1957
71d Sicks' Rainier Brewing Co. 1957-1970
aka Highlander Brewing Co. (1965-1970)
aka Rheinlander Brewing Co. (1965-1970)
71e Rainier Brewing Co. (Majority owner- Molson Brewing, Canada) 1977-
aka Highlander Brewing Co.
aka Rheinlander Brewing Co.
71f Rainier Brewing Co., Subs. of G. Heileman Brewing Co., LaCrosse, WI

Selah

WA 72 Yakima Valley Brewing Co. 1938-1954

Slaughter (see Auburn)

Snohomish

WA 73a Zweifelhofer & Wohlgethan 1890-1890
73b Zweifelhofer & Jehli 1891-1892
73c Carl C. Wagner 1892-1893

Spokane (Spokane Falls)

WA 74 American Brewing Co. (1124 E. Sprague Ave.) 1902-1903

WA 75a Galland-Burke Brewing and Malting Co. (901 Broadway & 726 Lincoln St., Spokane Falls) 1892-1902
75b Spokane Brewing and Malting Co., Galland-Burke Brewery 1902-1915
75c Spokane Brewing and Malting Co., Inc. 1934-1937
75d Spokane Breweries, Inc. 1937-1940
75e The Spokane Brewery, Inc. 1940-1944
75f Sicks' Spokane Brewery, Inc. 1944-1962
aka Sicks' Rainier Brewery (1958-1962)

WA 76a Goetz Breweries, Inc. (1107 N. Pearl St.) 1934-1937
76b Spokane Breweries, Inc. 1937-1937

WA 77a Rudolph Gorkow, New York Brewery (Front Ave. & 303 Washington St., Spokane Falls) 1886-1896
77b Rudolph Gorkow's Estate, New York Brewery 1896-1900
77c Spokane Brewing and Malting Co., New York Brewery 1900-1904

WA 78a Henco Bros. (Theodore & Charles), Henco Brewery (1705/1706 5th Ave. & Ash St., Spokane Falls) 1886-1897
78b Theodore Henco, Henco Brewery 1897-1899
78c Reinhard Martin, Henco Brewery 1899-1900
78d Spokane Brewing and Malting Co., Henco Brewery 1900-1915

WA 79a John G. F. Hieber 1890-1894
aka Union Brewery & Malthouse (1892)
79b Hieber Brewing and Malting Co. (Spruce St. & 12th Ave.) 1894-1905
79c Inland Brewing and Malting Co. (1402/1430 2nd Ave.) 1905-1915
79d Bohemian Breweries, Inc., Plant 1 1934-1957
79e Bohemian Breweries Co. (br. of Atlantic Brewing Co., Chicago) 1957-1962
aka Best Brewing Co.
aka Durst Brewing Co.
aka K. C.'s Best Brewing Co.
aka Tuxedo Brewing Co.

WA 80 Palmtag & Wilson (Spokane Falls) 1884-1887

WA 81 Panhandle Brewing Co. (124 Pacific Ave.) 1913-1914

WA 82a M. Peterson & Co. (Spokane Falls) 1879- ?
82b L. Weisgerber ? -1884
82c Amelia Berry 1884-1888
82d R. E. A. Mueller 1888-1890
82e Mueller & Koehler 1890-1891

Spokane (cont.)

State	No.	Brewery		Dates
WA	83	Geo. Richter & Co.		1891-1891
WA	84a	B. Schade Brewing Co. (Sheridan & Front Sts.)		1904-1915
	84b	Golden Age Breweries, Inc. (301 N. Sheridan St.)		1934-1948
	84c	Bohemian Breweries, Inc., Plant 2 (528 E. Trent Ave.)		1948-1949
WA	85	Spokane Creme Beer (3104 Sprague St.)	NP	1934-1934

Sprague

State	No.	Brewery		Dates
WA	86a	R. O. Porak		1882-1884
	86b	Porak & Dessert, Sprague Brewery		1884-1887
	86c	Sprague Brewery		1887-1890
	86d	Adams & Moerder		1890-1890
	86e	R. O. Porak		1890-1902
	86f	Sprague Brewery		1905-1906
	86g	Sprague Brewing Co.		1906-1906

Steilacoom

State	No.	Brewery		Dates
WA	87a	Anton Mueller		1874-1875
	87b	Furst & Baumeister		1879- ?
	87c	Gambel & Kaufman		? -1882
WA	88a	Wolf Schafer		1874-1877
	88b	Schafer & Howard		1877-1890

Tacoma

State	No.	Brewery		Dates
WA	89a	Columbia Brewing Co. (2120/2142 S."C" St.)		1900-1915
	89b	Columbia Breweries, Inc.		1934-1953
	89c	Heidelberg Brewing Co.		1953-1958
	89d	Carling Brewing Co., Inc., Heidelberg Breweries aka Tuborg Brewing Co. (1973-1976)		1958-1976
	89e	Carling National Breweries, Inc., Heidelberg Breweries		1976-1979
	89f	G. Heileman Brewing Co., Heidelberg Brewery		1979-1979
WA	90a	Ignatz Fuerst		1884-1888
	90b	Donau Brewing Co.		1888-1893
	90c	Pacific Brewing and Malting Co., Donau Brewery		1899-1902
WA	91	Hermsen & Striegel (1914 S. 30th St.)		1904-1904
WA	92a	Anton Huth, Puget Sound Brewery		1888-1890
	92b	Scholl & Huth		1890-1891
	92c	Puget Sound Brewing Co. (25th & Jefferson Sts.)		1891-1897
	92d	Pacific Brewing and Malting Co., Puget Sound Branch		1897-1911
	92e	Pacific Brewing and Malting Co.		1911-1915
WA	93	Independent Ice Co., Inc. (5624 McKinley Ave.)		1940-1940
WA	94	Christopher Kopp		1904-1904
WA	95a	Lusthoff & Stegmann		1884-1886
	95b	Diedrich Stegmann		1886-1888
	95c	United States Brewing Co.		1888-1891
	95d	Milwaukee Brewing Co. (Jefferson Ave. & 23rd St.)		1891-1897
	95e	Pacific Brewing and Malting Co., Milwaukee Branch		1897-1899
WA	96a	Fredk. Neitzel		1884- ?
	96b	Hufeisen & Horning		1888-1890
WA	97a	Northwest Brewing Co., Inc. (105 E. 26th St.)		1934-1936
	97b	United Union Breweries	NP	1937-1937
	97c	Pioneer Brewing-Tacoma, Inc.		1946-1947
	97d	Silver Springs Brewing Co.		1950-1967

Tekoa

State	No.	Brewery		Dates
WA	98	Tekoa Brewing Co.		1908-1912

Twisp

State	No.	Brewery		Dates
WA	99	Twisp Brewing and Malting Co.		1902-1902

Uniontown

State	No.	Brewery		Dates
WA	100a	Peter Jacobs, Union Brewery		1884-1893
	100b	Mrs. Sophia Jacobs (Main St.)		1893-1897
	100c	Jacobs Bros. & Portz		1897-1899
	100d	Uniontown Brewery, Joseph Portz		1899-1900

Vancouver (formerly Fort Vancouver)

WA 101 L. Dampfhoffer 1879-1884

WA 102 Francis & Holtmann 1884-1884

WA 103 Moeckel & Huth 1882-1884

WA 104a Muench 1856-1859
104b Henry Weinhard (Fort Vancouver) 1859-1864
104c Anton Young 1864-1887
104d Anton Young & Co. 1887-1893
104e Star Brewery (6th & C Sts.) 1895-1897
104f Star Brewery Co. 1897-1904
104g Northern Brewery Co., Star Brewery 1904-1915
104h Star Brewery Co., Inc. (215 W. 7th St.) 1934-1939
104i Interstate Brewery Co. (615 Columbia St.) 1939-1950
104j Lucky Lager Brewing Co. 1950-1964
104k General Brewing Corp., Northern Div. 1964-1969
104l Lucky Breweries, Inc. 1969-1972
104m General Brewing Co. 1972-1975
104n General Brewing Co., affiliated w/Falstaff Brewing Corp. CA 1975-

Walla Walla

WA 105a Jacob Betz (S. 3rd & Alder Sts.) 1878-1880
105b P. F. Phillips 1880-1882
105c Jacob Betz 1882-1904
105d Jacob Betz Brewing and Malting Co. 1904-1910

WA 106a Albert G. Ernst (East End Main St.) 1882-1884
106b H. Schwarz, Washington Brewery 1885- ?

WA 107 Goesch & Huber 1891-1891

WA 108 Chas. M. Hecker 1882-1882

WA 109a Kleber & Stang 1874-1877
109b F. E. Kleber 1877-1880
109c Krekel & Hinger 1880-1882
109d F. E. Kleber 1882-1884

WA 110a Emil Meyer, City Brewery (S. 2nd St.) 1855-1870
110b John H. Stahl & Co., City Brewery 1870-1871
110c John H. Stahl, City Brewery (2nd & Birch Sts.) 1871-1884
110d Mrs. John H. Stahl, aka Mrs. Catherine E. Stahl, City Brewery 1884-1905
110e Stahl Brewing and Malting Co., City Brewery (346 S. 2nd St.) 1905-1912
110f Walla Walla Brewing Co. (350 S. 2nd St.) 1914-1926
110g Northwest Brewing Co., Inc. 1934-1936
110h United Union Breweries Co. 1936-1945
110i Pioneer Brewing Co., aka Pioneer Brewing Co. of Walla Walla 1945-1952

WA 111a George Seisser 1874-1877
111b Benjamin Scott 1877-1879
111c Gleim & Son, Walla Walla Brewery (Lower Main St.) 1879-1880
111d George Gleim 1880-1884
111e Harter Bros., Walla Walla Brewery (113 Main St.) 1884-1887

Waterville

WA 112a E. F. Hauch, Jr. 1890- ?
112b Geo. L. Forschner 1893-1897
112c Michael Schuster 1897-1899

Wenatchee

WA 113 National Brewing Co. NP 1934-1934

WA 114 Wenatchee Brewing and Malting Co. 1905-1905

Whatcom (became Bellingham in 1904)

WA 115 J. Beck 1886-1887

WA 116a Bellingham Bay Brewery, Br. of Olympia Brewing Co., WA 1902-1904
116b Bellingham Bay Brewery (Bellingham) 1905-1915
116c Whatcom-Skagit Brewing Co., (Squalicum Fill, Bellingham) NP 1934-1934

WA 117a Fritz Grathwohl 1899- ?
117b Whatcom Brewing and Malting Co. (Iowa St.) ? -1903

Yakima

WA	118	A. D. Eglin	1884-1884
WA	119a	North Yakima Brewing and Malting Co. (Front St., N. Yakima)	1905-1915
	119b	Yakima Brewing and Bottling Co. (924 Fenton St.)	1934-1935
	119c	Yakima Brewing and Bottling Works	1935-1938
WA	120	Perkins & Sandmeyer (N. Yakima)	1886-1887
WA	121	Charles Schanne	1878-1890
WA	122	Yakima Brewing and Malting Co. (25 N. Front St.)	1982-

WEST VIRGINIA

Benwood

WV	1	Benwood Brewing Co.	1906-1912

Bluefield

WV	2	Bluefield Brewing Co.	1905-1914

Central City (see Huntington)

Charleston

WV	3a	Capital City Brewing Co.	1902-1905
	3b	Charleston Brewing Co.	1905-1906
	3c	Kanawha Brewing Co. (Bullitt St. & K&M R.R.)	1907-1914
WV	4	Charleston Brewing Co. (Slack between Baker & Branch)	1874-1875
WV	5a	Jacob Haberer	1875-1877
	5b	H. Slack	1877-1878

Clarksburg

WV	6a	Clarksburg Brewing Co.	1905-1914
	6b	Old Tavern Brewing Co. (430/432 E. Pike St.)	1936-1937
	6c	The Mountain State Brewing Co.	1937-1941

Elkins

WV	7a	Elkins Brewing Co.	1906-1909
	7b	Elkins Brewing and Storage Co.	1909-1911

Fairmount

WV	8a	Charles Berns	1874-1877
	8b	W. F. Berns	1877-1888
	8c	Thomas Deveny	1888-1890
WV	9a	Fairmount Brewing Co. (5th & Virginia Aves.)	1898-1914
	9b	The North Pole Brewing Co. (414 Virginia & 5th Aves.)	1934-1938
WV	10a	Monongahela Valley Brewing Co. (838 Washington St.)	1934-1934
	10b	Old Tavern Brewing Co.	1934-1935

Grafton

WV	11	Louis Beyer	1874-1884
WV	12a	Home Brewing Co.	1905-1908
	12b	Tygart Valley Brewing Co.	1908-1912

Harpers Ferry

WV	13a	Harpers Ferry Brewing Co. (Market St.)	1895-1897
	13b	Belvidere Brewing Co.	1897-1903
	13c	Leder-Weideman Brewing Co.	1903-1906
	13d	Jefferson Brewing Co.	1906-1908
WV	14	Aug. Krueger	1898-1898

Huntington

WV	15a	Huntington Brewing Co. (Central City)	1893-1895
	15b	American Brewing Co.	1895-1896
	15c	American Brewing and Ice Co.	1896-1899
	15d	West Virginia Brewing Co.	1899-1902
	15e	West Virginia Brewing Co. (14th & Madison Sts., Huntington)	1903-1914
	15f	Fesenmeier Brewing Co. (14th St. W. & Madison Ave.)	1934-1968
	15g	Little Switzerland Brewing Co.	1968-1970

Lubeck

WV	16	Hebrank & Rapp	1878-1884

Martinsburg
WV 17 F. T. Rossmarck 1875-1880

Mason City
WV 18 Godfrey Capito 1874-1875

Parkersburg
WV 19a Hebrank & Rapp 1874-1875
19b Hebrank & Rapp 1888-1890

WV 20a Parkersburg Brewing Co. (648 7th St.) 1889-1914
20b American Brewing Co. (George & Depot Sts.) 1934-1938

Sistersville
WV 21a Sistersville Brewing Co. 1906-1908
21b Ohio Valley Brewing Co. 1908-1911

Wellsburg
WV 22 Andrew Hebrank 1874-1882

Wheeling
WV 23a P. P. Beck 1847-1848
23b (P. P.) Beck & (A.) Reymann 1848-1863
23c Anton Reymann (Wetzel & Warren Sts.) 1863-1880
23d Reyman Brewing Co. 1880-1914

WV 24 Benwood Brewing Co. (4148 Water St.) NP 1934-1934

WV 25a Hagener 1840- ?
25b Frank Rodacker ? - ?
25c J. P. Brockhardt & Co. 1874-1875
25d Brockhardt Bros. 1875-1877
25e (John) Kinghorn & Smith (840 Market St.) 1877-1879
25f Alfred E. Smith 1879-1891
25g Smith Brewing Co. 1891-1902

WV 26 Kinghorn & Co. 1874-1875

WV 27 Henry Knoke 1874-1875

WV 28a John Pfarr 1854- ?
28b Kilian Kress, Eagle Brewery (1425 Smith St.) 1878-1884
28c Kenney & Blum (700/702 Market St.) 1884-1895
28d John J. Kenney, aka Kenney Brewery 1895-1901

WV 29a Unknown 1822-1845
29b George W. Smith 1845-1870
29c George W. Smith & Son 1870-1873
29d Smith & Co. (1700 Chapline St.) 1873-1877

WV 30 Uneeda Brewing Co. (31st & Jacob Sts.) 1903-1914

WV 31 Louis Weisgerber 1874-1875

WV 32a Frederick Ziegler 1855-1873
32b Nail City Brewing Co. (33rd & Wetzel Sts.) 1873-1882
32c Schmulbach Brewing Co. 1882-1914

WV 33a Peter & Th. Zimmer (25th ST.) 1860-1875
33b Maurus Balzer 1875-1887
33c Joseph Balzer 1887-1890
33d Catherine Balzer 1890-1897
33e Balzer's Brewery 1897-1914

WISCONSIN

Addison (see St. Lawrence)

Ahnapee (later: Algoma)
WI 1a H. Stansky, Ahnapee Brewery 1870-1873
1b Stransky & Swatz, Ahnapee Brewery 1873-1875
1c Ahnapee Brewing Co. 1875-1884
1d Henry Shmiling, Ahnapee Brewery 1884-1886
1c John Skala, Ahnapee Brewery 1886-1890
1d Klogner & Pitlik, Ahnapee Brewery 1890-1893

Allouez (see Green Bay)

Alma

WI	2	L. Becker	c1870
WI	3	William Briggeboos, Alma Brewery (Main St.)	1866-1888
WI	4a	John Hemrich	1855-1884
	4b	Wm. Hemrich	1884-1886
	4c	Wm. Hemrich & Co.	1886-1888
	4d	Alma Brewing Co.	1890-1920

Antigo

WI	5a	Frank Chaloupsky	1890-1892
	5b	John Benishek	1892-1893
	5c	(John) Benishek & (Albert) Fish	1893-1894
	5d	Frank Hanzal	1894-1895
	5e	Antigo Brewing Co. (Edison St.)	1895-1920
WI	6	Citizens Brewing Co. (Superior St.)	1899-1920
WI	7	Northern Lakes Brewing Co.	NP 1934-1934

Appleton

WI	8	L. Becker	c1870
WI	9a	Fisher (701/715 Lake St.)	1858-1860
	9b	Carl Muench	1860-1882
	9c	Mrs. Wallie Muench	1882-1884
	9d	Muench Brewing Co.	1884-1893
	9e	Mrs. Wallie Heid, Muench Brewery	1893-1899
	9f	Appleton Brewing and Malting Co.	1899-1917
WI	10	Nicholas Kirsch (Pacific & Bateman)	1896-1897
WI	11a	George Muench	1862- ?
	11b	Michael Fries, Star Brewery	1870- ?
	11c	Wing & Fries, Star Brewery (Walnut St.)	1878-1880
	11d	(George) Walter & (Frank) Fries, Star Brewery	1880-1885
	11e	Geo. Walter, Star Brewery (534/556 Walnut St.)	1885-1900
	11f	Geo. Walter's Estate, Star Brewery	1900-1903
	11g	Geo. Walter Brewing Co.	1903-1920
	11h	Geo. Walter Brewing Co. (200/220 S. Walnut St.)	1933-1972
WI	12	Unruth & Meyers	c1870

Arcadia

WI	13a	(Sanford) Bills & (Nick) Mergener (3rd & Main Sts.)	1872-1875
	13b	Nick. Mergener & Co.	1875-1876
	13c	(C.) Wolf & (John) Bion	1876-1876
	13d	Sherbert & Bion	1876-1877
	13e	John Bion	1877-1878
	13f	John N. Fertig	1878-1884
	13g	Fugina Bros. (Joseph & Marcx) & (John N.) Fertig	1884-1886
	13h	John Bion	1886-1890
	13i	(T.) Courtney & (Wm.) Fricker	1890-1892
	13j	William Fricker aka Hohmann & Fricker (1895)	1892-1897
	13k	Fricker & Hugn	1897-1898
	13l	William Fricker	1898-1900
	13m	Arcadia Brewing Co.	1900-1908
	13n	Arcadia Brewery, Peter Kronschnabl	1908-1920
	13o	Arcadia Brewing Co. (101/109 N. 3rd St.)	1934-1949

Ashland

WI	14a	Goeltz & Miller	c1870
	14b	Ashland Union Brewing Co.	1875- ?
WI	15a	(Frederick W.) Miller & Co. (107/123 10th Ave. E.)	1888-1899
	15b	Ashland Brewing and Malting Co.	1899-1901
	15c	Ashland Brewing Co.	1901-1920
WI	16a	Frank X. Schottmueller, Ashland Brewery	1872-1885
	16b	Philip Becker, Ashland Brewery (2nd St.)	1885-1892
	16c	Ashland Brewing Co. (900 E. 2nd St.)	1934-1937
WI	17	John Waegerle	1888-1888

Auburn			
WI	18	Langenbosch & Bros.	c1860
WI	19	B. Myer	c1860
Augusta			
WI	20	Kasper Ueher & Co.	1874-1875
Aztalan			
WI	21	Charles Bairenther	1888-1888
WI	22a	George Foster	c1870
	22b	Leissegger & Burns	1874-1875
Baldwin			
WI	23	John P. Mueller	1874-1875
Bangor			
WI	24a	Joseph Hussa	1858-1891
	24b	Estate of Joseph Hussa	1891-1895
	24c	Hussa Brewing Co. aka Hussa's Bangor Brewery (1897)	1895-1920
	24d	Hussa Brewing Co.	NP 1934-1934
Baraboo			
WI	25a	George Bender (331/335 Lynn St.)	c1870
	25b	Anna Bender	1875-1880
	25c	(Anna) Bender & (Ferdinand) Effinger, Baraboo City Brewery	1880-1885
	25d	Ferdinand Effinger	1885-1911
	25e	F. Effinger Brewing Co.	1911-1920
	25f	The Effinger Co.	1933-1949
	25g	Effinger Brewing Co.	1949-1966
WI	26a	George Ruhland (235 Lynn St.)	1867-1902
	26b	Ruhland Brewing Co.	1902-1915
Beaver Dam			
WI	27	George Amman	c1860
WI	28a	Mike Biersach, Beaver Dam Brewery (516 Madison Ave.)	1853-1855
	28b	(Mike) Biersach & (Frank) Liebenstein, Beaver Dam Brewery	1855-1856
	28c	(John) Goeggerle & (Joseph) Patzberger, Beaver Dam Brewery	1856-1859
	28d	John Goeggerle, Beaver Dam Brewery	1859-1901
	28e	J. Goeggerle Brewing Co.	1901-1902
	28f	Julia Goeggerle, Beaver Dam Brewery	1902-1904
	28g	Louis Ziegler, Beaver Dam Brewery	1904-1920
	28h	Louis Ziegler Brewing Co.	1933-1953
WI	29	Bernard Niehoff	c1860
WI	30a	Pfestel, New Brewery (Spring St.)	1868-1870
	30b	George Steil, New Brewery	1870-1875
	30c	Franz X. Steil, New Brewery	1875-1882
	30d	Xavier Steil, New Brewery	1882-1884
WI	31	Charles Schnettle	c1860
WI	32a	George Schutte, Farmer's Brewery	1857-1866
	32b	Philip Binzel	1866-1884
	32c	J. Philip Binzel	1884-1898
	32d	Binzel & Baum	1898-1899
	32e	J. Philip Binzel	1899-1902
	32f	Louisa Binzel (Madison St.)	1902-1904
	32g	Binzel Brewery	1904-1906
	32h	R. P. Binzel	1906-1907
	32i	J. Ph. Binzel Co.	1907-1920
WI	33	Thomas Young	c1850
Beloit			
WI	34	Bernard Cunningham, Beloit City Brewery (Liberty St. nr. 4th)	c1850
WI	35a	George J. Schlenk, Beloit Brewery (134 State St.)	1873-1878
	35b	Schlenk & Co., Beloit Brewery	1878-1879
	35c	August Schlenk, Beloit Brewery	1879-1887
	35d	Augustina Schlenk, Beloit Brewery	1887-1898
	35e	Frank Schlenk, Beloit Brewery	1898-1918

Berlin

WI	36a	August Buhler (Broadway)	1867-1875
	36b	Schmidt & Schunk	1875-1879
	36c	Louis Schunk	1879-1896
	36d	Jacobina Schunk	1896-1901
	36e	Berlin Brewing Co.	1901-1920
	36f	Berlin Brewing Co. (277/283 Broadway)	1933-1964
WI	37	Oscar B. Caswell	c1850
WI	38	C. W. Styer (408 Huron St.)	1899-1906

Berry

WI	39	George Esser	1874-1882

Black River Falls

WI	40a	Ulrich Oderbolz, Black River Falls Brewery (Spring St.)	1856-1900
	40b	Ulrich Oderbolz Estate, Black River Falls Brewery	1900-1901
	40c	Anna Oderbolz, Black River Falls Brewery	1901-1907
	40d	Oderbolz Brewing Co., Black River Falls Brewery	1907-1911
	40e	Badger Brewing Co.	1911-1920
	40f	Badger Brewing Co.	NP 1934-1934

Bloomer

WI	41a	Wendland & Adler (Bloomer & High Sts.)	1874-1875
	41b	John Wendland	1875-1878
	41c	John Wendland & Co.	1878-1880
	41d	John Wendland	1880-1890
	41e	Liehe & Kopp	1890-1893
	41f	Charles Liehe	1893-1899
	41g	Bloomer Brewing Co.	1899-1920
	41h	Bloomer Beverage Co.	1933-1935
	41i	Bloomer Brewery, Inc. aka Bloomer Brewing Corp. (1938-1940)	1935-1943
	41j	Bloomer Brewery	1943-1948

Boscobel

WI	42a	George Ziegelmaier	1866-1884
	42b	William Bruer	1884-1886
	42c	George Reiner	1886-1888
	42d	(Frank) Schuler & (Joseph A.) Dobler	1895-1908
	42e	Joseph A. Dobler	1908-1912
	42f	Dobler Brewery	1912-1913
	42g	Boscobel Brewing Co.	1913-1920
	42h	Boscobel Brewing Co.	1920-1942
WI	43	Frank Wunderly	c1880

Branch

WI	44a	Gottfried Kunz	c1870
	44b	Elizabeth Kunz	1878-1882
	44c	Peter Hermann	1882-1884
WI	45	D. B. Pierce	c1870

British Hollow

WI	46a	(Samuel) Stephens & (Wm.) Mohrenburg	1870-1872
	46b	Henry Macke	1872-1882
	46c	Joseph Vogelberg	1882-1888

Buchanan (see Kaukauna)

Burlington

WI	47a	Anton Finke (425 McHenry St.)	1865-1873
	47b	William J. Finke	1873-1884
	47c	W. J. Finke & Co.	1884-1897
	47d	(Wm. J.) Finke - (John) Uhen Brewing Co.	1897-1920
	47e	Burlington Cereal Products Co.	1920-1933
	47f	Burlington Brewing Co.	1933-1953
	47g	Van Merritt Brewing Co.	1953-1955
	47h	Wisconsin Brewing Co., subs.of Weber Waukesha Brewing, Waukesha	1955-1957
WI	48	Francis G. Klein & Co. (Pine & Mill Sts.)	1891-1901
WI	49	Jacob Muth, Sr.	1852-1872

Burlington (cont.)
WI 50 Old Dutch Brewing Co. NP 1934-1934

Buttes des Mortes
WI 51 Fred Bogk c1870

WI 52 C. Clenk c1850

Carlton (see Norman)

Cassville
WI 53a Derichs Bros. 1890-1890
53b Derichs & Geisen c1890

WI 54a Schmitz & Scherer c1870
54b F. Scherer & Co. c1870
54c Scherer & Alrath 1878-1879
54d (Wm.) Schmitz & (Hugo) Grimm 1879-1880
54e Alois Grimm 1880-1891
54f Mathias Lorscheter 1891-1895
54g Habermann & Lorscheter, Cassville Brewery 1895-1899
54h George Scheibl, Cassville Brewery 1899-1904
54i Mrs. Mary Scheibl, Cassville Brewery 1904-1907
54j Cassville Brewery, Andrew J. Lindner 1907-1920
54k The Cassville Brewing Co. (Brewery Ave.) 1933-1938

WI 55 Seitz & Co. c1850

Cato
WI 56 John Geo. Faatz 1875- ?

Cazenovia
WI 57 Alois Fix 1874-1875

Cecil
WI 58 E. W. Buche, Cecil Brewery (Lake Dr.) 1893-1906

Cedarburg
WI 59a Engels & Schaffer 1844-1850
59b August Runge c1850

WI 60a Dr. Fricke & Co. 1869-1874
60b John Weber (Water St.) 1874-1910
60c Cedarburg Brewery, John Weber 1910-1920

Cedar Creek
WI 61 A. Lekner c1850

Centreville
WI 62 Krausse & Co. c1880

WI 63a Christian Scheibe, Centreville Brewery 1867-1884
63b C. Scheibe 1884-1888
63c Centreville Brewing Co. 1888-1891
63d Hoffman & Mill 1893-1893
63e Gartzke Bros. Brewing Co. 1905-1911
63f Centreville Brewing Co. 1911-1915

Chilton
WI 64a Fred R. Gutheil, aka F. R. Gutheil & Co. 1853-1882
64b Jackeis & Thomas 1882-1883
64c Nicholas Thomas 1883-1888
64d Thomas & Freyer 1888-1890
64e Albert Freyer 1890-1891
64f Freyer & Hoch 1891-1893
64g (Herman) Gierow & Hoch 1893-1901
64h Gierow & Hoch Brewing Co. 1901-1906
64i Chilton Brewery, (Walter) Kroehnke & (M.) Landgraf 1906-1907
64j Calumet Brewing Co. 1907-1920
64k Calumet Brewing Co. (125 E. Commerce St.) 1933-1937
64l Henry Rahr Brewing Co. (br. of Green Bay, WI) 1937-1938
64m Calumet Brewing Co., Inc. 1938-1942

WI 65a J. Paulus 1860-1875
65b Philip Becker 1875-1885
65c Gutheil Bros. 1885-1888

Chippewa Falls

WI	66	Huber & Neher	? -1878
WI	67a	(Jacob) Leinenkugel & (John) Miller, Spring Brewery	1867-1883
	67b	Jacob Leinenkugel's Spring Brewery	1883-1898
	67c	J. Leinenkugel Brewing Co.	1898-1920
	67d	Jacob Leinenkugel Brewing Co. (1/3 Jefferson Ave.)	1933-
WI	68	T. X. Schmidmayer	1874-1875

Christiana (later Cross Plains)

WI	69	Henry Mehels	? -1878

Clarks Mills

WI	70a	Clark Bool	c1870
	70b	Faatz & Schweitzer	C1875-1880

Cleveland (see Centreville)

Cold Springs

WI	71	Marshall & Co.	c1850

Columbus

WI	72a	Alois Brauchle (Ludington St.)	1874- ?
	72b	Peter Brauchle	1888-1897
	72c	August Nothhelfer	1897-1900
	72d	Agnes Brauchle	1900-1901
	72e	City Brewing Co.	1901-1902
WI	73a	Stephen Fleck	1874-1880
	73b	Hayden Bros.	1880-1881
WI	74a	Henry Kurth	1859-1880
	74b	John H. Kurth	1880-1886
	74c	John H. Kurth & Co. (Ludington St.)	1886-1904
	74d	The Kurth Co.	1904-1920
	74e	The Kurth Company (Park Ave.)	1933-1949

Cross Plains

WI	75a	Geo. Esser & Son	1873-1885
	75b	Jacob Esser	1885-1910
	75c	Esser Bros.	1910-1913

Darlington

WI	76	Collins & Christ	1870s

Deerfield

WI	77	E. Silferson	1870s

Delafield

WI	78	Christian Christianson	c1870
WI	79	Dietrick, Delafield Brewery (Mill St.)	? -1870

Denmark

WI	80	Denmark Brewing Co. (Main St.)	1934-1947

De Pere

WI	81	De Pere Brewing Co. (did not brew)	1933-1933
WI	82	Alexander P. Schmidt	1874-1908

De Soto

WI	83a	George Eckhardt	1870-1884
	83b	Charles Reiter & Co.	1884-1885
	83c	Connelly, Kane & Co.	1885-1886

Dodgeville

WI	84a	John G. French	1870s
	84b	John G. Treutzech	1878-1880

Dundas

WI	85	Valentine Schaefer	1850s

Duplainville

WI	86	J. Wertz	1850s

Durand

WI	87a	Harstoff & (G.) Stending	1863-1866
	87b	Philip Lorenz	1866-1890
	87c	Bauer & Mertes	1890-1891
	87d	Bauer & Breunig (Warsha St.)	1891-1908
	87e	Durand Brewing Co.	1908-1920
WI	88a	Gustav Stending	1874-1876
	88b	John Stimger	1876-1880

Eagleton

WI	89	Charles Liche	1890s

Eau Claire

WI	90	Carstens & Hartwig, West Hill Brewery (Randall)	1882-1884
WI	91a	Ebner & Oliver	1875-1876
	91b	E. Robert Hantzsch (Barstow St.)	1876-1877
	91c	Emily M. Hantzsch	1877-1879
	91d	Frase & Lissack	1879-1880
WI	92	Heyson & Co.	1850s
WI	93a	H. J. Leinenkugel	1874-1875
	93b	Welter & Leinenkugel	1875-1876
	93c	Caroline Leinenkugel	1876-1878
WI	94a	Joseph Matthias Leinenkugel, Eagle Brewery (Farwell & Madison)	1855-1874
	94b	Theresa Leinenkugel, Eagle Brewery	1874-1885
	94c	Joseph M. Leinenkugel, Eagle Brewery	1885-1888
	94d	Henry Michels	1891-1904
	94e	Michels Brewing Co.	1904-1912
WI	95a	Henry Sommermeyer & Co., Dells Brewery (Hobart & Elm Sts.)	1878-1884
	95b	Henry Huebner, Dells Brewery	1884-1890
	95c	John Walter & Co., City Brewery	1890-1915
	95d	John Walter Brewing Co.	1915-1920
	95e	Walter Brewing Co. (318 Elm & 700 Barstow Sts.)	1933-
WI	96	Taylor & Son	1850s

Ellsworth

WI	97a	Nicholas P. Husting	1893-1897
	97b	Ellsworth Brewing Co.	1897-1901

Elroy

WI	98	J. Schorer	1880-1884

Fairchild

WI	99	Napoleon Santo	1903-1904

Farmersville

WI	100a	Michael Lepner	1870s
	100b	George Schmidt	1880s

Farmington

WI	101a	Ernest Klessig, Farmington Brewery	1860-1864
	101b	Ernest W. Jaehnig, Farmington Brewery	1864-1875
	101c	L. Jaehnig, Farmington Brewery	1875-1884

Fond Du Lac

WI	102a	A. G. Bechaud (515 Main St.)	1871-1875
	102b	A. G. Bechaud & Bros., Empire Brewery (11th St. near Hickory)	1875-1891
	102c	Bechaud Brewing Co.	1891-1920
	102d	Adolph Bates Bechaud (457/481 W. 11th St.)	1933-1934
	102e	Bechaud's, Inc.	1934-1941
WI	103	Hiram W. Eaton, Spruce Beer Brewery	1874-1887
WI	104a	Jacob & Charles Frey (Macy & Division Sts.)	1849-1880
	104b	P. & N. Seresse	1880-1882
WI	105a	Hauser & Dix (Portland St. near Division)	c1850-1870s
	105b	Paul Hauser & Co.	1870s
	105c	Anthony Voght	1880s
WI	106a	Moritz Krembz, Weiss Beer Brewery (Taycheedah Road)	1860s
	106b	F. Peter Severin	c1870-1883

Fond Du Lac (cont.)

WI	107	Almon W. Lockman, Spruce Beer Brewery (Johnson St. near Juneau)	1880-1903
WI	108a	James T. O'Halleran, Excelsior Spruce Beer Co. (235 E. 2nd St.)	1907-1908
	108b	Mrs. Mary O'Halleran, Excelsior Spruce Beer Co.	1908-1914
	108c	O'Halleran & Finnegan, Excelsior Spruce Beer Co.	1914-1918
WI	109a	Adam Sander	1873-1897
	109b	Sander Bros. (Albert & Edwin)	1897-1920
	109c	Pioneer Brewing Co. (S. Main St.)	1933-1933
WI	110a	Jos. Schussler, West Hill Brewery (172 Hickory St.)	1872-1884
	110b	Schussler Bros., West Hill Brewery	1884-1892
WI	111	Philip Stamm, Weiss Beer Brewery (401 Main St.)	1870s
WI	112	John S. Ziegenfuss	1878-1878

Forest Junction

WI	113	H. Rohr Sons & Co.	1903-1914

Fort Atkinson

WI	114a	George Lewis (W. Milwaukee St.)	1850-1851
	114b	(H. S.) Pritchard & (O. S.) Morrison	c1850-1879
	114c	A. Dalton & Co., aka Dalton & Grassmuck's Brewery	1879-1880
WI	115a	Louis Liebscher (German St.)	1861-1864
	115b	Charles Hasslinger	1869-1872
	115c	M. Huscher	1872-1873
	115d	Henchel & Grow	1873-1874
	115e	Christoph Regelin	1874-1876
	115f	John C. Regelin	1876-1878
	115g	Nicholas Klinger (br. of Whitewater, WI)	1878-1882
WI	116a	William Spaeth, City Brewery (26 S. Water St.)	1883-1920
	116b	Carl Ebner Brewing Co.	1933-1946
	116c	Louis Ziegler Brewing Co. (br. of Beaver Dam, WI)	1946-1948
	116d	Ziegler's Old Tap Brewing Co.	1948-1950

Fountain City

WI	117a	Eder & Ritcher	1850s
	117b	H. Erhardt	1860s
	117c	Eddie & Bros.	1870s
	117d	F. Moethwig & Co. aka Koschitz & Moethwig (1874)	1870s
WI	118	Erve & Kruger	1870s
WI	119a	(Henry) Fiedler & (Henry) Behlmer	1870s
	119b	Fiedler & Leonhard	1875-1877
	119c	Henry Fiedler	1877-1879
	119d	John Koschitz, Eagle Brewery	1879-1908
	119e	John Koschitz Brewery, Eagle Brewery, aka John Koschitz Estate	1908-1915
WI	120a	Fountain City Brewery, Philip Eder	1868-1878
	120b	Fountain City Brewing Co.	1886-1920
	120c	Fountain City Brewing Co., Inc. (436/444 Main St.)	1933-1965
WI	121	Hoefelin & Herley	1850s
WI	122	Alois Katler	1850s
WI	123a	George P. Ziegenfuss	1855-1880
	123b	John S. Ziegenfuss	1880-1882

Fox Lake

WI	124a	Frank A. Liebenstein, Fox Lake Brewery	1856-1870s
	124b	John Shlep, Fox Lake Brewery	c1870-1879
	124c	J. A. Williams, Fox Lake Brewery	1879-1880
	124d	Catherine Liebenstein, Fox Lake Brewery	1880-1893
	124e	Fox Lake Brewing Co. (Mill St.)	1904-1912
	124f	Fox Lake Brewery, John C. Brodesser	1912-1920
	124g	Fox Lake Brewing Co. (Mill & Trenton Sts.)	1933-1937

Francis Creek (see Kossuth)

Franklin

WI	125	Jacob Cromaner (St. Martins)	1870s

Franklin (cont.)

WI	126a	Sinderman & Pfeil	1870-1872
	126b	Gustav Sinderman & Son	1872-1874
	126c	Philip Gross	1874-1876
	126d	A. Koellner	1876-1878
	126e	Philip Gross	1878-1882

Freestadt

WI	127	L. Bodendorfer	1870s

Fussville

WI	128	Adolph Birkhauser	1849-1850

Geneva

WI	129	A. Shaw	1850s

Germantown

WI	130a	Milwaukee-Germantown Brewing Co. (1801 N. Marshall)	1933-1941
WI	131a	A. H. Reingrueber (South Germantown)	1890-1904
	131b	Milwaukee-Germantown Brewing Co.	1904-1906
	131c	Vogel's Independent Brewing Co.	1906-1916
WI	132a	Henry Runkel	1870s
	132b	John Staats	1874-1884
WI	133a	J. Schlicht	c1850-1860
	133b	Charles Reidenbach	? -1870
	133c	George Regenfuss & Co.	1870-1877
	133d	John Sieben	1877-1880

Golden Lake

WI	134a	Jacob Grubb	1858-1874
	134b	Michael Siverling	1874-1875
	134c	John Link	1875-1880
	134d	Mrs. Margaret Link	1880-1882
	134e	Louis C. Kuhry	1882-1887

Grafton

WI	135	Kusting & Co.	1882-1882
WI	136a	Charles Querngafar	1870s
	136b	Henry Diedrich	1882-1884
	136c	Sphen	1884- ?
WI	137a	J. B. Steinmetz	c1850-1875
	137b	Klug & Co.	1878-1880
	137c	Grafton Brewing Co.	1880-1884
	137d	John Weber, Grafton Brewery	1884-1890
	137e	William Weber, Grafton Brewery	1890-1920
	137f	Blessing Beverage Co.	1920-1933
	137g	Grafton Brewing Co.	1933-1935
	137h	Wisconsin Co-operative Brewery, Inc.	1935-1941

Grand Rapids (became Wisconsin Rapids c1920)

WI	138	Michael Eberle	c1870-1875
WI	139a	Grand Rapids Brewing Co.	1905-1920
	139b	Grand Rapids Products Co.	1920s
WI	140a	Nicholas Schmidt	c1870-1880
	140b	Jacob Lutz & Bro.	1880-1891
	140c	Scheibe & Stahl	1891-1893
	140d	Twin City Brewing Co.	1893-1894

Granville

WI	141	Ferdinand Wagner	1860s

Gravesville

WI	142	F. Sussenguth	1880s

Green Bay

WI	143	Anton Blasch (Pearl St. between Walnut & Hubbard)	1851-1879

Green Bay (cont.)

WI	144a	(Franz H.) Hagemeister & Co., Union Brewery (Manitowoc Road)	1866-1873
	144b	F. H. Hagemeister, Union Brewery	1873-1882
	144c	F. H. Hagemeister & Son, Union Brewery	1882-1886
	144d	Hagemeister Brewing Co.	1886-1926
	144e	Valley Brewing & Refrigerating Co.	NP 1934-1934
WI	145a	(August) Hochgreve & (Henry) Rahr, Bellevue Brewery (Lower De Pere Road, Allouez)	1857-1865
	145b	August Hochgreve, Bellevue Brewery	1865-1879
	145c	Christian Kiel	1879-1882
	145d	C. Hochgreve & Son, Bellevue Brewery	1884-1893
	145e	Caroline Hochgreve, Bellevue Brewery	1893-1894
	145f	Hochgreve Brewing Co.	1894-1920
	145g	Hochgreve Brewing Co.	1933-1949
WI	146	Christian Kiel (Allouez)	1860s
WI	147a	Landwehr & Beyer	1870s
	147b	Sebastian Landwehr, City Brewery (178 Chicago St.)	1872-1876
	147c	Louis Van Dycke, Green Bay Brewery	1876-1878
	147d	Octavia Van Dycke, Green Bay Brewery	1878-1884
	147e	O. Van Dycke Brewing Co. (Chicago & S. Jackson Sts.)	1884-1908
WI	148a	Henry Rahr, East River Brewery (1317 Main St.)	1866-1888
	148b	Henry Rahr & Co., East River Brewery	1888-1891
	148c	Henry Rahr's Sons	1891-1900
	148d	Henry Rahr Sons Co.	1900-1913
	148e	Rahr Brewing Co.	1913-1920
	148f	Rahr Green Bay Brewing Corp, aka All Star Brewing Co. (1317/1343 Main St.)	1933-1966

Greenwood

WI	149a	Ludwig & Norg	1891-1897
	149b	Joseph Bulin	1897-1902

Hammond

WI	150	Weyhe & Son	1874-1875

Hartford

WI	151	D. & J. Baum	1870s
WI	152	Laubenstein Brewery	1910-1910
WI	153a	Jacob Portz, Hartford City Brewery	1874-1890
	153b	Jacob Portz Brewing and Malt Co.	1890-1896
	153c	(George) Portz & Werner, Hartford City Brewery	1896-1900
	153d	Geo. Portz, Hartford City Brewery	1900-1902
	153e	Joseph Schwartz, Hartford City Brewery	1902-1904
	153f	Joseph Schwartz Brewing Co.	1904-1933
	153g	Joseph Schwartz Brewing Co. (220 E. Wisconsin St.)	1933-1937
WI	154	Whitman & Metzer, aka Metzer & Co.	1870s

Hartland

WI	155a	C. Christianson	1870s
	155b	Chas. Haslinger	1874-1875
	155c	Koeding & Krause	1875-1877

Herman

WI	156	John Hills	1850s

Highland

WI	157	Charles Gillmann	1860s
WI	158a	Schaffra & Meyer	1860s
	158b	Victor & Schaffra	1870s
	158c	J. Schaffra	c1870-1880s
WI	159a	(John) Topp & (Henry) Lampe & (F.) Imhoff	1867-1877
	159b	John Schaffer	1877-1887
	159c	John A. Semrad	1887-1893
	159d	John A. Semrad & Bros.	1893-1904
	159e	Semrad Bros. & Pusch Brewing Co.	1904-1920
	159f	Semrad-Pusch Brewing Co.	1933-1942

Hillsboro

WI	160a	Carl Ludwig & Joseph Landsinger	1870-1874
	160b	Frederick Schell	1874-1890
	160c	C. Ludwig & Co.	1890-1891
	160d	Joseph Bezucha	1891-1910
	160e	Hillsboro Brewing Co.	1910-1920
	160f	Hutter Brewing Co.	1933-1936
	160g	Hillsboro Brewing Co.	1936-1943

Horicon

WI	161a	Paul Deierlein	c1860-1882
	161b	Chas. H. Deierlein	1882-1884
	161c	John S. Deierlein	1884-1891
WI	162	Herman Muth	1901-1902
WI	163a	Lawrence Wolffram	c1870
	163b	John Grosskopf	1878-1884

Hortonville

WI	164a	Charles Hoier	1899-1900
	164b	Hortonville Brewing Co.	1900-1920
WI	165	Miller & Co.	c1870

Hudson

WI	166a	William Montmann (St. Croix River Bridge)	1874-1888
	166b	A. & J. Hochstein, Artesian Brewery	1888-1905
	166c	Henry M. Singelman Brewing Co.	1905-1910
WI	167a	Louis Yoerg (Buckeye St.)	1874-1890
	167b	George Riedel, City Brewery	1890-1896
	167c	Joseph A. Casanova	1896-1898
	167d	Casanova Brewing Co.	1898-1920

Huilsburg

WI	168a	John Huels	1850-1865
	168b	August Thielke	1865-1870
	168c	H. Sherman	1870-1874
	168d	H. Eifert	1874-1880s

Humbird

WI	169a	Andrews, Hay & Co.	1870-1870
	169b	Andrews & Gunderson	1870-1871
	169c	Ernest Eilert (Hales Creek Branch)	1871-1885

Huntingburgh

WI	170	J. H. Arensmann	1875- ?

Hurley

WI	171a	Philip Becker, Hurley Brewery	1888-1895
	171b	Gogeobic Grange Spring Brewery	1895-1896
	171c	M. E. Lennon, Gogeobic Range Spring Brewery	1896-1898
	171d	McGeehan Bros.	1898-1898

Inerton

WI	172	R. Fredrickson	1874-1875

Jackson

WI	173	John Hellenschmidt	1866-1874

Janesville

WI	174a	John Buob, South Side Brewery (329 S. Main St.)	1882-1890
	174b	Buob Bros. (John & Michael), South Side Brewery	1890-1897
	174c	Michael Buob, South Side Brewery (Main St. & Beloit Ave.)	1897-1904
	174d	M. Buob Brewing Co. (822 Beloit Ave. & Main St.)	1904-1915
	174e	Badger State Brewing Co.	1915-1920
WI	175	Charles C. Gray (15 Locust Ave.)	1903-1912
WI	176	John Grovier, Eagle Brewery (N. Milwaukee St.)	1860s
WI	177a	William Hemming (58 N. Franklin St.)	1880-1883
	177b	Wm. Hemming & Son (55 W. Milwaukee St.)	1883-1901
	177c	Wm. Hemming's Sons	1901-1912
	177d	Hemming's Ale Brewery, Geo. H. Esser	1912-1915
	177e	Esser's Ale Brewery (106/110 N. Franklin St.)	1915-1920
WI	178	Samuel Hocking (W. Main St. between N. 1st & 2nd)	1860s

Janesville (cont.)

WI	179a	Hodson & Co. (69 N. Main St.)	1870s
	179b	Nicholas Kramer	-1884
WI	180a	John Roethinger & Co. (Racine & Beloit Roads)	c1860-1870s
	180b	John Roethinger	1874-1877
	180c	C. Rosa & Co. (20 Main St. & Beloit Road)	1877-1879
	180d	A. B. Roethinger	1879-1882
WI	181a	A. Rogers, Janesville Brewery (N. River & Mineral Point Sts.)	1850s
	181b	Buob & Rogers	1860s
	181c	John Buob & Bro. (Michael)	c1860-1882
	181d	Gezelschap & Knipp, City Brewery	1882-1886
	181e	Knipp Bros. (Louis F. & Wm. Ph.), City Brewery	1886-1888
	181f	Louis F. Knipp, City Brewery	1888-1891
	181g	Louis F. Knipp Brewing Co.	1891-1893
	181h	Louis F. Knipp	1893-1904
	181i	Croak Brewing Co. (500 N. River St.)	1904-1920
	181j	Bower City Beverage Co. (500/520 N. River St.)	1933-1939
WI	182	Jacob Singer (Main St. & Racine Road)	1850s
WI	183a	John J. Todd (16 E. Milwaukee St.)	1868-1873
	183b	John G. Todd	1873-1889
	183c	Fardy & Norton	1889-1890
	183d	(Matt) Fardy & (Norton B.) Robinson	1890-1891
	183e	N. B. Robinson & Co.	1891-1898
	183f	James Smith	1898-1899
	183g	N. B. Robinson Brewing Co.	1899-1908

Jefferson

WI	184a	Jacob Breunig (Main & Racine Sts.)	1855-1890
	184b	Jefferson Brewing and Malting Co.	1895-1920
WI	185a	Forest Danner (Johnson Creek Road)	c1860-1873
	185b	George Foster	1873-1876
WI	186a	Christian Illing (N. Center St. opposite Mechanic)	1857-1862
	186b	Henry Long	1862-1873
	186c	(Henry) Danner & (Rudolph) Heger, City Brewery	1873-1880
	186d	Rudolph Heger, City Brewery	1880-1908
	186e	R. Heger Malt and Brewing Co.	1908-1920
	186f	Saxon Brewing Co.	1933-1939
	186g	Perplies Brewing Co. (1008 Center St.)	1940-1953
WI	187a	Jefferson Brewing Co. (Milwaukee & 1st Sts.)	c1880-1890
	187b	(Adam) Schmidt & Co., aka Jefferson Brewing Co.	1890-1895
WI	188	John Kemmeter (E. Racine St. between Dewey & Marion Sts.)	1870s
WI	189a	Stephen Neuer (E. Racine St. opposite Marion St.)	c1850-1874
	189b	Christian Neuer	1874-1878
	189c	Neuer & Georgelein	1878-1880
	189d	Christian Neuer	1880-1882
	189e	(Joseph) Berens & (John) Stephan, Jefferson Brewery	1882-1884
	189f	Berens Bros. (Joseph & Adolph), Jefferson Brewery	1884-1886
	189g	Jos. Berens, Jefferson Brewery	1886-1888
	189h	Charles Baireuther	1888-1891

Jefferson Junction

WI	190	Lytle-Stoppenbach Co.	1905-1906

Johnstown

WI	191	M. D. Waters	1850s

Kaukauna

WI	192	Peter Dedrich	1850s
WI	193a	Helf Bros. (John P. & Jacob), (10th St. near Hendricks Ave., South Kaukauna)	1888-1890
	193b	(Jacob) Helf & (John) Brill	1890-1892
	193c	Jacob Helf (Buchanan)	1892-1897
	193d	Jacob Helf & Co.	1902-1905
	193e	Jacob Helf Estate	1905-1911

Kaukauna (cont.)

WI	194a	(John) Helf & (Charles H.) Ristau, City Brewery (729 Desnoyer)	1893-1897
	194b	Helf Bros. Brewing Co.	1897-1902
	194c	Peter Helf	1902-1906
	194d	Regenfuss Brewing Co. (North Kaukauna)	1906-1920
	194e	Regenfuss Brewing Co.	1920-1933
	194f	Electric City Brewing Co. aka Mellow Brew Brewing Co. (1939)	1933-1947
WI	195	(Michael) Kline & (Adam) Hilz	1880s

Kenosha

WI	196	Brand Brewing Co. of Chicago and Kenosha	1910-1910
WI	197	N. A. Brown (Ann St.)	1860s
WI	198a	Jacob G. Gottfredson	1858-1877
	198b	J. G. Gottfredson & Son	1877-1890
	198c	Edwin Griesbach Brewing Co.	1890-1893
WI	199	V. Hughes	1850s
WI	200	Montanye & Graff, aka Brown's Ale Brewing Co. (Between Maiden & Lake)	1860s
WI	201a	Conrad Muntzenberger (6 N. Main & Water Sts.)	1847-1873
	201b	Muntzenberger & Co.	1873-1879
	201c	A. Muntzenberger	1879-1884
	201d	Muntzenberger Brewing Co.	1884-1885
WI	202	New Era Brewing Co. (non-alcoholic beer producer)	1883-1889
WI	203a	Wisconsin Brewing Co. (2111 63rd Place)	1933-1935
	203b	Kenosha Brewing Co.	1935-1936

Kewaunee

WI	204a	William Blackwell	1850s
	204b	Deitloff & Wenger	1860s
	204c	Joseph Werner & Co.	1870s
WI	205a	Adolph Ebel	1860-1864
	205b	Charles Brandes, Kewaunee Brewery	1864-1882
	205c	Frank Nuhlicek, Kewaunee Brewery	1882-1888
	205d	(Anton) Mach & (Joseph) Langer, Kewaunee Brewery	1888-1902
	205e	Anton Mach, Pilsen Brewery	1902-1907
	205f	Anton Mach Estate, Pilsen Brewery	1907-1909
	205g	Mach's Pilsen Brewery, Mrs. Katherina Mach	1909-1916
	205h	Pilsen Brewery, Raymond Rauch	1916-1920
WI	206a	Lutz & Trottman	1864-1866
	206b	Ritter	1866-1868
	206c	Charles Deda, Bavaria Brewery	1868-1885
	206d	Charles Deda & Son, Bavaria Brewery	1885-1886
	206e	Bergman & Deda, Bavaria Brewery	1886-1889
	206f	Wallner & Deda, Bavaria Brewery	1889-1893
	206g	(Fred) Wallner & (Thomas) Hlinak, Bavaria Brewery	1893-1895
	206h	Kewaunee Brewing Co.	1895-1916
	206i	Kewaunee Brewing Co. (324 Ellis St.)	1933-1942

Kiel (see Schleswig)

Kilbourn City

WI	207a	T. Hoffman, City Brewery (Broadway & Oak Sts.)	1860s
	207b	Julius Leuthe, City Brewery	1872-1891
	207c	Philip Klenk	1891-1893
	207d	Paul Keller	1899-1904

Knowles

WI	208	George Smith	1889-1890

Kossuth

WI	209	Mathias Dolegal	1874-1875
WI	210a	J. Robes	1870s
	210b	Anna Warm	1874-1877
	210c	A. Chloupek	1877-1879
	210d	Franz Jentsch	1879-1884

La Crosse

WI 211 Fritz Diefenthaler 1856-1870s

WI 212 Ignatz Furst 1850s

WI 213 John Gund (Front & Division Sts.) 1854-1858

WI 214a John Gund, Empire Brewery (9th St. & Mormon Cooley Road) 1873-1880
214b John Gund Brewing Co. 1880-1920

WI 215a (John) Gund & (Gottlieb) Heileman, City Brewery (1018 S. 3rd) 1858-1872
215b Gottlieb Heileman, City Brewery 1872-1878
215c Johanna Heileman, City Brewery 1878-1890
215d G. Heileman Brewing Co. 1890-1962
215e G. Heileman Brewing Co., Inc. 1962-
aka Ace Brewing Co.
aka Blatz Brewing Co. (1969-)
aka Duluth Brewing Division
aka Foxhead Brewing Co. (1966-1975)
aka Gluek Brewing Co. (1954-1965)
aka Heidelbrau Brewing Co.
aka Kingsbury Brewing Div.
aka Pioneer Brewing Co.
aka Weber-Waukesha Brewing Co.
aka Wisconsin Brewing Co.

WI 216a (Jacob) France, Eagle Brewery (1301 LaCrosse St.) c1850-1862
216b (Jacob) France & (Frederick) Miller, Eagle Brewery 1862-1866
216c Frederick Miller, Eagle Brewery 1866-1869
216d Kappes & Miller, Eagle Brewery 1869-1870
216e Kappes & (John) Hofer, Eagle Brewery 1870-1875
216f J. & J. Hofer, Eagle Brewery 1875-1879
216g John Hofer, Eagle Brewery 1879-1886
216h Franz Bartl 1886-1904
216i Franz Bartl Brewing Co. 1904-1920
216j George Kunz Company (1201/1217 La Crosse St.) 1933-1937
216k Louis Ziegler Brewing Co. (br. of Beaver Dam, WI) 1948-1948
216l Ziegler's Old Fashioned Brewery of La Crosse, Inc. 1948-1950

WI 217 Emil G. Kohn 1896-1897

WI 218a Charles & John Michel, La Crosse Brewery (727 3rd & Division Sts.) 1857-1882
218b C. & J. Michel Brewing Co. 1882-1920
218c La Crosse Breweries, Inc. (700/718 3rd St.) 1933-1956

WI 219 Gustavus Nicholai 1850s

WI 220a G. F. Voegele & Bro., North La Crosse Brewery (210 Mill St.) 1888-1893
220b Voegele Bros., North La Crosse Brewery 1893-1900
220c Jacob L. Erickson, North Side Brewery 1900-1901
220d Jacob L. Erickson, Monitor Brewery 1901-1920
220e Monitor Brewing Co. NP 1934-1934

WI 221 Warninger & Houthmaker, Berlin Weiss Beer Brewery 1896-1906

WI 222a (George) Zeisler & (Otto) Nagel, Plank Road Brewery (3rd St. between Grove St. & La Crosse River) 1867-1869
222b George Zeisler, Plank Road Brewery (718 N. 3rd St.) 1869-1890
222c Geo. Zeisler & Sons, Plank Road Brewery 1890-1902

Lake (see Milwaukee)

Lake Mills

WI 223 Abendroth & Co. 1870s

Leroy

WI 224a William Kole 1870s
224b George Schmidt 1874-1875

WI 225a Nic. Weidig 1878-1884
225b Michael Platzer 1884-1891

Lima

WI 226 Charles Foast 1893-1893

Lincoln			
WI	227	John Eisenbeis & Co.	1884-1884
WI	228	George E. Loux	1878-1878
Lisbon (see Sussex)			
Lock Haven			
WI	229	F. Davidson	1850s
Lomira			
WI	230a	Star Brewing Co.	1911-1920
	230b	Star Brewing Co. (Pleasant Hill Ave.)	1933-1945
	230c	Harold C. Johnson Brewing Co. aka A. B. P. Brewing Co. (1950-1952)	1945-1954
Lowell			
WI	231	Jolling, Brick House Brewery	1857-1860
WI	232	George J. Schmieg	1856-1880
Mackford (later Markesan)			
WI	233	John Hale	1850s
Madison			
WI	234a	Mathias Breckheimer (215 King St. btwn. N. Wilson & Clymer)	c1860-1901
	234b	Breckheimer Brewing Co.	1901-1916
WI	235a	John Hess (State & Gilman Sts.)	1875-1877
	235b	Hess & Moser	1877-1881
	235c	John Hess	1881-1882
	235d	Hess & Loehrer	1882-1884
WI	236	Barnhard Mauz (84 State St.)	c1860-1872
WI	237	Miller & Keiser	1870s
WI	238	Reeves & Waddle, Middleton Brewery	1860s
WI	239a	John Roedermund, Madison Brewery (Yahara Canal, Sherman Ave. & Lodi Road)	c1850-1875
	239b	Rodermund Brewing Co.	1875-1880
WI	240	Henry Schulkamp (Weiss Beer)	c1880-1900
WI	241a	Adam Sprecher (651/653 Williamson & Blount Sts.)	1848-1859
	241b	(Mathias) Breckheimer & (Joseph) Hausmann	1859-1864
	241c	George Rockenbach	1864-1868
	241d	Peter Fauerbach	1868-1886
	241e	Maria Fauerbach	1886-1890
	241f	Fauerbach Brewing Co.	1890-1920
	241g	Fauerbach Brewing Co.	1933-1966
WI	242a	William Voight, Capital Brewery (333 State & Gorham Sts.)	1854-1864
	242b	James Hausmann, Capital Brewery	1864-1877
	242c	Jos. Hausmann, Capital Brewery	1877-1891
	242d	Hausmann Brewing Co.	1891-1920
Manitowoc			
WI	243	Thurn & B. Carl	1874-1875
WI	244a	Chr. Dobert	1879- ?
	244b	Engels Brewing Co. (Washington St. near 21st St.)	? -1884
WI	245a	William Fricke (Main & Washington Sts.)	1862-1873
	245b	Christian Fricke	1873-1875
	245c	Carl Fricke	1875-1879
	245d	John Schreihart	1879-1884
	245e	(John) Schreihart & (George) Kunz	1884-1885
	245f	Schreihart Brewing Co.	1891-1920
	245g	Bleser Brewing Co. (1004 Washington St.)	1937-1942
WI	246a	Charles Hottelmann (Marshall & 9th Sts.)	1849-1865
	246b	George Kunz	1865-1874
	246c	F. Pautz & Co.	1874-1878
	246d	Fred Pautz	1878-1885
	246e	(George) Kunz & (Daniel) Bleser	1885-1890
	246f	Kunz, Bleser & Co.	1890-1913

Manitowoc (cont.)

WI	246g	Kunz-Bleser Co. (902/910 Marshall St.)	1913-1920
	246h	Manitowoc Products Co. (901 Marshall St.)	1920-1933
	246i	Kingsbury Breweries Co. (br. of Sheboygan, WI)	1933-1949
WI	247a	William Rahr, Eagle Brewery (6th & Washington Sts.)	1849-1880
	247b	Wm. Rahr's Sons, Eagle Brewery	1880-1893
	247c	William Rahr Sons Co.	1893-1911
	247d	William Rahr Sons Brewing Co.	1911-1920
WI	248	Riverview Brewing Co. (1100/1106 S. Water St.)	1933-1937
WI	249a	Roeffs & Hagen	1850s
	249b	John Roeffs	1860s
	249c	Charles Schirbe	1870s
	249d	J. Richter	c1870-1878
WI	250	Martin Schmidt	1874-1874
WI	251a	Albert Wittenberg (8th St.)	c1860-1870s
	251b	Frank Willinger	1870s

Manitowoc Rapids

WI	252a	Gottfried Kunz, Branch Station Brewery	1858-1878
	252b	Elizabeth Kunz, Branch Station Brewery	1878- ?

Marathon

WI	253a	Marathon City Brewing Co. (868 Lincoln Ave.)	1881-1889
	253b	Frank R. Sindermann	1889-1896
	253c	Stuhlfauth Bros.	1896-1900
	253d	Marathon City Brewing Co.	1902-1920
	253e	Marathon City Brewing Co. (Pine & 2nd Sts.)	1933-1964
	253f	Marathon Brewery, Inc.	1964-1966

Marinette (East)

WI	254	Swedish Brewing Co. (near Ogden & Bay Shore)	1897-1899

Markesan (see Mackford)

Marshfield

WI	255a	M. Bourgeois	1878-1882
	255b	(Emil P.) Scheibe & (Albert) Schneider (500 N. Pine St.)	1890-1893
	255c	Marshfield Brewing Co.	1893-1920
	255d	The Marshfield Brewing Co. (509 N. Pine St.)	1933-1966
	255e	J. Figi Brewing Co., Inc.	1966-1967

Mauston

WI	256a	Henry Runkel & Co.	1870s
	256b	Maria Runkel	c1870-1874
	256c	Maria Runkel & Co.	1874-1884
	256d	Runkel & Miller	1884-1888
	256e	Charles Miller	1888-1895
	256f	(Charles) Miller & (John) Hauer	1895-1901
	256g	J. Hauer Brewing Co.	1901-1903
	256h	John Hauer	1903-1904
	256i	J. Willens	1904-1906
	256j	Chas. Ellison, Mauston Brewery	1906-1911
	256k	Mauston Brewery, Jos. Vogl	1911-1916

Mayville

WI	257a	William Darge	1878-1884
	257b	Louis Darge	1884-1886
WI	258a	B. Kladen	1870s
	258b	Kroesing & Co.	1870s
	258c	Funke Bros.	c1870-1880s
WI	259a	Benjamin Mayer	1853-1855
	259b	Martin Bachhuber	1855-1868
	259c	John Henninger	1868-1869
	259d	E. Bachhuber	1869-1870
	259e	Leonard Uhl	1870-1872
	259f	Matheus Ziegler	1872-1880
	259g	M. Ziegler & Co.	1880-1892
	259h	M. Ziegler Brewing Co. (Main St.)	1892-1920
	259i	Mayville Brewing Co. (331 S. Main St.)	1934-1936

Mayville (cont.)

WI	260	Mayville Brewing Co.	1880-1882
WI	261	John Steger & Co.	1882-1920
WI	262	John Weringer	1850s

Mazomanie

WI	263a	Peter Weard, Mazomanie Brewery	1851-1870s
	263b	Tinker & Slough, Mazomanie Brewery	c1870-1880
	263c	Ambrose Lang, Mazomanie Brewery	1880-1895
	263d	Caroline Lang, Mazomanie Brewery	1895-1897
	263e	Edward M. Lang, Mazomanie Brewery	1897-1902

Medford

WI	264a	Carl Kuhn (3rd St.)	1888-1890
	264b	Kuhn Bros. Brewing Co.	1890-1893
	264c	Leo Kuhn	1893-1895
	264d	Medford Brewing Co.	1895-1897
	264e	William Kurz	1898-1900
	264f	Estate of William Kurz	1900-1901
	264g	Medford Brewery Co.	1901-1906
	264h	Medford Brewery	1906-1908
	264i	Wm. Gehring	1908-1910
	264j	Taylor County Brewing Co., aka Wm. Gehring	1910-1915
	264k	Medford Brewing Co. (132 N. Wisconsin Ave.)	1934-1935
	264l	Medford Brewing Co.	1940-1948

Menasha

WI	265a	Caspari, Island City Brewery	1860-1868
	265b	Jacob F. Mayer & Co., Island City Brewery	1868-1875
	265c	Joseph Mayer, Island City Brewery	1875-1879
	265d	Habermehl & Mueller, Island City Brewery	1879-1882
	265e	George Habermehl, Island City Brewery	1882-1888
	265f	Walter Bros. & Fries, Island City Brewery	1888-1891
	265g	Walter Bros. Brewing Co., Island City Brewing Co.	1891-1920
	265h	Walter Bros. Brewing Co. (134/144 Nicolet Blvd.)	1933-1956
WI	266	J. Dudler	1850s
WI	267a	Hall & Loescher	c1850-1870s
	267b	Merz & Behre	-1879
	267c	Winz & Loescher	1879-1882
	267d	Werner Winz	1882-1888
	267e	Menasha Brewing Co. (501/505 Manitowoc St.)	1888-1920
	267f	Menasha Brewing Co.	NP 1934-1934
	267g	Valley Brewing Co.	1935-1936
	267h	Fox Valley Brewing Co.	1938-1942

Menominee

WI	268a	Burkhardt Bros.	1888-1893
	268b	Gottfried Burkhardt	1893-1895
	268c	Louis Burkhardt	1895-1897
	268d	Burkhardt & Son	1897-1912
	268e	Josef Niedermair	1912-1916
WI	269	Virginia French	1850s
WI	270	Christian Fuss	1874-1884
WI	271a	Roleff & Wagner	1874-1880
	271b	Fred Wagner	1880-1884

Menominee Falls

WI	272	Jacob Stolz	1870s

Mentor

WI	273	Ernest Eilert	1874-1875

Mequon

WI	274a	Adolph Zimmermann	1874-1878
	274b	Franz Zimmermann & Co.	1878-1884

Merrill

WI 275 Erick Nelson 1905-1905

WI 276a Geo. Ruder (br. of Wausau, WI) (River & Nast Sts.) 1883-1888
276b Geo. Ruder Brewery, Emil Ruder 1888-1895
276c Louis Leidiger Brewing co. 1895-1896
276d Leidiger Brewing Co. (1609 River St.) 1896-1920
276e Leidiger Brewing Co. 1933-1948

Merton

WI 277 R. Frederickson 1878-1882

Middleton (see Pheasant Branch)

Milwaukee (including Wauwatosa)

WI 278 Phillip Altpeter, Northwestern Brewery, Weiss Beer (601/605 3rd & Sherman Sts.) 1856-1884

WI 279 Peter & Charles Anderson (281 S. Pierce St.) 1896-1896

WI 280a John Arnold (4th & Chestnut Sts.) 1881-1881
280b Ferd. Arnold 1881-1882

WI 281 Louis Arras (5th between Chestnut & Poplar Sts.) 1859-1860

WI 282 William Aschmann (9th & Cedar Sts.) 1859-1860

WI 283a Baker, Eagle Brewery (8th & Prairie Sts.) 1841-1843
283b Miller & Pawlett, Eagle Brewery 1843-1844
283c Miller & Hanson, Eagle Brewery 1844-1848
283d Alonzo Blossom, Eagle Brewery 1848-1852
283e Middlewood & Gibson, aka Pearson Gibson & Co. 1857-1858
283f Isaac Gibson & Co., Spring Brewery 1858-1860
283g Sand's Spring Brewery, John G. Sands 1860-1867

WI 284 Banner Brewing Co. (2302/2312 W. Clybourn St.) 1933-1935

WI 285a Bast & Nunemacher, Wisconsin Brewery (91 Knapp St.) 1850s
285b Bast & Klinger, Wisconsin Brewery c1850-1861
285c Christopher Bast, Wisconsin Brewery 1861-1869
285d Wilhelmina Bast, Wisconsin Brewery 1869-1871
285e Meeske Bros. & Hoch, Wisconsin Brewery 1871-1875
285f (Charles) Meeske & (Reiner) Hoch, Wisconsin Brewery 1875-1878
285g (Joseph) Grisbaum & (Jacob) Kehrein (607/613 Cherry St.) 1878-1890

WI 286a (Jacob) Best & Co. (Sons: Jacob, Jr., Charles, Lorenz, Philip), Empire Brewery (917 Chestnut St.) 1844-1853
286b Empire Brewery, Jacob Best, Jr. & Philip Best 1853-1860
286c Empire Brewery, Philip Best 1860-1864
286d Phillip Best & Co., Empire Brewery 1864-1873
286e Ph. Best Brewing Co., Empire Brewery 1873-1879
286f Pabst Brewing Co. 1889-1920
286g Premier-Pabst Corp. (917 W. Juneau Ave.) 1933-1939
286h Pabst Brewing Corp. 1939-1943
286i Pabst Brewing Co. 1943-

WI 287a Charles Best, Plank Road Brewery (Wauwatosa) 1850-1851
287b Best Bros. Brewery (Charles & Lorenz), Plank Road Brewery 1851-1853
287c Frederick Miller, Plank Road Brewery 1853-1878
287d Frederick Miller, Menomonee Valley Brewery 1878-1888
287e Fred Miller Brewing Co. (W. State St.) 1888-1920
287f Miller Brewing Co. (4002/4026 W. State St.) aka Miller High Life Co. (1932-1933) 1920-

WI 288a Johann Braun, City Brewery 1846-1851
288b Valentine Blatz, City Brewery (Broadway & Division Sts.) 1851-1889
288c Val. Blatz Brewing Co., United States Brewing Co. of Chicago 1889-1890
288d Val. Blatz Brewing Co., United States Brewing Co., Milwaukee and Chicago Breweries Co. (609 Broadway) 1890-1911
288e Val. Blatz Brewing Co., U. S. Brewing Co. 1911-1920
288f Blatz Brewing Co. (1120 N. Broadway) 1933-1958
288g Pabst Brewing Co., dba Blatz Brewing Co. 1958-1959

Milwaukee (cont.)

WI	289a	Felix Calgeer, Phoenix Brewery (189/195 Sherman St.)	1852-1854
	289b	Felix Calgeer, Phoenix Brewery	1858-1864
	289c	F. & Davis Calgeer, Phoenix Brewery	1864-1865
	289d	Felix Calgeer, Phoenix Brewery	1865-1868
	289e	Louis Liebscher, Phoenix Brewery	1871-1881
WI	290	Capitol Brewing Co. of Milwaukee, Inc. (3778 N. Fratney St.)	1933-1948
WI	291	Castalia Bottling Works, George Schweickart, Weiss Beer Brewery (Wauwatosa)	1893-1895
WI	292a	Century Brewing Co. (2318/2332 N. 30th St.)	1933-1934
	292b	Old Lager Brewing Co.	1934-1938
	292c	Milwaukee Beer Co.	1938-1939
WI	293a	John P. Engelhardt, Main St. Brewery (37 Main & N. Chicago)	1859-1861
	293b	Elizabeth Engelhardt, Main St. Brewery	1861-1862
WI	294	T. W. Falbe & Co., Weiss Beer Brewery (1312/1320 3rd St.)	1878-1878
WI	295	Fischbach Brewing Co. (3045 W. Walnut St.)	1933-1936
WI	296	Alois Gallagger, Washington Brewery (Johnson & Main Sts.)	1850s
WI	297	Germantown Spring Brewery and Soda Co., Arthur Warschauer (904 1st St.)	1916-1916
WI	298	Peter Gerstner (Walnut & 9th Sts.)	1861-1863
WI	299a	David Gipfel, Union Brewery, Weiss Beer (417 Chestnut St.)	1843-1849
	299b	Chas. W. Gipfel, Union Brewery	1849-1892
	299c	Herman Schliebitz, Weiss Beer Brewery	1892-1894
WI	300a	(Frederick) Goes & (Franz) Falk, Bavaria Brewery (8th & Chestnut Sts.)	1855-1866
	300b	F. Falk & Co., Bavaria Brewery	1866-1872
	300c	Franz Falk, Bavaria Brewery (Menomonee Rd., Wauwatosa)	1873-1882
	300d	Franz Falk Brewing Co. (merged with Jung & Borchert)	1882-1889
	300e	Falk, Jung & Borchert Brewing Co.	1889-1892
WI	301a	Charles Goerke (293 3rd St.)	1878 1879
	301b	Charles Goerke (324 Chestnut St.)	1879-1882
	301c	Chas. Goerke & Co. (1823 3rd & Burleigh Sts.)	1883-1888
WI	302a	(John) Graf & (Philip) Madlener, Weiss Beer Brewery	1874-1877
	302b	Graf & Madlener, South Side White Beer Brewery (530 National Ave.)	1877-1883
	302c	John Graf, South Side White Beer Brewery	1883-1884
	302d	John Graf (901/903 Greenfield Ave. & 17th St.)	1884-1913
	302e	John Graf Co.	1913-1920
WI	303	William H. & Joshua C. Gray (Ferry St. between S. Water & Lake)	1863-1863
WI	304	Green Bay Road Brewery	1859-1860
WI	305	William Grunert (Mineral & N. Jones St.)	? -1858
WI	306a	J. F. Gruszczynski (845/847 10th Ave.)	1895-1896
	306b	Oscar Altpeter	1896-1897
WI	307	John Hess	1840s
WI	308	The Home Brewery	c1912
WI	309	William L. Hopkins & Co. (Martin St. between Market & Fish)	1850-1855
WI	310a	Eugene L. Husting (454 5th & 432 Vliet Sts.)	1877-1900
	310b	E. L. Husting Co.	1900-1918
WI	311a	Independent Milwaukee Brewery (9th & Cleveland Aves.)	1901-1920
	311b	Independent Milwaukee Brewery (2701 S. 13th St.)	1933-1964
WI	312a	Phillip Knippenberg (3rd St. near Williamsburg)	? -1860
	312b	(Carl) Knoblauch & (John) Schreiber	1860-1866
	312c	Carl Knoblauch (Hopkinson)	1866-1868
WI	313a	John Kohl & Co., Weiss Beer Brewery (507 21st St.)	1893-1893
	313b	John Kohl	1893-1900
WI	314	Anton Korb (3rd & North Sts.)	1860s

Milwaukee (cont.)

WI	315a	Ben Kornburger & Bro. (John), Weiss Beer Brewery (578 23rd St.)	1901-1911
	315b	Ben Kornburger & Bro. Co.	1911-1920
WI	316a	August Krug	1849-1858
	316b	Joseph Schlitz	1858-1874
	316c	Joseph Schlitz Brewing Co. (3rd & Galena Sts.)	1874-1920
	316d	Joseph Schlitz Beverage Co.	1920-1933
	316e	Joseph Schlitz Brewing Co. (235 W. Galena St.)	1933-1981
WI	317a	Louis Liebscher, Weiss Beer Brewery	1859-1859
	317b	(Louis) Liebscher & (John) Berg (517 Chestnut St.)	1865-1866
	317c	Liebscher & Berg (936 Winnebago St.)	1866-1871
	317d	John Berg	1871-1877
	317e	John Berg (917 Vliet St.)	1877-1881
WI	318a	(John B.) Maier & (Lorenz) Winkler, aka John Maier & Co., Western Brewery (7th & Cherry Sts.)	1860-1862
	318b	Maier & (Fred) Hohl, Western Brewery	1862-1868
	318c	F. W. Manegold, Western Brewery	1868-1869
	318d	John Kargleder & Co., Western Brewery	1869-1875
	318e	Milwaukee Brewing Association	1875-1881
WI	319a	A. H. Manske Brewing Co. (626 18th St.)	1896-1897
	319b	Henry Fahl Brewing Co.	1897-1898
WI	320	J. Simon Meister, Weiss & Syphon Beer (406 Chestnut St.)	1860-1868
WI	321a	F. Meixner, Lemon Beer Brewery (1112 Vliet St.)	1873-1878
	321b	John F. Meixner, Lemon Beer Brewery	1878-1879
WI	322	Ludwig Mesow (Chestnut St. between 6th & 7th Sts.)	1861-1863
WI	323	Milo Beverage Co. (4008 State St.)	1919-1919
WI	324	Michael Muehlschuster (Old Line Rd. & W. Fon Du Lac Ave.)	1859-1860
WI	325	Conrad Muntzenberger	1842-1847
WI	326a	Munzinger & Koethe (184/186 Burrell St.)	1891-1892
	326b	Christian H. Munzinger	1892-1895
	326c	Munzinger & Gerlinger	1895-1897
	326d	Christian H. Munzinger	1897-1900
WI	327	Mutual Brewing Co. (418 Grove St.)	1913-1916
WI	328a	(Gustav A.) Obermann Brewing and Bottling Co. (787 24th St. & North Ave.)	1897-1900
	328b	West Side Brewery	1900-1901
WI	329a	Jacob Obermann, Germania Brewery (502 Cherry & 5th Sts.)	1854-1861
	329b	Obermann & Caspari, Germania Brewery	1861-1864
	329c	J. Obermann & Co., Germania Brewery	1864-1880
	329d	J. Obermann Brewing Co.	1880-1896
	329e	(Phillip) Jung Brewing Co.	1896-1920
WI	330a	(Richard G.) Owens, (William) Pawlett & (John) Davis, Milwaukee Brewery (222 Huron St.)	1840-1845
	330b	Owens & Pawlett, Lake Brewery	1845-1850
	330c	Richard G. Owens & Co., Lake Brewery	1850-1864
	330d	M. W. Powell & Co.	1864-1875
	330e	Powell's Ale Brewing Co.	1875-1880
WI	331	Albert Platz (Main & Division Sts.)	1859-1860
WI	332a	Herman Reuthlisberger, German Brewery (425 Virginia & Hanover Sts.)	1840-1841
	332b	J. B. Maier, Lake Brewery	1841-1844
	332c	Francis Neukirch, Lake Brewery	1844-1848
	332d	(Francis) Neukirch & (C. J.) Melms, Menomonee Brewery (Virginia & Oregon Sts.)	1848-1859
	332e	C. T. Melms, Menomonee Brewery	1859-1869
	332f	Ph. Best Brewing Co., South Side Brewery	1869-1886
WI	333a	Rheude & Co. (3rd & Walnut Sts.)	? -1858
	333b	John M. Davis & Co.	1863-1866
	333c	Pfeifer Brewery	1866-1873

Milwaukee (cont.)

WI	334a	Roedel Brewing Co. (Hubbard St. & Reservoir Ave.)	1897-1899
	334b	Badger Brewing Co.	1899-1901
WI	335a	Frederick Schunck (Cherry & 7th Sts.)	? -1858
	335b	(Nicholas) Schunck & (Louis) Hellberg (9th & Galena Sts.)	1858-1859
	335c	(Louis) Hellberg & (Maria) Schunck	1859-1860
WI	336a	Schwartz Brewery (3rd, Cedar & Tamarack Sts.)	c1856
	336b	Frederich Fritz	c1863
WI	337	Frederick Schwarz (Chestnut & 3rd Sts.)	1862-1864
WI	338a	John H. Senne (Prairie St. between 5th & 6th Sts.)	? -1858
	338b	Frederick Schwarz & Co., Prairie Street Brewery	1858-1861
	338c	Frederick Schwarz, Prairie Street Brewery	1861-1862
	338d	John Enes, Prairie Street Brewery	1862-1863
WI	339	Stock Brewing Co. (West Virginia St.)	NP 1933-1933
WI	340a	Stoltz & Krill	1840-1848
	340b	Henry Stoltz, Union Brewery (110/123 Odgen St.)	1848-1850
	340c	(Henry) Stoltz & (E.) Schneider, Union Brewery	1850-1862
	340d	Henry Stoltz, Union Brewery	1862-1865
	340e	Margaret Stoltz, Union Brewery	1865-1868
	340f	(David) Knab, (M.) Sprey & Co., Union Brewery	1868-1870
	340g	Paul Degan, Union Brewery	1870-1873
	340h	Joseph Fuss, Union Brewery	1873-1873
	340i	Jacob Stoltz. Union Brewery	1873-1874
	340j	Fred Borchert & Son, Union Brewery	1874-1879
	340k	(Philip) Jung & (Ernst) Borchert, Union Brewery	1879-1884
	340l	Jung & Borchert Brewing Co.	1884-1889
	340m	Falk,Jung & Borchert Brewing Co.	1889-1892
WI	341a	Strohn & Reitzenstein	1854-1854
	341b	George Schweickhart, Menomonee Brewery	1855-1871
	341c	Schweickhart & (Adam) Gettelman, Menomonee Brewery	1871-1874
	341d	Adam Gettelman, Menomonee Brewery	1874-1887
	341e	A. Gettelman Brewing Co. (4400 State St.)	1887-1920
	341f	A. Gettelman Brewing Co.	1933-1961
	341g	Gettelman Brewing Corp., div. of Miller Brewing Co.	1961-1964
	341h	Miller Brewing Co., Gettelman Div.	1964-1970
WI	342	Taylor & Bro., Lake Brewery	1850-1851
WI	343a	Town of Lake Brewing Co. (Clarence & 8th Aves.)	1892-1893
	343b	Milwaukee Brewing Co.	1893-1900
	343c	Milwaukee Brewing and Bottling Co.	1900-1901
	343d	Milwaukee Brewery Co.	1901-1920
WI	344a	(George) Wehr & (Christopher) Forster, West Hill Brewery (13th between Cherry & Galena Sts.)	1853-1858
	344b	George Wehr, West Hill Brewery	1858-1860
	344c	(Stephen) Weber & (John) Beck, West Hill Brewery	1860-1863
	344d	John Beck	1863-1877
	344e	Jacob Veidt & Co.	1877-1879
	344f	Cream City Brewing Co. (490/510 13th St.)	1879-1920
	344g	Cream City Products Co.	1920-1933
	344h	Cream City Brewing Co. (1512/1544 N. 13th St.)	1933-1937
WI	345	Louis Werrbach, Weiss Beer Brewery (89 Biddle St.)	1869-1897
WI	346	Jacob Wind (Near Broadway & Chicago Sts.)	c1870
WI	347	Wisconsin Cooperative Brewery, Inc. (S. 20th St. & W. Morgan Ave.)	NP 1934-1934
WI	348	Mary Wolf (757 N. Water St.)	1888-1888
WI	349	Geoge Zeiger (S. Main St.)	1901-1908
WI	350a	Jacob Ziegler (Tamarack St. between 8th & 9th Sts.)	1858-1860
	350b	John Ennes (810 State St.)	1860-1876
	350c	John Ennes & Co.	1876-1879
WI	351a	(Otto) Zwietusch & (Christopher) Forster, Weiss Beer Brewery	1858-1862
	351b	Otto Zwietusch (705/709 Chestnut St.)	1862-1864

Mineral Point

WI	352a	James Argall	c1850-1884
	352b	James Argall & Co.	1884-1886
	352c	Maurice J. Minor	1896-1898
	352d	Ballo Bruetting	1898-1902
	352e	Mineral Springs Brewing Co. (272 Hoard St.)	1902-1920
	352f	Mineral Spring Products Co.	1933-1936
	352g	Mineral Spring Brewing Co. (272 Shake Rag Road)	1936-1961
WI	353	Gillman & Spellman	1860s
WI	354a	Gillman Bros., Wisconsin Brewery	c1850-1870s
	354b	Charles Gillman, Wisconsin Brewery	-1898

Mishicot

WI	355a	Julius Linstadt	1874-1884
	355b	John George Scheuer	1884-1904
	355c	Mishicot Brewing Co.	1904-1920
	355d	Mishicot Brewing Co.	1933-1934

Monroe

WI	356a	Bissinger	1845-1848
	356b	John Knipschilt	1848-1867
	356c	Ed Ruegger	1867-1868
	356d	(Ed) Ruegger & (Jacob) Hefty	1870s
	356e	Jacob Hefty (102/106 Emerson St.)	-1890
	356f	Hefty & Son (Fred)	1890-1891
	356g	Hefty & Blumer	1891-1892
	356h	Adam Blumer, Monroe Brewery	1892-1906
	356i	Blumer Brewing Co.	1906-1920
	356j	Blumer Products Co.	1920-1933
	356k	Blumer Brewing Corp. (1200/1208 14th Ave.)	1933-1943
	356l	Blumer Brewing Co.	1943-1947
	356m	Joseph Huber Brewing Co. aka Associated Brewing Co. (1960-1965) aka Heim-Brau Brewing Co. (1970-1975) aka Swiss Brewing Co. (1959-1965)	1947-
WI	357a	(Gottlieb) Luenberger & Co. (Jefferson & Racine Sts.)	1874-1879
	357b	G. Luenberger	1879-1880
	357c	G. Luenberger & Co.	1880-1884
WI	358a	Pastel & Huppler	1878-1879
	358b	J. Z. Pastel	1879-1880

Montello

WI	359	H. Wild	1850s

Mount Calvary

WI	360a	Matthias Bourgeois	1875-1884
	360b	Henry Michels	1884-1886
	360c	John A. Wirth, aka Mount Calvary Brewing Co.	1886-1890
	360d	John A. Wirth & Co.	1890-1900
	360e	Neiss Bros. (John & Matt)	1900-1914
	360f	Mt. Calvary Brewing Co.	1914-1915
	360g	Plymouth Brewing Co. (depot only)	1915-1920

Mount Pleasant (see Racine)

Muscoda

WI	361a	Joseph Boggy & Co.	1851-1868
	361b	Postell & Huppler	1868-1882
	361c	John G. Postell	1882-1886
	361d	Philip Geiser	1886-1894
	361e	(William) Lampe & (Joseph) Kaiser	1894-1898
	361f	William Lampe, Muscoda Brewery	1898-1904
	361g	George Lampe, Muscoda Brewery	1904-1906
	361h	Muscoda Brewing Co.	1906-1907
WI	362	Meyer & Pess	1870s

Namur

WI	363a	Charles Marchant	1870s
	363b	Charles Mexime	1870s

Neenah
WI 364a J. Lachrman c1850-1870s
364b Ehrgott Bros. -1879
364c Adam W. Ehrgott, Neenah Brewery 1879-1902
364d Henry Angermeyer, Neenah Brewery (Lake St.) 1902-1905
364e Estate of Henry Angermeyer, Neenah Brewery 1905-1906
364e Neenah Brewery, Louis P. Sorenson 1906-1910
364f Neenah Brewing Co. 1911-1914

Neilsville
WI 365a William Neverman & Co. (John Foster), Neilsville Brewery 1869-1872
365b Neverman & Sontag, Neilsville Brewery 1872-1879
365c William Neverman, Neilsville Brewery 1879-1882
365d John Forster, Neilsville Brewery 1882-1885
365e Ernst Eilert, Neilsville Brewery 1885-1898
365f Kurt Listemann, Neilsville Brewery 1898-1898
365g Neilsville Brewing Co. (State & 6th Sts.) 1898-1920

Neosho
WI 366a F. Keoline 1870-1875
366b Jacob Binder, Neosho Brewery 1875-1912
366c Neosho Brewing Co. 1912-1914
366d Sebastian Niedermaier 1914-1916
366e Neosho Brewing Co. 1934-1937

Newburg
WI 367a Robert Schwalbach 1874-1893
367b Henry Schwalbach 1893-1899

New Cassel
WI 368 John P. Husting 1873-1891

Newfane
WI 369 Benedict Myer 1850s

New Glarus
WI 370a Jacob Hefty 1866-1894
370b Gabriel Zweifel, New Glarus Brewery 1894-1912
370c New Glarus Brewing Co. 1913-1920
370d Alpine Brewing Co. NP 1934-1934

New Lisbon
WI 371a Joseph Hausmann, New Lisbon Brewery 1857-1859
371b (Henry) Bierbauer & (Peter) Fauerbach, New Lisbon Brewery 1859-1862
371c Henry Bierbauer, New Lisbon Brewery (Monroe St.) 1862-1902
371d Henry Bierbauer Estate, New Lisbon Brewery 1902-1911
371e Bierbauer Brewery 1911-1916
371f Christmann Brewing Co. (8 Monroe St.) 1933-1937
371g Million Brewery, Inc. 1937-1941

New London
WI 372 Edward Becker, City Brewery (Main & S. Water Sts.) 1876-1898

WI 373a Loescher, New London Brewery 1860-1870
373b Becker, Beyer & Knapstein, New London Brewery 1870-1875
373c Theodore Knapstein & Co., New London Brewery 1875-1908
373d Knapstein Brewing Co. (505/511 E. Cook St.) 1908-1920
373e New London Products Co. 1920-1933
373f Knapstein Brewing Co. 1933-1959

Norman
WI 374 Anton Langenkamp & Bro. 1875-1884

North Lake
WI 375a Erasmus Frederickson, North Lake Brewery 1867-1910
375b Carl Hanson, North Lake Brewery 1910-1920

Oak Creek
WI 376 T. T. Luin 1850s

Oconomowoc
WI 377a Peter Binzel, City Brewery (Fowler St.) 1868-1912
377b Philip Binzel, City Brewery (219 Fowler St.) 1912-1920
377c Oconomowoc Brewing Co. 1933-1936
377d Binzel Brewing Co. 1936-1942

Oconto

WI	378a	Anton Link & Co. (Louis P. Pahl)	1858-1863
	378b	Louis P. Pahl, Oconto Brewery (N. Superior St.)	1863-1891
	378c	Oconto Brewing Co.	1891-1920
	378d	Oconto Brewing Co. (1009/1023 Superior Ave.)	1933-1965
		aka Fox Brewing Co.	
		aka Silver Cream Brewing Co.	
		aka Van Merritt Brewing Co.	
	378e	Van Merritt Brewing Co., Inc.	1965-1967

Onalaska

WI	379a	Milton G. Moore	1874-1880
	379b	Adolph Knecht, Onalaska Brewery	1880-1884
	379c	Onalaska Brewing Co.	1895-1899

Osceola Mills

WI	380	Veit Geiger	1874-1884

Oshkosh

WI	381a	Adolph Andrae, Lake Brewery (Ceape St.)	c1850-1860s
	381b	Ecke & Newman, Lake Brewery	1870s
WI	382	Tobias Fischer	1850s
WI	383a	(John) Glatz & (Christian) Elser, Union Brewery (Doty St.)	1869-1879
	383b	John Glatz, Union Brewery	1879-1886
	383c	John Glatz & Son, Union Brewery	1886-1894
	383d	Oshkosh Brewing Co., John Glatz & Son Brewery	1894-1899
	383e	Oshkosh Brewing Co., Union Brewery (31/34 Doty St.)	1899-1911
WI	384a	(August) Horn & (Lenhardt) Schwalm, Brooklyn Brewery (Doty St.)	1866-1894
	384b	Oshkosh Brewing Co., Horn & Schwalm Brewery	1894-1933
	384c	Oshkosh Brewing Co. (1631/1642 Doty St.)	1933-1971
		aka Rahr-Green Bay Brewing Co. (1967-1971)	
		aka Two Rivers Brewing Co. (1967-1971)	
WI	385	Christian Kaehler, Bush Brewery (160 Algoma Blvd.)	c1850-1880
WI	386a	Kuenzl & Walter, Gambrinus Brewery (Harney St.)	1875-1879
	386b	Lorenz Kuenzl, Gambrinus Brewery	1879-1894
	386c	Oshkosh Brewing Co., Lorenz Kuenzl Brewery	1894-1902
WI	387a	Leonard Loescher, Oshkosh Brewery (River & Frankfort Sts.)	c1850-1880
	387b	George Loescher, Oshkosh Brewery	1880-1884
	387c	William J. Loescher, Oshkosh Brewery	1884-1891
WI	388a	People's Brewing Co. (1506/1513 S. Main St.)	1911-1920
	388b	The Peoples Brewing Co.	1933-1972
WI	389a	Charles & August Rahr (91/103 Rahr Ave.)	1864-1875
	389b	August Rahr	1875-1882
	389c	Charles Rahr, Jr., City Brewery	1882-1904
	389d	Rahr Brewing Co.	1904-1920
	389e	The Rahr Company	1920-1933
	389f	Rahr Brewing Co.	1933-1956
WI	390	L. Schiffman	1880-1880

Palmyra

WI	391	John Buzzell	1850s
WI	392	J. F. Smith	1850s

Peshtigo

WI	393	Ferdinand Hoppe	1870s

Pewaukee

WI	394a	Mathias Schock	1878-1879
	394b	John Schock	1879-1884

Pheasant Branch (later Middleton)

WI	395a	Lenz & Hess	1870s
	395b	Jacob Lenz	1870s
	395c	Hubert Bernard	-1880
	395d	Bernard & Findorf	1880-1882
	395e	John Findorf	1882-1884
	395f	Brunkow & Mueller	1884-1905

Pheasant Branch (cont.)

WI	395g	Brunkow & Mueller, Pheasant Branch Brewery (Middleton)	1905-1912
	395h	Verten Bros., aka Middleton Brewery	1912-1920

Pierce

WI	396	John Vaser	1878-1879

Plainfield

WI	397	D. Wilson	1850s

Platteville

WI	398a	Dennis Centliver, Platteville Brewery	1868-1871
	398b	John Kemler, Platteville Brewery	1871-1875
	398c	(Richard) Briscoe & (H. F.) Rhemstedt, Platteville Brewery	1875-1878
	398d	H. F. Rhemstedt, Platteville Brewery	1878-1882
	398e	Wedel & Helberg, Platteville Brewery	1882-1884
	398f	George T. Wedel, Platteville Brewery	1884-1886
	398g	John Kemler, Plattville Brewery	1886-1890
	398h	(Fritz) Hoppe & (Charles) Mueller, Platteville Brewery	1890-1892
	398i	Fritz Hoppe, Platteville Brewery	1892-1913
	398j	List Brewing Co.	1913-1920
	398k	Platteville Brewery, Inc. (1001 E. Mineral St.)	NP 1934-1934
	398l	Platteville Brewery, Inc.	1937-1941

Plymouth

WI	399a	Buckel & Brahmer	1861-1873
	399b	Gottfried Weber	1873-1885
	399c	Ferdinand Streblow	1885-1886
	399d	Plymouth Brewing Co.	1886-1894
	399e	Anton Schreiner, Schwanstein Brewery, aka Anton Schreiner & Son	1894-1901
	399f	Plymouth Brewing Co.	1901-1916
	399g	Plymouth Brewing and Malting Co.	1916-1920
	399h	Plymouth Brewing Co. (2/16 E. Main St.)	1933-1937
WI	400a	(Andrew) Sander & (Adam) Schneider (Mill St.)	1857-1864
	400b	Andrew Schneider	1864-1884
	400c	A. Schneider & Sons (Otto & Richard)	1884-1890

Portage (Fort Winnebago until 1852)

WI	401a	Charles Haertel, City Brewery (Clark & W. Conant Sts.)	1851-1876
	401b	Charles Haertel Estate, City Brewery	1876-1880
	401c	Chas. Haertel Brewing Co.	1880-1884
	401d	Eulberg Bros. (Adam & Peter) (Cook & Clark Sts.)	1884-1907
	401e	Eulberg Brewing Co.	1907-1920
	401f	Eulberg Products Co.	1920-1933
	401g	Eulberg Brewing Co. (112/122 W. Conant & Clark Sts.)	1933-1957
	401h	Eulberg Beer Sales Co.	1957-1958
WI	402a	John M. Hettinger, Fort Winnebago Brewery	1851-1875
	402b	Nauer & Klecker, Fort Winnebago Brewery	1875-1875
	402c	Hettinger, Fort Winnebago Brewery	1875-1876
	402d	Henry Epstein, Winnebago Brewery	1876-1901
	402e	Epstein Bros. (Jefferson & Canal Sts.)	1901-1918

Port Washington

WI	403a	Jacob Moritz, Lake Side Brewery (419 Lake St.)	1847-1870
	403b	Nicolas Welter, Lake Side Brewery	1870-1874
	403c	Welter & Mallinger, Lake Side Brewery	1874-1875
	403d	Henry Dix & Co., Lake Side Brewery	1875-1881
	403e	Gottlieb Biedermann & Co., Lake Side Brewery	1881-1904
	403f	Port Washington Brewing Co.	1904-1920
	403g	Old Port Brewing Co. (220 E. Valley St.)	1933-1947
WI	404a	Geo. Wittmann	1865-1877
	404b	John Wittmann	1877-1894

Potosi

WI	405a	Albrecht & Hail	1852-1872
	405b	Gabriel Hail	1872-1884
	405c	Adam Schumacher	1886-1905
	405d	Potosi Brewing Co.	1905-1920
	405e	Potosi Brewing Co. (Van Buren Addition) aka Alpen Brau Brewing Co. (1963-1972)	1933-1972

Potosi (cont.)

WI 405e aka Alpine Brewing Co. (1963-1972)
aka Bohemian Club Brewing Co. (1967-1972)
aka Garten Brau Brewing Co.
aka Holiday Brewing Co. (1962-1972)
aka House of Augsburg (1968-1972)
aka La Crosse Brewing Co. (1957-1964)
aka Monarch Brewing Co. (1960-1971)
aka Van Merritt Brewing Co. (1970-1972)

WI 406 Henry Meeke 1878-1882

WI 407 Joseph Udlehoven 1850s

Prairie du Chien

WI 408 Georgi & Co. 1850s

WI 409 Schibb 1850s

WI 410a Theodore Schumann (Church St. near Bluff St.) c1870-1876
410b Schumann & Menges 1876-1891
410c Schumann & Menges Brewing Co. 1891-1909
410d Schwarz Bros. Brewery (George L. & Cornelius) 1909-1911
410e Schumann & Menges Brewing Co. 1911-1918
410f Prairie du Chien Brewing Co. 1918-1920

Prescott

WI 411a C. Haeffner c1850-1866
411b Nicholas P. Husting, Prescott Brewery 1866-1892

Princeton

WI 412a August Weisl (36 Farmer St.) 1866-1870s
412b William Forster 1870s
412c Lutz & Messing 1870s
412d (Jacob) Messing & (John) Ernst 1880-1894
412e John Ernst 1894-1896
412f John Ernst Estate 1896-1901
412g John Ernst Brewing Co. 1901-1914
412h Princeton Brewing Co. (Farmer & Harvard Sts.) 1933-1937

Racine (including Mount Pleasant, Sagetown)

WI 413 Atlas Brewing Co. (924/926 Garfield St.) 1918-1920

WI 414a Belle City Brewing Co. (1210 State St.) 1895-1901
414b Belle City Brewing Co. (1506 State St.) 1901-1910
414c Olsen & Feddersen, Temperance Beer Brewery, Racine Malt Co. 1910-1912
414d Andrew Feddersen, Temperance Beer Brewery, Racine Malt Co. (1502/1504 May St.) 1912-1920s
414e Racine Brewing Co. NP 1934-1934

WI 415a Buhler & Wolf (Harriet St. & Rapids Road) 1850s
415b Charles Wolf (Mt. Pleasant) c1858-1882
415c Casper Bertram 1882-1884

WI 416 John Dearsley & Orrin Barker, Badger Brewery (State St., Sagetown) 1857-1860

WI 417a Henry Frey (620 Stannard St. near 6th St.) 1852-1866
417b Jacob Goehring & Ferdinand Steiner, Star Brewery 1866-1868
417c Jacob Goehring, Star Brewery 1868-1873
417d George Schlenk, Star Brewery 1873-1879
417e (Valentine) Engel & Co., Star Brewery 1879-1883
417f Dorus Lyman, Star Brewery 1883-1884
417g (Henry) Wedemeyer & (John) Maas, Star Brewery 1884-1885
417h John Maas & Co. (Joseph Bezucha), Star Brewery 1885-1887
417i Joseph Bezucha, Star Brewery 1887-1889
417j Vincent Bezucha, Star Brewery 1889-1891

WI 418a Robert Grant, Lake Shore Brewery (78 N. Michigan) c1870-1874
418b George Paradis 1875-1876
418c Edmund Dotten, Lake Shore Brewery 1876-1878
418d William H. Weber, Lake Shore Brewery (1501/1507 N. Michigan) 1878-1901
418e William H. Weber Estate, Lake Shore Brewery 1901-1904
418f Weber Brothers (Ernst & Charles), Lake Shore Brewery 1904-1914

Racine (cont.)

WI	419a	(Frederick) Heck & (F.) Beebe's (8th & Center Sts.)	1852-1858
	419b	(Frederick) Heck & Co. (Philip Heck)	1858- ?
	419c	Fred Heck	1874-1882
WI	420a	(Frederick) Heck & (John) Brown, City Brewery (8th St. & Western Plank Road)	1848-1851
	420b	(John) Gnadt & (Thomas) Green's City Brewery	1851-1862
	420c	(Adolph) Fleisher & (Peter) Zirbe's City Brewery	1862-1866
	420d	Phillip Erhard Schelling, City Brewery	1866-1877
	420e	Schelling & Klinkert, City Brewery	1877-1879
	420f	John Klinkert, City Brewery	1879-1880
	420g	Ernst C. Klinkert, City Brewery (800/828 Washington Ave.)	1880-1904
	420h	Ernst Klinkert Brewing Co.	1904-1920
	420i	Old Dutch Brewing Co.	NP 1933-1934
WI	421	E. Henkel	1880s
WI	422	Phillip E. Schelling (Old Milwaukee Road)	1880-1904
WI	423	Service & Co., Racine Brewery, Peter & Phillip Service (6th & Barnstable Sts.)	1858-1858
WI	424a	James Stephanson & Hans Anderson (Old Milwaukee Road)	1875-1877
	424b	Anton R. Deinken, Northside Brewery (1627 Douglas Ave.)	1877-1879
	424c	Deinken & (Jacob) Schad, Northside Brewery	1879-1880
	424d	Deinken & (Peter) Reiplinger, Northside Brewery	1880-1881
	424e	Deinken & (Peter) Bower	1881-1883
	424f	Deinken & (Valentine) Engel, Northside Brewery	1883-1885
	424g	Valentine Engel, Northside Brewery	1885-1891
WI	425	C. Stephenson	1884-1884
WI	426	William Williams, Hope Brewery (Chippecotton St.)	1862-1870
WI	427	Phillip Zirbes (Chippewa & 6th Sts.)	1857-1860

Random Lake

WI	428a	Julius Siefert, Silver Creek Brewery (Sherman)	1866-1881
	428b	Carl Hamm, Silver Creek Brewery (Sherman)	1881-1904
	428c	Chares Hamm, Silver Creek Brewery (Racine)	1904-1910
	428d	Chas. Hamm Brewing Co.	1910-1920
	428e	Jung Beverage Co.	1920-1933
	428f	William G. Jung Products Co. (Carroll St.)	1933-1935
	428g	William G. Jung Brewing Co.	1935-1958

Reedsburg

WI	429a	(Francis) Mechler & (Fred) Schroeder, Reedsburg Brewery	1872-1879
	429b	John H. Hagenah, Reedsburg Brewing Co.	1879-1883
	429c	Henry Geffert, Reedsburg Brewing Co.	1883-1885
	429d	(Henry G. & John H.) Geffert & (P.) Pahl, Reedsburg Brewing Co.	1885-1895
	429e	Albert Fuhrmann, Reedsburg Brewery	1895-1920
	429f	Reedsburg Brewery, Inc. (401 N. Walnut St.)	1933-1947
	429g	The Reedsburg Brewing Co.	1949-1951

Reeseville

WI	430	Philipp Jaeckel	c1860-1870s

Rhinelander

WI	431a	Rhinelander Brewing Co.	1893-1907
	431b	Rhinelander Brewing and Bottling Co.	1907-1909
	431c	Rhinelander Brewing Co.	1909-1920
	431d	Rhinelander Brewing Co.	1933-1967

Rice Lake

WI	432a	Antone Mueller, Rice Lake City Brewery, aka Southside Brewery	1887-1896
	432b	Jacob Dick, Rice Lake City Brewery aka Rice Lake Brewing Co. (1900)	1896-1902
	432c	James Kozel, Rice Lake City Brewery	1902-1903
	432d	Schimmel & Glasbrenner, Rice Lake City Brewery	1903-1905
	432e	Phoenix Brewing Co.	1905-1920
WI	433	Rice Lake Brewing Co. (816 Hammond St.)	1936-1974

Rice Lake (cont.)

WI 434a Charles Saile c1870-1884
434b Elizabeth Saile 1884-1888
434c Gieser & Mueller 1888-1890
434d Gieser Bros. (August & William) 1890-1892
434e Mueller & Dick 1892-1893
434f Scharbilling Bros. & Co. 1895-1896
434g Frederick Baier 1896-1902
434h Burton & Baier 1902-1902
434i Baier & Baier (Joseph & Adam) 1902-1903
434j Baier, Baier & Co. 1903-1906
434k Joseph Baier 1906-1910

Richfield (see Germantown)

Richland City

WI 435 M. E. Lewis 1850s

Ripon

WI 436a Haas & Fischer, City Beer Brewery (130 Jefferson St.) 1865- ?
436b John Haas, Ripon City Beer Brewery 1878-1907
436c C. J. Haas 1907-1915
436d Ripon Brewing Co. 1933-1937

WI 437 W. R. Pearson c1850-1870s

River Falls

WI 438a Carl Krauth 1874-1877
438b Hickey & Meyer 1877-1879
438c Carl Krauth 1879-1882
438d (John) Henry & Albert 1882-1884
438e John Schneider 1884-1888

WI 439 S. T. Lobach 1870s

Rockfield

WI 440 Jacob Regenfuss 1870s

Rome

WI 441 August Dorsch 1870s

Roxbury

WI 442 Foshenden 1850s

Ryan

WI 443 John Frazier c1870-1880s

St. Croix Falls

WI 444 Miller & Bros. 1850s

St. Lawrence (Addison)

WI 445 Benedict Zeigelbauer c1850-1890s

St. Martins (see Franklin)

Sauk City

WI 446a Conrad Deininger c1850-1860s
446b Drossen & Molitor 1870s
446c Nicholas Drossen 1874-1875
446d Anna Drossen 1875-1882
446e Robert Zapp 1882-1883
446f Geo. Schlenk 1883-1884

WI 447 F. Frangel 1850s

WI 448a Matthias Leinenkugel 1845-1870
448b F. L. Leinenkugel 1874-1878
448c Robert Zapp 1878-1880
448d George Roeser (Phillips Blvd.) 1880-1895
448e Casper Roeser 1895-1898

WI 449a William Lenz, Sauk City Brewery 1874-1882
449b Mrs. Mary E. Lenz, Sauk City Brewery 1882-1889
449c Sauk City Brewing Co. 1889-1920
449d Sauk City Brewery, Inc. NP 1934-1934

WI 450 Joseph Schorrer 1870s

Sauk City (cont.)

WI	451	M. Stingelhammer	1850s

Schleisingerville (now Slinger)

WI	452	John Klinger	c1860-1870s
WI	453a	Benedict Kornburger	1868-1870
	453b	L. Rosenheimer	1870-1877
	453c	(Chas.) Storck & (Wm.) Hartig	1877-1884
	453d	Chas. Storck & Co.	1884-1888
	453e	Chas. Storck	1888-1895
	453f	Chas. Storck's Brewery	1895-1903
	453g	Estate of Chas. Storck	1903-1904
	453h	Storck Brewing Co.	1904-1912
	453i	Storck Co-operative Brewing and Malting Co.	1912-1913
	453j	Storck Brewing Co.	1913-1920
	453k	Storck Products Co. (201 S. Storck St., Slinger)	1933-1953
	453l	Storck Brewery, Inc.	1953-1958

Schleswig (now Kiel)

WI	454	J. Dimler	1865-1870s
WI	455a	Gutheil & Bro. (Bernhard & Ferdinand)	1858-1880
	455b	Gutheil Bros. (Bernhard & Lewis)	1880-1890

Sevastopol (see Sturgeon Bay)

Shawano

WI	456a	George Dengel	1878-1884
	456b	E. Raddant & Bro.	1884-1886
	456c	Emil T. Raddant	1886-1898
	456d	Emil T. Raddant Brewing Co. (5th St.)	1898-1920
	456e	Shawano Specialty Co.	1920-1933
	456f	Milwaukee-Shawano Brewing Co.	1933-1934
WI	457a	Farmers' Brewing Co.	1914-1920
	457b	Farmers Brewing Co. (713 S. Main St.)	1934-1948
	457c	Van Dyck Brewing Co., Inc.	1948-1950

Sheboygan

WI	458a	Gutsch Bros. (Leopold, Franz & Anton) (1012 New York Ave. & Water St.)	1847-1878
	458b	L. Gutsch	1878-1885
	458c	Adolph F. Gutsch	1885-1888
	458d	Gutsch Brewing Co.	1888-1920
	458e	Gutsch Products Co.	1920-1926
	458f	Gutsch Products Co., aka Manitowoc Products Co.	1926-1933
	458g	Kingsbury Breweries Co. aka Heidel Brau Brewing Co. (1960-1962) aka Ace Brewing Co. (1960-1962) aka Weber-Waukesha Brewing Co. (1959-1962)	1934-1962
	458h	G. Heileman Brewing Co., Inc. (br. of La Crosse, WI) (739 N. 11th St. & 1012 New York Ave.) aka Ace Brewing Co. (1963-1970) aka Blatz Brewing Division aka Fox Head Brewing Co. aka Heidel Brau Brewing Co. (1963-1973) aka Independent Milwaukee Brewery Co. (1964-1972) aka Kingsbury Brewers aka Weber aka Weber-Waukesha (1963-1968) aka Geo. Wiedemann Brewing Div.	1962-1974
WI	459a	Jacob Muth (Michigan Ave. between 14th & 15th Sts.)	1848-1852
	459b	Binz Bros. (Joe & August)	1860s
	459c	Thomas Schlachter	-1880
	459d	Thos. Schlachter & Co.	1880-1885
WI	460a	Charles Osthelder	1850s
	460b	Joseph Osthelder	1874-1875
	460c	Henry Dick	1875-1877
	460d	David Durow	1877-1879

Sheboygan (cont.)

WI	461a	August Rentz	1850s
	461b	Koepl & Gruebner, Sheboygan Brewery	1860s
WI	462a	(Leonard) Schlicht & (Konrad) Schreier (1504 New Jersey Ave. & 15th St.)	1854-1872
	462b	Konrad Schreier	1872-1895
	462c	Konrad Schreier Co.	1895-1920
	462d	Sheboygan Brewing Co.	1933-1934
WI	463	Frank Tasche, Weiss Beer Brewery (8th St. near Niagara Ave.)	1870s
WI	464	August Thamer (Ontario & 12th Sts.)	1875- ?
WI	465a	Wellhoefer, Kroos Brewery (Calumet Rd. & 24th St.)	1870s
	465b	Richard Weidenenser, Kroos Brewery	-1875
	465c	Martin Kuhl, Kroos Brewery	1875-1879

Sherman Township (see Spencer)

Shullsburg

WI	466a	Philip Marx, Shullsburg Brewery	c1850-1860s
	466b	S. Schulte, Shullsburg Brewery	1870s
	466c	Schulte & Lauterbeck, Shullsburg Brewery	1878-1879
	466d	Mahoney & Stephens, Shullsburg Brewery	1879-1882
	466e	Jacob Blotz, Shullsburg Brewery	1882-1885
	466f	John Schock, Shullsburg Brewery	1885-1890
	466g	Carl Steiner, Shullsburg Brewery	1890-1893
	466h	Wm. Buexton, Shullsburg Brewery	1893-1895
	466i	Moritz Hofmann, Shullsburg Brewery	1895-1902
	466j	Fred W. Langenberg, Shullsburg Brewery	1902-1904
	466k	Shullsburg Brewing Co., Louis Zimmerer	1904-1905
	466l	Michael Littl, Shullsburg Brewery	1905-1910
	466m	Fred W. Goetz, Shullsburg Brewery	1910-1912
	466n	Frank O. Moesmer, Shullsburg Brewery	1912-1914
	466o	Ludwig Meindl, Shullsburg Brewery	1914-1916

Silver Creek (see Random Lake)

Slinger (see Schleisingerville)

South Germantown (see Germantown)

South Grove

WI	467	William J. Arnold	1850s

Sparta

WI	468a	Whipple, Sparta Brewery (N. Water St.)	1860s
	468b	J. N. Wagner, Sparta Brewery	1870s

Spencer (Sherman Township)

WI	469a	Joseph Mayer	1878-1879
	469b	Eichert & Frothinger	1879-1879
	469c	Kuethe & Eichert	1879-1880
	469d	Kuethe & (John) Walter	1880-1883
	469e	John Walter	1883-1889

Spring Green

WI	470	Fredk. Frenzel	1884-1884

Stephensville

WI	471	Charles Graelz & Co.	1872-1877
WI	472a	Wolf, Wunderlich & Co.	1870s
	472b	George Wunderlich	1870s
	472c	Anton Fischer	1882-1889

Stevens Point

WI	473a	George Illenberger	1888-1893
	473b	Frank Michalski	1893-1896
WI	474a	Adam Kuhl (Brown & Prentice Sts.)	1867-1884
	474b	Stanley E. Kellar	1884-1891
WI	475	Frank Mehalsky (2nd & Market Square)	1870s
WI	476a	Polish Brewing Co.	1907-1914
	476b	National Brewing Co.	1914-1916

Stevens Point (cont.)

WI	477a	Frank Wahle & George Ruder	1857-1859
	477b	Wahl & Smith	1859-1867
	477c	Andrew Lutz & Bro. (Jacob)	1867- ?
	477d	Andrew Lutz & Son	? -1880
	477e	A. Lutz	1880-1884
	477f	A. Lutz & Bro.	1884-1888
	477g	Andrew Lutz	1888-1897
	477h	Gustav Kuenzel, Stevens Point Brewery	1897-1901
	477i	Gustav Kuenzel Brewing Co.	1901-1902
	477j	Stevens Point Brewing Co. (1061 Water St.)	1902-1924
	477k	Stevens Point Beverage Co. (1106 Water St.)	1924-1958
	477l	Stevens Point Brewery (2617 Water St.)	1958-1979
	477m	Stevens Point Beverage Co., dba Stevens Point Brewery	1979-

Sturgeon Bay (including Sevastopol)

WI	478a	Herman Seidemann	1874-1877
	478b	L. Lindemann & Bro.	1877-1879
	478c	Herman Leidemann	1879-1887
WI	479a	Wagner Bros., Sturgeon Bay Brewery	1874-1879
	479b	Leidiger Bros. (Louis & Ernest), Sturgeon Bay Brewery, aka L. Leidiger & Bro.	1879-1887
	479c	Sturgeon Bay Brewery (br. of Hagemeister Brewing Co., Green Bay)	1888-1920
	479d	Schonbrunn Brewing Co., Inc. (Bay Shore Road & George St.)	1933-1939

Summit Centre

WI	480	L. C. Kuhry	1888-1888

Superior (West Superior annexed in 1905)

WI	481a	Klinkert Brewing Co. (702 N. 8th St. & Catlin Ave., W. Sup.)	1890-1898
	481b	Northern Brewing Co. (Superior)	1898-1920
	481c	Northern Brewing Co. (702/724 N. 8th St. & Catlin Ave.)	1933-1967
WI	482	Klinkert Brewing and Malting Co. (24th St. & Scranton Ave.)	1898-1908
WI	483a	L. Kuchli	1860s
	483b	Thomas Shiels	1870s
	483c	Klein & Co.	1870s
WI	484	West Superior Brewing Co. (215 Hammond Ave.)	1891-1904

Sussex (Lisbon Township)

WI	485a	Ephraham Boots, aka Ephraham Boots & Co.	c1870-1880
	485b	Jos. Dvorak	1880-1884
WI	486	Bernard Hephen	1850s
WI	487	Weaver & Stone	1850s

Taycheedah

WI	488a	John W. Winfield	1850s
	488b	Paul Hauser	c1850-1870s

Theresa

WI	489a	Ulrich Oberley	1850s
	489b	Miller & Hartmann	1850s
	489c	Berthold & Co. (Hazheim)	1870s
	489d	John Quast	1878-1892
	489e	Luhn & Asenbauer	1892-1894
	489f	Luhn & Bandlow	1894-1896
	489g	Fred W. Bandlow	1896-1910
WI	490a	Benedict Weber	1850s
	490b	Gebhard Weber	1878-1906
	490c	G. Weber Brewing Co.	1906-1920
	490d	G. Weber Brewing Co. (Menomonee & Henni Sts.)	1934-1961

Thiensville

WI	491a	J. Harz	1870s
	491b	August Gerlach	1888-1900

Tirade

WI	492	Hiram Downer	1850s

Tisch Mills

WI	493	Frank Klinick	1890s
WI	494a	Frank Lufter	1880s
	494b	James Lodel	-1887
	494c	Anton Langenkamp & Bro.	1887-1898
	494d	Walecka & Kulhanek	1898-1901

Tomah

WI	495	Ignatz Gondrezick (Glendale Ave.)	1874-1889

Trempeleau

WI	496a	Jacob Melchior	1872-1872
	496b	S. W. Melchior	1872-1877
	496c	Jacob Melchior	1877-1882

Trenton

WI	497	R. Schwalbeck	1878-1884

Two Rivers

WI	498a	Edward Mueller, City Brewery (1608 Adams St.)	1848-1871
	498b	Richard E. Mueller, City Brewery	1871-1895
	498c	Mueller Bros., City Brewery	1895-1896
	498d	Mueller Bros. Brewing Co. (Charles E. & Edward R.)	1896-1920
	498e	Two Rivers Beverage Co.	1933-1966

Union

WI	499	S. Marchant	1874-1875

Washburn

WI	500a	Washburn Brewing Co.	1890-1899
	500b	Washburn Brewing Association	1899-1904
	500c	Pure Beer Brewing Co.	1904-1914

Washington Harbor

WI	501	Peter Bridham	1850s

Waterford

WI	502a	John Beck & Bros., Waterford Brewery	1874-1880
	502b	John Beck, Waterford Brewery	1880-1890

Waterloo

WI	503a	L. Schwager (Monroe St. near Madison St.)	1870s
	503b	William Schwager	1874-1880

Watertown

WI	504a	Joseph Bursinger, City Brewery	1854-1884
	504b	(Wm.) Hartig & (Charles) Manz, City Brewery (100 Cady St.)	1884-1895
	504c	William Hartig, City Brewery	1895-1920
	504d	The Hartig Co.	1933-1947
WI	505	C. M. Ducasse	1840s
WI	506	Albert Fuermann, aka Watertown Bottling Works (1026 N. 2nd)	1899-1901
WI	507a	August Fuermann, Empire Brewery (100 Jones St.)	1848-1886
	507b	A. Fuermann Brewing Co.	1886-1898
WI	508	Langenberg & Kypke	1875- ?
WI	509a	Raasch	1850s
	509b	Woodward & Bros.	1860s
	509c	Fred Schwartz & Co.	c1865-

Waukesha

WI	510	Fox River Brewery, Jacob Gettleman (Fox River)	c1860
WI	511	Charels Kreiner, Hickory Grove Brewery (Main St. near High)	c1870-1880s
WI	512a	Henry A. Meyer (140/141 North St. opposite Mary St.)	1859-1862
	512b	Stephan Weber, West Hill Brewery	1862-1885
	512c	(Wm. A.) Weber & (John C.) Land, Bethseda Brewery	1885-1886
	512d	Wm. A. Weber, Bethseda Brewery	1886-1899
	512e	Estate of Wm. A. Weber, Bethseda Brewery	1899-1903
	512f	Weber's Brewery, Stephan F. Weber	1903-1906
	512g	Weber Brewing Co.	1906-1920
	512h	Weber Waukesha Brewing Co. (210/220 E. North St.)	1934-1958

Waukesha (cont.)

WI	513	John M. Schock, Fountain Brewery (Main St. nr. Broadway)	1872-1890
WI	514a	C. Steiner	1891-1893
	514b	Waukesha Spring Brewing Co. (227 Maple & Grand Aves.)	1893-1895
	514c	Waukesha Imperial Spring Brewing Co.	1895-1899
	514d	Milwaukee-Waukesha Brewing Co.	1899-1920
	514e	Fox-Head Waukesha Corp.	1933-1946
	514f	Fox Head Brewing Co.	1946-1962
		aka Eulberg Brewing Co. (1947-1962)	
		aka Peter Fox Brewing Co. (1958-1960)	
		aka Noramco, Inc. (1962)	
		aka One-Two Brewing Co. (1958-1961)	
		aka Spring City Brewing Co. (1956-1958)	
		aka Wisconsin Brewing Co. (1956-1962)	
		aka Zeman Brewing Co. (1957-1959)	
		aka Ziegler Brewing Co. (1957-1959)	
	514g	Fox Head Brewing Co. (purchased & closed by G. Heileman Brewing Co., La Crosse, WI)	1962-1962
WI	515	Supreme Bottling Co., Weiss Beer Brewery	1907-1920

Waupaca

WI	516a	Leonard Arnold, Waupaca Brewery (Waupaca River)	1858-1890
	516b	Arnold Bros. (Leonard, Jr. & Albert), Waupaca Brewery	1890-1892
WI	517	Mrs. Amelia Padgham	1890s

Waupun

WI	518a	John M. Schroeck (Main St.)	c1850-1863
	518b	Philip Binzel	1863- ?
	518c	Peter Seifert (Main St. near Brandon Road)	1876-1894
	518d	John Skala (Franklin & Brandon Sts.)	1894-1896
	518e	Auguste Skala	1896-1902
	518f	John Skala	1902-1912
	518g	Waupun Brewing Co.	1912-1916

Wausau

WI	519a	Crowley Brewery (623 Forest St.)	1850s
	519b	Loeffler & Zastrow	1870s
	519c	John Williams	-1884
WI	520a	Mathie & Huebner (408/416 Grand Ave.)	1869-1870
	520b	Frank Mathie	1870-1888
	520c	Frank Mathie Brewing Co.	1888-1892
	520d	Mathie Brewing Co.	1892-1920
WI	521a	George Ruder (516 Grand Ave.)	1859-1888
	521b	George Ruder Brewery, Louis & Herman Ruder	1888-1892
	521c	Geo. Ruder Brewing Co.	1892-1920
	521d	American Brewing Co.	1920-1925
	521e	American Products Co. (504/516 Grand Ave.)	1925-1934
	521f	Mathie-Ruder Brewing Co.	1934-1955
WI	522a	Wausau Brewing Co. (622/644 7th & Porter Sts.)	1913-1920
	522b	Wausau Brewing Co.	1933-1961

Wauwatosa (see Milwaukee)

Wayne

WI	523a	Philip Pies	1878-1879
	523b	Kreutzer & Groeschel	1879-1880
	523c	John Bertram	1880-1882
	523d	Wenzel Beisbier & Co.	1882-1884
	523e	Wenzel Beisbier	1884-1888

Wequiot

WI	524a	Philip Annon	1850s
	524b	John Mason	1850s

West Bend

WI	525a	Christopher Eckstein (River St.)	1850-1860s
	525b	A. Artzbacher	1870s
	525c	Jansen & Co.	c1870-1873
	525d	Kuehlthau & Jansen	1873-1875
	525e	Adam Kuehlthau	1875-1883
	525f	West Bend Brewing Co.	1883-1920
	525g	West Bend Lithia Co. (415/459 N. Main St.)	1933-1972
WI	526a	Balthasar Goetter (River St. between Ash & Beech)	1849-1851
	526b	Mayer Bros. (Stephen & Charles)	1851-1872
	526c	Stephen F. Mayer & Co.	1872-1883
	526d	West Bend Brewing Co.	1883-1920
WI	527	Slippen & Mayer	1850s

West De Pere (see De Pere)

Westfield

WI	528	Dahlke Brewing Co.	1934-1943

Westford

WI	529a	Schott, Saltzenberger & Co.	1875-1877
	529b	Joseph Justin	1877-1879

West Granville

WI	530	Henry Stolz	1870s

West Lindo

WI	531	John Gross & Son	1878-1879

West Prairie

WI	532	John Pederson	1890s

Weyauwega

WI	533a	George Griel	1878-1886
	533b	Klipsmeyer & Schloesser	1886-1890
WI	534	Louis Herzinger	1879-1885
WI	535a	Jacob Konrad	c1860-1870s
	535b	Joseph A. Duerr	-1892
	535c	Loose & Quady	1892-1893
	535d	(Wm.) Quady & (Gustav) Schoeneck	1893-1899

Whitewater

WI	536a	George Streng	1859-1862
	536b	William Marshall	1862-1864
	536c	Nicholas Klinger (200 Jefferson & North Sts.)	1864-1905
	536d	Finke-Hoheisel Brewing Co.	1905-1906
	536e	Whitewater Brewing Co.	1906-1916
	536f	Whitewater Brewing Co., aka Whitewater-Manhattan	1933-1942

Windsor

WI	537	Archelaus Hobbs	1850s

Winneconne

WI	538a	Theodore Yaeger	1878-1882
	538b	Mrs. Catherine Yaeger	1882-1884

Wiota

WI	539a	John Glicker	1870s
	539b	Peter Ede	1878-1884

Wisconsin Dells (see Kilbourne City)

Wonewoc

WI	540	Hamburg Brewing Co.	NP 1934-1934

Wrightstown

WI	541a	(Otto) Gutbier & (C. G.) Miller, Fox River Brewery	1868-1871
	541b	Gutbier & Miller, Fox River Brewery	1873-1880
	541c	George W. Kaufman	1880-1884
WI	542	Mangold Gutbier	1870s

Yuba (see Greenwood)

Atlantic City

WY	1a	H. B. Macomber	1875-1877
	1b	Macomber & Huff	1877-1882
	1c	H. B. Macomber	1882-1884

Basin

WY	2	Williams & Parkhurst	1902-1904

Buffalo

WY	3	Fischer Brewing Co.	1882-1893

Casper

WY	4a	Casper Brewing Co.	1915-1920
	4b	Casper Brewing Co. (1740 S. Poplar St.)	1938-1948

Cheyenne

WY	5a	Charles Beno	1874-1877
	5b	C. Kapp	1877-1879
WY	6	Jaques Braun	1874-1882
WY	7a	Kabis & Zehner	1875-1877
	7b	L. Kabis	1877-1880
	7c	Herbert Kimm	1880-1884

Evanston

WY	8a	Becker Brewing and Malting Co.	1918-1920
	8b	Becker Brewing and Malting Co. (300 Front St.)	1933-1951
WY	9a	Longprey & Largilliere	1882-1883
	9b	Longprey & Kast	1883-1884

Green River

WY	10a	Adam Brown	1872-1879
	10b	Pelikan & Spinner	1879-1882
	10c	Karl Spinner	1882-1891
	10d	Hugo Gaensslen	1891-1897
	10e	Gaensslen & Rauch	1897-1899
	10f	Sweetwater Brewing Co.	1899-1920
	10g	Sweetwater Brewery, Inc. (46 W. Railroad Ave.)	1934-1937

Hyattville

WY	11	Downer & Carrothers	1896-1900

Lander

WY	12a	Charles Hart	1876-1877
	12b	Hart & Marcum	1877-1880
	12c	Charles Hart	1880-1882
	12d	Hart & Stockinger	1882-1884
	12e	Harris & Kongress	1884- ?
	12f	Mike J. Crowley & Co.	1890-1891
	12g	Charles Hart	1891-1893
	12h	Wm. H. Spaulding	1893-1893
	12i	Kuehl & Bordeaux	1893-1894
	12j	John R. Sampson	1894-1895
	12k	Lander Brewing Co.	1895-1899
	12l	Lander Brewing and Bottling Co.	1899-1903

Laramie

WY	13a	John J. Fein	? -1874
	13b	Ecoffey & Co.	1874-1875
	13c	Fred Barth	1875-1882
	13d	Henry Goetz	1882-1884
	13e	John A. Burman	1884-1888
	13f	J. J. Shore aka Shore & Meyers (1890)	1888-1891
	13g	Karl Schmidt	1898-1901
	13h	Charles Hilbig	1903-1904
	13i	Laramie Brewery, Henry Widmann, aka Laramie Malting and Brewing Co.	1904-1911
WY	14	John C. Huober	1890-1890

North Fork

WY	15	W. H. Spaulding	1890-1891

Rawlins

WY 16	G. Fischer & Co.	1879-1882

Sheridan

WY 17a	Sheridan Brewing Co. (202 Paul St.)	1887-1920
17b	Sheridan Brewing Co.	1933-1953

A.A. MI 16
A.B. PA756
A.B.C. CA168 MO131
A.B.P. WI230
Aab NY612
Abadie AZ 50
Abbe CA381
Abbott NY 93 PA505 PA506
Abendroth WI223
Abendschoen NJ 60
Aberdeen WA 2
Aberhart MD 51
Aberle MN 2 MN 48 OH226
Abner DC 1
Abraham KY 23
Ace IL133 WI215 WI458
Ace Hi IL133
Achauer OH340
Ackerman IL353
Ackermann KY 39 NY651
Acme CA142 CA291 CA338 CA444 GA 8 IL250 PA 33
Adam MN200 NJ 61 NJ 66 OH 41 OH 59 PA796
Adams CA298 NJ135 WA 86
Addicken IA 74
Addison NY 1
Adirondack NY272
Adler AL 1 MD 26 NJ118 WI 41
Adloff CA 2
Adolph ID 12 OR 92
Adrian MI145 MI200
Adrian City MI 2
Adt DC 14
Aenis OH100 OH106
Aetna CT 17
Agate NY240
Agri IA102
Aherns OH276
Ahlers IA174
Ahles MN 42 NY346 NY347 NY348
Ahnapee WI 1
Ahrens CA305 MI144 OK 7 OR 49 OR 91
Ahrentz MN 38 MN183
Ainsworth NY548
Aiple MN162 MN190
Airline OH174
Ajax IN 69
Akerblad OR 29
Akron OH 1
Aktien NY349
Alabama AL 1 CA367
Alameda CA 2
Alamo TX 73
Alamosa CO 1
Alaska AK 10 AK 23 AK 26
Alaskan AK 30
Albany CA357 NY 5 OR 2
Albers IN159
Albert DC 1 IA 61 MI 60 WI438
Albiez ID 19
Albion CA300 CA308 MD 62
Albrecht CA292 IL 35 IL322 MD 6 NY171 PA230 PA331 WI405
Albuquerque NM 1
Albus CO 92 CO123
Aldinger CO 61
Aleschleger OH174
Alexander MO112 NY539
Alexandria MN 2 MN 4
Algiers LA 3
Alqonquin CT 8
All Star WI148
Allegheny PA635 PA636 PA672
Allen IA 51 NY 63 OH101 OR 55 PA361 PA410
Allentown PA 2
Allerman IA 56
Alley MA 2 MA 3
Allgeier MI126 PA 56
Alliance OH 5
Allied IL133 NY408
Alma WI 3 WI 4
Alpen Brau WI405
Alpena MI 8 MI 9
Alert NY652
Alpine WI371 WI405
Alrath WI 54
Alten KS 32
Altenbrand NY 64
Altes CA285 MI110
Althen IL218 IA141
Altherr OH171
Alton IL 2
Altoona PA 13 PA 19
Altpeter WI278 WI306
Altstaetter OH199 OH314
Altvater MD 92
Alvatar MD 7
Alvery IN104
Amana IA136
Amann OH324
Ambassador CA143
Amber MA 56 PA670
Amberg CA 94
Ambridge PA 20 PA140
Ambron PA362
Ambrosia IL119
Amend NY480
Ament NY237
American CA 27 CA144 CT 51 FL 8 HI 5 ID 75 IL 36 IL241 IL308 IN 62 LA 4 LA 23 MD 14 MD112 MD124 MA 4 MI 52 MI 85 MO 92 MO131 MT 30 NY207 NY430 NY591 OR 11 PA 15 PA453 PA637 PA657 RI 5 TX 42 WA 70 WA 74 WV 15 WV 20 WI521
Amery NY338
Amesbury MO195 MO198
Amfahr NV 4
Amman WI 27
Ammann KY 6
Amory MA 24
Amott NY546
Amrhein PA364
Amsdell NY 2 NY326
Amsler TX 30 UT 4
Amsterdam NY 38
Amthor NY126
Amtmann NY617
Anaconda MT 1
Anaheim CA 7
Anchor CA227 CA297 CA364 NY242 PA798
Andersen MN107
Anderson CA 82 CA108 CA279 CT 12 MN196 NY350 WA 1 WA 28 WI279 WI424
Anderton OH192 PA 11 PA 24
Andrae WI381
Andre IA 45
Andres CA 82 IL258
Andresen IA 51
Andrews NJ 9 NJ138 OH 93 WI169
Andriessen NM 3
Angelbeck MO184
Angele NY596
Angeles WA 46
Angels CA 9 CA 10
Angermeyer WI364
Anheuser CA 79 CA145 FL 4 FL 8 FL 11 MO153 MO165 NH 4 NJ 64 NY 50 OH149 TX 43 VA 23
Aniser MO 76
Ankenbauer PA180 PA211
Ann Arbor MI 14 MI 16 MI 17
Annapolis MD115
Annon WI524
Anschutz IA157
Ansell CA317
Anselmo OR 13
Ansonia CT 15
Antelope NE 24
Anthe AL 4
Anthony MO130 MO133 OH 21 OH187 OH284
Anthracite PA241 PA333 PA756
Antigo WI 5
Anton MO203 PA323
Antricht MO 71
Antsch KY 14
A-One OR 53
Apel MO133
Apex WA 65
Apfel MO186 NY114
Apperger KS 37 MO 13
Appleton MA 86 MN 5 MO 67 WI 9
Arba NY684
Arbes MN 76
Arcade AZ 26
Arcadia IL 5 WI 13
Arcand MA 48
Arctic AK 17 AK 32
Arend NY 47
Arens MI 48 MI282
Arensdorf IA215
Arensmann WI170
Argall WI352
Arizona AZ 23 AZ 33 AZ 34 AZ 44
Arkansas AR 2
Arlington PA 40 VA 21

Armbruster LA 5 OH343
Armstrong CA293 NY684 WA 70
Arndt MI 53
Arnholt PA 15 PA409 PA470 PA591
Arnold AZ 13 AZ 41 AZ 43 AZ 57 CA358 ID 94 MI266 NE 3 NE 13 NY253 NY531 OH 20 OH192 OR 43 OR 61 PA206 PA242 UT 38 WI280 WI467 WI516
Arnoldi TX 23
Arnoldt NJ 10
Arnoldy MN 16
Arras KS 1 WI281
Arrowhead CA146 CA280 MN 24
Arsenal IA 67 MO178
Artesian WI166
Artsman KY 54
Artzbacher WI525
Asahi CA144 WA 68
Asbeck WA 23
Aschbacher TX 78
Aschmann WI282
Asenbauer WI489
Ash MT 7 MT 22
Ashby PA403
Ashcraft OH 63
Ashland PA 22 WI 14 WI 15 WI 16
Aslesen MN117 ND 7
Associated IL150 IN 33 IN137 MD169 MA 88 MI100 MN175 NY139 OH152 OH153 OH158 OH161 WI356
Astor IL296
Astoria OR 5
Atkins IN112
Atkinson NY 65
Atlanta GA 3
Atlantic FL 9 GA 3 ID 11 IL 66 IL119 IL163 IL345 IN137 IA141 MO183 NJ 1 NY351 NC 1 TN 2 VA 6 WA 79
Atlas IL 48 IL150 IN137 PA638 WI414
Attee OH 42
Atz NJ 11
Aubertine NY224
Auburn NY 47
Auen PA639
Auer LA 6 MD 8 MD 86
Auf NY606
Aufricht MO 71
Augie's MN126
Augsberg IL 37 IL107 WI405
Augusta GA 5
Auker CA 49
Auldrick NY352
Aull CO 47 CO107
Aulmann IA 76
Ault MI161
Aummermann MD 89
Aumuller AZ 33 KS 29
Aurnhammer NJ 62
Aurora IL 7
Austin NY622 PA451
Auto City MI 54
Auun IA195
Axtmann NJ 28
Ayers OR 46
Aztec CA285
B.B. IL150
B.B.B.B. PA341
B.B.S. PA447
B & O IL224
B & Y CO 23
Babler AK 11
Babrink OH207
Baccigalapi CA411
Bach IA 57 NY645 OH 59 PA206
Bacher PA 50 PA282
Bachhuber WI259
Bachman OR 49
Bachmann NY618
Bachrach TX 68
Backman CA 89
Bacon NE 28 NY442
Bader CA 43 CA 44 CA423 CA448 IN 83
Badger WI 40 WI174 WI334 WI416
Baehr IA149 OH102 OH133
Baemle IA194
Baer MA141 MD158 PA842
Baetzel NY600
Baeuerlein PA640
Baeumle IA194
Bagen CA385
Bagley CO 39
Bahr NY643
Baier CA 50 CA191 IL224 MD 9 NJ 63 UT 4 WI434
Baierle IL 38
Bailey CA260 IL275
Baird IA 87
Bairenther WI 21
Baireuther WI189
Baker ID 57 IA 44 IA169 OH287 PA154 WI283
Bakersfield CA 15 CA 16
Bakewell CT 30
Balboa CA157 CA288
Balder MN157
Baldwin NY253
Ball NY570 PA840
Ballantine NJ 68 NJ 86 NJ103 NY 12 NY680 RI 14
Ballard IN143
Ballon NE 28
Ballou MA 22
Ballweg KY 30
Balser OH 34 OH273
Baltic PA551
Baltimore MD 10 MD 11 MD 16 MD 24 MD 69 MD 77 MD 99
Baltz PA365
Balz IN 63
Balzer WV 33
Bammerling OH233
Bandleon IA 25
Bandlow WI489
Bang MN148
Bangor WI 24
Banholzer MN170
Banker AZ 16
Banlow IL368
Banner IL 39 MI247 NJ145 OH 43 VA 7 WI284
Bannister PA351
Bannock ID 45
Baraboo WI 25
Barbarossa IL150
Barber CO 30
Barbey PA714
Barker WI416
Barmann NY298
Barnard NY286
Barnes CO 6 CO 80 NY703
Barney AZ 56
Barnitz MD 11 PA194
Barnum CT 8
Barrett MO 37 OH135 PA116
Barry NY353
Bartalls MO 93
Bartel PA184
Bartelme IL132
Bartels NY 43 NY659 OH 43 OH 87 PA843
Barth CA205 SD 26 WY 13
Barthel AK 14 AK 31
Bartholdus CA278
Bartholomae IL 40 IL165
Bartholomay IL108 NY567 NY597 NY599 NY608
Bartholomew CT 26
Bartl WI216
Bartlesville OK 2
Bartlett IN105
Bartusch KS 11
Baruth CA297 CA317
Basil OH103
Basin MT 5
Basler OH291 OH294
Bassemeier LA 7
Basserman CT 31
Bassler IL361
Bast WI285
Bastendorff PA245
Batavia NY 51
Bates CO 31 NY554 WI102
Batt NY722
Battle Creek MI 23
Batz MN123
Bauder PA366
Bauer CA294 CO111 IL 17 IN 52 IA 32 IA202 KY 16 MD 12 MI 75 MN 48 NV 3 NY368 NY568 NY574 ND 12 OH 59 OH148 OH186 PA198 WI 87
Bauerfeind MD 53
Bauerfind MD 13
Bauernschmidt MD 9 MD 11 MD 14 MD 15 MD 16 MD 17 MD 18 MD 24 MD 50 MD 69 MD 79 MD105 MD108
Bauersachs NE 18
Baulston CT 32 RI 6
Baum WI 32 WI151

Bauman CA412 IL285 MI183
MI203
Baumann NE 32 NE 37
NJ 75 OH256
Baumeier IA 64
Baumeister MO 30 WA 87
Baumgartner IL265 NY178
PA712
Baumler PA294
Baumner PA367
Baur CA390 NY479 PA844
Baurhauser KS 29
Bausch CO 90 CO 92 MN160
PA124
Bautenstrauch MO152
Bavaria CA312 MI 15
WA 8 WI206 WI300
Bavarian CA312 DE 4
IL 98 IL154 IN 33 IN137
KY 5 KY 8 MI 92 MI192
MO 41 MO153 MO165 NJ 43
NY487 OH150 OH161 OH306
OH345 PA714 PA810
Bay CA295
Bay City CA286 MI 30
Bay St. MA 40
Bay View MD 35 WA 60
Bayard NY354
Bayer OH337
Bayley MD 66
Bayview MD 18
Baxter MN 43
Bazel MN113
Beadleston NY451 NY687
Beal KS 26
Beamer MO 13
Beamly PA236
Bear CA281 IL225 NY532
Beattie NY311
Beaty IN 23
Beaumont TX 7
Beauvais IL 29
Beaver PA735
Beaver Dam WI 28
Beaver Falls PA 26
Beaver Valley PA735
Beaverhead MT 26
Bechaud WI102
Becher AZ 24
Becherer OH315
Bechler OH314
Bechtel NY618 NY639
OH269
Bechtold MT 26
Beck CA141 CA198 CA381
CA391 CA392 IA 26 MD 19
MD 20 MD 21 MD 22 MD115
MD119 MD120 MD121 MD123
MI 10 MI 16 MN 74 NY133
NY178 NY264 NY333 OH 44
OH 59 OR 92 TX 70 WA115
WV 23 WI344 WI502
Becker CA 4 CA115 CA182
CO129 ID 31 IL331 IL373
IN141 IN144 IA 44 IA 51
KS 28 MI 33 MI 58 MI 81
MI102 MN202 MN205 MO 94
NV 35 NV 36 NJ 43 NY281
NY653 NY716 OH 87 OH216
Becker cont. PA591 UT 14
WA 18 WI 2 WI 8 WI 16
WI 65 WI171 WI372 WI373
WY 8
Beckler PA368 PA369
PA510
Beckman IL259
Beckstrum CA 82
Bedford CA 1 NY120
Beebe WI419
Beecher MT 13
Beehrer MT 34
Beekman NY414
Begstin IA150
Beh MD 38 MD 98
Behlmer WI119
Behloradsky TX 69
Behmler CA349
Behney PA275
Behr KS 39 NY 86
Behre WI267
Behrend IL320
Behringer IL 41
Behrle CA401 CO 15
Beider MI 55
Beierle KY 23
Beihl AK 6
Beirzel MT 11
Beisbier WI523
Beiser CA124
Belfast NH 9
Bellaire OH 14
Bellanger OR 1
Belle City WI414
Bellefontaine MO151
Bellenstein MI243
Beller NY337
Belleville NV 5
Bellevue OH 72 WI145
Bellingham WA116
Bellner OH299
Bellows Falls NH 14
Belmont OH231 PA736
Beloit WI 34 WI 35
Belser IN 97
Beltz OH 45 OH104
Belvidere WV 13
Belz NJ 4
Bemidji MN 10
Bemis IL 42 IL 72 IL 74
IL157 NE 30
Bendecker KS 15
Bender IL306 MN 48 MN122
NY355 OH 17 OH281 PA 12
PA212 WI 25
Bendleburg CO 24
Benedict UT 19
Benedictine PA266 PA820
Benfield MD170
Bengele PA288
Benicia CA 18
Benishek WI 5
Benjamin NY133
Benk PA370
Benke PA805
Bennann PA852
Bennett KS 8 MI 39
Beno WY 5
Benson MA 77
Bentler CA381 MI162
Bentleyville PA 33
Bentlich OH249
Benton Harbor MI 32
Bentz IA187 PA371
Benwood WV 1 WV 24
Benz CT 2 MT 28 MT 48
PA 36 PA289
Benzberg MN161
Benzinger PA745
Bercher CO 8
Berens WI189
Berg IN 23 MI125 MN 33
OR 16 WI317
Bergdoll PA372 PA373
PA381
Bergen MD 23 NJ 58
Berger AZ 47 IL332 KY 45
MD 32 MD 43 MD 62 MD 98
NJ 75 NJ115 OH255
Berges MO139
Bergheim PA396 PA718
Berghoff IN 39 IN 40
Bergschicker CA197
Bergman OH168 WI206
Bergmann OH168 PA377
TX 70
Bergner PA374 PA375
PA376 PA509
Bergstrom IL283
Berkin NE 51
Berkshire MA 77
Berlin CA147 CO 25 IL133
MO170 WI 36
Berlin Weiss IL159 MI 56
MO170 WI221
Berlina OH 46
Berliner IL 43 MD 10
MO169 NY195 NY494 OH 50
Bermes NJ146
Bernal CA135
Bernard WI395
Berne OH 22
Berner ID 50
Bernhardt AZ 44 OH 24
Bernheimer NY357 NY358
NY359 NY416 NY492 NY719
Berning IL216
Berns WV 8
Bernzen NE 46
Beroun MN 11
Berquist IL 80
Berridge IL305
Berrien MI 32
Berry CA 63 OR103 PA 88
WA 82
Berryman NV 9
Bertchey IL376
Berthold MI217 WI489
Bertina NY360
Bertolet PA715
Bertram WI415 WI523
Berwick PA 35
Besant NY 53
Bescher OH169
Besley IL371
Bessemer IL 59 MI 33

Best IL 44 IL 45 IL123 IA123 KY 4 NY674 WA 79 WI286 WI287 WI332
Beth PA 40
Bethseda WI512
Bettendorf NY634
Betting OH285
Betz MN 8 MN124 NV 2 NJ 46 NY361 NY389 NY410 NY416 NY479 PA451 WA105
Beuber MO 92
Beurlen MN 22
Beutel NJ154 NY356
Beuter OH285
Beveridge NY339
Beverly IL135
Beverwyck NY 4
Bevier NY585
Beyer MN193 NJ 16 UT 20 WV 11 WI147 WI373
Beyrer MN 20 MN 79
Beyschlag NE 25
Bezucha WI160 WI417
Bick NV 6
Bickta DE 1
Biddington MD143
Biddle MO 95
Biebesheimer IA230
Biederbeck PA447
Biedermann DE 7 WI403
Biegel NY560
Biegen NY242 NY410
Biehl OH151
Biela NJ 23
Bielfeldt IL360
Bienville AL 6
Bierbauer MN 82 NY222 NY696 NY703 WI371
Biersach WI 28
Bierwalter MN200
Bierworth IA 56
Biester PA195
Biewer MI221 MI260
Big Rapids MI 34
Big Tress CA391
Biggi MI245
Bihlmaier WA 42
Bihlmeier KS 16
Bilger IA 10
Bill NY150
Billan IN 20
Billings MT 8
Billiod OH 47
Billion PA133
Bills WI 13
Binder CA148 CA275 PA292 PA447 PA730 WI366
Bing IA188
Bingel CO 21
Binghamton NY 54
Bingle CO 2 CO 16 CO108 CO113
Bingmann OH250
Binklemann CA 95
Binswange OR 38
Binz IL 46 NY171 WI459
Binzel MT 36 WI 32 WI377 WI518
Bion MN131 WI 13
Birk IL 42 IL 47 IL 67 IL160 IN108 MN 9
Birkenhaeuser NJ111
Birkenhauer NJ 75
Birkenstock PA 8
Birkhauser WI128
Birkhofer MN 96
Birmingham AL 1
Bischoff IN132 NY641
Bisek MN 72
Biser IN 69
Bishop OH105 OH194
Bis-Mac MD 88
Bismarck IL 65 IL133 MD 88
Bissig AZ 15
Bissinger SD 5 WI356
Bissontza PA118
Bitter MD 90
Bittner ID 52 MI246
Bitz IL309
Bitzenhofer CO100
Bitzer CA258
Bixel CA 50 NV 14
Black Hills SD 4
Black Malt NY 66
Black River Falls WI 40
Blackburn AZ 35
Blackhawk IL206 IA 66 IA 69
Blackhorse MA 64 NJ145 NY244
Blackwell WI204
Blaisdell NY262
Blaise LA 8
Blake NH 14 VT 3
Blakey MD 66
Blankly NY 67
Blasauf CA208
Blasch KS 12 WI143
Blasford OR 53
Blass MN134 PA146
Blatt MN 83
Blattner IL 47 IA200 IA206 OR 56
Blatz KY 53 NJ 84 WI215 WI288 WI458
Blee OH289
Bleimer PA112
Blemen IA 17
Bleser WI245 WI246
Bless PA377
Blessing WI137
Blight RI 12
Blin IA234
Bliss SD 18
Blitz IN 33 MT 30 NJ 84 NJ103 OR 76 OR 82
Bloch NY224
Blocher OH166
Block CO 26 KS 26 MO 96 OR 9
Blohm CA 65
Blome MO 93
Blomquist WA 17
Blondberg CA367
Bloom CA278 UT 8
Bloomer WI 41
Bloomsburg PA 42
Bloss MI 86
Blossom WI283
Blotz WI466
Blouth DE 6
Blowser MO 97
Blue Grass KY 59
Blue Island IL 18
Bluefield WV 2
Bluff City IL 1
Blum ID 45 IL229 PA 71 WA 1 WV 28
Blume ID 59 SD 14 SD 26
Blumenauer IA 88 IA 98
Blumer WI356
Blumle PA144
Boca CA 31
Boche CO 68 CO119
Bockemuehl WA 32
Bode CA372
Bodendorfer WI127
Bodenschatz MD 24
Bodmer NM 8
Boeck MN206
Boefflins PA378
Boehler MN 83
Boehm MI 16 NE 16 NY613
Boehmer PA409
Boehn MD 25 MD 38
Boemecke NJ147
Boemer CA413 NY362
Boerner NE 5 NE 47
Boernstein MO159
Boes OH165
Bofinger CA 1 CA251 CA417
Boggy WI361
Bogk WI 51
Bogner CA 5
Bogue IL348
Bohemian CO109 CO127 ID 11 IL 48 IL107 IL251 MN 11 NY324 OH106 PA641 WA 79 WA 84 WI405
Bohle NV 6 NV 41
Bohler NJ 65
Bohn IL 49 OH 28 OH279 OH341
Bohr TN 1
Bohrer IN 80
Boise ID 12 ID 73
Boley IL275
Bolig IA 61 IA 62
Bollig IA 62
Bollinger PA344
Bolton NY675
Bolzing MI210
Bomhauser KS 53
Bommer MI105
Bomper NY363
Bond RI 25
Bonetti CA105
Bongo TX 70
Bonham CA 72
Booke NY681
Booken CA108
Bool WI 70
Bools OH328
Boos IN 60

Booth NY633 PA 70 PA324
PA693
Boots MT 7 WI485
Borchardt IN108
Borchers CA266
Borchert WI300 WI340
Bordeaux WY 12
Borden PA379 PA396
Borell PA715
Borhaeser ID 69
Bormann PA136
Born NY172 OH152 PA608
Bornhauser KS 29
Borntraeger IL366
Borser MN 61
Bosch AZ 14 CA 64 IA 24
IA 25 IA 26 MI161 MI191
Bosche AZ 14
Boscobel WI 42
Bose CA365
Boss OH 71
Bossert NY147
Bossinger PA276
Boston MA 5 MA 16
Bosworth IL163
Both TX 94
Bothe OH275
Bott KY 17
Botzett ID 1
Bouland IL170
Boulder CO 9 CO 94
Boulevard NJ146 NY144
Boulton NY525
Bourgardes WA 11
Bourgeois WI255 WI360
Bower PA380 PA381 WI181
WI424
Bowers CA 5 OH 17
Bowkley PA845
Bowler MA 89 NY 38
Bowlsby OH121
Bowman IA176 MT 14 OH 41
PA176
Boxleiter IA 95
Boyd MO140 NY 5
Boye NE 34
Boyen CA385
Boyer PA194
Boyertown PA 45
Brackenridge PA 46
Brackhahn NE 10
Braddock PA 47
Bradford PA 51
Bradly PA280
Brady IL207 NY292 TN 7
Braen PA642
Braendle MI269
Brahm IL 95
Brahmer WI399
Brainerd MN 13
Branch NY 68
Brand IL 18 IL 50 IL 51
IL 52 IL 58 IL 68 IL133
MI 10 OH303 OH308 WI196
Brandel MD 26
Brandenberger MO 98
Brandenburger IL372
Brandes WI205
Brandle MI269
Brandon KS 26 MO206
Brands KY 31
Brandstetter OH200
Brandt MD 92 MI145 MN 43
OR 56
Brauchle WI 72
Braun CA175 CA191 CA247
IL250 NJ 66 NJ122 OH 7
OH175 OR 40 WA 53 WI288
WY 6
Braunwarth PA382
Bray ID 87
Brazil IN 6
Brechesisen NY 42
Brecher NY364
Brecht PA176 PA703 PA791
Breckheimer WI234 WI241
Breckle CA296 CA297
Brede IA 96
Bredhoff CA222
Brehm MD 77 PA383
Breidenbach KY 56 MO 95
MO163
Breidt NJ 16
Breining PA562
Breistenstein OR 54
Breitkopf NY156 NY160
Bremen MO176
Bremenkampf NV 17
Bremer MO 38 PA384
Brennecke SC 4
Brenner KY 3 MO207
NE 7 ND 10 OH342
Brennes MN 81
Brennfleck IL 32
Brentle MN207
Bressel CA 90
Bressler IL 11
Brettler AK 18
Breunig WI 87 WI184
Brewer IL 53 MO 91 NY 39
PA202 PA339
Brewers Unlimited CA347
Brewery MI136 NE 30
NY433
Brewing Corp. OH108 OH113
Brewster NY654 NY716
Breyer OR 18
Bricht OH281
Brick MI280 MN 78 MN156
Brick House WI231
Brickmiller UT 15 UT 16
Bridesburg PA415
Bridgeport CT 2 CT 8
Bridham WI501
Briem NY 42
Brierly MA 60 MA 88
Brigel OH 70
Briggesboos WI 3
Briggs NY250 PA762 SD 18
Bright PA717
Brighton OH 67
Brill WI193
Brilliant City OH195
Brink IA119 PA101
Brinkle OH335
Brinkman NV 41
Brinkwirth IL330 MO139
Brinzing CA 40 CA187
Brinzing cont. CA241
Brisach IL 54
Briscoe WI398
Brisselbach MO100
Bristol MA 48
Britton NY110
Brizins IN117
Broad Street PA478
Broadbent MA 6
Broadway CA298 IL 55
MO194 NY171
Brobst PA716
Brock NY323
Brockett NY718
Brockhardt WV 25
Brockman TX 38
Brodbeck ID 11
Broderick MD 5
Brodesser WI125
Broeg IL290
Broese WA 20
Brohm IA178 KY 18
Brokorsch ND 8
Bron CO 70
Bronx NY547
Brooklyn CA222 MD 27
NY 85 NY106 NY154 WI384
Brooks NY 69 PA 43
Brookville PA 57
Brosemer NY539
Brouwer NY 6
Brown CA220 CO 27 ID 55
IN109 IA 20 KS 47 MN 46
NV 29 NY 70 NY 80 NY497
NY697 OH107 OH287 PA203
PA643 SD 19 TX 70 WI197
WI200 WI420 WY 10
Brownsville PA 58
Bruce TX 24
Bruck OH 67
Bruckman PA191
Bruchmann OH 48 OH 78
Brueck NJ147 OH 49
Bruenning MO124
Bruer WI 42
Bruetting WI352
Brugg ID 53
Bruggeman MN162
Brunig CA299
Bruning MO124
Brunkow WI395
Brunner IL320 NE 34
Bruno OR 13
Brunswick GA 6
Bruton MD 77
Bryden PA127 PA846
Bub MN209
Bube PA334
Buch MT 46
Buche WI 58
Bucher CA402 IL 56 OH180
Buchheit IN109
Buchler OR100
Buchner UT 2
Buckberger PA212
Buckel NY479 WI399
Buckeye OH 73 OH109
OH306

Buckhorn CA250 CA347 MN168
Bucyrus OH 21
Bud MI247
Buddencrock CO 21
Budlong IL333
Budweiser NY120
Buechler MD 12
Bueck PA291
Buehler OH292 PA851
Buelle TX 8 TX 71
Buena Vista MO101
Buerger MI197
Buexton WI466
Buffalo CA149 CA263 NY173 NY174 NY189 NY566
Buffington PA 5
Bugbee CA370
Buhl IN128
Buhler WI 36 WI415
Bulin WI149
Buller UT 28
Bundschuh NJ 38
Bunker Hill MA 10
Bunn NJ 75
Buob WI174 WI181
Burchnall MI177
Burckhalter OH224
Burd PA385
Burelbach OR 78
Burfeind MT 26
Burgemeister IL363
Burger NY 70 OH 2 OH 95
Burgermeister CA295
Burgess PA741
Burgie CA347 MN168
Burginger MN188
Burgweger IL108 MD 43
Burgy MI212 MI235
Burke NY320 NY329 WA 75
Burkhardt CA120 MA 7 MN 26 MN146 OH 2 PA215 PA386 TN 28 WI268
Burkholder OH202
Burkholtz OH 62
Burlington IA 32 WI 47
Burman WY 13
Burnell CA300
Burnham VT 4
Burns CA301 MA 66 NY549 SC 5 UT 23 WI 22
Burr NY489
Burrough MI131
Burroughs CT 8 IL 57
Burrows NY544
Burschel PA168
Burschell PA697 PA754
Bursinger WI505
Burster IA120
Burt NY 7 NY 8 PA139
Burtis NY 43 NY569
Burton CA442 CT 38 MA 8 MO 94 NJ124 NJ125 NY177 NY596 WI434
Busch CA 79 CA145 FL 4 FL 8 FL 11 IL 18 IL 58 MN 57 MO101 MO204 NH 4 NJ 64 NY 50 NY180 NY673 OH149 TX 43 VA 24
Buscher CA111
Buscherr OH170
Buschick TX 18
Buschmann IL 34
Buschoff NY248
Buselmeier MN134
Buselmeyer MN134
Bush CA414 NY294 SC 5 WI385
Bushkill PA138 PA543
Bushwick NY156
Busold IN133
Buss CA302
Bussald IN 8
Busse MN 28
Butcher KY 53 KY 54 MO 15 OH266
Butler KY 54 MO 39 NJ116 PA 59
Butschky MD 28
Butt CA108
Butte MT 16 OH292
Butterfield MD 11
Buttner MO102
Butz IN 94 MD149 MT 37 OH183 PA387 PA401 PA402
Buzzell WI391
Byra MI262
Byrne NY556 PA201
C.V. IL163
Cable OH281
Cache UT 8
Cadillac MI112
Cairns MO103
Cairo IL 23
Calder NY365
Caldwell IL148 NY570
Caley NE 54
Calgeer WI289
California CA147 CA185 CA201 CA291 CA303 CA338 CA350 CA386 ID 56
California Sake CA152 CA304
Callahan NJ 66 NY697
Calledonian MO156
Calumet IL 59 MI 38 WI 64
Calvert NE 19
Camack NY366
Camahl MN 28
Cambria PA231
Cambridge OH 23
Camden NJ 3 NJ 79
Cammert KS 19 KS 48
Camp Spring MO187
Camp Washington OH 41
Campbell CO115
Canadian RI 22
Canadian Ace IL133 IL319 NJ 27
Canajoharie NY222
Canandaigua NY223
Canavan NY519
Canon KS 30
Cantierri WA 54
Canton OH 28 OH 35
Cantrini WA 33
Cantwell IL 98
Cape MO 7
Cape Nome AK 27
Capital CA185 CA265 IL244 IN 64 KY 11 MT 37 NJ139 NY 24 OH152 WA 36 WV 3 WI242
Capito WV 18
Capitol AL 10 CO 29 CT 17 MO 33 TX 1 WI290
Carbon County MT 56
Cardes CA224
Cardinal MO 74
Carey PA401
Carion CA 32 CA219
Carl AZ 10 CO129 MN 51 MN199 NM 16 WI243
Carle KY 33
Carling AZ 23 GA 2 IL 12 MD 9 MD 29 MA 71 MI138 MO147 NJ 39 OH108 OH113 OH135 TX 33 WA 89
Carlson IL164
Carlton SD 2
Carnagie PA147
Carney IL 60 NH 3
Carolina SC 2
Carondelet MO104 MO115
Carpenter CA197
Carroll OH264
Carrollton MD 30
Carrothers WY 11
Carry DC 6
Carson NV 10
Carstens WI 90
Carter IA 63
Carthans PA342
Cartwright OR 67
Cary NY 43
Casanova WA167
Cascade PA166
Case PA204
Casey CA 92 ID 3 MA 17 PA755
Caspari WI265 WI329
Casper PA249 WY 4
Cass River MI139
Cassville WI 54
Castalia WI291
Castania PA283
Castel OR 41
Castle CO 30 IL 61
Catalina CA149
Cataract NY519 NY604
Catasauqua PA 75
Cavaness AZ 25
Cave MO136
Cecil WI 58
Cedarburg WI 60
Cellmer TX 95
Centennial MT 19 NY457 PA198
Centliver WI398
Centlivre IN 41 IA179 IA227
Central ID 9 IL211 KY 50 MI 17 MI213 NJ 40 NY367 NY388 NY616 PA175 PA206 PA216 PA697 PA700 PA755 PA759 PA762 PA763

Central cont. PA764
PA783 PA848
Central Sake CA150
Centreville WI 63
Century VA 7 WA 58
WA 71 WI292
Cereal Products CA338
Cerowski NY324
Certia IN 42
Chalapsky MN113
Chaloupsky WI 5
Chalupsky MN 75 MN187
Chambers MO157
Champ PA697
Champagne Velvet IL163
MO131
Champale NJ145 VA 7
Champion MI 75 NY438
TX 76
Champlain NY551
Chang WA 18
Channsley's NY175
Chapman CA385
Charleroi PA 86
Charleston WV 3 WV 4
Charlotte MI 39
Charlton MD139
Chartiers PA 69
Chase Gulch CO 4
Chautauqua NY290
Chatfield NY716
Chattahoochee AL 11
Chattanooga TN 2
Cheboygan MI 41
Chelan Falls WA 6
Chemung NY251
Cherokee MO129
Chesapeake MD 77 VA 22
Chesborough NY676
Chester PA 88
Chewton PA 89
Chicago CA305 CO 5
IL 20 IL 40 IL 42 IL 45
IL 47 IL 52 IL 62 IL 63
IL 71 IL 79 IL115 IL130
IL132 IL165 IL182 IL193
IL291 WI288
Chicago Heights IL196
Chico CA 44 CA234
Chicopee MA 46
Childs NY434
Chilton WI 64
Chippewa MI201
Chloupek WI210
Choate WA 40
Chod ID 34
Chormann OH136
Choteau Ave. MO163
Christ CA 21 CA306 KS 41
KY 19 KY 48 MN142 PA 57
WA 24 WI 76
Christianson WI 78 WI155
Christman OH258
Christmann PA388 WI371
Christoph IA 94 PA389
Chrystal OR 53
Chute CT 21
Cincinnati OH 43 OH 50
OH 78 OH 95 OH205 OH274

Circle NJ 27
Citizens IL 65 IL251
IN 64 NJ 94 NY 2 WI 6
City AZ 35 CA266 CA388
CO 45 CO121 CT 2 ID 16
ID 76 ID 83 IL 45 IL 71
IL230 IL241 IL312 IN 27
IN 77 IA 26 IA 29 IA 65
IA 78 IA101 IA151 IA231
LA 8 MD126 MI 18 MI 58
MI184 MI193 MN116 MN132
MN176 MN 28 MO 79 MO 98
MO111 NE 54 NJ 16 NY243
NY448 NY543 OH 51 OH 65
OH128 OH183 OH287 OH292
OH300 OH306 OH318 OR 62
OR 82 PA 13 PA313 PA804
PA851 TN 9 TN 14 TN 25
TN 26 WA 7 WA 15 WA110
WI 72 WI 95 WI116 WI147
WI153 WI177 WI181 WI186
WI194 WI207 WI288 WI372
WI377 WI389 WI401 WI420
WI432 WI436 WI498 WI504
City of Chicago IL 45
IL 71
City Springs NY586
Clark OR 45 PA694
Clarke PA845
Clarksburg WV 3
Clarkson OH167
Class PA390 PA588
Class A NJ145
Claus MD114 NY 71
Clausen NY368 NY369
NY421
Claussen SC 1 WA 64
WA 67
Clay NY571
Clay Street KY 20 KY 46
Clearfield PA 98
Clears IL207
Clemens MI 59 MI 88
Clemensen OR 50
Clement OH320
Clements PA391
Clemishire NY 30
Clenk WI 52
Clerff WA 9
Cleveland OH102 OH104
OH106 OH107 OH112 OH115
OH132 OH133 OH135 OH137
OH139 OH143 OH222 OH281
OH283 OH305
Clifford NY 43 NY225
NY257 NY325
Clifton KY 47 NY618
Clinton IA 50 IA 53
NY216
Clipson MI265
Cloner OR 15
Close MI121
Closner OR104
Clough CO 37
Cloverdale CA 49 MD 27
Club PA188
Clyffside OH 89
Coalport PA100
Coates MA 69

Cobe MA 26
Cochran NV 11
Cockade VA 11
Cody IL311
Coenin IA174
Coeur d'Alene ID 21
Coffin NE 2
Coggins PA695
Coghlin OH305
Cohalan NY329
Cohannet MA 84
Cohen AK 21 AK 30
Cohoes NY231
Coke MD150
Cold Brau IL133
Cold Spring MA 62 MN 24
MN 82 NY226 NY676 PA793
Cold Springs NY 48 NY175
Cold Stream MI184
Colden NY232
Cole IN125 NY421
Coleman NY 49 NY370
PA583
Coles NY144
Colfax WA 11
Collman IA177
Collins CA243 ID 12
KS 46 NJ 68 PA398 WI 76
Colonial NJ 27 NY487
NY724
Colony NJ145
Colony House NJ 27
Colorado CO 28 CO 46
CO 69 CO127
Colorado-Columbine CO 86
Colorado Sake CO 23
Columbia CA 51 CA319
CA382 CT 17 ID 75 IL173
IL189 IL211 IL250 IL309
IN 92 LA 9 MD 31 MI 61
MO105 MO106 NJ 43 NY 59
NY205 NY696 OH143 OR 97
OR 98 PA105 PA470 PA777
WA 44 WA 89
Columbus CA264 IL 66
NE 7 OH152 OH153 OH158
OH161
Colville WA 12
Colyer NC 6
Commercial MA 32
Commodities NJ 27
Common MD119
Commonwealth MA 83 PA382
Condon OH 48
Conemaugh PA108
Coney NY271
Conger MO185
Congress NY147
Connecticut CT 2 CT 24
CT 54
Connecticut Valley CT 24
CT 58
Connellsville PA110
Connelly WI 83
Conner NH 3 SD 4
Conners NY677
Connor PA174 PA392
Conrad CA 7 CT 8 PA151
PA393

Conradi OH 68 OH 89
Conshohocken PA115
Consolidated CA151
Constans KY 54 MN171
Constanz NY357 NY719
Consumers CA362 CO 29
GA 11 KY 50 LA 10 MD 16
MA 46 MA 67 MN 38 MO182
NV 16 NV 22 NJ 25 NJ108
NJ140 NY 5 NY 24 NY 72
NY133 NY151 NY199 NY251
NY285 NY321 NY371 NY372
NY388 NY476 NY519 NY618
NY660 NY703 NY711 OH 12
OH 25 OH 43 OH251 PA149
PA198 PA479 PA491 PA503
PA504 PA584 PA598 PA756
RI 20 RI 23 VA 7 VA 21
Contancier MT 24
Continental CA307 IN 49
MA 14 MI 89 NY502 PA582
Contra Costa CA247
Conville NY373 NY406
Conway IL 87 NY691
Cook AZ 13 CA130 CO 7
DC 2 IN 27 IN 33 MA 9
MA 17 MA 40 MI282 NY 10
Cooke IL 53 IL 64
Coolidge NY 5
Cooney RI 12
Coons MO107
Coop IA245
Cooper MA 10 MI147 MO185
PA 52 PA117 PA394 PA493
PA864 RI 2
Cooperative CA297 NY521
NY722 OH143 WI137 WI347
Coors CO 72
Coos Bay OR 50 OR 57
Copeland NM 14
Copper City AZ 9
Copper Country MI160
Corcoran PA696
Cordes TN 19
Corkings IL205
Corlett PA826
Cornell IL347
Cornish AZ 36
Cornnell NY530
Corper IL 67 IL 68 IL 69
Corporation PA395
Coste MO108
Costello NY189
Cottonwood ID 23
Coulson UT 13
Coulter NY374
Courtrenny PA396
Coutts MO190
Covington KY 8
Cowmans MI142
Cox NJ 41 PA348
Coyne MA 88
Cozzens NV 31
Crabtree OH325
Cramer SC 1
Crawford WA 13
Creagh MD 1
Cream City WI344
Creede CO 20
Cremo CT 28
Crescent ID 66 IN 4
LA 11 MO 34 MO 61 NH 14
PA132 PA223 PA799 PA826
Cresson PA123
Crest IL133
Crete NE 8
Creutzberg MD116
Crichton WA 55
Criterer OR 90
Croak WI181
Crockery OH190
Croenne NM 15
Croft MD 88 MA 35 RI 14
Croghan NY338
Croissant CA 44
Cromaner WI125
Crone MO133
Cronemeyer NE 31
Cropp CA 49
Croskey PA397 PA619
Crossley UT 7
Crossman TN 24
Croton NY442
Crout MI 39
Crowley IN 2 WY 12
Crown IN 23 OH 59 PA382
Crown Point IN 24
Cruckwith IA130
Crumbach MD150
Crump OH110
Cruse CA334
Crusius CA 57
Crystal MI 19 MT 57
Crystal Spring CO 8
NY655 NY661 NY664 NY669
PA115
Crystal Top OH339
Cuddy NY 10
Cullen UT 30
Cumberland MD122 MD124
PA 66
Cumming NJ 68
Cummings NY296
Cumminsville OH 48
Cunningham WI 34
Curiaux NV 41
Curieux NV 15 NV 41
Curtheth CO117
Curty PA313
Cuyahoga Falls OH167
Cziner IL 70
Dabszinsky AK 11
Daemgen CO129
Daeufer PA 5
Daeweritz CA274
Daffing MN 58
Dages AZ 10
Dahlbender NY 73
Dahlke WI528
Dahme MD 11
Daley MI134
Daily PA697
Dakota ND 1 SD 14
Dallas TX 25 TX 27
Dallin UT 39
Dallow NE 32
Dalton NY656 WI114
Dalzell NY621
Dambmann IA 26
Damgard IL275
Dammrich IN134
Dampfhoffer WA101
Damskey MI158
Dandelet MD 11
Dandelinger MN 58
Dangleisen OH 24
Danguire AZ 17
Danhakl DC 8
Daniel IA 36 OH 61
Daniels MI201
Danne ND 13
Dannels PA675
Dannenberg NY144
Danner WI185 WI186
Dannert CA 39
Dannhauser CA 5
Dansville NY241
Danville IL202 PA124
Danzer's MO 31
Darge WI257
Darley MD 69
Darlington PA644 PA645
Darmstaetter MI 60 MI 61
MI248
Darusmont OH 47
Dauch OH281
Daucher AZ 18
Dauterich PA424
Davenport IA 65 IA 67
IA 68 IA 69 IA 70
Davidson CA312 WI229
Davis CT 3 ID 2 IL339
MD144 MI 62 NY375 OH145
OH237 VA 5 WI330 WI333
Davison CA 34 NV 26
Dawes MI287
Dawson MA 72 MA 88 MI240
NJ 27 PA398
Dayton OH174 OH175 OH177
OH178 OH179 OH182 OH183
OH184 WA 14
De Criznius NY334
De Forest NY377
De Heck MI215
De La Vergne NY489
De Lay OR 60
De Pere WI 81
Dearsley WI416
Debakker CA221
Decatur IL204
Deck MT 55
Decker IL357 MA 11 MI260
MO102 NY376
Deckert AZ 21 AZ 32
NM 4 NM 8 NY719
Deda WI205
Dedrich WI192
Dee IL207
Deer Park NY557
Deetsen ID 50
Degan WI340
Degen TX 72
Degginger WA 4
Deglow KY 4
Dehler UT 4
Dehm IL246
Dehring MI 11

Deibel IL 27
Deierlein WI161
Deily PA 3
Deininger CA432 NV 45 WI446
Deinken WI424
Deitloff WI204
Del Norte CO 21
Delabar IL324
Delafield WI 79
Delaney NY553 OR 90
Delatron OH274
Delavon NY 74
Delaware OH188
Delbert PA399
Dells WI 95
Delphos OH189
Delta ID 27 MI128
DeLuxe ID 93
Delva WA 10
Delvin KY 13
DeMars NM 2
Demaugeot NY303
Demongo NY649
Demont ID 30
Dengel WI456
Denicke CA376
Denison NY 75 NY159
Denlacker CA414
Densler MI243
Dentler PA698
Denver CO 31 CO 32 CO 33
Deppe KY 55
Deppen PA720 PA725
DePue NY378
Derby CT 15 PA660
Derichs WI 53
Derr PA772
Dersil OH313
Desch PA102
Des Moines IA 77
DeSoto FL 12
Dessert WA 86
Deter OR 77
Detroit MI 89 MN 27
Deuber MO126
Deuscher OH204
Deutsch PA769
Deutsche NJ 37
Deutschmoser MO130
Deutz DC 3
Devell NY 76
Deventhal NY 77
Deveny WV 8
Devereaux IL 75
Devine MT 59
Devry IL169
DeWald PA644
Dewes IL 71
Dewey NH 14
Dewiscourt WA 20
Dewitt WA 51
Dexter MN172
Diamond IL335 IA165 MA 64
Diamond Spring CT 33
Diamond State DE 1
Dick IL325 IN 83 IN103 MN 50 MN159 OH 21 WI432
Dick cont. WI434 WI460
Dickinson IL 72 IL157 IL172
Dickler MN 29
Dickman IN 35 IN 37
Dickson DC 4 NY627 NY679 PA127 WA 19
Didas NY550
Diebolt OH136
Diedrich WI136
Diefenthaler PA148 WA211
Diehl CA290 IL261 MN183 NV 55 NY379 OH186
Diehm NJ138 PA400
Dier NY176
Diercks CA253
Diersen KY 21
Diesing CA155 CA276 OR 71
Dieter CA352
Dieterle OH 80
Dietrich MN144 MO 77 OH220
Dietz NY 11 PA149
Dietzel CA 2
Dieves CA226
Dilger OH223
Dill ID 59
Diller PA142
Dillman AZ 10
Dillmann OH 76
Dillon MT 26
DiMarco CA152
Dimler WI454
Dimmick WA 40
Dingeldein MO199
Dinkel OH287
Dinter RI 7
Diogenes NY 78
Diplomat CT 28
Dippel PA646 PA647
Dippold PA308
Disbrow CA194
Distler PA205
Dithmar PA401 PA402
Dittman MD 43
Dittmann MD 13
Dittmer MI 63
Ditz PA827
Diversey IL130
Dix WI105 WI403
Dixie AL 11 GA 7 LA 12 VA 21
Dixon IL207 IL208 MA 63 MT 52 MT 60
Dluser PA 80
Doberneck PA222
Dobert WI244
Dobler CA287 NY 34 WI 42
Doblin CA 46
Dobmeier ND 11
Dodge CA137 MN 91
Doehne PA196
Doelger NJ 79 NY 79 NY292 NY380 NY405
Doelker MT 23
Doemich NY381
D'Oench MO165
Doern KY 42
Doerr CA373 MT 35
Doerrbecker NY382
Dold IA189
Dolegal WI209
Doll MI 46 PA 30
Dolling CA132
Donald NY487
Donau WA 90
Donnenwirth OH 21
Donohue NY677 NY685
Donra PA128
Donovan IL 73
Donse UT 29
Dorey PA403
Dorman CO 69
Dormann IL344
Dorn AZ 51 IA190
Dorsch NY537 WI441
Dosch MI229
Dostal CO 50 IL 7 IA142 IA172 OH 21
Dotten WI418
Dotterweich NY241 NY243 NY533
Doty VT 2
Douglas City AK 8
Douty PA770
Dover CT 17 OH 24
Downer IL 42 IL 74 IL172 IA 96 NE 33 PA149 PA311 SD 6 WI492 WY 11
Downing NY545
Downs NY216
Doxey IN 1
Doyle IL 75 NY237 NY318 NY540
Dozenbach IN 25
Drachter IN 91
Rake CO 17
Drankowski TX 70
Draper MI155 NY313 NY318 NY631 OH 52
Drerupp OH263
Drescher MN149
Dressell NY292 PA198
Drewry IL 48 IL150 IN137 MA188 MI100 MN171 MN172
Dreyfuss CA209
Dries IA 64
Drischel MN144
Driskel NY177
Dronsutowicy MI246
Drossen WI446
Drostle MI 48 MI282
Drucker TN 24
Drum OH 52
Drummond KY 22
Drury DC 1
Dubacher AZ 3
Dubler PA282
Dubois PA130 PA654
Dubuque IA 89 IA 90 IA 91 IA 98 IA101 IA102 IA104
Ducasse WI505
Ducker CA186
Dudenhoeffer PA309 PA821
Dudler UT 24 UT 40 WI266
Duell NY 80

Duer IL 98 IL154
Duerr WI535
Dugas AZ 37
Dukehart MD 22 MD101
Dulla CA236
Dullea CA443 MI 64
Duluth MN 30 WI215
Dumville NY318
Duncan FL 1
Dunes IN101
Dunkel WA 14
Dunlop NY 12 NY680
Dunn NH 2 NY628 NY684
Dunton NY383
Dunville NY314
Dupax UT 11
Duquesne CA153 OH108 OH142 PA 24 PA 69 PA132 PA268 PA304 PA322 PA648
Durand WI 87
Durango CO 52
Durkee NY263
Durlam NY722
Durow WI460
Durrstein IL329
Durrwachter WA 51
Durst WA 79
Dutch Country PA718
Dutch Treat AZ 23
Duvel OH219 OH220
Dvorak WI485
Dyer PA403
Dyett OH 63
E & B MI 81
Eagar NY 51
Eagle AK 13 AK 23 AK 36 CA308 CA373 CO 34 CO 69 CT 25 CT 61 ID 32 IL 40 IL 76 IL 98 IL115 IL218 IN158 IA 70 IA158 MI158 MN 38 NJ 46 NJ 76 NJ127 NY361 NY565 NY698 OH 83 OH204 OH308 OK 31 OR 50 PA 8 PA 42 PA 78 PA132 PA156 PA259 PA403 PA649 RI 13 TN 21 WV 28 WI 94 WI119 WI176 WI216 WI247 WI283
Eagle Rock ID 45 ID 48
Eagle Run PA770
Eason MI 1
East Buffalo NY192
East Grand Forks MN 37 ND 6
East Idaho ID 75
East India MI 62
East River WI148
East St. Louis IL212 IL213 IL296
East Side IL193 MI 59
East Tennessee TN 5
Easter IN145
Easterly NY657
Eastern CT 61 MT 47 NJ 27 NY 93 NY487
Eastern Oregon OR100
Eastside CA165
Eaton WI103
Ebel WI205
Ebenbauer IL356
Eber IL326 IA225
Eberhardt PA649 PA650
Eberle KS 4 MI173 WI138
Eberlein IL118 MI269
Eberly PA243
Ebermann MN129
Ebert OH 98 OH208
Eble PA404
Ebling NY132 NY384
Ebner IN158 MN199 WI 91 WI116
Echnoz PA313
Eck MI280
Eckart CT 4
Ecke WI381
Eckerle MO153
Eckert CA154 NJ 15 NY385 PA 36 PA717
Eckhardt OH305 WI 83
Eckhoff NY466
Eckstein IN 76 MD141 NY330 NY719 WI525
Ecoffey WY 13
Economy PA 20 PA140
Eddie WI117
Ede WI539
Edel PA690
Edelbrau NY109
Edelbrew NY109
Edelstein PA 75
Edelweiss IL 48 IL150 IL178
Eder IL256 WI117 WI120
Edgar OH289
Edwards ID 45 MI192
Effinger MI211 PA244 WI 25
Egan AK 7
Eger MO 89 OH204 PA 72
Egg Harbor NJ 11
Eggleston ID 33
Eggspliveler IA219
Eglin WA118
Ehehalt NJ 69
Ehemann NY624
Ehinger PA405 PA406
Ehlers NJ 56
Ehresman NY 55
Ehret NJ151 NY 85 NY100 NY386 PA596
Ehrgott WI364
Ehrich CA107
Ehrmann NM 4 NY 47
Eich PA407
Eichenlaub OH 53
Eichenseher IL 77
Eichert MI216 WI469
Eichhammer NY309
Eichhorn IL351 MD 32 OH249
Eichler NY387 NY429
Eickmann MN 52 MN136
Eifert WI168
Eigenbrot MD 50
Eigenmann IA191
Eilert OH111 WI169 WI273 WI365
Eisele IL273 PA408 PA409
Eisenbeis WA 48 WI227
Eisenbeiss DC 5
Eisenmenger DC 14
Eisfelder KY 13 MD145
Eisfeller PA314
Ekhardt MI 58 MI 81 MI102
Elbett PA201
Elbreder CA415
Elco PA141
El Dorado CA414
Eldredge NH 5 NH 10
Electric City WI194
Elgin Eagle IL218
Elgin National IL217
Eli IA 27
Elias NY388 NY389 NY390
Eliel IL266
Elizabeth NJ 16
Elk PA732 PA743
Elk Run PA710
Elkins WV 7
Ellenburger IA170
Ellensburg WA 21
Eller NJ 16
Ellinger MI 6
Ellinghaus IA 13
Elliot MO112
Elliott CA370 CO 4
Ellis IA238 OR 97
Ellison MI 36 WI256
Ellspas MI259
Ellsworth WI 97
Elm NY118
Elm City CT 34 CT 38
Elm Street OH 76
Elmira NY253
Elmwood MA 37
El Paso CO 18 TX 28
El Rey CA308
Elsas OH 54
Elsasser PA409
Elschlager PA 94
Elser WI383
Elshire NE 48
Elsner KS 45
Elspass MI 65
Elwell CO 18 CO 93
Ely MI 7 NV 16
Embassy FL 10 VA 7
Embree OH 55
Emerald NJ 85 NY 38 NY435
Emich NY596
Emmerling PA232
Emmert MN176
Emmet MO147
Empire CA309 CA438 IL133 MD 13 MA 12 MO109 NV 56 NY 81 NY180 NY451 PA 13 PA 65 PA253 WI102 WI214 WI286 WI507
Empire State NY423 NY533
Ems IL211
Ende IA 34
Enderle MN155
Endlich CO 44 IL 78
Endres MI170 NJ 42 PA 96
Endrifs PA410

Endriss MI 63 MI 66
Enes MN 63 WI338
Engel IN113 MD 33 NY629 PA173 PA197 PA375 PA376 PA411 PA412 PA509 WI417 WI424
Engelfritz IL291
Engelhardt NY391 VA 1 VA 23 WI293
Engelhorn MN 54 MN185
Engelke PA413
Engels WI 59 WI244
Engert OH204 OH287
Engesser MN180
Engle MA 18 MA 37
Englehorn MN 66
Engler NE 34
Englert IA139 NY575
English MD 11 MO110 MO151
Ennes WI350
Enright NY573
Enser PA414
Ensslen PA422
Enterprise CA318 MD 26 MA 16 MA 49 MA 55 NY448 OR 26 PA480 PA658
Entress PA233
Enz PA657
Enzbrenner PA 13
Eppel IL265
Eppig NY 82 NY 85
Epstein WI402
Erath LA 2 LA 13
Erb NV 46 PA133
Erbrich PA651
Erdrich PA415
Erford WA 11
Erhardt MI271 OH234 WI117
Erickson MI 34 MN117 WI220
Erie NY722 OH142 PA149 PA150 PA151 PA156 PA158 PA168
Erikson PA652
Erisman PA345
Erlanger PA598
Ernst IL 79 NY 60 NY392 WA 10 WA106 WI412
Erpelding CA 86
Erpelt MD171
Errickson IL 80
Ertie OR 49
Erve WI118
Erwin PA416
Escanaba MI128
Esch IA 94 IA105
Esmeralda NV 1
Esselborn NY497 OH272
Esser TX 73 WI 39 WI 75 WI177
Essex IL133 MA 58 NJ 77
Esslinger MI273 MI274 PA417 PA418 PA523 PA714
Esteven CA438
Etna CA 70
Euchenhofer OH171
Eucker IL 11
Euker VA 12
Eulberg IL235 WI401 WI514
Eureka AK 19 CA254 CA258 CA353 CA428 MI284 PA784 SD 10 SD 25
Eurich NY114 NY118
Evanoff OR 50
Evans MA 63 MT 28 NY 57 NY287 NY615 NY681 OH289
Evansville IN 28 IN 29 IN 33
Everard NY393 NY394 NY513
Everett WA 22
Evergreen NY160
Evers NY395
Evertsen NY396
Ewald DC 10 MD 33
Excell IL163
Excelsior AZ 37 AZ 52 DE 4 IL 87 IL181 IL356 IN 76 IA 87 MO131 MO187 NY102 NY155 NY189 OH111 PA260 PA479 TX 22 WI108
Exchange PA 42
Exner ID 34
Exposition MI 52 MI 67
Extel MD 56
Eydt NY283
Eyman IL364
Eyppert NJ 23
Eyre NY397
Eyring PA721
Eysenbach OH189
Eyth PA 60
Faatz WI 56 WI 70
Faber CA 61 NV 6 PA 67 PA125
Fable NY574 PA283
Fabrichs NY629
Fackler MN 15
Faden CO120
Fahel PA131
Fahey CA 33
Fahl WI319
Fahrenbach IL 81
Fahrenger PA793
Fahrenholz MN152
Faig CA 47
Failey NY697
Fairbanks AK 15 AK 17
Fairhill PA436 PA590
Fairmount OH 87 WV 9
Fairnan OR 83
Fairview PA728
Falbe WI294
Falcon PA714
Falk PA 28 WI300 WI340
Fall River MA 50
Fallert NY 83
Falliers MI140
Falligan WA 50
Fallon NE 38
Falls MN 48
Falls City KY 22 NE 11
Falls Mountain NH 14
Falls Park PA591
Falstaff CA295 CA315 CA376 IL211 IN 39 LA 19 MO105 MO113 MO182 MO188 NE 40 RI 14 TX 28 TX 39 WA104
Fanning NY 44
Fantino ID 20
Fantz CA113 CA238
Farabaugh PA 72
Farber OR 2
Fardy WI183
Farley MI192 NJ105
Farmers WI 32 WI457
Farmington IA113 WI101
Farnham NY 42
Farnsworth ID 5
Farrell MI 68 NY 84 OH335
Farren NY 13
Fassert NY398
Fassnacht OH193
Fastnacht MI 69
Fauerbach WI241 WI371
Faul MT 1
Faulkins NY287
Faulkner SD 4
Fauss CA310
Fautz CA275
Faux IN 75
Fay IN105
Fayette PA816
Featherston MN142
Fechter GA 3
Fecker IL 82 IL 83 IL202
Feddersen WI414
Federal NY 80
Fehleisen NJ 70 NJ 87
Fehr KY 18 KY 36 KY 50 LA 14 OH 86
Fehrenbach DE 2 MI142
Fehrenbacher CA100
Fehy NJ 29
Feigel IL 84
Feigenspan CT 41 IN 39 NJ 86 NJ103 NY 34 NY324 NY448 RI 14
Feil PA419
Feilke MT 61
Fein WY 13
Felix PA725
Fell PA782
Feller NY 62 NY309 OH228
Fellows PA699
Fells Point MD 98
Felner IL321
Fenelich OH100
Fenker MD 10
Fenner MT 23 PA 36
Fensterer IA 28
Fenway MA 27
Fenzel NY719
Ferber MN135
Ferdinand IN 37 IA171 MD 34
Ferger NJ 43
Fergg NJ 94
Fergus MN 48
Ferl NY528
Fernbach CA117

Ferneding OH335
Fernwood PA265
Ferring IA194
Ferris NY399
Fertig WI 13
Fesenmeier MD123 WV 15
Festle IA196
Fette FL 13
Fetter MO 73
Fetzner MN 15 MO 78
Feuchter IL 24
Feuer OH 19
Feuerbacher MO164
Feuerstein CO 87
Feurer OR 14 OR 68
Fey IA245 MN129 OH 47
Feyh NY400
Ficker MN 58
Fiddler NY 14
Fidelio NY427
Fiedler WI119
Fielke NE 49
Fielmeyer PA420 PA421
Fiji WA255
Finck NV 8 NV 52 NJ 21 NY244 NY246 NY481
Finder IL 15 IL336
Findon MI236
Findorf WI395
Finegan NY279
Finger IL 30
Fink CA383 MI 28 MN 31 MN194 NY278 PA194 PA422
Finke WI 47 WI536
Finkenauer PA423 PA481
Finkler IL 35
Finkmann MO199
Finlay OH301
Finleyville PA172
Finnegan MA 48 WI108
Finney MO111
Finning CA 82
First Bohemian NY324
First National PA304 PA653
Fisch MI246
Fischbach MO 73 MO 74 WI295
Fischer CA 73 CA213 CA405 CO 8 CO 75 CO 79 CO 82 CO120 CT 22 FL 1 ID 7 IL 85 LA 19 MD124 MI 2 MI 16 MO183 NJ 27 NJ115 NM 16 NY 85 NY151 NY273 ND 3 OR 23 PA153 PA424 PA425 TX 39 UT 2 WI382 WI436 WI472 WY 3 WY 16
Fish AZ 41 MT 24 NY 51 WI 5
Fishel OH112
Fisher AK 23 CO 18 CO 82 CO 85 ID 39 IL337 IA 8 IA 29 MD151 MD152 MI 2 NH 5 NJ142 NY722 OH343 PA 90 PA246 PA561 PA583 PA728 UT 25 WI 9
Fitch CA 44
Fitger MN 32
Fitzgerald MD 80 MD 88 NE 24 NY233 NY682
Fitzsimmons MA 48 MN 74
Fix IL220 WI 57
Fizaine PA468
Flach PA453
Flagstaff AZ 10
Flaiber IN 22
Flaig PA284 PA720
Flamingo FL 6
Flanagan NY369 NY421
Flanigan NY541 NY668
Fleck WI 73
Fleckenstein MN 12 MN 44 MN 45 MN163
Fleigner ID 75
Fleiner MT 44
Fleischman OH 56
Fleishbein MO 95
Fleisher WI420
Fleming IL 86 IL 87 MO 99 NY 23 NY656
Fletcher OH262 RI 8
Flin AZ 19
Flint MI136
Flock PA338 PA851 PA853
Florida FL 1 FL 8 FL 14
Florin CA 78
Floto PA718
Flower City NY535 NY575 NY592
Floyd OH 57
Flynn MA 51
Foast WI226
Foegele MI182
Foehrenbach NY476
Foerster MI193 MI287 NE 27 SD 25
Fogarty NY457
Fogeli CA210
Fogt PA155
Foller MT 35
Folstaff IL123
Fontenelle NE 35
Food City MI 24
Ford ID 9
Fordham MD 2
Forest NJ119
Forest Castle PA168
Forest City OH113
Forest Park MO113
Forge NY274
Fornecker OH 2
Forrest MA 72 NY119
Forschner WA112
Forster NY 86 WA 8 WI344 WI351 WI365 WI417
Fort Dearborn IL133 MI 50
Fort Edward NY263
Fort Hamilton NY114
Fort Marshall MD111
Fort Orange NY 24
Fort Pitt MD112 PA227 PA776 PA784
Fort Schuyler NY697
Fort Spokane WA 32
Fort Stanwix NY615
Fort Winnebago WI402
Fort Worth TX 25
Fortman CA311
Fortmann CA311 OH 58 OH 81
Fortney PA 81
Fortune IL 88 IL 89
Foshenden WI442
Foss OH 85
Fossberger PA 88
Fossdick NY401
Fosselmann IA239
Foster AZ 33 CO 27 MO147 NY155 WI 22 WI185
Foulds NY609
Fountain WI513
Fountain City OH 20 WI120
Fountain Springs PA173
Four Flags MI230
Fovargue OH114
Fowler IL284
Fox IL111 IN 99 OH281 OH282 OK 6 WA 10 WI378 WI514
Fox DeLuxe IN 99 MI154
Fox Head NJ 27 WI458 WI514
Fox Hill NJ 30
Fox Lake WI124
Fox River WI510 WI541
Fox Valley WI267
Foxhead WI215
Frackville PA175
Frahm IA 65
Frampton PA426
France WI216
Francis WA102
Franciscus PA247
Frangel WI447
Frank CA 96 ID 49 MI186 NY 17 NY448 NY561 OH 18 OH 98 OH225 OH227 PA248 PA557 TX 5
Franke IL356 IN 91 PA249 TX 57
Frankenberger CA 34
Frankenmuth IN137 KY 28 MI100 MI136 MI138 OH195
Frankford Ave. PA547
Frankfort KY 11
Frankl ID 61
Franklin ID 75 MA 13 MO 99 NV 47 NY124 OH154 PA 4 PA847
Franks PA427
Franz CA423 IL226 IA216 MO 32
Frase WI 91
Frasier NY402
Fraudenberger PA124
Frauenheim PA654
Frauenholz CA313
Frazier WI443
Freche NJ 71
Freda ID 82
Frederick CA314 IL119 IL360 IN 85 IA 21
Fredericks CA302 MD163

Fredericksburg CA376
Frederickson WI277 WI375
Free MI176 PA860
Free State MD 14
Freed NJ 34
Freeland PA178 PA780
Freelinger KS 48
Freeman KS 17
Freeze OH 28 TX 65
Freiler PA318
Freimann NY496 NY636 NY640 OH314
Freinscht MD 92
Freiseis AR 1
Fremont NE 14 OH198
French ME 1 PA811 WI 84 WI269
French Creek PA313
Frenier VT 1
Frenzel WI470
Fresenius CT 33
Fresno CA 87
Freuger PA340
Freund NJ 45
Frey MA 14 MI 20 MI 88 MI146 MI173 MN159 PA 68 PA150 PA153 PA428 UT 17 WI104 WI417
Freyer CA258 CA349 OH266 OR 58 WI 64
Friara PA223
Friars MI243
Frick OH 80
Fricke MI237 MI279 NE 10 WI 60 WI245
Fricker WI 13
Friderici IA 18
Friedel PA655
Friederich MO 28
Friedman MI199
Friedmann NY178
Friedrich IL273 NY518
Frieman NY371 OH155
Friend WA 4
Fries ID 61 MO114 NY 87 WI 11 WI265
Frietschel MN 75
Frisch CO109
Fritch IN 57
Friton MN123
Fritsch PA429
Fritsche PA 37
Fritz CA 97 CA155 CO 76 CO 78 IL227 MI282 MO115 MT 46 NJ 78 PA770 WI336
Froehler MN118 MN119
Froelich PA705
Froelking OH 84
Froescher NJ 71
Frohmeyer OH 52
Frohwitter NJ 50
Fromm AL 5
Frommer AZ 33 CA448
Frontier NY673
Frost IN 92
Frostburg MD146 PA 88
Frothinger WI469
Fruch OH220
Frye PA 13
Fryman CA385
Frzaskowsky KS 20
Fuchs CO129 ID 18 IL288 NV 31 OH 59
Fuermann MN132 WI506 WI507
Fuerst WA 90
Fuerstahl CA255
Fuess PA151 PA310
Fugina WI 13
Fuhrmann PA770 PA771 WI429
Fuji Sake HI 7
Fulcher CA 83 CA416
Fulda MI105
Fuller AK 30 NY 88 NY403 UT 26
Fullgraff NY 24
Fullhart MT 58
Fulton IN 33 MO190
Fulton County NY291
Funk CA341 IL 90 MN164 MN176 PA555
Funke WI258
Furniture City MI149
Furst OR 24 WA 87 WI212
Fuss WI270 WI340
Futterer CA421
Gabel PA152
Gabler IL105
Gack IN 69
Gackle PA284
Gaegler PA180
Gaenssler WY 10
Gaertner IA114 IA201 NJ148
Gaff IN 4
Gaffigan NY683
Gaheen NY616
Gahr ND 11
Gail NE 27
Galena IL235
Galeton PA179
Galion OH199
Gallagger WI296
Galland WA 75
Gallatin MT 12
Galler MI194 TX 58
Gallivan PA551
Galveston TX 39
Gambel ID 55 WA 87
Gambell CA452
Gamble NY 51 NY 52
Gambrinus IL 91 MO133 NY190 NY433 OH 71 OH156 OH306 OR 68 PA345 WI386
Gambs MI275
Gamma MO 22
Gangwisch PA647 PA656 PA685
Gankman MO116
Gans ID 16 PA285
Ganser MN132
Gansneder AK 33
Ganz IA 26
Garber NY272
Garcis NY273
Gardella MA 58
Garden City CA372 IL 92 IL 93 IL158 MT 48
Garden State NJ 7 NJ 27
Gardine NY343
Gardiner PA582
Gardner NY252 NY404
Garfield OH264 WA 43
Garger PA282
Garner MN 92 MT 19 MT 40
Garnier IN 85 IN 86 IN 87
Garrett WA 28
Garrotte CA104
Garschutz NJ 20 NJ138
Garser NY 89
Garst IN105
Garten Brau WI405
Gartner IA227 RI 9
Gartzke WI 63
Gasa ND 14
Gass NY562
Gassler MN 84 OH 2
Gassner PA787
Gast IL247 MO117 MO118 MO200 PA657 PA658
Gaster CO 74
Gastriech IL109
Gatens TN 9
Gateway IA 53
Gauch IL 94 IL 95 MI217 RI 7
Gaul MO167 PA401 PA449 PA451 PA721
Gausner CA 35
Gavagan OH145
Gaw CO 80 CO 88
Gaylord CT 38
Gebert CA269
Gebhard KY 13 KY 23 MO119
Gebhardt IL286 IL376 MD 10
Geck NY598
Gecman NY179
Geeman IL 97
Geffert WI429
Gegen ND 3
Gehl MD 35
Gehler IL 13
Gehling NE 12
Gehre MO 54
Gehrhardt NY 90
Gehri NJ 93
Gehrig CA118 CA137 CA209
Gehring CA403 IL 98 IN157 IA 94 MN 70 NE 12 OH115 OR 13 PA628 WI264
Geib OH116
Geier PA742
Geiger CO102 ID 29 IA140 MN129 OH272 OR 86 PA417 PA839 WI380
Geis SD 23
Geisbauer KY 5
Geise IA 58 TN 2
Geisel MA 82 PA 76 PA834
Geisen WI 53
Geiser WI361
Geisin OH197

Geisler NY133
Geisman MO 19
Geisser IL238
Geitner CA350
Gelbke AL 7
Geltz IA190
Gelwicks MD153 MD174
Gem City IL327 OH178
Gem State ID 93
General CA 14 CA168 CA295 CA315 CO109 IN 39 MO182 NE 40 NJ 44 RI 14 TX 39 TX 69 UT 25 WA104
Genesee ID 29 NY 51 NY597 NY671
Geneseo IL238
Geneva NY268 NY708
Genkinger PA342
Gentner PA430 PA431
Geoffroy CA372
George OH302
Georgelein WI189
Georgi WI408
Georgia GA 15
Georgian MO206
Gerard IA 51 ND 2
Gerber MT 48 NY180 NY253
Gerckens CA 19 CA240
Gerhard NY312
Gerhardt AZ 7
Gerhart OH211
Gerhauser MT 36 NV 10
Gerke OH 83
Gerken PA480
Gerlach OH218 OH272 WI491
Gerlinger KY 13 WI326
German MD124 MO153 NY207 NY542 WI332
Germania IL129 IA 94 IA165 MD105 MI 70 MN109 NY 85 NY183 NY423 NY659 OH 60 PA 13 PA124 PA234 PA487 SC 1 WI329
Germantown PA491 WI130 WI131 WI297
Germershausen CA450
Gerst CA235 TN 28
Gerstacker MT 23
Gerster CO 74 PA301
Gerstlauer PA432
Gerstner PA125 WI298
Gerter CO 74
Gessler MI145
Gessner MD125
Gettelman WI341
Getter MI 46
Gettleman WI510
Getzloff NE 2
Geyer IL284 MI139 MI249 NV 39 NJ 95 NJ136
Geyser MN 33
Geywitz PA770
Gezelschap WI181
Gibbons PA849
Gibson MD 3 NY315 WI283
Giebenhain CA243
Giehl NY615
Gierow WI 64
Gies NV 56
Gieschen CA222
Giese IL300
Giesecke TX 10
Giesel PA176
Gieser WI434
Giessen OH 28
Gilbert MA 44 MT 62 NJ 54
Gilbride CO 42
Gilbridge MN 96
Gilg MT 29
Gilger MN 67 MN165 MN204
Gill CO 89 CO 96
Gillen IL 98
Giller IL363
Gillig NY 91 NY405 NY406 NY641
Gilligan PA433
Gillman NY563 WI353 WI354
Gillmann NY563 WI157
Gilmak WA 56
Gilmore MN 67 MN207 PA684
Gilroy CA 92
Gilt Edge NJ145
Gimlich MA 77
Gindele MA 90 PA434
Gindroff ID 25
Gines OH 38
Ginsberg MN 5 MN 91 MN201
Ginthner MN196
Gipfel WI299
Gipps IL133 IL310 IL311
Girard IA121
Gisselbrecht PA113
Glaab IA 91
Glab IA 91
Glade IL182
Glanz PA136
Grasbrener IA220
Glasbrenner WI432
Glaser NY649 OR 30
Glasgow VA 6
Glasman AZ 51
Glasser NV 5
Glatz WI383
Gleed IA101
Gleim ID 95 WA111
Glen NY714
Glencoe MN 52
Glennon NY271 PA168 PA697 PA700
Glick IN145
Glicker WI539
Globe CA291 IL 68 IL132 MD 11 MD122 MD124 NY258 NY370 NY699 PA323
Glock TX 88
Gloninger MD 11 MD 92
Glossner OH 61
Gloucester NJ 18
Glover PA153
Gluck NJ133 NY 92 NY 93
Glueck CA338 IL237
Gluek MN 98 WI215
Gnadt WI420
Gnam IA185
Gnauck CA 18
Godde WA 15
Goebel CA223 MI 66 MI 71 MI 82 MI 87 MI 92 MI109 MI224
Goedricke NV 33
Goeggerle WI 28
Goehring WI417
Goelert WA 48
Goeltz WI 14
Goelz PA492
Goelze PA364
Goenner PA 64 PA233
Goenwein MI270
Goeppert CA450
Goerke WI301
Goerl CA 3 CA385
Goerner PA271
Goerres IL329
Goes WI300
Goesch WA107
Goetter WI526
Goetz MI150 MO 40 MO 79 NY120 WA 76 WI466 WY 13
Gogeobic WI171
Gogreve OH 81
Gold Brau IL133
Gold Label CO109
Gold Medal IN 65 PA842
Gold Top FL 2
Goldbeck PA409
Goldberg NV 22
Golden CO 72 MI132 MI143
Golden Age WA 84
Golden Brew MA 64
Golden City CA297 CO 70
Golden Eagle AZ 47 PA478
Golden Gate CA316 CA336
Golden Horn NY114
Golden West CA 27 CA109 CA223 CA227
Goldenrod NY109
Goldicke NV 7
Goldkaefer CA387
Goldsmith MI155 NY280
Goldstein CA 8 IA236
Goldtree AZ 51
Goliath NY116
Gondrezick WI495
Good CO 3 CO 41 CO 44 CO 90 MD158 OH 3
Goodale CA 8
Goodbook NV 30
Goodbrod PA290 PA855
Goodfellow CO 9 CO 35
Goodhue MN148
Goodman CA202 ID 84
Goodwin OH 37
Goos OR 46 PA435
Gordon NY585
Gorkow WA 77
Gorman PA757
Gorney MI131
Gorsuch MD 44
Gortler MD 36
Gory MO202
Goscinsky CA359
Gossner CA188

Gottfredson WI198
Gottfried IL 78 IL 99
Gotthard NY564
Gottlieb MD 9 MD 11
MD 15 MD 16 MD 50 MD 69
MD 79 MD105 MD108
Gotto CO 36
Gottsberger NY407
Gould FL 17 NY526 NY555
Goundie PA 39 PA137
Gower CO 91
Graber CA311 OH223 OH333
Grace CA 87 CA149 CA263
CA396 NY311
Graeber MN 85
Graelz WI471
Graf CA442 IN144 IA104
IA140 MI269 MN 92 TN 4
WI302
Grafe PA235
Graff IN146 WI200
Grafmueller MN128
Grafton WI137
Graham MD 11 NJ123 NJ124
Graie MN171
Grain Belt MN108 NE 32
Gramer MI214
Grammel MI125
Grampp MT 9
Grams MN145
Grand Island NE 16
Grand Junction CO 73
Grand Lager MO 74
Grand Rapids MI152 MI224
WI139
Grand Valley MI170
Graner AZ 8
Granger MN 54 NY 23
NY286 NY411
Grangeville ID 31
Granite Lake NY275
Granshed MD 37
Grant NY340 NY408 WI418
Grass MN196 NY103
Grasser OH303 OH308
Grassmuck WI114
Grathwohl WA117
Gratten PA810
Grauch PA436
Grauer NY 94
Graupner PA198
Graus PA437
Grausch PA436
Graves UT 35
Gray AK 22 NY 95 PA403
PA438 PA439 PA489 WI175
WI303
Gray's Harbor WA 2
Grazer CA127 CA425 NV 13
Great Eastern NJ 57
Great Falls MT 30
Great Lakes IL 25 IL150
IN 39 MI151 NY181
Great Northern NY658
Great Western CA207
IA142 MO120
Greater New York NY427
Greeling IA237
Green MD 62 MA 46 WI420
Green Bay WI304 WI384
Green Tree MO164
Greenburg NV 53
Greener NY 73
Greenham PA 25
Greensburg PA187
Greentrees MO104
Greenville NJ 43
Greenway NY543 NY654
NY659
Greenwood MD 15 OH191
Greg IA112
Gregg NY286 PA781
Gregory CO 37 KY 31
NY 15 RI 3
Greif AK 20
Greiner IL123 IN 95
MO 85 NY 73 OH308
Grenay VA 7
Grentzinger NY584
Greiss CA239
Grete ID 85
Gretz PA441 PA553
Grey CT 58
Griebel OH117
Griel WI533
Grieme NY643
Griesbach CA439 WI198
Griesedieck IL 12 IN 39
MO 42 MO 95 MO113 MO139
MO147 MO182
Grieser MI 72
Griessmaier MO 4
Griffin MI 51
Griffith NJ106
Grim PA568 PA569 PA570
Grimm WI 54
Grimmer MD 38
Grinding NY409
Grisbaum WI285
Grob MI286
Groeber OH 29
Groene OH 66
Groeninger MO112
Grosche WI523
Grogan CA317
Groger WA 51
Groh NY410 NY482
Grohe NM 17
Grohs CA 11
Grone MO121
Gronenbold MO 95
Gross IA 82 IA193 MO106
MO203 NY685 PA440 WI126
WI531
Grosskopf WI163
Grossman PA177
Grot IL275
Grovier WI176
Grow WI115
Grub MN 58
Grubb WI134
Grubel KS 21
Gruber IL277 MN183 OH323
Gruebner WI461
Gruenberg NV 25 NY168
Gruendler MA 80
Gruenewald PA523
Gruhler CA264 MI257
Grummel OH297
Grun NJ 20
Grunbaum ID 10
Grunberg NY168
Grund KS 27
Grundel MD137
Grundler PA441 PA569
Gruner AZ 10
Grunert WI305
Gruszczynski WI306
Gsell MO115
Guam IA162
Gubelmann IN160
Guckenberger PA217
Guckes PA442 PA443
Guenther CO115 IN 83
MD 35 MD 39 NY 96 TX 60
Guethler DC 14
Guffee TX 13
Gugel IA 28 MO 26
Guggemos MO122
Guggenmos NE 35 NE 36
Guiden IA166
Guidorff ID 4
Guillaume OH313
Guindon NY551
Guinness NY320
Guldager NV 14
Gulf NY699 PA115 PA190
TX 44
Gullick IA145
Gun IL230
Gund IL231 OH123 WI213
WI214 WI215
Gunderson WI169
Gundlach CA312 IL200
Gundorf ID 49
Gundrum IA191
Gunnison CO 75 CO 77
Gunther MD 39
Gutbier WI541 WI542
Gute MI233
Gutekunst SC 5
Guth MT 49
Gutheil MN 4 WI 64
WI 65 WI455
Gutknecht PA127
Gutmann PA444
Gutsch CA158 IL100 WI458
Guttenberg MO 39
Guyer MN200
Haag IL298 PA250 PA711
PA865
Haas IL101 IL277 IA163
MA160 MI163 MI165 MN 47
MT 41 NJ 73 NJ141 NY182
NY659 NY720 PA 30 PA 31
PA332 PA445 PA446 PA456
PA737 WI436
Haase MN189
Hab MO 2
Haberer WA 5
Haberkorn IA146 IA214
Haberle NY655 NY660
NY661 NY664 NY669
Habermann WI 54
Habermehl WI265
Haberstroh NY207
Haberstumpf MI170 OH204

Habich MA 15
Habig IN 76
Hack IN158
Hackenberg NJ 31
Hacker MA 62
Haddock NY411
Hadlee CA258
Hadler CA258
Haeben PA277
Haeberle PA447
Haeffer IA124
Haeffner PA296 PA448
PA531 WI411
Haefner PA253 PA797
Haegele IL223
Haegelin KS 1
Haehnle MI 35 MI172
MI174
Haemen MN 24
Haertel WI401
Hafele MI 73
Hafenbrank OH255
Haffen NY412
Haffenreffer MA 4 MA 16
MA 33 RI 14
Hafner KS 53 MI229 NY413
Hagely CO 99
Hageman OR 27
Hagemann CA357 TX 64
Hagemeister NY390 WI144
WI479
Hagen WI249
Hagenah WI429
Hagener WV 25
Hagensick IA180
Hager IN146 MD 40 MD154
NY650
Hagerstown MD155
Hagg IA 59
Hagl PA187
Hagle PA823
Hagner CA277
Hahn IL319 MI166 OR 9
TX 45
Haibel CA337
Haid OH337 PA 14 PA213
Hail WI405
Hailey ID 34
Haines IL 22 PA449
Haisch PA479
Haischer NY238
Hait NY 56
Hajicek MN 66
Halbysan OH235
Hale MA 57 WI233
Haley OH135
Hall CA 97 CT 48 IL334
MI178 NY414 UT 20 WI267
Hallaher CO129
Haller OH106 OH218 PA 14
Hallgren PA334
Halm IL 4 MO 95 MO123
OH 20
Hals MD 11
Halthnorth OH118
Haltinner CA 74 CA396
Halz CA101
Hama MO124
Haman CO 19
Hamann CA419
Hamburg WI540
Hameister SD 26
Hamilton MA 68 OH204
Hamm CA142 CA347 MD 39
MN166 MN168 MO 66 MO125
NH 6 NY 91 TX 44 WI428
Hammel IL268 NM 19
Hammelef MI 74
Hammer CA437 MO165 NY183
TX 8
Hammerle IN130
Hammersen NJ 21
Hammond IN 51 MD 11
OH119
Hampden MA 88 NJ 27
Hamper MT 52
Hanauer NY532
Hanbrick CO 65
Hanbury IL302
Hand IL102 RI 4
Handloeser MD 73
Handschigl SD 3
Handschuh MN114 MN116
Hanekamp MD163
Hang IN 37
Hanley IN 39 LA 19 MA 17
RI 12 RI 13 TX 39
Hanly IL259 IL261
Hannan IN 22
Hannemann MO126
Hanney MO 8
Hannibal MN 29
Hanover PA125 PA847
Hansen CA338 MT 12 OH207
Hanson IL103 WI283 WI375
Hantzsch WI 91
Hanzal WI 5
Hapsburg IL133
Harberdier OH296
Harby MT 3
Hard Rock NY295
Hardcastle UT 35
Hardinghaus MI 20 NY289
Hare OH 62 PA450 PA451
Hargelsheimer IA135
Hargrave CT 21
Hargraves NY293
Harinz NE 22
Harke IL 43
Harkins NY 97
Harland MI179
Harman OH 41
Harmony PA 20
Harney OR 17
Harold CA309
Harp PA337
Harper CA 75
Harpers Ferry WV 13
Harpstrite IL204
Harries OH172
Harris NH 7 NY 98 OH 63
WY 12
Harrisburg PA198
Harrison NJ 79 PA325
Harryhousen CA211
Harstoff WI 87
Hart MA 61 WY 12
Hartdorn NJ 74
Harter MI215
Hartford CT 16 CT 21
WI153
Harth NJ 75 NJ 76
Hartig WI453 WI504
Harting IN 66
Hartka PA 95
Hartman AZ 51 CA 93
CA284 CA454 KS 7 MO 72
NY515
Hartmann CA373 CT 8
DE 2 IL 11 IL213 MN139
MO193 NE 37 NJ 77 NY662
OR 59 WI489
Hartmetz IN 29 KY 24
Hartung MD127 MA217
MO 17 PA216 PA800
Hartwig WI 90
Harvard MA 67 MA 88
Harvey CA446 ID 33 OH226
Harz WI491
Haser IL234 PA 88
Hashimoto CA444
Haskins NY 65
Haslinger WI155
Hasse MN 54
Hasslinger WI115
Haster NJ 78
Hastings MN 59 NE 20
Hastreiter NY309
Hatfield PA714
Hathaway NY585
Hau PA 80
Haubert IA152
Haubrich CO 5 ID 70
Hauch AZ 38 NY292 PA659
WA112
Hauck MI 75 MT 51 NJ 79
OH 64 OH313
Hauenstein MN124 NJ 21
NJ150
Hauer WI256
Haug ID 40 MI204
Kaungs KY 25
Hausberg IL 19
Hauschild MO 92
Hauselt CA404
Hauser CA156 CA199 CA383
MD141 OH 80 PA229 PA389
PA452 WI105 WI488
Hausman KS 38 PA236
Hausmann IL294 IA202
WI241 WI242 WI371
Hauswald NM 18
Havana NY136
Haven VA 5
Havre MT 33
Hawaii HI 3 HI 4
Hawkes NY318
Hawkeye IA 27
Hawkins NY415
Haxel MO 93
Hay MO127 WI169
Hayashi CA374
Hayden WI 73
Hayek NE 57
Hayenah CA182
Hayer IL305

Hayes AZ 15 ID 75 MI 45 MT 48
Hayes Valley CA365
Hazelwood PA660
Hazen MO182
Hazheim WI489
Hazleton PA206 PA207
Head IA 5 NV 57
Healey MA 50
Healt MA 70
Health CT 28 PA718
Healy IL104
Heath ID 45
Hebe RI 10
Hebel IL320
Hebrank KS 17 WV 16 WV 19 WV 22
Hechelmann PA661
Hecht MD 18 NY 99
Heck MD138 WI419 WI420
Hecker OH173 WA108
Heddendorf NY309
Heckmann SD 12
Hedrick MA 88 NJ 27 NY 16
Hedwig IL221
Heeley OR 37
Hefft PA294
Heft WA 20
Hefty WI356 WI370
Heger WI186
Hegner AK 2
Hehner MO131 MO178
Heiberg IA240
Heibrau MD112
Heid WI 9
Heidbreder MO 94
Heidel Brau WI458
Heidelberg KY 8 PA 719 WA 89
Heidelbrau WI215
Heil IA 32 MN 71 MO 28
Heiland MN 71
Heileman AZ 23 FL 1 GA 10 IL 12 IN 33 KY 53 MD 9 MD 29 MI138 MN175 OR 81 TX 76 WA 71 WA 89 WI215 WI514
Heiligenstein IL273
Heilman PA154
Heim CA157 IL214 MO 41 MO 47 MO 60 OH312
Heim-Brau WI356
Heime UT 27
Heimel MD156 MD157
Heimenz MO131
Heimgaertner PA547
Hein SD 13
Heinbockel MT 29
Heindel NY416
Heindl NY428
Heine IA 2
Heinerath CA188
Heinickel NJ 80
Heinike IA 61
Heinold NY184
Heinrich MN102
Heins NY417
Heintz CA235 PA720
Heinze CO 38 IN154
Heippele NE 55
Heirboldscheimer MI180
Heisel NE 45
Heiselmann NY227 NY294
Heiser NY185
Heising MN140
Heist MD156 MD157
Heitcamp MO180
Heitz MO128 NY663
Heitzmann NJ108
Helb PA863
Helberg WI398
Helbert PA 87
Held MI 33 MT 45
Helena MT 37
Helf WI193 WI194
Hell Gate NY386
Hellburg WI335
Helldorfer MD 12
Hellenschmidt WI173
Heller MN185
Hellinger MT 12
Hellmann CT 62
Hellmick NY280
Helm MO197 NJ 81
Helmke CA223
Helmle IL354
Helms IL356
Helmuth ID 73
Helwig OH238
Hemming WI177
Hemmisch MN 95
Hempfling IA 20
Hemrich IA153 MT 29 WA 57 WA 60 WA 65 WI 4
Henall OR 70
Henchel WI115
Henckel MD167
Henco WA 78
Hendel ID 36
Henderson KY 13
Hendricks ID 23 PA186
Hendrickson CA 74
Henes MI215 MI217
Hengeler NE 7
Henius MN154
Henke CA 89 CA223
Henkel OH200 WI421
Henn IL105
Henne OH310
Hennepin MN103
Henning IL277 MI 45 PA185
Henninger MO 9 WI259
Henry IL 91 IL163 MI133 NY344 NY724 PA729 WI438
Hensel PA292
Henser MI 76
Hensler CA302 CA358 NJ 83 NJ 89
Hentschel MI 40
Hentschell MI169
Henze MI171
Henzler PA453 PA454
Hepburn ID 15
Hephen WI486
Herancourt OH 65 OH 66 OH158
Herb OH239
Herber IL275
Herberger MN156
Herbert IN 80 IN 82 NY331 NY642
Herbig IA206
Herbold IL320
Herboldsheimer KS 43
Herbolsheimer OH246
Herder MI122 NY706
Herdt PA662
Herl MO 27 MO 29
Herley WI120
Herman CA375 CO 98 IA 51 NY233
Hermann ID 60 ID 61 IL273 IL356 IA 16 MN189 MO 31 OH 32 TX 49 WI 44
Hermsen WA 91
Hermuesch MN 95
Hernig PA552
Herold CA 92 CT 17 MO129
Herrall OR 80
Herrberg IN 61
Herrman RI 11
Herrmann IL356 NY100 OH 9 OH 17 PA455
Herrn IA 64
Herschel TN 28
Herschfeld MO130
Herschle CA120
Hert PA 80
Hertel NY418
Herter PA404
Herterich NY537
Hertlein MD 49
Hertrich IL224
Hertwig IN147
Hertz MN 19
Herzinger WI534
Herzog KY 6 KY 7 MD 42
Hess CA 57 CA319 KS 9 MN 95 PA414 PA487 PA508 PA516 PA584 PA598 PA614 WA 20 WI235 WI307 WI395
Hessemer IL 54
Hessell MI271
Hessner CO 42
Hetherington PA311
Hetiman NV 19
Hettinger WI402
Hetzel NJ 26 NJ142
Heubach PA237
Heubisch MI139
Hermann NY328
Heurich DC 17
Heuser MI204 MI228
Hevenin ID 17
Hewel PA809 PA810
Hewlitt MA 74
Hey IN 46
Heyer CA109 CA144
Heyson WI 92
Heywood IL 15
Hialeah FL 2
Hiawatha MN 99
Hibernia CA343
Hickey WI438
Hickory MO112 WI511

Hicks NY271
Hieber WA 79
Hiemenz NY186
Hieronimus CA209 CA216
Hierp IA 78
Higgins NY576
High Ground NY166
Highhouse PA817
Highland IL247 MA 35
MA 82 MT 48 NY341
Highlander WA 71
Hilbert CA266 NY304
PA134
Hilbig MI250 WY 13
Hildebrandt CA318
Hildenbrand PA624
Hilderbrand PA372
Hilger MN 94
Hilgers MN 70
Hilknie PA289
Hill CO 17 MI155 NJ 63
NJ 66 NJ142 PA465 PA587
RI 2
Hill Top MI174 PA335
Hillberg IA 51
Hiller IL 56 IN156 NY625
Hills WI156
Hillsboro WI160
Hillside IL254 PA353
Hillyer MO 14
Hilo HI 1
Hilt MN 24 MN 95
Hilz WI195
Himelien NY229
Himelspach KS 51
Himminghofer CA195
Himmler MD126 MD128
MD133
Hinchcliffe NJ127
Hinckel NY 28 NY522
Hind NY709
Hinde CA 8
Hinds NY538
Hiner MO 68
Hines MA 91
Hinger WA109
Hinkey NV 55
Hippe PA285
Hippely PA658
Hippler CO121
Hirsch NY233 OH 8
Hirschberg NJ 45
Hirschle CA 6
Hirt CO 83
Hittleman NY109 NY719
Hitz IL106
Hitzelberger IN 67
Hitzrodt MD 43
Hladovec IL107
Hlinak WI206
Hoag PA 4
Hoard NY531
Hobelmann MD 11
Hoboken NJ 32
Hoburg MD 44
Hobyberger PA456
Hoch IN 60 MI209 MI225
MI287 PA317 PA363 PA508
PA727 WI 64 WI285
Hochberger MO 65
Hochenluther OH 67
Hochgesang IN 76 OH209
Hochgreve WI145
Hochstein WI166
Hochstrasser IL265 NE 2
Hockenberger PA122
Hocking WI178
Hocking Valley OH248
Hodecker NY 42
Hodel MD129
Hodge CA 97 OH145
Hodges AZ 51
Hodskins MA 76
Hodson WI179
Hoedt IN 33
Hoefelin WI121
Hoeffling IL260
Hoefle CA388
Hoeflein ID 41
Hoefling PA663
Hoehl PA664
Hoehn MI 34
Hoelle PA 19
Hoelscher CA320
Hoelzle MO131 PA 68
PA271
Hoenervogt MD111
Hoenig PA804
Hoerber IL108 IL109
IL110 IL369
Hoering IL326
Hoerl NY 17
Hoevler PA654
Hof NY577
Hofbrau PA 2
Hofburg CA 22
Hofen MI167
Hofer PA802 WI216
Hoffbauer IA 21
Hoffbrau IN 40
Hoffer IA 48
Hofflein OH 68
Hofflin NY189
Hoffman CA138 CA212
CO 59 CO109 ID 68 IL246
IN 54 MD 45 MD 46 MD 47
MO 80 NV 3 NV 37 NJ 84
NY203 PA537 PA851 VA 25
WI 63 WI207
Hoffmann IA172 IA203
IA204 MD 48 MN 37 MN 58
MN141 MO 57 NY295 NY419
NY660 OH120 OH139
Hoffmeier CA206
Hoffmeister MO138
Hoffstaedter MI207
Hofmann IL 53 IL111
IL257 PA313 WI466
Hofreiter NY265
Hofstaetter MI141
Hofstetter WA 12
Hogl ID 30
Hogrefe CA 85
Hogue RI 1
Hoheisel WI536
Hohenadel PA457 PA458
PA591
Hohing MD164
Hohl CA 13 CA261 WI318
Hohlberg WA 15
Hohler PA119
Hohmann MN181 WI 13
Hoier WI164
Hokuf NE 57
Holderer CO 18
Holiday WI405
Holihan MA 64
Holl MN125
Holland MI164
Hollen RI 23
Hollencamp OH174 OH335
Holler IA 7 OH 69
Hollingworth IA 52
Hollister CA111
Holloway KY 13
Hollywood CA160
Holmes MI181 PA 26 RI 12
Holshuh TN 25
Holste NY391
Holtmann WA102
Holweck NY660
Holyoke MA 88
Holzappel OH326
Home CA158 CO 67 CT 8
IL 35 IL112 IL113 IL114
IL196 IN 68 LA 15 MD124
MI 98 MI272 MO 31 MO 35
MO 81 MO153 NJ 1 NJ 95
NJ130 OH 30 OH 78 OH104
OH250 OH288 OH304 PA 22
PA 47 PA778 TX 5 TX 86
VA 16 WV 12 WI308
Homestead PA215
Homig OH217
Honer MI 25 MI 53
Honig MD 76
Honolulu HI 5 HI 6
Hony IL232
Hoos IL296
Hoosick Falls NY282
Hoover OH 99
Hop Beer MA 69
Hope WI426
Hopedale PA146
Hopf PA659
Hopke CT 26
Hopkins AZ 51 WI309
Hoppe MO182 MT 15 ND 19
WI393 WI398
Horix OH 3
Horlacher PA 2
Horluck WA 58
Hormann MO 16
Horn AZ 41 OH342 WI384
Hornberger MI212
Hornell NJ145 NY285
Hornier CA321
Hornig CT 13
Horning IN 43 MN177
UT 21 WA 96
Hornung IN112 MN167
PA459
Horowitz NY495
Horrmann NY641 NY645
Horsfield NY420
Horsky MT 37
Horst IN 23

Hortman PA460
Horton NY416
Hortonville WI164
Hoscheid WA 20
Hosfield IA130
Hoskin CA213
Hosneder WA 37
Hosp ID 79
Hossle CO 95
Hoster OH152 OH153 OH158 OH159 OH161
Hottelmann WI246
Hottenstein PA 10
Hottos LA 8
Hotz IA140 IA216 NJ 75
Houghton MA 18 MA 19
House IL334 NY578 NY579 NY662 PA 43
House of Augsberg IL107 WI405
Houston PA398 TX 46
Houthmaker WI221
Howard NY 18 NY 88 NY434 PA149 PA461 WA 88
Howarth ID 50 PA700
Howell PA702
Hower NY 70 NY101 NY102 NY648
Hoyer PA720
Hoyt CO 39
Hub MA 20
Hubach IN 44 OH298
Hubel OR 59
Hubelheimer OH 17
Huber ID 42 IL242 IL312 IL345 IN 14 IA 27 KY 26 KY 40 MO 85 MO133 MT 20 NE 12 NY109 NY584 WA107 WI 66 WI356
Hubert TX 32
Hubinger MI251
Hubler CA 10 CA159
Hubner MN 48
Huck CA 77 IL115 IL261 PA773
Huckenstein PA665
Huckle CA385
Hudepohl OH 51 OH 73
Hudson NJ 33 NJ 41 NY242 NY286
Huebner IL245 MD 49 OH301 OH303 OH307 WI 95 WI520
Huels WI168
Huelsman CA235
Huemmer NJ 75
Huerstel LA 5
Hufeisen WA 96
Huff WY 1
Huffner OH272
Hufnagel PA352
Hug MN116 OH247
Hughes NY103 OH121 OH135 OR 24 PA168 PA692 PA697 PA700 WI199
Hugn WI 13
Hulery OR 38
Hulka MO 71
Hull CT 33 CT 34
Hult ND 7
Humbel OR 70
Humboldt CA 74 CA341 NV 44
Hummel IL 51
Hump ID 38
Hundhausen TN 14
Hunt ID 86 MA 21 OR 24
Hunter's IL 65 IL135 IL159
Huntingburg IN 56 IN 57
Huntington IN 60 WV 15
Huntley IL248
Huober WY 14
Hupfel NY408 NY465
Huppeler ND 19
Huppler WI358 WI361
Hurley WI171
Huron MI269 SD 14
Hurst MA 52
Hurstfield NY684
Hurt MO 42
Huscher WI115
Husmann MN185
Huss NY335 OH233
Hussa WI 24
Husting WI 92 WI310 WI368 WI411
Huth WA 92 WA103
Huthsteiner IN141
Hutter WI160
Hutzler TX 74
Hux MI130 MI136
Huxbold MN 7
Huxhold IA223
Hybschman NV 14
Hyde NY580
Hyde Park MO147 PA219
Hydraulic NY187 OH175
Hygeia NJ120
I.J. Enterprises MN108
Ibach MN 86
Ibert NY 82 NY104
Icke NJ149
Idaho ID 7 ID 11 ID 31 ID 41 ID 44 ID 62
Idaho Falls ID 46 ID 47
Ideal MO135
Idlewild PA 44 PA279
Igarashi CA139
Iida CA380
Ijoni NY630
Ilawley NV 15
Iler MO 43 NE 32
Ilg OH284
Illenberger WI473
Illig NY105 NY106
Illing WI186
Illinois IL116 IL308 IL360 NM 19
Imberg OH122
Imbery IN148
Imhoff WI159
Imkamp ID 71
Immen NY107
Imperial CA158 CA260 IL132 MD 88 MD112 MI124 MI153 MN100 MO 45 OH314 PA156 PA789
Independent CA225 IL117 IL211 IL241 IA 66 KY 53 MD 19 MI 77 MO105 MO109 MO118 MO131 MO149 MO153 MO182 NY 45 NY 47 NY616 PA 24 PA 47 PA 59 PA 69 PA 86 PA215 PA268 PA304 PA322 PA323 PA335 PA346 PA363 PA637 PA648 PA672 WA 59 WA 93 WA131 WI311 WI458
Indeweiss CA 52
India Wharf NY108
Indian PA220
Indiana IN 70 IN 99 IN112 PA220
Indianapolis IN 69 IN 70 IN 73
Ingermann IN 12
Ingham PA848
Inland WA 79
Innis PA462 PA463
Interboro NY 72 NY 85
Intercoast PA760
International FL 16 KY 5 MI138 NY192 NY201 NY206 OH195 PA443
Inter-State IA217 WA104
Ionia MI170
Iowa IA 28 IA 98 IA142 IA177
Irmer IA110
Iron City PA273 PA654
Iron Mountain MI171 MO119
Iron Range MN194
Ironwood MI172
Iroquois NY173 NY201 NY216 NY244 OH156 OH305
Irr NY722
Irvin IL172
Isengart NY685
Island City WI265
Islaub MO 82
Ittis MN 21
Iwan NV 42
Jackeis WI 64
Jackson AZ 33 CA124 CA314 KY 45 LA 16 MI173 MI197 MO102 NY724 OH 70
Jacksonville FL 5
Jacob IA168 IA199 MO147
Jacobi OH305 PA154 PA155 PA464
Jacobs IA 1 PA 30 WA100
Jacobson CA 62 PA344
Jacoby AZ 33
Jacquillard NJ 89
Jaeckel PA465 WI430
Jaeger IN 73 IA 19 IA106 KY 51 MO112 MO133 PA521 PA728
Jaehnig WI101
Jaensch NE 54
Jaissle OR 40
Jakobi MT 36
Jamaica PA714
Jameson CO116
Jamestown NY290 ND 13

Jammerthal OR 46
Janak TX 29
Jans PA466
Jansa NE 54
Jansen IA 54 WI525
Janesville WI181
Japan CA 23 CA 69 CA322
Jarger NY338
Jarvis MN 37
Jax FL 5
Jeannette PA226
Jefferson KY 27 MI 58
MO124 MO134 MO144 WV 13
WI184 WI187 WI189
Jehle IL 2
Jenkins ID 59 NC 4
Jenner PA 44
Jensen AZ 30 WA 7
Jentes SD 15
Jentsch WI210
Jersey NJ 53
Jerusalem IL118
Jersy PA186
Jesse CO 74
Jessup NY421
Jester IL133 MO 83
Jetter NE 6 NE 39 NY346
Jeudy MD 4
Joast CA396
Jochimsen NV 34
Jockers KS 13
Joerger AZ 4 NY109
Joh MD 50 MD 79
John NJ143
Johnson CA 73 CO 31
IL 26 MD 11 MA 40 MA 80
MI 78 MI224 MN 34 MT 31
NE 53 NY110 NY111 PA137
PA347 WI230
Johnston MI229
Joliet IL251 IL252
Jolling WI231
Jonas CA 1
Jones MA 40 NH 3 NH 10
NY144 NY259 NY345 NY422
PA467 PA784
Jonte OH 71
Joos CA406
Joplin MO35
Jordan CA135 MI 28 MN 70
MN 71 PA 90
Jost NY188
Joyce NY697
Jubitz OR 69
Judd PA137
Judwitsch MN 47
Juenemann DC 6
Jugenheimer IA231
Jugenhutt TX 21
Juliaetta ID 50
Jumbo NJ 76
Juneau AK 23
Jung IA 80 KY 3 TX 4
WI300 WI329 WI340 WI428
Jungens CA365
Jungk IA131
Junk IL119
Junker CA452 IN156
Junkert CA405
Jurgen ID 31
Jurgens NV 55
Justin WI529
K.C. WA 79
Kabis WY 7
Kacher OH207
Kadish NE 56
Kaehler WI385
Kaelin CA223
Kagebein IL223
Kaier PA293
Kaiser CA 11 IL319 LA 18
MI 3 MI 12 MI 75 MN 70
MN121 OH267 WI361
Kaisha HI 2
Kalamazoo MI182 MI183
MI184 MI189
Kalb MD 51 PA797
Kalberer ND 4
Kalispell MT 40
Kalmbach MA 82
Kaltenbach NY189
Kaltenborn KS 33
Kaltenhaeuser PA666
Kaltenmeir NY619 NY635
NY643
Kalvelage PA156 PA161
Kambich ID 29
Kamenk NJ 21
Kamm IN103 OH204
Kammerer CA 54 IA 30
Kampf IA 11
Kanawha WV 3
Kanda HI 7
Kane NY691 WI 83
Kankakee IL259
Kansas City MO 44 MO 45
MO 47
Kantenberger MI145
Kantz IA 22
Kanzig OH105
Kapizky OH 16
Kapp PA468 WY 5
Kappes WI216
Kappler CA 70 MI 46
Karasinski NY581
Karcher MN 22
Kargleder WI318
Karlson MN101
Karn NY176
Karsch NY233
Karst OH186
Kasche CA368
Kase NY614
Kasper PA446 PA470
Kassens IL120
Kast WY 9
Kastner MI142 NJ 85
Katlein OH 10
Katler WI122
Kattine OH 10
Katz IL 88 NJ125 NY 93
PA848
Kauffman IL335 OH 53
Kauffmann PA425
Kaufman MN 92 SC 6
TN 9 WA 87 WI541
Kaufmann IN135 IN150
Kaupp MI159
Kawaguchi CA380
Kayser OH212 PA382
Kazmaier PA105
Keany NY110
Kear PA319
Kearney NY664 PA758
Keck IL204
Keefer ID 45
Keeley IL 46 NJ 59 PA706
Keenan NY113
Kegel PA244
Kegley CA401
Kehbein WI285
Kehoe PA178
Kehrer NY234 NY306
Kehrhoffer MN 58 MN 59
Keiff IL299
Keil OH331
Keiley RI 13
Keilhofer CO103
Keilman PA704
Keine IA 98
Keinzle MD 18
Keiser WI237
Keisler UT 11
Kellar MI 88 WI474
Keller CA 36 CA384 CO 8
IL121 IL270 IL349 MD 52
MN168 OH245 PA145 PA471
PA721 PA808 SD 25 WI207
Kellermann PA479
Kelley MI245 NY616
Kellogg NY709
Kelly NJ125 NY438 PA755
Kemler WI398
Kemmeter WI188
Kemp NJ144
Kempel OH 3
Kemper MD 81 MD108
Kempf IA 92 PA229
Kempker IA246
Kenilworth DC 7
Kennedy IA160 NY283
PA439
Kenney MA 22 MA 23 MA 24
MA 25 NY684 WV 28
Kenosha WI203
Kensington PA547
Kent MA 79 RI 26
Kenton OH214
Kentucky KY 28
Keokuk IA152
Keoline WI366
Keppeler NY241
Keppler PA472
Keppley PA473
Kerber IL122
Kerchmer CO123
Kerchner CO123
Kern CA 16 ID 30 MI243
OH171 OR 30 PA 4 WA 25
Kerner PA474
Kernwein DC 8
Kerr MD 11 NY423 PA475
Kersenbrock NE 7 NE 8
Kersten SC 1 VA 13
Kerth CA267 NV 37
Kertzinger MO136

Kessler MT 34 NV 56 PA216
Ketcham IA197
Ketterer MO 95
Kewanee IL262
Kewaunee WI205
Key City IA 93
Keym CA392
Keys OH126
Keyser UT 30
Keystone PA149 PA194 PA393 PA640 PA667 PA720 PA760 PA863
Kickenbaugh OH259
Kiefer ID 45 NY112 OH267 OR 3
Kieffer CA406 PA251 TX 12
Kiel WI145
Kielhofer CA426
Kielmeyer IA141
Kiene MN 35
Kienlen OR 32
Kiernan MA 44 NY296
Kiesche UT 11
Kieseler NV 7
Kiewel MN 26 MN 47 MN 78
Kihm KS 28
Kiley IN 99
Kilkenny NY 61
Kille NY266 NY528
Killinger PA 88
Kim PA219
Kimball ME 1
Kimm WY 7
Kimmel PA 18
Kimmick MN190
Kinast MI183
Kindler IA 79
Kindsvater OH123
King IL275 IL343 MA 14 MO106 MT 37 PA149 PA150 PA702 TN 3
King Cole IL187
King Philip MA 53
Kinghorn NY224 WV 25 WV 26
Kings IL133 NY102 OH111
Kings County NY114
Kings Tavern MI136
Kingsbury IA217 KY 53 WI215 WI246 WI458
Kingsley PA733
Kingston NY295
Kinsinger OH 72
Kinsley IA 79 NY259
Kinzel IL274
Kip NY424
Kipp CT 62
Kips Bay NY486
Kirby CA323 CA339 CO 6
Kirchgessner IN 77 KY 23
Kirchmer CO125
Kirchner CT 56 NV 32 NM 17 NY 19 NY686
Kirk NY 20 NY226 NY438
Kirker AZ 45
Kirmeyer KS 26
Kirsch WI 10
Kirst NY601 PA344
Kissel NY115
Kistner OH 89
Kitsap WA 47
Kittinger KY 45
Kittiwell IN146
Kitzinger IL320
Kiushel TX 41
Kladen WI258
Klady NY561
Klaiber IN 83 OH275
Klaibert OH275
Klamath Falls OR 42
Klant IN 53 IN149
Klas OH337
Klasi NY653
Klauder KY 13
Klaus CT 8 NV 45 OR 44
Klausmann IL200
Klear CO117
Kleber WA109
Klecker WI402
Kleffner OH272
Klein CA389 IN 93 IA 75 IA244 MO 5 NV 10 NV 28 NV 34 NJ115 NY116 NY566 OH292 OH336 PA446 VA 2 WI 48 WI483
Kleine MO 27
Kleiner CA125 IL370 MI282 NM 3 NM 10 OH 70
Kleinclaus CA310
Kleinlein IA 38 IA224
Kleinmann MN 66
Kleinschroth NY425
Klemmert PA 15
Klempp CA454
Klenk MN 15 PA477 WI207
Klenzing PA 81
Kler CO124
Klessig WI101
Kley IN 45
Klier MI272
Klinckhammer OH 80
Klindt IA 70
Kline WI195
Kling CA 91 MI 79 MI134 OR 51 PA142
Klinger OR 92 WI115 WI285 WI452
Klinick WI493
Klink NY241
Klinkers MN 6
Klinkert ND 9 WI420 WI481 WI482
Klipsmeyer WI533
Klockgeter IL123
Kolgner WI 1
Kloidt PA105
Klondike AK 5
Klopfenstein OH 31 OH296
Klopfer PA478
Kloster NY156
Klotter OH 72 OH 89
Klueg NY114
Kluetsch IL292
Klug ID 18 WI137
Klumpp PA479
Knab WI340
Knam OH 6
Knapp PA252 PA253
Knapstein MI 33 WI373
Knauer CA268 ID 43
Knaus PA 77
Knauss PA 10
Knaust MI139
Knecht KS 1 MD 55 OH 39 WI379
Kneipp IL277
Knell IL 8
Knepper IA 67 IA173 IA232
Knibe PA157
Knickerbocker NY487
Knight AZ 14 IL124 NY271
Knipers KY 29
Knipp IN 60 WI181
Knippenberg WI312
Knips MN191
Knipschild IL223
Knipschilt WI356
Knivel MI123
Knoblauch MI 28 WI312
Knobloch MN132 OH 32 PA148
Knoedler CT 5
Knoke WV 27
Knoll CA119
Knopf OH223
Knorr MD172
Knott OH337 SD 20 TX 54
Knox OH213
Knoxville TN 5
Knust NV 35
Kobes NE 8 NE 57
Koch CA160 CA220 CO 92 IL125 IL125 IL132 MI 80 MI 81 MI200 MI282 MN165 MN171 MO137 NV 24 NJ 61 NY244 NY426 OH318 PA 21 PA343 PA812 PA852
Kocher ND 15
Kodedek MN121
Koebel IL 26
Koeding WI155
Koegel OH 49
Koehler ID 61 ID 62 IL204 IL273 IN 66 IA 67 IA122 MO131 NJ 21 NY427 OH 73 OH308 PA149 PA156 PA158 PA249 TX 93 WA 82
Koehm CA392
Koehn CA393
Koehne NY388
Koehnle PA480
Koellner WI126
Koenecke IL 18
Koenemann CO 71
Koenig CO 70 IL133 NM 2 NY 45 NY428 PA 5 PA198 PA300 PA670
Koeniger ID 53
Koeninger ID 20
Koenneker AL 3
Koepl WI461
Koerber OH304
Koering IA129

Koerner IL 6 IL328 MO 84
Koestle OH124
Koethe WI326
Koevenig IA 47 IA208
Kohl IA 94 MI 45 MI225 NJ 43 WI313
Kohlepp ID 34
Kohler MI 28 PA 61
Kohles MD 53 MD 54
Kohlkase TN 5
Kohn TN 2 WI217
Kohnle PA543
Kohny ID 74
Kokes MN 62 MN120
Kokusui HI 2
Kol CO109 FL 16 IL133 MO 74
Kolb MD130 MI 27 NJ 86 NJ 87 NY117 NY253 NY429
Kolberg MD116
Kolbs MI 22
Kole WI224
Kolkschneider MO168
Koll IA116
Koller IL127 WA 39
Kollmer IL309
Kolter OH318
Kondolff NY582
Kongress WY 12
Koniger ID 53
Konrad WI535
Kopf NJ 13
Kopp ID 20 OH234 OR 6 PA590 WA 60 WA 94 WI 41
Koppitz MI 82
Korb WI314
Kording MI281
Korn IN 23 IN156
Kornburger WI315 WI453
Korner NY644
Korzenborn OH250
Koschel MN 71
Koschitz WI117 WI119
Kossuth CT 29
Kost PA108 PA238
Kostenbader PA 78
Koster CA324
Kothe IN 30
Kotter CA121
Kowitz MN 18 MN 25
Kozel DC 10 DC 11 WI432
Krack NJ 8 NJ106
Kraenzlein ND 9
Kraft MI116 MN201 NY723 OH 17 OH198 PA292
Krahenberg CA376 CA389
Kraijcek NE 1
Krall ID 11
Kramer IA202 MN 80 MN188 OH174 PA481 WI179
Kramm CA226 CA227 NY133
Kraner IA204
Krantz NY253 OH195 PA783 PA800
Kranz PA216
Kranzlein MN102
Krasman NY643
Kratockvil MI276

Kratz OR 70
Kratzer IN 78
Kraus CA 11 NY105 OH143 PA155 PA482 PA483 PA484 PA712
Krause DE 3 MI 20 OH206 PA485 TX 83 WA 9 WI155
Krauss CA251
Krausse WI 62
Krauth WI438
Krautter PA414 PA584
Krebs MD 56 PA808
Krein PA555
Kreiner WI511
Kreis GA 3 PA143
Kreisch TX 51
Kreiss CA256 CA257
Kreiter MI163
Krekel WA109
Krell PA206
Krembz WI106
Kremer ID 45 NJ 21
Kremkow CA 20
Kress NY 58 NY346 OH125 PA109 PA237 WV 28
Kreter IA181
Kretz PA705
Kreutzer PA 78 WI523
Kreuzner AK 9
Kreuztscher OR 88
Krick MO 15
Krieg IL358
Krieger MI195
Krill WA340
Krinkle NV 57
Krochling MO108
Kroedel IN 54
Kroeger CA418
Kroener IN 31
Kroenke CA317 CA346 WI 64
Kroesing WI258
Kroetz OR 70
Kroger MT 6 MT 50 OH275
Kroll MI269
Kronenberg CA366
Kroner IN 31
Kronschnabl WI 13
Kroos WI465
Kropf OH 32 OH210 OH253 OH265 OH278
Kropp MO 31
Krother IL 28
Krotter IL264
Krouse MD 11
Krueger DE 4 NJ 66 RI 14 WA 12 WV 14
Krug IL214 MO182 MT 12 NE 40 NY645 WI316
Kruger NE 51 WI118
Krulish WA 20
Krumb CA377
Krupp KY 30
Kruse CA121
Kuchler CA124
Kuchli WI483
Kuck MI200
Kuebeler OH281 OH283 PA382

Kuebler CA 57 PA136 PA852
Kuech MT 37
Kuechle MO 85
Kuehlthau WI525
Kuehn OH236
Kuehne KS 45
Kuenzel WI477
Kuenzl WI386
Kuepfert MO119
Kuester MO 94
Kuethe WI469
Kugel CA 55
Kuhl MI 83 OR 18 WA 51 WI465 WI474
Kuhlitz CA443
Kuhlmann NY249 NY715
Kuhn CA450 IL354 MD141 MN 95 MO130 MO133 NY190 NY290 PA569 TN 28 WI264
Kuhry WI134 WI480
Kulhanek WI494
Kump MO 46 MO 47
Kumpf PA552
Kunkler IN 37 IN154
Kunster NJ137
Kuntz MO138 MO139 NY430
Kunz KS 29 MO206 TN 3 WI 44 WI216 WI245 WI246 WI252
Kupfer NJ 91
Kurley OH188
Kurt ID 45
Kurth IL128 NE 51 WI 74
Kurtz IA103 MI 96 PA 82 PA861
Kurz IA154 WI264
Kurzenberger NJ 88
Kuser NJ145
Kusterer MI152
Kusting WI135
Kutruff PA100
Kutscher CT 6 CT 35 CT 36
Kypke WI508
La Crosse WI218 WI220 WI405
La Grande OR 43
Labadie NY 21
Labor PA 38 PA818
Lace PA729
Lachner OR 10
Lachrman WI364
Lachs OR 10
Lackawanna PA759
Lackman OH 51
Laclede MO181
Ladenburger KY 44
Laderer NJ 74
Ladner PA605
Laekauf MD 57 MD 58
Lafayette CA317 IN 82 LA 1 MO139 NY703 OH 47
Lafrantz CA325
Lage IA 70
Lagerhausen CO121
Lahey NM 7
Laible NJ 16 NJ 66
Laier MT 45

Lail NM 2
Lais OH261
Laitenberger TN 26
Lake AZ 48 WI330 WI332
WI342 WI343 WI381
Lake Shore WI418
Lake Side WI403
Lake View NY202
Lakeside MI242 MN129
Lakeview IL123 OR 46
Lambert NE 55 PA109
PA237
Lambrecht OR 61
Lamm IL129 NE 49
Lammel MN 52 MN129
Lampe IA246 WI159 WI361
Lancashire NC 5
Lancaster NY303 OH216
PA253 PA259
Land WI512
Landeck NY528
Lander WY 12
Landgraf WI 64
Landis PA245 PA294
Landkowski MN 15
Landregan CA229
Landsinger WI160
Landt MT 43
Landwehr WI147
Landzer NY139
Lang CA203 CA359 IN 60
IN 77 IA188 KY 8 MA 14
MT 27 MT 48 NY172 NY191
OH308 OH332 OR 61 PA668
WI263
Langan NV 48 NV 50 SD 13
SD 15
Langdon NY411
Lange IA 67 NE 16 OH242
OH268
Langen MN 73
Langenberg IL313 WI466
WI508
Langenbosch WI 18
Langendorf CO121 ID 82
WA 28
Langenkamp WI374 WI494
Langer WI205
Langlotz MD164
Langston MI 84
L'Anse MI192
Lansing MI193 MT 46
LaParle IL 46
Lapeer MI197
Laramie WY 13
Lareoda TX 75
Larer PA486
Largay CT 19 CT 62
Largilliere ID 89 WY 9
Larkin MN117
Larquier CA161
Larsen MN153
LaSalle IL208 IL266
Las Vegas NM 11
Lashbrook IA238
Lasse LA 17
Latrobe PA267
Laube PA750
Laubenstein WI152
Lauber PA487
Lauck CA 41 CA389
Lauckhardt PA488
Lauer IN 51 IA 54 MD 86
NY544 PA217 PA669 PA706
PA722 PA723 PA801 PA857
Lauffer KY 31
Laurel MO112
Laurent MN 57
Laurenzi CA128
Laurer NY 57 NY253
Lauritzen MN103
Lautenschlager NV 18
Lauterbeck WI466
Lauth CA162
Laux KY 32 MT 41
Lauzendoerfer MA 26
Law PA700
Lawrence KS 25 MA 63
NY431
Lawyer CO 82
Layer NJ138 PA522
Layman CA195
Leach NY283
Leadville CO 92 ID 53
Leavy NY110
Lebanon IL269 PA272
Leber TX 19
LeBeau MO140
Lechner NY 60
Lechsmger CO 57
Leder WV 13
Lederer IL163 IA155
NJ 22
Lee CA326 IL263
Leeds PA489
Leeland KS 30
Leetonia OH218
Leggett NY519
Legle PA641
Legler MN156 TN 10
Lehigh PA796
Lehmann CA126 CA246
CA316 IL 45 IL139 IA108
KY 45 MI 3 OH305 PA405
PA424 PA548 PA557
Lehmkuhl CO 10
Lehn NE 21
Lehner PA770
Lehr OH133
Lehrkind IA 68 IA 69
MT 12 MT 42 MT 54 MT 56
Lehrter OH275
Leibe CA389
Leiber CA163
Leibinger NY118
Leible WA 10
Leibold MD157
Leicht IL 40 NJ 49 NY341
NY465
Leidemann WI478
Leidich MD173
Leidiger WI276 WI479
Leigh PA490
Leighmann CA179
Leiling PA491
Leimbach PA199 PA364
PA492
Leinenkugel WI 67 WI 93
WI 94 WI448
Leininger NM 11
Leins MI 13
Leipoldt PA 97
Leisegger WI 22
Leisen MI215 MI217
Leiss MO178
Leister PA142
Leisy IL133 IL312 IA149
OH118
Lekner WI 61
Leman MN 23
Lembeck NJ 46
Lemmert CA164
Lemon WI321
Lemp ID 12 ID 90 IL211
MO182
Lenhard PA334
Lengel DE 4 PA622
Lenhardt MN 77
Lenk OH307
Lennon WI171
Lenz WI395 WI449
Leonard IN118 IA 24
MD 11 MD131 MT 46
Leonhard MI252 PA670
WI119
Leonhardt MI137
Leonhart PA114 PA824
Leonori MO162
Lepner WI100
Leppens NY583
Lepstein AZ 44
Leptein AZ 44
Le Roy KS 31
Leslin MN196
Lessmann CA112
Leubert PA275
Leuger NE 27
Leusler MO108
Leussler MO108
Leuthe WI207
Leuthner OH227
Levante AK 3
Leverens IL 88
Levi AK 30
Levin AZ 51
Levinger NY261
Lewis MI 13 MI136 WI114
WI435
Lewisburgh KY 8
Lewistown MT 41
Lexington KY 15 KY 17
MO 57 NJ103
Lexius OH105
Leybold MT 61
Liberty MD 59 MD124
MA 81 MI287 MO 94 NY517
PA671 PA697 PA796
Liche WI 89
Lucht NY324
Lichtenwalner PA 10
Lichter CO 92
Lickert PA100 PA792
Liddell PA692
Liden MN104
Lidenman MT 27

Liebenstein MI225 WI 28 WI124
Lieber CA185 IN 69
Lieberman PA 5 PA 8
Liebert PA493
Liebig MO 86
Liebmann CA338 NJ119 NY119 NY136 NY429
Liebner PA708
Liebscher WI115 WI289 WI317
Liehe WI 41
Liesiewski NJ 76
Light MI 39
Ligonier IN 90 PA279
Lill IL130
Lilly IA 41
Lima OH220
Limburger NY120
Linck CA180
Lincoln IL198
Lindemann WI478
Linden NY309
Lindenhurst NJ 55
Lindenmeyer AZ 49 CA384
Lindenschmitt MI263
Linder IL240
Lindlahr MT 40 MT 45
Lindner MI212 WI 54
Lindstrom CO 54
Lindvall IL281
Lingley ID 97
Link CT 18 CT 57 KS 28 MO121 WI134 WI378
Linke OR 40
Linker IN 46
Linnerman NY121
Linnett NJ134
Linnewerth NJ150
Linser OH340 OH343
Linstadt WI355
Lintz WA 28
Linxweiler NY307
Linze MO124
Lion CO 40 CT 49 MD 79 MI109 MO191 NY199 NY492 NY591 OH 95 OH123 PA206 PA245 PA257 PA661 PA849
Lipp IA220
Lipps MD140
Lips PA494
Lipsius IA232 NY 71
Lispenard NY432 NY503
Lissack WI 91
List WI398
Listlemann WI365
Listman NY584 OR 59
Litchfield MN 77
Lithuanian PA125
Litsch CA401
Littig AZ 33 IL344 IL345 IA 35 IA 70 MD 60
Littl WI466
Little MA 75
Little Falls MN 78
Little Rock AR 3 AR 4
Little Switzerland WV 15
Liverman MN 23
Livermore CA135
Lloyd OH126
Loacker WA 7
Loaker WA 10
Lobach WI439
Lochbaum CA327
Lochner OR 16
Lock City NY319
Locker OR 85
Lockman WI107
Lockport NY319 PA286
Lodel WI494
Loder PA105 PA807
Loeb WA 59
Loeble PA116
Loebs MO129 NY591
Loeffler WI519
Loehr CT 10 MD 61 NY376
Loehrer PA294 WI235
Loemer MO202
Loepel OH 39
Loerzel NY625
Loesch PA495
Loescher MI180 PA496 WI267 WI373 WI387
Loeser IL 11 KY 33
Loewer NY433
Lofthouse OH 42
Loftus PA783
Logan IA207 UT 9
Logansport IN 92
Lohmueller MO 92
Lombardi RI 24
Lommert NE 51
London CA 68
Lone Star OK 5 TX 76
Long NY 23 NY602 OH226 PA702 WI186
Long Island NY 80
Long Prairie MN 79
Longevine MT 28
Longmuir NY585
Longprey WY 9
Longuemare MO141
Loos MO142
Loose WI535
Lorain OH222
Lorenz MO 23 NJ 89 WI 87
Lorscheter WI 54
Los Angeles CA165 CA166
Losty NY221
Lott NY122
Loudenschlager IA156
Louisiana LA 14 LA 28
Louisville OH223
Loux WI224
Lowell MO162
Lowenstein MO 87
Lowertown IA 25
Loyalhanna PA268
Lubbermann PA535
Lubeck IL133 OH306
Lubken CA136
Lubkin CA237
Luby CT 25
Lucas MD 11 MD 65 NY 46 PA283
Luchsinger OR 3
Luckhardt NY345
Lucky CA 14 CA315 UT 25 WA104
Ludewig NY123
Ludwick IL131
Ludwig MD 58 MD 62 MD 63 MO 67 OR 70 PA 83 PA 84 WI149 WI160
Lueders MN202
Luenberger WI357
Luers IL221
Lufter WI494
Luhmann MN136
Luhn WI489
Luhr PA746
Luin WI376
Luippold CT 3 NY192
Luke AZ 26
Luksch NY328
Lund IA 40
Lundquist MN101
Lungstras IL293 MO125 MO143
Lurmann CA295
Lurz CA277 MD 57
Luscher KY 11
Luss CA242
Lusthoff WA 95
Luther IL329 PA202 PA284 PA798
Lutz CA359 CO120 IL 66 IN 42 MA 83 MI214 NJ 20 NY144 NY236 NY636 NY638 PA484 PA497 PA498 PA661 PA672 WI140 WI206 WI412 WI477
Lux CA297
Luxberger DC 4
Luzerne PA849
Lykens PA291
Lyman NY434 NY435 NY586 WI417
Lynch MO144 NH 3 NY587
Lynsky MA 47
Lynwood CA183
Lyon CA109 CA328 NJ 90 NY268 PA249
Lytle WI190
Maack DC 11 NY416
Maar IL301
Maas WI417
Maass PA499
Mabbett NY340
MacDonald IL134
Mach WI205
Machaltz AZ 2
Mack CO 3 CO 11 CO 41 CO 66 CO 90 CO 92 IL246 MO206 NE 7 OH127 TX 89 TX 90
Mackay MI 85
Macke KS 10 WI 46
MacKubbin MD 5
Macomber WY 1
Macon GA 8 MO 59
Mader IL132 OR 59
Maderer MO 23
Madison IN 95 WI239
Madlener WI302
Maehl CA330

Magee PA489
Magenan NE 15
Maggio CA 66
Magna Carta PA654
Magnolia AZ 55
Magnus IA261 IA 42
Mahl OR 84
Mahlstedt CA168
Mahoney CA443 WI466
Maiden MT 44
Maier CA168 CA123 OH272
PA191 PA255 PA500 PA516
WI318 WI332
Main St. WI293
Mair CO123
Makenthum IL347
Malcolm NY124
Malinowski PA847
Mall OH123
Mallinger WI403
Mallon ID 63 ID 92 NE 2
Mallows CA 66
Maloney MO 55
Malt CO 60
Malt Brew NY588
Malt Diastase NY 78
Malt Maid IL133
Malt Marrow IL123 IL133
Malt Sinew IL 71 IL193
Maltz OH 17
Manchester MI200
Mander NJ 81 NY254
Manegold WI318
Mang NY665
Manger OH 17 PA629
Manhattan IL133 NY416
NY476 WI536
Manila NH 14
Manilla NY242
Maning IA165
Manistee MI201
Manistique MI202
Manitowoc WI246 WI458
Mankato MN 70 MN 82
Manlick PA297
Mann CA248 MI 86 MI 87
NV 19 NY529 PA141 PA858
Mannell NY100
Manney KS 52
Mannheim MN132 MT 29
Manning MD 76
Mansfield NY436
Manske MN 94 WI319
Mantel NY659 NY666
Mantsch NY 10
Mantorville MN 91
Manuel ID 98
Manz PA501 WI504
Marathon WI253
Marbacker PA502
Marburger NY589
Marchant WI363 WI499
Marcum WY 12
Marganstern MD159
Margetts UT 28
Marhofer OH 74
Mariano NY324
Marieska MN 62
Marietta OH228
Marin MN 78
Marine City MI204
Marinette MI215
Marion IA174 NJ 50 OH229
Mark NY125
Marke IA210 PA770
Markel PA326 PA770
Markell MD141
Markert IL375
Markgraf IL 16 NY126
NY154
Markle PA 99
Marks CA331 CA332 MI208
PA 68
Marlin FL 9
Marquardt NY 87 NY448
Marr MD 16 MD 19
Marsch KS 5 KS 35
Marsden OR 50
Marsh MI 88
Marshall IA176 MI205
NJ150 NY 24 WI 71 WI536
Marshfield OR 50 WI255
Martens NY127 NY360
OH314
Marth MO 95
Martin AZ 51 CO 90 CO 96
CT 62 MD132 MI 16 MT 48
NH 8 NY128 NY590 OH 25
UT 35 VA 3 WA 78
Martischang IN129
Martz MD 64 MI 79 MI 89
Marvin AZ 54
Marx CT 55 MI 90 MI285
WI466
Mary WA 15
Maryland MD 9 MD 11
MD 12 MD 15 MD 16 MD 18
MD 22 MD 24 MD 50 MD 62
MD 69 MD 79 MD 99 MD101
MD105 MD108 MD111
Marysville MT 45
Mascoutah IL273
Maser IL233
Mason CA333 OH204 WI524
Mason City IA178
Masontown PA299
Massachusetts MA 3
MA 4 MA 13 MA 14 MA 15
MA 17 MA 24 MA 31 MA 37
MA 38
Massey PA398
Massilon OH234
Massolt MN105
Mast IL265
Mather NY220 NY707
Mathewson CT 58
Mathie CA157 WI520 WI521
Mathis IA 51
Matlock AK 23
Matson ME 3
Matsuo CA329
Matt CA394 NY264 NY696
Matter OR 65
Mattes IA 80 IA 81 NE 25
Matthern IA226
Matthew OH 75
Mattmann NY 41
Matz OH 14
Matzen CA 89
Mauch IA237
Mauch Chunk PA303
Mauer CA282 PA152 TX 37
Maui Sake HI 8
Maulbach CA 82
Maumee OH306
Maupai NY129
Maus IN 70 TN 28
Mauston WI256
Mauz WI236
Mawbray MI253
Maxheim IA 53
May IA 37 NM 18
Mayer CO 84 IL 16 IL 25
IN 50 IN150 MD147 MI213
NY453 NY602 NY618 OH209
OH279 OH310 PA516 TX 24
WI259 WI265 WI469 WI526
WI527
Mayetto UT 29
Mayfield CA186 UT 12
Mayhoffer CA 58
Mayor PA 16
Mayville WI259 WI260
Maywood NJ 58
Mayworth MI161
Mazomanie WI263
McAleenan CA 77
McArthur PA620
McAlpin CA 32
McAvin NE 12
McAvoy IL 42 IL360
McCaffrey PA594
McCann CT 21
McCarthy UT 17
McCausland MD 65
McClane MT 46
McCord NY546
McCormick MA 27
McCoy PA714
McCulloch NY 5
McDermott IL135
McDevitt IA178
McDonald IL172 MA 85
McDowell AZ 5
McEniry NY231
McFadden NJ132
McGee IL224
McGeehan WI171
McGettigan CA433
McGinty PA796
McGlinchy ME 4 MA 28
McGlynn ID 50
McGoldrich NY116
McGonagle CA102
McGovern MO 61 MO 67
McGowan NY540 NY543
McGrath MI 91 NY679
McGraw WA 40
McGregor OR 58
McHenry IL275
McHose PA 6
McInhill IL 9
McKay PA692
McKechnie NY223
McKee CA154
McKeesport PA305
McKenzie CA 32

McKernan MI192
McKnight NY 22 NY437 NY438
McLain OH234
McLaughlin ME 5 NY 23
McLean PA403
McMahon NY723
McNair PA159
McNally PA792
McNamara MA 92 NY 23
McNirney MA 88
McNulty MD168
McPherson NY487
McQuade NY 20 NY 30 NY699 PA760
McVey CA 33
Mead MN111
Meadowbrook PA761
Meadville PA312
Mears NJ 34
Mechler WI429
Meckel CA218 CA447
Meckert NJ 23
Medford OR 53 WI264
Medina NY328
Medler AZ 15 IL287
Medlin OH106 OH128 OH129
Medoed MN 78
Medtart MD 66 MD 92 MD101
Meeke WI406
Meeske MI209 MI224 MI225 WI285
Mehalsky WI475
Mehels WI 69
Mehl OR 13 OR 58
Mehlhorn WA 55
Mehlhose MI284
Mehrer CA334
Meier CA 98 IN162 PA239
Meierdierck NJ 24
Mein PA718
Meindl WI466
Meiner MN 79
Meingassner ID 51
Meinhofel IA235
Meisler MI192
Meister KY 1 PA302 WI320
Meisterbrau CA295 IL102 LA 16 OH305
Meixner WI321
Melander MN142
Melchers MI 82
Melchior WI496
Meller IL234 IL235
Mellett PA706
Melley PA 22
Mellow WI194
Melms WI332
Melrose MN 95 NY358
Melsheimer CO 41
Meltzer NY131
Melyn NY439
Melzer OR 25
Memphis TN 11 TN 12 TN 13
Menars MN120
Menasha WI267
Menass MN 62
Mendelsohn NY552
Mendenhall CA395
Mendes NV 20
Mendota IL277
Mengay OH223
Menge MO 69 NJ 19
Mengel IA 70
Menger TX 77
Mengert WA 10
Menges WI410
Meninger NY130
Menk CA427 KY 17
Menke CA181 CA277
Menken NY646
Mennel NJ122 NJ128
Menominee MI215 MI216
Menomonee WI287 WI332 WI341
Mentges NY440
Mentzel CT 8
Mercer MD165 PA171
Mergener WI 13
Meriden CT 23 CT 24
Merkel NY419
Merkle OH344
Merrifield CA335
Mersenhetter IN126
Mertes WI 87
Mertins MO 66
Merz CO111 LA 12 LA 18 MN155 WI267
Mesch CO 74
Mescher IA194
Mesenbrink MN 71
Mesha WI267
Mesier NY441
Mesmer IA 26
Mesow WI322
Messing WI412
Messner NY721
Metcalf OH 96
Metcalfe MO145
Metropolis FL 10 NJ145 NY285 NY427
Metropolitan IL136 NY112
Mette IL137
Metz CO109 IL 20 IL138 NE 35 NE 37 NY244 OH175 TN 27
Metzer WI154
Metzger CA396 IL232 IN 71 IA 26 NV 54 NY649 NY703 PA167
Metzler CA336 IN131
Metzner KY 14 NJ 12
Meuser IA 98
Meussner PA655
Mexicali CA 37
Mexime WI363
Meydenbaur ID 39
Meyer CA 41 CA 66 CA127 CA136 CA186 CA237 CA365 CO125 IL 16 IL222 IL259 IN115 IA126 IA182 IA227 KS 34 KY 4 KY 5 KY 12 KY 50 NY334 NY546 OH254 OR 7 OR 89 OR 90 SD 17 WA110 WI158 WI362 WI438
Meyer cont. WI512
Meyers NY591 NY597 NY630 WI 12 WY 13
Meyersdale PA315
Meyn CA454
Mezger NV 16 NV 51
Miami FL 2 FL 7 OH175
Miamisburg OH236
Michael MD 7
Michaels MD 10
Michaelson WA 11
Michalski WI473
Michel IA 12 IA127 NY132 PA809 WI218
Michelie CA239
Michels WI 94 WI360
Michenfelder MI 92
Michigan MI 16 MI 81 MI 93 MI154 MI247 MI269
Mick IL215 MO123
Mickus MN121
Mid-City IL281
Middle West MO 35
Middlekauff MD158
Middleton WI238 WI395
Middlewood OH 75 WI283
Midland MI218
Mid-West IL116 IN 69 MN142
Midwest MO 48
Miexner PA181
Miksch MN 53
Milan OH239
Mile High CO 29
Miles NY442 NY443 OR 85
Mill WI 63
Millard NY286
Millbank NY443
Miller AK 34 CA 14 CA 17 CA 89 CA123 CA450 CO103 CT 26 GA 1 ID 68 IL139 IL140 IL141 IL312 IL333 IN 21 IA248 KY 48 MD 13 MD 18 MD 42 MD 67 MD 68 MD 69 MD 70 MD 81 MI 4 MI 44 MI 94 MI206 MI222 MO182 MT 23 MT 37 NE 8 NE 15 NY232 NY592 NY593 NY594 NY637 NC 3 OH130 OH262 OH293 OH309 OR 27 PA 62 PA 78 PA 94 PA258 PA308 PA405 PA503 PA654 PA809 TX 33 TX 66 VA 10 WI 14 WI 15 WI 67 WI165 WI216 WI237 WI256 WI283 WI287 WI341 WI444 WI489 WI541
Milles MI175
Million WI371
Millot NY543
Mills MI175
Millschlauer NY 52
Millstadt IL279
Millstine PA 53
Milner IL225
Milo WI323
Milster MO207
Miltzer WA 13

Milwaukee CA295 CO 41
ID 45 ID 50 IL 40 IL 52
IL 79 IL165 IL182 MI114
NY324 ND 3 TX 34 WA 41
WA 95 WI130 WI131 WI288
WI292 WI311 WI318 WI330
WI343 WI456 WI458 WI514
Minahan CA434
Minard MI183
Minars MN 14
Minck IN128
Mineral Springs WI352
Miners ID 43 IA 95 PA321
Minette MN183
Minger AZ 1 KS 41
Mingus TX 59
Mink IN128
Minneapolis MN102 MN108
MN109 MN110
Minnesota MN 57 MN169
Minor WI352
Minuet NY444
Mischler OH277 PA475
Mishicott WI355
Misselt ID 13
Mission CA165 CA286
CA337
Mississippi IA157 MN 98
MO180
Missoula MT 48
Missouri MO 61 MO106
MO146 MO152 MO173
Miswald MI 38 MI192
MI232
Mitchell CA 66 CA 97
CA 99 ID 53 IL142 IL280
TX 28
Mittler IL309 OH266
Moat NY 40
Mobile AL 8
Moeckel WA103
Modesto CA192
Moehn IA 27 IA 31
Moelle CO102
Moeller NY193
Moenkhaus IN 57
Moens OR 61
Moerder WA 86
Moerlbach NY595
Moerlein OH 76 TN 28
Moersberger MT 28
Moerschel MO 74 MO196
Moes MN128
Moeschlin PA290 PA349
PA793
Moesmer NY133 WI466
Moessner PA308
Moethwig WI117
Moffat NY194
Mogger IN150
Mohawk NY173 NY280 NY288
NY303 NY628 OH 89 PA701
VA 8
Mohrenburg WI 46
Mokelumne CA195
Molitor CO 57 MN 95
WI446
Moll IA208 NY445
Moller MD 71
Moloney MI 41 MI 85
Molson OR 71 WA 71
Molt NJ 4
Molter MN 26 RI 20
Monahan MN106
Monarch CA157 IL107
MD 72 WI405
Monessen PA322
Mongey OH333
Monitor WI220
Monocacy PA 36
Monongahela PA 93 PA326
WV 10
Monroe IL200 NY600 WI356
Montague CT 7
Montana MT 31
Montanye WI200
Montauk NY324
Monterey CA169 CA197
CA277
Montezuma NM 12
Montgomery AL 10 MN113
MN116
Monticello VA 7
Montmann WI166
Monumental MD 72
Moody MA 79
Mooney CA437
Moore MA 76 NY446 NY667
NY705 OH 26 PA504 WI379
Moose PA738
Moran MO147
Moravian PA 39 PA 92
Morbach IN107
Morgan NJ 62 NY531 NY538
Morgenthaler NJ 4
Morgenthau PA287
Moritz SD 26 UT 30 UT 31
WI403
Morris AL 1 PA120 PA449
PA505 PA506 PA507
Morrison PA172 PA327
PA398 WI114
Morrow OH244
Morton NJ 68 NJ 91 PA762
Moscow ID 61
Moser IL143 IN 16 KS 44
WI235
Mosey CA420
Mosler ID 26
Moss OK 3 SD 26
Motlow ID 2
Mott PA589
Moulton MI121
Mound MO136
Mound City IL296
Mount MD 24
Mt. Calvery WI360
Mount Carbon PA706
Mt. Carmel PA333
Mount Clemens MI223
Mt. Hood OR 72
Mt. Hope MA 50
Mount Joy PA334
Mt. Morris NY527
Mt. Penn PA728
Mount Pleasant IA186
MD 26 PA336
Mt. Royal MD 47
Mt. Tamalrais CA 24
Mount Vernon MD 16 NY476
Mountain CA 41 VA 20
Mountain Dew NY227
Mountain Spring NH 14
Mountain State WV 6
Mowz IA157
Moyer IA 32
Moyers OH240
Moyses WA 58
Mucci NY618
Muchow NE 8
Muck NV 49
Muehlbauer NY195 NY196
Muehlberger PA 4
Muehlebach MO 42 NE 35
TX 76
Muehlig NJ 47
Muehling OH 39
Muehlschuster MO 5
WI324
Mueller CA104 CA110
CA388 ID 64 IL144 IL145
IL146 IL147 IL271 IL272
IL312 IA 32 KY 1 KY 26
MD 73 MD 74 MI235 MN 43
MN102 MN109 MN154 NY406
NY528 NY596 NY647 NY703
OH 81 OH 84 OH 99 OH104
OH119 OH131 OH297 PA508
PA509 PA658 WA 82 WA 87
WI 23 WI395 WI398 WI432
WI434 WI498
Muellerschoen PA511
Muench NY117 NY120 WA104
WI 9 WI 11
Muenchener TX 70
Muenchner NY133
Muennig MO 35
Muenzenberger OH 58
OH 81
Muenzenmeier IA 82
Muessel IN137
Muff NE 8 OH280
Mugler CA407 KS 25 KS 40
Muheim AZ 3
Muhlbach CA103
Muhlenberg PA724
Muhlhauser OH 95 OH272
Muhlheim PA714 PA778
Muldowney PA333
Mulgren CA 32
Mulhauser MD 26 MD 62
Mullanphy MO154
Mullen IL137
Muller CA104 CA388 CO121
IL154 NY648 PA357
Mullholland CO120
Mulligan MI 4
Mumm NY316
Munch NY447
Muncie IN106
Mundelius AZ 53
Mundigel MN 37
Mundus MI 60
Munger IL148
Munich PA724
Municipal NY 24
Munn CO114

Muntzenberger WI201 WI325
Muntzer MT 16
Munz CA189
Munzenmaier IA212
Munzinger CA 30 CA137 CA237 IA212 WI326
Murata CA445
Murche MO203
Murisch MN 60
Murphy IA117 MO154 NJ139 NY668 NY684
Murphysboro IL290
Murray MA 76 NJ132 NY277
Murzenbach MI 63
Muscatine IA191
Muschett MD117
Muscoda WI361
Muskegon MI224
Muth IN 22 MD 75 MD 88 OH132 PA673 WI 49 WI162 WI459
Mutschler IN 92
Mutual IL151 MI105 MO148 NY233 PA491 WA 21 WI327
Mutual Union PA 1 PA224
My NE 35
Myer IN 69 WI 19 WI369
Myers NY683 NY700
Myndartsen NY449
Myrick ND 16
Nacey NY541
Nachod PA390 PA588
Nachtman IA 94
Nack NY450
Nadorff IN113 KY 29 KY 34
Naecker MI 88
Naegeli MN 91
Nagel IA152 MI 95 PA512 PA725 WI222
Nagengast MD 76
Nager WA 27
Nagle MO154 PA739
Nail City WV 32
Nangle IL149
Napa City CA204
Napa Valley CA201
Naperville IL291
Narr PA437 PA513 PA514 PA515
Narragansett MA 35 RI 14
Narrows MD128
Nase NY612
Nash NY451 NY687
Nashville TN 28
Nass DC 12 NE 2
Nassau NY120
National AZ 23 CA338 DC 14 FL 8 FL 9 IL 99 IL123 IL150 IL154 LA 19 MD 9 MD 29 MI110 MI150 MI254 MO127 MO149 MO193 MT 31 NJ 92 NY430 NY655 NY669 NY704 PA151 PA226 PA789 WA113 WI476
Natter OR 34
Nau MD172
Naudascher PA456 PA516
Naudauscher PA456
Nauer WI402
Nauman RI 7
Nay NY421
Neale MA 29
Nealon PA783
Nebecker DE 1
Nebraska NE 35 NE 37
Nectar NY255
Neef CO 50
Neenah WI364
Neff CA107 CA400 MO112 MO180
Neher NE 8 WI 66
Neiderhofer PA192
Neiderstadt ID 62
Neifert MN205
Neilan OH204
Neilsville WI365
Neimann MO94
Neinau PA354
Neisendorfer MD 49 MD 77
Neiss CT 14 IA134 WI360
Neistrath CA415
Neitzel WA 96
Neitzer NJ 93
Neller CA 25
Nelson AZ 20 CA 51 WI275
Nentzel PA517 PA518
Neosho WI366
Nes PA861
Ness IA134
Nessler CA 65
Nestler UT 22 UT 32
Netzhammer IL 1
Neu IL 12 NJ 94
Neuer WI189
Neugass AZ 52
Neuhaus IA178
Neuhoff IL 11
Neukam IN 55
Neukirch WI332
Neumaier MI183 MI184
Neuman NY452
Neumayer TX 90 TX 91
Neumeister MI224
Neunert OR 71
Neurath OR 32
Neurich OH 43
Neustadtl PA790
Neuweiler PA 7
Neuwirth OH259
Nevada CA209
Neverman WI365
New IL151 WI 30
New Albion CA409
New Athens IL296
New Bethlehem PA341
New Braunfels TX 61
New Bremen MO176
New Brunswick NJ115 NJ116
New Castle PA342
New England CT 19 MA 16 MA 33 MA 42 MA 65
New Era WI202
New Freeland PA178
New Glarus WI370
New Hampshire NH 3
New Haven CT 38 CT 41
New Kensington PA346
New Knoxville TN 5
New Lebanon PA272
New Lisbon WI371
New London CT 51 WI373
New Mountain NH 14
New Orleans LA 11 LA 14 LA 18 LA 20 LA 26
New Philadelphia OH255
New Prague MN121
New South KY 52
New State OK 4
New Ulm MN127
New Vienna IA194
New York CA170 CA339 MD 10 NY106 NY154 NY369 NY380 NY421 NY427 NY448 NY452 NY492 NY641 WA 77
Newark NJ 95
Newberry VA 11
Newbrand IA200
Newburgh NY341
Newkorn CA229
Newlin PA506
Newman AL 1 IN 80 NV 11 NJ 38 NY 36 OH114 PA621 WI381
Newton CA194
Niagara NY316
Niagara Falls NY520
Niagara River NY673
Nibbe CA340
Nichnitz UT 1
Nicholai WI219
Nichols MA 2 NY277
Nichter PA706
Nichterlein PA470 PA479
Nickel NY134
Nicklas CT 37
Nicola ID 61
Nicolaus CA268
Niebauer PA100
Niedermaier WI366
Niedermair WI268
Niederstadt ID 61
Niehaus OH 80
Niehoff WI 29
Nielson SD 8
Niemann MO150
Niemeyer CO 56 KY 9
Nienstadt IA 13
Nies IA134
Nightman OH 34
Nikolas SD 1
Niles City MI229
9-0-5 IL133 IL150 IN137
Nippon CA304 CA379
Nirmaier IN108
Nisch ID 35
Nisher IA221
Nishwitz SD 7
Nissler MT 57
Nitzel MD 78
Noble NY212
Nockin IL 67
Nockles IA222
Noebling UT 36
Noelp OH 45

Noethig CA341
Nohrenberg MN110
Nolan NY 4 NY 26
Nolden MI128
Nolker MO139
Noll OH 77
Noller NY453
Nolte OR 61
Nome AK 28
Non-Alcoholic IL152
Nonnemann MI214
Noramco WI514
Norberg ID 36
Norfolk MA 15 VA 14
Norg WI149
Norman IL 13 NY317
Normann OH342
Norris PA850
North American IL163 NY135
North Bay CA149 CA396
North Beach CA352
North Bend OR 57
North Bergen NJ118
North Judson IN121
North La Crosse WI220
North Lake WI375
North Mississippi MN170
North Pacific OR 6
North Pole WV 9
North Side NY430 WI220
North Star CA342 IL 72 IL172 MN171
North State NC 2
North Western IL105 IL153
North Yakima WA119
Northampton PA350
Northern IA 91 MI 20 MI239 MN 24 NY711 WA104 WI481
Northern Indiana IN121
Northern Lakes WI 7
Northern Pacific MN133 WA 41
Northfield MN128
Northport WA 34
Northside WI424
Northwest OR 73 WA 61 WA 97 WA110
Northwestern WI278
Norton IN 2 IN155 WI183
Norwich NY524
Noth IA 64
Nothhelfer WI 72
Nothnagel MI 96
Noway CT 10
Nuding PA 7
Nuhlicek WI205
Nuhn CT 62 TX 80
Null PA747
Numano CA 26
Nunan CA343
Nunemacher WI285
Nunemann KY 35
Nuner NY303
Nunn NY596
Nunning MO 88
Nuss OH236
Nusser PA674
Nutt Terrace NY629
Nutz ID 81
Nyssen MN186
O K MN120 NJ 24
Oakland CA226 CA228
Oakman MI 97
Ober PA649 PA650 PA670
Oberer NV 19
Oberholz OH 3
Oberholzer CA 63
Oberley WI489
Oberly PA 8
Obermann WI328 WI329
Obermeyer NY136
Obernburg NY528
Oberschelp MO130
Obert MO178 PA493
Oberting IN 87
O'Brien CT 1 MN 48 NY 59 OR 8
Ochs CA269 NY154 NY233 OH216 PA803 PA835 TX 78
Ochsenhirt MI 98
O'Connor CA438
Oconomowoc WI377
Oconto WI378
Odenwald MD 79
Oderbolz WI 40
O'Donnell IL 98 IL154
Oechsle MN153
Oehlschlager MN 49
Oehm NY118 RI 20
Oertel KY 24 KY 53
Oester MN 24
O'Fallon TN 3
Offer MO 22
Offermann CA258
Ogden DC 13 MA 54 PA201
Ogren IL155
O'Halleran WI108
Ohio OH157
Ohio Union OH 78
Ohio Valley WV 21
Ohlendorf IL224
Ohnesorg MO 89
Ohse PA519
Oil City PA355
Oklahoma OK 4
Olarich NY600
Old IN 31 KY 36 NY539
Old Abbey IL156
Old Bohemian NJ145
Old Capitol OH 39
Old City NJ145
Old Colony MA 49 MA 53 MA 55
Old Crown IN 41
Old Dominion VA 5 VA 9
Old Dutch IN137 MI100 NY137 OH195 PA 2 WI 50 WI420
Old Economy PA169
Old England CT 15
Old Fashion NJ 96
Old Fashioned NJ 75 WI216
Old Hickory PA 19
Old Holland MI 99
Old Indian PA220
Old Kent MI153
Old Lager WI292
Old Lancaster PA259
Old Missouri IL133 IL194
Old Monroe IL201
Old Munich FL 3 OH 76
Old Port WI403
Old Reading PA718
Old Reliable PA187
Old South NC 7
Old Tap WI116
Old Tavern WV 6 WV 10
Old Tyme CA260
Old Vienna IL133
Old Vincennes IN158
Olean NY535
Ol-Fashion OH174
Olferman KS 45
Oliver WI 91
Olsen MN107
Old OH176
Olympia MN168 MT 17 TX 76 WA 36 WA116
Omaha NE 32
Onalaska WI379
One Horse CO 42
One-Two WI514
Oneida NY616 NY701
O'Neil OR 87 PA401
O'Neill IL 60 IL157 MD 79
Oneonta NY536
Onondaga NY660
Ontario NY541
Oothout NY454 NY569
Opdyke NY455
Oppenlander CO 45 CO120
Oppermann NY406 NY456
Oppmann OH133 OH145
Opposition AZ 52
Orange NJ119 NY332
Ordeng OH 79
Oregon OR 74 OR 90 PA675
Oregon City OR 59
O'Reilley PA594
O'Reilly IL302 NJ 62
Orbit FL 8
Ordish PA590
Oriental MD 38 NY419
Oriskany Falls NY538
Ormound UT 10
Oroville WA 38
Ortel MO 10
Orth MN 13 MN108 PA520
Ortlieb PA293 PA302 PA303 PA396 PA630 PA771
Ortonville MN129
Oshkosh WI383 WI384 WI386 WI387
Osten SD 14
Osterhaut PA721
Osterstock PA137
Osthelder WI460
Oswald PA 15 PA631
Oswego NY540 NY542 NY543
Otoe NE 25

Ott NE 16 OH 36 OH262 OR 26 OR 35 OR 96
Ottawa IL303
Otterbach PA521
Ottis MN 22
Otto KY 36 MN 91 MT 48 NY458 NY494 PA522 SD 24
Ottumwa IA205
Ouray CO102 CO104
Overbeck KY 52
Overland ID 66
Owen MI204
Owens MN 68 WI330
Owensboro KY 56
Owosso MI234
Owyhe ID 85
Oxley NY138
Ozark MO199
P.B. NJ145
P & H PA273
Pabst GA 10 IL252 IL318 MD 81 MD 82 MN168 NJ 84 NY 41 OR 82 WA 36 WI286 FL 15 WI288
Pacific AZ 40 CA223 CA311 CA344 CA345 CA376 CA447 CA452 ID 42 IA 64 MO138 NV 36 OR 11 WA 55 WA 90 WA 92 WA 93
Padgham WI517
Paducah KY 58
Paeltzer PA714
Pafendorf MT 45
Pagels MI144
Pagenstecker PA344
Pahl WI378 WI429
Palace CA 3
Palm AZ 42 NE 53
Palmer KY 47
Palmetto SC 1
Palmtag CA109 CA444 WA 80
Palo PA299
Palouse WA 40
Pamperin CO122
Panhandle ID 21 WA 81
Pank IN112
Papmahl OR 9
Paradis WI418
Paris NY 23
Parisel MT 45
Park AZ 51 MA 25 MI160 MI168 MN208 NY133 NY172 OH 80 PA558 RI 15
Park Circle NY140
Park Row CT 33
Parker IL158 MN111 NY553 WA 40
Parkersburg WV 20
Parkhurst CO 43 SD 8 SD 19 TN 11 WY 2
Parks SD 5
Parr NY423
Parsons MA 30
Partenheimer PA620
Partzwick CA 20
Passaic NJ123
Pastoor NY 25
Pathe NH 1
Paterson NJ122 NJ123 NJ124 NJ125 NJ127 NJ128
Patsch MI 45
Patterson AZ 51 NJ 68
Pattison OH 70
Patton PA358
Patzberger WI 28
Patzsch MI 45
Paul IN 79 MD 71
Pauli IN 48
Paulson IA115 NJ 48
Paulus NJ133 OH198 WI 65
Pautz WI246
Pavek MN203
Pawlett WI283 WI330
Payette NY552
Peabody NY286
Peacock IL338
Pearl MO 79 TX 69
Pearson ID 8 MO151 WI283 WI437
Peaslee IA 96
Pechstein IA152
Peck NY712 ND 10
Peckham CO120
Pederson WI532
Peeples AZ 55
Peerless IL 11 MO205 PA523
Peifer IA 85
Peipe KS 27
Pelican LA 20 LA 21 NY264
Pelikan MT 48 WY 10
Pelkes ID 96 WA 40
Pells CO126
Pels NY688 NY689
Peltzer PA720
Pemberton PA524
Pembina ND 17
Penar NY724
Pendlebury CO 36
Peninisular MI 79
Penn PA220 PA360 PA738 PA789
Penn-Star PA262
Penn-State PA262
Pennsylvania PA127 PA206 PA216 PA697 PA700PPA755 PA759 PA762 PA763 PA764 PA783 PA848
Penrose NY231
Peoples IN151 MD142 MN 36 NJ 97 NJ140 NJ142 NJ145 NY197 NY705 PA132 WI388
Peoria IL315
Pepin CA392 MN115
Pepper PA525 PA534
Pequod CT 51
Perchal MN113
Periolat IL374
Perkins CA326 MD166 WA120
Perkiomen PA186
Perot PA526
Perpente RI 16
Perplies WI186
Perry PA146
Peru IL320
Pehek MN 67
Pess WI362
Petaluma CA239
Peter CA390 GA 9 NJ151 TX 79
Peters CA 71 CA453 ID100 IL 2 NY459 OR 51
Petersen AK 24 MI158 MN 87
Peterson CA193 ID 23 IL339 IA 46 IA195 MN 88 NJ131 WA 82
Petoskey MI238
Petri IN 72
Petruschak PA809
Petzold TX 86
Pexa MN114
Peyinghaus MO152
Pfaender PA381 PA705
Pfaff MA 31
Pfahler PA527
Pfannebecker NJ126
Pfarr WV 28
Pfau OR 3
Pfaulder UT 33
Pfeffer PA282 PA287
Pfeifer IL159 WI333
Pfeiffer CA205 IN137 IA 39 MI100 MI134 MN153 MN175 PA446 PA529 PA788 PA862 TN 28 TX 80
Pfeifle MI 21
Pfeil WI126
Pfestel WI 30
Pfester MN154
Pfether CA346
Pfister IA106
Pfleiderer OR 24
Pflitschinger NJ 98
Pfohl NY253 NY651 NY670
Pforr IL160
Pframmer PA532
Pfuhl PA768
Pfund MO153
Phelps CT 38
Philadelphia CA168 CA369 MO130 NV 26 PA501 PA530 PA591
Philippay CA 30
Philipsburg MT 50 PA633
Philipson MO154
Phillipbar NY198
Phillips PA713 WA105
Phipps NY287
Phoenix AZ 27 CA323 IL161 KY 5 KY 49 MD 76 MI 28 MI 63 MO 95 NJ 85 NY192 NY434 OH133 PA692 WI289 WI432
Pickett IA102
Pie NY318
Piel MA 88 NY139 NY160 NY645 PA 9
Piemeisl MN120
Piemeisle MN125
Pieper AZ 15 AZ 22
Piequet CA196
Pier IA101 PA675

Pierce IA198 WI 45
Pierson MO 15 MO 36
Pies WI523
Piez NJ 63 NJ 99
Pillig CA320
Pilsen IL 20 IL133 IL162 WI205
Pilsener AK 25 ID 47 MO155 NY416 OH128 OH154 OR 75 PA208 PA396 PA654 WA 62
Pilser NY408
Pilsner OH142
Pinal AZ 15
Pink IA132
Pioche NV 34
Pioneer AK 16 AZ 51 ID 6 IL254 MI 8 OH180 WA 2 WA 97 WA110 WI109 WI215
Piper MN190
Pitlik WI 1
Pitts CO 12
Pittsburgh MN168 MO108 PA110 PA226 PA267 PA305 PA336 PA640 PA644 PA649 PA654 PA659 PA667 PA669 PA670 PA674 PA676 PA685 PA686 PA690 PA692 PA752 PA819
Pittston PA697
Pitzel MN119
Placer CA 12 CA 66
Plagemann CA434
Planck PA531
Plank Road WI222 WI287
Platteville WI398
Plattsburgh NY553
Platz NE 17 NE 51 PA163 WI332
Platzer WI225
Playmate PA714
Plein IL208
Pleitner CA 66
Plentz ID 83
Ploch OH266
Plocher OH194
Ploshke NV 2
Plotzer MN 66
Plumb CA258
Plummer PA 43
Plymouth WI360 WI399
Pocono PA849
Poggenklas IA183
Poggensee IL125 IL132 IL314 NE 41
Pohl IL163
Pohle WA 10 WA 12
Pointer IA 53
Polar NJ 27
Polish PA125 WI476
Pompe IA 3
Pontiac MI241
Poock OH185
Popel IL363
Popp CA 44 CA 98 CA243
Porak OR 99 WA 86
Port Angeles WA 46
Port Huron MI242
Port Jervis NY558
Port Townsend WA 49
Port Washington WI403
Portage MI188
Porter IL253 OH110 PA461
Portland OR 76 OR 77
Portmann IL167
Portner VA 4
Portsmouth NH 7 NH 9 OH272
Portz WA100 WA153
Post NJ123
Postell WI361
Poth NJ 3 PA371 PA533
Potosi WI405
Potter NY691
Potts PA534
Pottstown PA705
Poultney PA398
Powell IL101 WI330
Power City NY519
Powers AZ 10 NY631
Pra PA382
Prafcke IL323
Prairie KS 22 WI338
Prairie du Chien WI410
Prairie Queen SD 14
Pratt NY 5
Preiss MN136 MN156
Prell OH 59
Premier IL318 MI256 OH238 PA598 WI286
Premium LA 16
Prendergast PA794
Prentiss OH243
Prescott AZ 39 WI411
Presque Isle MI246
Presser PA535
Pressler TX 2
Preston MN136
Preuss CA171
Price NY368 NY451 OH 96
Pride of Missouri MO 61
Priemer MI278
Prima IL 50 IL 65 IL117 IL133 IL194
Primalt IL117
Princeton WI412
Prinderville IL174
Prinz AK 1
Prior PA349
Pritchard PA126 WI114
Probst NM 17 TX 36
Producers IL 50
Progress OK 5
Prospect Park NY140
Pros't MI101 MI113
Prost IL150 MI101
Proto PA547
Providence RI 5
Pruden OH171 OH177
Psotta PA372 PA373 PA629
Pudey PA536
Pueblo CO109
Puegg CA394
Pueschel CA200
Puget WA 92
Puissant IN 83
Pukownik MI231
Pulkrabek MN 5
Pullman NY228
Punxsutawney PA712
Pupka KS 4
Pure Aqua PA784
Pure Beer WI500
Pure Springs PA173
Puritan MA 32
Purity TN 2
Purkiss MI198
Pusch WI159
Putnam MI133 MN172
Quady WI535
Quaker City PA596
Quality FL 10
Quandt NY686
Quast MI 40 WI489
Queen Co. MD124
Queen City MD122 MD124 NY205
Queens County NY324
Quer MO 6
Querin PA792
Querngafar WI136
Quigg MO 50
Quilna OH220
Quinaults WA 3
Quincy IL325
Quinlivan MO151
Quinn CT 25 NY 4 NY 26 NY667
Quinnipiac CT 41
Quist IL164
Raab CA120 PA720
Raasch WI509
Rabe DC 14
Rabenschlag PA 14
Rabenstein IL304
Raber NY106
Rablin CA 66
Rabolt CA420
Rachenberger WA 52
Rachor WA 51
Racine WI414
Rack TX 52
Raddant WI456
Raddatz CA420
Raddy MN121
Radeke IL259
Radford VA 15
Radly MN 75
Raether NY 86
Rahn CA114 PA796
Rahr MI128 WI 64 WI145 WI148 WI247 WI384 WI389
Raiber MD 26
Raible AZ 40 IL343
Rail OH292
Rainer IA 39
Rainier CA178 CA347 WA 64 WA 71 WA 75
Raithel NM 4
Ralph NY701
Ralston OH 43
Rambour ID 85 NE 51
Ramharter IA243
Rammelmeyer ID 65
Ramming MD 83
Rammchuger MT 9

Rampart AK 29
Ramsdale MN200
Ramsey OH333 PA 19
Ramspeck MT 25
Ramstetter NY564
Range MN 65
Rankert IN 42
Ransom Canyon AZ 4
Rantzau CA348 CA382
Rapp CA 48 MT 57 NV 50 NY 24 OH229 OH243 WV 16 WV 19
Raquet MI253 MI254
Raspiller CA 27
Rast OR 90
Rath MN207
Rathberger IA 23
Rathgeb CA278
Rathman MI157
Rau NY597 NY598 OH193
Rauber NY597
Rauch MN 26 PA214 WI205 WY 10
Raulston VA 11
Raupfer IN 17
Rausch CA214 IL320 MN170
Rauschkolb IL312
Rautert IL356
Ravensburg CA121
Ray MO198 OH 71
Raycraft NV 10
Read NY411 NY460 NY684
Reading OH335 PA396 PA718
Real OH134
Real Ale MI 43
Rebstock OH 80
Rechenmacher CA 11 CA432
Reck ID 29 IL 2
Record NY251 NY714
Red Bluff CA252
Red Fox VA 7
Red Hook WA 63
Red Lion CA359 OH 95
Red Lodge MT 53
Red River ND 9
Red Star NJ125
Red Top IL163 OH 64 OH 89
Red Wing MN142
Redeker NY559
Reden NY318
Redford PA414
Redig PA796
Redle KY 26
Redmond MI176
Redwood CA258
Reed OH224
Reed City MI244
Reedsburg WI429
Rees NY502
Reeves WI238
Regal CA344 FL 8 MI 81 MI102
Regelin WI115
Regenfuss WI133 WI194 WI440
Regent FL 10
Reger CA 49
Reges PA537
Regional MA 88
Regitz IL104
Regli NV 17
Reh IA 98
Rehberg MI 20
Rehberger NY461
Reher UT 6
Rehfuss CA 60 NV 56 OH 49 OR 59
Rehm IL165
Rehn PA462 PA538
Rehorn WA 44
Reiber CO120
Reich CA408
Reichard PA848
Reichart CO 62
Reichel IL246 MN200
Reichenbach PA306 PA676
Reichert IL222 IL228 MD 76 OR 50
Reichmann KY 13 PA316
Reichow MN173
Reick CA408
Reid MO156
Reidel MN 28
Reidelberger IL166
Reidenbach WI133
Reidmiller IN 47
Reilly NY679
Reily OH 81
Reiman OH226
Reimer MN166
Reimers NY 86
Reimsland NY392
Reindl MI216
Reinecke NY332
Reiner IL307 WI 42
Reingruber NM 13
Reingrueber WI131
Reinhard OH203
Reinhardt MO167 NY648
Reinheit PA765
Reiniger ID 22 ID 76
Reinold IA154
Reiplinger WI424
Reis NY186
Reisch IL354
Reiser CA 8 IL167 NJ108 PA539 PA720
Reising IN110 MO157
Reisky NY597
Reissinger CA185
Reitman IN 33
Reitter PA540 PA559
Reitzenstein WI341
Reitzner NY144
Reiver CO120
Rekers IN161
Remde NY328
Remely MN157
Remensperger CA318
Remmler MN140
Rendlen MN 27 MN 29
Rengers PA 28
Renner IN 41 KY 4 OH 3 OH 67 OH226 OH333 OH338
Rennert TX 62
Rennig PA749
Reno NV 37 NV 38
Rentschler PA541 PA577
Rentz WI461
Renz MI195 MI200
Reof IA 49
Reppe PA587
Republic PA731 WA 50
Resen IA 51
Rettig IN125 IN159 PA708
Rettner KY 32
Reuter CA387 MI 75
Reuther MA 90
Reuthlisberger WI332
Reutlinger IL298 KY 13
Reutti OH205
Rex CT 39 MN 30 PA784
Reyber IL126
Reyer MI 18
Reyle PA371
Reymann WV 23
Rheinboldt OH 53
Rheinbrau MI267
Rheingold CA142 MA 72 NJ119 NY119 OH142 PA396
Rheinlander WA 71
Rhemstedt WI398
Rheude WI333
Rheudy IA158
Rhinelander WI431
Rhode IA 73
Rhode Island RI 4 RI 12
Rhodes PA677
Rhomberg IL210 IA 98
Rhomburg MO 13
Rialto NJ145
Rice AK 12 CA380 ID 91 IN 27 IN 31 IA107 MA 78 PA 75
Rice Lake WI432 WI433
Rich MN 88 OH 11 OH241 OH290 OH333
Richards CA208 CO 13 NJ103 RI 14
Richardson KS 15
Richenmacher MO202
Richman PA256
Richmond IN128 VA 13 VA 16
Richter DC 14 MI127 MN116 PA 85 PA798 TX 31 TX 41 UT 15 UT 17 WA 20 WA 83 WI249
Rick IL249 IA 6 IA111
Ricke OR 64
Rickrich OH252
Ridelsperger PA824
Ridgewood Park NY 94
Riedel IL330 MN136 TX 96 WI167
Riedesel MN 26
Riedlin KY 5
Rieffenstein AK 4
Rieger PA116 PA441 PA542
Riehl CA 92 PA401
Rieker PA105 PA257 PA262
Riepe NV 7
Ries PA 98
Riley CO 75 OR 23
Ringer MN200

Ringgenberg CA229
Ringler CT 38 NY390
Rink IL 10
Rintoul NY440
Rinz MN170
Rio CA149
Rio Grande NM 2
Rioppelle MI284
Ripon WI436
Rippele NE 45
Ripsam NY598
Rising Sun NJ 17 PA384
Risley NY 49
Risser IL364
Ristau WI194
Ritcher WI 17
Riter NY 35
Rithmann IL269
Rittenhouse NY462
Rittenmeyer IA139
Ritter MD125 MA 46 MN 64 PA 4 WI206
Rittmaier PA543
Rittman PA 14
Ritz CA288
Ritze IN 88
River City CA270
Riverside IL168 IL259 OH154 OH179 OH345
Riverview NY520 PA328 PA734 WI248
Rivinius NY453
Roast OH220
Roberts NY 59
Robertson CA134 NY463
Robes WI210
Robinette WA 9
Robinson CA240 MA 24 NY287 NY349 OR 58 PA763 PA764 PA774 WI183
Robson VA 17
Rochevot NY199
Rochester MN149 MO 43 MO 44 NY568 NY592 NY595 NY599
Rock Island IL343 IL344 IL345 IL346 IA 68
Rock River IL338
Rock Spring MD 22 NJ115 NY666
Rocke MA 82
Rockenbach WI241
Rockford IL338
Rockwood PA736
Rocky MO 93
Rocky Mountain CO 44
Rodacker WV 25
Rodebank SD 8
Rodemeyer IL169
Rodenberg OH207
Rodenburg AZ 33
Rodener MT 46
Rodermund WI239
Rodney RI 3
Roe NY464
Roedel WI334
Roeder MI219 PA741
Roedermund WI239
Roeffs WI249
Roehm PA478 PA598
Roehrich PA720 PA728 PA809
Roelke MN174
Roell IN123
Roemer MN 38 MN121 NY361
Roemheldt DC 15
Roemmelt NJ 49 NY465
Roemmich PA544
Roesch MD 42 OR 34 OR 43 OR 62 WA 48
Roeschel MO 4
Roeshman NJ 4
Roeser WI448
Roesing IL165
Roesner PA804
Roesser NJ100
Roessing OH246
Roessle MA 33
Roessner PA 98
Roetger MN 77
Roethinger WI180
Roettcher OH272
Rogers NV 12 OH135 WI181
Rogner PA221
Rohner MN 79 MT 59
Rohr MO173 WI113
Rohrer CA298 MD154 NY200 OH201
Rohrman OR 16 OR 39 OR 97
Roland NJ118
Roleff WI271
Roll CA 11
Roller MN199
Rollison CA151
Rolls OH 82
Rolver IN 26
Rome NY615
Romer MN 38
Romey WA 55
Rood ID 40
Roos MN137 NE 26 NY201
Roosevelt IL171 NJ101
Root AZ 48
Rooth IL170
Ropkins CT 21
Ropenscher SD 26
Rorig NY717
Rosa MI 28 MI255 MI264 WI180
Rose PA618
Rose City OR 68
Roseburg OR 90
Rosenbauer IL260
Rosenberger IL239
Rosenegk VA 13
Rosenheimer WI453
Rosenkranz SD 4
Rosenmund MO 89
Roser NY237
Rosita CO112
Roslyn WA 51
Ross IN 97
Rossdeutscher MD 17 MD 84
Rossmarck MD 85 MD 86 MD 87 MD114 WV 17
Rossmeisel MN 95
Rost ID 40 MD 88 MO192
Roth CO109 DC 15 IL223 IL297 IL365 IA132 IA147 IA175 OH223 OH270 OH333 PA 90 PA329 PA343 PA656 PA658
Rothacker PA545 PA563
Rothengerger IA 26
Rothenburg CA435
Rothenbush CA414
Rotherngerber IA220
Rother MN 94 NJ118 PA186
Rotherburger IA 86
Rothert OH 66
Rothfuss MA 83
Rothgeb NM 11
Rothweiler MO150
Rottler MO 75
Rottmann NY466
Rowe MN170
Roxbury MA 34
Royal IL 50 IL133 LA 12 MI 53 MO158 MO206
Rubel NY132
Ruble OH136
Rublein MI141 MI209 MI283
Rubsam NY639 NY645
Ruch OH 26 OH233
Ruck MI 16
Ruckelhausen AZ 2
Ruckäuber MN145
Ruder WI276 WI477 WI521
Rudman PA403
Rudolph PA511 PA546
Rueckeisen PA678
Ruedi CO 96
Rueger CA 18
Ruegger WI356
Ruehl IL108 IL171
Ruenzi MO 73
Rueter MA 35
Ruff IL330
Ruffer OH213
Rufley NM 6
Rugers NY469
Rugg CA398
Ruh KY 4
Ruhkamp IN 36
Ruhland WI 26
Ruhstaller CA266
Rule WA 64
Rumelhort OR 94
Rummelmann MD 88
Runge CA419 MO 74 NY141 WI 59
Rumpf WA 14
Rungle MO 1
Runkel WI256
Runnels WA 12
Runzi IL 3
Ruoff IL111 MI103 PA547 PA589
Rupello MI178
Rupert IA142
Ruppert MA 72 NJ119 NY119 NY349 NY467 PA396 PA714
Rupprecht MD108 MI140

Rupthuer CT 40
Ruser TN 14
Rush CO 26 NY620
Rush City MN152
Ruscher CA 48 NY690
NY692
Russel NY468
Russell CT 20 GA 9
NY502
Russert IN 83 NJ115
Rust OR 11 OR 20
Rustenbach PA548
Rutgers NY470 NY471
NY472 NY473 NY474
Rutgerson NY475
Ruthardt CA 2
Rutishauser CA 84 CA398
Rutledge MA 44
Ryan CT 1 IL 98 NY660
Rybok MN120
Ryckman NY 18
Ryerson NY516
S.C. FL 8
Saake AK 35 WA 55
Saal PA841
Saberton IL172
Sabinas TX 76
Sachs NE 34 OH177
Sacramento CA263 CA266
CA267 CA268
Saddle Mountain CO106
Safranek NE 54
Saggen NE 41
Saginaw MI248 MI256
Sahner NJ150
Saile MT 18 WI434
St. Albert's ID 23
St. Anthony ID 80
St. Boniface PA160
St. Claire CA378
St. Cloud MN156
St. Genevieve MO 75
St. Helena CA274
St. Joseph MO 88
St. Louis AZ 16 CA349
CA356 IL214 IL247 MI 91
MO 94 MO 95 MO111 MO120
MO121 MO137 MO139 MO140
MO144 MO147 MO154 MO163
MO164 MO179 MO182 MO185
MO187 MO189 MO194 NV 27
OR 9 WA 21
St. Marys PA743
St. Paul MN175
St. Vincent PA267 PA747
Sake CA374 CA445
Saladin IL 78
Salber PA437
Salem OR 2 OR 92
Sales AZ 52
Salinas CA277
Salls TN 15
Salmon IN 96
Salomon PA549
Salt Lake UT 30
Salter PA550
Saltsman PA813
Saltzenberger WI529
Saltzmann NE 50 PA355
Salvator KY 42 MO159
NY443
Salzburg MI 27
Salzig MD 90
Samarkand CA230
Samberg MI242
Sampson WY 12
Samuelsohn TX 2
San Antonio TX 69
San Bernardino CA283
San Diego CA286 CA289
San Francisco CA222
CA226 CA295 CA305 CA310
CA311 CA356 CA366 CA369
CA376
San Francisco Sake CA354
San Jose CA231 CA379
San Juan NJ 27
San Luis CO 21
San Mateo CA259
San Rafael CA385
Sandbach WA 35
Sander NY142 WI109 WI400
Sanders CA381 CO 3
Sandkuhler MD 91
Sandler IA 55
Sandmeyer WA120
Sands IL173 NY691 WI283
Sandt PA 94
Sandusky MD122 OH102
OH106 OH107 OH112 OH115
OH132 OH133 OH135 OH137
OH139 OH143 OH222 OH281
OH283 OH305
Santa Barbara CA388
Santa Clara CA389
Santa Cruz CA391
Santa Fe NM 16
Santa Rosa CA396
Santo IA121 WI 99
Saratoga MD 66 NY327
Sargel MN 24
Sarowski CA187
Sarton MO 23
Sass CA242
Saub NJ102
Sauk City WI449
Sauk Rapids MN184
Saumenig MD 92
Saunder WA 40
Saunders CO 62 NY143
WA 40
Sauter CA331 MI 5 NY284
NY337
Saux ID 99
Savage MO198
Savana CA127
Savannah GA 12 GA 13
Savior UT 6
Savoy IL163 IA 66
Sawyer DC 16
Sax PA330
Saxon WI186
Say OH160
Sayert NY288
Sayles AZ 24 AZ 52
Sayre PA751
Scalusser IA221
Scanlan NY670
Scanlon IL174
Schaaf KS 6 PA161
Schabel CT 25
Schad WI424
Schade WA 84
Schaefer DE 3 IA192
IA203 KY 30 KY 50 MD 39
MO 73 NV 16 NV 34 NE 40
NY 4 NY135 NY145 NY346
NY476 NY490 NY497 NY498
OH142 OH271 OR 78 PA 9
PA302 PA409 PA510 PA551
PA657 WI 85
Schaeffer CA 49 MO159
MO160 NY202 OH294 PA721
Schafer PA 49 PA 98
PA270 WA 88
Schaffer IN 17 WI 59
WI159
Schaffhauser PA521
Schaffner IA 32
Schaffra WI158
Schaibold OR 56
Schaler PA676
Schalk NJ 85 NJ103 NY 77
NY452 OH204
Schaller MN 61 OH 83
OH 84
Schalten CA 29
Schamberger CA271 IL291
Schancie OH 17
Schandler MO 49
Schane MN 22
Schanno OR 99
Schantz OH175 OH178
OH179
Schanz IL276 IL326 IL329
Schanzenbecker KY 37
Schanzlin NY203 NY204
Scharbilling WI434
Scharmann NY 92 NY 93
Scharmong MI 74
Scharnagle NY144
Schatz-Brau MN 95
Schaub MO201
Schaubacker MO 29
Schauble NY286 WA 26
Schauermann OH141
Schaufel OR 52
Schauffele PA514 PA529
Schaufler PA552 PA553
PA554
Schaupp MN153
Scheef PA281
Scheer OH244
Scheffel IL175
Scheffels NJ129
Scheffer PA836
Scheibe WI 63 WI140
WI255
Scheibl WI 54
Scheidt IL255 IL256
PA349
Scheily IA 67
Scheiner NJ104
Scheland OR 79
Scheld CA272
Schell MN126 MO197 WI160
Schellhas UT 18

Schelling NJ 62 WI420 WI422
Schellinger IN103
Schemm MD 93 MI257 PA373 PA452 PA629
Schemmel IA 97
Schenectady NY629
Schenk IL295 MO 90 MO203
Schepps TX 25
Scherer MN207 WI 54
Scherhold CA312
Scherr IA 98
Scherrer CA373
Scheu MI104 NY205 NY206 NY207
Scheuer WI355
Scheuermann MI161
Scheufele NJ 13 NY215 NY351 NY418
Scheurer PA544
Scheyer NY553
Schibb WI409
Schibi MO 73 MO 74
Schick MI280 PA555 PA559
Schieck NY297
Schiemann IL132
Schierling IN122
Schierlitz MD 94
Schiff OH 83
Schiffer MO179
Schiffman WI390
Schill IL219 IL328
Schiller PA521
Schilling MO137 PA 40 PA225
Schillinger AL 2 KY 49
Schilpp OH192
Schimke OH234
Schiml OH180
Schimmel WI432
Schimminger PA 19
Schimpff PA217
Schindler KS 18 MN148 NY 27 WA 6
Schinkel CA297
Schinner CA138
Schinnerer NY 28
Schips WA 12
Schirbe WI249
Schittinger PA556
Schlachter CA245 WI459
Schlaffer MD 28 MD 38
Schlaffner PA670
Schlapp IA122
Schlather OH137
Schlatter CA250
Schlecht PA557
Schlee OH161
Schlegel MI 45 MI273 MT 38 OH162 OH232 OR 46 PA863
Schleicher NY130
Schleifer ID 85
Schleippman CT 41
Schlemmer PA558
Schlenk IL 15 IL340 WI 35 WI417 WI446
Schlesinger IL277
Schleucher NY208
Schlicht WI133 WI462
Schlickeisen OR 10
Schliebitz WI299
Schlinkert MI260
Schlitz CA295 CA436 FL 15 HI 3 MO 42 NY 50 NY 85 NC 8 OH138 TN 16 TX 55 WI316
Schloesser WI533
Schloetterer NJ 26 PA559
Schlop MO137
Schlosser IN109
Schlosstein MA 58 MO164
Schlotfeldt WA 51
Schlotter MI195
Schlotterer NJ143
Schluckebier MI140
Schmal NJ 50
Schmasse MN210
Schmedjte NY477
Schmeer OR 61
Schmelz PA680
Schmersahl NY230
Schmich IL226 IL227
Schmick IL227
Schmid IA 98 NJ 79 NY 1 NY357 NY358 NY359 NY719 PA181 PA561 PA587
Schmidheiser PA447
Schmidlapp OH267
Schmidmayer WI 68
Schmidt CA122 CA172 CA222 CA424 ID 89 IL 88 IL 98 IL176 IL177 IL182 IL345 IN 73 IN 92 IN112 IA 98 IA109 IA117 KS 31 MI 75 MI 81 MN118 MN171 MN175 MO 50 MO161 MT 19 NE 21 NV 27 NY134 NY156 OH 59 OH108 OH139 OH142 OH297 PA 91 PA173 PA209 PA349 PA396 PA534 PA560 PA590 PA634 PA706 PA770 PA771 PA798 TX 84 UT 1 UT 17 WA 8 WA 11 WA 15 WA 40 WI 36 WI100 WI140 WI187 WI224 WI250 WY 13
Schmitz NJ 14 WI 54
Schmohl MN 17 MN143
Schmucker MN127
Schmuhl MI272
Schmulbach WV 32
Schmultzer OH227
Schnabel CA376
Schnaderbeck NY146
Schnagl MN 26 MN 91 MN152
Schnaider MO163 MO164
Schnarderer PA828
Schneider CA235 CA349 CO127 IL115 IL259 IN140 IA174 KY 23 KY 38 MD 62 MD 95 MI 85 MI140 MO137 MO165 MO166 MT 44 NE 21 NJ115 NJ137 NY 29 NY147 NY217 NY267 OH 27 OH 84 OH 85 OH107 OH140 OH207 OH217 OH229 OH266 OH287 PA218 PA274 PA562 PA712
Schneider cont. PA728 WI255 WI340 WI400 WI438
Schnell DC 17 NY381 OH266 PA189 PA791
Schnepel TN 17
Schnerr MO161 MO167
Schnettle WI 31
Schneyer OH268
Schnitz MN 95
Schnitzel PA563
Schnitzer CA337 CA408 PA564 PA597
Schnitzins IL189
Schnurr NJ 5
Schobel CA135
Schober ID 23 ID 62 TX 81
Schoch PA565
Schock IL169 WI394 WI466 WI513
Schoenberger NY478 PA258
Schoeneck WI535
Schoenewald NY148
Schoenfeld TX 20
Schoenfelder CA222
Schoenheit MI185 MI257
Schoenheiter PA566
Schoenhofen IL 48 IL 99 IL150 IL178
Schoenling OH 86
Schoenith MI164
Schoeplen DC 18
Schoettle PA569
Scholl CA 44 IA172 WA 44 WA 45 WA 92
Schomer CA 63
Schonbrunn WI479
Schonegg PA 20
Schoppe IL200
Schorer WI 98
Schori IA108
Schorr IL367 MO 28 MO168
Schorrer WI450
Schott IL 44 IL133 IL247 IL364 PA155 PA170 WI529
Schottmueller WI 16
Schottmuller MN193
Schrader ID 79
Schraf PA156
Schraishuhn PA561
Schramm CA376 MD116 MI 29
Schrecker KY 56
Schreiber IN 18 NY209 WI312
Schreier MD 33 WI462
Schreihart WI245
Schreiner NE 4 WI399
Schrempp NE 49
Schrey AZ 45
Schriber CO 45
Schrieder PA141
Schriker MO128
Schriner MD 96
Schroder CA 80 CA233
Schroeck WI518

Schroeder CO124 CO128 IL213 IA228 IA249 MI186 MI261 MN133 MN148 MO169 NV 47 PA854 WI429
Schrope AZ 41
Schroth NY600 NY601
Schrotte PA 73
Schrudd NY601
Schub NY214
Schubert CA106
Schubler IN 58
Schuchart SD 9
Schuchmann MD 33
Schuebel PA479
Schueler CO 72 UT 35
Schueller MN188
Schuerley CA450
Schuff IL 33
Schuhmacher MN 63
Schuler CA 3 CA 13 CA 80 CA266 CA440 WI 42
Schulkamp WI240
Schull OR 63
Schulte IN 33 TX 47 WI466
Schultheis CT 42 MD 97 MD106 WA 13
Schultz CA312 CA350 ID 32 IL133 KS 12 MD125 MI 46 MI 88 MO170 NJ152 OH 87 OH 88 OH 93 OR 64 PA567 WA 11
Schulz CO120 MN121 NJ 72 PA 48 PA215 TN 18 VA 5
Schulze TX 67
Schumacher IL261 IA126 WI405
Schumaker TX 63
Schuman OH319
Schumann MN 91 MO171 NY479 OH297 PA435 WI410
Schunck WI335
Schunk WI 36
Schuppert CA351
Schusler NY210
Schussler WI110
Schuster CA346 MD160 MN149 MT 10 OH215 OH234 WA 31 WA112
Schustrich NV 34
Schut PA244
Schutte WI 32
Schuykill PA 22
Schwab NY211 NY528 OH205 PA 55 PA312 PA822
Schwabn MI261
Schwachow IL 20
Schwaderer PA792
Schwaebel KS 42
Schwager WI503
Schwalbach NY298 WI367
Schwalbeck WI497
Schwalm WI384
Schwamb PA440
Schwanenfluegel NY388
Schwaner NY480
Schwanitz IL 24
Schwanstein WI399
Schwartshoff IA 85
Schwartz AZ 51 CA164 CA190 CA266 CA352 IA 19 MN 40 NY216 NY416 PA805 TX 17 WI336 WI509
Schwarz PA441 WA106 WI337 WI338 WI410
Schwarzenbach NY285 PA179 PA182 PA183 PA837
Schwebach MN 16
Schweibers MN119
Schweibinz PA303
Schweickart WI291 WI341
Schweikhart NY247
Schweinfurth MO 21
Schweiss NV 23 NV 45
Schweitzer CA353 PA568 PA569 PA570 WI 70
Schweizer MN176
Schwela IA220
Schwenk NM 5 SD 26
Schwerdfeger PA478
Schwerin CA135
Schwers OH254
Schweyer NY481
Schwind IA104 OH178 OH181 OH182 OH310
Schwing NY100
Schwinger MD 98
Schwitzgable OH238
Schwoeri NJ 6 PA571
Scioto OH 39
Scobell NY214 NY224
Scofield NY149
Scotch Hop MO172
Scott CA189 ID 97 NY524 NY632 OH 90 TX 87 WA 15 WA111
Scottdale PA752
Scotten MN171
Scranton PA762
Scully IA213
Scurz MI125
Seattle OR 92 WA 53 WA 58 WA 60 WA 64 WA 71
Sebald OH238
Sebewaing MI269
Seckel PA534 PA572
Seckinger MI200
Sedalia MO197
Sedgwick MA 36
Seeber NJ 17
Seeger IL189 IA101 MD 99 MD100 MD105 MI 88 OH218 OH257 OH338 OR 40
Seegers SC 3
Seeland IA137
Seelig ID 65 MT 9 SD 15
Seeling IN 19
Seelinger PA150
Seemann PA516 PA573 PA574
Seeser IA 54
Seewald PA 49
Segal OH145
Sehring IL250
Seibel IL281 IN 9
Seibert NE 51 NY710
Seible CA441
Seibold OH255
Seibt IL179 OH317
Seidel NJ 69 PA715
Seidemann WI478
Seidenschwanz IL 47
Seidensticker CO118
Seidler IL306 NY141
Seif MI164
Seifert IN 79 WI518
Seiferth PA690
Seigmann IL278
Seikel OH296
Seiler CT 8 KY 3 KY 8 NY602
Seip PA138
Seipp IL 45 IL139
Seiser ID 57
Seisser WA111
Seitz MO 64 NY150 NY482 NC 1 PA137 PA575 WI 55
Sekrit MO 20
Selak CO 63
Selbitz PA 55
Selg NY151
Selig NE 23
Sell PA 98 PA210 PA829
Sellinger NY308 PA705
Sels OR 18
Selva NM 2
Selzer IA218 ND 2
Semrad WI159
Seneca NY268 NY535
Seng IN 77
Senger OH252
Senn IN161 KY 39 KY 40 KY 45 PA262
Senne WI338
Sepaman MI187
Seresse WI104
Service NY194 WI423
Settel NY334
Setz NY719
Setzler MO 51
Seubert OH185
Seubold IN 57
Seventh Street IN143
Severin WI106
Severn IA 63
Sewanee FL 10
Sexton NY483
Seyer IL189
Seyfarth IL224
Seyfferth MI188
Seyler OH141
Seymour NY531
Shaefer MO 89
Shafer IA113 PA 98
Shaffery NJ105
Shakopee MN186
Shamokin PA771
Shannon CT 21 WA 42
Sharp NY322 NY702
Sharswood PA576
Shary NE 57
Shasta CA364 CA402
Shaw MA 83 NJ127 WI129
Shawano WI456
Shea MA 45 TN 5
Sheboygan WI461
Sheehan ME 2

Sheer IL144
Sheerer AZ 40
Sheffield AL 21 OH 37
Shefield MN 43
Sheik IL 97
Sheip IL371
Shelby TN 17
Shelby Street KY 50
Shelden MI226
Sheldon NY271
Shelley IA 40
Shepley MI128
Sheridan WY 17
Sherman WI168
Shettle MD101
Shider PA858
Shiels WI483
Shieman NY485
Shilburne TX 50
Shiley IA 67
Shillof PA103
Shiner TX 86
Shioji CA354
Shiras PA682
Shireoaks PA781
Shirmer IA 14
Shirtz OH213
Shlaudeman IL204
Shlep WI124
Shmilling WI 1
Shoemaker NY212
Shokai HI 7
Sholl MD154
Shomer PA287
Shook NY513
Shore MD169 WY 13
Showalter IA159
Shreveport LA 27
Shullerr WA 20
Shullsbury WI466
Shurr PA577
Sibley MD119
Sichler CT 18 CT 20
CT 22
Sicken MI204
Sicks MT 30 MT 48 OR 92
WA 58 WA 71
Siddell PA135
Siebel MO 24 MO197
Sieben IL109 IL180 IL181
WI133
Sieber AZ 23 CA 63 CA185
Siebert IL182 IL183
OH 49
Siebolt PA578
Siefert WI428
Siegel NY237 NY322
Siegle OH218 PA814
Siegler IL132
Siegmann MD 69
Siegrist OH298
Siemon IL214 MO153 NE 29
Sierra CA126 CA173
Sierra Nevada CA 45
CA213 CA349
Siersdorfer KY 2
Sievers PA809
Sigerald IL261
Sigg IA164
Sigi CO 46
Silbernagel OH152 OH158
Silferson WI 77
Silkinson SD 13
Silver Cream WI378
Silver Creek WI428
Silver Foam MI 25
Silver Lake MN187
Silver Springs WA 47
WA 97
Silverbow MT 57
Silverton CO120
Silvey MD 11
Simmersbach MI126
Simon CT 9 IN158 MI 49
NJ 51 NY210 PA579
Simons CA227
Simonsen AZ 33
Simpson CO105
Sinderman WI126
Sindermann MN 15 WI253
Sineman IA 15
Singelman WI166
Singer WI182
Sinzer PA797
Sioux City IA216 IA217
Sioux Falls SD 20
Sipfle MT 58
Sistersville WV 21
Siverling WI134
Skagit WA116
Skagway AK 36
Skala MI216 WI 1 WI518
Skandia IL341
Skelly NY457 NY486
Skooner MO 74
Slaby MN 79
Slack WV 5
Slagle ID 88
Slaughter WA 5
Slippen WI527
Sloan MO 56 NY213
Slorah WA 65
Slough WI263
Smales MN 41
Small MD141 MO173 PA489
Smelter CO 52
Smith AZ 5 AZ 52 CA 82
CA133 CA355 CA419 CA434
IN 3 MA 27 MA 38 MA 58
MA 59 MA 73 MI155 MI277
MO151 MO174 MO175 MO176
MT 62 NV 41 NJ137 NM 18
NY 49 NY152 NY153 NY225
NY245 NY290 NY423 NY487
NY488 NY538 NY617 NY723
OH339 PA290 PA308 PA451
PA452 PA534 PA580 PA581
PA643 PA852 WA 40 WV 25
WV 29 WI183 WI208 WI392
WI477
Smraker MN 51
Smutney IA229
Smyth NY 20 PA582
Snowden PA583
Snyder IA 43 KY 56 PA111
PA295 PA356 PA740 WA 33
Sobocinski DE 3
Soderholm IL282
Soemann NY305
Soergel IL362
Sohn IN113 OH 51 OH 89
OH205
Solano CA435
Solaro OR 18
Solly CT 43
Solmon NY387
Solomon CO 44 OR 85
Somer IA 83
Sommer NY489 OH 59
Sommerfeld MD 79
Sommerhaeuser MO 72
Sommerkamp ID 87
Sommermeyer WI 95
Sommers NY490 OH265
Sonderegger NE 2
Sonnenmaier PA515
Sonnleitner ID 36
Sonoma CA410
Sonoma Valley CA397
Sontag WI365
Soo MI266
Sorensen CA108 CA193
WI364
Sorg NY491
Soss NY584
Soule LA 22
Soulek MN113
South Bend IN139
South Bethlehem PA 41
South Chicago IL 51
South Cottonwood UT 12
South Fork ID 96 PA785
South Nashville TN 28
South Omaha NE 39
South Rondout NY359
South San Francisco
CA320 CA356
South Side IL119 MO 27
WI174 WI302 WI332
Southeastern TN 2
Souther MA 8 MA 40
Southern CA149 FL 16
LA 18 MO151 NC 1 PA137
TX 48
Southern Indiana IN110
Southern Oregon OR 53
Southern States GA 4
Southside IL355 WI432
Southwestern NM 2 OK 6
Soyer AZ 15 AZ 16
Spaeth PA414 PA584 PA598
WI116
Spahn DE 4 ID 15 ID 82
Spangler PA786
Spanknebel IL122
Sparks NY603
Sparta WI468
Spaulding WY 12 WY 15
Specht DE 4 IL236 OH 13
PA134 PA585 PA586
Spedding NY288
Speidel CT 10
Speier IL233
Speiler NY 62
Speiser CT 11
Spellman WI353
Spellmire WA 66

Spencer OH121 PA692
Spengler MD 28 MD102 MO176
Sperri MO176
Speyers NY492
Sphen WI136
Spiegel MD157 NY493
Spielman ID 7 ID 44
Spielmann ID 7
Spies NY589 NY597
Spieth MT 12
Spink NY269
Spinner NY294 OH 90 WY 10
Spittler CT 41 IA233
Spitzbarth MO177
Spitzig MI268
Spoehrer NY494
Spoerl CA258
Spoetzl TX 86
Spohn PA717 PA727
Spokane WA 75 WA 76 WA 77 WA 78 WA 85
Sponagl CO 97
Spori MO176
Spowden PA398
Sprague WA 86
Sprang NY614
Sprattler NJ122 NJ128
Sprecher NY274 WI241
Spreckles CA357
Sprenger CT 44 PA213 PA249 PA259 PA260
Spreter PA118
Sprey WI340
Spring IA184 PA 56 PA 90 WI 67 WI283
Spring City WI514
Spring Garden MD 16 PA725
Spring Hill DE 7
Spring Water TN 24
Springbrook MI 3
Springer PA214
Springfield IL355 MA 46 MA 80 MA 81 MA 82 MA 83 MA 88 MO199 OH287 OH288 OH289
Springman UT 28
Springmeyer NY495
Spruce Beer WI103 WI107 WI108
Spunger PA628
Squibb OH 70
Srandt NJ106
Staats NY154 WI132
Stab MD 42
Stachlen MO 73
Stack OR 10
Stackere IA 94
Stadelhofer NJ 72
Stadler IL 82
Stadtmiller ID 72 MT 55 PA222
Staeblin MO 19
Staeheli NY496
Staehle NY281 PA748
Staehler NV 1
Staehlin MO 95
Staehly CT 39
Staemmle IA172
Stag IL 12 PA323
Stahl AZ 6 MI 26 MI140 NV 4 OH204 OR 18 WA110 WI140
Stahlmann IA 95 IA 99 MN175
Stainthorpe NY319
Staley PA439
Stallman IN 37
Stallmann IN 37
Stallnecker MI 39
Stamm CO 14 KS 1 MO142 WI111
Standard CA273 IL184 IA100 LA 23 MD 88 MN 89 NJ 23 NJ 25 NY592 NY595 NY604 OH142 PA344 PA766 WA 67
Stang OH281 OH283 OR 65 WA109
Stanley MA 65 OR 47
Stanton NY678
Stapff NY391
Staples WA 30
Star CA 38 ID 37 IL 11 IL144 IL145 IL267 IA102 KY 23 MA 41 MI253 MO 90 MO150 MO167 NY133 NY155 NY182 NY216 NY691 OH132 OH242 OH261 OH343 PA188 PA627 PA640 PA830 PA855 TN 19 WA104 WI 11 WI230 WI417
Star Union IL133 IL319
Stark CT 45 IN152 OH 24 OH 28 OH 35 OH234 OH255
State MT 5
State Cereal NY724
State Street IN108
Staten Island NY641
Staubler IA 20
Staudacher MI 39 NY256
Staudaucher NY299
Stauf OR102
Stauff OR 50 PA848
Steadman PA806
Steam CA364 IA218 MO140 MO150
Stecher IL290
Stecker CA162
Steeb PA125
Steffen IL253 MN 59 MN188
Stege IL122 IL185 LA 71
Steger IL307 PA587 WI261
Stegmaier PA338 PA842 PA845 PA848 PA849
Stegmann WA 95
Stegmueller NJ 77
Stegner KY 41
Stehle PA 17
Stehlin IL 10 NY160
Steiger MT 48 PA587
Steil MD 19 WI 30
Stein IL 4 IL203 KY 42 MI243 NY171 NY497 NY498 PA372
Steinacher CA452
Steinbach IL328 PA588
Steinback MI192
Steinberger NJ 52
Steinbrecher IA209 MO 59
Steinbrenner NY237
Steinkauler MO178
Steinemann MO 62 OH242
Steiner MI105 WI417 WI466 WI514
Steinhaus MN126
Steinhauser NY 89
Steinle OH189
Steinmann NY224
Steinmetz WI137
Steinrude KY 10
Stelzer MN182
Stemmer AZ 10
Stending WI 87 WI 88
Stengel IL343 NY499 PA492 PA589 PA590
Stenger IL291 IA 33 MN150 OR 19
Stengert PA626
Stenson IL 64 IL 82
Stephan CA 36 IN136 NY300 OH305 OH307 WI189
Stephanson WI424
Stephany OH207
Stephens IL256 WI 46 WI466
Stephenson WI425
Steppacher PA592
Sterilern IA122
Sterling IL227 IL357 IN 33 NE 42 OH145 PA303
Stern MO141
Sterrett MD104
Steuben OH292
Steuber MO102
Steurer KY 43
Stevens Point WI477
Stevenson IA148 NY500 OR 34
Stewart MO 73
Steyert PA593
Stich PA 74
Stichel NY605
Stick PA 18
Stickle OH183
Stickler OR101
Stiefel MD105 PA595 TN 28
Stier MD 13
Stifel MO111 MO179 MO188
Stiles ND 18
Stillmover CA 54
Stilwell NY157
Stimger WI 88
Stingelhammer WI451
Stirm ID 68 PA 83
Stiven MI155
St. Vrain MO 2
Stock IN 10 MO180 WI339
Stockberger PA 79
Stockbridge CO 18 CO 93
Stocker PA728
Stockinger WY 12
Stocklasa MO 71

Stoeckle DE 1 DE 5
Stoegle IL 14
Stoehr CT 10
Stoekle MI199
Stoelzle IL 14
Stofft ND 5 OR 12
Stoker OH163
Stokes NY277
Stoll CA425 NY692 NY693
Stollsteimer PA554
Stoltz WI340
Stolz FL 16 WI272 WI530
Stolzh MO181
Stonder MI106
Stone CT 59 IA101 NY270 WI487
Stoolmiller OH235
Stoppel OH143
Stoppenbach WI190
Storck WI453
Storm MO 25
Storms IL 31
Stortz MT 49
Story NY 23
Storz MI 47 NE 32
Stough CA 42
Straits MI107
Stransky WI 1
Strasbourg IN119
Strasser CO 53 NY100
Stratton NY158
Straub IN 13 NY596 PA 34 PA647 PA684 PA685 PA745
Straubel NY606
Straubmiller PA516 PA596
Straubmueller PA612
Straus MD 9 MD 11 MD 15 MD 16 MD 18 MD 26 MD 35 MD 50 MD 69 MD 79 MD105 MD108
Strausch MN 5
Strauss OH 54 PA597
Streator IL359
Strebel KS 24
Streblow WI399
Streeter NY159
Streib MD106
Streigel MN 55
Streit AZ 10
Strelinger MI108
Streng WI536
Streuli CA358
Stricht TX 9
Strick PA162
Stricker OR 64
Strickfaden IN 59
Striebel MD 98
Strieberger OH144
Striegel WA 91
Strobel MO 31 MO 70 NY606 OH284 PA262
Stroebele PA598
Stroh FL 15 AI 51 IA201 MI 71 MI109 MO 71 PA 9 MN168 TN 16 TX 55
Strohl AZ 12
Strohm CA124
Strohman MO 19
Strohn WI341
Strom NY703
Strothmann IA246
Stroudsburg PA790
Strunk MN186
Stuber CA359 KY 31 NY651
Stucki IN 5
Stucklauser MD126 MD133
Stuckman IA 28
Stuhlfauth WI253
Stulz MO 52
Stumpf CO 47 CO 55 CO107 IN 32 MO182 OH145 OH146 VA 16
Stumph PA599
Sturcken LA 24
Sturgeon Bay WI479
Sturm TN 6
Stutz IL186
Stuzenacker ID 14
Styer WI 38
Suckfield IN 23
Suess IA 12 IA 91 IA110
Suessdorf CA195
Suffolk MA 42 NY336
Sugar Loaf MN209
Sugita CA380
Suiler NY602
Sulliman MI274
Sullivan IN 2 PA134 RI 13
Summ MI170
Summer CO 42 CO 48 CO 57 CO 64
Summercamp ID 87
Sunbury PA793
Sundbeck MN104
Sunrise OH123 PA 8
Suset ID 93 PA 8
Sunshine FL 17 PA714
Superior IL133 IL159 MI172 NJ107 TX 35 WI484
Supple OH235
Supreme WI515
Susanville CA418
Susquehanna PA338
Suss CT 18
Sussenguth WI142
Sutcliffe NY 47 NY 48
Sutor TX 3
Sutter CA420 MO 63 MO 72 MO150
Sutton MI164
Svenson IL187
Swan CA129 CA232 CA360
Swartz NY 60
Sweatman PA600
Swedish IL282 MO 53 WA254
Sweeney IL137 WA 64
Sweetwater WY 10
Swenk PA770
Swift ID 96
Swindel NH 10 NH 11
Swiss CA358 WI356
Switehard NY568
Swope PA 72
Sykes MI182
Syme NY609
Syphon WI320
Syracuse NY651 NY671
Szomaski NY 30
T.S.B. NY549
Tabor IL163 IA241
Tacke IA 85
Tacoma CA361
Tain NJ 68
Taixe CA381
Tallant NM 18
Talmon PA601 PA602
Tama City IA226
Tamasaki CA445
Tampa FL 14
Tanana AK 17
Tann PA692
Tanner MN192
Tannhaeuser WA 67
Tarr PA799
Tasche WI463
Tascher CO 40
Taylor CT 46 IA230 IA236 NV 9 NY 14 PA357 PA603 WA 20 WI 96 WI264 WI342
Tazewell IL218
Tedele PA604
Teegarden MO206
Teichler NY301
Tekoa WA 98
Tell City IN141
Telluride CO121
Temperance NY547 WI414
Templeton KY 44
Tener MO183
Teneson NJ115
Tennessee TN 12 TN 24
Teodozia NJ121
Tepass MN190
Terre Haute IN150
Terry ND 10
Terstegge IN114
Tesch CO 49
Teschner MD 97
Teshima CA174
Tettman OH168
Tetzner NY623
Teufel PA206 PA261 PA503
Teunison NJ 35
Texas TX 35
Thalheimer AZ 26 CT 47
Thamer MO182 WI464
Thaney IN154
Thatcher OH 63
Thau MD 26
Thayson CA382
Theilen CA421
Theimer MN 39
Theis PA605
Theising OR 36
Theobald PA804
Theurer PA414 UT 8
Theysohn CA382
Thied UT 1
Thiel MI129
Thiele NY310
Thielke WI168
Thieme IN 82
Thierey MN157
Thierse MN157
Thies IL170

Thistlethwaite PA141
Thode CA280 CA319
Thoebes IL 30
Thoma MO 38
Thomas AL 9 CA428 ID 48 MO184 OH175 PA504 SD 16 WI 64
Thompson AZ 32 NY 42 OH244 PA506 WA 16
Thomson MI125
Thoreson MN 1
Thornton IL360
Thorp IL209
Thousand Oaks CA 28
Thrasher MI280
Thurn WI243
Thurston PA308
Thwaites NY268
Tice PA275
Tiemann OH 91
Tiesse IA170 IA171
Tietjens OH246
Tierney MI 7 NY685
Tiffin OH297
Tilinski PA178
Tillman CA274
Time TX 25
Timmings PA 26
Tinker MO 99 WI263
Tioga PA459
Tip Top OH123
Tippmann PA112
Tischhauser CA175
Tischner WA 13
Tiverton RI 21
Tivoli CO 41 CO 44 CO109 MI110 MT 20 NJ108
Tjernald MN101
Tobener CA 52
Toberer MN124
Tobin MA 87
Todd WI183
Toelle MI 53
Toeller IA110
Tognini CA105
Toledo OH301 OH303 OH306 OH307 OH308
Tolle OR 21
Tollen MI171
Tomasini CA105
Tona FL 17
Tonawanda NY673
Tonningsen CA 83 OR 46
Top Hat OH 86
Topp WI159
Topping CT 48
Torch Lake MI191
Torge NY214
Tornberg CA308 CA352 CA362
Tosetti IL188
Towgood MN 2
Town of Lake WI343
Townsend CO 58 CO112 NY501 PA781
Tracy CA424 NY502 NY672
Trainer PA504 PA598
Trap CA181
Traudt NJ 62
Trausch MN 94
Trausdale CA 66
Trautmann IA143
Traverse City MI275
Trefz NJ 69
Tremont PA809
Trenor NY684
Trenschel CA363 IA122
Trenton IL363 NJ145
Treser PA814
Treutzech WI 84
Tribaldt AZ 3
Tribolet AZ 3 AZ 47
Trilling NV 42
Trimborn MT 26
Tri-State AZ 28 SD 22
Tritschler IA170 IA171
Trockenbrod MI274
Trommer NY160
Trophy IL150
Trost MD 81
Trottman WI206
Troup IA247
Troy IN154
Troyner MN176
Truckee CA426
Trueman MO 18
Truman KS 17
Trumbour MO185
Trunk NY235
Tschann NM 12
Tschirgi IA103 IA104
Tsugi WA 68
Tubbs CO110
Tube City NJ 27 PA307
Tuborg MD 29 MA 71
Tuchen CA431
Tucker NM 3
Tudor IL133 NJ145 VA 7
Tullman CA383
Tunnah PA779
Turk CA341
Turtle Bay NY349
Tuscara OH 35
Tuscarawas OH 25 OH 28 OH 35 OH234 OH255
Tuscarora NV 41
Tusch MI156
Tuxedo IL163 VA 7 WA 79
Twells PA449 PA632
Twenty-Sixth Ward NY161
Twin Bridge MT 61
Twin City WI140
Twisp WA 99
Twitchell PA606
Two Rivers WI384 WI498
Twohig TN 20
Tygart WV 12
Tyler PA 27
Tyrone PA810
Tyrrell PA326
Ubel AZ 46
Uchtorff IA 66
Udermann MN158
Udlehoven WI407
Uebel UT 3
Uebelhoer NY720
Ueher WI 20
Uehlein OH136
Uerlings OR 48
Ufken IL356
Uhen WI 47
Uhl MO 11 PA 40 WI259
Uhler AK 20
Uhrig MO186 MO187
Uhrman PA240
Ukiah CA429
Ullrich CO 81
Ulmer IN 33 MN 23 NY162 PA199 PA206
Ulrich ID 77 IL312 NY319 PA861
Ulrichs CA108
Umatilla OR 66
Umbach MD 13
Umlang TX 40 TX 85
Underhill NY724
Underwood NY 43
Uneeda WV 30
Union CA 7 CA319 CA324 CA346 CO 45 IL 64 IL138 IL315 IL319 IN 98 IA 34 IA 83 IA140 IA149 IA171 IA202 KY 16 LA 25 MD 97 MA 43 MI 8 MI 16 MI 62 MI111 MI161 MI184 MI189 MN185 MO179 MO188 MT 39 NE 43 NV 4 NJ 63 NJ150 NY600 OH 32 OH 78 OH107 OH227 OH228 PA269 PA274 PA312 PA321 PA344 PA607 PA685 PA702 PA740 PA753 PA760 PA775 PA799 RI 18 TN 6 TN 29 WA 79 WA100 WI 14 WI144 WI291 WI340 WI383
Union City NJ152
Uniontown PA819 WA100
United IL 18 IL 51 IL 69 IL 83 IL105 IL108 IL145 IL153 IL161 IL180 MI215 NJ 63
United States AZ 24 CA176 CA239 CA252 CA366 IL 40 IL 52 IL 63 IL 65 IL 79 IL133 IL165 IL182 NJ 66 NJ 69 NJ 79 NJ150 NY 5 NY408 OR 24 OR 80 WA 97 WI288
United Union WA 97 WA110
Unruth WI 12
Unschuld NY246
Upham MN177
Upper Michigan MI171
Upper Peninsula MI171 MI209 MI225
Upper Sandusky OH314
Urbach NY495
Urban MO165 NY 93 NY101 OH242
Urfer AZ 33
Urff NY151
Utah UT 28
Utica NY697 NY699 NY704
Utsch ID 37
Vager MO167
Valdez AK 38
Valiton MT 24

Vallecito CA431
Vallejo CA432 CA435
Vallentine UT 2
Valley MI136 MI153 TX 56 WI144
Valley Forge OH108 PA349 PA396
Valley Mead OH313
Van Briesen CA137
Van Buren NY216 NY316
Van Cortlandt NY503
Van Couwenhoven NY504 NY505
Van Dinter IN102
Van Dyck WI457
Van Dycke WI147
Van Dyke MO 74
Van Gundy MT 23
Van Lauter AZ 23 MD 9 MI110
Van Meter MI 30
Van Merritt IL107 IL251 WI 47 WI378 WI405
Van Nostrand MA 10
Van Rensselaer NY 31
Van Schakk NY688
Van Schoenderwoerdt NY688
Van Soes NY 32
Van Staden IA244
Van Steenwyck NY506
Van Vleck NY504
Van Wert OH316
Vance IN 22
Vanderveer NJ120
Varcoe CA111
Vardman OH275
Varrelmann OR 29
Vaser WI396
Vassar NY565
Vedell IL187
Vefer AZ 33
Veidt WI344
Veile PA137
Veit MI157 MI269
Veitel MI246
Veith MN130
Velott PA730 PA853
Verner PA643
Vernon CA178
Verten WI395
Vesser PA292
Vetter PA569
Victor MN152 PA187 PA219 PA227 WI158
Victoria VA 26
Vienna MA 19 MI 85 OH 71
Vigelius NY162
Viking CA364 PA 75
Vill MN112 MN151
Villhauer OH308
Vilsack PA654
Vincent NY446
Virginia MN195 VA 20
Vigne NY507
Vockerodt IA160
Voegele WI220
Voegtle CO 8
Voelke IN142 MN145
Voelker AK 37 OH147
Voetsch NY192 NY215
Vogel IA177 MI199 OH 15 PA298 UT 9 WI131
Vogelberg WI 46
Vogelberger DC 19
Vogelsang OH308
Voght WI105
Vogl OR 27 WI256
Vogt IL137 IA 37 KY 49 MD107 MI268 MI287 PA146 PA152 PA163
Voight WI242
Voigt MI101 MI113 MI114 NY685 PA163
Volk IL277 MN 3 MT 31 MT 32 PA 28 PA 30 PA745
Vollbrecht MN 76
Vollert CO 85
Vollmer PA447 PA521
Vollstedt IA 73
Volmer IL 21 PA608
Volz IL237 MI 17 MI 37
Von MI115
Von Berge ID 32
Von der Horst MD108
Von Fricken NY163
Von Hollen IL292
Vorce OH289
Vosberg NV 21
Vossler OH254
Vostoupal NE 56
Wabash IN159
Wabasha MN196
Wachter CA349 TN 21
Wack CA302
Wackenhuth NJ109
Wacker IL 42 IL 47 PA259 PA741
Wackerott IA 40
Waddle WI238
Wade IL224
Wadena MN199
Waeckerling CA275
Waegerle WI 17
Waful NY543
Wageman MI184
Wagemann MI189
Wagener UT 5 UT 34
Wagenhaeuser MO182
Wagenhauser TX 26 TX 27
Wager OH175 PA815
Wagner CA206 FL 8 IL126 IL189 IL190 IL191 IL199 IL241 IN 82 IN103 IN124 MD 78 MD161 MI 57 MI273 MN 16 MO 33 MO127 MO193 MT 48 NV 10 NV 26 NJ 17 OH 40 OH156 OH203 OH286 OH298 PA 29 PA 98 PA609 TX 49 WA 73 WI141 WI271 WI468 WI479
Wahl CA264 IL285 IL326 IL337 MI220 MO 58 MO178 PA 18 WI477
Wahlers NJ153
Wahlmuth CA365
Wahlruff MO206
Wainwright MO189 MO190 PA686
Wakefield CA 59
Wala NE 56
Walbridge PA807
Walch MI128
Waldberg MA 26
Waldeck IL 15 OH214 OH321
Waldeman MI 31
Waldenmeier CA 34 CA320
Walder IN 91 OH 9
Waldsauer PA610
Walecka WI494
Walford PA201
Walk KY 56
Walker ID 67 IA197 MI 42 MI190 MO195 MI198 NH 14 NY 20 ND 2 OH 52 OH 79 OH 92 OH 93 OH183 PA639 TN 28
Wall CO101
Walla Walla WA110 WA111
Wallabaut NY124
Wallace NH 3 NY342 NY443
Waller AZ 40 MN154
Wallner WI206
Walruff KS 25
Walsburga MO187
Walser CA 84 IN 53 OR 13 OR 87
Walsh CT 25 NY325
Walshe NY260
Walstadt MT 28
Walter CA 38 CA290 CA447 CO109 CO121 CO127 IN 17 KY 45 KY 46 MA 1 MA 79 MI198 MO 91 NY 20 NY120 NY694 ND 3 OR 33 PA 75 PA611 PA612 TX 15 TX 50 WI 12 WI 95 WI265 WI469
Walters MN138 ND 4 PA 63 PA129
Waltham MN154
Walther IL193
Walti CA390
Walz CT 3 IA 19 IA 26 MI 86 PA481 PA661 TX 70
Wandell NE 7
Wanemacher CA366
Wanger CA 77
Wanner SC 5
Ward MD166
Warm WI210
Warnecke ID 82
Warner OH264 TX 37
Warnholtz CA226
Warninger WI221
Warnke AZ 31
Warren IN146 NY586 PA825
Warsaw IL102 IL363
Warschauer WI297
Wartemburg ID 50
Warwick RI 25
Waseca MN200
Washa MN116
Washburn OR101 WI500

Washington CA223 CA371 DC 1 DC 6 IL329 MD 11 MD109 MD125 MO125 MO166 OH164 OH340 PA172 PA690 PA831 TN 22 WA 22 WA 66 WA106 WI296
Washoe MT 2 NV 35
Waterbury CT 61 NY286
Waterford WI502
Waterhill MA 70
Waterhouse MI235
Waterloo IL367
Waters WI191
Watertown NY711 WI506
Watry AZ 57
Waukee NJ 27
Waukegan IL371
Waukesha WI 47 WI215 WI458 WI512 WI514
Waupaca WA516
Waupun WI517
Wausau WI522
Waverly IA242
Waymin ID 78
Waymire ID 78
Wayne MI116
Waynesburg PA833
Wear NY508
Weard WI263
Weaver MD174 PA142 PA848 WI487
Webb OH190
Webben OH 74
Weber CA 11 CA 42 CA330 CT 27 CT 60 IL316 IN 98 IA 82 IA212 KY 47 KY 49 MD 62 MD110 MI 79 MI251 MN147 NJ 74 NM 9 NY 33 NY126 NY164 NY233 NY302 OH 70 OH221 OH225 OH226 OH227 OH311 OR 81 PA 68 PA687 TX 84 TX 92 WA 8 WI 47 WI 60 WI137 WI215 WI344 WI399 WI418 WI458 WI490 WI512
Webster MA 93
Weckerle IN 15 IN127
Weckerling LA 26
Weddle OH335
Wedel CA290 IA154 WI398
Wedemeyer WI417
Weedsport NY716
Wegenast KY 40 KY 45
Wegenburg NJ149
Wegener MI117 MN 4
Weger PA605
Wehile KS 53
Wehle CT 49
Wehn PA233
Wehner OH180 OH184
Wehr CO 64 MD 11 NJ 77 WI344
Wehrfritz AZ 47 NV 3
Wehrle NY244
Wehrsitz UT 3
Weibel CT 37
Weibold OH238
Weichmann MN 93
Weichselbaum KS 36
Weick AZ 51
Weickert CA367
Weidemaier KS 14
Weideman OR 28 WV 13
Weidemann CT 49 OR 40
Weidenenser WI465
Weidig WI225
Weidlich TX 9
Weidling IA189
Weidmair DE 7
Weidmann NY167
Weigand CA384 MO197 MT 59
Weigel KY 30
Weigert WA 69
Weigt NM 18
Weihmann PA543 PA613
Weikert CA359
Weiland NJ110
Weile MN 1
Weiler CA 84 PA630
Weilmunster CA 83 CA416
Weimann ID 48
Weinbender NY695 NY713
Weinhard IN 33 MT 30 NJ 84 NJ103 OR 76 OR 82 OR100 WA 14 WA104
Weinmann IN112 KS 1 NY607
Weirich CA319 MI158
Weis IA190 OH333 PA508 PA688
Weisbrod MN209 PA614
Weise IA211
Weisel MN 7
Weisenhorn CO 8
Weisenstein IL200
Weiser MT 26
Weisgerber ID 55 ID 58 PA 54 PA615 WA 82 WV 31
Weising PA689
Weiss CA215 CA217 CO 22 CO111 IA167 MN 50 MN 56 MN144 MO153 MO178 NJ 81 NJ111 NY633 OH 20 OR 90
Weiss Beer MD 55 MD 82 MD 90 MD109 MN169 MO 92 MO106 MO169 MO170 NY100 NY174 NY187 NY360 NY494 OH 46 OH 50 OH109 OH125 OH139 OR 77 PA511 PA621 PA630 TX 22 TX 70 WI106 WI111 WI221 WI278 WI291 WI294 WI302 WI313 WI315 WI317 WI320 WI345 WI351 WI463 WI515
Weissendorfer MO 63
Weisenrieder PA767
Weissert PA670
Weissig NV 13
Weist WI412
Welch MN 90
Welde PA164 PA504
Welder IA103
Weldon SC 5
Welker PA290 PA855
Weller MI142 NY239 SD 24
Wellhoefer WI465
Wellmann NY391
Wells UT 15 VA 18
Wellston OH327
Welscher CA223
Welte NY215 UT 37
Welter WI 93 WI403
Welti NV 16
Welz NY166
Welzhofer OH308
Wenatchee WA114
Wendland WI 41
Wenger WI204
Wengert IA138
Wenitzer PA 34
Wenner MN128 MN200 NY376
Wentworth NH 13
Wentz ND 15
Wentzler PA291
Wenzel IL205 PA768
Werford WA 11
Weringer WI262
Werley KS 28
Wernberg IN 72
Werner AZ 31 CA 5 CA125 CA127 CA236 CA250 KS 49 MD 76 MD148 NY327 NY509 NY510 NY619 PA 18 PA228 PA838 SD 4 WI153 WI204
Werneth ID 28 ID100
Wernz NY511
Werrbach WI345
Werrin NV 48
Wertmire IA118
Wertmueller IA 34
Wertz WI 86
Wertzig MN 66
Weschler PA153 PA165
Wesnitzer OH166 PA741
Wesp TX 82
West NY 58 WA 66 WA 70
West Bay City MI 28
West Bend WI525 WI526
West Coast CA151
West End MN 33 NY696 PA166 PA302 PA680
West Hammond IL 25
West Hill WI 90 WI110 WI344
West Hudson NJ 79
West India NY512
West Louisville KY 31
West Masontown PA299
West Point NE 56
West Side IL 45 IL193 MI 60 WI328
West Superior WI484
West Virginia WV 15
Westacott OR 93
Westchester NY547
Westermann CA222 CA223
Western CO 41 CO 50 IL 12 IL372 IA 31 IA104 IA154 IA170 IA171 IA192 MI 16 MO 42 MO147 MT 23 OH 42 TX 77 WA 57 WI318
Western Maryland MD 73
Western Reserve OH322
Western Steam IA 24
Westerhagen CA177
Westminster IL133 IL194

Westmoreland PA795
Weston MO206
Westover MI 27
Westphal MN109
Westphalia MI 58
Wet Mountain CO129
Wetekamp MO181
Wetsal IL283
Wetsell IL283
Wettekamp MO124
Wetterer OH 60 OR 37
Wettermann OH276
Wetzel IL231 IL288 IA 42 PA616
Weyand CA368 MO191 NY218 OH 94
Weygand MO191
Weyhe WI150
Weymuller IA 60 IA128 NE 44 SD 11
Weysser PA302
Wharton NY546
What Cheer RI 19
Whatcom WA117
Wheat IN153
Wheatcroft NY440
Wheeler IL173
Wheeling IL374
Whelan MO121 NY683
Whipple WI468
Whirlpool NY521
White IL302 MA 77 MN 37 NY 59 NY334 NY524 NY574 NY629 OH329 PA407 PA439
White Bear IL360 PA624
White Beer NY167
White Eagle IL116 IL195 MI120
White Rock OH 4
White Seal MI136
Whiteley CT 53
Whitesides PA619
Whitewater WI536
Whitman PA121 WI154
Whitmore MA 75
Whitney NY513 PA439
Whittle MI130
Wichman CO121
Wichmann CO121 IL317
Wickett CO 13
Wickstrom CA 73
Widder NJ 17
Widenmann CA435
Widman DC 20 OR 10 PA 36
Widmann PA233 PA282 PA859 WY 13
Wiedemann KY 53 KY 54 NJ 78 PA617 PA618 WI448
Wiedenmayer NJ112 NJ113 NJ114 NJ117
Wiedmaier NJ 20
Wiedmeier IL350
Wiegand KS 50 MI255 NY542 OH330
Wieland CA369 CA376 NY514
Wiesenfeld MD 97
Wiesenham IN 89
Wiesner MN 95
Wiessner MD 14 MD 42 MD111 MD112 MD113
Wigger MO 3
Wilber NE 57
Wilbers IN 38
Wilco NJ145
Wild WI359
Wildanger MI136
Wildermuth OH271
Wildner NY 48
Wile PA620
Wilhelm CA 95 CA 98 OR 95 PA 19 PA690
Wilke OH185
Wilkens NJ 91
Wilkins CT 26
Wilkstrom WA 9
Will AZ 11 NM 5 NY608
Willauer AL 3
Willebrand MI202
Willem IA 26
Willens WI256
Willers OK 1
William AZ 56
Williams CA137 CA420 ID 88 IN155 IA 43 KS 8 MI118 PA850 RI 17 WI124 WI426 WI519 WY 2
Williamsburg NY147
Williamson CA383 MO151
Williamsville NY722
Willinger PA798 WI251
Willmott CA140
Willoh CA349
Willow Grove PA657
Willow Springs NE 33
Willows CA310 CA449
Wilmer ID 2
Wilmington DE 6
Wilmot CA370
Wilmott CA349
Wilms MD 10
Wilson NY609 NY610 PA832 WA 80 WI397
Wilting NY217
Wimmer IA 18 MN119 MN156 PA747
Winckler ID 24
Wind WI346
Windber PA856
Windeck MO 93
Windecke MO180
Windeler CA318
Winderberger NY515
Windfelder PA746
Windisch OH 64 OH 76 OH 95 OH281
Windsor IL133
Windspear NE 31
Winfield WI488
Wing NY263
Winkel IL308
Winkelmeyer MO179
Winker MN 69 MN186
Winkler KY 56 MO 58 MT 4 MT 21 NY523 UT 38 WA 50
Winling NY 52
Winnebago WI402
Winnemucca NV 57
Winnig PA621
Winslow NY679
Winter GA 14 MI227 NJ119 NY385 PA676
Winterath IN154
Wintter CT 2
Winz WI267
Wirth CA413 CA451 PA622 WI360
Wisch CO 51
Wisconsin WI 47 WI137 WI203 WI215 WI285 WI347 WI354 WI514
Wise PA 10 WA 52
Wisemann PA261
Wishmann MN 92
Wisler PA104
Wissel IN 11
Wisser CA381 ID 50
Wissler CO129 OH 40
Wiswell NE 2
Witt IA 72 IA 73
Witte NY167
Wittekind IN 34
Witteman IA188
Wittemann MO192
Wittenberg WI251
Witter NY232
Wittig NJ 36
Wittlinger OH188 PA262
Wittman PA149
Wittmann OH235 WI404
Witz AK 30
Witzenbacher MD118 MD162
Wochner IL 16
Woelfel CA 76 RI 20
Woelffer IL183
Woerner MD 79 NY553 PA728
Woerz NY451
Woesler IA174
Woessner CA 64
Wohlgethan WA 73
Wohlieb NJ129
Wohlleber MD 86 MD114
Woldenberg OR 17
Wolf CA116 CA262 IL357 KS 9 MN192 NY566 NY611 PA193 PA369 PA411 PA623 PA624 PA625 PA691 WA 42 WI 13 WI348 WI415
Wolff CA249 CA399 CA422 IN 7 IA161 TX 23
Wolffram WI163
Wolter CT 50 IA133
Wolters GA 15 PA368 PA480 PA510 PA553 TX 6 TX 32
Woltmann CO 69
Wolverine MI241
Wood NY 34 OH 75 OH 96 PA681 PA692 WA 37
Wooden Shoe OH242
Woods CA426 OR 86
Woodside NY168
Woodstock IL376
Woodward WI509
Woolford WA 11

The Palo Alto Brewing Co. of Mountain View, CA started brewing in 1983.

One of the problems in gathering facts for this work was that more data very often conflicted with data already on hand. The scope of the endeavor precluded much conflict resolution by the authors alone. Where the information in this book is of the highest level, it is due to the collaboration of colleagues researching information most easily accessed in the locale of the individual breweries. Hundreds of people helped make this work the most complete volume on breweries published to date.

The following is a presentation of expressions of appreciation to certain dedicated individuals intermingled with information regarding the areas where they were most helpful.

The authors especially acknowledge the dedicated, intensive, and thorough scholarship of three individuals:

Henry Herbst   Robert Kay   Dale Van Wieren

They worked in concert with Robert Gottschalk to produce the most comprehensive and accurate information for the St. Louis, Chicago, and Philadelphia sections.

The following individuals were extremely helpful in supplying brewery directory information:

Will Anderson   Kenneth Kroeger   William D. Ross
Herbert A. Haydock   Reino Ojala   Lewis W. Thornburg
Henry W. Herbst   Tom Raub   William J. Vollmar

Through their assistance the following handbooks and directories became available to fill many of the gaps which existed in the first draft of this work:

AMERICAN BREWING TRADE LIST AND INTERNAL REVENUE GUIDE FOR BREWERS. 1915.
AMERICAN BREWER, ANNUAL DIRECTORY OF BREWERS. 1953/54, 1962/63, 1963/64.
ANNUAL SALES IN BARRELS. Research Company of America. 1939, 1942, 1949, 1955, 1959, 1968, 1969.
BREWERIES AUTHORIZED TO OPERATE. Treasury Department, Bureau of Alcohol, Tobacco, and Firearms. 1932-1983 issues and revisions.
BREWERS AND BOTTLERS UNIVERSAL ENCYCLOPEDIA. 1910.
BREWERS DIGEST ANNUAL BUYERS' GUIDE AND DIRECTORY. 1948, 1949, 1952, 1954, 1955, 1956, 1960, 1961, 1962, 1963, 1965, 1966, 1967, 1970, 1973, 1974, 1975, 1976, 1977, 1978, 1979, 1980, 1981, 1982, 1983.
THE BREWERS HANDBOOK, A DIRECTORY OF BREWERS. H. S. Rich & Co. 1888, 1890, 1891, 1895, 1896, 1898, 1899, 1900, 1901, 1902, 1905, 1906, 1907, 1908, 1910, 1911, 1912, 1913, 1914, 1916, 1918.
THE BREWERS HANDBOOK, BREWERS JOURNAL DIRECTORY. Gibson Publishing Co. 1938, 1943, 1947, 1951.
THE BREWERS HANDBOOK FOR 1876. Louis Schade.
BREWERY DIRECTORY AND SUPPLIES INDEX. Atlas Publishing Co. 1934, 1937.
BUYERS' GUIDE AND BREWERY DIRECTORY. Brewery Age. 1937, 1939.
MODERN BREWERY AGE BLUE BOOKS. 1941, 1944, 1945, 1946, 1948, 1949, 1950, 1957, 1958, 1959, 1968, 1969.
TOVEY'S OFFICIAL BREWERS AND MALSTERS' DIRECTORY. 1882, 1884, 1893, 1894, 1897, 1903, 1904, 1915.
WING'S BREWERS' HAND BOOK FOR 1880.

Martin Landey supplied a complete set of BREWERIES AUTHORIZED TO OPERATE for the period 1932 to 1981. The following were then used to cross check brewery information on hand:

BREWERIES AUTHORIZED TO OPERATE issues and revision dates for:
1932: October 31.
1933: May 1, 15, 31; July 1, 15; August 1, 3, 16; September 1, 16, 30; November 1, December 1.
1934: January 2; July 1.
1935-1983: July 1.

Charles Bacon supplemented this information by contributing copies of the annotated work sheets for the years 1942 to 1951 and 1956 to 1959. These work sheets showed the specific dates of deletions, and changes occuring since the previous annual listing.

Thank you to Carl A. Schwarzen for 1821 to 1920 St. Louis City Directory Data. Also to Herman Ronnenberg for supplying the Oregon, Washington, and Idaho Gazetteer and Business Directories for 1886-1887 and 1889-1890. And to William Ross for 1876-1877 information from the Kentucky State Gazetteer and Business Directory.

Many colleagues supplied in depth data from research they had done in specific areas:

Michael Ashendorf, Westchester, NY
John E. Bernhard, Washington State
Randy Carlson, Part of Iowa
Tom Cebula, New Haven, CT
Donna Christian, Kalamazoo, MI
William Frederick, Denver, CO
Robert Gottschalk, Rochester, NY
Henry W. Herbst, St. Louis, MO
Duke Jones, Sacramento, CA
Robert E. Kay, Chicago, IL
Glenn C. Kuebeler, Sandusky, OH
Martin Landey, Boston, MA
Shelby Meyer, Arizona
Ernest C. Oest, New York City
Scott Parzanese, Reading, PA
Edgar Provine, Memphis, TN
Thomas Raub, Allentown, PA
Walter Ronda, Milwaukee, WI
Herman Ronnenberg, Idaho
Leonard J. Rosol, Pittsburgh, PA
William D. Ross, Knoxville, TN
Donald Sarver, Baltimore, MD
Carl Schwarzen, St. Louis, MO
Ken Simon, West Palm Beach, FL
John Snyder, Erie, PA
Dale Van Wieren, Philadelphia, PA and Charleston, WV
Bernard Wallace, Reading, PA

Through their study of brewery artifacts such as letterheads, glasses, bottles, trays, and city directory advertising, the following individuals added to or corrected information originally published in THE REGISTER OF UNITED STATES BREWERIES 1876-1976:

Herb Ashendorf
Leon Beebe
John E. Bernhard
Peter Blum
Ed Kaye
Donald Kurtz
Stanley D. Loula
Reino Ojala
Ken Ostrow
John Pardee
William D. Ross
Charlotte Wright

The following are but a few of the many who supplied bibliographical data, newspaper article, magazine articles, and other information:

Fred H. Banks
Bob Bendula
Jeanette Bendula
Larry Biehl
Randy Carlson
Gordon Dean
Bill Frederick
Andy Growe
Henry Herbst
John Horn
Robert E. Kay
Irv Kennedy
Ken Kroeger
Pete Lundell
John Marx
Bill McKienzie
Charles Merrill
Lowell Owens
Ed Provine
John Pyrek
Tom Raub
Donald Reed
Harry Richards
Walter Ronda
Art Santen
Larry Sherk
Randy Schreck
John Snyder
Stuart Steggall
Jim Starkman
Richard Strisofsky
Jack Turner
Russ Van Nostrand
Robert Van Vactor
Dale Van Wieren
Verne Vollrath
Glenn Walling
Terry Warrick
Cathy Winkler

Last but not least, special recognition should go to all the authors and publishers of brewery information. Without their dedicated efforts to preserve the history of breweries, this work would not have been possible. A recommended reading list for further research by the serious brewerianist is on the following pages.

Robert Gottschalk, Penfield, NY

March, 1984

Recommended reading list for the brewerianist:

Anderson, Will. THE BEER BOOK. Princeton, N.J.: Pyne Press, 1973.
Anderson, Will. THE BREWERIES OF BROOKLYN. Croton Falls, N.Y., 1976.
Anderson, Will & Sonja. BEERS, BREWERIES AND BREWERIANA. Carmel, N.Y., 1969
Andreas, A. T. HISTORY OF CHICAGO., c1886.
Baron, Stanley. BREWED IN AMERICA. Boston: Little, Brown & Co., 1962.
Clint, Dave, COLORADO HISTORICAL BOTTLES, 1859-1915. Antique Bottle Collectors of Colorado, 1976.
Cochran, Thomas C. THE PABST BREWING COMPANY. New York: New York University Press, 1948.
Curtis-Wedge. HISTORY OF BUFFALO AND PEPIN COUNTIES. Wisconsin, 1919.
Downard, William L. THE CINCINNATI BREWING INDUSTRY: A SOCIAL AND ECONOMIC HISTORY. Athens: Ohio University Press, 1973.
Downard, William L. DICTIONARY OF THE HISTORY OF THE AMERICAN BREWING AND DISTILLING INDUSTRIES. Westport, Ct.: Greenwood Press, 1980.
Ehret, George. TWENTY-FIVE YEARS OF BREWING. New York, 1891.
Ford, Everett & Janice. PREPROHIBITION BEER BOTTLES AND BREWERIES OF BALTIMORE. Maryland, 1974.
Friedrich, Manfred and Donald Bull. THE REGISTER OF UNITED STATES BREWERIES 1876-1976, VOL. I & VOL. II. Trumbull, Ct., 1976
Jackson, Michael, ed. THE WORLD GUIDE TO BEER. Englewood Cliffs, N.J.: Prentice-Hall, Inc., 1977.
Karwowski, Gerald L. BOTTLED IN THE BELLE CITY, RACINE 1848-1920. Racine, Wis., 1979.
Kearse, William E. A HISTORY OF THE BREWERY AND LIQUOR INDUSTRY OF ROCHESTER, NEW YORK. 1907.
Kelley, William J. BREWING IN MARYLAND. Baltimore: John D. Lucas Printing Co., 1965.
Kobler, John. ARDENT SPIRITS: THE RISE AND FALL OF PROHIBITION. New York: Putnam, 1973.
Krebs, Roland, and Percy J. Orthwein. MAKING FRIENDS IS OUR BUSINESS: 100 YEARS OF ANHEUSER-BUSCH. Anheuser-Busch, Inc., 1953.
Kroll, Wayne L. BADGER BREWERIES, PAST AND PRESENT. Jefferson, Wis., 1976.
Lindhurst, James. HISTORY OF THE BREWING INDUSTRY IN ST. LOUIS 1804-1860. 1939.
Matthews, W. L. BRIEF HISTORY OF LONE STAR BREWING COMPANY. 1981.
Monette, Clarence. JOSEPH BOSCH AND THE BOSCH BREWING COMPANY. 1978.
Morin, Eugene C. THE QUEEN CITY BREWING CO., INC., CUMBERLAND, MARYLAND 1901-1974. 1978.
Muzio, Jack. COLLECTIBLE TIN ADVERTISING TRAYS. Santa Rosa, Cal.: 1972.
Ojala, Reino. 20 YEARS OF AMERICAN BEERS, THE 30's & 40's. Minneapolis: 1980.
Pfirman, Kenneth. ERIE BREWING INDUSTRY LISTING.
Pospychala, Phil and Joe McFarland. THE GREAT CHICAGO BEER CANS. Libertyville, Ill.: Silver Fox Productions, 1979.
Rich & Co., H.S. ONE HUNDREAD YEARS OF BREWING. Chicago and New York: 1903.
Salem, F.W. BEER, ITS HISTORY AND ITS ECONOMIC VALUE AS A NATIONAL BEVERAGE. Hartford, Ct.: F.W. Salem & Co., 1880.
Scott, Ed and Alexander Clark and R. L. Roffino. WHO'S WHO IN BREW. Paterson, N.J.: 1978.
Thomann, Gallus. AMERICAN BEER: GLIMPSES OF ITS HISTORY AND DESCRIPTION OF ITS MANUFACTURE. New York: U.S.B.A., 1909.

Brewery publications:

Anheuser-Busch. MARKET STATISTICAL REPORT APRIL 19, 1978.
Bartholomay. THE BARTHOLOMAY BREWING CO.
Blitz-Weinhard. ABOUT OUR BEER.
Burger. THE STORY OF BURGER.
Carling. THIS IS CARLING.
Coors. THE ADOLPH COORS STORY.
Erie. KOEHLER KOMMENTS.
Hawaii. THE PRIMO STORY.
Heileman, G. THE BLATZ BEER STORY. THE HOUSE OF HEILEMAN.
Hudepohl. A SHORT HISTORY OF THE BREWING INDUSTRY IN CINCINNATI. 1979.
Koch. FRED KOCH BREWERY.
Miller. HISTORY AND CURRENT OPERATION OF THE MILLER BREWING CO.
Oshkosh. THIS IS OUR STORY.
Pilsen. 50th ANNIVERSARY. 1953.
Pittsburgh. BREWING WITH THE TIMES.
Schaefer, F. & M. OUR ONE HUNDRETH YEAR. 1942.
Schlitz. THE BIOGRAPHY OF ERWIN C. UIHLEIN. 1963.

Schmidts of Philadelphia. TAVERNS OF YESTERDAY- 100th ANNIVERSARY. 1960.
Schoenhofen, Peter. EDELWEISS NEWS. 1916
Stroh. STROH'S, THE FIRE BREWING STORY.

Collector publications:

ALL ABOUT BEER. McMullen Publishing Co.
ANTIQUE TRADER WEEKLY. Babka Publishing Co.
BEER CAN COLLECTORS NEWS REPORT. Journal of the Beer Can Collectors of America.
THE BREWERIANA COLLECTOR. Journal of the National Association of Breweriana Advertising (NABA).
BREWERS DIGEST.
CANADIAN BREWERIANIST.
COLLECTIBLES ILLUSTRATED. Yankee Publishing Co.
COLLECTORS NEWS.
EASTERN COAST BREWERIANA ASSOCIATION NEWSLETTER. ECBA.
HOBBIES MAGAZINE.
JUST FOR OPENERS.
MAINE ANTIQUE DIGEST.
THE OLD BOTTLE MAGAZINE.
JOEL SATER'S ANTIQUES NEWS.
THE SPINNING WHEEL.
TRI-STATE TRADER.
BREWERIANA COLLECTIBLES MAGAZINE (formerly BEER CANS MONTHLY).
ANTIQUE GAZETTE.
SOUTHERN ANTIQUES.
ZYMURGY.

General interest publications which occassionally contain news of the brewing industry:

ADVERTISING AGE.
BUSINESS WEEK.
FINANCIAL WORLD.
FOOD ENGINEERING.
FORBES.
FORTUNE.
HIGH COUNTRY.
IDAHO YESTERDAYS.
MINNESOTA EARTH JOURNAL.
NEW JERSEY MONTHLY.
NEWSWEEK.
NORTHWEST.
PENNSYLVANIA ILLUSTRATED.
TIME.
WALL STREET JOURNAL.

We have made every effort to achieve accuracy in the listings in this book. If any errors or omissions are noted by the reader, we would appreciate hearing from you.

Robert Gottschalk
115 Peachtree Road
Penfield, NY 14526
USA

Donald Bull
P.O. Box 106
Trumbull, CT 06611
USA

Manfred Friedrich
D6900 Heidelberg
Zahringerstrasse 3
West Germany